LOWER AUSTRIA AND BURGENLAND
Pages 128–155
VIENNA
Pages 48–123
Krems
Klosterneuburg
Linz
St. Pölten
Wels
Wien
Steyr
LOWER AUSTRIA AND BURGENLAND
UPPER AUSTRIA
Eisenstadt
Wiener Neustadt
Leoben
STYRIA
Graz
St. Veit an der Glan
Klagenfurt
0 km
50
0 miles
50
STYRIA
Pages 156–185

EYEWITNESS TRAVEL

AUSTRIA

EYEWITNESS TRAVEL

AUSTRIA

MAIN CONTRIBUTORS: TERESA CZERNIEWICZ-UMER,
JOANNA EGERT-ROMANOWSKA
AND JANINA KUMANIECKA

DK

LONDON, NEW YORK,
MELBOURNE, MUNICH AND DELHI
www.dk.com

Produced by Wydawnictwo Wiedza i Życie S.A., Warsaw

ART EDITOR Paweł Pasternak
CONTRIBUTORS Janina Kumaniecka, Ewa Dan, Marianna Dudek, Konrad Gruda, Małgorzata Omilanowska, Marek Pernal, Jakub Sito, Barbara Sudnik-Wójcikowska, Roman Taborski, Zuzanna Umer

CONSULTANT Małgorzata Omilanowska

CARTOGRAPHERS Magdalena Polak, Olaf Rodowald, Dariusz Romanowski

PHOTOGRAPHERS Wojciech and Katarzyna Mędrzakowie

ILLUSTRATORS Michał Burkiewicz, Paweł Marczak, Bohdan Wróblewski

DTP DESIGNER Paweł Pasternak
EDITORS Teresa Czerniewicz-Umer, Joanna Egert-Romanowska
DESIGNERS Elżbieta Dudzińska, Ewa Roguska, Piotr Kiedrowski

Dorling Kindersley Limited
EDITOR Sylvia Goulding / Silva Editions Ltd.
TRANSLATOR Magda Hannay
DTP DESIGNERS Jason Little, Conrad van Dyk
PRODUCTION CONTROLLER Bethan Blase

Reproduced by Colourscan, Singapore
Printed and bound in China by L.Rex Printing Co. Ltd.

First published in Great Britain in 2003 by
Dorling Kindersley Limited
80 Strand, London WC2R 0RL

12 13 14 15 10 9 8 7 6 5 4 3 2 1

Reprinted with revisions in 2006, 2008, 2010, 2012

A CIP CATALOGUE RECORD IS AVAILABLE FROM THE BRITISH LIBRARY.
ISBN 978 1 4053 6886 5

Front cover main image: The town of Hallstatt and Hallstätter See

MIX
Paper from responsible sources
FSC www.fsc.org FSC™ C018179

The information in this DK Eyewitness Travel Guide is checked regularly.

Every effort has been made to ensure that this book is as up-to-date as possible at the time of going to press. Some details, however, such as telephone numbers, opening hours, prices, gallery hanging arrangements and travel information are liable to change. The publishers cannot accept responsibility for any consequences arising from the use of this book, nor for any material on third party websites, and cannot guarantee that any website address in this book will be a suitable source of travel information. We value the views and suggestions of our readers very highly. Please write to: Publisher, DK Eyewitness Travel Guides, Dorling Kindersley, 80 Strand, London, WC2R 0RL, Great Britain, or email: travelguides@dk.com.

◁ **Beautiful winter scenery in Seefeld, Tyrol**

CONTENTS

INTRODUCING AUSTRIA

Detail of the façade of a pharmacy in Obernberg in Upper Austria

12th-century Burg Clam in Upper Austria, seen from the Danube

Memorial on a tombstone in the church in Maria Saal in Carinthia

Grundlsee and Totes Gebirge (Dead Mountains) in Styria

Stained-glass window of a church in Bürserlberg, in Vorarlberg

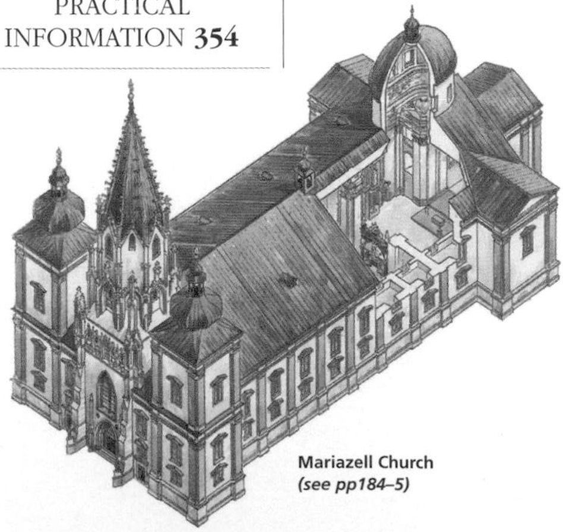

Mariazell Church

(see pp184–5)

HOW TO USE THIS GUIDE

This guide will help you to get the most out of a visit to Austria. The first section, *Introducing Austria*, locates the country geographically, and provides an invaluable historical and cultural context. Subsequent sections describe the main sights and attractions of the capital, Vienna, and the different regions. Information on accommodation and restaurants can be found in the *Travellers' Needs* section, while the *Survival Guide* provides many useful tips on everything you need to know during a visit to Austria.

VIENNA

This section is divided into three parts: Inner City, North of Mariahilfer Strasse and South of the Ring. Sights outside the centre are described in the *Further Afield* section. All sights are numbered and plotted on the area map. Detailed information for each sight is given in numerical order.

Pages referring to Vienna are marked with a red thumb tab.

A locator map shows where you are in relation to other areas of the city.

1 Area Map
For easy reference the sights are numbered and located on the area map as well as on the map of Vienna, on pp117–21.

Sights at a Glance lists the sights in an area by category: Historic Streets and Buildings, Museums and Galleries, Churches, Parks and Gardens.

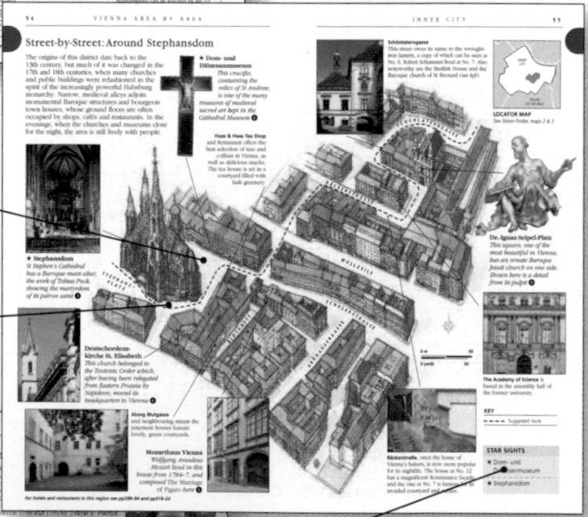

2 Street-by-Street Map
This gives a bird's-eye view of each sightseeing area described in the section.

A suggested route for sightseeing is indicated with a dotted red line.

Stars indicate the sights no visitor should miss.

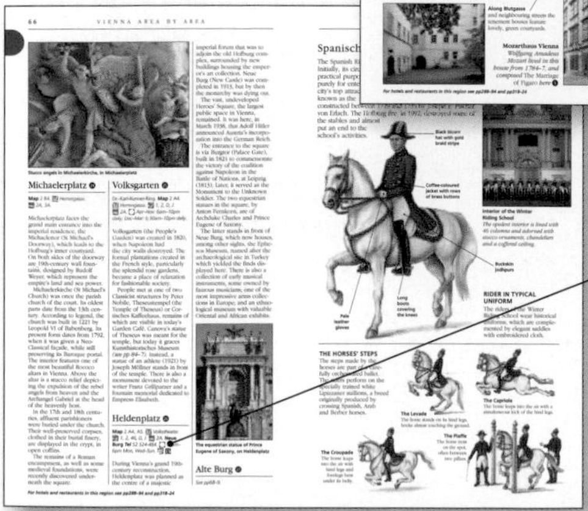

3 Detailed Information
All the sights of Vienna are described individually. The practical information includes addresses, telephone numbers, opening hours, admission charges, transport links and disabled access. The key to the symbols used is on the back flap.

AUSTRIA REGION BY REGION

In this guide Austria is divided into six regions, each of which is explored in a separate section. The most interesting cities, towns, villages and sights are shown on each Regional Map.

1 Introduction

The landscape, history and character of each region are described, showing how the area has changed through the ages, and the sights on offer for the visitor today.

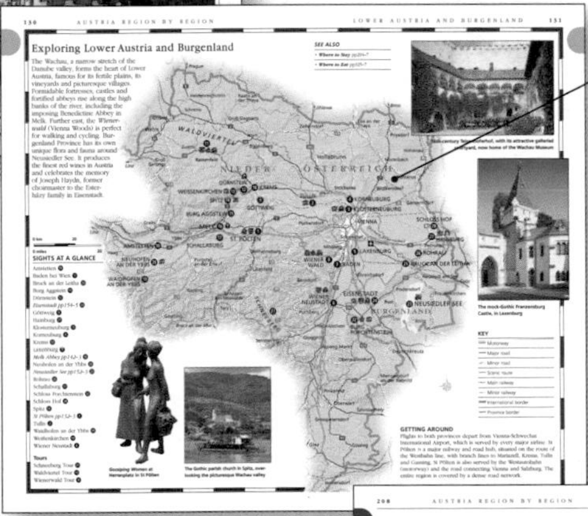

2 Regional Map

The regional maps show the main roads and the topography. All the important sights are numbered and details on how to get there are given.

Boxes highlight interesting aspects connected with a sight.

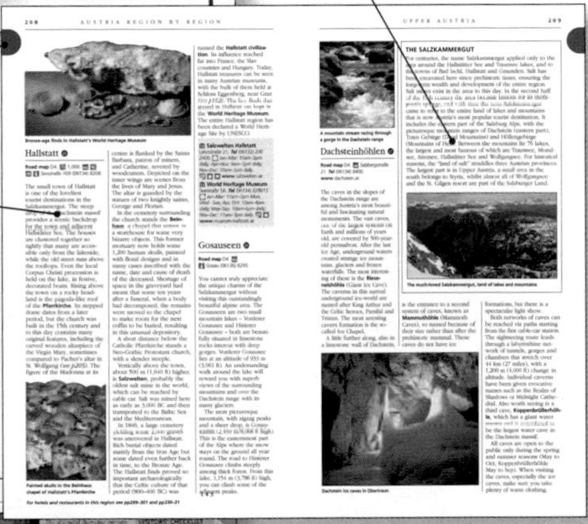

Colour coding on each page makes it easy to find a region; the colours are explained on the inside front cover.

3 Detailed Information

Major towns, villages and other tourist sights are listed in order and numbered as on the Regional Maps. Each entry contains detailed information on the main places of interest.

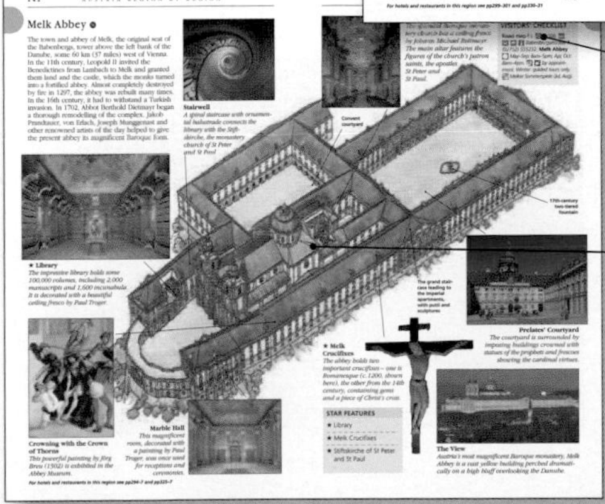

A Visitors' Checklist for each of the main sights provides practical information to help you plan your visit.

4 Major Sights

At least two pages are devoted to each major sight. Historic buildings are dissected to reveal their interiors. For interesting towns or town centres, street maps are provided, with the main sights marked and described.

INTRODUCING AUSTRIA

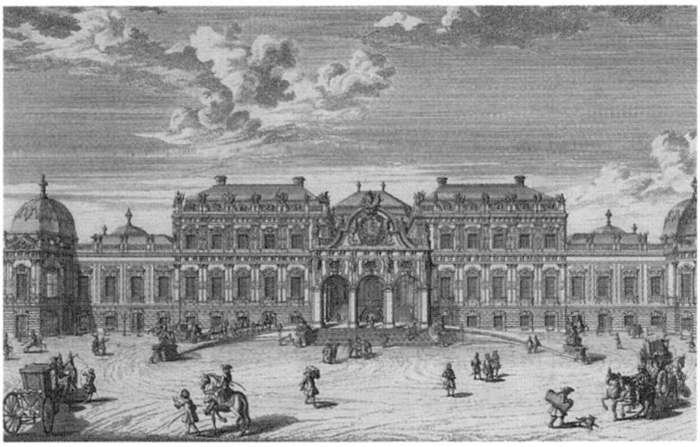

DISCOVERING AUSTRIA

Austria is a compact jewel at the heart of Europe. From the breathtaking Alpine scenery, enchanting forests and crystal clear lakes of the countryside to the cultural delights of the larger cities, there is something for every visitor. Outdoors enthusiasts will enjoy the spas, world-class winter sports, canoeing, mountain-biking and walking, and exploring the country's diverse flora and fauna. For lovers of museums, architecture, art and music, the pickings are richer still. Use these pages for an introduction to the things to see in each of the main regions.

Cherub statues at the Hofburg Palace, Vienna

VIENNA

- **Opulent palaces**
- **Gothic Stephansdom**
- **Elegant shopping on Kohlmarkt**
- **State Opera House**

Exploring Vienna's romantic cobbled streets, hidden courtyards, lavish churches and grand architecture is to take a fascinating journey through centuries of history. Marvel at the opulent splendour of the Habsburg Empire at the **Hofburg** *(see p240)*, **Belvedere** *(see pp98–9)* and **Schönbrunn** *(see pp110–11)* palaces. Another must-see is the city's beloved **Stephansdom** *(see pp58–9)*, a breathtaking Gothic cathedral at the heart of the Innere Stadt. To get a feel for Vienna's tragic past, visit the atmospheric **Jewish Quarter** and the Holocaust Memorial (see *pp60–61*). For shoppers, there are abundant opportunities along elegant **Kohlmarkt** *(see p64)*. People here also love to eat, so be sure to sample the delights on offer at the bustling **Naschmarkt** *(see p93)* or one of the city's legendary coffee houses. In the evening, join the Viennese in their love of music, art and other intellectual pursuits with a performance at the **State Opera House** or Musikverein *(see p96)*, home of the world-famous Vienna Philharmonic Orchestra.

Busy streets of Kohlmarkt, with its sophisticated stores

LOWER AUSTRIA AND BURGENLAND

- **Birdwatching at Seewinkel**
- **Spectacular Melk Abbey**
- **Romantic walking in the Wienerwald**

Although probably the least explored of the Austrian provinces, Lower Austria and Burgenland have much to offer. Take a stroll through the picturesque towns of **Rust** (*see p152*) and **Krems** (*see p138*) or the Baroque delights of **St Pölten** (*see pp132–3*) and enjoy a glass or two of the finest red wines produced in Austria. Unrivalled bird-watching opportunities abound in **Seewinkel National Park** *(see p153)* at Neusiedler See, Europe's largest steppe lake. Ride on the scenic Schneeberg Railway and Raxalpe cable car or enjoy a boat trip along the pretty stretch of the Danube known as the Wachau to see the stunning **Melk Abbey** *(see pp142–3)*. Follow in Beethoven's footsteps with a romantic stroll through the **Wienerwald** *(see pp136–7)* and perhaps relax at the spa and casino in **Baden bei Wien** *(see p136)*.

Rooftops of Graz's old town, a UNESCO World Heritage Site

STYRIA

- **World Heritage Site at Graz Altstadt**
- **Prestigious Styriarte and Autumn Festivals**

Known as the "province of variety", beautiful Styria is the place many Austrians choose to holiday in. With six nature reserves, one national park, five thermal spas, and around 800 mountain peaks above sea level, there's plenty to keep nature and sports lovers happy. Culture enthusiasts will enjoy Styria's capital city **Graz** *(see pp160–61)*, a UNESCO World Heritage Site, with one of the best-preserved *Altstadt* (old town) in Central Europe. Graz is also home to the **Styriarte** *(see p33)* **and Autumn Festivals** *(see p34)*.

◁ **Johannesbergkapelle, above Traunsee in Traunkirchen**

UPPER AUSTRIA

- **Cycling along the Danube**
- **Austria's oldest church – Martinskirshe**
- **Futuristic exhibits at Ars Electronica Center**

Upper Austria's pleasing backdrop of rich, undulating farmland, glacier-carved lakes, spectacular monasteries and chocolate-box towns make it worth a visit. Particularly beautiful is the **Danube Valley** *(see p194–5)*, where visitors can cycle along the banks of the river, admiring numerous historic sites. Despite its industrial appearance, the province's capital city, Linz, also has treats, including **Martinskirche** *(see p190)*, the oldest church in Austria, and the innovative **Ars Electronica Center** *(see p193)*, which houses some of the most futuristic technological wizardry in Europe.

Cascading Krimmler Wasserfälle, Salzburger Land

SALZBURGER LAND

- **Mozart's Salzburg**
- **Winter sports in Kaprun**
- **Natural beauty of Krimmler Wasserfälle**

Although Salzburger Land's most famous son is omnipresent, the region has more to offer than just Mozart. Nevertheless, a trip to the province would be incomplete without taking in **Salzburg** *(see pp214–23)*, the city of his birth. The **Salzburger Festival** *(see p221)* is also held there in summer. For year-round skiing and winter sports, head for the well-equipped resort of **Kaprun** *(see p232)*. For hikers, the long walk up the cascading **Krimmler Wasserfälle** *(see p233)* in Hohe Tauern National Park is a demanding, but extremely memorable experience.

Wintersport resort Going and the Wilder Kaiser mountains, Tyrol

TYROL AND VORARLBERG

- **Exclusive ski resorts**
- **Cable car ride at Ehrwald**
- **Rural charm of the Bregenzer Wald**

Craggy Alpine peaks and racing rivers characterize the landscape of this region. It has some of the best skiing in Austria and the Winter Olympics have twice been held in **Innsbruck** *(see p238–43)*, Tyrol's vibrant capital city. Close to the border with Germany, at **Ehrwald** *(see p253)*, take a ride in the terrifying, but magnificent cable car journey that scales the heights of Zugspitze. Walkers will enjoy the pristine **Bregenzer Wald** *(see pp258–9)*, with its many hiking trails and distinctive wooden architecture.

CARINTHIA AND EAST TYROL

- **Beautiful Hohe Tauern National Park**
- **Watersports at Wörther See**
- **Klagenfurt's Diözesanmuseum**

Proximity to Italy and long warm summers give this area a Mediterranean feel. Many Europeans are drawn by the mountain scenery and pristine lake resorts. One of the greatest attractions of the region is **Hohe Tauern National Park** *(see p278–8)* with its many indigenous species of flora and fauna, and breathtaking glaciers. Watersports enthusiasts will be kept busy around the shores of **Wörther See** *(see p276–7)*, Austria's warmest lake. **Klagenfurt** is home to Austria's oldest artifact at the **Diözesanmuseum** *(see p271)* – the 12th-century stained glass panel of Mary Magdalene. Nearby, **Villach** *(see p274)* and **Lienz** *(see p275)* offer plenty of interesting architecture and cultural attractions.

Bluethroat at Hohe Tauern National Park

Putting Austria on the Map

Located in the southeastern part of Central Europe, Austria covers an area of 83,858 sq km (32,378 sq miles), and spans five major geological formations: the Eastern Alps, the Alpine and Carpathian Foreland, the Pannonian Basin, the Vienna Valley and the Czech Massif. Its longest river is the Danube, which flows from west to east. Landlocked, Austria borders Germany, the Czech Republic, Slovakia, Hungary, Slovenia, Italy, Switzerland and Liechtenstein. It has over 8 million inhabitants, 1.7 million of whom live in Vienna.

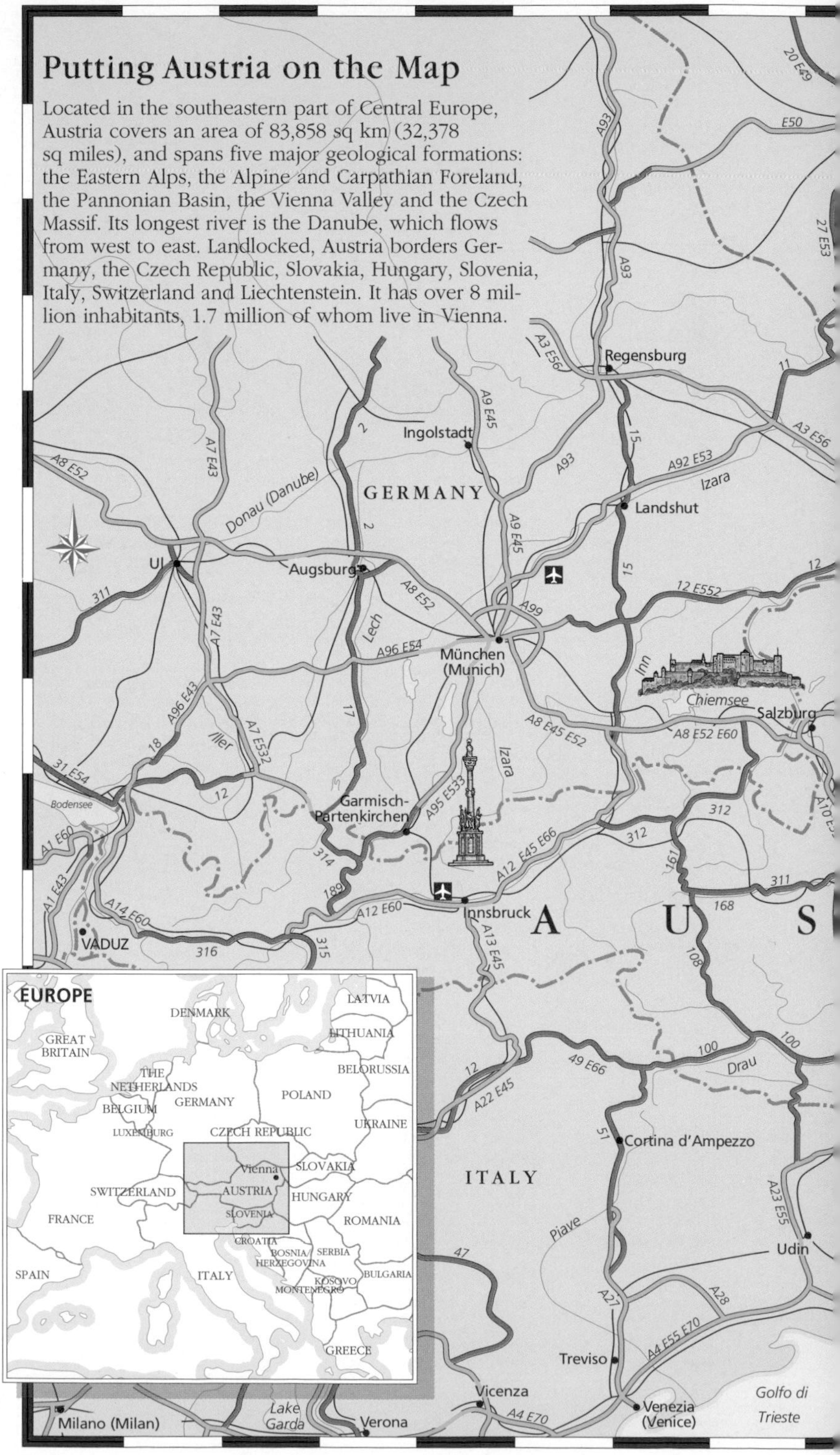

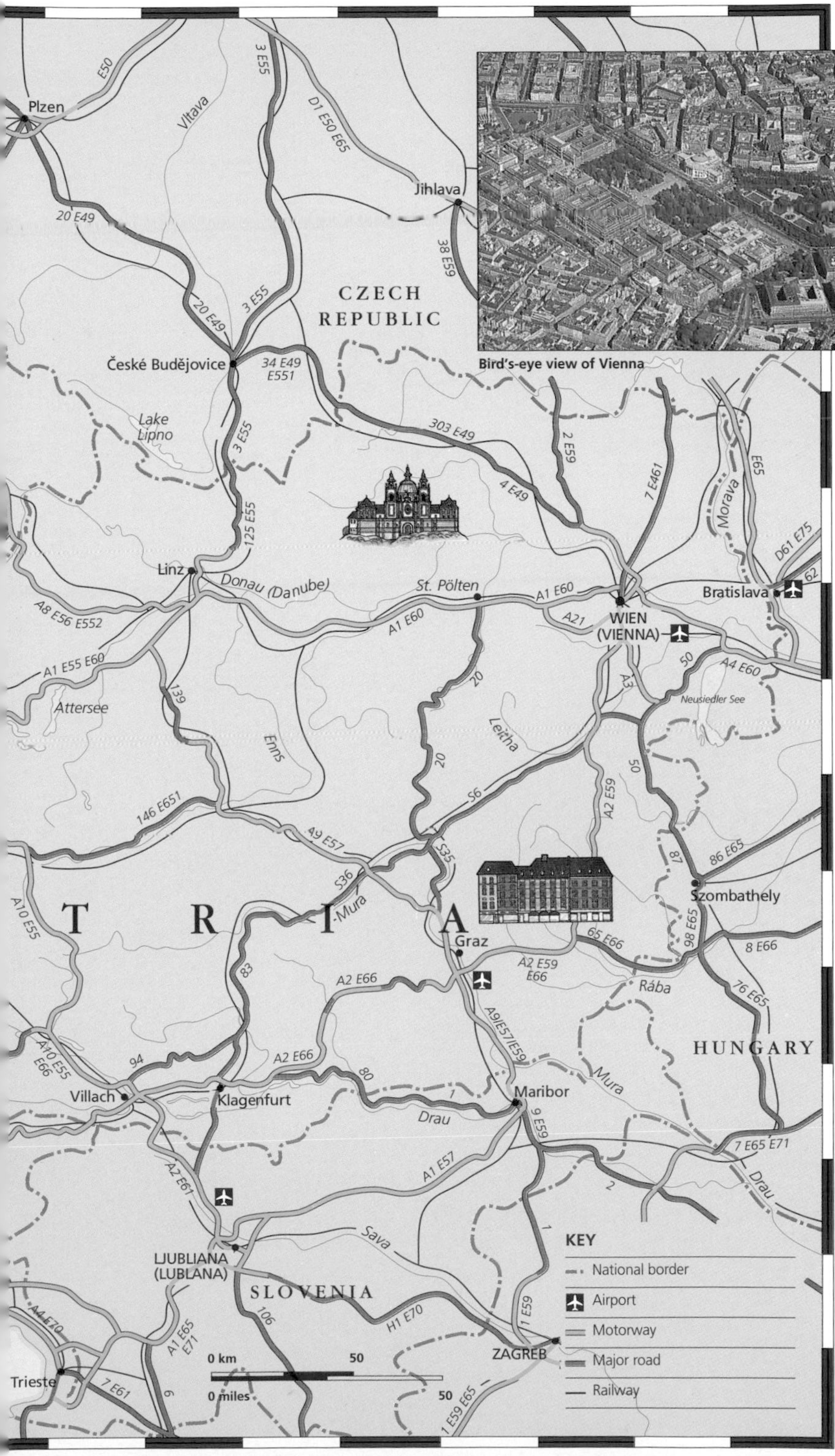
Bird's-eye view of Vienna
CZECH REPUBLIC
Plzen
Vltava
Jihlava
České Budějovice
Lake Lipno
Linz
Donau (Danube)
St. Pölten
WIEN (VIENNA)
Bratislava
Neusiedler See
Morava
Attersee
Enns
Leitha
Mura
T R I A
Graz
Szombathely
Rába
HUNGARY
Villach
Klagenfurt
Drau
Maribor
Sava
LJUBLIANA (LUBLANA)
SLOVENIA
ZAGREB
Trieste
0 km 50
0 miles 50
KEY
National border
Airport
Motorway
Major road
Railway

LX-HOT
CAMERA

A PORTRAIT OF AUSTRIA

Magnificent mountains span two-thirds of present-day Austria, gathering in a massif at the centre of the country. The breathtaking scenery of alpine peaks, lakes and enchanting valleys, together with excellent year-round facilities for a variety of sports, attracts many visitors. Innumerable cultural events and fascinating historical sights make every visit unforgettable.

Austrian eagle

Austria grew at a crossroads, when the main routes between northern Europe and Italy, and from western to eastern Europe, met at Vienna. The Habsburg kings and emperors, who ruled the country for almost seven centuries, pursued expansion via matrimonial alliances rather than sending troops into battle. Although not entirely without bloodshed, they managed to incorporate several provinces into Central Austria through a series of arranged marriages, beginning with the duchy of Tyrol, followed by the powerful Czech kingdom, the equally strong Hungary and a sizeable chunk of Italy. Austrian culture, while traditionally linked with that of Germany, also absorbed many Roman, Slav and Hungarian influences, thus creating its own unique combinations. As well as producing many outstanding artists and composers, such as Mozart, it also offered foreign artists the opportunity to further their talents.

Present-day Austria is a federal state, consisting of nine provinces *(Bundesländer)*. The head of state is the president, elected for a term of six years; the most important political figure is the head of the federal government, or Chancellor (as in Germany). Austria's legislative power rests with a two-chamber parliament. Parliamentary elections are held

View over the Hohe Tauern mountain range, from Heiligenblut in Carinthia

◁ The annual hot-air balloon festival held in Stubenberg, Styria, in mid-September

Europabrücke, connecting northern and southern Europe

every four years, when votes are cast for the candidates put up by the political parties. The present Austrian parliament includes representatives of five political parties: the Social Democratic Party of Austria (SPÖ), the Christian-Democratic Austrian People's Party (ÖVP), the Freedom Party of Austria (FPÖ), the Alliance for the Future of Austria (BZÖ) and a political alliance of various groups known as the Greens (die Grünen).

For modern-day Austrians, the might of their former empire is only a distant memory, yet their country continues to play an important role in international politics. Since 1955, when the Austrian State Treaty was signed and the country found itself at the centre between two worlds – Western capitalism and Soviet communism – it has often acted as an intermediary. Vienna has served as the venue for important summits, and is home to many UN agencies and international organizations, including the United Nations Industrial Development Organization (UNIDO), the International Atomic Energy Agency (IAEA) and the Organization of Petroleum Exporting Countries (OPEC) Central Office. A member of the European Union, Austria does not belong to NATO. The 1955 Treaty pledges neutrality for all time, and despite external and internal pressures, Austria retains this.

AT THE HEART OF EUROPE

Roads once trodden by foreign armies are today packed with sun-seeking tourists from the north. Travelling through Vienna and the Semmering Pass, they cross the Alps at the Brenner Pass, where the huge Europabrücke (European Bridge), a vast viaduct, connects northern Europe with the warm south. The heavy transit traffic constitutes a major problem for Austria, where great emphasis is placed on protecting the natural environment. Protest action by local ecology groups stopped the building of a nuclear power station in Zwentendorf and later prevented the destruction of the unique flora around Hainburg, the intended site for a hydroelectric power plant. The ecology movement gave rise to the Green Federation, which is winning ever more seats in Parliament. It is perhaps thanks to its activities that Austria remains a natural paradise for its many visitors.

TOURISM

Tourism revenue accounts for nearly half of Austria's GDP. The country has much to offer: winter sports on snow-covered slopes, or year-round on the glaciers, and beautiful mountains and lakes in summer all

Thermal pool in Lutzmannsburg

The Alpincenter ski station below Kitzsteinhorn Mountain in the Salzburger Land

attract large numbers of visitors. The impressive infrastructure offers superb conditions for rest and recreation. Nearly every resort boasts funicular railways and cable cars, chair and drag lifts, magnificent pistes and toboggan runs, outdoor and indoor swimming pools, well maintained river banks and lakes. There are plenty of places for eating, and overnight accommodation ranges from small pensions and private homes to luxury hotels, all guaranteeing a very pleasant visit.

A traditional horse-drawn carriage

The regional authorities take care to ensure that entertainments are not limited to large resorts, and organize sports events and art exhibitions, theatre and music festivals, as well as festivities devoted to individual towns, streets or even squares. Visitors may enjoy the traditional religious festivities, and the Giant Chocolate Festival in Bludenz and the Dumpling Festival in St Johann will prove memorable. Many restaurants organize special weeks when regional cooking or local game dishes feature on the menu. Although events are often local, Austria is also a venue for acclaimed international festivals, such as the famous music and theatre festivals in Salzburg and Bregenz, the Wiener Festwochen and the Viennale.

A typical alpine pension in Kartitsch, East Tyrol

LANGUAGE AND RELIGION

Modern Austria is virtually a one-nation state, but there are some Slovenians in Carinthia, Croatians in Burgenland, and Czech and Hungarian minorities in Vienna. Austria became a haven for refugees fleeing from the former Yugoslavia in the 1990s, as well as for people from other regions of the Balkan peninsula, and for Turks coming in search of work. Around 95 per cent of the country's population speaks German,

The annual church festival in Villach in Carinthia, a weekend of folk music and parades

although not every German speaker will find it easy to communicate with every Austrian. While the Vienna Burgtheater is regarded as one of the foremost German-language theatres in the world, many Austrians speak a pronounced local dialect. When travelling, the visitor needs to remember that many things have different names here than in Germany. A bread roll, for instance, is called a *Semmel* instead of a *Brötchen*, a tomato is a *Paradeiser* and not a *Tomate*, and the hospital is the *Spital*, rather than a *Krankenhaus*.

Austria is traditionally a Roman Catholic country, and some 80 per cent of its inhabitants today belong to the Roman Catholic church.

The hyper-modern Millennium Tower in Vienna

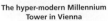

CULTURE

Austrian culture has reached acclaim and importance far beyond its borders. *The Good Soldier Schweik*, by the Czech writer Jaroslav Hašek, is a bawdy satire about the Habsburg monarchy. The Austrian film directors Ernst Lubitsch, Billy Wilder and Fred Zinneman played an important role in the creation of Hollywood shortly before and immediately after World War II. Today, the best-known Austrian is probably Arnold Schwarzenegger, star of action movies, governor of California and, by marriage, a member of the Kennedy clan. His fame is unmatched even by winter sports champions, who are so popular in Austria. Another prominent Austrian actor is Klaus-Maria Brandauer, who played Mephistopheles in Isztvan Szabo's film of the same name. The late Romy Schneider, revered star of French cinema, was also Austrian and won fame as the unhappy Empress Elisabeth, in the Austrian film *Sissi*.

Austria has also produced many Nobel Prize winners. Perhaps the most famous among them is Konrad Lorenz, a researcher into animal and human behaviour, who was awarded the Nobel Prize for Medicine in 1973. The work of Sigmund Freud, the Viennese psychiatrist who became the founding father of psychoanalysis, has heavily influenced modern psychology, as well as other domains of science and culture.

TRADITIONS

Austria is one of the most modern and efficiently run countries in Europe. However, while admiring the stunning landscapes or strolling along the streets of the impeccably tidy towns and villages, visitors may get the impression that time has stood still here, feeling immersed in the past, a bygone age of the Habsburg empire when

The traditional parade of Tyrolean hunters in Götzens

the benevolent Franz Joseph I was the guardian of stability and justice, and his unhappy wife Sissi fulfilled the public craving for romance.

The Austrians are very fond of their traditions. The most popular newspaper is the arch-conservative *Neue Kronen Zeitung*, which has offices in almost every federal province, while the highly respectable Viennese daily *Die Presse* represents the solid opinions of the Austrian centre. *Der Standard* is the leading liberal newspaper.

Child in folk costume

In Austria, as perhaps nowhere else in Europe, the *Tracht*, or traditional folk costume, is accepted as formal wear. The costumes, made of high-quality wool and natural linen, can be worn anywhere, even to an elegant ball at the Viennese Opera. An entire branch of the textile industry is devoted to their design and manufacture. Men wear green loden jackets and *Lederhosen* (leather breeches), the women *Dirndl* dresses.

Another Austrian speciality is the *Heurige*, wine taverns serving the year's new-vintage wines. Mostly found in and around Vienna, these taverns were originally attached to vineyards whose owners had a licence to sell beverages but not food. Secretly, though, they also offered home-produced meats, especially when a pig had been slaughtered. Today, they serve grilled pork knuckles – delicious, but very filling – as well as roast hams, grilled ribs and other specialities. As of old, the wine is brought to the tables by waiters who also take payment; the food is available from self-service buffet counters. The *Heurige* are characterized by a uniquely sociable ambience, with all the guests joining in the merriment. Many a dedicated beer-drinker has become a devotee of young wine at a *Heuriger* evening.

One of the many wine taverns *(Heurige)* around Vienna

The Formation of the Alps

About 70 million years ago, during the Cretaceous period, the African plate and the Adriatic microplate both began to move north. The Alpine range was thrown up when the latter collided with the European plate. The Tethys Sea that lay between them was almost entirely obliterated, and sediment deposited at its bottom over millions of years was carried far to the north, and tossed as vast nappes over the rigid block of indigenous rocks of the Central Alps. The formation of the present Alps ended in the Miocene period, some two million years ago, and subsequent erosion gave them their final shape.

The Krimmler Falls *in the Hohe Tauern National Park are the highest waterfalls in the Alps and the fifth highest in the world, dropping almost 400 m (1,312 ft).*

The Northern Limestone Alps *are formed of soft carbonate rock. The mountains, such as the Dachstein Group (2,995 m/9,826 ft), have characteristically steep slopes, yet their summits are rounded domes rather than sharp peaks.*

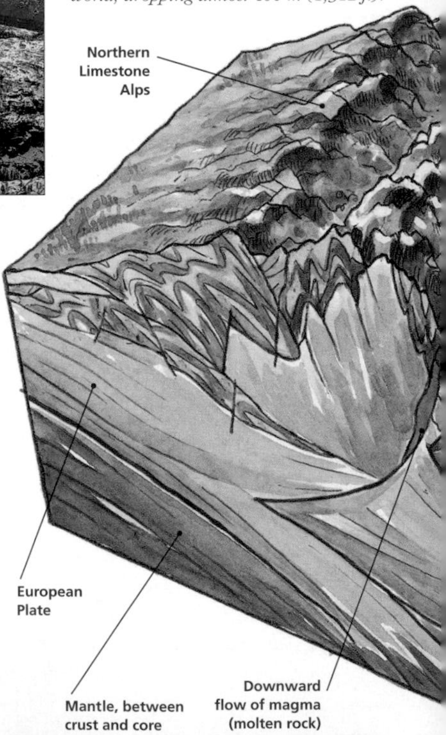

The central part of the Austrian Alps *consists of hard crystalline rock (gneiss, shale). The oldest and the hardest among them form the steep fells of the Hohe Tauern.*

The Alps *possess the right conditions for the formation of glaciers. Largest in the Eastern Alps is the Pasterze; together with 40 others it forms a thick mantle on the Grossglockner massif, covering 40 sq km (15 sq miles).*

The end of the Ice Age *marked the beginning of a new type of erosion. The Northern Limestone Alps have Europe's largest cave systems and underground streams, typical features in limestone regions.*

MOUNTAIN SCENERY

The current shape of the Alps was created during the Ice Age (between 600,000 and 10,000 years ago). It is characterized by distinctive post-glacial cirques, suspended valleys, moraines, thaw lakes and vast U-shaped valleys filled with material carried down the mountains.

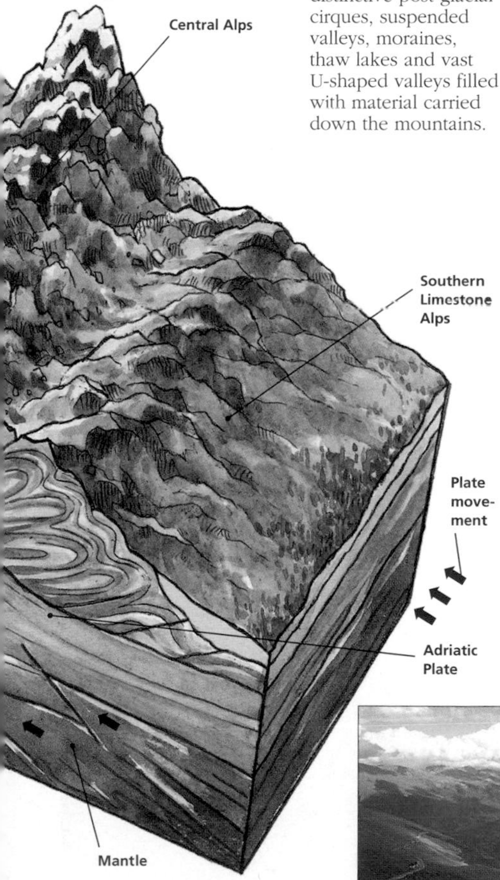

THE AUSTRIAN ALPS

The Austrian Alps lie in the European Alpides range, which rose between 70 million and two million years ago. In geological terms they form an entity known as the Eastern Alps. They occupy an area about 500 km (310 miles) long and 150 km (95 miles) wide. One of Europe's most fascinating regions, the Austrian Alps enchant visitors with their beautiful high peaks and the unique idyllic atmosphere in the mountain villages and small towns that nestle in vast, cultivated valleys. The most valuable ecological areas have been made into National Parks, including the Hohe Tauern – the largest in the Alps and one of the largest in Europe, featuring Austria's highest mountain range with some 300 peaks of over 3,000 m (9,800 ft) in height. In summer, the Alps are a magnificent area to explore on foot or bike, while in winter they provide an excellent base for winter sports.

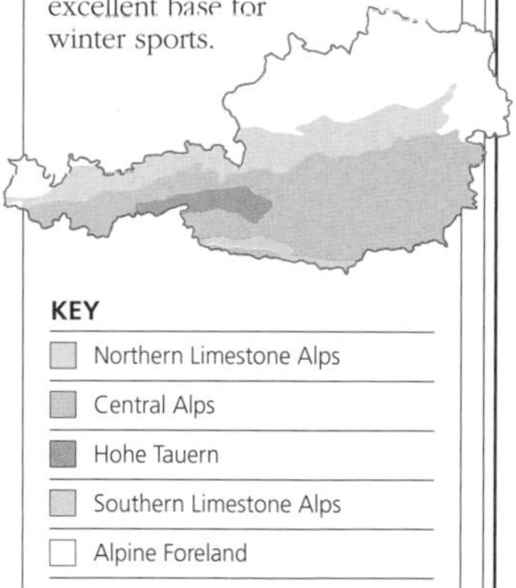

The majority of alpine lakes *have been created by retreating glaciers. Some of the most beautiful can be found in the Salzkammergut region, in the Northern Limestone Alps.*

The Landscape of Austria

Austria has a highly diverse landscape because of its location at the junction of four regions. The north of the country is part of the Central European natural region, originally dominated by deciduous and mixed forests, while the southern part belongs to the Alpine region. The southeast lies in the Illyrian region, which benefits from a Mediterranean climate, resulting in a rich flora and fauna including edible chestnuts and rare species of lizards and snakes. The northeastern part of the country belongs to the Pontian-Pannonian region, with surviving species of steppe flora and characteristic fauna including the suslik (a ground squirrel), hamster and great bustard.

The alpine belt stretches from the zone of the mountain pine up to the ice and snow fields. At altitudes of 2,500–3,200 m (8,200–10,500 ft), snow is present all year (this snow-line is called the "nival belt").

The transition zone between forests and alpine grassland is covered in scrub (dwarf mountain pine, rhododendron and alder). Here, the growing season lasts only 70–100 days.

Alpine high mountain grasslands *and low meadows include a wide variety of species and plant communities. Mountain arnica (in the foreground) avoids limestone soils; it is a highly regarded medicinal plant.*

In gulleys and hollows, in valleys and along the banks of the streams, Austrian flora is at its most magnificent.

Traditional grazing in the forest belt has preserved the natural fauna and flora of the alpine meadows and pastures.

MOUNTAINSCAPES

Climate and flora change with altitude, as is typical of mountain environments. The lower regions are covered with mixed forests (including beech). The upper parts have coniferous trees (Arolla pine, spruce and larch) up to about 1,800 m (5,900 ft) – above which are brush thickets and colourful alpine meadows.

Humid, *cool valleys are the perfect habitat to encourage the growth of herbaceous plants.*

Lakes *situated at higher altitudes are poor in nutrients and hence their surrounding flora and fauna are extremely sparse.*

AUSTRIAN FAUNA

Austrian fauna is typical of Central Europe. Along with invertebrates (primarily insects: beetles and butterflies), it features a rich avifauna, small numbers of amphibians (newts, salamanders, fire-bellied toads and frogs) and reptiles (Aesculapian snake, grass snake, lizards), and mammals, including rodents, marten, fox, weasel and hoofed animals. Mountain animals – insects, rodents (marmots) and deer (red deer, chamois) – are particularly fascinating.

The marmot, *a rodent, burrows deep into mountain meadows and alpine pastures. When disturbed, it emits a high-pitched whistle.*

Chamois *are ideally adapted for moving over steep rocks.*

Red deer (above) *live in the deciduous and mixed forests in the high mountains. They have a fawn-coloured coat. The male sheds its antlers in spring.*

The Alpine ibex (right, a female) *came close to extinction towards the end of the 20th century, but is now being successfully reintroduced.*

AUSTRIAN FLORA

Some 60 per cent of Austria's territory is mountainous, which determines the country's key flora. Forests occupy as much as 39 per cent of the country's entire area, occurring mainly in the Alps and in the Czech Massif. Many areas of special environmental interest enjoy some form of legal protection as nature reserves, nature monuments and national parks. One of the first was the Hohe Tauern National Park.

The Arolla pine (Pinus cembra), *along with the larch, forms large tree populations in the upper forest regions.*

Swiss Rock Jasmin (Androsace helvetica) *and its rounded clusters are typical on limestone soil.*

Bitterwort (Gentiana lutea) *is common in meadows, clusters of herbaceous plants and forest verges. Bitterwort liqueur has long been used in folk medicine.*

The Music of Austria

Austria was – and remains to this day – a world-renowned centre for music. Musical life in present-day Austria has typically been closely linked with that of Germany, as well as the Habsburg Empire. Composers belonging to the old Viennese school contributed to the emergence of the Viennese Classical style, with Joseph Haydn, Wolfgang Amadeus Mozart and the German composer, Ludwig van Beethoven, its main proponents. Their work guided 19th-century composers such as Franz Schubert, Johann Strauss, Anton Bruckner, Hugo Wolf and Gustav Mahler.

Franz Schubert, *one of the earliest exponents of the Romantic style, is best-known for his* Lieder, *or songs. He also composed piano music, chamber music and symphonies.*

Arnold Schönberg, *together with his students, Alban Berg and Anton Webern, developed the Viennese dodecaphonic school after 1918. His best-known work is the sextet* Verklärte Nacht.

Joseph Haydn, *one of the Viennese Classicists, was a court composer to Count Esterházy. In 1790, he moved to Vienna. His works include over 100 symphonies, 83 string quartets, 52 piano sonatas, 14 masses and many other compositions.*

Wolfgang Amadeus Mozart

Mozart's sister, Maria Anna, known as Nannerl

WOLFGANG AMADEUS MOZART, a child prodigy, had the gift of perfect pitch and an unrivalled memory. He achieved musical perfection with his symphonies, operas *(The Marriage of Figaro, Don Giovanni, The Magic Flute)*, and his masses including the unfinished *Requiem*, which is shrouded in mystery.

TIMELINE

1700 – 1725 – 1750 – 1775 – 1800 – 1825 – 1850

- **1715–77** Georg Christoph Wagenseil
- **1732–1809** Joseph Haydn
- **1739–99** Karl Ditters von Dittersdorf
- **1756–91** Wolfgang Amadeus Mozart
- **1791–1857** Carl Czerny
- **1797–1828** Franz Schubert
- **1801–43** Joseph Lanner
- **1804–49** Johann Strauss (father)
- **1819–95** Franz von Suppé
- **1824–96** Anton Bruckner
- **1825–99** Johann Strauss (son)
- **1852–95** Joseph Schrammel
- **1860–1903** Hugo Wolf
- **1860–1911** Gustav Mahler

Wolfgang Amadeus Mozart

Joseph Haydn

Johann Strauss (son) *has been proclaimed the king of the waltz, thanks to his compositions including* The Blue Danube *and* Tales from the Vienna Woods.

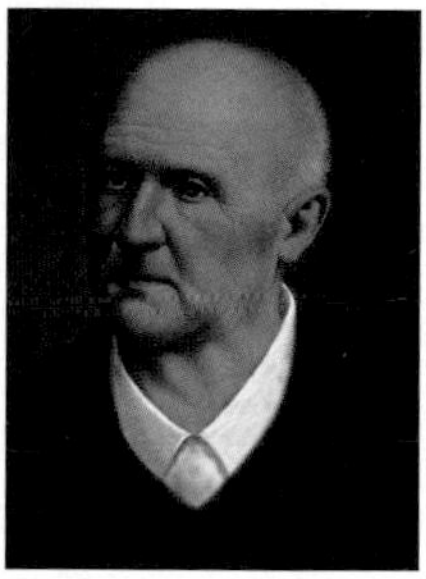

Anton Bruckner *is probably best known for his nine symphonies but he also wrote church music, in particular choral works.*

Gustav Mahler *started his career as a conductor and only in later years devoted himself to composing music. His most important work is the cycle of ten monumental symphonies.*

FOREIGN MUSICIANS IN AUSTRIA

Vienna, an important cultural centre on the European map, has always attracted musicians and composers from other countries. The Renaissance brought Flemish artists, the Baroque period attracted Italians. Vienna was home to Christoph Gluck, Ludwig van Beethoven, Johannes Brahms and others. The main exponent of the New Viennese operetta was the Hungarian, Franz Lehár.

Johannes Brahms *(1833–97), German composer, outstanding creator of traditional symphonies, piano and chamber music, was unsympathetic towards progressive trends.*

Ludwig van Beethoven *(1770–1827), German composer and one of the Viennese Classicists, battled from 1798 with his progressive deafness. His best-known work is perhaps the Ninth Symphony, with the Ode to Joy in its finale.*

1874–1951 Arnold Schönberg

1900–1991 Ernst Křenek

1926 b. Friedrich Cerha

1935 b. Kurt Schwertsik

1941 b. Dieter Kaufmann

1956 b. Herbert Willi

1971 b. Michael Huber

2006 Mozart Year

2009 Haydn Year

1875 | 1900 | 1925 | 1950 | 1975 | 2000 | 2025

1874–1949 Edmund Eysler

1885–1935 Alban Berg

1883–1945 Anton von Webern

Edmund Eysler

1943 b. Heinz Karl Gruber

1960 b. Karlheinz Essl

1971 b. Bernhard Gál

1998 Arnold Schönberg Center opened in Vienna

The Architecture of Austria

Since the Middle Ages, Austria has been at the forefront in the development of architecture. Particularly typical of the Austrian architectural landscape are the vast abbeys built in medieval times and modernized during the late Baroque period, as well as the multi-storey town palaces and large country residences built for the aristocracy in the 17th and 18th centuries. The late 1800s and early 1900s marked the birth of modern town architecture, with public buildings such as theatres, banks and government offices. These and other buildings displayed typical Habsburg-era features – monumentality and a distinctly ornamental character.

Cupolas crowned with openwork lanterns, inspired by Renaissance domes in Italy.

Pediment with an early-Renaissance statue of Christ blessing the people.

Windows with grab-frames, typical of the early Baroque period.

Statues of saints by Michael Bernhard Mandel

Heiligenkreuz Abbey (see p136) *was built in the 12th to 13th centuries, but only the Romanesque church remains from that period. The abbey itself is a magnificent Baroque structure erected in the 17th century. The courtyard has an imposing St Mary's column.*

Schwaz church, *dating from the 15th century* (see p245), *with its opulent star vaulting resting on slender columns, and its interior illuminated by vast windows, typifies the lightness of Baroque architecture.*

The decorative railings *of the famous staircase at Mirabell Palace in Salzburg* (see p215) *are the masterpiece of architect Johann Lukas von Hildebrandt and sculptor Georg Raphael Donner.*

The octagonal layout of the top storey of the tower is a typical feature of the Lombardy style.
Statues of Moses and Elijah
Oval tower windows serve to amplify the sound of the bells.
Vast clock faces

The Vienna State Opera House *(see p92)*, conceived by August von Siccardsburg and Eduard van der Nüll, was completed in 1869. Its façade and interior, particularly the auditorium, the foyer and the grand staircase, are examples of the opulence, ornamentation and pomposity typical of 19th-century Austrian architecture.

Melk *is one of the most famous Benedictine abbeys and the largest surviving abbey complex in Europe. The spectacular Baroque abbey was designed by J. Prandtauer* (see pp142–3).

SALZBURG DOMKIRCHE

The cathedral, begun in 1614 to a design by Santino Solari and finished in 1657, is one of the earliest twin-towered churches of the modern era found anywhere north of the Alps. It is also the earliest and most magnificent example of the Early Baroque style in the entire Danube region *(see p220)*.

FRIEDENSREICH HUNDERTWASSER

The Rogner Bad Blumau resort complex *(see p170)*

A painter, graphic designer and architect with the real name of Friedrich Stowasser, Hundertwasser (1928–2000) was an organizer of provocative "happenings". His decorative style of painting was close to that of abstract artists, with subject matter often associated with the natural environment. His buildings *(see pp104–5)* are distinguished by their highly experimental, extravagant shapes, combining colourful new architectural ideas with the artist's vision of structures that blend with the natural environment. Irregular in shape, they employ a variety of unusual materials, including ceramics.

Austrian Art

Austrian painting, like the country's literature, cannot be considered in isolation from artistic movements in neighbouring countries. Art in Austria developed in close relationship with German art, but it was also influenced by the Italian, Hungarian and Czech cultures. Over many centuries, the imperial court in Vienna acted as a strong magnet for artists from all over Europe. In the 19th century, the artists of the Viennese Secession produced outstanding works of art. Some of Austria's painters have gained international acclaim, but it is well worth becoming acquainted with its lesser artists, too.

***The Entombment*, Albrecht Altdorfer**

MEDIEVAL

The earliest examples of pictorial art in Austria include illuminations and wall paintings. The late 8th-century *Codex Millenarius Maior*, kept in Kremsmünster Abbey, is regarded as the oldest illuminated manuscript. The Austrian art of illumination flourished during the 11th and 12th centuries, particularly thanks to the Salzburg monastery scriptoria, which, among other works, produced the famous Admont Bible (c1130–40).

The oldest wall paintings in Austria, dating from the first half of the 11th century, are found in the Church of St Ulrich in Wieselburg. The Benedictine Abbey church in Lambach has original wall paintings of Old Testament scenes, created in the last quarter of the 11th century. Paintings dating from the 12th century can be seen in St John's Chapel in Pürgg, the Benedictine abbey church in Nonnberg and in the castle chapel of Burg Ottenstein, near Zwettl.

From the 14th century, panel painting flourished, particularly in Vienna under Rudolph IV. The 15th century is notable for the works of Jakob Kaschauer and Thomas Artula von Villach. At the turn of the 16th century, Austrian painting was influenced by Italian *Quattrocento* art, especially the works of Michael Pacher and his students. The Danube School, influential in the early 1500s, was represented by Wolf Huber and Albrecht Altdorfer of Regensburg, who painted the altar in the abbey of St Florian, near Linz.

RENAISSANCE

The Renaissance style entered Austrian painting around 1530. Interesting wall paintings, created soon after that date, include the secular decoration of the Knights' Room in Goldegg Castle near St Johann (1536), and the paintings devoted to Reformation themes in Pölling Church, near Wolfsberg. Hans Bocksberger, one of the most outstanding Renaissance artists, decorated Freisall Castle and the castle chapel in Burg Strechau. Until the 16th century, Austrian painting was strongly influenced by Italian artists such as Giulio Licinio, Teodoro Ghisi and Martino Rota, who worked at the court in Graz, and Donato Arsenio Mascagni in Salzburg. Local artists, such as Anton Blumenthal, whose paintings adorn the presbytery of Gurk Cathedral, and Jakob Seisenegger, a portrait-painter, were also influenced by Italian art.

BAROQUE

In the 17th century, Italian art continued to influence Austrian painting. One of the most important painters of the Baroque period was Pietro de Pomis.

The Austrian victory in the Battle of Vienna in 1683 was a historic event that proved very influential in the development of art. It brought about political and economic stability and with it many new artistic initiatives. The capital, Vienna, began to attract foreign artists, such as Andrea Pozzo, the Italian master of illusionist painting. Vast interior compositions were created to complement the magnificent architectural works by Johann Bernhard Fischer von Erlach and Johann Lukas von Hildebrandt. This particular style of fresco painting flourished thanks to artists such as Johann Michael Rottmayr, Martino Altomonte and, in

***The Holy Family with St Joachim and St Anna*, F.A. Maulbertsch**

the following generation, Paul Troger, Daniel Gran and Bartolomeo Altomonte. Great portrait-painters of the 18th-century included Johann Kupetzky, Martin van Meytens and Johann B. Lampi.

A prominent representative of late Baroque painting, Franz Anton Maulbertsch created frescoes as well as numerous works on religious and secular themes. The last great artist of the Baroque era was Martin Johann Schmidt, who produced magnificent wall paintings, for example for Melk Abbey.

***Portrait of Hanna Klinkosch*, Hans Makart**

19TH-CENTURY

The most important Neo Classical painters in Austria were Heinrich Friedrich Füger and Joseph Anton Koch. In 1809, the Brotherhood of St Luke was formed at the Vienna Academy of Fine Arts. Its members, the Nazarenes, mostly German painters, including Julius Schnorr von Carolsfeld, and only a few Austrians, set out to revise religious art.

An important figure during the Biedermeier and Realism periods in Austria was Ferdinand Georg Waldmüller, creator of small-scale genre paintings. The most outstanding academic painter was undoubtedly Hans Makart, who created vast compositions on allegorical or historic themes, as well as brilliant portraits. In the town of Szolnok, in today's Hungary, an artists' colony was established by a group of landscape painters inspired by the French Barbizon School.

***Time of the Rose Blossom*, F.G. Waldmüller**

Probably the best-known of all Austrian painters was Gustav Klimt, the founding member and main representative of the Vienna Secession. He used gold in his paintings and embellished them with striking "mosaics". The subject matter was often allegorical, infused with a subtle eroticism.

MODERN

Expressionism played a major role in early 20th-century Austrian art. The foremost artists associated with this movement included Egon Schiele, Richard Gerstl and Oskar Kokoschka, and, in Upper Austria, Alfred Kubin. An important figure of the 1930s and the period following World War II was Herbert Boeckl. A versatile artist – he also produced wall paintings – Boeckl drew his inspiration from fantasy realism, popular in post-war Vienna. Ernst Fuchs, Anton Lehmden and Wolfgang Hutter were members of the Vienna School of Fantastic Realism, which was inspired by surrealism. Abstract art was represented by Max Weiler and Josef Mikl. An unusual late 20th-century figure who escapes easy classification was Friedensreich Hundertwasser, who became famous with his architectural project of unusual buildings erected in and around Vienna.

The artists of Viennese Actionism achieved considerable notoriety in the 1960s. "Happenings" organized by the group revolved around the use of the body as a sculptural medium. Their fascination with self-mutilation and sado masochism culminated in the death of one of the group's members, Rudolf Schwarzkogler.

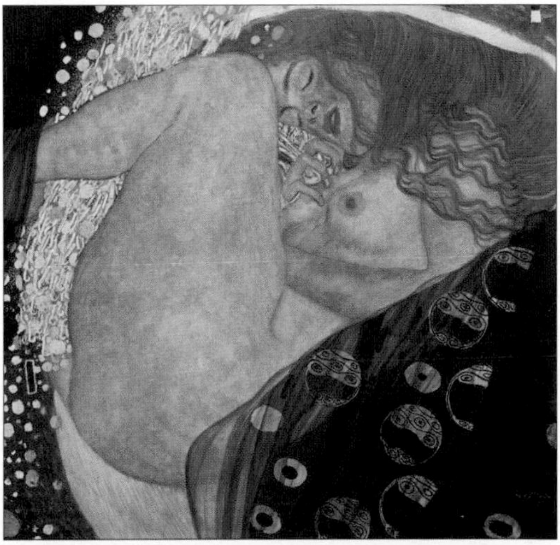

Gustav Klimt's *Danae* (1907/08), one of his famous erotic paintings

Sport in Austria

Austria is one of the most sports-loving nations in Europe, a fact reflected in the great popularity of recreational sports as well as in the country's success in international competitions – relative to its small population, the number of European and world champions, as well as Olympic medallists, in Austria is very high.

Some three million people – members of 27,500 sports clubs – participate actively in various sports and sports contests. The most popular and widely pursued sport is downhill skiing, followed by soccer, nordic (or cross-country) skiing, tennis, swimming, golf, cycling and windsurfing. New sports, such as snowboarding, are also becoming more popular.

ALPINE SKIING

Alpine or downhill skiing has been the number one national sport in Austria for over 100 years. Matthias Zdarsky (1856–1940) wrote the first handbook of skiing in 1897, invented the first ski bindings worthy of mention, and organized, in 1905, the first slalom race.

The Winter Olympics have twice been held in Innsbruck (1964 and 1976), and European and world championships are hosted by other resorts. The best-known venues for downhill skiing contests are Arlberg in Tyrol, St. Anton (which hosts the Alpine World Championships), Kitzbühel and St. Christoph, with its Ski Academy, the training centre for ski instructors. The international Hahnenkamm races in Kitzbühel are famous the world over. In January, the spectacular World Cup Men's Downhill and Slalom race takes place here; past Austrian champions have included Toni Sailer, Franz Klammer and Hermann Maier.

Austria's eight glacial regions permit year-round skiing. Most popular are the glaciers situated above Kaprun and Stubai.

Up-to-date information on snow cover and the running of some 3,500 ski lifts and cable cars is available from the Alpine Association's website at www.alpenverein.at (in German only).

Hermann Maier on his final slalom run, in Hinterstoder

NORDIC SKIING

It is no coincidence that, in 1999, the World Championships in nordic or cross-country skiing events were held in Styria, in the beautiful town of Ramsau. The local glacier, Dachstein, is a popular year-round training ground for cross-country runners from around the world. Even the national teams of Finland and Norway practise here in summer, polishing up their techniques and developing stamina dressed only in their swimwear – or less: famously, nude cross-country skiing is permitted in this resort.

Two of the prestigious Four Hills ski jump tournaments take place in Innsbruck and Bischofshofen. The event, straddling the last week of December and the first week in January, sees the final event in Bischofshofen.

Record-breaking ski jumper Andreas Goldberg

TOBOGGANING

Tobogganing is another winter sport at which Austria excels on the international stage; worldwide, only Germany and Italy achieve comparable results. Over the last decades, Austrian competitors have won several medals in this discipline at the Olympic Games, as well as various World Championships and World Cup events in all age categories.

The reason for this great Olympic and international success is the widespread popularity of the sport in Austria. Competitors train in some 310 tobogganing clubs and associations, represented in all provinces, with the exception of Burgenland.

Johann Wolfmayr and team in the World Championship in pair driving

SOCCER

The days when Austria ranked as one of the world's great soccer nations, in the 1920s and 1930s, are now buried deep in the past, along with the names of its former stars, including Matthias Sindelar, Toni Polster and Hans Krankl. Yet, although the national team did not qualify for the World Cup 2010 in South Africa, soccer remains the second most popular spectator and participation sport in Austria after skiing.

The present star of the national squad is the midfielder Andreas Herzog, who plays for Rapid Wien. As in other countries, many football players are "bought" in from other countries to play in Austrian football clubs, while the best Austrian players join clubs in other countries. Many play in the German Bundesliga, with just a few going to Italy or Spain.

As the Austrian clubs have little success in international competitions, most of the spectators prefer to watch the matches of the Austrian league. The most famous football stadiums are the Ernst-Happel-Stadion and the Hanappi-Stadion, both in Vienna. The First Division consists of ten soccer teams, including two from Vienna and two from Graz, but other teams are ready to take on the challenge.

Roman Mählich of Sturm Graz, playing against Bayer Leverkusen

HORSE RIDING

The first sports riding club in Austria, the Campagnereiter-Gesellschaft, founded in 1872, had the Emperor Franz Joseph I, himself a keen rider, as a patron. It consisted mainly of military personnel, and is now considered to be the predecessor of the Bundesfachverband für Reiten und Fahren (Federal League for Riding and Driving), established as recently as 1962.

Austrian riders have achieved many international successes. One of its legends is the pre-war master of horse dressage, Alois Podhajsk. The greatest character among Austrian riders in the 1980s and 1990s was showjumping champion, Hugo Simon. In the 1980s, Austrian competitors began to achieve considerable success in harness racing, involving one- and two-horse carts.

Rodeos – known as *Westernreiten* (wild west riding) – have been introduced from America, and are very popular across the country.

CANOEING AND MOUNTAIN BIKING

With its many rivers and lakes and its superb mountain scenery, Austria boasts the perfect natural conditions, as well as a well-developed infrastructure, for both these disciplines (though this does not always translate into international medals). The huge popularity of summer mountain sports among Austrians and visitors is nevertheless very noticeable. Mountain canoeing is practised on turbulent mountain streams.

Mountain biking is well-liked throughout Austria: the 2012 World Championships will be held in Saalfelden.

Helmut Oblinger competing in the individual slalom in Sydney

AUSTRIA THROUGH THE YEAR

Austria is a conservative country and Austrians value their traditions highly. In many regions the population maintains such ancient customs as the rites of spring and ritual re-enactments of death and resurrection, as well as various festivals associated with the grape harvest. Carnival festivities and parades are also big crowd-pullers, and many festivals are associated with the main religious holidays, such as Easter, Corpus Christi and Christmas. Labour Day (1 May) is the traditional day for workers' processions. These national festivities, plus scores of regional and local cultural events catering for the arts, fill the Austrian events calendar almost every day of the year. Many festivals enjoy an international reputation, including the Salzburg Festival, the Bregenz Festival and the Vienna Viennale. Information on all events is available from tourist offices or the Internet.

A Tyrolean in regional costume

SPRING

Spring sees the re-opening of regional museums that were closed for the winter. The Viennese Prater funfair starts up at full steam. Traditionally, Lent is a period of abstinence and anticipation, but the shops are already full of Easter specialities, their shelves laden with chocolate bunnies, giant Easter eggs and other sweet delicacies.

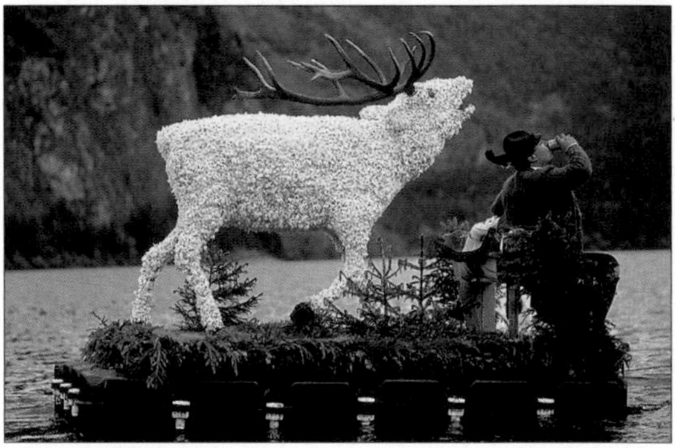

Narzissenfest on Altausseer See

MARCH

Palmprozessionen Palm Sunday processions, such as the one in Thaur, in Tyrol, based on ancient traditions, yet highly imaginative.
Passionsspiele During Holy Week and in the run up to Easter, many towns and villages stage Passion plays. Some of the most famous plays can be seen in Pongau (Salzburger Land), Tressdorf (Carinthia) and Traunkirchen (Upper Austria).
Frühlingsfestival Vienna. Classical music festival.

Palm Sunday procession, in Thaur

Osterfestspiele *(Holy Week and Easter)* Salzburg. Easter Festival with opera and classical music concerts.

APRIL

Easter On Easter night, many mountain slopes are lit with Easter bonfires called **Osterfeuer**. Easter Sunday begins with the traditional chocolate Easter egg hunt, **Eiersuchen**. A pastry in the shape of a lamb (*Osterlamm*) is also traditionally given to children on Easter by their godparents.
Donaufestival *(mid-April–mid-May)* Krems, Korneuburg. Festival of contemporary theatre and music.

MAY

Wiener Festwochen *(early May–early June)* Vienna. The biggest arts festival.
Labour Day *(1 May)*. Day of workers' marches and demonstrations; also of numerous shows and sporting events.
Passionsspiele Erl in Vorarlberg. Passion plays organized every six years (the next event is in 2014). Following the May première, the plays are then performed every Saturday and Sunday until early October.
Musikwochen Millstadt *(mid-May–early October)* Millstadt, in Carinthia. International music festival.
Gauderfest *(1st weekend in May)* Zell am Ziller, in Tyrol. Festival of strong beer, with animal fights and wrestling.
Kufenstechen *(Whit Sunday/ Monday)* Gailtal, in Carinthia. Jousting tournament.
Internationale Barocktage *(Whit Friday–Monday)* Melk Abbey. Baroque music days.
Narzissenfest *(late May–early June)* on the banks of the Altausseer See in Salzkammergut. Narcissus flower festival, music and processions.

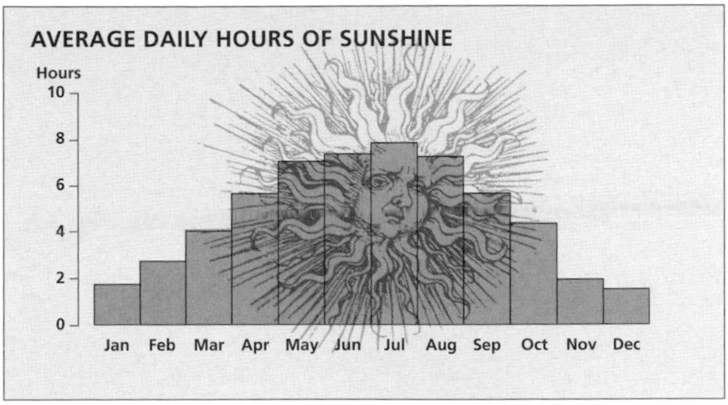

Sunshine Chart
The largest number of sunny days occurs in July, but May, June and August are also sunny. The cloudiest month is December.

SUMMER

Summer is the height of the tourist season. Theatres close for the summer, but the most important arts festivals, including the Salzburg and Bregenz Festivals, take place during this season. There are also numerous popular entertainment events and traditional village festivals.

Corpus Christi procession in Hallstatt, Salzkammergut

JUNE

Corpus Christi Processions throughout Austria; the best take place in Salzkammergut, Gmunden, Hallstatt and Traunkirchen.
St Pauler Kultursommer *(June–mid-August)* St Paul's Abbey, in Carinthia. Festival of classical music.
Schubertiade *(June, August, September)* Schwarzenberg, in Vorarlberg. Festival of Schubert's music.
Styriarte *(end June–end August)* Graz. Festival of early and contemporary music.
Donauinselfest *(late June)* Danube Island, Vienna. A three-day pop music event.
Orgelfest Stift Zwettl *(late June–late July)*. Zwettl, in Lower Austria. Festival of organ music.

JULY

Oper Klosterneuburg *(July)* Klosterneuburg, north of Vienna. Throughout the month, a programme of opera performances is held in the courtyard of the palatial Kaiserhof.
Jazzfestival *(mid-July)* Wiesen, Burgenland. Jazz festival.
Salzburger Festspiele *(July–late August)* Salzburg. Festival of music, opera and theatre; most important event of the summer.
Seefestspiele *(end July–late Aug)* Bregenz. Performances of theatre, opera and music on the stage in Bodensee.
Rathaus Film Festival *(July–August)* Vienna. Opera and music films, shown on a big screen in front of the town hall.
Kammermusikfest Lockenhaus Schloss Lockenhaus, in Burgenland. Chamber music.
Samsonumzug *(late July)* Tamsweg, Salzburger Land. Samson's procession; saints' statues are paraded in town.
Operettenfestival Baden *(late July–early September)* Baden, near Vienna. Festival of operetta.
Operettenfestspiele Mörbisch, on Neusiedler See, Festival of operetta.
Carinthischer Sommer Ossiach, Villach, in Carinthia. Carinthian summer festival.
Operettenfestival *(July–August)* Bad Ischl, Salzkammergut. Festival of operetta.
Innsbrucker Festwochen der Alten Musik *(July–August)* In and around Innsbruck. World-renowned festival of early music and Baroque opera.

AUGUST

Jazzfestival Saalfelden. Jazz concerts, performed by several hundred artists.
Internationales Chopin Festival *(mid-August)* Gaming Abbey. International Chopin Festival.
Piratenschlacht *(early August)* Oberndorf. Pirates fight it out on the Salzach River.
Assumption of the Virgin Mary *(15 August)*. Colourful processions all over Austria. The most interesting is the **Schiffsprozession** (procession of ships) on Wörther See.
Internationaler Brahms Wettbewerb Velden and Pörtschach on Wörther See. International Brahms Contest.

Fire dance during the Salzburg Festival

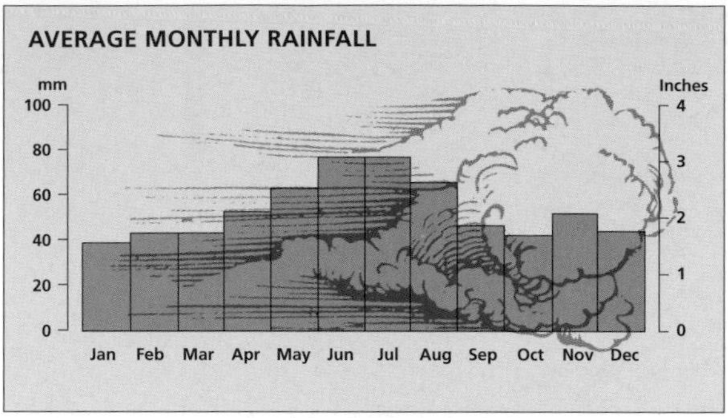

Rainfall Chart
The summer months are not only the hottest but also the wettest time of the year. Western regions tend to be wetter than central areas of Austria.

AUTUMN

In the towns, autumn marks the start of the theatre and opera season. In the mountains, the sheep and cows are rounded up and brought back down from their summer pastures, accompanied by various festivities. Grape harvest festivals are held in the wine-producing areas, mainly in Lower Austria and Burgenland. The lightly fizzing *Sturm* appears on the tables, quickly followed by new-vintage wines. Numerous music events attract music lovers throughout the country.

SEPTEMBER

Ars Electronica *(early September)* Linz. Technology exhibition accompanied by concerts of electronic music.
Haydn Tage *(early September)* Eisenstadt. Festival of Music by Haydn.
Festlicher Almabtrieb *(mid-September–mid-October).* Flocks return from the mountains. Various festivities, and the mountains echo to the sound of cows' bells.
Brucknerfest Linz *(September)* Linz. The Bruckner festival starts with **Klangwolken** (sound clouds), a series of concerts on the banks of the Danube with laser light shows.
Badener Beethoventage *(September–October)* Baden. Festival of Beethoven music.
Internationale Woche der Alten Musik *(early September)* Krieglach, in Styria. International Week of Early Music.
Internationales Musikfest Brahms *(mid-September)* Mürzuschlag. International Brahms festival.

Start of Bruckner Festival, Linz

OCTOBER

Winzerumzüge *(mid-October)* Weinviertel and Wachau Valley, Lower Austria; wine-producing regions of Burgenland. Grape harvest festivals.
Niederösterreichischer Weinherbst Lower Austria. The "Wine Autumn" is a time of increased eating and drinking in the old inns of ancient wine-producing villages, often regarded as historic architectural treasures.
Steirischer Herbst Graz. The Styrian Autumn is an avant-garde arts festival, one of the most prestigious events of the season, taking place over four weeks. Festival-goers are mainly young people, and the events include theatre and opera productions, performance arts, films, music concerts, talks and art exhibitions.
National Day *(26 October).* Celebration of the Declaration of Neutrality in 1955.
Viennale *(late October)* Vienna. Two-week International Film Festival.
Wien Modern *(end October–end November)* Vienna. Contemporary Music Festival, initiated by Claudio Abbado.

Krampus Devil and St Nicholas at a St Nicholas party

NOVEMBER

Salzburger Jazz-Herbst *(early November)* Salzburg. Ten days of traditional jazz concerts and films.
St Martin's Day *(11 November).* This is the day when all Austria feasts on *Martinigans* – roast St Martin's goose.
Voicemania *(November–December)* Vienna. A capella festival in unusual venues.
Weihnachtsmärkte *(late November–December).* Start of the Christmas market season. On offer: tree decorations, gifts, food and drink; best in Vienna, Salzburg, Klagenfurt, Spittal an der Drau and Villach.

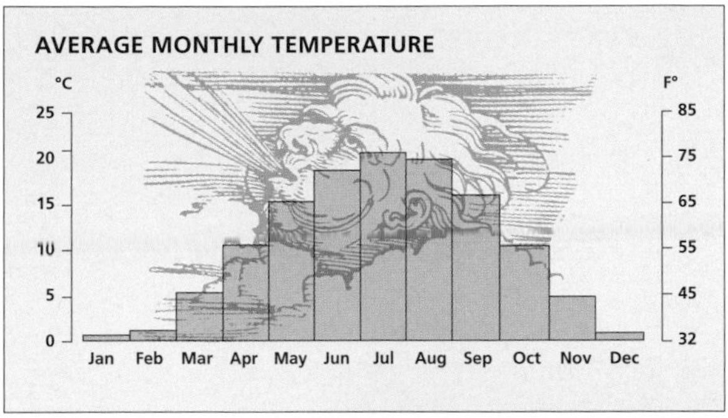

Temperature Chart
The hottest month is July, with August and June being only slightly cooler. Winters are cold, particularly in January when temperatures often drop below the freezing point.

WINTER

Winter begins with the pre-Christmas shopping rush. Christmas figures and decorations adorn every shop window. The main shopping streets in the towns and villages sparkle with lights. As soon as Christmas is over, fresh festivities get under way: New Year's Eve marks the beginning of the carnival season, celebrated in Austria with numerous balls.

The famous Vienna Opera Ball, in February

DECEMBER

St Nicholas parties *(early December)* Tyrol. The most interesting of these include **Klaubaufgehen**, a masquerade in Matrei, and **Nikolospiel** in Bad Mittendorf. In Thaur (Tyrol), people traditionally display cribs in their homes.
Adventsingen Advent concerts held in Salzburg.
Steyrer Kripperl, one of the last stick-puppet theatres, performs nativity plays using the various crib displays. The crib display in Bad Ischl is also worth seeing. Nativity plays are staged throughout the country.
St Stephen's Day (Stefanitag) *(26 December).* Colourful festival in the Lavanttal Valley (**Stefaniritt**) in Carinthia.

Christmas lights in Getreidegasse, Salzburg

JANUARY

New Year's Day *(1 January).* Austria welcomes the New Year with champagne and fireworks; people dance in the streets and squares, regardless of the weather.
Neujahrskonzert *(1 January).* Traditional New Year's concert of the Vienna Philharmonic Orchestra transmitted throughout the world from the Golden Hall of the Wiener Musikverein.
Epiphany *(6 January). Dreikönigssingen* (singing for the Three Kings) – Austria bursts into song on the Day of the Three Magi.
Perchtenlauf Carnival procession marking the start of the party season, held in four towns of the Pongau region: St Johann, Altenmarkt, Bischofshofen and Badgastein.
Salzburger Mozartwoche *(late January)* Salzburg. Mozart Week.
Resonanzen. A festival of early music held at Vienna's Konzerthaus.

FEBRUARY

February is the main carnival season. Masquerades and magnificent balls are held throughout the country.
Opernball *(last Thursday of Carnival)* Vienna Opera Ball.
Villacher Fasching *(end of Carnival)* Villach.
Maschkerertanz *(end of Carnival)* Steinfeld, Carinthia. Colourful festivities mark the end of the carnival season.

PUBLIC HOLIDAYS

Neujahr New Year (1 Jan)
Dreikönigsfest Epiphany (6 Jan)
Ostern Easter
Tag der Arbeit Labour Day (1 May)
Fronleichnam Corpus Christi
Pfingsten Pentecost
Mariä Himmelfahrt Assumption of the Virgin Mary (15 Aug)
Nationalfeiertag (26 Oct)
Allerheiligen All Saints (1 Nov)
Mariä Empfängnis (8 Dec) Immaculate Conception
Weihnachten/Stefanitag Christmas (25/26 Dec)

THE HISTORY OF AUSTRIA

During the Middle Ages, Austria was only one of several small duchies within the Holy Roman Empire, but during 600 years of Habsburg rule it rose to the ranks of a world power and was a determining factor in Europe's fate. The Austro-Hungarian Empire ended with World War I. Since the end of World War II, Austria has been a central element in European democracy.

PREHISTORY AND EARLY MIDDLE AGES

The geographic nature of Austria's territory, opening up towards the Bohemian-Moravian Valley and the Hungarian Plains, meant that, from the 7th century BC, this area was regularly raided and populated by belligerent Scythians, Celts and Germanic tribes. At the end of the 1st century BC, the land south of the Danube was occupied by the Romans, who in the middle of the 1st century AD, during the reign of the Emperor Claudius, founded the Province of Noricum here, with its main centres in Carnuntum (near Hainburg) and Vindobona (Vienna).

Stone-age Venus, discovered in Willendorf

The influence of the dominant Roman culture and civilization over the entire region began to wane in the 2nd century AD, during a period of increased German raids. In AD 180, Emperor Marcus Aurelius died in Vindobona, in the war against the Marcomanni and Quadi tribes.

From the 4th century onwards, during the Great Migration of Nations, the territories of present-day Austria saw successive waves of invading Huns, Goths and Avars. Later arrivals included Slav and Bavarian settlers. The Bavarian tribal state, established and consolidated during the 7th and 8th centuries, was crushed in 787 when Charlemagne deposed his vassal Tassilo III, the last Prince of Bavaria, and annexed his territories. In 803, Charlemagne also defeated the Avars and established a margravate (territory) on the banks of the Danube, between Enns River and Vienna Woods, which became the nucleus of the Austrian state. Its existence was cut short by Magyars, who raided it in the early 10th century.

BABENBERG AUSTRIA

Following the defeat of the Magyars in 995, on the banks of the Lech River near Augsburg, the German King Otto I restored the margravate; his successor, Otto II, handed it as a fief to Leopold I of the Babenberg dynasty (976–94). The centre of the margravate was Melk, on the Danube river. Having defeated the Magyars, Leopold extended the frontiers of his province up to the

TIMELINE

170 Raid by the Germanic tribes of Marcomanni and Quadi

493 Raid by Theodoric, King of the Ostrogoths

739 Founding of the bishopric of Salzburg

803 Charlemagne founds the eastern margravate

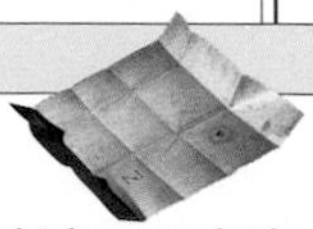

The "Ostarrichi Urkunde" document of 996

AD 1 | 500 | 650 | 800 | 950 | 1100

AD 4th–7th century The Great Migration of Nations. Raids by Huns, Goths, Avars, Slavs and Bavarians

45 Foundation of the Roman province, Noricum

Tassilo's chalice of 777

787 Charlemagne deposes the last independent Bavarian prince, Tassilo III

976 Leopold I Babenberg becomes the first Margrave of the margravate

◁ **Emperor Franz Joseph I, who ruled 1848–1916**

Vienna Woods. In 1156, Henry II Jasomirgott was given the title of Duke, and Austria became a hereditary fief of the Empire. Vienna began to assume its role as capital.

BOHEMIAN AUSTRIA

In 1246, the Babenberg line died out and Austria fell into the hands of the Bohemian kings, Vaclav I and Ottokar II. The latter, having annexed Carinthia and Carniola (1269), became the most powerful duke in the Empire. He had his eyes on the German crown, but in the 1273 election a more modest feudal lord rose to the German throne, the landgrave (count) of Upper Alsace, Rudolf von Habsburg (1273–91). He defeated his opponent, Ottokar II, in 1278, took the Austrian territories and handed them to his sons as hereditary fiefs. From then on, for the next 640 years, the fate of Austria became tied to that of the Habsburg dynasty.

Death of Frederick II Babenberg

Stone ducal throne in Maria Saal

THE HABSBURG RISE TO POWER

Rudolf I and his successors pursued a very successful policy of acquiring new territories. During the 14th century, in addition to Austria, Styria, Carinthia and Carniola, the Habsburgs gained control of Tyrol (1363) and Trieste (1382). An important contribution to the strengthening of the dynasty was made by Rudolf IV, called the Founder (1358–65), who founded Vienna University and laid the foundation stone for St Stephen's Cathedral, the church that to this day remains one of the symbols of the Austrian capital. Rudolf signed a treaty with the Emperor Charles IV – Bohemian king of the Luxemburg dynasty – stating that in the event of one of the dynasties (Habsburgs or Luxemburgs) dying out, the other would reign over both territories. This situation arose in 1438, when, following the death of Emperor Sigismund of Luxemburg, both the imperial crown of Germany and the throne of Hungary and Bohemia passed to the Austrian Duke Albrecht II of Habsburg, and on his death to his cousin Frederick III (1440–93), who was regarded as the last emperor of the Middle Ages. His motto was written as the five vowels – AEIOU – which were variously interpreted, for example as "Austriae Est Imperare Orbi Universo" (The Entire World is Austria's Empire).

THE EMPIRE OF CHARLES V

This maxim appeared close to becoming true during the reign of Maximilian I (1486–1519), who by his marriage to Maria of Burgundy in

TIMELINE

1156 Thanks to privileges granted by Frederick Barbarossa, Austria is elevated to the status of a Duchy of the Reich. Margrave Henry II Jasomirgott becomes its first duke

1251 Austria ruled by Ottokar II

1358 Rudolph IV, the Founder, ascends to the throne

1100 | 1150 | 1200 | 1250 | 1300 | 1350

Fragment of a medieval altar from Verdun, 1185

1246 End of the Babenberg line. Vienna occupied by the Bohemian King Vaclav I

1278 Rudolf von Habsburg defeats Ottokar II in the Battle of Dürnkrut. Austria becomes a hereditary fief of the Habsburgs

Gothic altar in Zwettl Abbey

1477 gained control of Alsace, Lorraine and the Netherlands, one of the richest countries in Europe. He also entered into a treaty with the Jagiellons – thus reviving his claims to the Bohemian and Hungarian crowns – and, by arranging the betrothal of his son Philip to the Spanish Infanta Joan, extended Habsburg rule over the Iberian Peninsula and the South American dominions. In 1519, Maximilian's successor, his grandson Charles V (1519–56), heir to the Spanish and Austrian territories, succeeded to the throne of an empire over which, it could be said, "the sun never set". Following the abdication of King Charles in 1556, the imperial crown passed to his brother Ferdinand (1556–64); he represented the younger line of Habsburgs, taking control of Austria, Styria, Carniola, Carinthia and Tyrol and the Jagiellon inheritance, Bohemia, Moravia, Silesia and western Hungary.

Panel inscribed "AEIOU", Frederick III's motto

REFORMATION AND TURKISH THREAT

During the Reformation, the state, now with a population of seven million, became the scene of fierce religious conflicts. Ferdinand and his successor, Maximilian II (1564–76), pursued a policy of tolerance towards the Protestants, but Rudolf II (1576–1612), brought up in the staunchly Catholic Spanish court, declared himself in favour of the Counter-Reformation. The growing religious conflict led to the Thirty-Years' War (1618–48), which ravaged large areas (51 castles, 23 towns and 313 villages in Austrian-ruled countries alone).

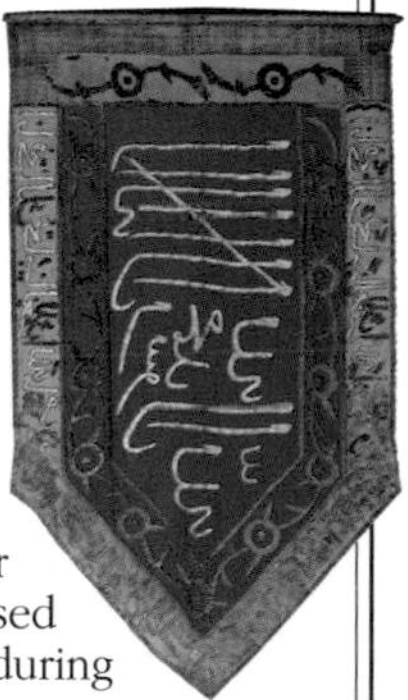

Turkish banner, captured in 1683

Even greater destruction was caused by the wars fought during the 16th and 17th centuries against the Turks, who twice tried to conquer Vienna (1529, 1683). The crushing defeat suffered by the Sultan's army during the second siege of Vienna allowed the Habsburgs to take control of the whole of Hungary, Transylvania and Croatia.

1438 Albrecht II becomes the first Habsburg emperor

1469 Founding of the bishopric of Vienna

1556 Abdication of Charles V and ascension to the throne of his brother, Ferdinand I

1683 Outbreak of Great Turkish-Austrian war

1400 | 1450 | 1500 | 1550 | 1600 | 1650 | 1700

1493 Coronation of Maximilian I

1519–1556 Reign of Charles V. Height of Habsburg territorial power

Maximilian I

1618–48 Thirty Years' War

1697 Prince Eugene of Savoy becomes the chief commander of the imperial army

The First Habsburg Monarchy

The Habsburgs rose to the ranks of the most influential German feudal families during the first half of the 1300s, and in the following centuries they became the rulers of one of Europe's most powerful countries. This advancement was due mainly to their far-sighted dynastic policy and expedient marriages. Strategic matches brought under their control territories far beyond their native Austria and Styria, to include Tyrol, Flanders, the Netherlands, Bohemia, Hungary and the possessions of the Spanish crown in both Europe and South America. The Habsburgs' marriage policy was later summed up in the motto "Let others fight wars, you, lucky Austria, get married".

AUSTRIA OF RUDOLF I

Austria in 1278

Sauce Boat of Rudolf II
The sauce boat from the famous collection of objets d'art from the Mannerist period, collected by Rudolf II, can be seen in Vienna's Kunsthistorisches Museum (see pp84–7).

Regalia of Rudolf II
The intricate sceptre, orb and crown became the insignia of the Austrian Empire.

Ferdinand I, grandson of Maximilian I, ruled Bohemia, Austria and Hungary.

Maximilian I

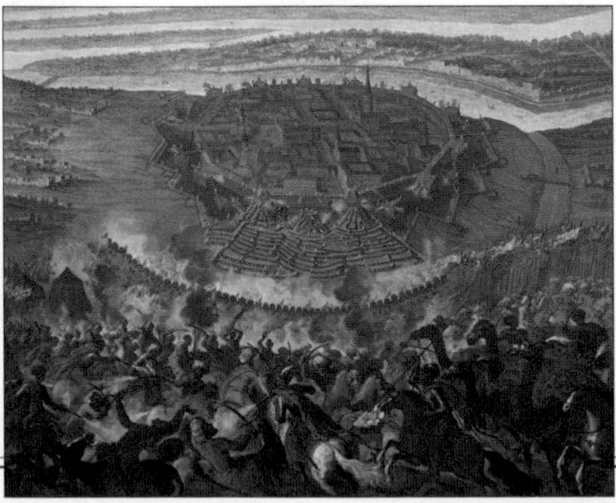

Relief of the Siege of Vienna in 1683
The 70,000-strong Christian army, led by the Polish King Jan III Sobieski, broke through the ring around Vienna and forced the 110–115,000 Turkish troops of the Grand Vizier Kara Mustapha to flee.

Rudolf II
During his reign, Rudolf II attracted scholars such as Kepler, as well as famous sorcerers, alchemists and seers to the imperial court.

Philip I, son of Maximilian I, gained control of Spain as the result of his marriage to Joanna the Mad.

Mary of Burgundy, wife of Maximilian I

Karl V, grandson of Maximilian I, inherited Spain from his mother.

FAMILY OF MAXIMILIAN I
This painting by Bernhard Strigel (c.1520) depicts Maximilian I with his family, a dynasty that turned Austria into a powerful empire.

Rudolf I
The first Habsburg king of Germany, having defeated Bohemian King Ottokar II in 1276, seized Austria, Carinthia and Styria.

Rudolf IV the Founder
Rudolf IV died very young (only 26 years old) and was buried in St Stephen's Cathedral – the church he had founded in Vienna.

WHERE TO SEE GOTHIC AUSTRIA

The most interesting early-Gothic remains to be found in Austria, dating back to the 13th–14th centuries, are the cloisters of the Cistercian abbeys in Heiligenkreuz *(see p136)* in the Wienerwald, as well as Lilienfeld and Zwettl, both in Lower Austria. Among the best examples of Gothic architecture are the impressive Stephansdom (St Stephen's Cathedral) in Vienna, the Franciscan church in Salzburg *(see p220)*, and the four-nave parish church in Schwaz *(see pp244–5)*, in Tyrol. The most famous late-Gothic (1481) winged altar, an outstanding work by the Tyrolean artist Michael Pacher, is found in St Wolfgang *(see p205)*, in the Salzkammergut. Many churches feature original Gothic sculptures.

Stephansdom *(St Stephen's Cathedral) in Vienna* (see pp58–9) *is Austria's best-known Gothic building.*

Goldenes Dachl *The "Golden Roof" in Innsbruck* (see p240) *is an attractive example of secular Gothic architecture.*

THE STRUGGLE FOR SPANISH AND AUSTRIAN SUCCESSION

The expiration of the Spanish line of Habsburgs led to the Spanish War of Succession (1701–14), which brought further territorial gains for Austria, including Belgium, Milan, Naples and Sardinia. Soon the problem of succession also arose in Austria, where Emperor Charles VI (1711–40) had died without a male heir. The so-called Pragmatic Sanction, established by Charles in 1713, stipulated that the Habsburg Austrian territories remain an integral, indivisible whole, with female members of the house also eligible for succession. The Emperor's only daughter, Maria Theresa (1740–80), however, was forced to defend her rights by fighting Prussia, France, Spain and a number of German states in the War of Austrian Succession (1740–48), during which she lost Silesia to Prussia. In 1772 and 1775, Austria participated in the first and third Partitions of Poland, annexing that country's southern territories.

Apotheosis of Eugene of Saxony

ENLIGHTENED ABSOLUTISM

Maria Theresa and her son Joseph II (1780–90) embarked on an extensive course of reforms, in the spirit of enlightened absolutism. They curtailed the rights of the Church, abolished serfdom, created a new administrative structure of the state and declared German the official language for all institutions. Their aim was to obliterate the differences between the individual countries of the Empire, to unify the multi-ethnic state and to centralize power.

REVOLUTION AND RESTORATION

During the revolutionary changes that took place in Europe at the turn of the 18th century, the Habsburgs joined the anti-French coalition forces. Initially they suffered major territorial losses (Belgium, Lombardy, southern Poland). Franz II, Maria Theresa's grandson, relinquished his title of Holy Roman Emperor and in 1806 declared himself Emperor Franz I of Austria. Following the defeat of Napoleon and the Congress of Vienna where proceedings were dominated by the Austrian Foreign Minister, Klemens Metternich, the Habsburg Empire became once again a European superpower. Metternich, who from 1821 held the office of Chancellor, and in fact ruled Austria, became the main ex ponent of absolutism and the policy of ethnic oppression; hence his nickname, "Europe's coachman".

Emperor Franz I of Austria and Maria Theresa surrounded by their children

TIMELINE

1701–14 War of Spanish Succession. Austria acquires Belgium, Milan, Naples, Parma and Sardinia

1740–48 War of Austrian Succession. Prussian-French-Spanish Coalition opposes Maria Theresa's right to the imperial throne

1700 | 1720 | 1740 | 1760 | 1780

Maria Theresa

1756 Birth of Wolfgang Amadeus Mozart

Wolfgang Amadeus Mozart

1795 Austria participates in Third Partition of Poland

1772 Austria participates in First Partition of Poland

The Congress of Vienna in 1815

THE 1848 REVOLUTION

In 1848–9, a wave of revolutions swept across Europe and the Austrian Empire. Uprisings against absolute government broke out in Vienna, Milan, Venice, Budapest, Cracow and Prague; the Hungarian revolution was suppressed only with the help of the Russian army. Emperor Ferdinand I saw himself forced to grant several concessions, including giving Austria a constitution (1848). Badly affected by the revolutionary events, the Emperor abdicated in 1848 and the Austrian throne passed to his 18-year-old nephew, Franz Joseph I (1848–1916), who quickly reintroduced absolute rule, thus inviting increased resistance, particularly in the Hungarian part of the empire.

THE AUSTRO-HUNGARIAN EMPIRE

Defeat suffered in the wars with Sardinia and France (1859), and with Prussia and Italy (1866), testified to the weakening position of Austria, particularly when confronted with the growing power of the unifying Germany. Defeat in the international arena also brought about changes in internal policy. In 1867, the emperor signed a treaty with Hungary and transformed the Austro-Hungarian Empire into a state consisting of two parts, united under one common ruler as well as a common army, finances and foreign policy. The adopted model of government eased the tensions in Austro-Hungarian relations, but did not contribute to the solution of other conflicts, including those with the Czechs, who revolted afresh, led by nationalist feelings.

Internationally, the Empire's attention was focused on the Balkans where, with Russian approval, it occupied Bosnia and Herzegovina (1878). Key to Vienna's political strategy was the political-military treaty signed in 1882 with Germany and Italy, the Triple Alliance.

In the late 1800s, Vienna developed as a centre of fashion and became the birthplace of the avant-garde Viennese Secession style.

Vienna during the revolution of 1848

Johann Strauss (son)

1805 Napoleon defeats the Austrian and Russian armies in the Battle of Austerlitz

1806 Franz II relinquishes title of Holy Roman Emperor

1815 Congress of Vienna

1825 Birth of Johann Strauss (son)

1848 Revolution in Vienna

1848 Ferdinand I abdicates and Franz Joseph I ascends the throne

1866 Defeated by Prussia, Austria loses its status as the main German power

1867 Austria becomes Austro-Hungarian state

1889 Death of the Crown Prince, Archduke Rudolf

1898 Assassination of Empress Elisabeth, by an Italian anarchist

1800 | 1820 | 1840 | 1860 | 1880 | 1900

The Monarchy of Franz I

At the turn of the 19th century, Austria had to face social and political changes brought about by the French Revolution. Franz II ascended the Austrian throne as Holy Roman Emperor in 1792, and Austria entered a 22-year-period of war with France. Franz II declared his opposition to all reformist ideas and, in response to Napoleon's self-coronation, he established the Austrian Empire in 1804. As Emperor Franz I, and with his all-powerful chancellor Klemens Metternich, his main concern in the field of domestic policy, was the preservation of the monarch's absolute power.

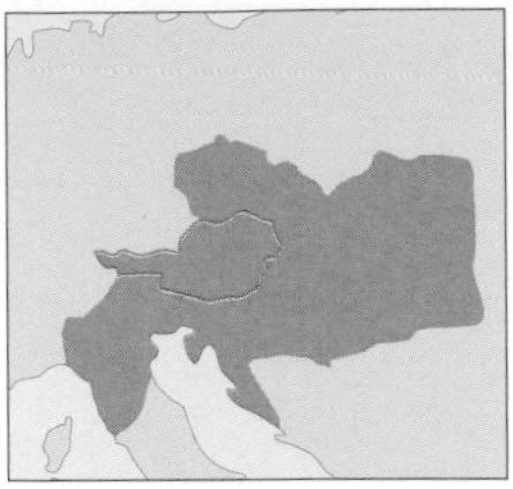

AFTER THE VIENNA CONGRESS

Austria in 1815

Franz I Crosses the Vosges Mountains
Following Napoleon's defeat at Waterloo in 1815, Franz I marched into France at the head of troops belonging to the coalition's occupying forces.

The coffin contains the body of Franz I, which was later laid in a sarcophagus in the crypt of the Capuchin Church in Vienna.

An officer in Austrian uniform

The Imperial crown of Austria – once the crown of Emperor Rudolf II. Alongside lie other regalia.

Radetzky Statue
Johann Radetzky was one of the most outstanding commanders in Austrian history. After the victory over Italy in the Battle of Custozza (1848), the 82-year old became famous as the mainstay of the Habsburg monarchy.

Emblem of the Empire
In 1836 Austria's national emblem combined Lorraine's two-headed eagle, with imperial crown, sword, sceptre and a shield with the Habsburg family crest.

Technological Progress
The first railway line on the European continent was built in Austria, in 1832. It linked Linz with České Budejovice.

An officer in Hungarian uniform

FUNERAL CEREMONY OF FRANZ I

When Napoleon declared himself Emperor of France in 1804, Franz II countered by proclaiming himself Franz I, Emperor of Austria. He was the last ruler of the Holy Roman Empire of the German Nation. He died in 1835.

Franz I in his Coronation Robes
In 1804, Franz I took on the newly created role of Emperor of Austria and King of Hungary. Two months later, he added the title King of Bohemia.

WHERE TO SEE BIEDERMEIER STYLE IN AUSTRIA

The Biedermeier style of furniture, interior design and painting, popular during the early 19th century, reflected the virtues and aspirations of the middle classes. Draped curtains, patterned carpets, bureaus and glazed cabinets became standard features. Domestic architecture flourished. Typical interiors can be seen in Vienna, in the Geymüller Schlössl (home to the Biedermeier Museum), the Museum of Applied Arts (MAK – *see p60)* and the Dreimäderlhaus. Works of prominent artists such as Ferdinand Waldmüller, Josef Danhauser and Moritz M. Daffinger can be found in the Belvedere *(see p98)*, the Wien Museum Karlsplatz *(see p97)*, and in the Schlossmuseum in Linz *(see p190)*, among others.

Biedermeier-style furniture *was highly valued by the prosperous middle classes, particularly in the first half of the 19th century.*

The Dreimäderlhaus, *at No. 10 Schreyvogelgasse, is one of the most beautiful examples of Viennese Biedermeier.*

Depiction of the assassination of Archduke Ferdinand

WORLD WAR I

In 1908, Austro-Hungary decided on a formal annexation of Bosnia-Herzegovina, leading to increased tensions with Russia, which had begun to strengthen its position in the Balkans, and with Serbia, which pursued its own expansionist aims. On 28 June 1914, in Sarajevo, the Serbian student Gavrilo Princip shot dead the heir to the Austrian throne, Franz Ferdinand. His assassination resulted in the outbreak of World War I. Germany, Austria's old ally from the Triple Alliance, declared itself on the side of Austria (Italy remained neutral for a while), while the Entente countries – Russia, France and England – sided with Serbia. The war exposed the weakness of the Habsburg monarchy and brought about its collapse. Charles I, Austria's last emperor, was exiled to Madeira in 1921.

THE FIRST REPUBLIC

On 12 November 1918, the Provisional National Assembly proclaimed the birth of the Austro-German Republic. Its first elected chancellor was the socialist Karl Renner. The peace treaty, signed in St-Germain-en-Laye (1919), imposed war compensations on Austria and forbade unification with Germany. During the 1920s, Austria's economic situation steadily worsened, giving rise to radical sentiments. The worsening internal problems were exploited by nationalist circles calling for Austria to join with Germany. Chancellor Engelbert Dollfuss, elected to office in 1932, tried to counteract such dangers by introducing "strong-arm government", repressing the Social-Democratic opposition and dissolving Communist and Nazi parties. These steps led to bloody riots in Vienna and Linz, in February 1934. In July of that year, the Nazis unsuccessfully attempted a coup, and murdered Dollfuss in the process. The new chancellor, Kurt Schuschnigg, under pressure from Adolf Hitler, agreed in February 1937 to admit Nazi politicians into his government, but

German troops marching into Austria during the annexation

TIMELINE

1908 Annexation of Bosnia and Herzegovina

1916 Death of Franz Joseph I. Emperor Charles I ascends the throne

1934 Workers riot in Vienna and Linz; bloody suppression by the police

1938 Anschluss – Austria's integration into the Third Reich

1943 Moscow Conference

1900 | 1910 | 1920 | 1930 | 1940 | 1950

Archduke Ferdinand's jacket

1914 Assassination of Archduke Ferdinand, in Sarajevo. Outbreak of WWI

1918 End of WWI. Collapse of Austro-Hungary. Creation of the Republic of Austria

Engelbert Dollfuss

1934 Nazi coup failed. Engelbert Dollfuss killed

1955 Treaty of State restoring full sovereignty to Austria. Parliament declares Austria to be neutral for all time

Soldiers of the occupying forces in Vienna in 1951

resigned in the face of demands for Austria to be incorporated into Germany. His successor, the Nazi activist Arthur Seyss-Inquart, proclaimed Austria's integration into the Third Reich *(Anschluss)* on 13 March 1938, which met with the approval of the majority of the Austrian population. German troops marched into the country. In 1938, some 200,000 Jews lived in Vienna, yet after the Holocaust only 7,000 remained.

WORLD WAR II AND THE SECOND REPUBLIC

Following the *Anschluss*, Austria became a part of Greater Germany until the end of World War II. Opposition against the Nazi administration was negligible. Before the end of the war, at the Moscow Conference in 1943, the Allied forces decided to restore an independent Austrian state. In April 1945, Karl Renner formed the first provisional government of the restored Second Republic, and in December he was elected president. In July 1945, Austria was divided into four occupation zones by the Allied powers.

The first parliamentary elections, in November 1945, were won by the Christian-Democratic Party (ÖVP), with the Socialist Party (SPÖ) coming second. Both parties were to control the political life of the country for the next 50 years. De-Nazification continued until 1948. In 1955 the Austrian State Treaty was signed, restoring Austria to full sovereignty. Foreign troops were withdrawn from its territory and Parliament proclaimed permanent neutrality. In December 1955 Austria became a member of the United Nations, and in 1995 joined the European Union.

In the 1990s, the nationalist and anti-immigration Austrian Freedom Party (FPÖ) gained in popularity. It formed a coalition government with the Christian-Democratic ÖVP in 2000, arousing fears of a resurgence of Nazi activity in Austria. However, the coalition soon collapsed, and in 2002 the nationalist vote plummeted to around 10 per cent. In 2007, a coalition government was formed between the Socialist Party (SPÖ) and the Christian-Democratic ÖVP.

Simon Wiesenthal and Ariel Musicant, Austrian investigators into Nazi crimes, at the Jewish memorial

1973 Konrad Lorenz receives Nobel Prize in Physiology and Medicine

1995 Austria joins the EU

2004 Elfriede Jelinek receives Nobel Prize for Literature

2006 Austria heads EU Presidency

2008 Far-right leader Jörg Haider dies in car crash

0 | 1970 | 1980 | 1990 | 2000 | 2010 | 2020

961 Vienna ummit of John . Kennedy and ïikita hrushchev

1972–1981 Austrian diplomat Kurt Waldheim holds office of UN Secretary General

Austrian anti-globalization protest

2000 Nationalist Austrian Freedom Party enters government coalition

2010 Heinz Fischer of the Social Democractic Party wins the presidential elections with just under 80 per cent of the vote

REISEBÜRO

VIENNA AREA BY AREA

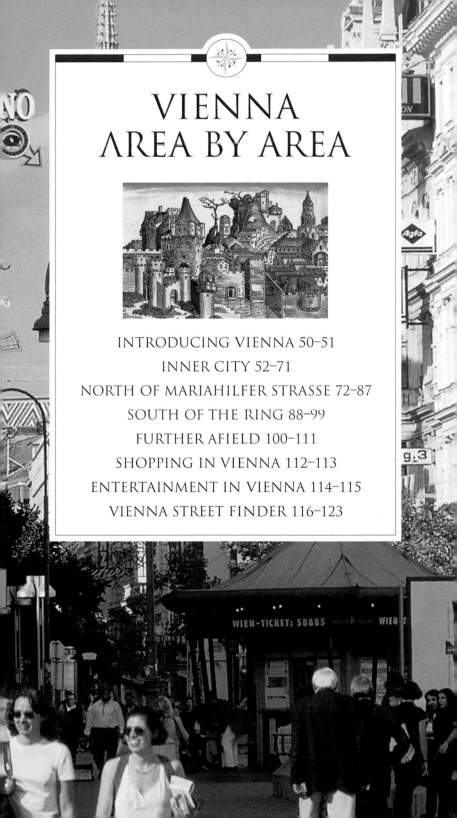

Introducing Vienna

Central Vienna includes the Inner City demarcated by Ringstrasse (often shortened to Ring) and Franz-Josefs-Kai, plus the area between Ring and Gürtel. Gürtel is Vienna's second ring road, running almost parallel with the Ring. In this guide, central Vienna is divided into three districts, in line with its administrative sectors. The most interesting sights outside the centre are also featured.

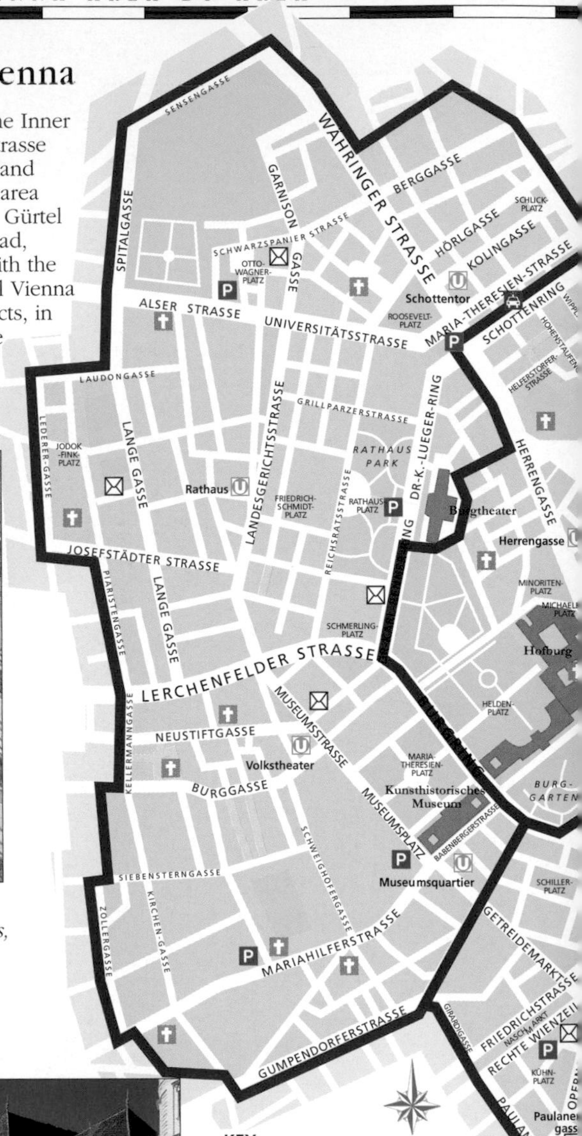

KEY

- Major sight
- Tourist information office
- Police
- Church
- Synagogue
- Parking
- U-Bahn station
- Post office
- Railway station
- Pedestrian street

Majolikahaus Façade
The façade of Majolikahaus, at No. 40 Linke Wienzeile, was designed in 1899 by Otto Wagner, one of the foremost representatives of Viennese Secession style.

Freyung
Freyung Square is dominated by the Austria Fountain; in the background is the Schottenkirche, the church of Vienna's Benedictine monks.

◁ **Graben Street in Vienna**

Pallas Athene Fountain

The statue of goddess Pallas Athene by Karl Kundmann was placed on the fountain in front of the Parliament building in 1902.

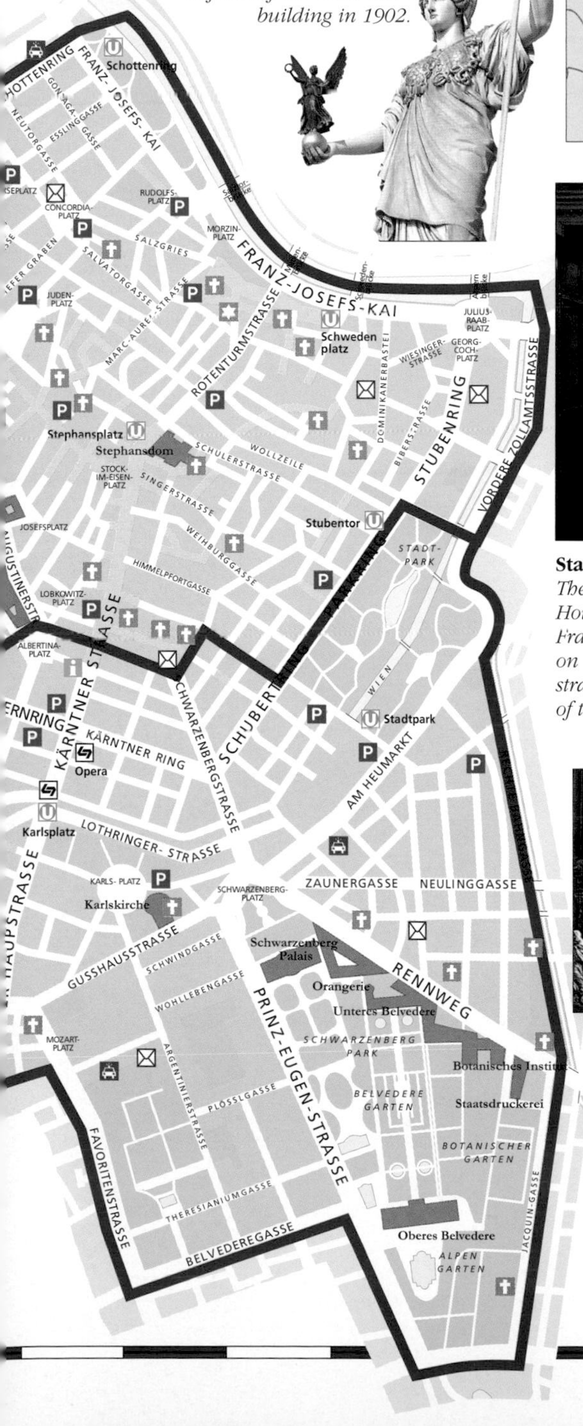

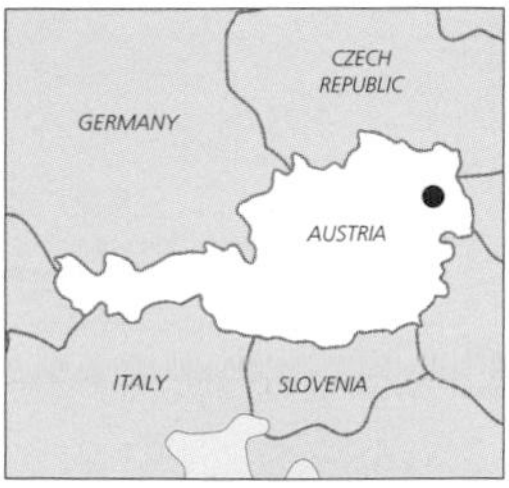

Staatsoper

The Vienna State Opera House was the first building Franz Joseph I had erected on the prestigious Ringstrasse, built on the grounds of the old city walls.

Stephansdom

The interior of the Gothic St Stephen's Cathedral has been modified many times through the centuries, and Baroque elements have been added.

INNER CITY

Vienna's old town, the Innere Stadt or "inner city", developed in the area enclosed on one side by the present-day Danube canal, and on the other three sides by fortifications. In the 19th century, these were replaced by the town's elegant artery – the Ringstrasse. The Ring encircles many splendid historic remains, bearing witness to Vienna's turbulent history from Roman times until the present day, while numerous museum collections convey Austria's rich heritage. It is also one of Vienna's liveliest areas, where the smartest cafés and restaurants and most expensive shops await the visitor, and where bars and clubs stay open until the early hours.

Statues on a portal in Josefsplatz

SIGHTS AT A GLANCE

Streets and Squares
Am Hof 20
Dr.-Ignaz-Seipel-Platz 8
Freyung 21
Graben 2
Heldenplatz 26
Herrengasse 22
Hoher Markt 17
Jewish Quarter 14
Josefsplatz 29
Kärntner Strasse 34
Michaelerplatz 24
Minoritenplatz 23
Schulhof 19
Schwedenplatz 12

Historic Buildings
Alte Burg pp68–9 27
Altes Rathaus 16
Böhmische Hofkanzlei 18
Mozarthaus Vienna 5
Spanische Reitschule p67 28
Urania 11
Winterpalais des Prinzen Eugen 33

Churches
Augustinerkirche 30
Deutschordenskirche St. Elisabeth 6
Dominikanerkirche 9
Franziskanerkirche 7
Kapuzinerkirche, Kaisergruft 32
Maria am Gestade 15
Peterskirche 1
Ruprechtskirche 13
Stephansdom pp58–9 3

Museums
Albertina 31
Dom- und Diözesanmuseum 4
österreichisches Museum für Angewandte Kunst 10

Parks and Gardens
Volksgarten 25

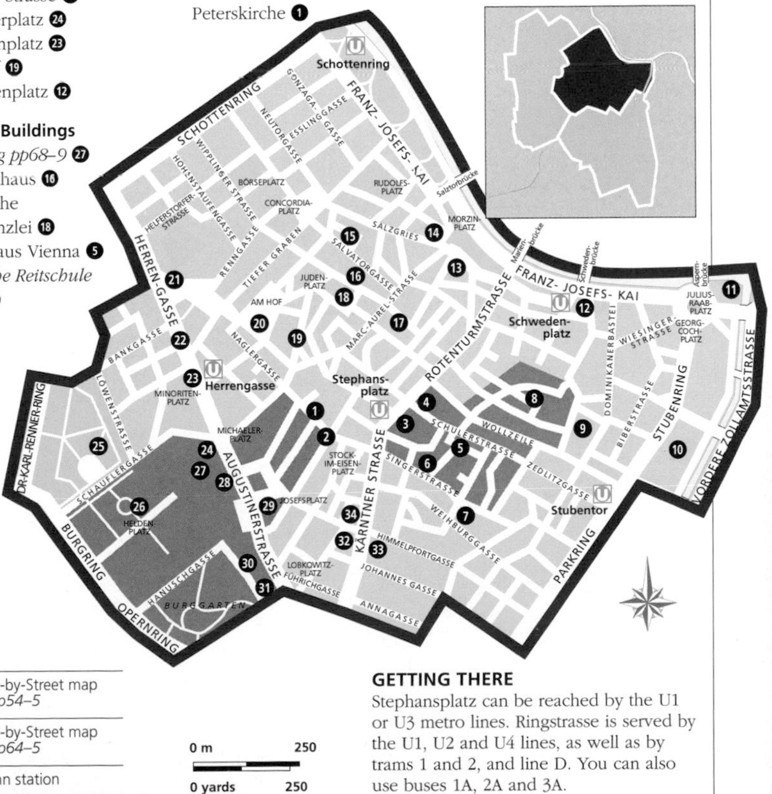

KEY

Street-by-Street map *see pp54–5*

Street-by-Street map *see pp64–5*

U-Bahn station

0 m 250
0 yards 250

GETTING THERE
Stephansplatz can be reached by the U1 or U3 metro lines. Ringstrasse is served by the U1, U2 and U4 lines, as well as by trams 1 and 2, and line D. You can also use buses 1A, 2A and 3A.

◁ **Sculpture in the Peterskirche by Lorenzo Mattielli (1729), of St John Nepomuk's martyrdom**

Street-by-Street: Around Stephansdom

The origins of this district date back to the 13th century, but much of it was changed in the 17th and 18th centuries, when many churches and public buildings were refashioned in the spirit of the increasingly powerful Habsburg monarchy. Narrow, medieval alleys adjoin monumental Baroque structures and bourgeois town houses, whose ground floors are often occupied by shops, cafés and restaurants. In the evenings, when the churches and museums close for the night, the area is still lively with people.

★ Dom- und Diözesanmuseum
This crucifix, containing the relics of St Andrew, is one of the many treasures of medieval sacred art kept in the Cathedral Museum ❹

Haas & Haas Tea Shop and Restaurant offers the best selection of teas and coffees in Vienna, as well as delicious snacks. The tea house is set in a courtyard filled with lush greenery.

★ Stephansdom
St Stephen's Cathedral has a Baroque main altar, the work of Tobias Pock, showing the martyrdom of its patron saint ❸

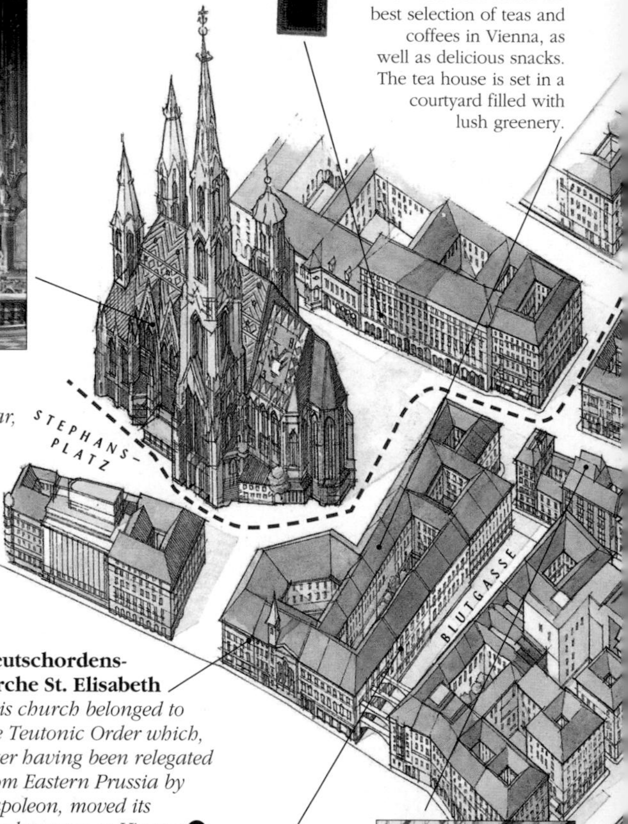

Deutschordens-kirche St. Elisabeth
This church belonged to the Teutonic Order which, after having been relegated from Eastern Prussia by Napoleon, moved its headquarters to Vienna ❻

Along Blutgasse and neighbouring streets the tenement houses feature lovely, green courtyards.

Mozarthaus Vienna
Wolfgang Amadeus Mozart lived in this house from 1784–7, and composed The Marriage of Figaro *here* ❺

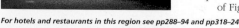

For hotels and restaurants in this region see pp288–94 and pp318–24

Schönlaterngasse
This street owes its name to the wrought-iron lantern, a copy of which can be seen at No. 6. Robert Schumann lived at No. 7. Also noteworthy are the Basilisk House and the Baroque church of St Bernard *(see left)*.

LOCATOR MAP
See Street Finder, maps 2 & 3

Dr.-Ignaz-Seipel-Platz
This square, one of the most beautiful in Vienna, has an ornate Baroque Jesuit church on one side. Shown here is a detail from its pulpit ❽

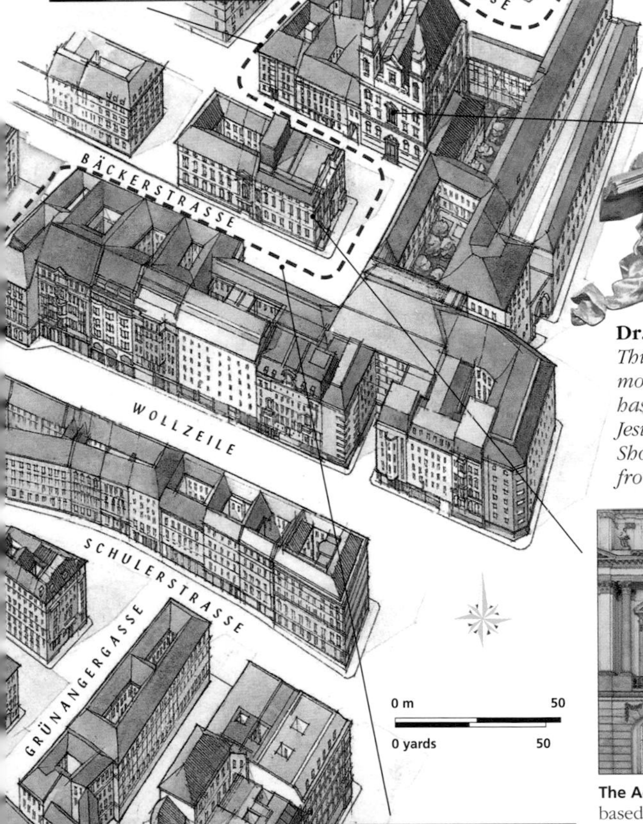

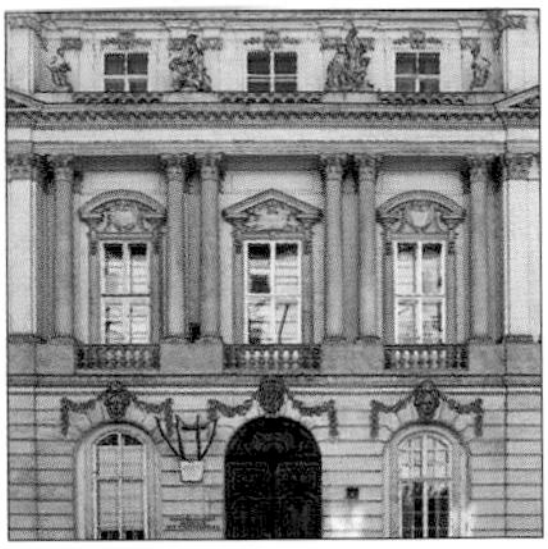

The Academy of Science is based in the assembly hall of the former university.

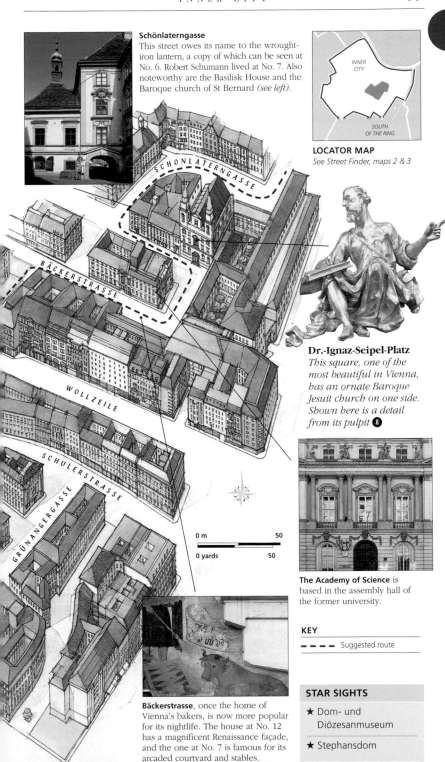

Bäckerstrasse, once the home of Vienna's bakers, is now more popular for its nightlife. The house at No. 12 has a magnificent Renaissance façade, and the one at No. 7 is famous for its arcaded courtyard and stables.

KEY

- - - - Suggested route

STAR SIGHTS

★ Dom- und Diözesanmuseum

★ Stephansdom

Peterskirche ❶

Petersplatz 6. **Map** 2 B4.
Tel *53 36 443.* *Stephansplatz.*
1A, 2A, 3A. *6:30am–7pm Mon–Fri, 8am–7pm Sat, Sun.*

St Peter's church, one of Vienna's oldest, was, according to legend, founded in 792 by Charlemagne, as commemorated in a marble relief on the church's façade, *The Placing of the Cross by Charlemagne*, by Rudolf Weyr (1906).

The site was occupied by a Roman basilica as early as the 12th century. The present Baroque church was built in the 18th century to designs by Gabriele Montani. It received its final form from Johann Lukas von Hildebrandt, who also gave the church its magnificent green patina-covered dome, which towers over the whole district. The frescoes inside the dome, depicting the Assumption of the Virgin Mary, were created by J.M. Rottmayr.

The Chapel of St Michael, the first on the right, holds a glass coffin containing the relics of St Benedict.

The striking patina-covered copper dome of Peterskirche

Graben ❷

Map 2 B4, C4. *Stephansplatz.*
1A, 2A, 3A. **Jewish Museum**
Tel *53 50 431.* *10am–6pm Mon–Wed, Fri, Sun, 10am–8pm Thu.*
www.jmw.at

This fully pedestrianized street, running through a bustling part of the city centre, is one of the most fashionable shopping areas in Vienna, full to bursting with lively restaurants and cafés. There are two identical fountains in the square, St Joseph Fountain on the northwestern side and St Leopold Fountain on the southeastern side.

The Baroque plague column in Graben

In the centre of the square stands the Baroque Pestsäule (Plague Column), also known as the Dreifaltigkeitssäule (Trinity Column), which the Emperor Leopold had erected after the end of the plague that decimated the town in 1687–93. It depicts the Holy Trinity, with a statue of the praying emperor at the top. A carved group, entitled *Faith Conquers the Plague*, adorns the southern side of the column. A short distance from here, towards Stephansplatz, stands a modest statue of St John Nepomuk, which is a favourite spot with buskers.

The modern Haas Haus on Graben, at Stephansplatz, was built in 1985–90 on the site of older buildings destroyed during a bombing raid. Made from glass and aluminium, it is the most controversial building at the heart of the city. Its windows beautifully reflect the cathedral towers. The top floor is a café-restaurant, from where you get a great view over Vienna.

One of the original Baroque structures is the Bartolotti Palace, at the corner of Dorotheergasse. Next to it is a popular Trzesniewski Sandwich Buffet. Further along Dorotheergasse, at No. 11, is the **Jewish Museum** (Jüdisches Museum), which moved into the former Eskeles Palace from the old synagogue. The museum chronicles the history of Jews in Vienna.

Otto Wagner, an outstanding architect of the Viennese Secession, had his studio at Graben No.10; in the 1980s, the house belonged to the eccentric Austrian artist Friedensreich Hundertwasser.

Stephansdom ❸

See pp58–9.

Dom- und Diözesanmuseum ❹

Stephansplatz 6. **Map** 2 C4.
Tel *51 552-35 60.* *Stephansplatz.*
1A, 2A, 3A. *10am–5pm Tue–Sat.* **www**.dommuseum.at

The cathedral museum contains a large collection of sacral paintings and sculptures, as well as fascinating examples of folk art. Many pieces were donated to the cathedral by Duke Rudolf IV. Star exhibits include the famous portrait of the duke (c.1360), and the *Erlacher Madonna,* a life-size statue of the Madonna and Child, a Gothic masterpiece (c.1330) from Lower Austria. The Cathedral Museum also holds sacral vessels and reliquaries from St Stephen's Cathedral, valuable masterpieces of the Gothic, Baroque and Romantic eras, and the Otto Mauer collection of 20th-century Austrian art.

Gothic Madonna and Child, Cathedral Museum

For hotels and restaurants in this region see pp288–94 and pp318–24

Mozarthaus Vienna ❺

Domgasse 5. **Map** 2 C4.
Tel *51 21 791.* *Stephansplatz.*
1A. *10am–7pm daily.*
www.mozarthausvienna.at

Domgasse 5 is the most famous of Mozart's various homes in Vienna. He lived here with his family in 1784–7, and composed many of his masterpieces here, including *The Marriage of Figaro*. Restored for the anniversary year of 2006, the Mozarthaus Vienna has exhibitions on two upper floors as well as the Mozarts' first-floor flat.

Deutschordenskirche St. Elisabeth ❻

Singerstrasse 7. **Map** 2 C4.
Tel *51 21 065.* *Stephansplatz.*
1A. **Church** *7am–6pm daily.*
Treasury *10am–noon Mon, Thu, Sat, 3–5pm Wed, Fri, Sat.*

The knights of the Teutonic Order arrived in Vienna in the 13th century. They established their quarters near the Stephansdom, but only the tower still stands today. In the 15th century, they built the present Gothic **church** of St Elizabeth. Its Baroque façade, added between 1725 and 1735, hides the original Gothic features.

In 1807, when Napoleon abolished the Order of Teutonic Knights in Eastern Prussia, the knights moved their headquarters to Vienna and brought the Order Treasury here. The four rooms of the **Treasury** hold collections of objects associated with the history of the Order: insignia of the Grand Masters, coins, medals, seals, sacral vessels and tableware, as well as masterpieces of European art collected by the knights.

The walls of the church are hung with the coats of arms of the Teutonic knights. The beautiful winged altar (1520) is made from elaborate carved and painted panels depicting scenes from the Passion, surrounded by intricate tracery.

Within the complex of buildings belonging to the Order is the apartment where Mozart first lived in Vienna, later occupied by Johannes Brahms (1863–5).

The impressive winged altarpiece in Deutschordenskirche

Franziskanerkirche ❼

Franziskanerplatz 4. **Map** 2 C4.
Tel *51 24 578.* *Stephansplatz.*
7:30–11:30am, 2:30–5:30pm daily.

In the 14th century, the Franciscans took over this church, originally built by wealthy citizens as a "house of the soul" for prostitutes wishing to reform. The present church, designed in the South German Renaissance style by Bonaventura Daum, was built in 1601–11. Its façade is topped by a scrolled gable with obelisks and carvings. The interior was decorated by Austrian and Italian masters of the Baroque, including Andrea Pozzo and Johann Georg Schmidt. An axe has been stuck in the wooden statue of Madonna and Child above the tabernacle, known as *Madonna and Axe*, ever since an attack during the religious wars. The Moses Fountain in front of the church dates from 1798.

A charming 18th-century wall fountain, Academy of Science

Dr.-Ignaz-Seipel-Platz ❽

Map 3 D4. *Schwedenplatz.* *1A.*

Dr. Ignaz Seipel, a conservative politician, was twice Chancellor of Austria in the 1920s. The square bearing his name is one of the most attractive in Vienna. At its centre (at No. 2) stands a Rococo structure designed by Jean Nicolas Jadot de Ville-Issey, originally intended as part of the Old University. Since 1857 it has served as the headquarters of the Österreichische Akademie der Wissenschaften (Austrian Academy of Sciences). The frescoes on the ceiling of the Rococo assembly hall, painted by Gregorio Guglielmi, show an allegory of the four academic faculties. Damaged by fire in 1961, they have been meticulously restored, together with the rest of the hall.

Opposite the Academy of Sciences stands the impressive High Baroque Jesuitenkirche. The Jesuits took over the university in the 1620s and, from 1703–5, rebuilt the church next to it, with a new façade and interior, the works of the Italian painter Andrea Pozzo.

Stephansdom ❸

Rudolf IV the Founder

Situated in the centre of Vienna, the cathedral, dedicated to the first Christian martyr, St Stephen, is the very soul of the city. Although built on this site some 800 years ago, the present building is mainly late-Gothic in style – the only fragments remaining of the original 13th-century Romanesque church are the Giants' Doorway and the Towers of the Heathens. Largely destroyed during World War II, the cathedral was restored to its former glory by the efforts of the entire nation. In a vault beneath its main altar are urns containing the internal organs of some of the Habsburgs – other body parts were kept elsewhere in Vienna.

★ Giants' Doorway
This masterpiece of late-Romanesque art, with its richly carved portal and the twin Towers of the Heathens, stands on the site of an earlier heathen shrine.

★ Cathedral's Pulpit
The pulpit in the main nave is decorated with portraits of the Four Fathers of the Church. The sculptor himself looks on from a "window" below, under the stairs.

Singer Gate
At one time, this was the entrance for male visitors. The superb sculptures depict scenes from the life of St Paul, and Duke Rudolf IV the Founder.

For hotels and restaurants in this region see pp288–94 and pp318–24

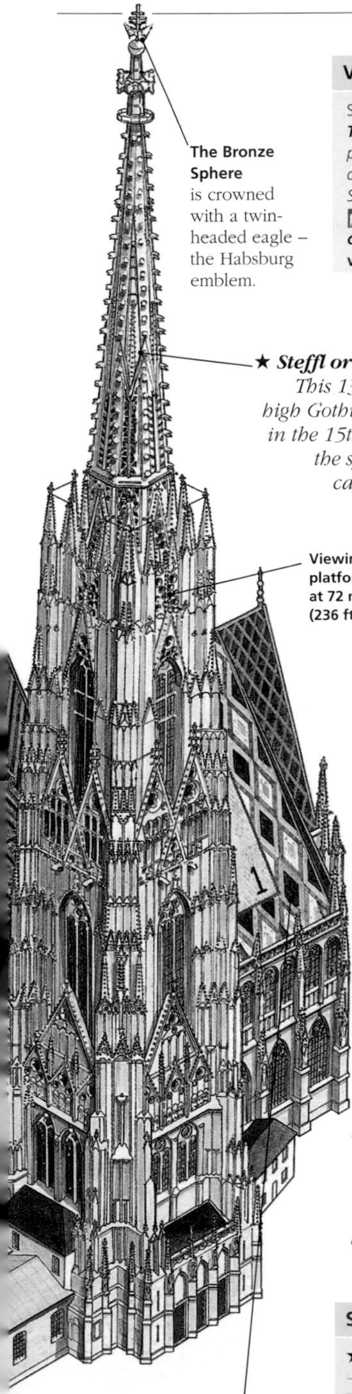

The Bronze Sphere is crowned with a twin-headed eagle – the Habsburg emblem.

Viewing platform, at 72 m (236 ft)

The mosaic roof is covered with almost 250,000 glazed tiles.

VISITORS' CHECKLIST

Stephansplatz 1. **Map** 2 C4. ***Tel*** *51 552-3526.* *Stephansplatz.* *1A, 2A.* *6am–10pm daily.* *10:30am, 3pm Mon–Sat, 3pm Sun and public holidays.* ***Organ concerts*** *May–Nov: 7pm Wed.* **www**.stephanskirche.at

★ ***Steffl or South Spire***
This 137 m (450 ft) high Gothic spire, built in the 15th century, is the symbol of the cathedral and of Vienna.

Wiener Neustädter Altar
Commissioned in 1447 by the Emperor Friedrich III, this elaborately carved altarpiece is situated to the left of the main altar.

STAR FEATURES

★ Cathedral's Pulpit

★ Giants' Doorway

★ *Steffl* – the South Spire

Dominikanerkirche ❾

Postgasse 4. **Map** 3 D4.
Tel *51 29 174.* *Stephansplatz, Schwedenplatz, Stubentor.* *2.* *1A.* *7am–7pm Mon–Sat, 7:30am–9pm Sun.*

The Dominican monks came to Vienna in 1226, at the invitation of Duke Leopold VI. They built and consecrated their first church and convent here in the second half of the 13th century. The church that stands now, built between 1631 and 1674, was designed by Ciprian Biasino and Antonio Canevale.

The church has a richly ornamented interior, with a ring of chapels surrounding the nave, with early-Baroque frescoes on the ceiling and a painting by Franz Geyling inside the dome. The second chapel on the right, St Vincent Chapel, has swirling Rococo grilles and candelabra, and a very beautiful gilt organ above the west door, set within a mid-18th century decorative enclosure.

Niches in the majestic façade contain statues of Dominican saints. The two statues in the corner recesses commemorate two great scientists and medieval religious figures, St Albert the Great and St Thomas Aquinas.

Worth seeing are the frescoes by Tencala and Rauchmiller, and the high altar (1839–40) by Karl Rösner, with a painting by Leopold Kuppelwieser.

The majestic Baroque façade of Dominikanerkirche

Österreichisches Museum für Angewandte Kunst ⑩

Stubenring 5. **Map** 3 D4.
Tel *71 136-0. 2. 74A.*
Stubentor, Landstrasse.
Landstrasse. 10am–midnight Tue, 10am–6pm Wed–Sun.
Admission free Sat. **www**.mak.at

The Austrian Museum of Applied Arts (MAK), founded in 1864, the first of its kind in Europe, exercised a strong influence on the development of the applied arts for some time. It houses the archives and collections of the Wiener Werkstätte – workshops famous for their promotion of good design.

The building was designed by one of the Ring architects, Heinrich von Ferstel, in Florentine Renaissance style. A new wing was added in 1909, and in 1994 the Arenbergpark flak tower became an annexe of the museum. Each room is unique, designed by a different artist, thus creating a fine setting for the items on display.

The permanent collection includes glass, pottery, porcelain, jewellery, metalwork, furniture, textiles, Eastern carpets and decorative items from the Far East. Separate rooms are devoted to the Secession period.

Biedermeier-style sofa, in MAK

Urania ⑪

Uraniastrasse 1. **Map** 3 E3.
Tel *71 26 191–15. 1, 2, 21, N.*
Schwedenplatz. **Planetarium**
Apr–Sep: 9pm Tue, Fri, Sat; Oct–Mar: 8pm Tue, Fri, Sat.
www.urania-sternwarte.at

On the south side of Julius-Raab-Platz, on the banks of the Danube Canal, stands a round building with a distinctive dome that is visible from afar. Urania, named after the Greek muse, was built in 1910 to designs by Max Fabian. It is the home of Vienna's oldest educational establishment that is not a school. Inside the building are lecture halls and a theatre for visiting theatre performances as well as the resident puppet theatre; it is also home to a cinema and a **planetarium**. Every year, Urania holds a symposium devoted to the outstanding Austrian writer and Nobel prize winner, Elias Canetti.

Schwedenplatz ⑫

Map 3 D3. *Schwedenplatz.*

Schwedenplatz, the Swedish Square, is one of Vienna's busiest spots. Here, on the banks of the Danube Canal, under Schwedenbrücke, is a landing stage with riverboats inviting visitors on to a variety of pleasure cruises.

Another attraction awaits at No. 13: an Italian ice-cream parlour, reputed to sell the best ice cream in Vienna.

In Laurenzberg, on one side of Schwedenplatz, remains of the old town wall can be seen, with a metal ring that was used to tie up horses and an old sign with traffic regulations. Steep, narrow steps lead down to Griechenbeisl, a small cosy Greek bar. Visitors are welcomed by a board showing the *Lieber Augustin*; from the entrance hall you can see down to a small, illuminated cellar where his statue is on display. The story of Augustin, a piper, goes back to the times of the Great Plague in Vienna. In a drunken stupor, he slumped into the gutter. When undertakers mistook him for dead and threw him into a plague pit, he woke up and terrified them by singing: *O du lieber Augustin…* (Oh, dear Augustin). Miraculously, he survived, and today, tourists wishing to return to Vienna throw a coin into the cellar.

Ivy-clad façade of Ruprechtskirche

Ruprechtskirche ⑬

Ruprechtsplatz. **Map** 2 C3.
Tel *53 56 003. Schwedenplatz.*
2A, 3A. Sep–Jun: 10am–1pm Mon–Fri, during mass: 5pm Sat, 10:30am Sun; Jul–Aug: 10am–1pm Mon–Fri, during mass: 6pm Sat, 10:30am Sun.

The church of St Ruprecht, rising on an escarpment overlooking Ruprechtsplatz, is Vienna's oldest church. At one time, an arm of the Danube flowed nearby with a landing stage for salt transported from Salzburg. According to legend, the church was founded in 740 by disciples of the Salzburg bishop, St Ruprecht, patron saint of salt merchants. The Romanesque nave and three lower floors of the tower date from the 11th century. In the choir is a 12th-century stained-glass window, Vienna's oldest, depicting the Crucifixion and the Virgin Mary on the throne.

Jewish Quarter ⑭

Map 2 C2, 3. *Schwedenplatz, Herrengasse. 1A, 2A, 3A.*
Jewish Museum Palais Eskeles, Dorotheergasse 11. ***Tel*** *535 04 31. Stephansplatz.*
10am–6pm Sun–Fri, 10am–8pm Thu.
Museum Judenplatz Misrachi-Haus, Judenplatz 8. *Schwedenplatz, Herrengasse. 10am–6pm Sun–Thu, 10am–2pm Fri.*

A tangle of narrow streets west of Rotenturmstrasse makes up the earliest Jewish quarter in Vienna. Today, the

For hotels and restaurants in this region see pp288–94 and pp318–24

Jewish quarter is a busy area of discothèques, bars and kosher restaurants, but during the Middle Ages, Judenplatz was the site of the Jewish ghetto, with a synagogue, the remains of which can be seen under the square. There was also a Jewish hospital, rabbi's house, bathhouse and school.

Stadttempel, the beautiful present synagogue, is hidden on Seitenstettengasse and guarded by armed police after an attack in 1983.

In 1895, the first **Jewish Museum** in the world was founded here. It was closed down by the Nazis, but a new museum opened in 1993 in Palais Eskeles in Dorotheergasse *(see p56)*. In 2000, the **Museum Judenplatz**, devoted to medieval Jewish life, was opened in Misrachi House. A modern monument by Rachel Whiteread at the centre of the square commemorates the victims of the Holocaust.

The Gothic interior of the church Maria am Gestade

Maria am Gestade ⓯

Salvatorgasse 12. **Map** 2 C3. ***Tel*** *533 95 94.* *Schwedenplatz, Stephansplatz.* *1A, 3A.* *7am–6pm daily.*

The church of St Mary's on the Riverbank was once flooded by the waters of an old Danube canal, but today it rises on a steep escarpment, its lofty, 56-m (180-ft) high Gothic steeple dominating the town. The stone helmet at the top of the steeple is a masterpiece of Viennese Gothic art.

First mentioned in the 12th century, the present building dates from the late 1300s. It was used as an arsenal during Napoleon's occupation of the city in 1809, but later restored.

Inside, the stained-glass panes behind the main altar are mostly original medieval features. The pillars are adorned with six Gothic statues, plus some from the 17th and 19th centuries. To the left of the main altar is a chapel with a Renaissance stone altar, adorned with colourful painted carvings. The church also holds the tomb of Clemens Maria Hofbauer, the city's patron saint.

Altes Rathaus ⓰

Wipplingerstrasse 8. **Map** 2 B3. *Schwedenplatz, Stephansplatz.* *1, 2.* *1A, 3A.* **Archives and Museum of the Austrian Resistance** ***Tel*** *228 9469 319.* *9am–5pm Mon–Thu.* *by appointment.*

Vienna's oldest town hall probably first stood at neighbouring Tuchlaubenstrasse. The building at Wipplingerstrasse was once owned by the rich and influential brothers Otto and Heymo Neuburg, who headed a burghers' rebellion against the Habsburgs. In 1309, Prince Friedrich the Fair confiscated the building and gave it to the town. It served as the town's main administrative centre until 1883.

Ironwork at the entrance to Altes Rathaus, in Wipplingerstrasse

The entrance of Altes Rathaus is festooned with beautiful Baroque ironwork. In the courtyard stands the Andromeda Fountain (1741), the last work of the sculptor Georg Raphael Donner. A door leads from the courtyard to Salvatorkapelle (St Saviour's chapel), the former Neuburg family chapel, which has a Renaissance portal (1520–30), facing Salvatorgasse, a rare example in Vienna of the Italian Renaissance style.

Today, the Old Town Hall houses the **Archives and Museum of the Austrian Resistance**, devoted to the memory of those who risked their lives by opposing National Socialism in Austria, in the years 1934–45.

VIENNA'S JEWS – PAST AND PRESENT

A Jewish merchant community thrived in Vienna from the 12th century, with the original Jewish quarter centred around Judenplatz. During the 1421 persecutions many Jews were murdered, while others were forced to convert to the Christian faith or to leave the town. The 1781 Edict of Tolerance, issued by Joseph II, lifted legal constraints on Jews, and the centre of Jewish life gradually moved to the opposite bank of the Danube Canal, around the Prater. In 1938, some 200,000 Jews lived in Vienna, contributing to its cultural and intellectual life. After Nazi genocide, only 7,000 remained. Now Eastern European immigrants are again adding to their total number.

The lavish interior of Stadttempel

Anker Clock in Hoher Markt, with cut-out historical figures

Hoher Markt 17

Map 2 C3. *Stephansplatz, Schwedenplatz.* *1A, 3A.*

Hoher Markt is the oldest square in Vienna. After World War II, the foundations of the Roman military camp of Vindobona, where Emperor Marcus Aurelius died in AD 180, were discovered under the square. The ruins are now a popular tourist attraction.

In medieval times, fish and cloth markets as well as executions were held in the square. Since the early 18th century, it has been a venue for town court trials.

The Ankeruhr (Anker Clock), above the way to Bauernmarkt, is a copper and bronze sculptural clock designed in 1911 by Franz von Matsch. It features 12 historical figures who contributed to Vienna's development and reputation. Every hour one of these emerges, and at noon the entire set parades past. The procession is headed by Marcus Aurelius, followed by Rudolf IV, and closes with the composer Joseph Haydn.

In the centre of the square stands the Baroque Josephsbrunnen (Joseph's fountain) or Vermählungsbrunnen (nuptial fountain), commissioned by Leopold I and designed by Johann Bernhard Fischer von Erlach, depicting Joseph and Mary's betrothal.

Böhmische Hofkanzlei 18

Judenplatz 11. **Map** 2 B3. ***Tel*** *53 122.* *Stephansplatz.* *1A, 3A.* *7:30am–3:30pm Mon–Fri.* **www**.vfgh.gv.at

The Habsburg rulers were also kings of Bohemia, which was initially governed from Prague; in 1627, however, Emperor Ferdinand II transferred the administration to Vienna. In 1714, the Bohemian Court Chancery moved into this grand palace, designed by Johann Bernhard Fischer von Erlach, and henceforth the Austrian emperors ruled Bohemia from here.

The vast original Baroque portals, with sculptures added later by Lorenzo Mattielli, create a harmonious exterior, which is subtle yet powerful. Also noteworthy are the beautiful carved and elegantly curved window frames.

Schulhof 19

Map 2 B3. *Stephansplatz, Herrengasse.* *1A, 2A, 3A.* **Clock Museum** ***Tel*** *53 32 265.* *10am–6pm Tue–Sun.* *1 Jan, 1 May, 25 Dec.* *Free admission – 9am–12pm Fri.*

Schulhof is a small alley connecting the imperial Am Hof square with the elegant, Baroque residential area of Kurrentgasse. The building at No. 2, the former Obizzi Palace (1690), now houses a fascinating **Clock Museum**, which has more than 3,000 exhibits. The museum provides its visitors with a comprehensive account of the history of chronometry through the ages and of clock technology from the 15th century to the present day. The Biedermeier and Belle Epoque periods are particularly well presented. A major highlight is the 18th-century astronomical clock by the Augustinian friar David Cajetano.

Entrance to the Clock Museum in Schulhof

At every full hour the three floors of the museum resound to the striking, chiming and playing of numerous clocks. All are carefully maintained to keep the correct time. This is something of an ear-ringing experience, although quite enchanting.

A short distance from here, at No. 10 Kurrentgasse, is the bakery Grimm, one of the most famous in Vienna.

Am Hof 20

Map 2 B3. *Stephansplatz, Schottentor.* *1A.*

The name of the square (meaning "by the Court") refers to the medieval princes' residence nearby. It later housed the mint, and then the royal military chancery. Today it is a bank.

The main architectural gem of present-day Am Hof is the chapel of the Nine Angel Choirs, built in the late 14th century by the Carmelite Friars and rebuilt after the fire of 1607. It was adorned with a Baroque façade crowned with a triangular pediment featuring Our Lady, the queen of the nine angel choirs. The dissolution of the Holy Roman Empire was proclaimed from the chapel's terrace on 6 August 1806.

There are a number of other interesting houses in the square. The building at No. 10 with a magnificent façade incorporating sculptures by Mattielli, is the former citizens' armoury, today housing the headquarters of

Statue on top of No. 10 Am Hof, the former citizens' armoury

the city's fire services. No. 14 is the Collalto Palace, where, in 1762, the six-year-old Mozart gave his first performance.

In front of the church stands the Mariensäule (Column of Our Lady), a monument commissioned by Ferdinand III to commemorate the end of the threat of the Swedish invasion, at the conclusion of the Thirty Years' War.

Austria Fountain in a courtyard in Freyung Passage

Freyung ㉑

Map 2 B3. *Herrengasse.* *1A.* *1, D.*

The square derives its name from the right of sanctuary (frey is an old word for "free") granted to any fugitive seeking refuge in the Schottenkirche (Scottish church), now at No. 6. The priory church was founded by Irish Benedictine friars, who came to Vienna in 1177. Although much altered, the church has a Neo-Classical façade and a magnificent Baroque interior, which still bears features of its former Romanesque decor. Above the tabernacle stands the 13th-century statue of Our Lady, the oldest Romanesque sculpture in Vienna.

The adjacent abbey buildings house a picture gallery with an interesting collection of medieval art.

Other interesting buildings in Freyung include the Baroque Harrach Palace at No. 3, designed by Domenic Martinelli (1690) and, at No. 4, the Kinsky Palace, designed by Johann Lukas von Hildebrandt, who became the court architect in 1700.

Nearby is one of the few remaining, largely unaltered Renaissance buildings, the Porcia Palace of 1546, one of the oldest in Vienna.

At the centre of the square, in a glass-roofed, hexagonal atrium, stands the Austria Fountain. Erected in 1846, it shows an allegorical figure of Austria surrounded by four mermaids representing the major rivers (Danube, Elbe, Po, Vistula) in the Habsburg Empire at the time.

Herrengasse ㉒

Map 2 A3, B4. *Herrengasse.* *2A, 3A.*

Herrengasse was once one of the smartest addresses in Vienna, where the nobility had their palaces. Nowadays, most buildings are occupied by government offices. Herrengasse's name, meaning gentlemen's alleyway, dates from the 16th century, when the Landhaus at No. 13 was the seat of the Provincial Government of Lower Austria, the province surrounding Vienna. It fulfilled this function until 1986, when the small town of St Pölten became the new capital of the province. Some very old parts of the Landhaus still remain; the chapel is believed to have been built by Anton Pilgram, one of the architects of Stephansdom. The present building was rebuilt in 1837–48, under the supervision of Ludwig Pichl. In the courtyard, a tablet from 1571 warns visitors not to carry weapons or fight here. The injunction was famously ignored when the 1848 Revolution was ignited on this very spot. In 1918 the Republic was proclaimed from the Landhaus.

Liechtenstein Palace, seen from Minoritenplatz

Minoritenplatz ㉓

Map 2 B4. *Herrengasse.* *2A, 3A.*

The dominant feature of the square is Minoritenkirche. Built originally by Minor Friars in 1224, the present structure is a Franciscan church from the 14th century. It was rebuilt during the Baroque period, and restored to its original Gothic form in the 19th century. The church retains a fine west portal (1340). The tower acquired its unusual pyramid shape during the Turkish siege of Vienna in 1529, when a shell sliced the top off the steeple. Inside the church is a mosaic copy of Leonardo da Vinci's *Last Supper*.

Between Minoritenplatz and Bankgasse is the town palace of the Liechtenstein family.

On the south side of the square, at No. 3, is the former palace of the Dietrichstein family. This palace, an early work in 1755 by Franz Hillebrand, now houses the Austrian Chancellor's Office and the Foreign Office. Its rooms have witnessed many historic events.

Street-by-Street: The Hofburg Complex

The Hofburg Complex, the former Emperor's residence, is a permanent reminder of the glory of the Habsburg Empire, with its majestic palace – particularly impressive when seen from Heldenplatz – and the harmony of the squares and palaces in Augustinerstrasse. This part of Vienna is one of the capital's most fashionable and lively areas, both during the daytime and at night, when the former palace rooms serve as theatre and concert halls.

Michaelerplatz
The Michaelertrakt, on the site of the former court theatre on the south side of the square, was commissioned by Franz Joseph as a passageway and built to designs by Ferdinand Kirschner 24

Heldenplatz
The square between Ring and Hofburg is used for large public gatherings 26

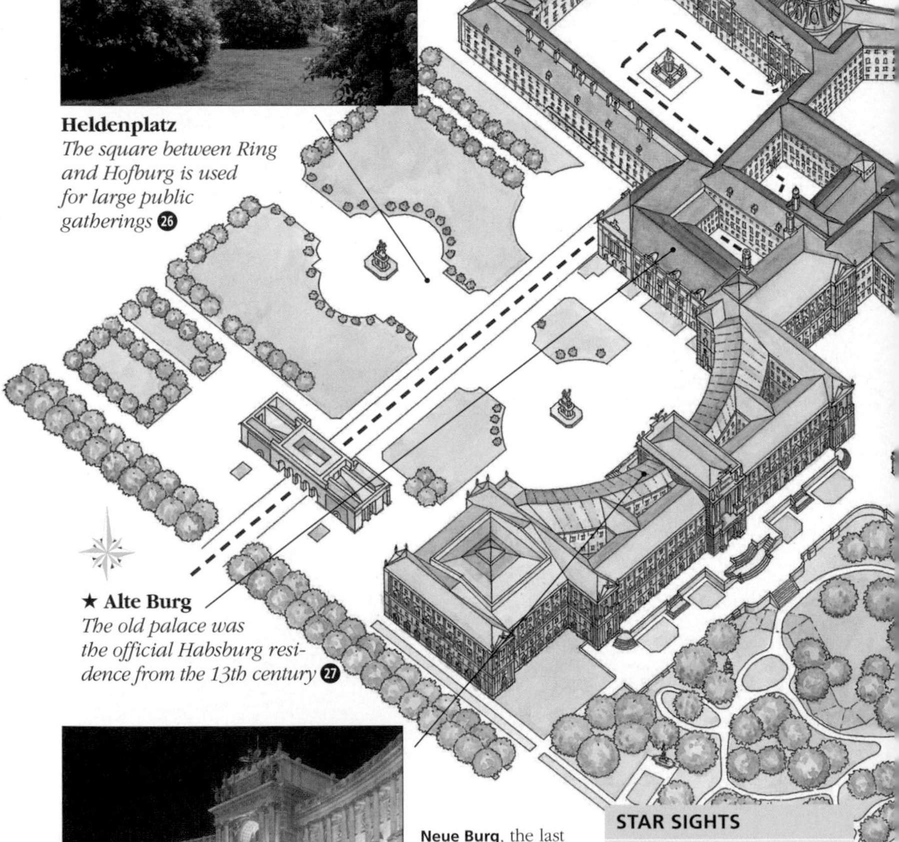

★ Alte Burg
The old palace was the official Habsburg residence from the 13th century 27

Neue Burg, the last wing of Hofburg, was built just before the outbreak of World War I, during the final days of the monarchy.

STAR SIGHTS

- ★ Albertina
- ★ Alte Burg
- ★ Josefsplatz

Kohlmarkt has some of the smartest shops in town, including some designed by the renowned architect Hans Hollein.

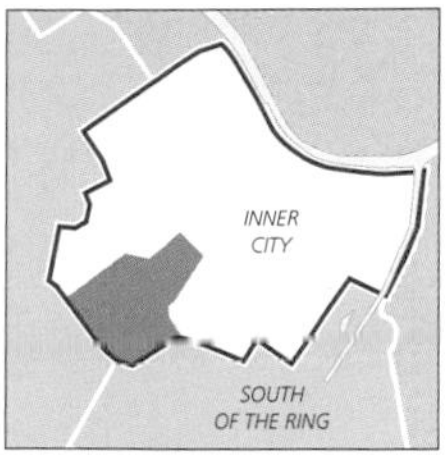

LOCATOR MAP
See Street Finder map 2

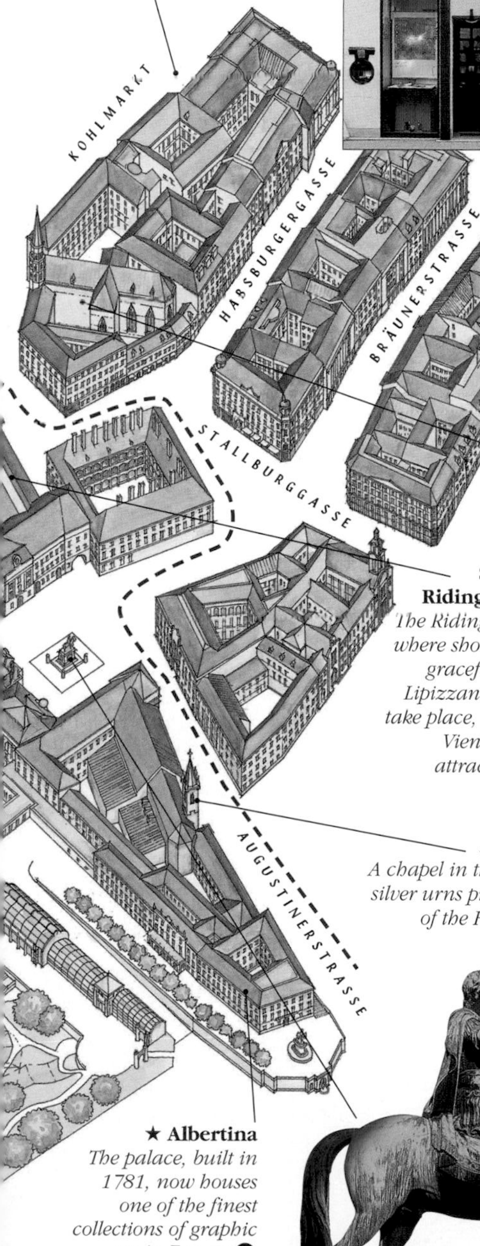

Inside Michaelerkirche the Rococo main altar and the 14th-century Renaissance frescoes are spectacular.

Spanish Riding School
The Riding School, where shows of the graceful, white Lipizzaner horses take place, is one of Vienna's star attractions ㉘

Augustinerkirche
A chapel in the church contains silver urns preserving the hearts of the Habsburg family ㉚

★ Albertina
The palace, built in 1781, now houses one of the finest collections of graphic art in Europe ㉛

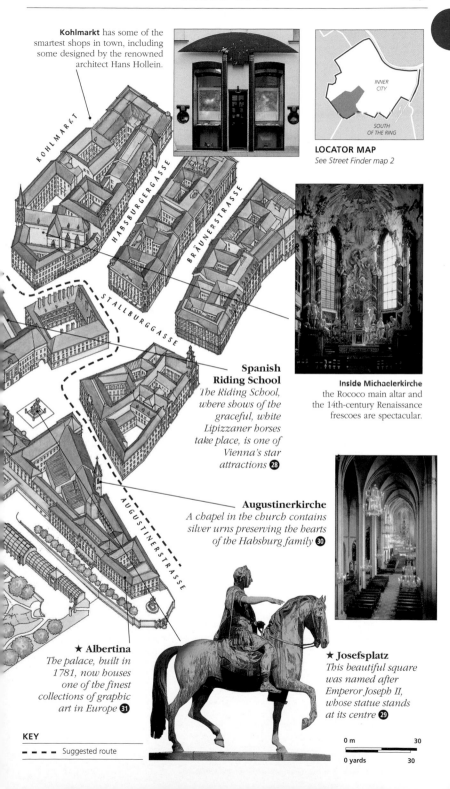

★ Josefsplatz
This beautiful square was named after Emperor Joseph II, whose statue stands at its centre ㉙

KEY

- - - Suggested route

0 m 30
0 yards 30

Stucco angels in Michaelerkirche, in Michaelerplatz

Michaelerplatz ㉔

Map 2 B4. *Herrengasse.* *2A, 3A.*

Michaelerplatz faces the grand main entrance into the imperial residence, the Michaelertor (St Michael's Doorway), which leads to the Hofburg's inner courtyard. On both sides of the doorway are 19th-century wall fountains, designed by Rudolf Weyer, which represent the empire's land and sea power.

Michaelerkirche (St Michael's Church) was once the parish church of the court. Its oldest parts date from the 13th century. According to legend, the church was built in 1221 by Leopold VI of Babenberg. Its present form dates from 1792, when it was given a Neo-Classical façade, while still preserving its Baroque portal. The interior features one of the most beautiful Rococo altars in Vienna. Above the altar is a stucco relief depicting the expulsion of the rebel angels from heaven and the Archangel Gabriel at the head of the heavenly host.

In the 17th and 18th centuries, affluent parishioners were buried under the church. Their well-preserved corpses, clothed in their burial finery, are displayed in the crypt, in open coffins.

The remains of a Roman encampment, as well as some medieval foundations, were discovered underneath the square in 1990.

Volksgarten ㉕

Dr.-Karl-Renner-Ring. **Map** 2 A4. *Herrengasse.* *1, 2, D.* *2A.* *Apr–Nov: 6am–10pm daily; Dec–Mar: 6:30am–10pm daily.*

Volksgarten (the People's Garden) was created in 1820, when Napoleon had the city walls destroyed. The formal plantations created in the French style, particularly the splendid rose gardens, became a place of relaxation for fashionable society.

People met at one of two Classicist structures by Peter Nobile, Theseustempel (the Temple of Theseus) or Cortisches Kaffeehaus, remains of which are visible in today's Garden Café. Canova's statue of Theseus was meant for the temple, but today it graces Kunsthistorisches Museum *(see pp84–7)*. Instead, a statue of an athlete (1921) by Joseph Möllner stands in front of the temple. There is also a monument devoted to the writer Franz Grillparzer and a fountain memorial dedicated to Empress Elisabeth.

Heldenplatz ㉖

Map 2 A4, A5. *Volkstheater.* *1, 2, 46, D.* *2A.* **Neue Burg** ***Tel*** *52 524-484.* *10am–6pm Mon, Wed–Sun.*

During Vienna's grand 19th-century reconstruction, Heldenplatz was planned as the centre of a majestic imperial forum that was to adjoin the old Hofburg complex, surrounded by new buildings housing the emperor's art collection. Neue Burg (New Castle) was completed in 1913, but by then the monarchy was dying out.

The vast, undeveloped Heroes' Square, the largest public space in Vienna, remained. It was here, in March 1938, that Adolf Hitler announced Austria's incorporation into the German Reich.

The entrance to the square is via Burgtor (Palace Gate), built in 1824 to commemorate the victory of the coalition against Napoleon in the Battle of Nations, at Leipzig (1813). Later, it served as the Monument to the Unknown Soldier. The two equestrian statues in the square, by Anton Fernkorn, are of Archduke Charles and Prince Eugene of Saxony.

The latter stands in front of Neue Burg, which now houses, among other sights, the Ephesos Museum, named after the archaeological site in Turkey which yielded the finds displayed here. There is also a collection of early musical instruments, some owned by famous musicians; one of the most impressive arms collections in Europe; and an ethnological museum with valuable Oriental and African exhibits.

The equestrian statue of Prince Eugene of Saxony, on Heldenplatz

Alte Burg ㉗

See pp68–9.

Spanish Riding School ㉘

The Spanish Riding School was founded in 1572. Initially, its circus-style training of horses served a practical purpose, but today performances are staged purely for entertainment, and have become one of the city's top attractions. Shows are held in the building known as the Winterreitschule (Winter Riding School), constructed between 1729 and 1735 by Joseph E. Fischer von Erlach. The Hofburg fire, in 1992, destroyed some of the stables and almost put an end to the school's activities.

VISITORS' CHECKLIST

Michaelerplatz 1. **Map** 2 B4. ***Tel*** *53 39 031.* *Herrengasse, Stephansplatz.* *2A, 3A.* *Jan–Jun, Aug–Dec: 10am–noon Tue–Sat.* **www**.srs.at

Interior of the Winter Riding School
The opulent interior is lined with 46 columns and adorned with stucco ornaments, chandeliers and a coffered ceiling.

RIDER IN TYPICAL UNIFORM

The riders of the Winter Riding School wear historical uniforms, which are complemented by elegant saddles with embroidered cloth.

THE HORSES' STEPS

The steps made by the horses are part of a carefully orchestrated ballet. The riders perform on the specially trained white Lipizzaner stallions, a breed originally produced by crossing Spanish, Arab and Berber horses.

The Levade
The horse stands on its hind legs, hocks almost touching the ground.

The Capriole
The horse leaps into the air with a simultaneous kick of the hind legs.

The Croupade
The horse leaps into the air with hind legs and forelegs bent under its belly.

The Piaffe
The horse trots on the spot, often between two pillars.

Alte Burg ㉗

The Imperial Palace is a vast complex. Its construction was started by the Babenbergs, but the Neue Burg (New Castle) was not completed until 1913. Apart from housing several museums, including in the royal apartments a museum dedicated to Empress Elisabeth, the Alte Burg is today also a conference centre. Different architectural styles are represented in individual parts of the complex: the Gothic Schweizerhof, the Renaissance Stallburg courtyard and the Baroque Josefsplatz.

In der Burg
This large inner courtyard, called "inside the fortress", has a large statue of Franz I, built by Pompeo Marchesi, in 1842–46.

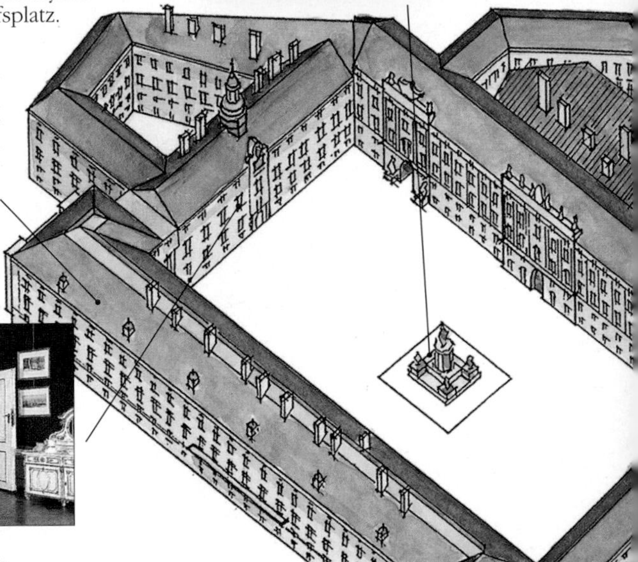

The Leopoldinischer Trakt, dating from 1660–70 and built by Leopold I, today houses the offices of the President of Austria.

Amalienburg
In the 19th century, this Renaissance palace, built for Rudolf II in 1575, was the home of Empress Elisabeth. Shown above is her dressing room with gymnastic equipment.

The Silberkammer
The Silver Chamber displays stunning silver, gold and porcelain tableware, and vessels used at official receptions, such as this 1821 goblet.

STAR FEATURES

- ★ Reichskanzleitrakt
- ★ Schatzkammer
- ★ Schweizertor

★ Schweizertor
The 16th-century Baroque Swiss Gate leads to the oldest parts of the castle, originally a four-tower stronghold.

For hotels and restaurants in this region see pp288–94 and pp318–24

★ Reichskanzleitrakt
Franz Joseph's apartments in the Imperial Chancery Wing, built in 1726–30, are open to visitors. This portrait of Empress Elisabeth (1865) hangs in the Sisi Museum.

VISITORS' CHECKLIST

Michaelerplatz 1. **Map** 2 B4. ***Tel*** *533 75 70.* *Stephansplatz, Herrengasse.* *1, 2, D.* *57A.* **Imperial Apartments** ***Tel*** *533 75 70.* *9am–5pm daily.* **Treasury** ***Tel*** *525 24 4031.* *10am–6pm Wed–Mon.* **www**.hofburg-wien.at **www**.khm.at

★ Schatzkammer
The collection of sacred and secular treasures, including this 10th-century crown, is regarded as the most magnificent of its kind in the world.

Michaelertor, **leading to Hofburg**

The Spanish Riding School stages its world-famous horse riding performances at the Winterreitschule (Winter Riding School).

Stallburg, a Renaissance palace, houses the stables.

Redoutensäle, the former ballrooms.

The Burgkapelle
The Gothic Royal Chapel was completed in 1449. The Wiener Sängerknaben (the Vienna Boys' Choir) sings here on Sundays.

Nationalbibliothek
The showpiece of the Austrian National Library (1722–35) is the opulent Prunksaal, or Hall of Honour, panelled in wood.

The magnificent Prunksaal in the National Library, on Josefsplatz

Josefsplatz ㉙

Map 2 B4. *Stephansplatz, Herrengasse.* *2A, 3A.*

In the centre of Josefsplatz stands an equestrian statue (1807) of Joseph II portrayed as a Roman emperor, by Franz Anton Zauner.

Behind the statue, to the right, is the entrance to the National Library building designed by Johann Bernhard Fischer von Erlach. Its Prunksaal (Hall of Honour) is regarded as the most beautiful library in Europe. Frescoes by the Baroque painter Daniel Gran adorn its vault. The walls of the historic reading room are graced by Johann Bergel's frescoes.

Perhaps the grandest items in the library's rich collection are the cartographic treasures exhibited just behind the Prunksaal.

The Redoutensäle, in the wing adjacent to the library and once the Court Ballrooms, now serve as the head office of the Vienna Congress Centre.

On the opposite side of Josefsplatz are two interesting palaces: at No. 5 is the 18th-century Pallavicini Palace by Ferdinand von Hohenberg, and at No. 6 the 16th-century Palffy Palace by Nikolaus Pacassi. They now serve as cultural venues for the city.

Augustinerkirche ㉚

Augustinerstrasse 3. **Map** 2 B5. ***Tel*** *53 37 099.* *Stephansplatz, Karlsplatz, Oper.* *3A.* *7am–6pm Mon–Sat, 9am–7pm Sun.* **Mass** *11am Sun & church hols.*

The 14th-century Gothic Augustinian church was refurbished in the Baroque style, but some 100 years later was restored again to its original character. Inside is one of the most powerful works by Antonio Canova (1805), the tomb of Maria Christina, Maria Theresa's favourite daughter. It is shaped like a pyramid, approached by a funeral procession. St George's Chapel, on the right, contains the tomb of Emperor Leopold II and, further along, is a small crypt with silver urns containing the hearts of the Habsburg family as well as the heart of Napoleon's son, the King of Rome, who died when young.

Tomb of Maria Christina in Augustinerkirche

The church was once the Court Chapel and, as such, the scene of many historic events including the wedding of Marie Louise (1812) to Napoleon, and that of Elisabeth of Bavaria (Sisi) to Franz Joseph (1854).

Albertina ㉛

Albertinaplatz 1. **Map** 2 B5. ***Tel*** *534 830.* *Stephansplatz, Karlsplatz.* *1, 2, D, 62, 65.* *2A, 3A.* *10am–6pm daily, 10am–9pm Wed.* **www**.albertina.at

The Albertina was once the Habsburg palace of Duke Albert of Sachsen-Teschen and his wife Archduchess Marie-Christina, the favourite daughter of Maria Theresa.

The beautiful Neo-Classical Historic State Rooms in the palace are among the most valuable examples of Classical architecture. They have been opened up to visitors.

The Albertina houses one of the world's finest collection of graphics, including works by Leonardo da Vinci, Michelangelo, Dürer, Rubens, Manet and Cezanne, as well as by Schiele, Klimt and Picasso. It has a million prints, over 65,000 watercolours and drawings and some 70,000 photographs. It is also home to the Sammlung Batliner, a collection of paintings under the motto "Monet to Picasso".

Kapuzinerkirche and Kaisergruft 32

Neuer Markt. **Map** 2 C5. ***Tel*** *51 26 853.* *Stephansplatz, Karlsplatz.* *3A.* *10am–6pm daily.*

The Capuchin church stands at the southwestern corner of Neuer Markt, formerly a cereal and flour market. In 1617, Anna of Tyrol, wife of Emperor Matthias, founded a crypt in its vaults in which the Habsburg family members were laid to rest. Today, the Kaisergruft (imperial crypt) contains the earthly remains of 138 family members. The only Habsburg monarchs not present are Ferdinand II, whose vast tomb-mausoleum is in Graz, and Charles I, the last Austrian emperor who died in exile and is buried on Madeira. The only non-Habsburg buried here is Maria Theresa's governess, Countess Caroline Fuchs.

The double sarcophagus of Maria Theresa and her husband Franz Stephan I, the work of Balthasar Ferdinand Moll, is worth looking at. It bears the statues of the imperial couple and four figures with the crowns of Austria, Hungary, Bohemia and Jerusalem (the Habsburgs were also the titular Kings of Jerusalem).

Tomb of Karl VI, by Balthasar Moll

The most poignant tomb is the crypt of Franz Joseph I, where the long-lived monarch rests flanked by separate tombs containing the remains of his wife Elisabeth, assassinated by an Italian anarchist, and their only son Crown Prince Rudolf, who committed suicide in 1889.

The last person to be buried in the imperial crypt was the Empress Zita, wife of Charles I, last Emperor of Austria, who was interred in 1989.

It is worth noting that, on their death, the Habsburgs were dismembered; their hearts are kept in silver urns in Augustinerkirche *(see p70)*, their entrails are held in the catacombs of Stephansdom *(see pp58–9)*, and only what remained is in the Kaisergruft.

Grand stairway in the Winterpalais des Prinzen Eugen

Winterpalais des Prinzen Eugen 33

Himmelpfortgasse 1A. **Map** 2 C5. ***Tel*** *51 433.* *Stephansplatz.* *I8.*

The palace was commissioned in 1694, by Prince Eugene of Savoy, one of the most brilliant military commanders of his day, who entrusted the task to Johann Bernhard Fischer von Erlach. It was subsequently extended by Johann Lukas von Hildebrandt. Its central part includes the original magnificent staircase, adorned with sculptures by Giovanni Giuliani. The central portal reliefs depict the figure of Aeneas carrying his father out of the burning city of Troy, and the hero Hercules who is slaying a monster.

From 1848 until 2006, the palace was home to the Ministry of Finance. It is not open to the public, but visitors may view the famous staircase and glance into the courtyard with its Rococo fountain.

Nearby, at Seilerstätte No. 30, is the Haus der Musik (House of Music). This is a museum dedicated to the Wiener Philharmoniker (Vienna Philharmonic), it also houses a high-tech exhibition on the nature of sound, which allows visitors to see and feel as well as hear music.

Kärntner Strasse 34

Map 2 B5, C4, C5. *Stephansplatz, Karlsplatz.* *1A, 2A, 3A.* *1, 2, 62, 65, D.*

Kärntner Strasse was once the main road running south across town to Kärnten (Carinthia), hence its name.

Today, the view down the street is blocked at its Ring end by the silhouette of the opera house, and at the Stock-im-Eisen-Platz end by the modern Haas-Haus, which reflects the spires of the Stephansdom. At Stock-im-Eisen-Platz there is a wooden block into which every passing apprentice ironworker used to drive a nail, in the hope that this would ensure his safe return.

In the mid-section, at No. 37, stands the Malteserkirche (Church of the Knights of Malta). The Maltese Knights came to Vienna in the early 13th century, and the church remains under their jurisdiction to this day. The church walls display the coats of arms of the Grand Masters of the Maltese Order.

Malteserkirche is one of the few older buildings in the street. When Kärntner Strasse was widened during the 19th century, to transform it into the old town's main artery, most of the buildings were demolished.

Today, the pedestrianized street is one of Vienna's most fashionable and expensive shopping streets. Here, you can shop at one of many exclusive boutiques, eat and drink in busy restaurants, bars and outdoor cafés, and listen to street musicians or just watch others stroll by.

Frauenhuber, a café near Kärntner Strasse

NORTH OF MARIAHILFER STRASSE

This district, to the north of Mariahilfer Strasse and along the Ring, includes some of the most magnificent and monumental buildings in Vienna. The semicircular Ring or Ringstrasse, developed during the 1870s and 1880s, is a grand boulevard divided into nine sections, each named after architectural landmarks or prominent politicians from the Habsburg era. Today, it is still Vienna's most prestigious street. In this district visitors will find many of the city's cultural institutions, including the biggest concentration of museums in Austria. Mariahilfer Strasse is also a very busy shopping street, with large department stores and many cafés and bars, concentrated especially in the cobbled, pedestrianized streets of the bustling Spittelberg area.

Figure of a saint in Sankt-Ulrichs-Platz

SIGHTS AT A GLANCE

Streets
Mariahilfer Strasse 18
Spittelberg 19

Historic Buildings
Burgtheater pp78–9 3
Josephinum 7
Old AKH – University Campus 8
Palais Trautson 13
Parlament 2
Neues Rathaus 1
Theater in der Josefstadt 12
Universität 4
Volkstheater 14

Churches
Dreifaltigkeitskirche 9
Maria Treu Kirche 11
Votivkirche 5

Museums and Galleries
Freud-Museum 6
Kunsthistorisches Museum pp84–7 16
Museum für Volkskunde 10
MuseumsQuartier 17
Naturhistorisches Museum 15

GETTING THERE

Parts of the Ring are served by tram lines 1, 2 and D. U3 U-Bahn trains run along Mariahilfer Strasse; Schottenring can be reached by U2. The district is also criss-crossed by many tramlines: 5, 33, 37, 38, 41, 42, 43, 44, 46, 48, 49, 52, 58, and bus lines Nos. 1A, 2A, 13A, 40A, 48A, 57A.

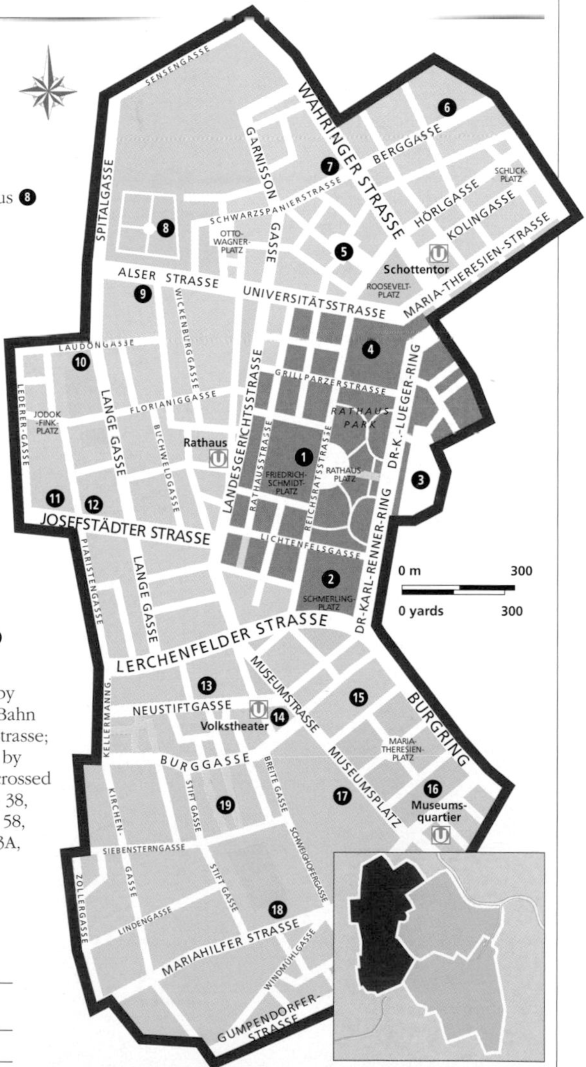

KEY

Street-by-Street map *see pp74–5*

U-Bahn station

◁ **The opulent façade of Neues Rathaus by night, in the pre-Christmas period**

Street-by-Street: Around the Town Hall

The most prestigious buildings in Vienna were erected in the second half of the 19th century, in Ringstrasse, at the command of Emperor Franz Joseph I. These include Neues Rathaus (the new town hall, seat of the town administration), the immense Parlament (the seat of Austria's Upper and Lower Houses), the magnificent buildings of the University, and the Burgtheater.

The square in front of the town hall, with its adjacent park, is Vienna's largest open-air arena, serving as a stage for theatre and concert performances, and in the summer for vast film screenings.

The Town Hall forecourt turns into a vast Christmas market in December, selling gifts and Christmas decorations.

★ Neues Rathaus
This Neo-Gothic building, modelled on Brussels' town hall, is the seat of the Vienna City and Provincial Assembly ❶

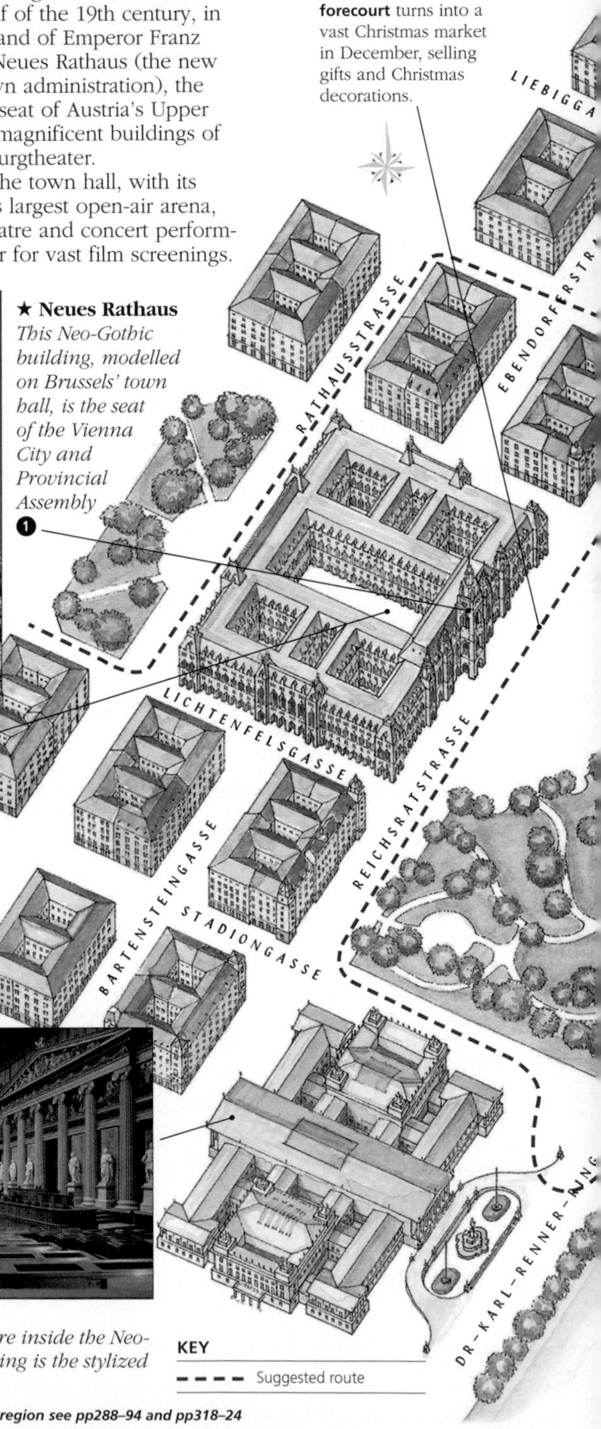

Arkadenhof, the courtyard of the town hall, serves as a concert venue in summer.

0 m 100
0 yards 100

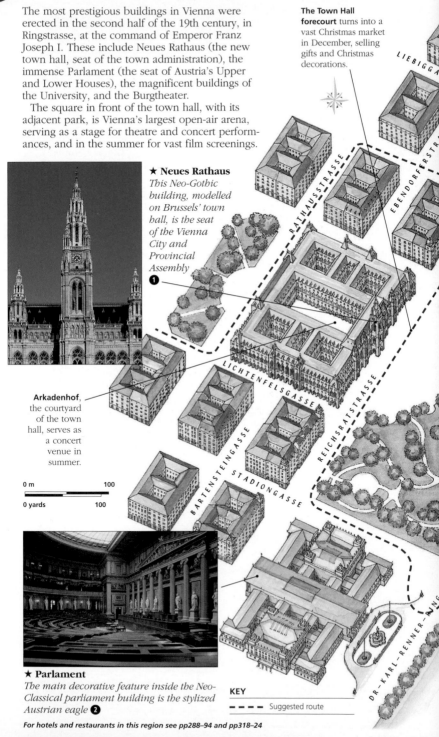

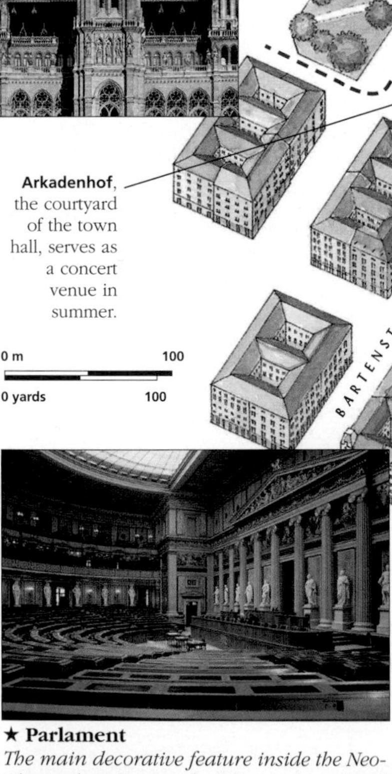

★ Parlament
The main decorative feature inside the Neo-Classical parliament building is the stylized Austrian eagle ❷

KEY

- - - - Suggested route

For hotels and restaurants in this region see pp288–94 and pp318–24

★ Universität
The University courtyard is surrounded by arcades lined with busts of its professors ❹

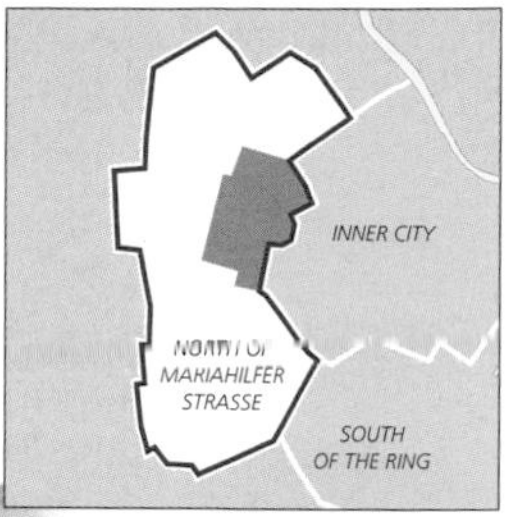

LOCATOR MAP
See Street Finder maps 1, 2

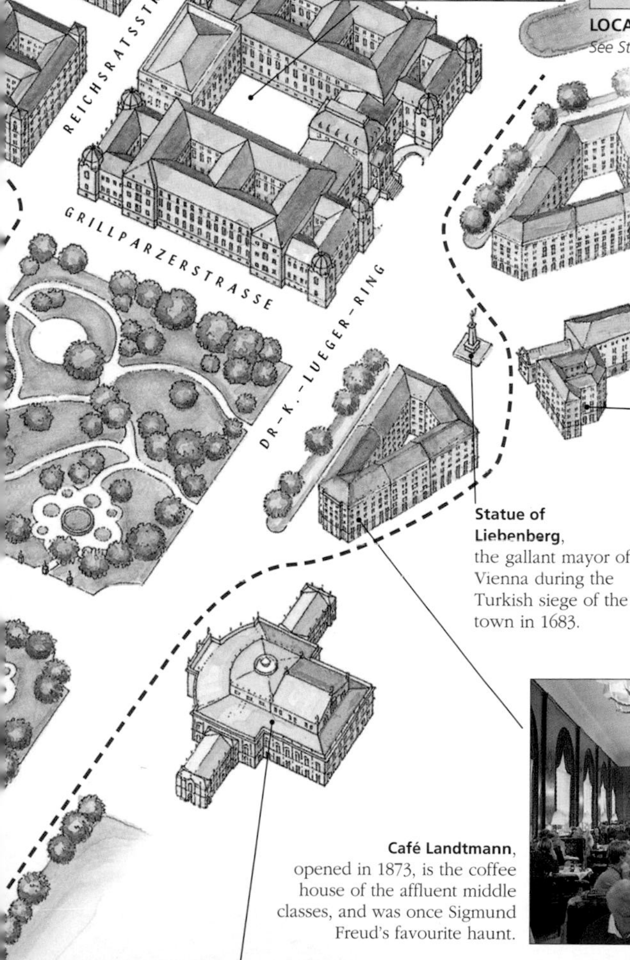

Plaque from the Pasqualati house at Mölker-Bastei No. 8, which, in 1804–8 and again in 1810–15, was the home of Ludwig van Beethoven. It was here that he composed his opera Fidelio, as well as Symphonies 4, 5, 7 and 8. Today, the house is a small museum.

Statue of Liebenberg, the gallant mayor of Vienna during the Turkish siege of the town in 1683.

Café Landtmann, opened in 1873, is the coffee house of the affluent middle classes, and was once Sigmund Freud's favourite haunt.

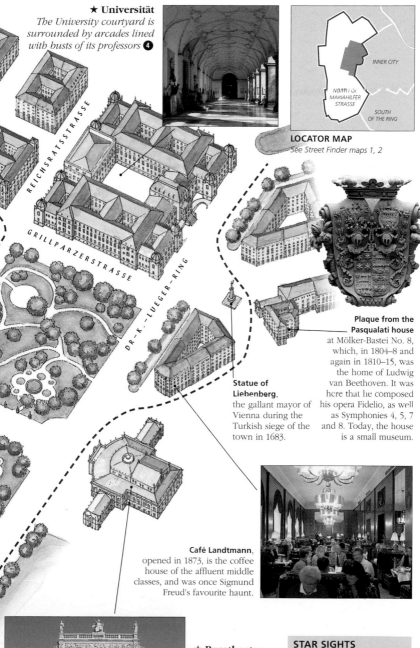

★ Burgtheater
The high attic above the centre of the building is decorated with a frieze depicting a Bacchanalian procession ❸

STAR SIGHTS

- ★ Burgtheater
- ★ Neues Rathaus
- ★ Parlament
- ★ Universität

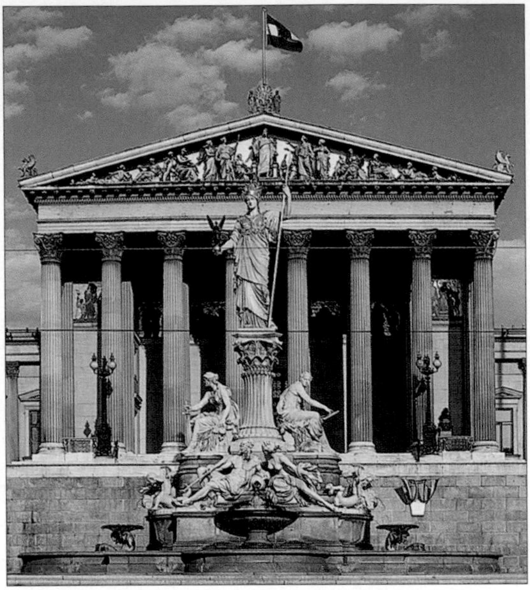

Pallas Athena monument in front of the parliament building

Neues Rathaus ❶

Friedrich-Schmidt-Platz 1. **Map** 1 C3. ***Tel*** *52 550.* *Rathaus.* *1, D.* *Sep–Jul: Mon–Sat. Telephone reservations for group visits.* *during meetings and public holidays.*

The new town hall, built in 1872–83 by Friedrich Schmidt, lies in an attractive park. The symmetrical, triple façade of the Neo-Gothic building faces Ringstrasse. Its huge central tower, 98 m (321 ft) high, is topped by the statue of a knight-in-armour, one of Vienna's symbols. The main tower is flanked by two smaller towers, 60 m (197 ft) high. The town hall cellar is a restaurant. The whole length of the first floor is taken up by a reception hall. The forecourt is used for many events, including the Christmas fair.

Parlament ❷

Dr.-Karl-Renner-Ring 3. **Map** 1 C4. ***Tel*** *40 11 00-25 70.* *Volkstheater.* *1, 2, D.* *11am, 3pm Mon–Thu; 11am, 1pm, 2pm, 3pm Fri.* **www**.parlament.gv.at

Today's assembly hall of Austria's two-chamber parliament originally served as the location of the highest legislative body of the Austrian part of the Austro-Hungarian Empire. An imposing Neo-Classical building, the Parlament was completed in 1883 to designs by the Dutch architect, Theophil Hansen.

The entrance is raised above street level. A gently sloping ramp leads to the main portico, which is modelled on a Greek temple. Both the ramp and the attic are adorned with carved marble figures of Greek and Roman historians, scholars and statesmen. The relief depicts the Emperor Franz Joseph I handing the constitution to the representatives of the 17 peoples of the Empire. The magnificently decorated state apartments and conference rooms can be visited in a guided tour. The lower vestibule contains busts of prominent members of the Austrian National Assembly.

The side wings have four bronze chariot groups, each driven by Nike, the Greek goddess of victory. Another, smaller statue of Nike is held aloft by her fellow goddess, of wisdom, Pallas Athena, whose 5-m (16-ft) statue is the main feature of the monumental fountain in front of the central portico, designed by Karl Kundmann and placed here in 1902. It is flanked by allegorical figures representing Law Enforcement (left) and Legislation (right), as well as figures symbolizing the major rivers of the empire.

Burgtheater ❸

See pp78–9.

Universität ❹

Dr.-Karl-Lueger-Ring 1. **Map** 2 A3. ***Tel*** *42 77 0.* *Schottentor.* *1, 41, 42, 43, 44.* *1A.*

Vienna University is the oldest university in the German-speaking world and the third oldest in Central Europe, after Prague and Cracow. It was founded in 1365, by Rudolf IV, and flourished and grew in the late 15th century. Its present

The main building of Vienna University

home, designed by Heinrich Ferstel in the style of the Italian Renaissance, was completed in 1883.

The university complex has its buildings arranged around one large and eight smaller courtyards. The courtyard arcades, modelled on the Palazzo Farnese in Rome, are adorned with statues of famous scholars associated with Vienna University, including one of Freud.

Neo-Gothic stone figures from the façade of Votivkirche

Votivkirche ❺

Rooseveltplatz 8. **Map** 2 A2. ***Tel*** *40 61 192.* *Schottentor.* *1, 37, 38, 43, 44, D.* *9am–1pm, 4–6:30pm Tue–Sat, 9am–1pm Sun.*

Opposite the spot where a deranged man tried to assassinate Franz Joseph I in 1853, stands this Neo-Gothic church with its two 99-m (325-ft) high, lacy steeples completed 26 years later as a grateful offering for sparing the Emperor's life. The architect was Heinrich von Ferstel.

The most beautiful historic relic in the Votivkirche is its late 15th-century Antwerpian altar, a masterpiece of Flemish woodcarving, representing scenes from the Passion. The main portal sculptures depict the four Evangelists and figures from the Old Testament, along with four patrons of the Empire's regions.

Many of the chapels inside the church are dedicated to the Austrian regiments and to military heroes.

Sigmund Freud's waiting room in the Freud-Museum

Freud-Museum ❻

Berggasse 19. **Map** 2 A1. ***Tel*** *31 91 596.* *Schottentor.* *37, 38, 40, 41, 42, D.* *40A.* *9am–5pm daily.* **www**.freud-museum.at

Berggasse No. 19, a typical 20th-century Viennese town house, was the home of Sigmund Freud, the famous doctor and father of psychoanalysis, from 1891–1938. Here he created his most acclaimed works and treated patients before he was forced to flee Austria at the arrival of the Nazis.

The room in which Freud received patients is on the mezzanine floor. In the small, dark lobby hangs Freud's frayed hat; in a corner stands his travel trunk. A cabinet contains some archaeological objects collected by Freud. The world-famous couch, however, now stands in the Freud museum in London.

A Foundation for the Arts was initiated in 1989 in order to confront a scientific institution with contemporary art.

Josephinum ❼

Währingerstrasse 25. **Map** 1 C2. ***Tel*** *40 160-26 000.* *Schottentor.* *37, 38, 40, 41, 42.* *10am–6pm Mon–Sat.* *public holidays.*

Designed by Isidor Canevale and built in 1783–85, this building once housed the Military Surgical Institute. Life-sized anatomical wax models, commissioned by Joseph II to teach human anatomy to his army surgeons, are now the main attraction of the medical museum based here today.

Old AKH – University Campus ❽

Alsergasse 4/Spitalgasse 2. **Map** 1 A1, B1. *Schottentor.* **Federal Museum of Pathological Anatomy** ***Tel*** *40 68 672.* *3–6pm Wed, 8–11am Thu, 10am–1pm 1st Sat of the month.* *Public holidays.* **www**.univie.ac.at

Vienna's Old General Hospital (AKH), built in 1784, was donated to the University of Vienna in 1988 and adapted to house the 15 academic faculties of the university.

It was inaugurated in 1998 as university campus. The complex consists of several buildings around one vast and 12 smaller courtyards. The Narrenturm (Madman's Tower) of the former lunatic asylum, designed by Canevale, now houses the **Federal Museum for Pathological Anatomy**.

FREUD'S THEORIES

With his theory of psychoanalysis, Sigmund Freud (1856–1939) has exerted a lasting influence not only on medicine but also on our culture generally. According to Freud, the unconscious psyche, driven by certain instincts and impulses, in particular the sexual instinct (libido), is the main engine behind all our conscious and unconscious actions. An imbalance in the psychological system, so posited Freud, could lead to very serious emotional disorders and might result in severe mental disturbance.

Various objects used by Sigmund Freud

Burgtheater ❸

The Burgtheater is one of the most prestigious stages in the German-speaking world. The original theatre, built in Maria Theresa's reign, was replaced in 1888 by today's Italian Renaissance-style building by Karl von Hasenauer and Gottfried Semper. In 1897, after the discovery that the auditorium had several seats with no view of the stage, it closed for refurbishment. A bomb devastated the building in 1945, leaving only the side wings and Grand Staircases intact, but subsequent restoration was so successful that today the damage is hard to see.

Busts of Playwrights
Lining the walls of the Grand Staircases are busts of playwrights whose works are still performed here, including this one of Johann Nepomuk Nestroy (left) *by Hans Knesl.*

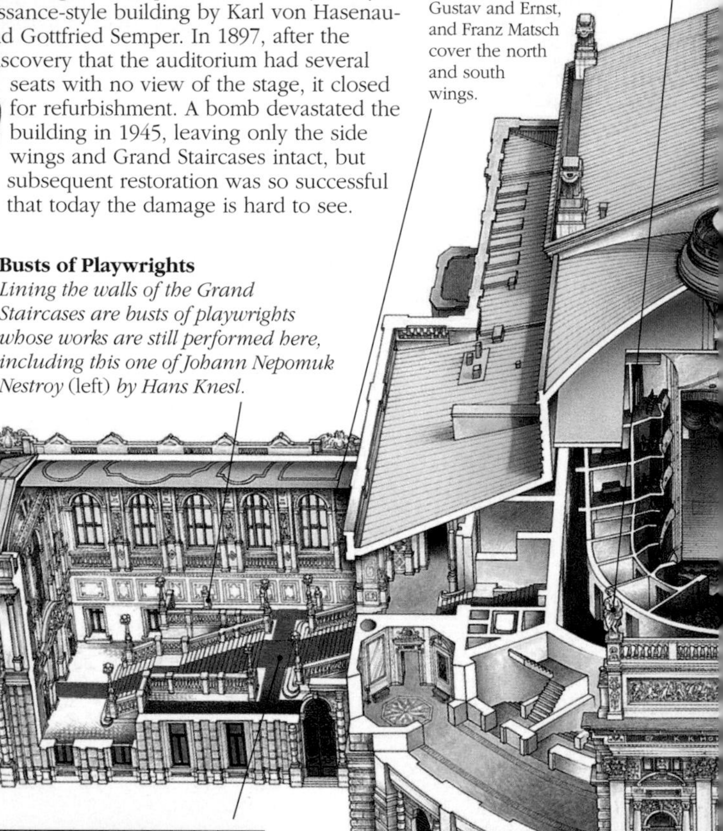

Statue of the muse, Melpomene

Ceiling frescoes
by the Klimt brothers, Gustav and Ernst, and Franz Matsch cover the north and south wings.

Main entrance on Dr.-Karl-Lueger-Ring

★ Grand Staircases
The two majestic gala staircases in the side wings are the only original parts of the building that escaped destruction in World War II.

STAR FEATURES
★ Der Thespiskarren
★ Front Façade
★ Grand Staircases

Foyer
The walls of the curving first-floor foyer are lined with the portraits of famous actors and actresses.

For hotels and restaurants in this region see pp288–94 and pp318–24

Auditorium
During rebuilding after the war, the original layout was kept in the auditorium with the imperial colours of red, gold and cream. It seats over 1,000 spectators.

VISITORS' CHECKLIST

Dr.-Karl-Lueger-Ring 2. **Map** 2 A3. ***Tel*** *51 444 41 40.* *Schottentor, Minoritenplatz.* *1, D.* *Guided tours 3pm daily; performances: Sep–Jun; tickets: 9am–6pm Mon–Fri, 9am–noon Sat.* **www**.burgtheater.at

★ **Der Thespiskarren**
The ceiling frescoes in the side wings are by the Klimt brothers and Franz Matsch. This one, by Gustav Klimt, depicts the cart of Thespis, first performer of a Greek tragedy.

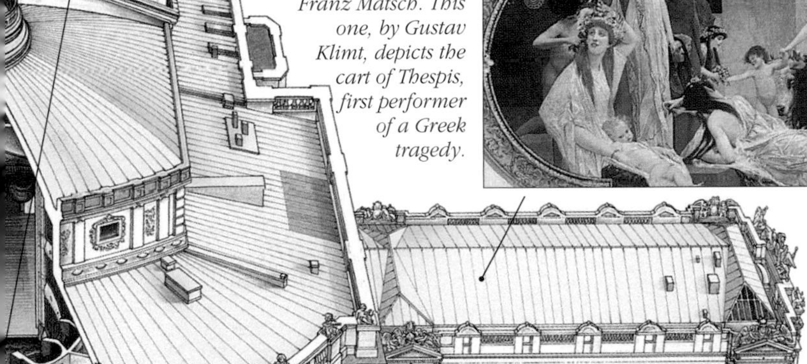

Statue of the muse, Thalia

★ **Front Façade**
The façade is crowned by a frieze of Bacchus and Ariadne, by Rudolf Weyr. Above the frieze towers the statue of Apollo.

TIMELINE

1741 Maria Theresa founds the Burgheater in an empty ballroom at the Hofburg, to stage mainly Italian operas

1874 Work on the present building begins

1955 After its destruction in World War II, the theatre reopens with Grillparzer's King Ottokar

1750 | 1850 | 1900 | 1950

1776 Joseph II reorganizes the theatre and promotes it to the status of a national theatre

The Old Burgtheater in the Michaelaplatz in Hofburg, in the mid-18th century

14 Oct 1888 The Burgtheater opens in the presence of the Emperor Franz Joseph I and family

Dreifaltigkeitskirche der Minoriten ❾

Alserstrasse 17. **Map** 1 B2. ***Tel*** *40 57 225.* *Rathaus.* *5, 33, 43.* *7:30am–noon Mon–Fri, Sun, 7:30–8:30am Sat.*

Built between 1685 and 1727, the church of the Holy Trinity is a typical Baroque structure, with a twin-tower façade. It contains an altarpiece (1708) in the north aisle by the painter Martino Altomonte, and a beautiful crucifix in the south aisle from the workshop of Veit Stoss.

In 1827, the body of the composer Ludwig van Beethoven was brought to this church, from Schwarzspanierhaus in neighbouring Garnisonsgasse, where he had died. Following the funeral service, attended by his contemporaries (including Schubert and the playwright Franz Grillparzer), the cortège conveyed his coffin to its final resting place, the cemetery in Währing, on the city outskirts.

16th-century crucifix in the Dreifaltigkeitskirche

Museum für Volkskunde ❿

Laudongasse 15–19. **Map** 1 B3. ***Tel*** *40 68 905.* *Rathaus.* *5, 33, 43, 44.* *13A.* *10am–5pm Tue–Sun.* **www**.volkskundemuseum.at

Near a quiet park stands the charming Austrian Folklore Museum. Founded in 1895, it

Entrance to the Museum für Volkskunde, in Schönborn Palace

moved in 1917 to its present premises, the former Schönborn Palace, built in 1706–11 to designs by Lukas von Hildebrandt as a homely two-storey mansion, and altered in 1760 by Isidor Canevale. The building has a rather imposing façade with statuary running along its top.

In the museum you will find artifacts reflecting popular culture in Austria and neighbouring countries that were once part of the Habsburg Empire. The collection includes furniture, textiles and ceramics, household and work tools, religious objects and two complete living rooms that illustrate the lifestyle, customs and rituals in the various regions. The core of the collection consists of objects from the 17th to 19th centuries.

On Lange Gasse, a couple of blocks along towards Josefstädter Strasse, you will pass the **Alte Backstube**, at No. 34. This old bakery is one of the loveliest town houses in Vienna. It was built in 1697 by the jeweller Hans Bernhard Leopold and was in continuous use until 1963. The rooms have been lovingly restored, retaining the old baking ovens, and house a traditional restaurant and café, and a small baking museum where baking equipment from the early 18th century can be seen.

Maria Treu Kirche ⓫

Jodok-Fink-Platz. **Map** 1 B3. ***Tel*** *40 50 425.* *Rathaus.* *J.* *13A.* *during mass or by appointment.*

Originally designed by Johann Lukas von Hildebrandt in 1716, Maria Treu Kirche (church of Mary the Faithful) acquired its present form in the mid-19th century, when twin towers were added.

The church, as well as the adjacent monastic buildings, was founded by fathers of the Piarist Order, one of whose main aims is education; they also founded a primary and a secondary school next door. The homely cellar of the former monastery is today a pleasant restaurant.

The interior of the church is one of the best preserved in Vienna. Its Baroque ceiling frescoes, the work of the great Austrian painter Franz Anton Maulbertsch, are very lovely. They depict scenes from the life of the Virgin Mary and events from the Old and New Testaments. In one of the chapels, to the left of the presbytery, you can see an altarpiece of the crucifixion, also painted by Franz Anton Maulbertsch.

The Chapel of Our Lady of Sorrows contains the *pietà* known as Our Lady from Malta, which was brought here by the Knights of Malta.

In front of the church is a Baroque pillar, topped with a statue of the Madonna (1713), one of many such plague columns erected in Vienna as thanksgiving at the end of the plague era. In this case the column commemorates the epidemic of 1713.

Baroque frescoes in Maria Treu Kirche

The opulent auditorium of Theater in der Josefstadt

Theater in der Josefstadt ⓬

Josefstädter Strasse 26. **Map** 1 B4. ***Tel*** *42 700.* *Rathaus.* *2.* *13A.* **www**.josefstadt.org

This intimate theatre, one of the oldest still standing in Vienna, has enjoyed a glorious history. First established in 1788, the theatre was later much altered. After renovation by Joseph Kornhäusel, for its reopening in 1822, Ludwig van Beethoven composed his overture *The Consecration of the House,* conducting it himself at the reopening gala.

In 1924, the directorship of the theatre was given to Max Reinhardt, one of the most outstanding theatre directors and reformers, who supervised its further restoration and introduced an ambitious modern repertoire as well as magnificent productions of classic drama. He transformed what was once a middle-of-the-road provincial theatre into the most exciting stage in the German-speaking world.

The theatre is worth a visit for viewing its interior alone. As the lights slowly dim, the crystal chandeliers float gently to the ceiling. It offers excellent productions of Austrian plays, with an emphasis on comedy, classics and the occasional musical.

Palais Trautson ⓭

Museumstrasse 7. **Map** 1 C4. *Volkstheater.* *48.* *48A.* *to the public.*

The Baroque Trautson Palace, built between 1710 and 1712 for Prince Johann Leopold Donat Trautson, to a design by Johann Bernhard Fischer von Erlach, was acquired by Maria Theresa in 1760. She then donated it to the Royal Hungarian Bodyguard, which she had founded.

The Neo-Classical façade, with rows of Doric columns, is heavily ornamented. Its finest sculptures, including that of Apollo playing the lyre, tower above the first-floor windows. The palace has a beautiful staircase, decorated with carvings of the sphinx, and columns of male figures who support the ceiling, by the sculptor Giovanni Giuliani. Since 1961 the palace has housed the Ministry of Justice, so there is no public access.

Volkstheater ⓮

Neustiftgasse 1. **Map** 1 C5. ***Tel*** *52 47 263.* *Volkstheater, Lerchenfelderstrasse.* *49.* *48.* **www**.volkstheater.at

Famed as a venue able to combine classic and modern drama with popular Viennese plays, the Volkstheater (People's Theatre) was, for many years, a staging post for directors and actors on their way from the provincial theatres to the estimable Burgtheater. Today, classic and modern, or even experimental drama dominate the repertoire. The Volkstheater presents many plays for the first time, or for the first time in the German language.

The Volkstheater was built in 1889 by the Austrian architects Ferdinand Fellner and Hermann Helmer. They employed the latest in theatre technology, including electric lighting throughout, and many theatre designers later copied their work. The auditorium, with more than 1,000 seats, is one of the largest in a theatre devoted to German-language drama, and is a great example of Viennese *fin-de-siècle* architecture. In front of the theatre stands a statue (1898) of the dramatist Ferdinand Raimund.

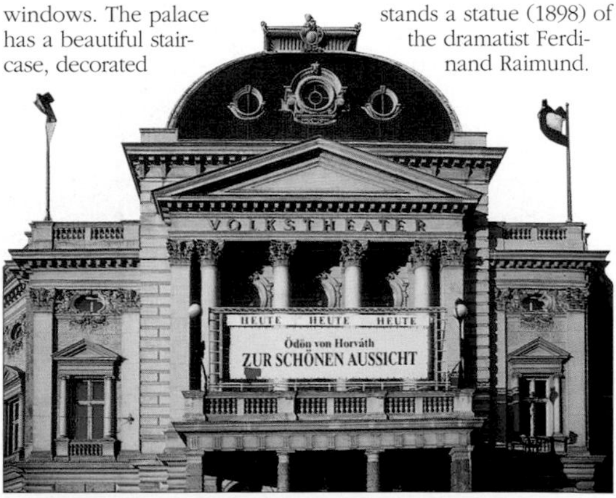

The majestic entrance to the 19th-century Volkstheater

The dinosaur room in the Naturhistorisches Museum

Naturhistorisches Museum ⓯

Burgring 7. **Map** 2 A5. ***Tel*** *52 177.* *Volkstheater.* *2, 46, 49, D.* *2A, 48A.* *9am–6:30pm Thu–Mon, 9am–9pm Wed.* *Tue, 1 Jan, 1 May, 1 Nov, 25 Dec.* **www**.nhm-wien.ac.at

On two sides of Maria-Theresien-Platz are two identical buildings, designed by Gottfried Semper and Karl von Hasenauer. They were both built as museums at the time of Franz Joseph I, as part of the Ringstrasse development. Today, one is an art museum (Kunsthistorisches Museum, *see pp84–7*), the other the Natural History Museum, home to one of the richest and most wide-ranging collections in the world.

Many exhibits originally belonged to Maria Theresa's husband, Francis Stephen of Lorraine. The present permanent exhibition occupies two floors and consists of archaeological and anthropological displays, reconstructed specimens of extinct animals and one of the best gem collections in the world.

Among the most famous exhibits are the Hallstatt archaeological finds, dating from the early Iron Age, and the famous Venus of Willendorf – a 24,000-year-old stone statuette of a woman.

The Natural History Museum plays a very important role within the education system and its temporary exhibitions are organized mainly with schools in mind. The once famous exhibition showing the imaginary life of dinosaurs toured much of the world in the wake of Steven Spielberg's film *Jurassic Park*. The museum holds several casts of dinosaur skeletons in its palaeontology department.

In the square between the buildings stands an imposing monument of Maria Theresa (1888) by Kaspar von Zumbusch. It shows the empress clasping the Pragmatic Section of 1713, enabling women to ascend to the throne. Below her are her generals and her principal nobles and advisors.

Kunsthistorisches Museum ⓰

See pp84–7.

MuseumsQuartier ⓱

Museumsplatz 1. **Map** 1 C5. ***Tel*** *52 35 81.* *MuseumsQuartier, Volkstheater.* *1, 2, 49, D.* *2A, 48A.* **Information** *10am–7pm daily.* **www**.mqw.at. **Museum of Modern Art** *10am–6pm daily (to 9pm Thu).* *Mon, 24–25 Dec.* *Admission free 26 Oct.* **Leopold Museum** *10am–6pm daily (to 9pm Thu).* *Tue, public holidays.* **Kunsthalle Wien** *10am–7pm daily (to 9pm Thu).*

Johann Bernhard Fischer von Erlach was commissioned by Emperor Karl VI to build the imperial stables on the escarpment behind the old town fortifications. In 1921, these Baroque buildings became a venue for fairs, and in the 1980s they were converted into a museum complex to designs by Laurids and Manfred Ortner. They changed the furnishings of the existing structures and added new ones, resulting in one of the world's largest cultural centres.

Rossbändiger **(1892), the tamer of horses, near the MuseumsQuartier**

The MuseumsQuartier (Museum District) includes the **Kunsthalle Wien** (Vienna Art Hall) opposite the main entrance, behind the former premises of the Spanish Riding School. Vienna's main showcase for international contemporary art, the Kunsthalle is one of the city's most important art spaces, focusing on transdisciplinary work including photography, video, film and new media, as well as modern-art retrospectives.

To the left of the Kunsthalle is the white limestone façade of the **Leopold Museum**, which houses the art collection of Rudolph Leopold. This encompasses over 5,000 works of art, including major pieces by Gustav Klimt, together with the world's largest Egon Schiele collection.

The **Museum of Modern Art Ludwig Foundation Vienna**, or **MUMOK**, to the right of the Kunsthalle, is clad in contrasting dark basalt. It contains one of the largest European collections of modern art, from American Pop to Cubism, Expressionism and Viennese Actionism, as well as contemporary art from Central and Eastern Europe.

The **Architektur Zentrum Wien** is a venue for interesting temporary exhibitions of modern architecture and architectural history. Its permanent exhibition features 20th-century Austrian architecture.

The **Tanzquartier Wien** is dedicated to dance, providing facilities and training to performers and choreographers, and presenting various types of dance and other performances to the public.

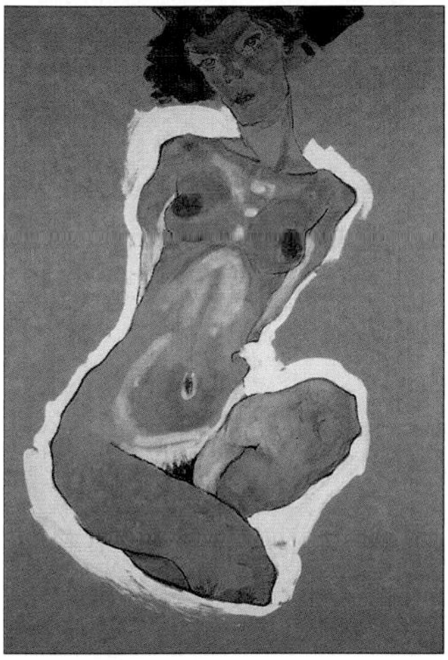

Schiele's *Kneeling Female Nude* (1910), in Museum of Modern Art, MuseumsQuartier

The MuseumsQuartier also has archives and facilities for lectures, workshops and seminars, as well as Austria's first centre for museum and exhibition studies. Children can play, explore and learn about a variety of subjects in the **ZOOM Kindermuseum**, an unconventional centre.

Amid this extraordinary cultural setting, numerous cafés, bars, green spaces, shops and bookstores invite visitors to relax.

Mariahilfer Strasse ⓲

Map 4 A1, B1. *Westbahnhof, Zieglergasse, Neubaugasse, MuseumsQuartier.* *2A, 13A.*

Mariahilfer Strasse is one of the longest streets in Vienna, a main artery running west from the town centre to the area around Schönbrunn.

The part between Getreidemarkt (Grain Market) and Westbahnhof (the Western Railway Station) is also the busiest shopping street in this part of the city. Here you will find Vienna's largest department stores and its best window displays. Shopping tends to be better value here than in Kärntner Strasse, but is still more costly than in Meidling or Favoriten, for instance. Mariahilfer Strasse took its name from the church of St Mary, Our Lady of Perpetual Succour, built in the late 17th century on the site of an older church, but was not consecrated until 1730. Its façade is an austere pyramidal structure, rising to a bulbous steeple, and there are lively Rococo reliefs set in its walls. In front of the church stands a monument to the composer Joseph Haydn *(see p108)*, who lived at this address for 12 years.

Mariahilfer Strasse No. 45 is the longest and most famous double-exit house in Vienna, the birthplace in 1790 of the popular Austrian playwright Ferdinand Raimund *(see p28)*.

Spittelberg ⓳

Map 1 C5. *Volkstheater.* *49.* *2A, 48A.* **Amerlinghaus** Stiftgasse 8. ***Tel*** *52 36 475.* *2–10pm Mon–Fri.* **www**.amerlinghaus.at

Spittelberg is the oldest and most colourful part of the elegant 7th District. In the 17th century, the cluster of streets between Siebensterngasse and Burggasse, around Spittelberggasse, was Vienna's first immigrant worker district. Its inhabitants were mainly craftsmen, merchants and servants from Croatia and Hungary, brought here to work at the court. Today, the district's crafts heritage lives on in the street market, held on the first weekend of each month and prior to Christmas. Among the stalls with wood carvings, tie-dyed fabrics and silver jewellery, waiters from the local bars negotiate the busy crowds; there are some 58 bars in this small area, which contains just 138 houses. The number of bars may change from one week to the next, but the bustling, festive party atmosphere can be experienced almost every evening. The Spittelberg area also comprises small art galleries, and artists display their work in the restaurants.

At one time, attractive bar maids offered "additional services", and legend has it that Emperor Joseph II once decided to explore the Spittelberg district for himself. However, when, in disguise, he entered the Witwe Bolte (Widow Bolte) restaurant, still open today, he was unceremoniously thrown out.

Nos. 18 and 20 Spittelberggasse are fine Baroque houses.

The beautifully restored **Amerlinghaus**, in which the painter Friedrich Amerling (1803–87) was born, is now a cultural and community centre, and a restaurant.

A little further along, between Siebensterngasse and Mariahilfer Strasse, is an enclosed area around former barracks now housing the Military Academy, and the Stiftkirche, topped with an onion-shaped cupola, which serves as a garrison church. Its walls are lined with very expressive Rococo reliefs.

Community centre in Amerlinghaus, in Spittelberg

Kunsthistorisches Museum ⑯

The world's fourth largest gallery, the Museum of Art History houses a collection based on works amassed over the centuries by generations of Habsburg monarchs. The public was given access to these art treasures when two museums were built in Ringstrasse to designs by Karl Hasenauer and Gottfried Semper. One was to house the art collection, a second, identical building the Natural History Museum *(see p82)*. Both opened in 1891. The art museum's lavish interior complements its exhibits, today seen by more than one and a half million people each year.

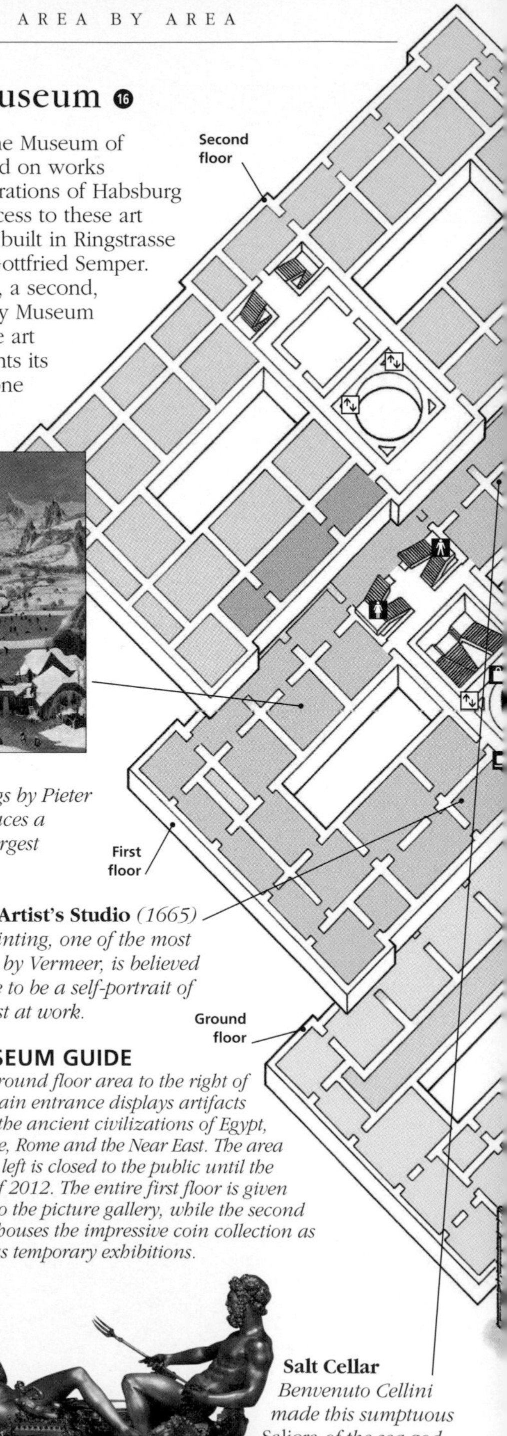

★ Hunters in the Snow *(1565)*
The last in a cycle of seasonal paintings by Pieter Bruegel the Elder, this winter scene graces a gallery room containing the world's largest collection of this artist's work.

★ The Artist's Studio *(1665)*
This painting, one of the most famous by Vermeer, is believed by some to be a self-portrait of the artist at work.

MUSEUM GUIDE
The ground floor area to the right of the main entrance displays artifacts from the ancient civilizations of Egypt, Greece, Rome and the Near East. The area to the left is closed to the public until the end of 2012. The entire first floor is given over to the picture gallery, while the second floor houses the impressive coin collection as well as temporary exhibitions.

KEY

- Egyptian and Near Eastern collection
- Collection of Greek and Roman Antiquities
- Sculpture and Decorative Arts
- Picture gallery
- Coin cabinets
- Non-exhibition space

Salt Cellar
Benvenuto Cellini made this sumptuous Saliera of the sea god Neptune and an earth goddess for the French King François I.

★ Velázquez's Infanta
The Spanish artist Diego Velázquez immortalized the eight-year-old Margarita Teresa (1659), the future wife of Emperor Leopold I.

VISITORS' CHECKLIST

Burgring 5. **Map** 2 A5. ***Tel*** *525 24-40 25.* Ⓤ *Volkstheater, MuseumsQuartier.* *D, 1, 2.* *2A, 57A.* *10am–6pm Tue, Wed, Fri–Sun, 10am–9pm Thu.* **www**.khm.at

★ Gemma Augustea
The famous Roman cameo, carved in great precision from onyx, shows the goddess Roma and Emperor Augustus welcoming his son Tiberius after his heroic victory over the barbarians in Pannonia.

King Thutmosis III
This king from the 18th Dynasty (c.1500 BC) was one of the foremost warriors of ancient Egypt. He is depicted in the style typical of the Late Kingdom period.

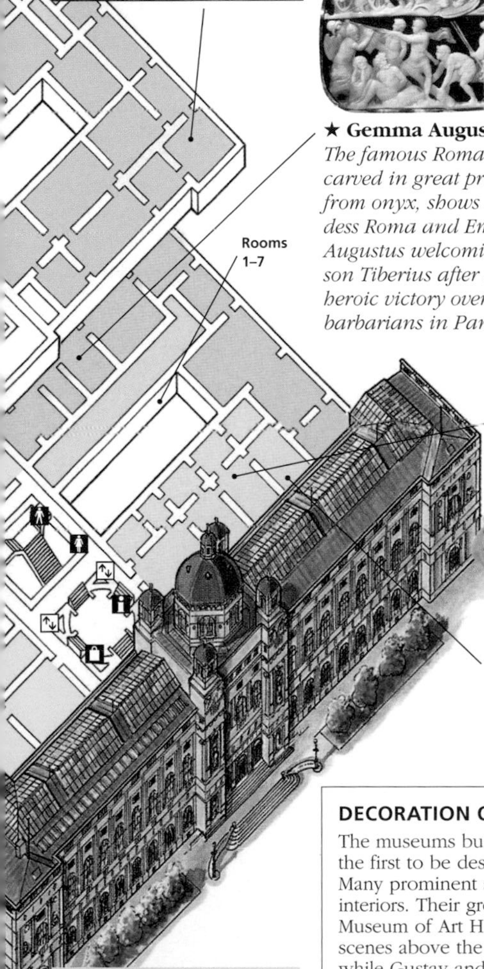

Hippopotamus
This blue ceramic figure from Middle-Kingdom Egypt (around 2000 BC) was placed in the tombs of important persons, to mark their status in society.

DECORATION OF THE MUSEUM

The museums built in Ringstrasse in the 1890s were among the first to be designed with particular collections in mind. Many prominent artists were employed to decorate the interiors. Their great masterpiece is the main staircase in the Museum of Art History. Hans Makart created the symbolic scenes above the windows, while Gustav and Ernst Klimt painted frescoes depicting stages in the development of art. The *Apotheosis of the Renaissance* (1890) is the fabulous *trompe l'oeil* ceiling fresco by Michael Munkácsy.

Apotheosis of the Renaissance

STAR EXHIBITS

- ★ *The Artist's Studio*
- ★ Gemma Augustea
- ★ *Hunters in the Snow*
- ★ Velázquez's *Infanta*

For hotels and restaurants in this region see pp288–94 and pp318–24

Exploring the Kunsthistorisches Museum

The Museum of Art History has a fine collection of Egyptian, Greek and Roman objects, which provide an intriguing record of the world's earliest civilizations. Most European sculpture and decorative art dates from the 15th to the 18th centuries, which is also the focus of the picture gallery, largely reflecting the personal tastes of its Habsburg founders. Venetian and 17th-century Flemish paintings are well represented, and there is an excellent display of works by earlier Dutch and German artists. There is also a vast coin collection.

ORIENTAL AND EGYPTIAN ANTIQUITIES

The core of this collection are the objects unearthed by Austrian archaeologists in Giza. Particularly fascinating are the well-preserved relics from the tomb of Ka-Ni-Nisut, dating from the Early Kingdom era, including a meticulously reconstructed burial chamber. The blue ceramic figure of a hippopotamus dates from the Middle Kingdom era. Such animal figures were placed in the tombs to mark the social status of the deceased – the hippopotamus was regarded as a royal beast and could be hunted only with the pharaoh's permission.

The exhibits from the Late Kingdom, mainly associated with the mortuary cult, include a papyrus book of the dead, the mummified corpses of people and animals, sarcophagi and Canopic jars used to preserve the entrails of mummified corpses.

Near-Eastern antiquities are represented in the museum collections by the Babylonian reliefs, a lion made of red ceramic brick and various exhibits from Arabia.

Room I of the Egyptian galleries

GREEK AND ROMAN ANTIQUITIES

Only part of the museum's Greek and Roman collection is housed in the main building; the finds from Ephesus and on Samothrace are on display in the Ephesus Museum in Neue Burg *(see p66)*. The main building in Burgring has a beautiful collection of early Greek urns, in a variety of shapes, including vessels presented to winners at the Panathenaean Games. The sculpture rooms house many examples of early Greek and Roman art. Some are of outstanding quality: for example, the *Youth from Magdalensburg*, a cast of a lost Roman statue found buried in an Austrian field; the huge *Head of Athena,* probably from the school of Phidias; and fragments of a frieze with a dying Amazon. The Hellenic era is represented by the magnificent *Head of a Philosopher*, likely to have been that of Aristotle. One of the most precious items in the entire collection of antiquities is *Gemma Augustea*, a Roman cameo depicting Emperor Augustus welcoming his son Tiberius on his return from war, together with Roma, the goddess of Rome.

The antiquities section also contains some Etruscan ceramics and statuettes from Tanagra. Early Coptic, Byzantine and German items are shown in the other rooms, but the true jewel among the antiquities is the Treasure of Nagyszentmiklós, a collection of 9th-century golden vessels with stunning reliefs, showing Far-Eastern influences, found in Romania in 1799.

SCULPTURE AND DECORATIVE ARTS

This collection (closed until the end of 2012) consists of magnificent works of art bought or commissioned by successive Habsburg rulers, scientific instruments and clocks regarded as masterpieces of applied art, as well as curiosities and artifacts from the rulers' *Kunstkammern* (chambers of art). Some of the royals worked in the studio; exhibits include, for example, glass blown by Archduke Ferdinand II and embroidery by Maria Theresa.

Virgin with Child (c1495) by Tilman Riemenschneider

Some of the most intriguing items, however, are splendid examples of craftsmanship, including pieces of jewellery and items made from gold. The showpiece of the collection is the golden *Saliera* or Salt Cellar *(see p84)*, made by the Italian goldsmith and sculptor Benvenuto Cellini for the French King, François I.

Other gems in these rooms include the magnificent chalice from the collegiate church in Wilten and the precious Burgundy cup of Friedrich III.

A separate section is devoted to wood and stone sculptures from the Middle Ages, mainly of religious subjects, among them the amazing *Madonna from Krumlowa* (c.1400), the poignant *Virgin with Child* by Tilman Riemenschneider

Susanna and the Elders **(1555) by Tintoretto**

(c.1495) and stone statues from the cathedral churches of Bamberg and Naumburg.

Highlights of the Italian Renaissance and Baroque rooms are the marble bust of a laughing boy, by Desiderio da Settignano, a marble relief of Bacchus and Ariadne, and a fine bronze and gilt figurine known as *Venus Felix*, after an antique marble statue.

The collection of decorative arts also includes fine pieces of furniture and tapestries, gilded table ornaments and vases, a number of statuettes and figurines, miniature clocks and jewellery.

PICTURE COLLECTION

Exhibits in the painting galleries are mostly hung according to regional schools or styles of painting, and arranged chronologically.

Summer **(1563) by Giuseppe Arcimboldo**

Paintings go back as far as the 16th century, and include several works by early Flemish masters, such as Rogier van der Weyden, Hans Memling and Jan van Eyck. The highlight is the collection of Pieter Bruegel the Elder's surviving works, the largest collection of his work and the museum's greatest treasure.

Two rooms are devoted to Rubens, with large-scale religious works and an intimate portrait of his wife. Antony van Dyck is represented by some outstanding works, and there are paintings by Dutch genre painters. All the Rembrandts on show are portraits. The only painting by Johannes Vermeer is *The Artist's Studio,* an enigmatic work.

The Italian collection of 16th-century paintings from Venice and the Veneto include works by Titian, from his early *Gypsy Madonna* (1510) to the late *Nymph and Shepherd* (1570–75). Other highlights are Giovanni Bellini's graceful *Young Woman at her Toilette* (1515) and Tintoretto's *Susanna and the Elders*, one of the major works of Venetian Mannerism. There is a series of allegorical portrait heads representing the elements and the seasons by Giuseppe Arcimboldo. Italian Baroque painting includes works by Annibale Carracci and Michelangelo Merisi da Caravaggio, including the huge *Madonna of the Rosary* (1606–7).

French treasures include the formal court portrait of the youthful Charles IX of France (1569) by François Clouet, and *The Destruction of the Temple in Jerusalem* (1638) by Nicolas Poussin.

Among the few British works are the *Landscape of Suffolk* (around 1750) by Thomas Gainsborough and paintings by Reynolds. The German collection contains several works by Albrecht Dürer, including his *Madonna with the Pear* (1512), and by Lucas Cranach the Elder and Hans Holbein the Younger.

There are several fine portraits of the Spanish royal family by Diego Velázquez, including his *Portrait of the Infanta* (1659).

COIN CABINETS

The coin and medal collection of the Museum of Art History comprises 500,000 individual items, making it one of the most extensive numismatic collections in the world. Its first inventory was compiled in 1547. The nucleus of the collection derives from the former possessions of the Habsburgs, but has been added to by modern curators.

The exhibits illustrate the history of money, with coins from ancient Egypt, Greece and Rome, examples of Celtic, Byzantine, medieval and Renaissance money, right up to present-day Austrian currency.

Medal of Ulrich II Molitor (1581)

Also on display is a collection of 19th- and 20th-century medals, with portraits that are often outstanding miniature works of art. Particularly noteworthy are the silver and gilt medals of Ulrich II Molitor, the Abbot of Heiligenkreuz, and the silver medallion engraved by Bertrand Andrieu and minted to commemorate the baptism of Napoleon's son, showing the emperor as proud father.

SOUTH OF THE RING

This part of town is an area of great diversity, ranging from the stateliness of the Opera House to the raucous modernity of bustling Karlsplatz, from the magnificence of Karlskirche, one of Johann Bernhard Fischer von Erlach's greatest churches, to the secular attractions of the Belvedere. Once Prince Eugene of Savoy's palace, the Belvedere is now the home of the Gallery of Austrian Art, which includes works by Gustav Klimt. The district also has beautiful buildings with façades decorated in the Vienna Secession style. The stalls of the bustling Naschmarkt are also a popular attraction.

Relief on the façade of the Secession Building

SIGHTS AT A GLANCE

Streets and Squares
Schwarzenbergplatz 13

Historic Buildings
Hotel Sacher 1
Karlsplatz Pavilions 9
Musikverein 11
Staatsoper 2
Technische Universität 7
Theater an der Wien 5

Museums and Galleries
Academy of Fine Arts 3
Belvedere see pp98–9 15
Künstlerhaus 10
Secession Building 4
Wien Museum Karlsplatz 12

Markets
Naschmarkt 6

Churches
Karlskirche see pp94–5 8

Parks
Stadtpark 14

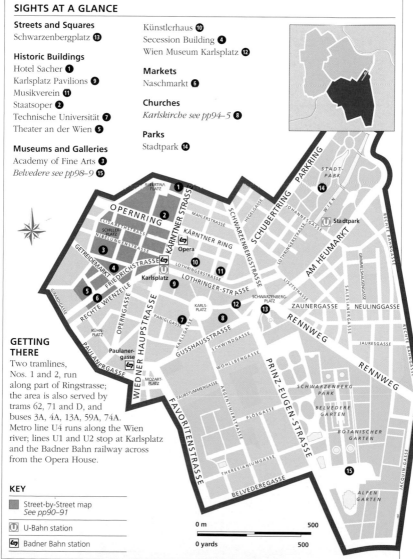

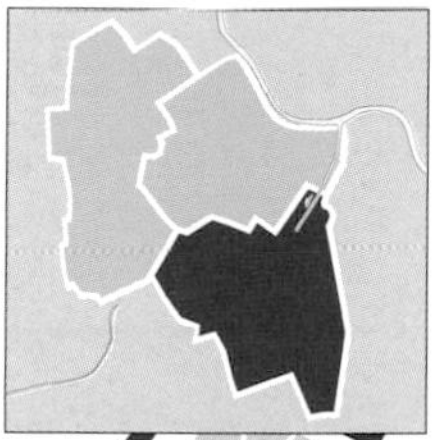

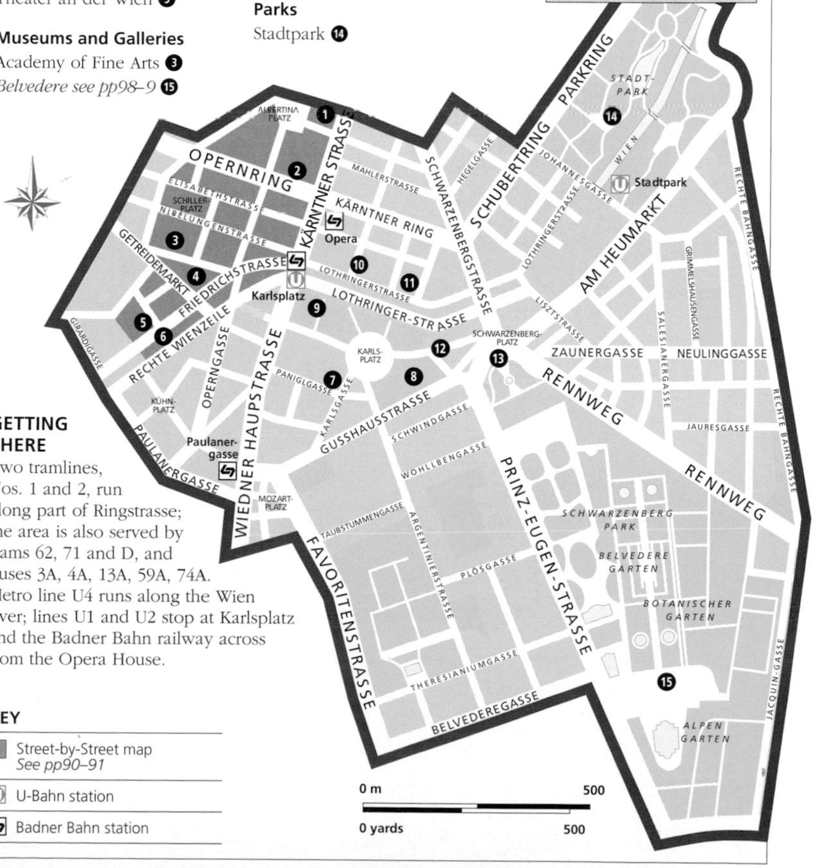

GETTING THERE

Two tramlines, Nos. 1 and 2, run along part of Ringstrasse; the area is also served by trams 62, 71 and D, and buses 3A, 4A, 13A, 59A, 74A. Metro line U4 runs along the Wien river; lines U1 and U2 stop at Karlsplatz and the Badner Bahn railway across from the Opera House.

KEY

Street-by-Street map *See pp90–91*

U-Bahn station

Badner Bahn station

◁ **The opulent central hall of the Opera House, seen from the main staircase**

Street-by-Street: Around the Opera

Between two of Vienna's key landmarks, the Opera House and Karlskirche, lies an area that typifies the varied cultural vitality of the city as a whole. Here, you will find cultural monuments such as an 18th-century theatre, a 19th-century art academy and the superb Secession Building, mixed in with emblems of the Viennese devotion to good living: the Hotel Sacher and the Café Museum, both as popular today as ever, and the colourful Naschmarkt, Vienna's best market for vegetables and exotic fruits.

Academy of Fine Arts
This Italianate building is home to one of the best collections of old masters in Vienna ❸

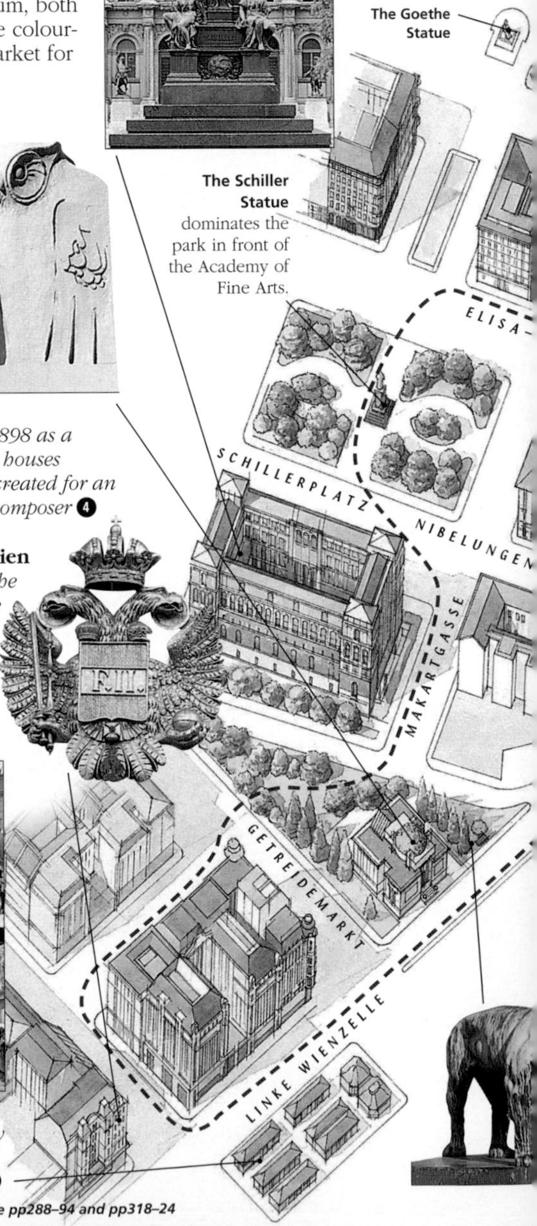

The Schiller Statue dominates the park in front of the Academy of Fine Arts.

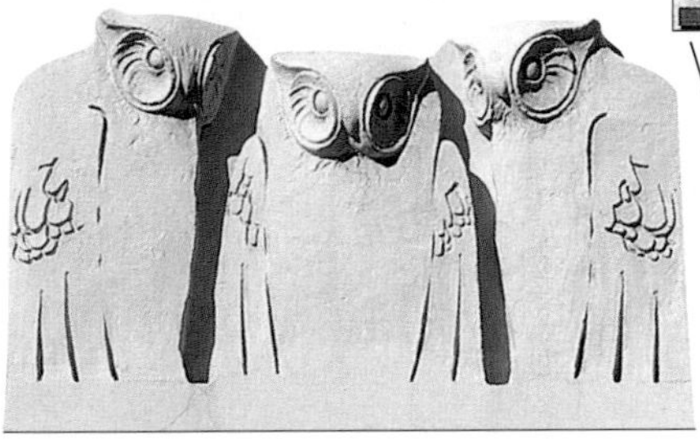

★ Secession Building
This delightful structure, built in 1898 as a showroom for the Secession artists, houses Gustav Klimt's Beethoven Frieze, *created for an exhibition in honour of the great composer* ❹

Theater an der Wien
The 18th-century theatre on the banks of the Wien river is a prime operatic venue in a historic setting. Their programme also includes ballet and concerts ❺

★ Naschmarkt
Fresh produce is sold here Monday to Saturday, and a flea market operates on Saturday mornings ❻

For hotels and restaurants in this region see pp288–94 and pp318–24

Hotel Sacher
This hotel is the home of the famous Sachertorte, which you can eat in its café ❶

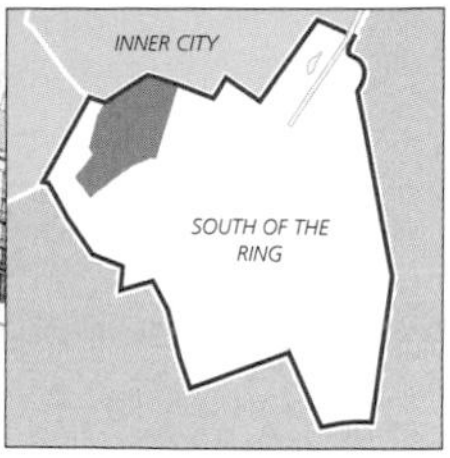

LOCATOR MAP
See Street Finder, maps 2 & 4

0 m 50
0 yards 50

★ Staatsoper
The majestic state opera, erected on this site in 1869, is still the hub of Vienna's glorious cultural life ❷

The Café Museum had been remodelled in the 1930s but it has been restored to its original late 19th-century appearance in accordance with Adolf Loos's forward-looking design.

The Mark Anthony Statue (1899), alongside the Secession Building, is a gloriously decadent bronze statue by Arthur Strasser. It depicts the Roman leader sitting in a chariot drawn by lions.

KEY

- - - - Suggested route

STAR SIGHTS

★ Naschmarkt

★ Secession Building

★ Staatsoper

The imposing building of the Vienna State Opera House

Hotel Sacher ❶

Philharmonikerstrasse 4. **Map** 2 B5. ***Tel*** *51 45 60. Karlsplatz. 1, 2, D, J.* **www**.sacher.com

The Hotel Sacher is one of the "must-see" places in Vienna. It was founded by the son of Franz Sacher, who was said to have created the famous *Sachertorte* in 1832. Although this cake can now be bought in any café, the genuine article is still the best.

The hotel came into its own under Anna Sacher, the founder's cigar-smoking daughter-in-law, who ran the hotel from 1892 until her death in 1930. She collected autographs, and, to this day, a vast white tablecloth signed by Emperor Franz Joseph I is on display. During her time, the Sacher became a venue for the extra-marital affairs of the rich and noble. It is still a discreetly sumptuous hotel with red velvet sofas, draped curtains and stylish furniture.

Staatsoper ❷

Opernring 2. **Map** 2 B5. ***Tel*** *51 444-2250. Karlsplatz. 1, 2, D.* **www**.wiener-staatsoper.at

In May 1869, when Vienna's State Opera House opened to the strains of Mozart's *Don Giovanni*, music lovers rejoiced that it would no longer be necessary to travel to Paris in order to hear good opera. Built in Neo-Renaissance style, the Opera House initially failed to impress the Viennese. The distressed interior designer, Eduard van der Nüll, committed suicide, and two months later, the architect, August Sicard von Sicardsburg, also died. Yet, when the opera was hit by an allied bomb in 1945, the event was seen as a symbolic blow to the city. With a new state-of-the-art auditorium and stage, the Opera House eventually reopened on 5 November 1955 with a performance of Beethoven's *Fidelio*. Its illustrious directors have included Gustav Mahler, Richard Strauss and Herbert von Karajan.

Each year, on the last Thursday of Carnival, the stage is extended to create a vast dance floor for the Vienna Opera Ball. This prestigious high-society event opens when Vienna's youth – well-to-do girls clad in white and their smartly dressed escorts – take to the floor.

Academy of Fine Arts ❸

Schillerplatz 3. **Map** 4 C1. ***Tel*** *588 16-225. Karlsplatz. 1, 2, D. 57A, 59A. 10am–6pm Tue–Sun and public holidays. 1 Jan, 1 May, 1 Nov, 24, 25, 31 Dec.* **www**.akademiegalerie.at

The Academy of Fine Arts is not only an educational establishment, but also one of the finest galleries of Old Masters. It was built in 1872–6, by Theophil Hansen, as a school and museum. In 1907, Adolf Hitler applied to be admitted but was refused a place on the grounds that he lacked talent.

Today, the gallery shows changing exhibitions. Its pride is late-Gothic and early-Renaissance works, including some pieces by Rubens, a winged altarpiece by Hieronymus Bosch depicting the Last Judgement and works by Titian, Cranach and Botticelli. It also has some 17th-century Dutch and Flemish landscapes and an Austrian collection.

Secession Building ❹

Friedrichstrasse 12. **Map** 4 C1. ***Tel*** *58 75 307. Karlsplatz. 59A. 10am–6pm Tue–Sun & hols.* **www**.secession.at

The unusual Secession Building was designed in *Jugendstil* style by Joseph Maria Olbrich, as a showcase for the Secessionist artists, including Gustav Klimt, Kolo Moser and Otto Wagner, who broke away from Vienna's traditional art scene. The almost windowless

OTTO WAGNER (1841–1918)

The most prominent architect at the turn of the 20th century, Wagner studied in Vienna and Berlin. Initially, he was associated with the historicist style, but in time he became the foremost representative of the Austrian Secession. He prepared plans for the re-routing of the Wien river and the modernization of the town's transport system. His most outstanding works include the **Majolikahaus** *(see Naschmarkt, opposite)*, train stations *(see p96)*, the Post Office Savings Bank building, a hospital and the Kirche am Steinhof *(see p108)*.

Detail of Otto Wagner's design

Façade of the Secession Building, with its golden filigree dome

building, with its filigree globe of entwined laurel leaves on the roof, is a squat cube with four towers. Gustav Klimt's *Beethoven Frieze* (1902) is its best known exhibit. Designed as a decorative painting running along three walls, it shows interrelated groups of figures thought to be a commentary on Beethoven's *Ninth Symphony*.

The Secession Building is Vienna's oldest independent exhibition space dedicated to showing contemporary and experimental Austrian and international art.

Theater an der Wien ❺

Linke Wienzeile 6. **Map** 4 C1. ***Tel*** *58 83 06 65 / 58 885 (tickets).* Ⓤ *Kettenbrückengasse.* 🚌 *59A.* **www**.theater-wien.at

The "Theatre on the Wien River", one of the oldest theatres in Vienna, was founded by Emanuel Schikaneder. A statue above the entrance shows him playing Papageno in the premiere of Mozart's *Magic Flute*. Schikaneder, who had written the libretto for this same opera, was the theatre's first director. The premiere of Beethoven's *Fidelio* was staged here in 1805, and for a while the composer lived in the theatre. Many plays by prominent playwrights such as Kleist, Grillparzer and Nestroy, and many Viennese operettas were premiered here, too, including works by Johann Strauss (son), Zeller, Lehár and Kalman. After many years as a venue for musicals, the Theater an der Wien now stages only opera.

The Neo-Classical entrance to the Theater an der Wien

Naschmarkt ❻

Map 4 C1. Ⓤ *Kettenbrückengasse, Pilgramgasse.* 🚌 *59A.* ◯ *6am–7pm Mon–Fri, 6am–5pm Sat.*
Schubert Memorial Apartment
Tel *58 16 730.* ◯ *10am–1pm, 2pm–6pm Wed & Thu*

The Naschmarkt is Vienna's liveliest market, selling all types of market goods as well as delicatessen food. The Saturday flea market is particularly popular.

Nearby, at Kettenbrückengasse No. 6, is the simple apartment where the composer Franz Schubert died in 1828. It displays facsimiles, prints and a piano.

Overlooking Naschmarkt, at Linke Wienzeile Nos. 38 and 40, are two remarkable apartment blocks. Designed by Otto Wagner in 1899 and known as the Wagner Apartments, they represent the peak of *Jugendstil* style. No. 38 has sparkling gilt ornament, mostly by Kolo Moser. No. 40 is known as **Majolikahaus**, after the glazed pottery used to weather-proof the walls. Its façade has subtle flower patterns in pink, blue and green, and even the sills are moulded and decorated.

Technische Universität ❼

Karlsplatz 13. **Map** 5 D1. ***Tel*** *588 01–0.* Ⓤ *Karlsplatz.* 🚋 *1, 2, D.* 🚌 *4A, 59A.*

Vienna's Technical University has a Neo-Classical façade, beautiful colonnades and attic statues by Joseph Klieber. It was built in 1816 by Joseph Schemerl von Leytenbach, to the designs of the Imperial Office of Public Works. Klieber also created the eight stone heads flanking the main entrance, featuring some of the university's famous professors.

Inside, the most beautiful room is the Assembly Hall, with carved wall panelling.

The University fronts on to Resselpark, which contains many busts and statues of Austria's most important scientists and engineers.

Karlskirche 8

An angel representing the New Testament

During Vienna's plague epidemic of 1713, Emperor Karl VI vowed that as soon as the city was delivered from its plight he would build a church dedicated to St Charles Borromeo (1538–84), the patron saint of the plague. Johann Bernhard Fischer von Erlach created a richly eclectic building, later completed by his son. At 72 m (236 ft), it is the tallest Baroque church in Vienna. The Neo-Classical giant dome and portico are flanked by two minaret-like towers and the Oriental-style gatehouses. The most striking features inside are the beautiful cupola frescoes, high altar and side altarpieces painted by the foremost artists of the day, Martino Altomonte, Daniel Gran and Sebastian Ricci.

The Pulpit
Two putti crown the canopy of the richly gilded pulpit, adorned with rocailles and flower garlands.

★ High Altar
A stucco relief by Albert Camesina shows St Charles Borromeo being assumed into heaven on a cloud laden with angels and putti.

The two gatehouses leading into the side entrances of the church seem to combine the architecture of Roman triumphal arches with that of Chinese pavilions.

Pediment reliefs by Giovanni Stanetti show the suffering of the Viennese population during the 1713 plague.

Main entrance

STAR FEATURES
★ Cupola Frescoes
★ High Altar
★ The Two Columns

VISITORS' CHECKLIST

Karlsplatz 8. **Map** 5 D1.
Tel *505 62 94.* *Karlsplatz.*
1, 2, 71, D. *4A.* *9am–6pm Mon–Sat, noon–5:45pm Sun & hols.*
(to cupola) **www**.karlskirche.at

★ Cupola Frescoes
Michael Rottmayr's frescoes, painted in 1725–30, depicts the Apotheosis of St Charles Borromeo. It was the painter's last commission.

JOHANN BERNHARD FISCHER VON ERLACH

An outstanding architect of the Austrian Baroque, Fischer von Erlach (1656–1723) designed many of Vienna's finest buildings, including the palaces of Schönbrunn, Prince Eugene of Savoy and the Trautson family. He died before he finished the Karlskirche; his son, Joseph Emanuel, completed it in 1737, and also took over as court architect.

★ The Two Columns
Inspired by Trajan's Column in Rome, these two columns feature scenes from the life of St Charles Borromeo, illustrating the qualities of Steadfastness and Courage.

St Charles Borromeo
Lorenzo Mattielli's statue of the patron saint and protector from the plague crowns the pediment.

Sunflower motif on the façade of the Karlsplatz pavilions

Karlsplatz Pavilions ❾

Karlsplatz. **Map** 5 D1. *Karlsplatz.* *1, 2, 62, D.* *3A, 4A, 59A.* *Kärntner Ring.* ***Tel*** *50 58 747-85 177.* *Apr–Oct: 9am–6pm Tue–Sun.*

Otto Wagner *(see p92)* was responsible for designing and engineering many aspects of Vienna's early underground system in the late 19th century. His plans, however, did not materialize until the 1960s, when work on the metro started. One of the underground lines, the U4, runs almost exactly along his train route linking the city centre with Schönbrunn *(see p110)*.

A few of Wagner's stations remain to this day – it is worth looking at the stations in Stadtpark, Kettenbrückengasse and Schönbrunn, for example – but none can match his stylish pair of underground railway exit pavilions (1898–9) alongside Karlsplatz. The patina-green copper roofs and the ornamentation complement the Karlskirche beyond. Gilt patterns are stamped onto the white marble cladding and eaves, with repetitions of Wagner's beloved sunflower motif. The greatest impact is made by the buildings' elegantly curving rooflines. The two pavilions face each other; one is now a café, the other is used for exhibitions.

Künstlerhaus ❿

Karlsplatz 5. **Map** 5 D1. ***Tel*** *58 79 663.* *Karlsplatz.* *1, 2, 62, 65, D.* *3A, 4A, 59A.* *10am–8pm daily (to 9pm Thu).* **www**.k-haus.at

Commissioned by the Vienna Artists' Society as an exhibition hall for its members, the Künstlerhaus (Artists' House) was built in 1868. The society favoured grandiose, academic styles of painting in tune with the historicist Ringstrasse architecture which was also being developed around that time. The Artists' House itself is typical of this style. Designed by August Weber (1836–1903) to look like a Renaissance *palazzo*, it is decorated with marble statues of the masters of art, including Albrecht Dürer, Michelangelo, Raphael, Peter Paul Rubens, Leonardo da Vinci, Diego Velázquez and Titian, symbolizing the timeless value of art.

Today, the Künstlerhaus still serves as an exhibition space, focusing on architecture, interdisciplinary themes and international cooperation. There is also a space for live performances, a cinema, theatre and restaurant.

Musikverein ⓫

Bösendorferstrasse 12. **Map** 5 D1. ***Tel*** *50 58 190.* *Karlsplatz.* *1, 2, 62, 71, D.* *3A, 4A, 59A.* *guided tours: please phone for details, box office: 9am– 6:30pm Mon–Fri, 9am–5pm Sat.*

Next to the Künstlerhaus is the Musikverein, headquarters of the Society of the Friends of Music. It was designed by Theophil Hansen in 1867–9 and features terracotta statues and balustrades.

The Musikverein is the home of the famous Vienna Philharmonic Orchestra, which performs both here and in the Opera House. The concert hall, seating almost 2,000, has excellent acoustics and superb decor. The balcony is supported by vast columns; the gilded ceiling shows nine muses and Apollo; along the walls are the statues of various famous musicians.

The most famous annual event here is the New Year's Day concert, which is broadcast live around the world.

The monumental, historicist façade of the Musikverein

Wien Museum Karlsplatz ⓬

Karlsplatz. **Map** 5 D1. ***Tel*** *50 58 747.* *Karlsplatz.* *1, 2, 62, 71, D.* *3A, 4A, 59A.* *9am–6pm Tue–Sun.* *Admission free – 9am–noon Fri.* **www**.wienmuseum.at

Visitors to the Historical Museum of the City of Vienna are greeted by a vast model of the city from the era when the Ringstrasse was developed. The exhibition covers nearly 3,000 years of urban history. It illustrates the lives of its first settlers and life in the Roman camp of Vindobona, and it chronicles the threat from Turkish invaders and the subsequent rise of Vienna to the magnificent capital of a great empire.

The museum has collections of memorabilia of many of Vienna's famous citizens. Perhaps the most interesting of these are the reconstructed apartments of the writer Franz Grillparzer (1791–1872) and the architect Adolf Loos (1870–1933).

Fountain and Soviet Monument at Schwarzenbergplatz

Schwarzenbergplatz ⓭

Map 5 E1. *Karlsplatz.* *71.* *4A.*

The elongated Schwarzenberg Square, one of the city's grandest spaces, is best seen from the Ringstrasse, from where several important structures come into view together. In the foreground is the equestrian statue of Prince Karl Schwarzenberg, who commanded the Austrian and allied armies in the Battle of Leipzig in 1813 against the French army under Napoleon.

The Hochstrahlbrunnen (high jet fountain) was built in 1873 to mark the connection of Vienna's first Alpine water supply. The fountain is floodlit in summer. It partly obscures the heroic-style Soviet monument to the Red Army that commemorates the Russian liberation of Vienna. Beyond the Russian monument, the beautiful Schwarzenberg Palace can be seen. It was built in 1697 by Johann Lukas von Hildebrandt and altered by the Fischer von Erlachs, Johann Bernhard and Joseph Emanuel. Part of it will be converted into a luxurious hotel and restaurant, and one wing houses the Swiss Embassy.

Stadtpark ⓮

Map 3 D5. *Stadtpark, Stubentor, Wien Mitte.* *Wien Mitte.* *2.* *74A.*

On the Weihburggasse side of the municipal park stands one of the most photographed sights in Vienna, the gilded statue of the King of Waltz, Johann Strauss the Younger. It was designed by Edmund Hellmer in the Neo-Romantic style of the 1920s. The park, opened in 1862, also contains the statues of the composers Franz Schubert and Franz Lehár, the painter Hans Makart and portraitist Friedrich von Amerling. Parallel to the Ringstrasse, along the Wien River, runs an attractive promenade designed in Secession style by Friedrich Ohmann. It includes several magnificent portals, part of a project to regulate the flow of the Wien river, as well as several pavilions, bridges and stone playgrounds.

A Secession-style portal in the Stadtpark, built in 1903–04

Belvedere ⓯

The Belvedere was built as the summer residence of Prince Eugene of Savoy by Johann Lucas von Hildebrandt. A brilliant military commander whose strategies helped vanquish the Turks in 1683, the Prince became a favourite at the Austrian court and with the people. Situated on a gently sloping hill, the Belvedere consists of two palaces linked by a formal garden designed in the French style by Dominique Girard. The garden is laid out on three levels, each conveying a complicated series of Classical allusions: the lower part represents the domain of the Four Elements, the centre is Parnassus and the upper section Mount Olympus.

Chapel
Prince Eugene's former chapel is now part of a gallery with works by Caspar David Friedrich, F. G. Waldmüller, Edvard Munch, Renoir and Monet.

Lower Belvedere
Houses temporary exhibitions.

Figures from the Providentia Fountain *(1739)*
The original lead figures that Georg Raphael Donner made for the Providentia Fountain in Neuer Markt are displayed in the Marble Hall; this central statue shows Providence. The figures that now stand in the market are copies.

STAR FEATURES

- ★ Gustav Klimt Collection
- ★ Hall of Mirrors
- ★ Sala Terrena

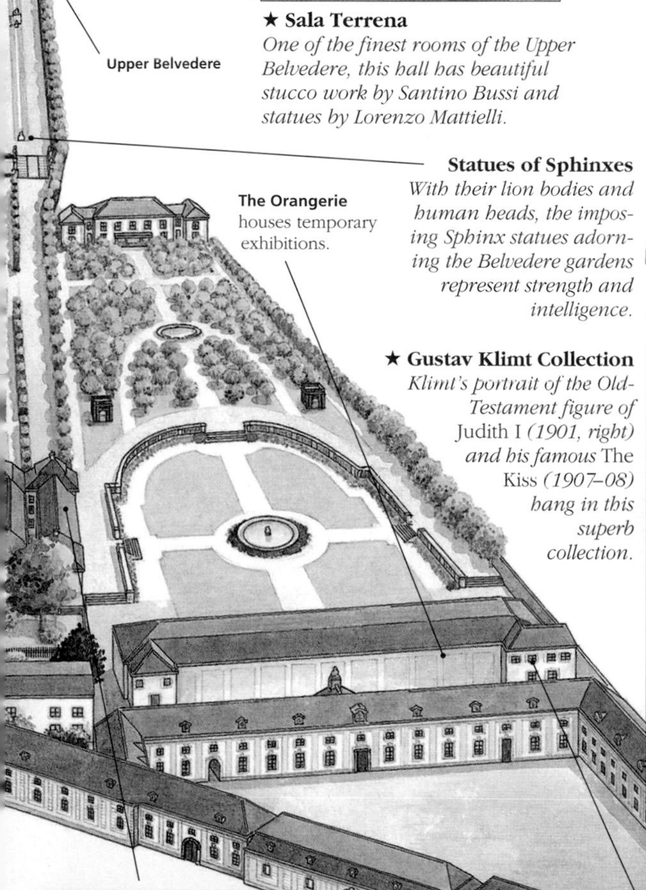

Entrance to the Upper Belvedere from Prinz-Eugen-Straße

★ Sala Terrena

One of the finest rooms of the Upper Belvedere, this hall has beautiful stucco work by Santino Bussi and statues by Lorenzo Mattielli.

VISITORS' CHECKLIST

Map 5 E2, F2, F3. **Lower Belvedere** Rennweg 6a. *Karlsplatz.* *71.* **Upper Belvedere** Prinz-Eugen-Strasse 27. ***Tel*** *79 55 70.* *Südbahnhof.* *18, D, O.* *13A.* *10am–6pm daily* **www**.belvedere.at

Upper Belvedere

Statues of Sphinxes

With their lion bodies and human heads, the imposing Sphinx statues adorning the Belvedere gardens represent strength and intelligence.

The Orangerie houses temporary exhibitions.

★ Gustav Klimt Collection

Klimt's portrait of the Old-Testament figure of Judith I *(1901, right) and his famous* The Kiss *(1907–08) hang in this superb collection.*

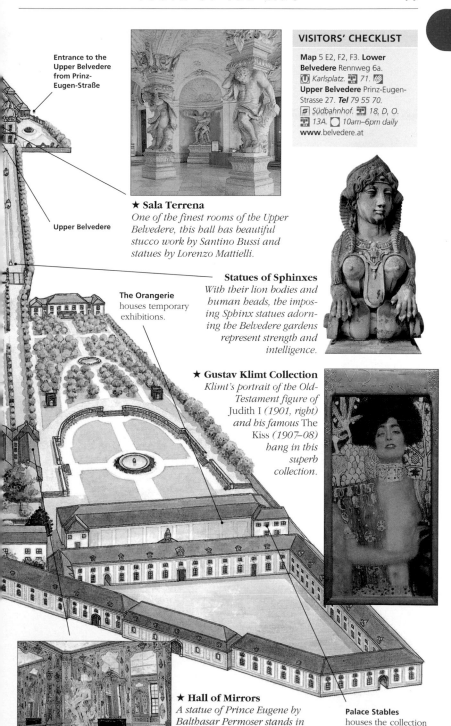

★ Hall of Mirrors

A statue of Prince Eugene by Balthasar Permoser stands in this richly ornamented Baroque room, whose walls are covered with huge gilt-framed mirrors.

Palace Stables houses the collection of Medieval Art (Study Collection).

FURTHER AFIELD

For a city of 1.6 million inhabitants, Vienna is surprisingly compact. Nonetheless, some of the most interesting sights are a fair distance from the historic city centre. At Schönbrunn sprawls the vast Neo-Classical palace of the same name, with its Rococo state rooms and superb gardens. The Habsburgs' summer residence, it was greatly beloved by Maria Theresa. It is also worth going to Kahlenberg, which offers the most splendid panoramic views of Vienna. You should spend at least one evening tasting the new-vintage wines in one of the *Heurigen* in Grinzing. Many parks and gardens, including the Prater, featured in the film *The Third Man* and one of Europe's best funfairs, as well as the Lainzer Tiergarten, are former Habsburg domains now open to the public.

Detail in Karl-Marx-Hof

SIGHTS AT A GLANCE

Historic Buildings
Amalienbad 11
Augarten 5
Hundertwasser-Haus 9
Karl-Marx-Hof 3
Liechtenstein Museum 4
Schönbrunn see pp110–11 15
Wagner Villas 17

Museums and Galleries
Haydn-Haus 13
Heeresgeschichtliches Museum 10
Museum of Technology 14

Parks and Gardens
Donauinsel 6
Lainzer Tiergarten 18
Prater 8

Interesting Districts
Grinzing 2
Kahlenberg 1
UNO-City 7

Churches
Kirche am Steinhof 16
Wotruba-Kirche 19

Cemeteries
Zentralfriedhof see pp106–7 12

KEY
Central Vienna
Greater Vienna
Railway station
Coach and bus station
Motorway
Motorway tunnel
Major road
Other road

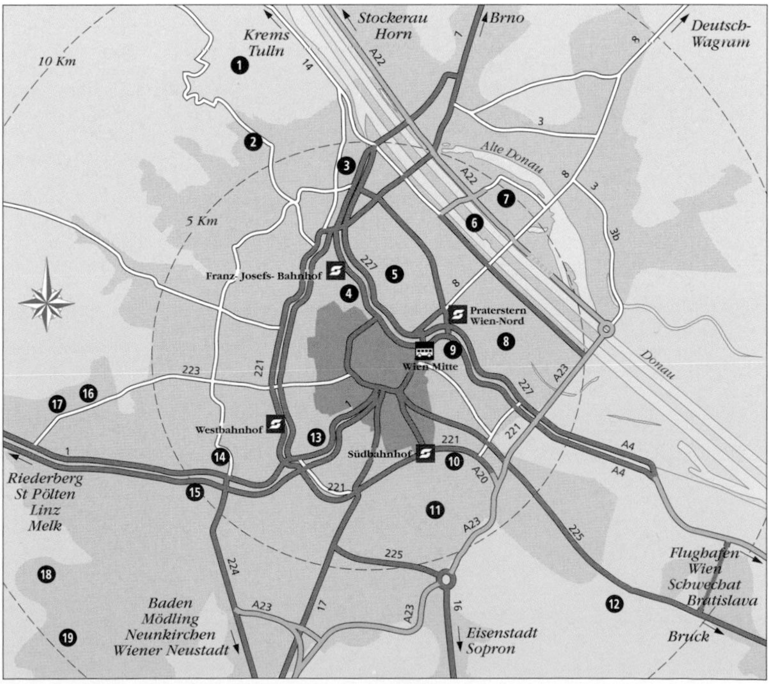

◁ **Part of the façade of the eccentric Hundertwasser Haus, built in 1985**

Cobenzlgasse, one of the charming streets in Grinzing

Kahlenberg ❶

38A.

North of the city, on the edge of the Vienna Woods, rise two almost identical peaks. The lower of the two, with ruins visible on top, is Leopoldsberg, the former seat of Margrave Leopold who ruled Austria in the 12th century. The second, with a television mast and the outline of a white church at the top, is Kahlenberg, the highest peak in Vienna.

It was from here, on the 12 September 1683, that the Polish King Jan III Sobieski led his troops to relieve the besieged city. Pope Innocent III's papal legate celebrated a thanksgiving mass in the ruins of the church that had been destroyed by the Turks.

The restored church of St Joseph on Kahlenberg is now maintained by Polish monks. Two tablets beside the church door commemorate the battle and the visit by Pope John Paul II, in 1983. Inside the church is a chapel with frescoes by the Polish artist, Henryk Rosen, and a display of the coats of arms of families whose members took part in the battle.

A short distance behind the church is an observation terrace and a restaurant. The views over the vineyards below and the city beyond are fabulous, with the Danube bridges to the left and the Vienna Woods to the right. No wonder then that Kahlenberg is a popular weekend destination.

Grinzing ❷

38. 38A.

The quiet villages scattered among the vineyards on the slopes of the Vienna Woods usually come to life during the wine-making season, when large groups of tourists descend on them to sample the new-vintage *Heuriger*. Originally, the vintners were licensed to sell their own wine, while snacks were offered for free. This tradition developed into today's *Heurigen* – new-vintage wine taverns, typical of Vienna.

Today, of course, such hospitality is no longer offered for free. At *Heurigen* inns, wine and other drinks are served at the table and food is available from self-service buffets. Guests sit on benches around wide wooden tables, where they can drink and enjoy themselves until the early hours.

A plaque on No. 31 Himmelstrasse in Grinzing

There are many such villages in the area around Vienna, but undoubtedly the most famous of all is Grinzing. Although it may have lost some of its original charm, this is still a nice place to spend an evening.

On the way to Grinzing, it is worth taking the time to visit the Heiligenstädter Testament-Haus at No. 6 in the narrow Probusgasse, Ludwig van Beethoven's most famous home in Vienna. It was here that the great composer tried to find a cure for his worsening deafness; when he failed, he wrote a dramatic letter to his brothers, known as *The Testament*.

Karl Marx-Hof ❸

Heiligenstädterstrasse 82–92.
Heiligenstadt. D. 10A, 11A, 38A, 39A.

In the 1920s, Vienna was governed by a social-democratic town council, elected mainly thanks to the votes of first-time women voters, a period known as Red Vienna. The council formed the ambitious plan to build houses for its entire working population. As a result, between 1923 and 1933 more than 60,000 new apartments, well-appointed for the time, were built. The programme was financed by a luxury tax imposed on wealthy citizens. Its execution was so strict that the municipal finance director, Hugo Breitner, earned himself the

The peach- and salmon-coloured façade of the Karl Marx-Hof

For hotels and restaurants in this region see pp288–94 and pp318–24

The Baroque building of the Wiener Porzellanmanufaktur

nickname the "financial vampire". Karl Marx-Hof is an immense complex of 1,382 council apartments and recreational facilities, and is the most celebrated of the municipal housing developments of that period. The project's architect, Karl Ehn, was a pupil of Otto Wagner.

The delightful ceiling frescoes in the Liechtenstein Museum

Liechtenstein Museum ❹

Fürstengasse 1. **Map** 2 A1. ***Tel*** *31 95 767 252.* *Friedensbrücke.* *40A.* *D.* *10am–5pm Fri–Tue.*

Completed in 1692 to designs by Domenico Martinelli in the Rococo style, this was the Liechtenstein family's summer palace. It has a monumental façade, with tall pilasters and typically Baroque windows.

Inside, the colourful ceiling paintings in the vast ground-floor room are the work of Michael Rottmayr. Vault paintings by Antonio Belucci can be seen on both sides of the stairway. The grand hall is decorated with frescoes by Andrea Pozzo, a masterpiece of Baroque interior design.

The museum houses the art collection of Prince Hans-Adam II von und zu Liechtenstein – one of the richest private collections in the world. The collection is centred on the Baroque with special focus on Rubens, and ranges from the Renaissance (for example, Raphael and the Breugels) through to the early 19th century (Waldmüller and Füger). The Liechtenstein family also acquired many masterpieces of modern art, dating from the early 20th century. The palace stands in an extensive garden, which was remodelled in the 19th century in the English style.

Augarten ❺

Obere Augartenstrasse 1. **Map** 3 D1. ***Tel*** *21 12 418.* *21, 31, N.*
Wiener Porzellanmanufaktur
guided tours 9:30am Mon–Fri.
public holidays, summer holidays.

There has been a palace on this site since the days of Leopold I, but it was destroyed by the Turks in 1683 and then rebuilt around 1700 to designs attributed to Johann Bernhard Fischer von Erlach. Since 1948 it has been the home of the world-famous Vienna Boys' Choir and is consequently closed to the public.

The surrounding park is one of the oldest in Vienna; it was first planted in 1650 by Emperor Ferdinand III, later renewed and opened to the public in 1775. Topiary lines long paths; the handsome gates were designed by Isidor Canevale. Mozart, Beethoven and Johann Strauss (father) all gave concerts in the park pavilion, which was once the imperial porcelain factory.

The **Wiener Porzellanmanufaktur**, established in 1718, is today run by the municipal authorities, but its products are still stamped with the imperial crest. The factory is open to the public, and there are displays on the history of Augarten porcelain.

Donauinsel ❻

Donauinsel, Handelskai.

The numerous side-arms and rivulets of the Danube river regularly flooded the town until it was first canalized between 1870 and 1875. The second period of canalization in the Vienna region began in 1972 and was completed in 1987. The New Danube, a 5-km (3-mile) canal that acts as an "overflow", dates from this period.

The wooded island created between the Danube and its canals by the first stage of canalization is known as Donauinsel, or Danube Island. It is Vienna's largest recreation area and a favourite with the local population, who come here to swim and sunbathe in the summer. The vast park is criss-crossed by dozens of avenues, walking and cycling paths, picnic areas with built-in barbecues as well as nudist areas. Even water-skiing and surfing are possible. Once the weather warms up, the Copa Cabana entertainment centre attracts visitors with its array of bars, restaurants, discos and the popular *Heurigen*.

The island hosts an annual festival, with open-air pop concerts and other events.

The vast, modern complex of UNO-City on the Danube

UNO-City 7

Wagramerstrasse 5. ***Tel*** *26026.* *Kaisermühlen, Vienna International Center.* *20B.* **UNO** *11am, 2pm Mon–Fri (ID required).* **Donauturm** ***Tel*** *263 35 72.* **www**.unvienna.org

On the left bank of the Danube is UNO-City, one of only three United Nations headquarters. The complex stands on international, non-Austrian territory; its post office uses its own special postage stamps and UN postmarks. UNO-City consists of four vast semicircular buildings and a large congress hall, one of the most strikingly modern pieces of architecture in Europe, designed by the architect Johann Staber and opened in 1979. Today, visitors can join one of the regular guided tours of the complex.

UNO-City is surrounded by a green park, covering an area of over 600,000 sq m (700,000 sq yds), with excellent recreational facilities. One of the main attractions is the Donauturm, a TV tower rising to 252 m (827 ft), with two revolving restaurants and an observation platform.

Prater 8

Tel *Praterverband 728 05 16. Ferris Wheel 72 95 430.* *Praterstern.* *5, O.* *Wien Nord.* *Funfair 15 Mar–15 Oct: 10am–midnight daily.* **www**.prater.wien.info

Originally an imperial hunting ground, the woods and meadows between the Danube and its canal were opened to the public by Joseph II in 1766. The Hauptallee (central avenue) was for a long time the preserve of the nobility and their footmen. During the 19th century, the western end of Prater became a massive funfair with booths, sideshows, shooting galleries, merry-go-rounds and beer gardens. Today, it is one of Europe's best-equipped amusement parks, with high-tech rides. Its most famous attraction is the giant Riesenrad (ferris wheel) built in 1896 by the English engineer Walter Basset. The setting for the tense final scene in Carol Reed's film *The Third Man* (1949), it is now one of the city's symbols.

The Prater is also a vast sports park, home to a soccer and a trotting stadium, the Freudenau Racetrack, swimming pools, tennis courts, a golf course and cycling trails, as well as a planetarium and open-air restaurants and bars.

Nearby are the pavilions and vast grounds of the annual Vienna Fair for numerous temporary exhibitions.

The Prater funfair at night

Hundertwasser-Haus 9

Löwengasse/Kegelgasse. *Landstrasse.* *1, O.* **www**.hundertwasserhaus.at *no admission to the public.* **Kunsthaus Wien** ***Tel*** *71 20 495-12.* *10am–7pm daily.*

Hundertwasser-Haus is a municipal apartment block created in 1985 by the artist Friedensreich Hundertwasser. An eclectic-style building, combining the elements of a Moorish mosque with features of Spanish villages and Venetian palaces, it has become one of Vienna's main attractions. The shopping centre opposite was designed by the artist, whose work is on show at the Kunsthaus Wien, Untere Weissgerberstrasse 13.

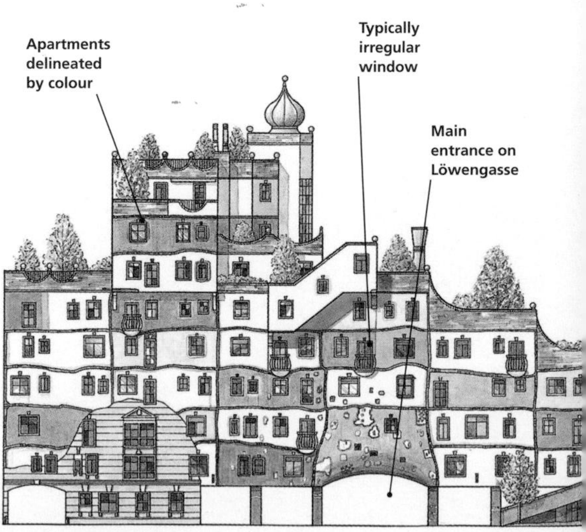

For hotels and restaurants in this region see pp288–94 and pp318–24

Heeresgeschichtliches Museum ⑩

Ghegastrasse Arsenal, Objekt 18. ***Tel*** *79 56 10.* *Südtiroler Platz, Schlachthausgasse.* *Südbahnhof.* *13A, 69A.* *18, O & D.* *9am–5pm daily. Guided tours (in English), call 0664 622 2248.* *1 Jan, 1 May, All Saints, 4, 25, 31 Dec.* **www**.hgm.or.at

The impressive Museum of Army History is housed in the military complex known as the Arsenal, built as a fortress in 1856. The museum, which chronicles Austria's military prowess from the 16th century, was designed by Theophil Hansen and Ludwig Förster.

Exhibits relate to the Turkish Siege of Vienna in 1683, the French Revolution and the Napoleonic wars. There are documents relating to the battles fought by the Habsburgs, a collection of arms, banners, uniforms and military vehicles. Among the most fascinating exhibits are memorabilia relating to Prince Eugene of Savoy, as well as a collection of model ships that illustrates the past glories of imperial power at sea – since it is landlocked, it is easy to forget that Austria was once a formidable naval power. A separate section is devoted to the events in Sarajevo on 28 June 1914, when Archduke Ferdinand and his wife Sophie von Hohenberg were assassinated by a Serbian nationalist, provoking a crisis that led to the outbreak of World War I.

Decorative tiling from the 1920s in Amalienbad

Amalienbad ⑪

Reumannplatz 23. ***Tel*** *60 74 747.* *Reumannplatz.* *67, 68A.* *9am–6pm Tue, 9am–9:30pm Wed, Fri, 7am–9:30pm Thu, 7am–8pm Sat, 7am–6pm Sun.*

Public baths may not seem like an obvious tourist attraction, but the *Jugendstil*-style Amalienbad (1923–6) is a fine example of a far-sighted municipal authority providing essential public facilities for the local working population, and doing so with style and panache. Named after one of the councillors, Amalie Pölzer, the baths were designed by Otto Nadel and Karl Schmalhofer, employees of the city's architectural department.

The magnificent main pool, overlooked by galleries, is covered by a glass roof that can be opened in minutes. There are saunas, smaller baths and therapeutic pools. When first opened, the baths were one of the largest of their kind in Europe. The interior is enlivened by fabulous Secession tile decorations. The baths were damaged in World War II but have been impeccably restored.

Corner of block with first-floor café and staircase topped by onion dome

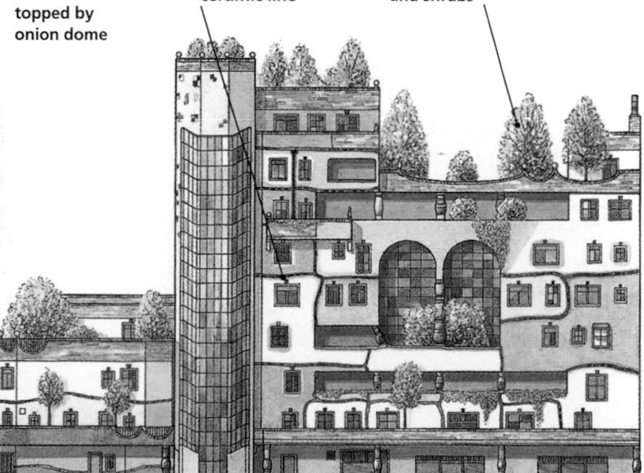

Zentralfriedhof ⓬

Headstone on Johannes Brahms' grave

Austria's largest burial ground, containing two and a half million graves and covering over 2.5 sq km (1 sq mile), was opened in 1874. The central section includes the graves of artists, composers, architects, writers and local politicians. Funerals in Vienna are often quite lavish affairs, and the cemetery contains a vast array of funerary monuments, from the humble to the ostentatious, paying tribute to the city's enduring obsession with death.

★ Dr.-Karl-Lueger-Kirche
This church and mausoleum is dedicated to Vienna's much-esteemed mayor of 1907–10.

Presidential Vault
This contains the remains of Dr Karl Renner, the first President of the Austrian Republic after World War II.

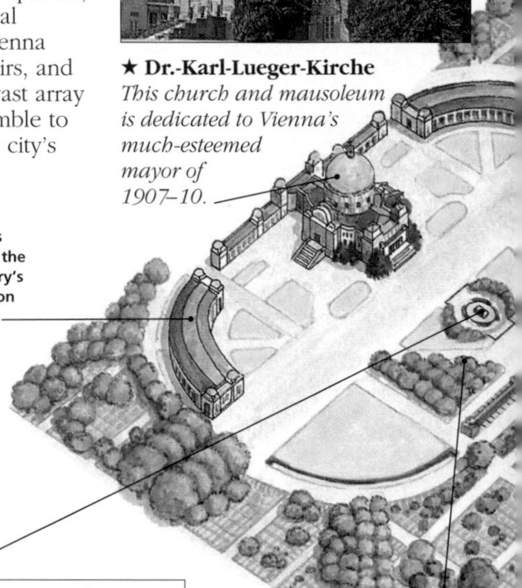

Arcades around the cemetery's Secession church

Arnold Schönberg's Cube
The grave of the modernist composer Arnold Schönberg, creator of dodecaphonic music, is marked with this bold cube by Fritz Wotruba.

CEMETERY LAYOUT

The cemetery is divided into numbered sections: apart from the central garden of honour (reached via gate II), where VIPs are buried, there are old (gate I) and new (gate IV) Jewish cemeteries, a Protestant cemetery (gate III), a Russian Orthodox section, and various war graves and memorials. It is easiest to explore the cemetery on board the circulating minibus.

The Monument to the Dead of World War II is a powerful representation of a grieving mother by Anton Hanak.

STAR FEATURES

- ★ Dr.-Karl-Lueger-Kirche
- ★ Musicians' Graves

Theophil Hansen's Grave
A Danish architect, Theophil Hansen, made Vienna his home and designed the city's Parliament building. He died in 1891.

VISITORS' CHECKLIST

Simmeringer Hauptstrasse 234. ***Tel*** *76 041.* *Zentralfriedhof.* *6, 71.* *Nov–Feb 8am–5pm daily; Mar, Apr, Sep, Oct, 1–2 Nov: 7am–6pm; May–Aug: 7am–8pm daily.*

Monument (1894) to Dr. Johann Nepomuk Prix, mayor of Vienna, by Viktor Tilgner.

The Arcades
Some spectacular monuments can be seen carved in the semi-circular arcades facing the main entrance, including this memorial (1848) to the miner August Zang. It shows the entrance to a mine.

The main entrance to the cemetery is from Simmeringer Hauptstrasse, with the Secession-style Gate II, designed by Max Hegele in 1905.

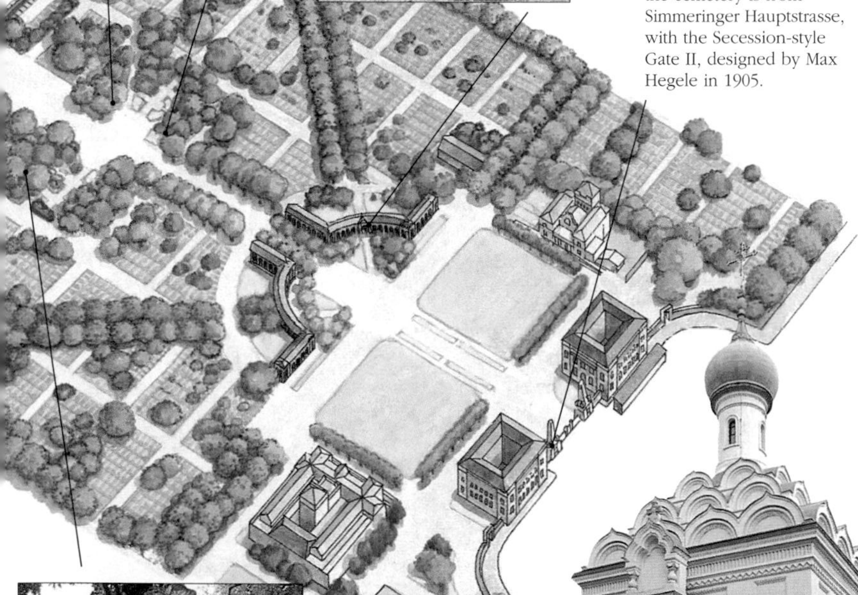

★ Graves of the Musicians
The musicians buried here include Johann Strauss father and son (shown left), *Brahms, Beethoven and Schubert. There is also a monument to Mozart.*

Russian Orthodox Chapel
This small chapel, built in traditional Russian Orthodox style in 1894, is used by Vienna's Russian community.

Brahms' Room in the Haydn-Haus

Haydn-Haus ⓭

Haydngasse 19. ***Tel** 59 61 307.*
Zieglergasse. 10am–1pm, 2–6pm Tue–Sun & hols. 1 Jan, 1 May, 25 Dec. Admission free – Fri am.

Haydn built this house in what was then a new suburb with money that he had earned on his successful trips to London between 1791 and 1795. He lived in the house from 1797 until his death in 1809, and composed many major works here, including *The Seasons* and *The Creation*.

The museum is not very comprehensive but it has a few portraits, autographs, documents and original scores on display. A separate room is devoted to another great composer, Johannes Brahms. Here, you can see some furniture and a few mementoes as well as the clavichord, originally Haydn's, that was bought by Brahms.

Museum of Technology ⓮

Mariahilfer Strasse 212. ***Tel** 89 998 6000. Schönbrunn, Johnstrasse. 52, 58. 10A, 57A. 9am–6pm Mon–Fri, 10am–6pm Sat, Sun and holidays.* **www**.tmw.at

Originally founded by Franz Joseph I in 1908, Vienna's Museum of Technology was completely renovated during the late 1990s, and now covers a massive area.

The museum documents technical progress over the past centuries, from domestic appliances to heavy industry, with a particular emphasis on Austrian engineers and scientists. Exhibits include the world's first sewing machine (Madersperger, 1830), the oldest typewriter (Mitterhofer, 1860), the ship's propeller, designed by Ressel in 1875, and the first petrol-driven car built in the same year by Siegfried Marcus. A major section features displays on computer technology and oil and gas refining, as well as a reconstructed coal mine.

The Railway Museum, which is an integral part of the museum, houses a large collection of imperial railway carriages and engines. Its prize exhibit is the carriage used by Franz Joseph I's wife, the Empress Elisabeth. The Post Office Museum displays the world's first postcard – an Austrian invention.

A huge lighthouse at the entrance recalls the Habsburg Empire's once formidable extent, from the Tatra Mountains to the Atlantic Ocean.

Schönbrunn ⓯

See pp110–11.

Kirche am Steinhof ⓰

Baumgartner Höhe 1. ***Tel** 91 060-11007. 3–5pm Sat. 47A, 48A. 3pm Sat.*

At the edge of the Vienna Woods rises the conspicuous copper dome of the astonishing Church at Steinhof. Built in 1902–7 by Otto Wagner, the church is considered to be one of the most important works of the Secession. It is an integral part of the large mental hospital complex, also designed by Wagner, who laid out the church to facilitate access for disabled churchgoers.

The church, dedicated to St Leonard, is clad in marble with copper nailhead ornament, and has spindly screw-shaped pillars topped by wreaths supporting the porch, and four stone columns. The light and airy interior is a single space with shallow side chapels. Its main decoration consists of gold and white friezes as well as gilt nailhead and beautiful blue stained-glass windows by Kolo Moser. The altar mosaics are by Rudolf Jettmar.

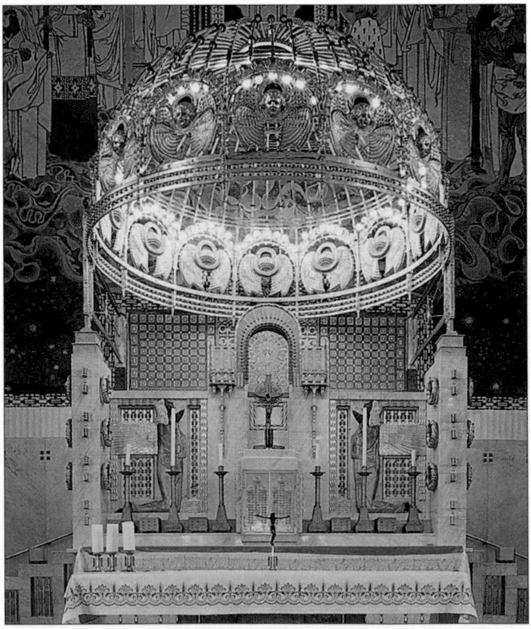

The Secession-style interior of the Kirche am Steinhof

Hermes Villa in Lainzer Tiergarten, retreat of the imperial family

Wagner Villas **⓱**

Hüttelbergstrasse 26 & 28. **Tel** *914 85 75.* Ⓤ *Hütteldorf.* 🚌 *148, 152.* **Fuchs Villa** ◯ *10am–4pm Mon–Fri.* 🎟️ 🛗

Hidden behind dense, leafy greenery, at the start of a road to Kahlenberg, stand two villas built by the architect Otto Wagner. The oldest, built for himself, still has some Classical elements such as Ionic columns, once favoured by Wagner. It was meticulously restored by the present owner, the painter Ernst Fuchs, who added his own colours and established a museum. The villa is now a famous meeting place for Vienna's artistic community as well as a venue for fund-raising auctions. The second villa, built some 20 years later, was completed in pure Secession style. Privately owned, it can be viewed only from outside.

Lainzer Tiergarten **⓲**

Hermesstrasse. 🚌 *60B.* **Hermes Villa Tel** *80 41 324.* ◯ *Apr–Oct: 10am–6pm Tue–Sun & hols.* ◉ *between exhibitions.* 🎟️ **www**.wienmuseum.at **www**.lainzer-tiergarten.at

The Lainzer Tiergarten in the Vienna Woods, once an imperial hunting ground, was enclosed within a 25-km (16-mile) long wall on the orders of Maria Theresa. The wall still stands today and successfully stops herds of deer and wild boar escaping as well as building development encroaching.

The Tiergarten was opened to the public in 1923, and in 1941 the entire area was declared a nature reserve. Walks in the woods and meadows of this large park will transport the visitor into another world. It is forbidden to disturb the animals; bikes and dogs are banned, turning the reserve into a true haven for wildlife.

There are now also bars and cafés here. From the observation platform on top of Karlbründl, there are great views over Vienna and the Vienna Woods.

Detail on the stables in Hermes Villa

A 15-minute walk along paths brings you to the **Hermes Villa**. In 1885, the Emperor Franz Joseph I ordered a hunting lodge to be built here and presented it to his wife Elisabeth, in the hope that this would keep her close to the court and stop her from perpetually seeking to escape the clamour of the city. He did not succeed, but the beautiful Hermes Villa was built by Karl von Hasenauer as a retreat for the imperial family. The couple's rooms were on the first floor; Elisabeth's quarters were designed with flourish and elegance; Franz Joseph's were much more spartan. The villa, named after a marble statue of Hermes, was fully equipped with electricity, and was served by one of the first lit-up streets. Bathtubs and toilets were added by the Empress in the 1890s. Attractive murals show scenes from *A Midsummer Night's Dream*, designed by Hans Makart and painted by the young Gustav Klimt.

Today, Hermes Villa holds exhibitions, while the stables act as summer quarters for the Lipizzaner horses from the Spanish Riding School.

Wotruba-Kirche **⓳**

Georgsgasse/Rysergasse. **Tel** *88 85 003.* 🚌 *60A.* ◯ *2–8pm Sat, 9am–5pm Sun and public holidays.* 🛗 *by appointment.*

Standing on hillside close to the Vienna Woods, this church was designed in uncompromisingly modern style in 1965 by the Austrian sculptor Fritz Wotruba (1907–75), after whom it is named. It was built in 1974–6 by Fritz Mayer. The church is made up of a pile of uneven concrete slabs and glass panels that provide its principal lighting and views for the congregation out onto the hills. The building is raw in style, but powerful and compact. The church looks different from every angle and has a strong sculptural quality. The central section, consisting of 152 concrete blocks, can accommodate a congregation of up to 250.

The sculptural Wotruba-Kirche

Schönbrunn ⓯

In 1695, Emperor Leopold I asked Johann Bernhard Fischer von Erlach to rebuild the former summer residence of the imperial family. However, it was not until the reign of Maria Theresa that the project was completed by Nikolaus Pacassi (1744–9). It is to him that the palace owes the magnificent Rococo decorations of its state rooms. Schönbrunn has been the scene of many important historic events.

Round Chinese Cabinet
Maria Theresa used this room for private discussions with her State Chancellor, Prince Kaunitz. The walls of the white-and-gold room are adorned with lacquered panels.

★ Great Gallery
Used for imperial banquets, this room has a lovely ceiling fresco by Georgio Gugliemi.

A hidden staircase leads to the apartment of the State Chancellor, above which he had secret conferences with the Empress.

Blue Chinese Salon
The last Austrian emperor, Karl I, signed his abdication in 1918 in this Rococo room with Chinese scenes.

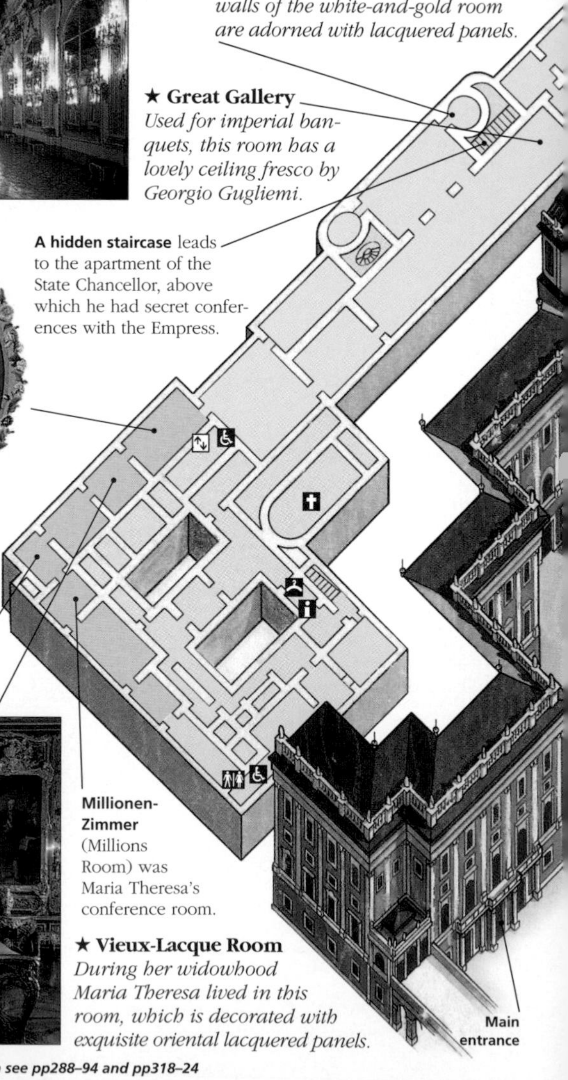

Napoleon Room

Millionen-Zimmer (Millions Room) was Maria Theresa's conference room.

★ Vieux-Lacque Room
During her widowhood Maria Theresa lived in this room, which is decorated with exquisite oriental lacquered panels.

Main entrance

For hotels and restaurants in this region see pp288–94 and pp318–24

Miniatures Cabinet
The paintings on the wall of Maria Theresa's breakfast room are copies of Dutch and German paintings by Franz Stephan and his daughters Maria Anna, Maria Christine and Maria Antonia.

VISITORS' CHECKLIST

Schönbrunner Schlossstrasse 147. ***Tel*** *81 11 32 39. Schönbrunn, Hietzing. 1 0, 58, 60. 10A.* **Palace** *1 Apr–30 Jun, Sep–Oct: 8:30am–5pm; Jul–Aug: 8:30am–6pm; Nov–Mar: 8:30am–4:30pm daily.* **Gardens** *morning till dusk.* **www**.schoenbrunn.at

Large Rosa Room
This is one of three rooms decorated with monumental Swiss and Italian landscape paintings by Josef Rosa, after whom the room is named.

PALACE GUIDE

On the first floor, the suite of rooms to the right of the Blue Staircase was occupied by Emperor Franz Joseph I and his wife Elisabeth. The rooms in the east wing include Maria Theresa's bedroom and rooms used by Grand Duke Karl.

STAR FEATURES

★ Great Gallery

★ Vieux-Lacque Room

The Blue Staircase leads to the entrance for all tours of the state rooms.

KEY

- Franz Joseph I's apartments
- Empress Elisabeth's apartments
- Ceremonial and reception rooms
- Maria Theresa's rooms
- Grand Duke Karl's rooms
- Closed to visitors

THE COACH MUSEUM

One wing of Schönbrunn Palace, formerly housing the Winter Riding School, now contains a marvellous collection of coaches – one of the most interesting in the world. It includes over 60 carriages dating back to the 17th century, as well as riding uniforms, horse tackle, saddles, coachman liveries, and paintings and drawings of horses and carriages. The pride of the collection is the coronation coach of Emperor Karl VI. Other exhibits include sleighs and sedan chairs belonging to Maria Theresa, among others.

Coronation coach of Karl VI

SHOPPING IN VIENNA

Since Vienna is a compact city, it is a pleasant place to shop. The main shopping area is pedestrianized and you can browse around at a leisurely pace. Austrian glassware, food and traditional crafts are all good buys. However, the shops tend to cater for fairly mature tastes and full purses. Vienna has a number of markets selling anything from produce to trinkets. The pedestrian shopping areas of Kärntner Strasse, Graben and Kohlmarkt have more expensive shops. The largest shopping centre is SCS (Shopping Centre Süd), in the suburbs. It can be reached on the southern motorway or the Baden train.

Augarten porcelain Lipizzaner

WHERE TO SHOP

The most elegant shops are found within the Ring, and the most attractive window displays can be seen in Kärntner Strasse, Graben, Kohlmarkt and the central shopping passage connecting Kärntner Strasse with Weihburggasse. The shops here are also the more expensive ones, although on Graben and Kärntner Strasse are chain stores such as H&M and Mango. You will find smaller shops, tastefully decorated, offering goods of guaranteed quality and which are often truly unique. This applies to clothes, glass and porcelain, as well as to confectionery and decorative items. There are also some excellent bookshops here.

The shops along Mariahilfer Strasse are more middle-of-the-range; this is where you will find many of the multinational chains, as well as large shoe shops, stationery and book shops, and a variety of food shops. A similar range of goods, but at lower prices, can be found in Meidlinger Hauptstrasse, and even less costly ones are on sale in Favoritenstrasse.

All of Vienna's shopping areas can easily be explored by public transport.

OPENING HOURS

Shops generally open at 8:30 or 9am and close at 6 or 7pm. Almost all stay open till 5pm on Saturday and close on Sundays and public holidays.

The supermarket chain Billa is open on Sundays at the main railway stations and Vienna airport. Most bakeries are also open. It is possible to buy some items at petrol stations too.

HOW TO PAY

In Vienna, most stores accept major credit cards, including Visa, MasterCard and American Express. Debit cards are also usually accepted, however, it is still wise to carry some cash. Visitors normally resident outside the EU are entitled to claim back the VAT (Mehrwertsteuer – MwSt) if the total value of goods purchased in any one shop exceeds €73. Take your passport when shopping and ask the shopkeeper to complete the appropriate form; keep the receipts. The VAT rate is 20 per cent and the goods listed in the form must be unused and available for inspection by Customs officers.

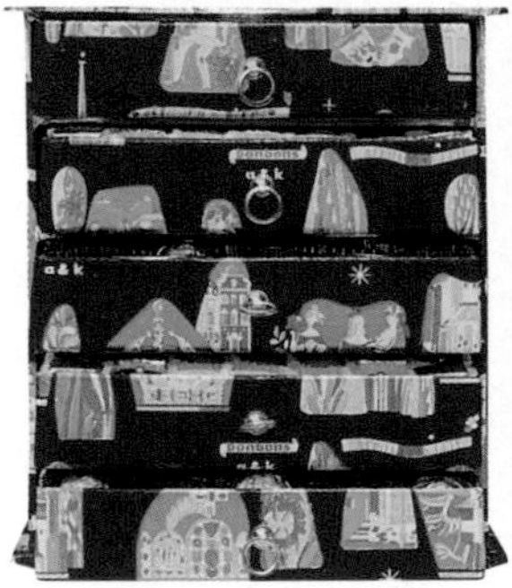

A chest of drawers with chocolates from Altman & Kühne

RIGHTS AND SERVICES

If you have purchased goods that turn out to be defective, you are usually entitled to a refund, provided you have kept the receipt. This is not always the case with goods bought in the sales – inspect them carefully before you buy. Many shops in Vienna will pack goods for you – and often gift-wrap them at no extra charge – and send them anywhere in the world.

ANTIQUES AND ART

A pawnshop established by Emperor Joseph I in 1703 has been transformed into Austria's largest auction house,

Opulent glassware in a shop on Kärntner Strasse

Dorotheum, one of the best known in the world. Items auctioned here include mainly antique furniture and objects of decorative value. Its vast store at Dorotheergasse No. 17 is open to the public and also conducts a non-auction sale. Dorotheum has several branches all over the city.

Lovely second-hand and antique items can also be bought at the flea markets that take place regularly in one part of town or other; the largest of them, but also the most expensive, is the **Naschmarkt** *(see p93).*

FOOD AND DRINK

Vienna is justly famous for its cakes, pastries and *Torten*, and any good *Café-Konditorei* (cake shop and café) will post cakes back home for you. In the pre-Christmas period, try the buttery Advent *Stollen* from **Meinl am Graben**, or the original *Sachertorte,* directly from the **Hotel Sacher**, at any time of year. The specialist chocolate shops are also worth a visit if you have a sweet tooth. And look out for *Eiswein,* a delicious dessert wine made from grapes left on the vine after the first frosts.

Kohlmarkt, one of Vienna's most fashionable shopping streets

SOUVENIRS

There are many things you can buy to remind you of Austria, from the kitsch, such as the giant Ferris Wheel in a snowstorm or drinking glasses playing *O du lieber Augustin*, to the classy, such as Biedermeier-style flower posies, handbags embroidered with folkloric designs or figurines and tableware from the **Augarten** porcelain manufactury. There are also cups with the profile of Romy Schneider in her role as Sissi, or pictures of the young Franz Joseph I. Traditional Austrian clothes or *Trachten* are sold by **Witzky** and others, including *Loden*, a felt-like fabric used to make warm coats, jackets and capes, and *Dirndls* (dresses). Zauberklingl is the place for practical jokers, with great party jokes.

DIRECTORY

ANTIQUES & ART

Dorotheum
Dorotheergasse 17.
Map 2 B4.
Tel *51 560.*

Galerie Rauhenstein
Rauhensteingasse 3.
Map 2 C4.
Tel *513 30 09.*

Kunst- und Antikmarkt
Donaukanal-Promenade.
Map 3 D3. ◯ *May–Sep: 2–6pm Sat, 10am–8pm Sun.* Am Hof. **Map** 2 B3.
◯ *10am–7pm Fri, Sat.*

Naschmarkt
Map 4 C1.
◯ *6am–7pm Mon–Fri, 6am–6pm Sat, Flea market: 6am–2pm Sat.*

FOOD & DRINK

Altmann & Kühne
Graben 30.
Map 2 B4.
Tel *533 09 27.*

Delikatessen Böhle
Wollzeile 30. **Map** 2 B4.
Tel *512 31 55.*

Hotel Sacher
Philharmonikerstrasse 4.
Map 2 B5.
Tel *514 56 0–0.*

Meinl am Graben
Graben 19.
Map 2 B4.
Tel *532 33 34.*

Vinothek St. Stephan
Stephansplatz 6.
Map 2 C4.
Tel *512 68 58.*

Zum Schwarzen Kameel
Bognergasse 5.
Map 2 B3.
Tel *533 81 25.*

SOUVENIRS

Augarten
Stock-im-Eisen-Platz 3–4.
Map 2 C4.
Tel *512 14 94.*

J. & J. Lobmeyr
Kärntner Strasse 26.
Map 2 C5.
Tel *512 05 08.*

Kalke Village
Kegelgasse 37–39.
Tel *710 46 16.*

Maria Stransky
Hofburg Passage 2.
Map 2 B4.
Tel *533 60 98.*

Metzger
Stephansplatz 7.
Map 2 C4.
Tel *512 34 33.*

Österreichische Werkstätten
Kärntner Strasse 6.
Map 2 C4.
Tel *512 24 18.*

Petit Point
Kärntner Strasse 16.
Map 2 C4.
Tel *512 48 86.*

Witzky Landhausmode
Stephansplatz 7.
Map 2 C4.
Tel *512 48 43.*

Zauberklingl
Führichgasse 4.
Map 2 C4.
Tel *512 68 68.*

ENTERTAINMENT IN VIENNA

Vienna offers a wide range of entertainment of every kind, from street theatre in the famous Prater funfair to classical drama in one of the opulent theatres. But most of all, Vienna is a musical town. There is grand opera at the Staatsoper, or the latest musical at the Theater an der Wien; dignified orchestral music and elegant waltzes; relaxed dances in the Stadtpark and free open-air concerts. Even the famous Lipizzaner horses perform to Viennese music. The city also takes pride in its Burgtheater, one of the most foremost stages in the German-speaking world, as well as its many smaller dramatic theatres. There are two excellent theatres performing in English and several cinemas which specialize in classic films. Restaurants tend to close early but you can still be entertained around the clock at one of the many nightspots: jazz clubs, discos, casinos and bars with live music all beckon within the Ringstrasse. Or you can end your day sipping coffee and indulging in the gorgeous pastries at one of the late-night cafés.

Papageno puppet

The giant Ferris wheel in the Prater funfair

PRACTICAL INFORMATION

Listings of current events and theatre, concert and cinema programmes can be found in most daily newspapers; check *Neue Kronen Zeitung, Die Presse, Standard* or *Kurier*. The weekly guide *Der Falter* (www.falter.at) is entirely devoted to the arts. The Vienna Tourist Office (Wiener Tourismusverband) publishes a monthly guide with listings of art and sports events taking place that month, and every hotel has a range of free leaflets with details of concerts, theatre performances and other artistic events. You can also check the fat round billboard columns all over the city, which have posters advertising the latest events.

Most theatres, concert halls and public buildings have been specially adapted to accommodate disabled spectators (ramps, lifts), and many museums also offer wheelchairs for hire. All have at least one disabled toilet.

BOOKING TICKETS

You can buy tickets directly from the appropriate box office, or reserve them by telephone or via the Internet. Hotel receptions can often help. Theatres offer various concessions and the opera house sells cheap tickets for standing-only places. Tickets bought in advance tend to be up to 10 per cent cheaper than those bought just before the start of a performance.

MUSIC

The principal venues for classical concerts, including the ever-popular waltzes, are the **Staatsoper** (State Opera), the concert halls of the **Musikverein**, where the Wiener Philharmoniker perform, and the **Konzerthaus**. Here you can hear the world's greatest performers. Classical music concerts are also held in many churches. Open-air concerts are very popular during the summer season. Another Viennese favourite is the **Wiener Kursalon**, where you can enjoy old and new tunes while overlooking the Stadtpark.

The **Donauinselfestival**, staged in the summer on the Danube island, is a great way to hear free pop concerts by some of the world's most popular performers. During local festivals, in wine bars

A young street musician entertaining with his cello

and cafés you can often hear Viennese folk music called *Schrammelmusik* after the music by the Schrammel Brothers. Kärntner Strasse is another kind of music venue – many street performers and buskers here hope for hand-outs from the generally well-to-do passers-by.

THEATRES

Vienna's **Staatsoper** enjoys an excellent international reputation. Opera is also shown at the **Wiener Volksoper** (Vienna People's Opera) and the **Wiener Kammeroper** (Vienna Chamber Opera). The **Raimund Theater** is one of the best places for musicals. The **Theater an der Wien** specializes in opera productions. The **Burgtheater** is still regarded by many as one of the most interesting theatres; a smaller and more intimate stage is called **Akademietheater**. The **Volkstheater** stages modern plays and the occasional classic drama, while the **Theater in der Josefstadt** specializes in subtle takes on comedy, both old and new, as well as performances of past and contemporary Austrian drama.

The famous Vienna State Opera Ball

CINEMAS

Most films are dubbed and shown in German; those that can be watched in their original language are always advertised as such in the programme. Some cinemas specialize in foreign films. The **Österreichisches Filmmuseum,** based in the Albertina building, screens classics of the silver screen, while the **Votivkino** and the **Filmhaus Stöbergasse** cinemas often put on a season of films devoted to one artist or subject; it is usually these art-house and repertory cinemas that show the most interesting films in the city.

Billboard column

CASINOS

Casino Wien is set in the fabulous Baroque Esterházy Palace, where you can play French or American roulette, baccarat and poker.

AFTER A NIGHT OUT

At night, public transport is provided by a network of half-hourly buses, departing from the central points at Schwedenplatz, Franz-Josef-Kai and the opera. It is worth buying a ticket in advance from the kiosk, as these are cheaper than the ones sold on the bus. The U-Bahn runs all night on weekends and the night before a public holiday. Taxis can be found outside all major venues and at taxi ranks.

DIRECTORY

BOOKINGS

Bundestheaterkassen
Operngasse 2.
Map 2 B5. ***Tel*** *513 15 13.*
8am–6pm Mon–Fri, 9am–noon Sat, Sun and public holidays.

CONCERT HALLS

Konzerthaus
Lothringerstrasse 20.
Map 5 D1. ***Tel*** *24 20 02.*
www.konzerthaus.at.

Musikverein
Bösendorferstrasse 12.
Map 5 D1.
Tel *50 58 190.*
www.musikverein.at.

Staatsoper
Opernring 2.
Map 2 B5. ***Tel*** *51444 2250.*
www.wiener-staatsoper.at.

Wiener Kursalon
Johannesgasse 33.
Map 3 D5. ***Tel*** *512 57 90.*

THEATRES

Akademietheater
Lisztstrasse 1. **Map** 5 E1.
Tickets: Opernring 2.
Tel *51444–4140.*

Burgtheater
Dr.-Karl-Lueger-Ring 2.
Map 2 A3.
Tel *51444–4400.*

Raimund Theater
Wallgasse 18–20.
Tel *59 9770.*

Theater an der Wien
Linke Wienzeile 6.
Map 4 C1. ***Tel*** *58 885.*

Theater in der Josefstadt
Josefstädter Strasse 26.
Map 1 B4. ***Tel*** *42 700.*

Volkstheater
Neustiftgasse 1.
Map 1 C5. ***Tel*** *52 47 263.*

Wiener Kammeroper
Fleischmarkt 24. **Map** 3 D3. ***Tel*** *51 201–0077.*

Wiener Volksoper
Währingerstrasse 78.
Map 1 C1.
Tel *51 444–3670.*

CINEMAS

Filmhaus Stöbergasse
Stöbergasse 11–15.
Map 4 A 4/5.
Tel *54666–30.*

Österreichisches Filmmuseum
Augustinerstrasse 1.
Members only.
Map 2 B5. ***Tel*** *53 37 054.*

Votivkino
Währingerstrasse 12.
Map 2 A2. ***Tel*** *31 73 571.*

CASINO

Casino Wien
Kärntner Strasse 41.
Map 2 B5.
Tel *51 24 836.*

VIENNA STREET FINDER

The map references given for all the sights, hotels, restaurants, bars, shops and entertainment venues described in this book refer to the maps in this section. Most of the city's famous sights, historic buildings, tram, bus, U-Bahn and railway stations, and river landing-stages have been marked on the map. Others are indicated by symbols, which are explained in the key below. The names of the streets and squares on the map are given in German. The word *Strasse* (Str.) translates as street, while *Gasse* is a smaller street, *Platz* means square, *Hof* means a courtyard, *Brücke* translates as bridge and a *Bahnhof* is a railway station.

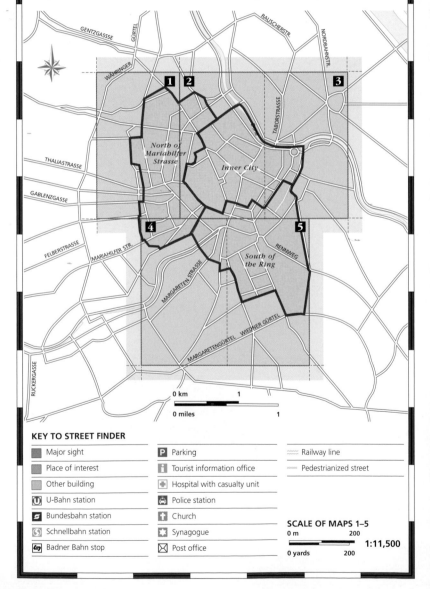

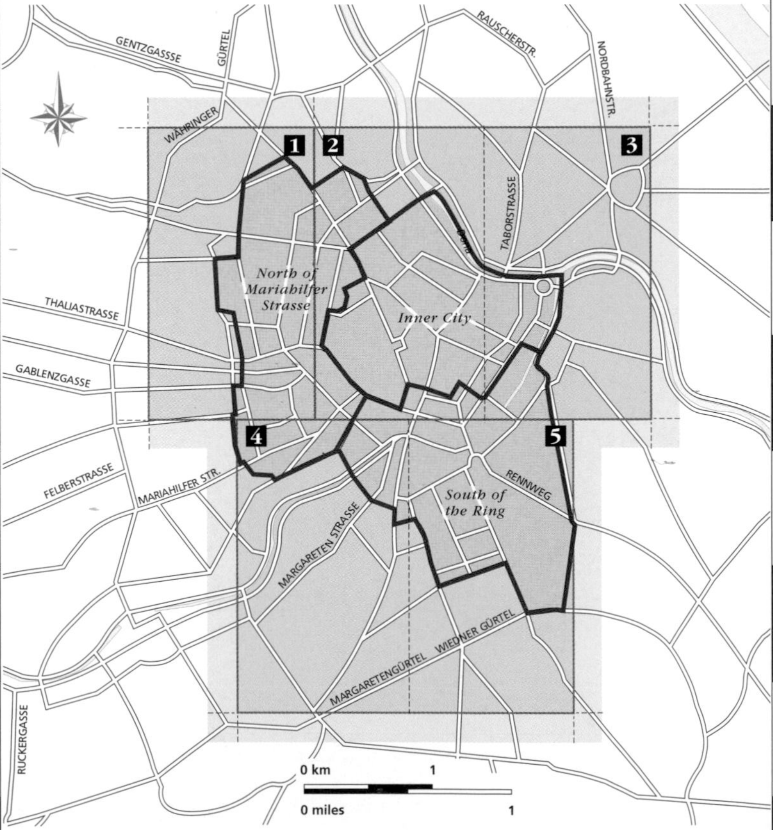

KEY TO STREET FINDER

- Major sight
- Place of interest
- Other building
- U-Bahn station
- Bundesbahn station
- Schnellbahn station
- Badner Bahn stop
- Parking
- Tourist information office
- Hospital with casualty unit
- Police station
- Church
- Synagogue
- Post office
- Railway line
- Pedestrianized street

SCALE OF MAPS 1–5

0 m 200

0 yards 200

1:11,500

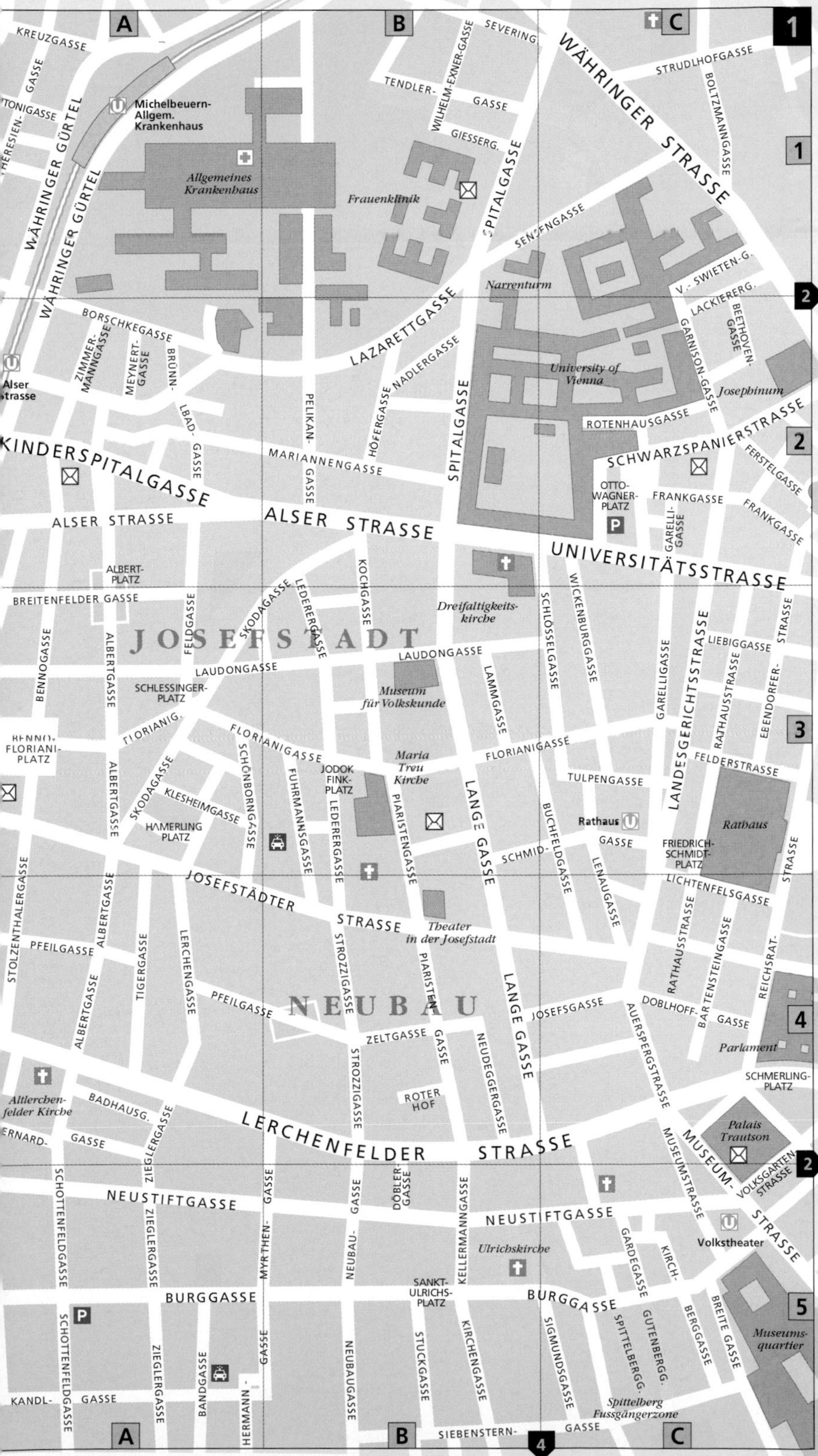

A
B
C
1
Kreuzgasse
Severing
Währinger Strasse
Strudlhofgasse
Boltzmanngasse
Wilhelm-Exner-Gasse
Tendler-Gasse
Giesserg.
Spitalgasse
Michelbeuern-Allgem. Krankenhaus
Währinger Gürtel
Allgemeines Krankenhaus
Frauenklinik
Sensengasse
Narrenturm
V.-Swieten-G.
Lackierergasse
Beethoven-Gasse
Garnison-Gasse
2
Lazarettgasse
Borschkegasse
Zimmermanngasse
Meynert-Gasse
Brünn-Lbad-Gasse
Alser Strasse
Nadlergasse
Höfergasse
Pelikan-Gasse
University of Vienna
Josephinum
Rotenhausgasse
Schwarzspanierstrasse
Ferstelgasse
Kinderspitalgasse
Mariannengasse
Otto-Wagner-Platz
Frankgasse
Garelli-Gasse
Alser Strasse
Universitätsstrasse
Albert-Platz
Breitenfelder Gasse
Skodagasse
Lederergasse
Kochgasse
Dreifaltigkeits-kirche
Schlösselgasse
Wickenburggasse
Garelligasse
Landesgerichtsstrasse
Liebiggasse
Strasse
Josefstadt
Feldgasse
Bennogasse
Albertgasse
Laudongasse
Laudongasse
Museum für Volkskunde
Lammgasse
Rathausstrasse
Ebendorfer-
Schlessinger-Platz
Florianig.
Benno-Floriani-Platz
Florianigasse
Florianigasse
Maria Treu Kirche
3
Felderstrasse
Tulpengasse
Jodok Fink-Platz
Skodagasse
Klesheimgasse
Hamerling Platz
Schönborngasse
Fuhrmannsgasse
Lederergasse
Piaristengasse
Lange Gasse
Buchfeldgasse
Rathaus
Rathaus
Gasse
Friedrich-Schmidt-Platz
Schmid-
Lenaugasse
Lichtenfelsgasse
Strasse
Josefstädter Strasse
Theater in der Josefstadt
Stolzenthalergasse
Albertgasse
Pfeilgasse
Tigergasse
Lerchengasse
Strozzigasse
Piaristen Gasse
Lange Gasse
Rathausstrasse
Bartensteingasse
Reichsrat-
Pfeilgasse
Neubau
Josefsgasse
Doblhoff-Gasse
Auerspergstrasse
4
Parlament
Zeltgasse
Neudeggergasse
Strozzigasse
Schmerling-Platz
Altlerchen-felder Kirche
Badhausg.
Roter Hof
Palais Trautson
Bernard-Gasse
Ziegler Gasse
Lerchenfelder Strasse
Museumstrasse
Museum-Strasse
Volksgarten-Strasse
Schottenfeldgasse
Neustiftgasse
Zieglergasse
Myrthen-Gasse
Neubau-Gasse
Döbler-Gasse
Kellermanngasse
Neustiftgasse
Gardegasse
Kirch-Berggasse
Volkstheater
Ulrichskirche
Burggasse
Sankt-Ulrichs-Platz
Burggasse
Breite Gasse
5
Museums-quartier
Schottenfeldgasse
Zieglergasse
Bandgasse
Hermann-Gasse
Neubaugasse
Stuckgasse
Kirchengasse
Sigmundsgasse
Spittelberg.
Gutenbergg.
Spittelberg Fussgängerzone
Kandl-Gasse
Siebenstern-Gasse
A
B
C

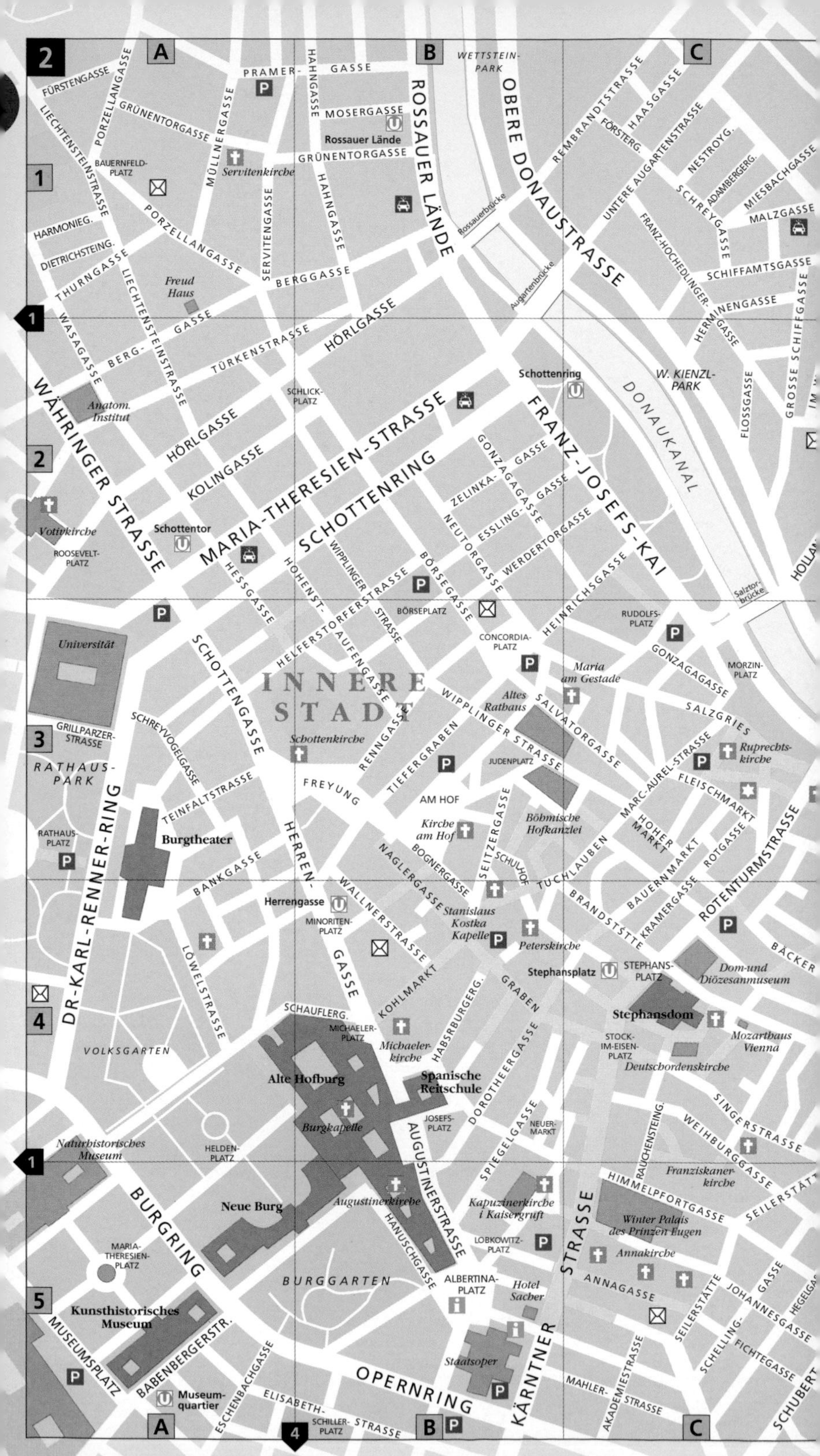
2
A
B
C
1
2
3
4
5
FÜRSTENGASSE
PORZELLANGASSE
PRAMER-
GASSE
HAHNGASSE
MOSERGASSE
ROSSAUER LÄNDE
WETTSTEIN-PARK
OBERE DONAUSTRASSE
REMBRANDTSTRASSE
HAASGASSE
FÖRSTERG.
UNTERE AUGARTENSTRASSE
NESTROYG.
ADAMBERGERG.
MIESBACHGASSE
MALZGASSE
SCHREYGASSE
FRANZ-HOCHEDLINGER-GASSE
SCHIFFAMTSGASSE
HERMINENGASSE
GROSSE SCHIFFGASSE
FLOSSGASSE
W. KIENZL-PARK
DONAUKANAL
LIECHTENSTEINSTRASSE
GRÜNENTORGASSE
MÜLLNERGASSE
Rossauer Lände
Servitenkirche
BAUERNFELD-PLATZ
SERVITENGASSE
HARMONIEG.
DIETRICHSTEING.
THURNGASSE
BERGGASSE
Freud Haus
Rossauerbrücke
Augartenbrücke
WASAGASSE
BERG-GASSE
TÜRKENSTRASSE
HÖRLGASSE
Schottenring
SCHLICK-PLATZ
Anatom. Institut
WÄHRINGER STRASSE
HÖRLGASSE
KOLINGASSE
MARIA-THERESIEN-STRASSE
SCHOTTENRING
FRANZ-JOSEFS-KAI
GONZAGAGASSE
ZELINKA-GASSE
ESSLING-GASSE
NEUTORGASSE
WERDERTORGASSE
Votivkirche
Schottentor
ROOSEVELT-PLATZ
HESSGASSE
HOHENST-AUFENGASSE
WIPPLINGER STRASSE
BÖRSEGASSE
HELFERSTORFERSTRASSE
BÖRSEPLATZ
HEINRICHSGASSE
Salztorbrücke
HOLLAN
RUDOLFS-PLATZ
CONCORDIA-PLATZ
Universität
INNERE STADT
SCHOTTENGASSE
Maria am Gestade
GONZAGAGASSE
MORZIN-PLATZ
Altes Rathaus
SALVATORGASSE
SALZGRIES
SCHREYVOGELGASSE
GRILLPARZER-STRASSE
RATHAUS-PARK
Schottenkirche
RENNGASSE
TIEFERGRABEN
WIPPLINGER STRASSE
JUDENPLATZ
MARC-AUREL-STRASSE
Ruprechts-kirche
FLEISCHMARKT
TEINFALTSTRASSE
FREYUNG
AM HOF
Böhmische Hofkanzlei
HOHER MARKT
ROTENTURMSTRASSE
RATHAUS-PLATZ
DR.-KARL-RENNER-RING
Burgtheater
HERREN-GASSE
Kirche am Hof
SEITZERGASSE
SCHULHOF
TUCHLAUBEN
BAUERNMARKT
ROTGASSE
NAGLERGASSE
BOGNERGASSE
BANKGASSE
Herrengasse
WALLNERSTRASSE
Stanislaus Kostka Kapelle
BRANDSTÄTTE
KRAMERGASSE
MINORITEN-PLATZ
Peterskirche
LÖWELSTRASSE
Stephansplatz
STEPHANS-PLATZ
Dom-und Diözesanmuseum
BÄCKER
GRABEN
KOHLMARKT
HABSBURGERG.
SCHAUFLERG.
MICHAELER-PLATZ
Stephansdom
Michaeler-kirche
STOCK-IM-EISEN-PLATZ
Mozarthaus Vienna
VOLKSGARTEN
Alte Hofburg
Spanische Reitschule
DOROTHEERGASSE
Deutschordenskirche
SINGERSTRASSE
Burgkapelle
JOSEFS-PLATZ
AUGUSTINERSTRASSE
SPIEGELGASSE
NEUER MARKT
RAUCHENSTEING.
WEIHBURGGASSE
Naturhistorisches Museum
HELDEN-PLATZ
Franziskaner-kirche
HIMMELPFORTGASSE
SEILERSTÄTTE
BURGRING
Neue Burg
Augustinerkirche
Kapuzinerkirche i Kaisergruft
Winter Palais des Prinzen Eugen
HANUSCHGASSE
LOBKOWITZ-PLATZ
KÄRNTNER STRASSE
MARIA-THERESIEN-PLATZ
Annakirche
BURGGARTEN
ALBERTINA-PLATZ
Hotel Sacher
ANNAGASSE
JOHANNESGASSE
HEGELGASSE
SEILERSTÄTTE
Kunsthistorisches Museum
SCHELLING-GASSE
FICHTEGASSE
MUSEUMSPLATZ
BABENBERGERSTR.
ESCHENBACHGASSE
Staatsoper
AKADEMIESTRASSE
OPERNRING
MAHLER-STRASSE
SCHUBERT
Museum-quartier
ELISABETH-STRASSE
SCHILLER-PLATZ

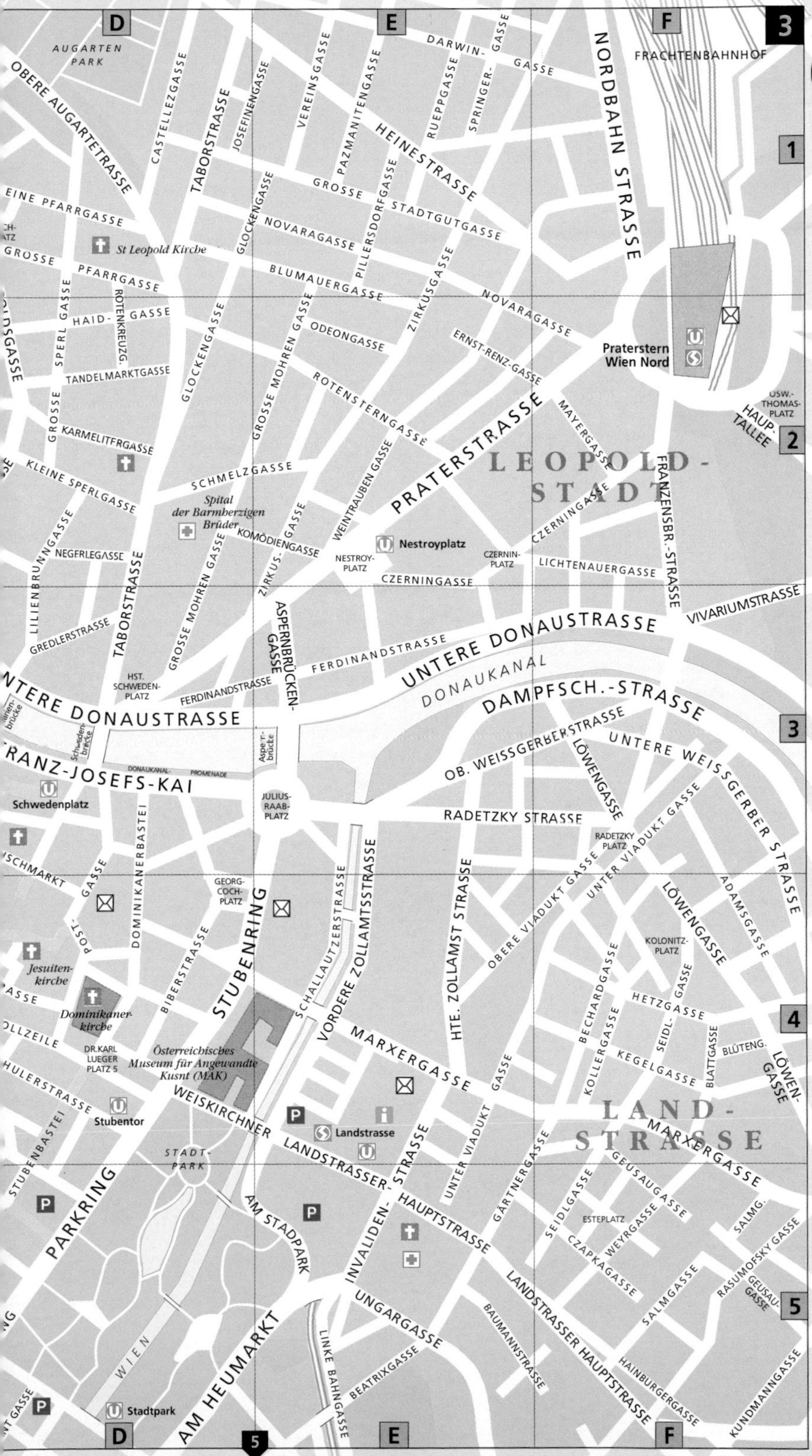
3
D
E
F
1
2
3
4
5
AUGARTEN PARK
OBERE AUGARTETRASSE
CASTELLEZGASSE
TABORSTRASSE
JOSEFINENGASSE
VEREINSGASSE
PAZMANITENGASSE
DARWIN-GASSE
RUEPPGASSE
SPRINGER-GASSE
NORDBAHN STRASSE
FRACHTENBAHNHOF
HEINESTRASSE
GROSSE STADTGUTGASSE
PILLERSDORFGASSE
KLEINE PFARRGASSE
GLOCKENGASSE
NOVARAGASSE
St Leopold Kirche
GROSSE PFARRGASSE
BLUMAUERGASSE
ZIRKUSGASSE
HAID-GASSE
SPERLGASSE
ROTENKREUZG.
ODEONGASSE
GROSSE MOHREN GASSE
ERNST-RENZ-GASSE
Praterstern Wien Nord
TANDELMARKTGASSE
ROTENSTERNGASSE
GROSSE SPERLGASSE
KARMELITERGASSE
PRATERSTRASSE
MAYERGASSE
USW.-THOMAS-PLATZ
HAUP. TALLEE
LEOPOLDSTADT
KLEINE SPERLGASSE
SCHMELZGASSE
Spital der Barmherzigen Brüder
KOMÖDIENGASSE
ZIRKUS-GASSE
WEINTRAUBEN GASSE
Nestroyplatz
NESTROY-PLATZ
CZERNINGASSE
CZERNIN-PLATZ
LICHTENAUERGASSE
FRANZENSBR.-STRASSE
LILIENBRUNNGASSE
NEGERLEGASSE
GROSSE MOHREN GASSE
ASPERNBRÜCKEN-GASSE
FERDINANDSTRASSE
UNTERE DONAUSTRASSE
VIVARIUMSTRASSE
GREDLERSTRASSE
HST. SCHWEDEN-PLATZ
DONAUKANAL
DAMPFSCH.-STRASSE
Schwedenbrücke
Aspernbrücke
FRANZ-JOSEFS-KAI
DONAUKANAL-PROMENADE
OB. WEISSGERBERSTRASSE
UNTERE WEISSGERBER STRASSE
LÖWENGASSE
Schwedenplatz
JULIUS-RAAB-PLATZ
RADETZKY STRASSE
RADETZKY PLATZ
DOMINIKANERBASTEI
FLEISCHMARKT
POST-GASSE
GEORG-COCH-PLATZ
STUBENRING
SCHALLAUTZERSTRASSE
VORDERE ZOLLAMTSSTRASSE
HTE. ZOLLAMST STRASSE
OBERE VIADUKT GASSE
UNTER VIADUKT GASSE
ADAMSGASSE
KOLONITZ-PLATZ
Jesuitenkirche
BIBERSTRASSE
Dominikanerkirche
HETZGASSE
SEIDL-GASSE
BECHARDGASSE
KOLLERGASSE
KEGELGASSE
BLATTGASSE
BLÜTENG.
WOLLZEILE
DR.KARL LUEGER PLATZ 5
Österreichisches Museum für Angewandte Kusnt (MAK)
MARXERGASSE
SCHULERSTRASSE
WEISKIRCHNER
Stubentor
Landstrasse
LANDSTRASSER-HAUPTSTRASSE
UNTER VIADUKT
GÄRTNERGASSE
LANDSTRASSE
STUBENBASTEI
STADT-PARK
INVALIDEN-STRASSE
GEUSAUGASSE
SEIDLGASSE
ESTEPLATZ
WEYRGASSE
CZAPKAGASSE
SALMG.
RASUMOFSKY GASSE
PARKRING
AM STADPARK
UNGARGASSE
BAUMANNSTRASSE
LANDSTRASSER HAUPTSTRASSE
SALMGASSE
GEUSAU-GASSE
WIEN
AM HEUMARKT
LINKE BAHNGASSE
BEATRIXGASSE
HAINBURGERGASSE
KUNDMANNGASSE
Stadtpark

4
A
B
C
1
2
3
4
5
Stiftskirche
St Josef Kirche
Mariahilfer Kirche
Akademie der Bildenden Künste
Secession
Theater an der Wien
KIRCHENGASSE
LINDENGASSE
MARIAHILFER STRASSE
SCHWEIGHOFERGASSE
RAHLGASSE
KÖNIGSKLOSTERG.
THEOBALDGASSE
GETREIDEMARKT
NIBELUNGENGA.
LEHÁRGASSE
FRIEDRICHSTRASSE
FILLGRADERGASSE
WINDMÜHLGASSE
LAIMGRUBENGASSE
KÖSTLERGASSE
GIRARDIGASSE
LINKE WIENZEILE
NASCHMARKT
RECHTE WIENZEILE
MÜHLG.
OPERNGASSE
KÜHNPLATZ
SCHLEIFMÜHLGASSE
PAULANERGASSE
NELKENG.
BARNABITENGASSE
SCHADEKGASSE
ESTERHAZYPARK
GUMPENDORFER STRASSE
STIEGENGASSE
JOANELLIGASSE
LUFTBADGASSE
DÜRERGASSE
KOPERNIKUSGASSE
KAUNITZGASSE
CORNELIUSGASSE
MÜHLGASSE
HEUMÜHLGASSE
PRESSGASSE
Kettenbrückengasse
Paulanergasse
MARGARETENSTRASSE
WIEDNER HAUPTSTRASSE
ESTERHAZYGASSE
MAGDALENENSTRASSE
WIENZEILE
RECHTE WIENZEILE
RÜDIGERGASSE
GRÜNGASSE
WEHRGASSE
FRANZENSGASSE
KETTENBRÜCKENGASSE
WAAGGASSE
GROSSE SCHÄFFERGASSE
RIENÖSSLGASSE
FLEISCHMANNG.
HOFMÜHLGASSE
SANDWIRTGASSE
TURMBURGGASSE
MOLLARDGASSE
LINKE
Pilgrambrücke
Pilgramgasse
PILGRAMGASSE
SCHÖNBRUNNER STRASSE
STROBACHGASSE
KLEINE NEUGASSE
KRONGASSE
NEUGASSE
MOSTG.
Mayerhofgasse
STRAUSSENGASSE
ZIEGELOFENGASSE
MITTERSTEIG
KLAGBAUMGASSE
LAMBRECHTGASSE
SCHAUMBURGERGASSE
Josefskirche
GROHGASSE
GARTENGASSE
HOFGASSE
SCHLOSSGASSE
Blumenmarkt
SCHÖNBURGSTRASSE
Reinprechtsbrücke
BRÄUHAUSGASSE
ZENTAGASSE
PHORUSGASSE
HARTMANNGASSE
Johann-Strauss-Gasse
TRAPELGASSE
RAINERGASSE
CASTELLIGASSE
BACHERPLATZ
VIKTOR-CHRIST-GASSE
RAMPERSTORFFERGASSE
NIKOLSDORFER GASSE
SEISGASSE
ALOIS DRASCHE PARK
GIESSAUFG.
KOHLGASSE
ARBEITERGASSE
REINPRECHTSDORFER STRASSE
SPENGERGASSE
SIEBENBRUNNENGASSE
WIMMERGASSE
ZENTAPLATZ
STOLBERGGASSE
St Florian Kirche
BLECHTURMGASSE
KRIEHUBERGASSE
OBERE
BRANDMAYERGASSE
STÖBERGASSE
Laurenzgasse
LAURENZGASSE
ANZENGRUBERGASSE
HÖGELMÜLLERGASSE
SIEBENBRUNNENGASSE
VOGELSANGGASSE
JAHNGASSE
HAUSLABGASSE
KLIEBERGASSE
GASSERGASSE
LEITGEBGASSE
AMTSHAUSGASSE
EMBELGASSE
FENDIGASSE
STORKGASSE
STAURACZGASSE
GEIGERGASSE
Kliebergasse
EINSIEDLERGASSE
SIEBENBRUNNENFELDGASSE
HOLLGASSE
LANDGUTGASSE

5
D
E
F
2
3
1
4
5
Opera
Imperial Hotel
BÖSENDORFERSTRASSE
Künstlerhaus
Musikverein
Karlsplatz
LOTHRINGERSTRASSE
Karlsplatz Pavilions
Wien Museum
Technische Universität
KARLS-PLATZ
Karlskirche
KARLSGASSE
SCHWARZENBERGSTR.
KANTG.
LOTHRINGER-STRASSE
AM HEUMARKT
LAGERGASSE
ÖLZELT-GASSE
BAYERNGASSE
SALESIANERGASSE
GRIMMELSHAUSENGASSE
GOTTFRIED-KELLER-GASSE
REISNERSTRASSE
RECHTE BAHNGASSE
LINKE BAHNGASSE
LISZTSTR.
MAROKKANERGASSE
ZAUNERGASSE
NEULINGGASSE
MATTIELLISTR.
SCHWARZENBERG PLATZ
TRAUNGASSE
VEITHGASSE
STROHGASSE
RENNWEG
Schwarzenberg Palais
Orangerie
JAURÈS-GASSE
METTERNICHGASSE
REISNER-STRASSE
Russische Kirche
SCHWINDGASSE
WOHLLEBENGASSE
ARGENTINIER STRASSE
PRINZ-EUGEN-STRASSE
Unteres Belvedere
SCHWARZENBERG PARK
BELVEDERE GARTEN
Botanisches Institut
TAUBSTUMMENGASSE
Taubstummengasse
PLÖSSLGASSE
MECHELGASSE
BOTANISCHER GARTEN
FAVORITENSTRASSE
DANHAUSERG.
SCHMÖLLERLGASSE
THERESIANUMGASSE
VIKTOR-STRASSE
Oberes Belvedere
BELVEDEREGASSE
MOMMSENGASSE
Elisabethkirche
KAROLINENGASSE
ALPEN GARTEN
JACQUINGASSE
FASANGASSE
GRAF-STARHEMBERG-GASSE
GOLDEGGASSE
ARGENTINIERSTRASSE
WEYRINGERGASSE
LANDSTRASSER GÜRTEL
Südbahnhof
WIEDNER GÜRTEL
KOLSCHITZKYGASSE
SCHELLEINGASSE
SCHWEIZER-GARTEN-STRASSE
ARSENALSTRASSE
SÜDTIROLER-PLATZ
Südtiroler Platz
Ostbahnhof
SCHWEIZER GARTEN
MARGARETENGÜRTEL
LAXENBURGERSTRASSE
SONNWENDGASSE
HINTERE SÜDBAHNSTRASSE
REISINGERGASSE
HUMBOLDTGASSE
RIEPLSTRASSE

Street Finder Index

AUSTRIA REGION BY REGION

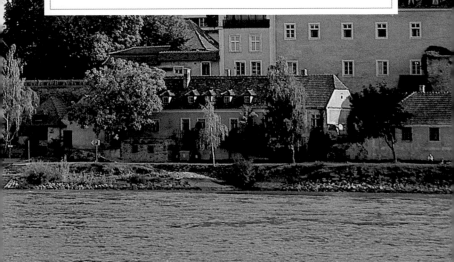

Austria at a Glance

This modest-sized country situated at the heart of Europe is a true paradise for visitors. There is its beautiful countryside – from Neusiedler Lake in the east, surrounded by vast, flat steppes, to the fertile plains of the Danube Valley; the scenic Vienna Woods; and three majestic alpine ranges that cut across the country from west to east. These glorious settings provide stunning backdrops for the historic sites and art treasures that form Austria's cultural highlights, and the names of great artists and Habsburg rulers will follow you wherever you go. There are also grand Baroque abbeys, and everywhere you can enjoy the work of Austria's outstanding musicians – Mozart, Strauss, Haydn and Beethoven, an adopted citizen of Vienna.

The Mirabell Palace in Salzburg *was built in the 17th century for Salome Alt, the mistress of Archbishop Wolf Dietrich. The magnificent stairway is adorned with sculptures by Raphael Donner.*

Innsbruck, *with its picturesque Old Town and church spires rising against the majestic backdrop of the snow-covered Alps, is the capital of the Tyrol, the picture-postcard province most popular with visitors.*

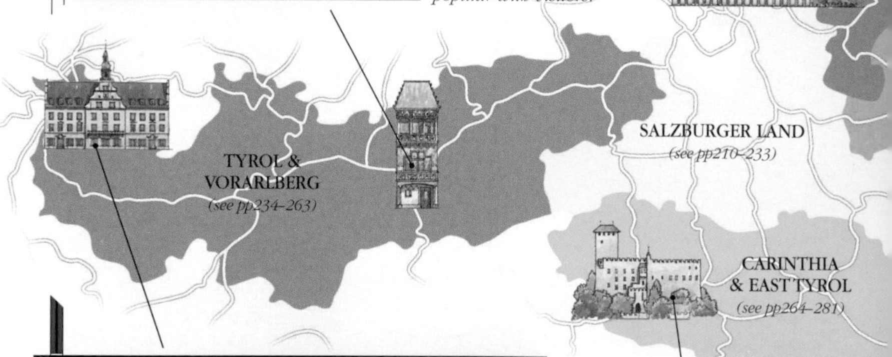

Houses in Bregenz, *capital of the Vorarlberg province, are decorated with early heraldic paintings and the figures of saints.*

Bruck Castle in Lienz, *in East Tyrol, was built in 1252–77 for the Görz family. Today, it is the home of the Heimatmuseum, with a fine collection of 19th- and 20th-century popular Austrian art and folklore items.*

◁ **Maria Himmelfahrtskirche and ruins of Künringerburg above Dürnstein**

Hauptplatz in Linz, *capital of Upper Austria, is one of the most beautiful architectural sights in Central Europe. In the centre of the square stands the marble column of the Holy Trinity (1723).*

A Monument to Strauss and Lanner *was erected in the spa park of Baden, a sleepy town close to Vienna, famous for its sulphuric baths and casino, one of the oldest in Austria.*

The Zeughaus in Graz, *capital of Styria province, is an impressive display of the city's armoury and former power.*

The Landhaus in Klagenfurt, *seat of the Carinthian provincial government, was built in the 16th century in an Italianate style, and is one of Klagenfurt's most attractive buildings. Its glorious galleried inner courtyard remains intact to this day.*

LOWER AUSTRIA & BURGENLAND

Lower Austria is the largest province in Austria, both in terms of area and population. It surrounds the Austrian capital, Vienna, which for many years doubled as capital of the province. Following a plebiscite in 1986, the provincial capital was moved to St Pölten. At the edge of Lower Austria, bordering Hungary along one side, is the low-lying province of Burgenland, with its capital Eisenstadt.

Lower Austria, together with Upper Austria, covers the area that was once the cradle of the country. The low-lying and gently undulating terrain make this region easily accessible. During Roman times, its southern reaches belonged to the provinces of Noricum and Pannonia, while the areas north of the Danube frequently changed hands as Slav and German tribes fought over them. From AD 791, Lower Austria belonged to the Franks and, in AD 970, it was given the name Ostmark (Eastern Margravate). Today, it occupies an area of 19,163 sq km (6,930 sq miles) and stretches along the Danube valley, from the German border in the west, to Hungary in the east. In the south it reaches the slopes of the limestone Rax Mountains, with their highest peak, Schneeberg, and the popular winter resort of Semmering.

Lower Austria's most important towns, beside St Pölten, are Krems, Mödling, Wiener Neustadt, Klosterneuburg and Baden bei Wien. In the north of the province, adjoining the Czech Republic and Slovakia, lies the vine-growing region of Weinviertel. Further west is the wooded Waldviertel.

To the southeast of Lower Austria, from Neusiedler See downwards, is the long province of Burgenland, covering an area of 3,965 sq km (1,530 sq miles), with a population of 278,000. Historically, it was a part of Hungary, but after the Turkish wars (1529–1791) it was settled by Germans and Croats, and finally included in Austria in 1921.

The main town in Burgenland is Eisenstadt, where the mighty Esterházy family established their seat; to this day they continue to play an important role in the region's development.

The ornate 19th-century casino in the spa town of Baden bei Wien

◁ **Schönbühel Castle on the Danube**

Exploring Lower Austria and Burgenland

The Wachau, a narrow stretch of the Danube valley, forms the heart of Lower Austria, famous for its fertile plains, its vineyards and picturesque villages. Formidable fortresses, castles and fortified abbeys rise along the high banks of the river, including the imposing Benedictine Abbey in Melk. Further east, the *Wienerwald* (Vienna Woods) is perfect for walking and cycling. Burgenland Province has its own unique flora and fauna around Neusiedler See. It produces the finest red wines in Austria and celebrates the memory of Joseph Haydn, former court musician to the Esterházy family in Eisenstadt.

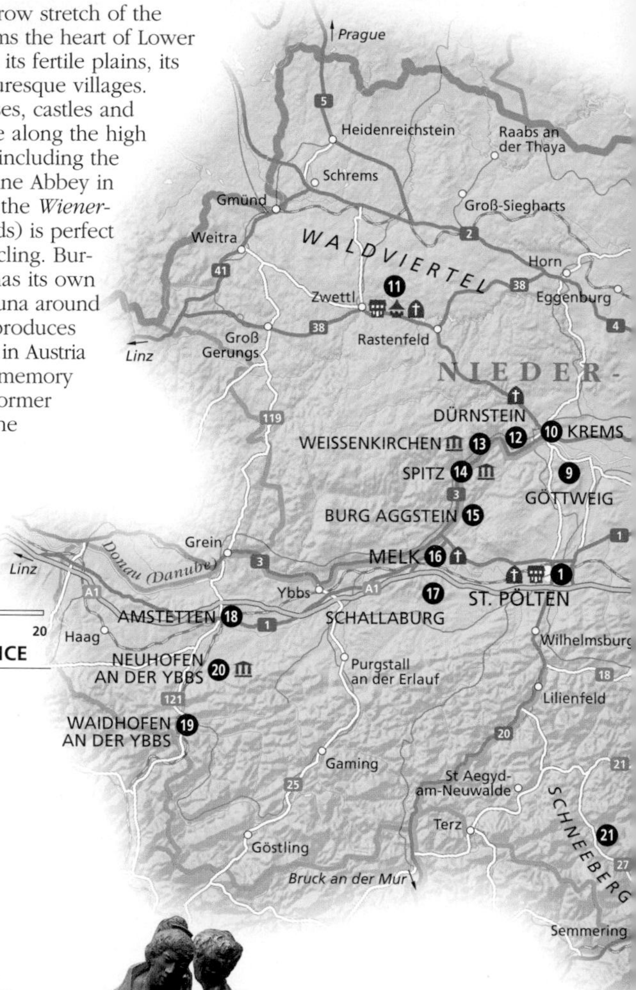

SIGHTS AT A GLANCE

Amstetten 18
Baden bei Wien 7
Bruck an der Leitha 25
Burg Aggstein 15
Dürnstein 12
Eisenstadt pp154–5 24
Göttweig 9
Hainburg 27
Klosterneuburg 3
Korneuburg 4
Krems 10
Laxenburg 5
Melk Abbey pp142–3 16
Neuhofen an der Ybbs 20
Neusiedler See pp152–3 23
Rohrau 26
Schallaburg 17
Schloss Forchtenstein 22
Schloss Hof 28
Spitz 14
St Pölten pp132–3 1
Tulln 2
Waidhofen an der Ybbs 19
Weissenkirchen 13
Wiener Neustadt 6

Tours

Schneeberg Tour 21
Waldviertel Tour 11
Wienerwald Tour 8

***Gossiping Women* at Herrenplatz in St Pölten**

The Gothic parish church in Spitz, overlooking the picturesque Wachau valley

SEE ALSO

- ***Where to Stay*** pp294–7
- ***Where to Eat*** pp325–7

16th-century Teisenhoferhof, with its attractive galleried courtyard, now home of the Wachau Museum

The mock-Gothic Franzensburg Castle, in Laxenburg

KEY

- Motorway
- Major road
- Minor road
- Scenic route
- Main railway
- Minor railway
- International border
- Province border

GETTING AROUND

Flights to both provinces depart from Vienna-Schwechat International Airport, which is served by every major airline. St Pölten is a major railway and road hub, situated on the route of the Westbahn line, with branch lines to Mariazell, Krems, Tulln and Gaming. St Pölten is also served by the Westautobahn (motorway) and the road connecting Vienna and Salzburg. The entire region is covered by a dense road network.

St. Pölten ❶

The capital of Lower Austria since 1986, St. Pölten was the first Austrian city to be granted municipal rights, in 1159. Its history dates back to Roman times, and it achieved considerable status under the Augustinian orders in the 8th century. St. Pölten's fastest period of growth, however, was during the Baroque period, when outstanding masters of that era, such as the architect Jakob Prandtauer and the painters Daniel Gran, Paul Troger and Bartolomeo Altomonte, made their home here. Economically, St. Pölten became the most important city in Lower Austria when trade switched from the Danube waterways to overland roads.

Rathausplatz in St. Pölten, with the Holy Trinity column

Exploring St. Pölten

The beautiful Baroque centre, with several older buildings, lies to the south of the railway station between Domplatz, Riemerplatz and Rathausplatz. The town centre is compact and easy to explore on foot, being largely pedestrianized. Apart from fascinating Baroque buildings and those associated with the town's administrative role, St. Pölten also has more recent architecture of interest.

A detail on the cathedral door

Domkirche Mariä Himmelfahrt

Domplatz 1. ***Tel** (02742) 324 331.*
Diocesan Museum ***Tel** (02742) 324 331. May–Oct: 10am–noon, 2–5pm Tue–Fri, 10am–1pm Sat.*

In the 12th century, a church dedicated to St Hippolytus stood on this site. After a devastating fire in 1278, the church was renovated and practically rebuilt in Baroque style to designs by Jakob Prandtauer. Deceptively plain on the outside, the cathedral's interior is a typical example of exuberant Baroque ornamentation. Daniel Gran and Bartolomeo Altomonte created the large wall and ceiling paintings, depicting scenes from the life of Jesus.

Adjoining the cathedral is the Bishops' Palace, once an abbey, with a lovely staircase, also by Prandtauer, and a magnificent library decorated by Paul Troger.

The **Diocesan Museum** houses a collection of sculptures, paintings and decorative art objects dating from the Gothic and Baroque periods. Behind the palace, at No. 1 Klostergasse, is the apartment of Jakob Prandtauer.

Franziskanerkirche

Rathausplatz.

The Franciscan church of the Holy Trinity, together with its friary, occupies the narrow, northern end of the square. A Rococo church with a delightful pink façade, it is unusual because it has no tower. The church interior, also decorated in Rococo style, features an altarpiece by Andreas Gruber. There are four wing paintings by another well-known Austrian Baroque artist, Martin Johann Schmidt, known as Kremser Schmidt.

Rathaus

Rathausplatz 1. ***Tel** (02742) 333 3000.*

The present town hall was built in the 16th century by combining two Gothic buildings in a mishmash of incongruous styles. The niches of the Gothic entrance gate abut a Renaissance portal, the Gothic tower has a Baroque onion dome on top, and the entire structure has been concealed behind a Baroque façade. Inside, however, it is worth seeing the ceiling stuccowork in the Mayor's Chamber and sculptures by Christoph Kirschner.

The town hall occupies the southern side of Rathausplatz, once considered the most beautiful square in Austria. Today, it is lined with modern buildings, and has lost some of its Baroque charm. Next to the town hall you can see the house where Franz Schubert once lived, and at No. 5 is the Montecuccoli Palace. The façades of both buildings were created by Prandtauer's nephew, Joseph Munggenast.

At the centre of the square stands the marble column of the Holy Trinity, with a fountain and statues of saints.

The Mayor's Chamber in the Rathaus

For hotels and restaurants in this region see pp294–7 and pp325–7

Institut der Englischen Fräulein

Linzer Strasse 9–11. ***Tel*** *(02742) 3521 88–0.* **Church:** *10am–5pm daily.*
The Institute of the English Ladies, founded by the English Catholic nun Mary Ward, established several schools in St. Pölten to educate the girls of aristocratic families. The institute, one of the most beautiful Baroque buildings in Lower Austria, was begun in 1715 and enlarged some 50 years later. Prandtauer created the beautiful white and pink façade, punctuated by black wrought-iron grills on the windows, with three groups of sculptures on two floors.

A statue on the façade of the Institut der Englischen Fräulein

St Mary column, in the centre of the Baroque Herrenplatz

Riemerplatz

Riemerplatz is another beautiful Baroque square, lined with exquisite buildings such as the striking Herbertstein Palace, at the wider end of Wiener Strasse. In Kremser Gasse, which runs north from the square, at No. 41, stands the delightful Stöhr Haus with its breathtakingly beautiful Art Nouveau façade. It is the work of the architect Joseph Maria Olbrich, who also designed the superb Secession Building in Vienna.

Herrenplatz

This is yet another attractive Baroque square in the city; its most outstanding features are the Baroque façades of the buildings around the square.

VISITORS' CHECKLIST

Road map F3. *50,000.*

Rathausplatz 1 (02742-353354). ***Fax*** *3332819.*
www.st-poelten.gv.at

Mostly attributed to Jakob Prandtauer, these façades often hide much earlier medieval niches and arcaded courtyards. On top of the house at No. 2 is a lovely sculpture by Georg Raphael Donner, called *Dispersing of Darkness by Light*. At the centre of the square stands St Mary's Column (1718).

Wiener Strasse

Wiener Strasse, adjacent to Herrenplatz, has been a main thoroughfare since Roman times, as is still obvious today from its many inns. There are a number of interesting historical buildings in this road, including St Pölten's oldest pharmacy, at No. 1, dating back to 1595. Its façade, built in 1727 by Joseph Munggenast, still displays the pharmacist's original coat of arms from 1607 and the 19th-century sign "Zum Goldenen Löwen" (To the Golden Lion).

ST. POLTEN CITY CENTRE

Domkirche Mariä Himmelfahrt ①
Franziskanerkirche ②
Herrenplatz ⑥
Institut der Englischen Fräulein ④
Rathaus ③
Riemerplatz ⑤
Wiener Strasse ⑦

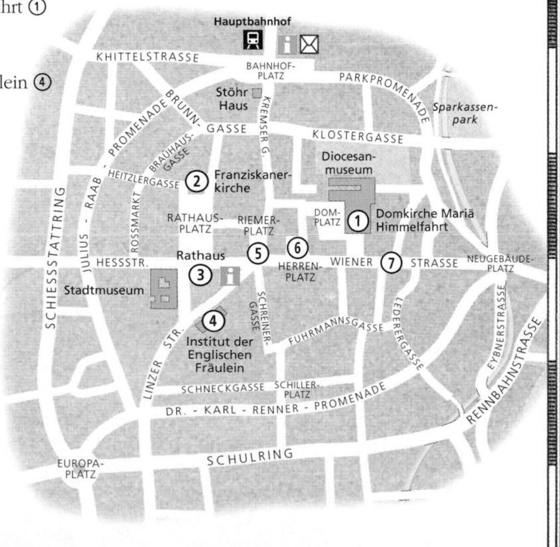

0 m 250
0 yards 250

Key to Symbols *see back flap*

The 13th-century funerary chapel of the Three Wise Men in Tulln

Tulln ❷

Road map F3. 12,300. *Tourismusverband Tullner Donauraum, Minoritenplatz 2 (02272) 67 566.* ***Fax*** *02272/67 566 44.* **www**.tulln.at

Tulln, on the right bank of the Danube river, was the site of the Roman camp of Comagena. Two structures remain from that period: the 3rd-century Roman Tower, probably the oldest structure in Austria, and a milestone.

Tulln is famous as the birthplace of Egon Schiele, one of the foremost painters of the turn of the 20th century, best known for his provocative nudes. The **Egon-Schiele-Museum**, housed in an old prison on the banks of the Danube, shows 90 original works by the artists and the permanent exhibition *Egon Schiele and his Times*.

In Minoritenkloster is a museum complex, the **Tullner Museen**, devoted to the small town's history.

The Romanesque **Pfarrkirche St Stephan**, the parish church of St Stephen, was built in the 12th century, but subsequently altered, first in Gothic, then in Baroque style. It has an interesting Romanesque portal with 12 reliefs, probably representing the apostles. Next to the church is the 13th-century mortuary, one of the more interesting historic sites in town. It holds the cemetery chapel of the Three Wise Men, the largest and most famous in Austria, combining elements of late-Romanesque style with early Gothic, and featuring a beautifully decorated portal and well-preserved murals.

The remains of the old city walls are also still preserved.

Egon-Schiele-Museum
Donaulände 28. ***Tel*** *(02272) 645 70.* *Mar–Nov: 10am–5pm Wed–Sun; guided tours on request.* **www**.egon-schiele.eu

Tullner Museen im Minoritenkloster
Minoritenplatz 1. ***Tel*** *(02272) 61 915.* *3–6pm Wed–Fri, 2–6pm Sat, 10am–6pm Sun & hols.*

Klosterneuburg ❸

Road map G3. *30,500.* *Niedermarkt 4 (02243) 320 38.* **www**.klosterneuburg.at.

This small town, just outside Vienna, was once the main seat of the Babenberg rulers. In the early 12th century, Margrave Leopold III built his castle here, and later the collegiate church, the magnificent **Stift Klosterneuburg**, supposedly in atonement for an act of treason he committed against Heinrich V.

A wine barrel in Klosterneuburg

The Romanesque church of the Augustinian Abbey was altered many times until the 17th and 18th centuries, when it acquired its present Baroque interior, designed by Joseph Fischer von Erlach and Felice Donato d'Allio, among others. Original features include the early-Gothic cloister and burial chapel of Leopold III; the latter contains the town's greatest treasure, an altarpiece by Nicolas of Verdun, a goldsmith and master of enamel from Lorraine. In 1181, the church acquired its altar, with 45 gilded and enamelled tiles depicting Bible scenes. The chapel also has fine stained-glass windows.

The museum in the former imperial residence holds a valuable collection of paintings and Gothic and Baroque sculptures. A highlight is the **Essl Collection**, an important museum specializing in Austrian art since 1945.

A small museum in nearby **Kierling** is devoted to the writer Franz Kafka, based in the former Hofmann Sanatorium where he died.

Stift Klosterneuburg
Tel *(02243) 411-212.* *9am–6pm daily.* *24, 25, 26 Dec.*

Essl Collection of Contemporary Art
An der Donau-Au 1. ***Tel*** *(02243) 37050.* *10am–7pm Tue–Sun, 10am–9pm Wed.* **www**.sammlung-essl.at

Korneuburg ❹

Road map G3. *8,500.* **www**.korneuburg.gv.at

Korneuburg once formed a single town with Klosterneuburg. In 1298 it became independent, and grew into an important trading and administrative centre. Hauptplatz, the main square, is surrounded by houses with late-Gothic, Renaissance and Baroque façades. Other interesting sights include the late-Gothic Ägidkirche (church of St Giles) and the Rococo Augustinerkirche (church of St Augustine), whose main altarpiece shows the sky resting on four columns, with God the Father sitting on his throne, holding the Earth in

The main altarpiece in Korneuburg

Franzensburg Castle, a mock-Gothic folly in Laxenburg

his hand. The altar painting of the *Last Supper* is the work of Franz Anton Maulbertsch.

Burg Kreuzenstein, on the road to Stockerau, is a fascinating folly of a Gothic castle. Built in the 19th century by Count Hans von Wilczek, on the site of a former fortress (1140) that was almost entirely destroyed by Swedish forces during the Thirty Years' War, it holds the count's extensive collection of late-Gothic art and handicrafts.

Laxenburg ❺

Road map G3. *Gemeindeamt (02236) 71101.* ***Fax*** *73150.* **www**.laxenburg.at

This small town, situated 15 km (9 miles) outside Vienna, is a favourite place for day-trips from the capital. It began as a hunting lodge, Lachsenburg, around which a settlement grew. Destroyed during the last Turkish wars, but restored and enlarged in the 17th century, it became a favourite retreat for Maria Theresa and other members of the imperial family. Laxenburg was chosen as a venue for the signing of many important state treaties, including the Pragmatic Sanction which made it possible for a woman, Maria Theresa, to accede to the throne. Today, the former imperial palace is the seat of the International Institute of System Analysis (IISA), and it also houses the Austrian Film Archives. The palace is surrounded by a landscaped, English-style **Schlosspark**, one of the grandest such palace parks in Europe at the time of Emperor Joseph II.

The park is dotted with many follies, and one particularly worth visiting is the early 19th-century **Franzensburg**, a mock-Gothic castle, built on an island in an artificial lake within the palace grounds at the height of the fashion for all things historic. It was furnished with original objects collected and pillaged from all over the empire, such as the 12th-century columns with capitals in the chapel, from Klosterneuburg, or the ceiling in the Hungarian Coronation Room from the Hungarian town of Eger. In the summer, open-air theatre performances take place on the castle island.

Wiener Neustadt ❻

Road map G3. *37,600.* *Hauptplatz 1–3 (02622) 373-311.* **www**.wiener-neustadt.at

This large town, some 40 km (25 miles) south of Vienna, is an industrial city and an important road and rail transport hub, and also the largest shopping city of Lower Austria.

In the centre of the town is the attractive Hauptplatz, with a part-Gothic **Rathaus** (town hall) rebuilt in Baroque style. Gothic houses line the northern side of the square, and the St Mary's Column (1678) stands in the centre. The **Dom** (Cathedral Church of the Ascension of Our Lady) was built in the 13th century. Its outstanding features include 12 wooden statues of the apostles by the columns of the central nave, and the Baroque main altar. The Brautportal (Portal of the Betrothed) dates from 1230.

In **Stift Neukloster** (Holy Trinity church) you can see a beautifully carved stone on the tomb of Eleanor of Portugal, wife of Emperor Friedrich III, by Niklas Gerhaert of Leyden, dating from 1467.

The former castle now houses the prestigious Military Academy, once commanded by General Rommel. In its west wing is the 15th-century **St. Georgs-Kathedrale** (St George's Cathedral), with the tomb of Maximilian I under the main altar. A corner tower, a remnant of the old fortified city walls, now houses a criminology museum and a gruesome exhibition of instruments of torture.

The town hall in Hauptplatz, Wiener Neustadt

One of many attractive villas in Baden bei Wien

Baden bei Wien 7

Road map G3. *28,000.* *Brusattiplatz 3 (02252) 22 600–600.* **www**.baden.at. *Operetta Festival (Jul); Festival of Roses (Jun).*

The spa town of Baden, on the eastern slopes of the Vienna Woods, was already known in Roman times, when it was called *Aquae Pannoniae*, and Emperor Marcus Aurelius praised its sulphuric springs. Today, its 15 hot springs make Baden a popular destination with older patients, but taking a hot sulphur bath is a relaxing experience for younger visitors too. In summer, you can swim in the open-air Art-Deco baths.

The small town was completely rebuilt after a fire in 1812, and many of its attractive Neo-Classical town houses and Biedermeier-style villas hail from this period. The main architect at the time, Joseph Kornhäusel (1786–1860), largely shaped the look of the town.

At one time, the list of Baden visitors read like a *Who's Who* of the rich and famous, and included such luminaries as Wolfgang Amadeus Mozart, who composed his *Ave Verum* here; Franz Schubert; and, most importantly, Ludwig van Beethoven. It was here that he composed his *Ninth Symphony*. Baden was frequented by the maestros of Viennese operetta as well: Strauss (father and son), Lanner and Zille. Napoleon also holidayed here with his wife Marie Louise.

Wienerwald Tour 8

The Vienna Woods (Wienerwald), to the west of the capital, are a favourite weekend destination for the Viennese. Crossed by numerous walking and cycling tracks, the wooded hills covering an area of 1,250 sq km (480 sq miles) are a perfect place for recreation. The main towns in the area are Klosterneuburg, former capital of the Babenbergs, Tulln *(see p134)* and Baden, one of Europe's most famous spa towns. There are also some interesting works of art and unique scenery worth seeing.

Heiligenkreuz ②
The Cistercian Abbey (1133) at Heiligenkreuz, founded by Leopold III of Babenberg, has retained its fine Romanesque-Gothic character and some Baroque furnishings to this day.

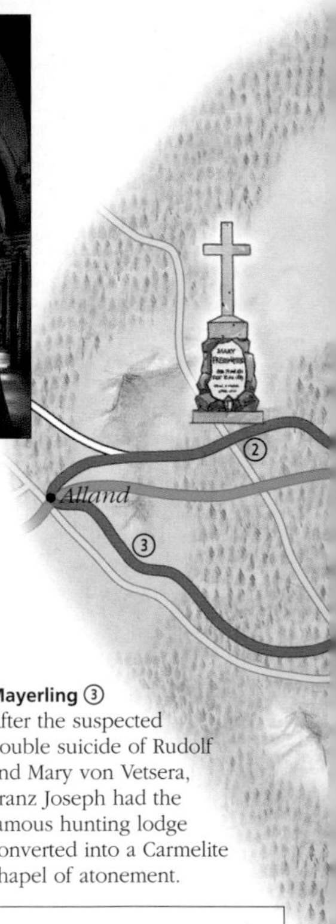

KEY

Suggested route

Scenic road

Other road

River, lake

Mayerling ③
After the suspected double suicide of Rudolf and Mary von Vetsera, Franz Joseph had the famous hunting lodge converted into a Carmelite chapel of atonement.

THE MAYERLING MYSTERY

Rudolf, the only son of Franz Joseph I and Elisabeth, was a restless man, unable to adjust to the rigours of court. After a fierce quarrel with his father, he went to Mayerling with his mistress, Mary von Vetsera. On 30 January, the two lovers' bodies were found in the lodge. They had seemingly committed suicide: Mary had drunk poison and Rudolf had then shot himself. The reason for the tragedy remains a mystery to this day.

The tombstone of Mary von Vetsera

Burg Liechtenstein ①
The castle in Maria Enzensdorf, originally built in 1166, has been altered many times and now resembles a Gothic castle, with imposing towers and battlements.

Mödling ⑦
This small, picturesque town, once a retreat for artists, is situated in beautiful natural scenery of limestone rocks.

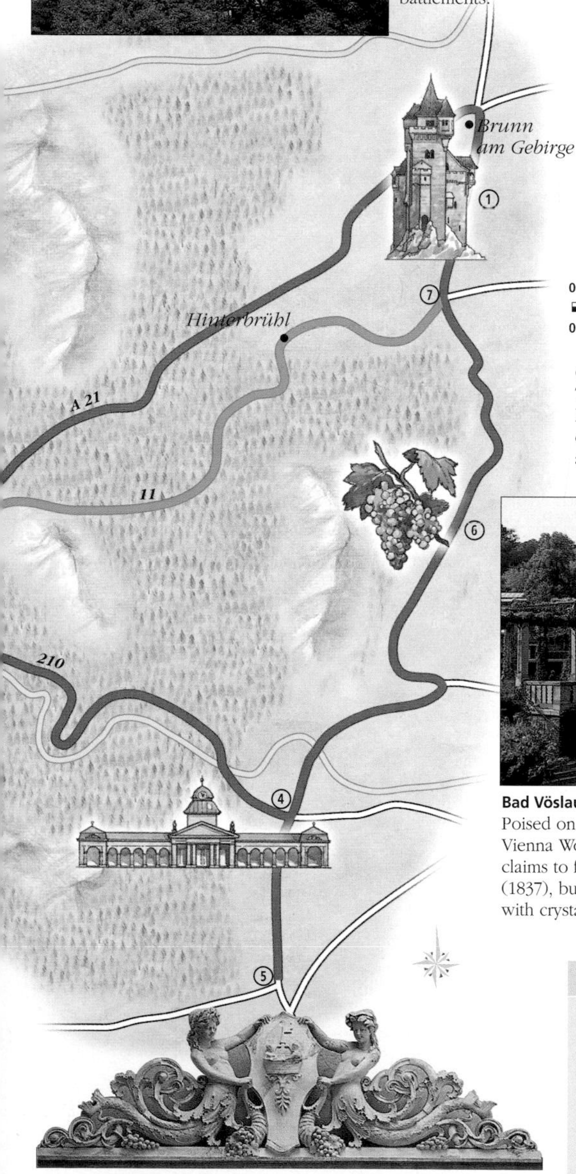

Gumpoldskirchen ⑥
This small wine-making town has become famous for its countless *Heurigen* wine bars and cheerful restaurants.

Bad Vöslau ⑤
Poised on the southern slopes of the Vienna Woods, this village has two claims to fame: its wines and its baths (1837), built by Count Moritz Fries, with crystal-clear natural mineral water.

Baden bei Wien ④
Frauenbad, one of the original 19th-century baths, is today no longer in use but makes an interesting historic sight.

TIPS FOR DRIVERS

Length of the route: *60 km (37 miles).*
Stopping places: *most of the best restaurants can be found in Gumpoldskirchen and Baden.*
Suggestions: *visit the abbey in Heiligenkreuz.* ***Tel*** *(02258) 8720; take a boat excursion on the underground lake in Seegrotte Hinterbrühl* ***Tel*** *(02236) 26364.*

The magnificent organ in Göttweig Abbey

Göttweig 9

Road map F3. *Furth (02732) 846 220. 10am–6pm daily (from 9am Jun–Sep). mid-Nov–mid-Mar.*

Stift Göttweig, a Benedictine Abbey, crowns a hilltop on the south bank of the Danube, near Krems. Founded in 1083, it was inhabited by Benedictine monks from St Blasien in the Black Forest in 1094. **Stift Göttweig** is sometimes referred to as the Austrian Monte Cassino because, superficially, it resembles the Benedictine mother abbey. The abbey was rebuilt after a fire in 1718, according to plans by Johann Lukas von Hildebrandt. The project was never completed, however, and the present abbey has an interesting but somewhat asymmetrical outline, with a Neo-Classical façade. In 1739, a magnificent flight of stairs, known as Kaiserstiege (imperial staircase) was added to the western section of the abbey. The stairs are lined with statues representing the 4 seasons and the 12 months of the year. Inside, the abbey is adorned with a fresco by Paul Troger, depicting the apotheosis of Karl VI. The abbey has an interesting collection of sculptures, paintings and graphic art. The abbey restaurant affords great views of the surroundings.

Stift Göttweig
Tel *(02732) 85581-0. 21 Mar–15 Nov: 8am–6pm daily.*
www.stiftgoettweig.or.at

Krems 10

Road map F3. *23,000. Utzstrasse 6 (02732) 82676. Folklore Festival (Jul), Niederösterreichische Landesmesse (Aug).*

During the 11th and 12th centuries, Krems, then known as *Chremis*, was a serious rival to Vienna. Today, this attractive town, together with neighbouring Stein, is a popular destination. Visitors are enchanted by the beautiful architecture of its town houses and courtyards, which give Krems a southern, Italian feel. There are remains of the old town walls, but the greatest attraction is the late-Gothic **Piaristenkirche**, an imposing Piarist church built on the foundations of an older church. It boasts a beautiful Baroque altarpiece by the local artist Johann Martin Schmidt, known as Kremser Schmidt. The **Veitskirche**, the parish church of St Veit, is the earliest Baroque church in Austria, the work of the Ciprian Biasin. The former Dominican abbey has a lovely early-Gothic cloister; it is now the History Museum. Krems also has a Renaissance town hall and the vast, 13th-century **Gozzoburg**, a palace built by Judge Gozzo.

The Minoritenkirche, the Church of the Minorite Monks in Stein dates from the same period. It is adorned with 14th-century paintings of the Virgin Mary on a throne. The parish church of St Nicholas has beautiful ceiling frescoes and an altarpiece painted by Kremser Schmidt.

Exhibit from the Wine Museum in Krems

Waldviertel Tour 11

See pp140–41.

Dürnstein 12

Road map F3. *1,000. Rathaus (02711) 219. 8am–noon, 1–4pm Mon–Fri.*

Much of the popularity of the idyllically situated town of Dürnstein is due to the adventures of the English King, Richard the Lionheart. On the Third Crusade, undertaken with the French King Philip August and the Austrian Margrave Leopold V, Richard fell out with his fellow crusaders. On his journey home through Babenberg territories, in 1192, he was imprisoned in the Künringerburg fortress above Dürnstein, whose ruins can still be seen today. As legend has it, the King's faithful French minstrel, Jean Blondel, discovered him with a song known only to the two of them. A ransom of 35,000 kg (77,100 lbs) silver was paid and Richard released. The Babenbergs used the money to fortify Enns, Hainburg, Wiener Neustadt and Vienna, while the name of the faithful servant lives on in many of Dürnstein's establishments.

The Baroque silhouette of the **Stiftskirche** (Collegiate Church of the Assumption of the Virgin Mary) towering above the town was created by the masters of the day. The courtyard is probably the work of Jakob Prandtauer;

For hotels and restaurants in this region see pp294–7 and pp325–7

the entrance is embellished with lovely, decorated portals.

The former convent of St Claire is now an inn; the Renaissance castle a hotel.

The Baroque tower of the Pfarrkirche in Dürnstein

Weissenkirchen ⑬

Road map F3. *1,060.* *(02715) 2600.*

The small village in the heart of the Wachau Valley has attracted artists since 1900, who come to paint the magnificent scenery of the Danube gorge and to enjoy the cosy inns. Today, their works can be seen in the **Wachaumuseum**, in the Teisenhoferhof, a Renaissance mansion. Another attraction is the Wehrkirche Maria Himmelfahrt (Church of the Assumption of the Virgin Mary), on a hilltop, fortified against Turkish raiders. The well-preserved defence towers are remains of those fortifications. The main entrance to the church is through the western portal, which has fine mouldings. Inside, on the rainbow arch, is a beautiful painting (1520) of the Madonna, from the Danube School.

Wachaumuseum
Tel *(02715) 2268.* *Apr–Oct: 10am–5pm Tue–Sun.* *Mon.*

Environs: Situated between Weissenkirchen and Spitz is the small village of **St Michael**, with another example of a fortified church. A few miles beyond Spitz is **Willendorf**, where the famous statuette of the *Venus of Willendorf* was found. This representation of female fertility is believed to be over 25,000 years old. The figure itself is now kept in Vienna's Natural History Museum *(see p82)*, while an over-life-sized copy stands in a field near Willendorf.

Spitz ⑭

Road map F3. *1,930.* *(02713) 23 63.* *2–4pm Mon–Fri.*

On the banks of the River Danube at the foot of the Tausendeimerberg (thousand bucket hill, so called because of the amount of wine it was said to produce), nestles the enchanting town of Spitz an der Donau. The river was once important to the town's economic life, and the **Schifffahrtsmuseum** tells the story of the Danube navigation.

Another famous sight is the **Pfarrkirche**, the early-Gothic parish church of St Maurice, furnished in late-Gothic style. The church has a presbytery (1508), criss-cross vaulting and elaborate window lacework. The altar painting is by Kremser Schmidt. Lovely wooden statues from around 1380, showing Christ and the apostles, are set in niches along the Gothic gallery.

High above the town looms the ruin of Hinterhaus Castle, with its Gothic bulwark and Renaissance fortifications.

Schifffahrtsmuseum
Auf der Wehr 21. ***Tel*** *(02713) 2246.* *Apr–Oct: 10am–noon, 2–4pm Mon–Sat, 10am–4pm Sun & hols.*

Ruins of the formidable 12th-century Burg Aggstein

Burg Aggstein ⑮

Road map F3.

The impressive ruins of Burg Aggstein, built into the rock, are poised high above the banks of the river. Today the castle lies in ruin, but once it measured some 100 m (330 ft) in length, with tall stairs leading to the Upper Castle. Built by the notorious Künringers, a band of robber barons, it served to repel attacks by Turks and Swedes during the 16th and 17th centuries, thus cementing its rank as one of the most important fortresses in the region.

Many gruesome stories are told about the castle's early days. Its owner, an unmitigated thief, was said to have laid in wait for passing barges and demanded a hefty toll to allow them passage. Those who refused to pay were imprisoned in the Rosengärtlein, a rose garden set on a rocky shelf, where they would either die of hunger or jump to their death.

Today, the picturesque Burg Aggstein and its café are popular destinations for a day trip from Vienna.

The romantic ruins of Hinterhaus Castle in Spitz

Waldviertel Tour ⓫

Bitterly fought over by Germans and Slavs, who both wanted to settle here and exploit the area's natural resources, Austria's northwest boasts numerous historic sights, from abbeys built as defensive structures to the magnificent residences of the nobility built during times of peace. The wooded region became known as an idyllic spot for hunting trips and excursions, and today it is still its natural beauty and recreational facilities which draw most visitors; the traditional crafts practised in the area's numerous villages are another attraction.

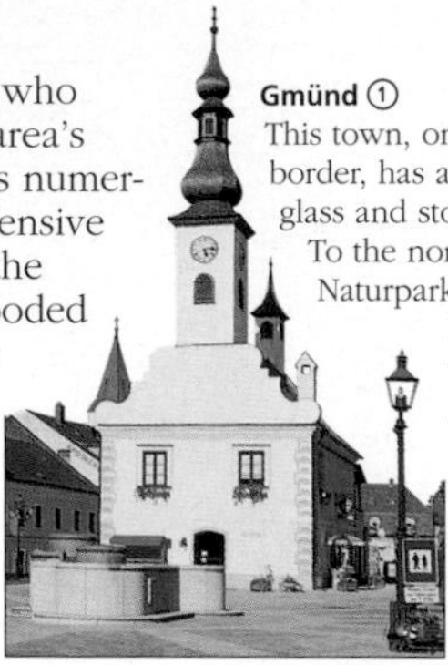

Gmünd ①
This town, on the Czech border, has a fascinating glass and stone museum. To the north is the Naturpark Blockheide-Eibenstein, with its vast granite rock formations and an unusual open-air exhibition of minerals.

Rosenau ②
First built in 1590 as a Renaissance palace, Rosenau was remodelled some 150 years later in Baroque style. Its owner, Leopold Schallenberg, set aside some rooms for use as a Masonic lodge; today, it is a Masonic museum.

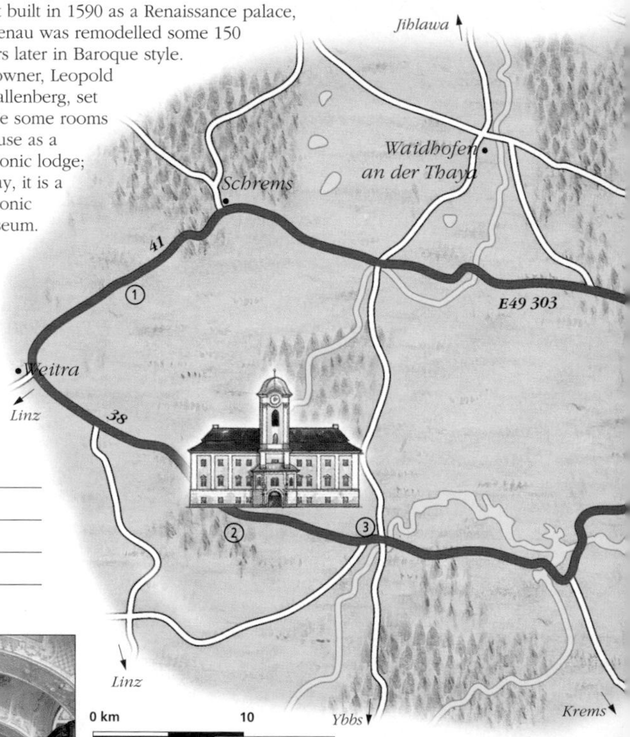

KEY

- Suggested route
- Other road
- River, lake

0 km 10
0 miles 10

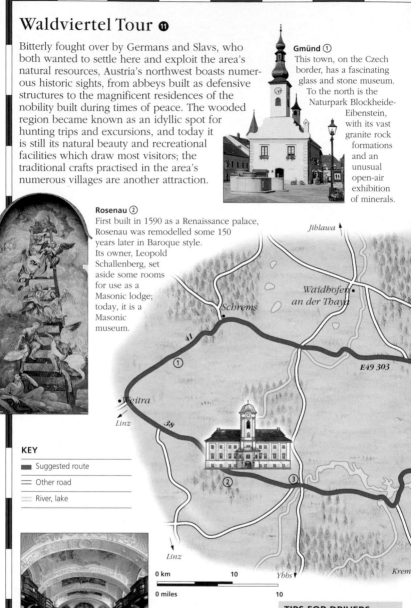

Zwettl ③
This lovely old town boasts several original Baroque houses with interesting pediments. Nearby is one of the region's gems, the magnificent Cistercian monastery (1137–8), with a Gothic church and Baroque interior.

TIPS FOR DRIVERS

Length of the tour: *210 km (336 miles).*
Stopping places: *there are numerous places offering accommodation at reasonable prices throughout the region.*
Suggestions: *visits to Altenburg Abbey and Schloss Greillenstein; falconry shows at Rosenburg.*

Greillenstein ⑦
Set in woodland in the Kamp river valley, this Renaissance castle features a beautiful arcaded courtyard and several tall chimneys.

Eggenburg ⑥
A small, medieval town, Eggenburg has two attractions: 1,900 m (6200 ft) of original town walls and towers, and the Museum of Motorcycles & Technology.

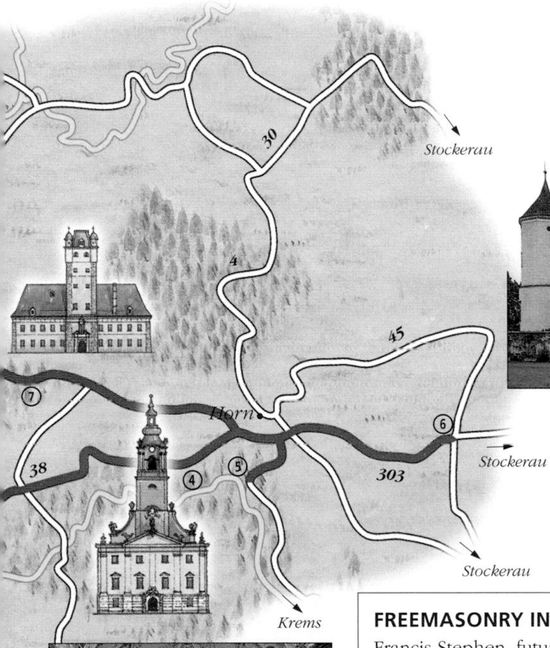

Rosenburg ⑤
One of Austria's most famous castles, Schloss Rosenburg was rebuilt in Neo-Classical style after a fire. The former state rooms house a splendid museum of old furniture, paintings and arms.

Altenburg ④
This gorgeous Benedictine Abbey (1144) has a great library, a treasury and, above all, a crypt entirely covered in stunning ceiling paintings depicting the dance of death.

FREEMASONRY IN AUSTRIA

Francis Stephen, future husband of Maria Theresa, introduced freemasonry to Austria from Holland. In the late 18th and early 19th centuries, it played a very important role in the Austro-Hungarian empire, with many prominent politicians and artists being counted among its members. An increasing desire for national self-determination and liberal thought slowly removed the masons from power. In 1945, the Grand Masonic Lodge of Austria renewed its activities. Today, it has some 2,400 members in 52 lodges, including many public figures, financiers and artists.

Masonic Lodge in Rosenau

Melk Abbey ⑯

The town and abbey of Melk, the original seat of the Babenbergs, tower above the left bank of the Danube, some 60 km (37 miles) west of Vienna. In the 11th century, Leopold II invited the Benedictines from Lambach to Melk and granted them land and the castle, which the monks turned into a fortified abbey. Almost completely destroyed by fire in 1297, the abbey was rebuilt many times. In the 16th century, it had to withstand a Turkish invasion. In 1702, Abbot Berthold Dietmayr began a thorough remodelling of the complex. Jakob Prandtauer, von Erlach, Joseph Munggenast and other renowned artists of the day helped to give the present abbey its magnificent Baroque form.

Stairwell
A spiral staircase with ornamental balustrade connects the library with the Stiftskirche, the monastery church of St Peter and St Paul.

★ Library
The impressive library holds some 100,000 volumes, including 2,000 manuscripts and 1,600 incunabula. It is decorated with a beautiful ceiling fresco by Paul Troger.

Crowning with the Crown of Thorns
This powerful painting by Jörg Breu (1502) is exhibited in the Abbey Museum.

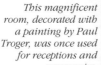

Marble Hall
This magnificent room, decorated with a painting by Paul Troger, was once used for receptions and ceremonies.

For hotels and restaurants in this region see pp294–7 and pp325–7

★ Stiftskirche

The splendid Baroque monastery church has a ceiling fresco by Johann Michael Rottmayr. The main altar features the figures of the church's patron saints, the apostles St Peter and St Paul.

VISITORS' CHECKLIST

Road map F3. 6,500. Babenbergerstrasse 1 (02752) 52307410. **Melk Abbey** May–Sep: 9am–5pm; Apr, Oct: 8am–4pm. by appointment. Winter: guided tours only. Melker Sommerspiele (Jul, Aug).

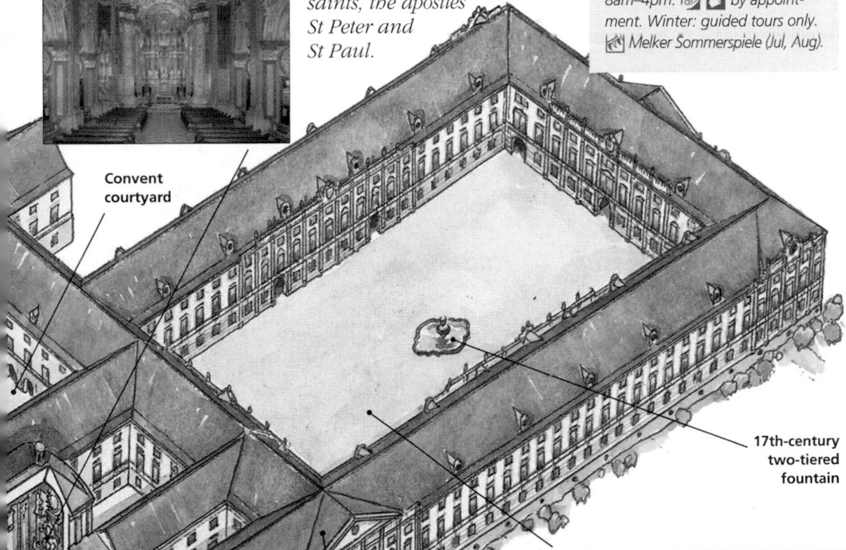

Prelates' Courtyard

The courtyard is surrounded by imposing buildings crowned with statues of the prophets and frescoes showing the cardinal virtues.

★ Melk Crucifixes

The abbey holds two important crucifixes – one is Romanesque (c.1200, shown here), the other from the 14th century, containing gems and a piece of Christ's cross.

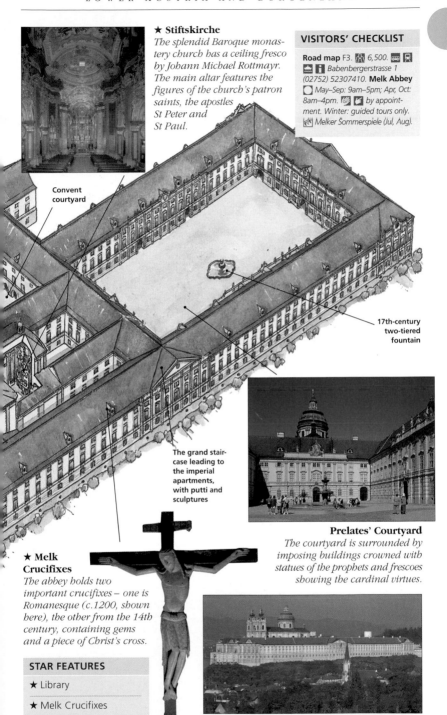

The View

Austria's most magnificent Baroque monastery, Melk Abbey is a vast yellow building perched dramatically on a high bluff overlooking the Danube.

STAR FEATURES

- ★ Library
- ★ Melk Crucifixes
- ★ Stiftskirche of St Peter and St Paul

A figure decorating an elevation of Schallaburg Castle

Schallaburg ⓱

Road map F3. (02754) 6317. *9am–5pm Mon–Fri, 9am–6pm Sat, Sun, public holidays.*

Schallaburg Castle counts as one of the most beautiful Renaissance castles in Lower Austria. It has some early remains of medieval Romanesque and Gothic architecture, but these are overshadowed by later additions. Particularly impressive are the Renaissance courtyard and the two-storey red and white terracotta arcades, the work of Jakob Bernecker. Carved terracotta atlantes support the second-storey arcades; sculptures and terracotta masks decorate the lower niches and walls of the castle. One of the best of these is the mask of a court jester holding a wand. Wilhelm von Losenstein, who owned the castle when the arcades were created, was a Protestant and a Humanist, a fact that is reflected in the works commissioned by him.

At the end of World War II, Schallaburg Castle was totally destroyed by the Russians, and it was not until 1970, when it came into state administration, that work began in order to return the castle to its former splendour.

Today, the Schallaburg houses Lower Austria's Cultural and Educational Centre, and serves as a venue for excellent exhibitions and lectures.

Amstetten ⓲

Road map E3. *21,989.* *(07472) 601 246.*

A major transport hub, the town of Amstetten is situated on the Ybbs River near the border with Upper Austria. Originally known as Amistein, the town witnessed the arrival of Illyrian, Celts and Roman settlers over time. It is the largest town in the Mostviertel region, and its regional museum tells the story of local country life in the days prior to the industrial revolution. Also worth seeing in Amstetten are the attractive town hall, the 15th-century parish church of St Stephen with frescoes depicting the Last Judgement, and the Gothic Church of St Agatha.

Environs: Some 6 km (4 miles) southwest of the town is the medieval **Burg Ulmerfeld**, first recorded in the 10th century. From the 14th century until 1803, the castle belonged to the bishops of Freising. Later transformed into a paper-mill, it is now an important cultural centre and has a collection of arms.

Waidhofen an der Ybbs ⓳

Road map E3. *11,744.* *(07442) 511255.*

In the 16th century, this little town in the Ybbs valley was an important centre of iron processing and arms production. Its medieval old town is dominated by church spires and two towers, remains of the medieval fortifications: the 13th-century Ybbsturm and the Stadtturm, which was raised by 50 m (164 ft) in 1534 to celebrate the town's victory over the Turks. Since then, the clock on its north side has shown 11.45am, the hour of victory. The former Capuchin church has an interesting painting by Kremser Schmidt from 1762. Another great attraction is the **Stadtmuseum Waidhofen**, one of the most modern in Lower Austria.

Stadtmuseum Waidhofen
Oberer Stadtplatz 32. ***Tel*** *(07442) 511 247.* *Easter–26 Oct: 10am–5pm Tue–Sun.*

Attractive houses and onion-dome spires in Waidhofen an der Ybbs

Environs: The Carthusian Marienthron Monastery in **Gaming**, the most important structure of its kind in Central Europe, was founded in 1332 by Prince Albrecht II. The monks' cells and the fortified walls with round turrets remain to this day. Its Baroque library has frescoes by the Prague painter Wenzel Lorenz Reiner, his only work on display outside his Czech homeland. Today, the Carthusian monastery is used as a venue for cultural events. One of the best Austrian concert halls, it is much-liked by pianists, and the annual International Chopin Festival is held at Marienthron in late summer.

The town also has an interesting Baroque church, several early buildings, St Mary's column and a pillory.

The Marienthron Monastery in Gaming, seen from the Prelates' Courtyard

For hotels and restaurants in this region see pp294–7 and pp325–7

Benedictine Abbeys

Benedictine monasticism was established in the 6th century, in Italy, by St Benedict of Nursia, and its mother abbey was Monte Cassino. The first Benedictine abbey in Austria was instituted in the 8th century, in Salzburg, but it was not until the 11th century that the order became a major force. Its growth was linked to the increased importance given to the Austrian state under the rule of the Babenbergs, whose history was chronicled by the Benedictines. Fortified abbeys were built on unassailable hilltops, and rural settlements grew up in the shadow, and under the protection of, the abbeys. The beautiful silhouettes of the abbeys tower over their surroundings. Stunningly decorated inside, they boast marvellous libraries that house outstanding records of the past.

Altenburg Abbey, (see p141) *from the 12th century, was altered in Baroque style in the 18th century. Its façade is adorned with statues and paintings.*

Kremsmünster Abbey (see p200) *houses a tombstone with the figure of Knight Gunther. The inscription tells the legend of how his father founded the abbey in 777, following his son's death.*

St. Paul im Lavanttal Abbey (see p268) *houses one of the most extensive Benedictine libraries with over 40,000 volumes and manuscripts.*

The grand imperial staircase in Göttweig Abbey (see p138), *lined with statues, was designed by F.A. Pilgram in 1739.*

The family tree *of the Babenberg dynasty, who brought the Benedictine monks to their seat in the stunning monastery of Melk, can be studied in Klosterneuburg Abbey* (see p134), *just outside Vienna.*

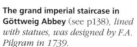

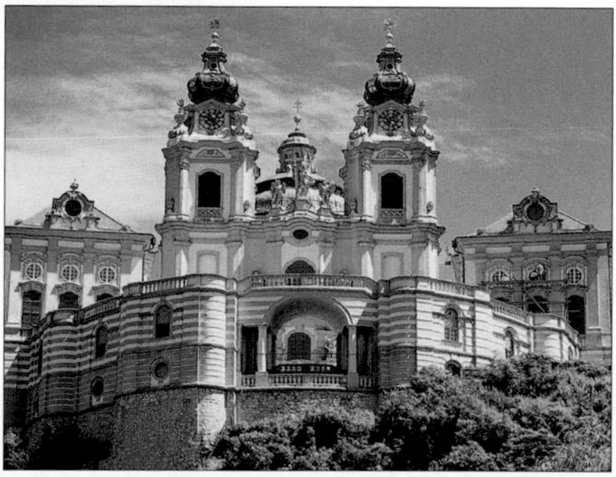

In front of the Stiftskirche in Melk (see pp142–3), *one of the most magnificent abbeys in Austria, extends a terrace affording fabulous views far across the Danube and the surrounding countryside.*

Neuhofen an der Ybbs ⓴

Road map E3. *2,550.*
(07475) 52700-40.
www.neuhofen-ybbs.at

Neuhofen is a small town on the Ybbs River, in the foothills of the Alps. Its centre is occupied by a Gothic church with a tall spire. The town was once a stopping place for pilgrims travelling to nearby Sonntagsberg, whose basilica is the central place of worship for followers of the cult of the Virgin Mary.

Today, the **Ostarrichi Kulturhof**, a museum of Austrian history on the outskirts of the village, is the town's top attraction. The modern building was erected in 1980 to designs by Ernst Beneder, who also landscaped the surroundings in an attempt to make new and old blend in a single composition. The museum was built in record time, at a cost of 28.8 million shillings, and in 1996 it became the focus of Austria's 1,000th anniversary celebrations.

The most important exhibit, from which the centre has taken its name, is the facsimile of a document which first mentions the term *Ostarrichi* (the original document is kept in archives in Munich). In this document, dated 1 November 996, Emperor Otto III, ruler of the German Roman Empire, presented the land around

Facsimile of the 996 document, Ostarrichi Kulturhof in Neuhofen an der Ybbs

Niuvanhof (present-day Neuhofen), known as *Ostarrichi* in the local language, to Gottschalk, Bishop of Freising in Bavaria. It was the first time that this name was used to describe the land that was controlled by the Babenbergs and which eventually, in the 11th–12th centuries, would become Austria. The Bishops of Freising had owned estates in this district from as early as the 9th century, and they regularly toured their territories. The names "Osterriche" and "Osterland", which appeared later, referred to the land east of the Enns River. It is fairly likely that originally the name referred to the entire country of Eastern Franconia. With time, Niuvanhof became Neuhofen, and if etymologists are to be believed, the present name of Austria (Österreich) derives from *Ostarrichi*. According to the most widely believed interpretation, it meant "eastern territories", but an alternative view also exists: at the time when the name *Ostarrichi* first appeared, the area in this part of the Danube valley was still populated by Slav tribes, and the names of many surrounding towns and villages reveal a Slav origin. *Ostarrichi,* as it was then, could come from the Slav word "ostrik", meaning a hill.

Whichever interpretation is accurate, the year 996 is recognized here as the beginning of Austrian history, and the Neuhofen Museum informatively presents the story of the remarkable rise of a small German duchy to the heights of European power as the multi-ethnic Habsburg empire, and the tangled web of history that eventually, in 1918, led to the creation of the Austrian Republic. It also documents the effects of such changes on the population, and demonstrates how the Austrians succeeded in preserving their national identity in the face of the strength of their German neighbours, a culture in many ways akin to their own.

The permanent exhibition in the Kulturhof consists of three parts. The first shows a facsimile of the *Ostarrichi* document in the original Latin version and in its German translation, together with photographs. The second is devoted to the etymological changes that the term has undergone, its geographical, linguistic and political transformations. The third part of the exhibition is devoted to present-day Austria and its provinces. It illustrates how the distinct areas grew together into the Austrian Republic of today, and how each provinces has managed to preserve its own regional identity, customs, traditions, arts and culture.

The Gothic church in the centre of Neuhofen an der Ybbs

Ostarrichi Kulturhof
Millenniumsplatz 1. ***Tel*** *(07475) 5270040.* ***Fax*** *(07475) 5270042.*
21 Apr–26 Oct: 9am–noon Mon, Tue, Thu & Fri; 10am–noon, 1–7pm Sat, Sun & hols.
www.ostarrichi-kulturhof.at

For hotels and restaurants in this region see pp294–7 and pp325–7

Schneeberg Tour ㉑

Both the Schneeberg and Raxalpen mountain ranges are popular with the Viennese for short winter breaks. Situated some 100 km (60 miles) from the capital, they offer excellent and well-developed skiing areas as well as many attractive walking trails for summer outings. The world's first high-mountain railway line was laid here, through the town of Semmering. To this day a ride on the railway is a thrilling experience.

TIPS FOR DRIVERS

Length of the route: *130 km (80 miles).* **Stopping places:** *hotels and restaurants can be found in Puchberg, Semmering, and at the upper station on Schneeberg.* **Suggestions:** *ride on the railway from Puchberg to Schneeberg (early April–early November).* ℹ *Puchberg (02636) 2256 11.* **www**.puchberg.at

Höllental – Hell Valley ⑤
The ravine along the Schwarza River starts from the slopes of Hirschwang, where the first-ever cable car in the world was built in 1926.

Schneeberg ④
The highest peak in the range and in Lower Austria, whose distinctive silhouette is clearly visible from the motorway between Vienna and Graz, rises to 2,076 m (6,811 ft). The summit affords magnificent views of the Raxalpe range.

Puchberg am Schneeberg ①
A rack-railway links Schneeberg with Puchberg, a popular resort which also boasts an old castle.

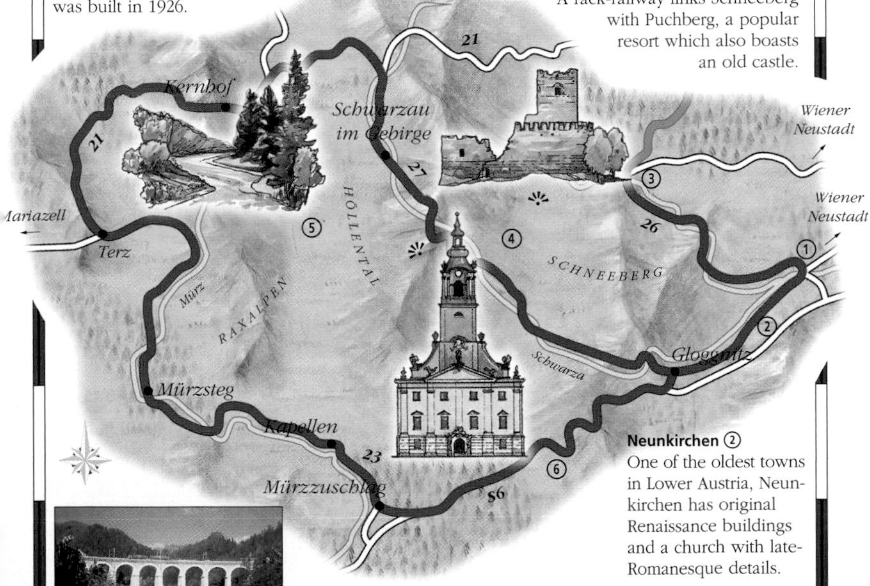

Neunkirchen ②
One of the oldest towns in Lower Austria, Neunkirchen has original Renaissance buildings and a church with late-Romanesque details.

Semmering ⑥
A popular health resort since the early 19th century, this town is known for its long sunshine hours, great views and interesting architecture.

Ternitz ③
This small town, in the Sierningbach valley, is a resort as well as a nature reserve. It has a modern church with a large mosaic.

KEY

- Suggested route
- Scenic road
- Other road
- River, lake
- Viewpoint

0 km 5
0 miles 5

Burg Forchtenstein ㉒

Road map G3. Mattersburg. Hauptstrasse 54 (02626) 63125. **Castle** ***Tel*** *(02626) 81212.* *Apr–Oct: 10am–6pm daily.* **www.** esterhazy.at

Perched unassailably on the rocky slopes of Rosaliengebirge stands Forchtenstein Castle, built in the 14th century by the Mattersdorfer family. Bought and extended by the Esterházys, it now houses a private collection of arms, one of the most magnificent and extensive in Austria. The castle armoury exhibits arms and war trophies dating from the 16th to 19th centuries as well as memorabilia and pictures from the wars with Turkey, France and Prussia. Forchtenstein Castle was one of the fortresses that defended the Habsburg state during the Turkish raids of 1529 and 1683. Other trophies from that period include a captured Turkish tent, one of the major attractions, as well as vast paintings of battle scenes and a tank, dug 142 m (466 ft) deep into the castle courtyard by the captive Turks. Having played its part in repelling the Turkish threat, the heavily fortified castle became a museum in 1815.

The equestrian statue in the courtyard is of Paul, the first Prince of the Esterházy family, which still owns the castle today. In summer the castle hosts a popular festival.

The birthplace of Franz Liszt in Raiding near Forchtenstein

Environs: In the village of **Raiding**, 24 km (15 miles) to the south of Forchtenstein, is a lovely cottage, the birthplace of the composer Franz Liszt (the **Liszt Geburtshaus**). The house has been turned into a small museum.

Liszt Geburtshaus
Lisztstrasse 46. ***Tel*** *(02619) 51047.*
Easter–late Oct: 9am–5pm daily. Other times by appointment.

Neusiedler See ㉓

See pp152–3.

Eisenstadt ㉔

See pp154–5.

Bruck an der Leitha ㉕

Road map G3. *7,000.* *Höfleinerstrasse 16 (02162) 6221.*

This small town, situated 30 km (19 miles) east of Vienna, was established as a Babenberg fortress in 1230, and formed the main border point between Austria and Hungary. Its present form dates mainly from the turn of the 17th century, but the remains of the medieval fortifications from the 13th century, as well as several old houses, remain in the main square today.

In Hauptplatz, the main square, stands an attractive town hall with a Rococo balcony and an arcaded courtyard. Also here is the Baroque Pfarrkirche (parish church of the Holy Trinity), built by

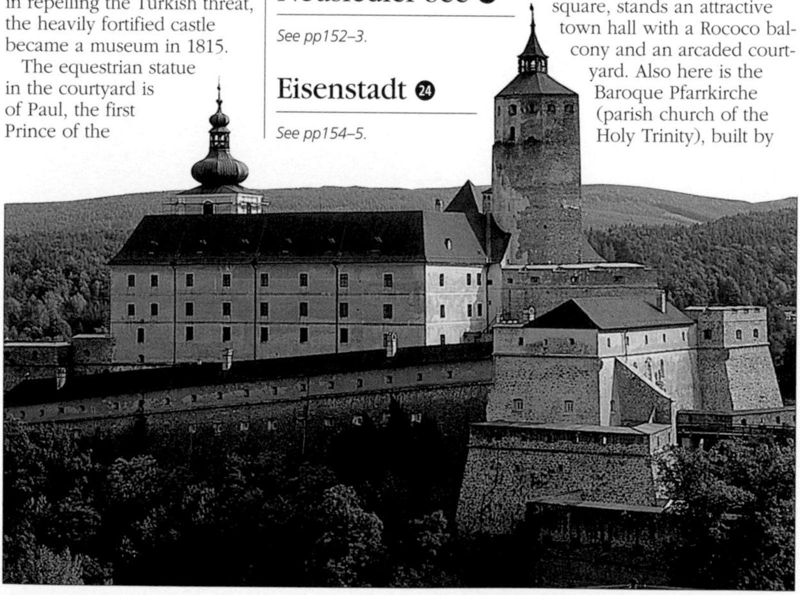

◁ The tranquil waters of Neusiedler, see jewel of Burgenland

Heinrich Hoffmann. In Friedrich-Schiller-Gasse stands the Kapuzinerkloster, the Capuchin Friary with its church dating from 1629.

The town's greatest architectural attraction, however, is the **Prugg**, a 13th-century castle with an original early-Gothic turret. In 1707, Lukas von Hildebrandt altered the castle in the Baroque style. The chapel also dates from this period.

At No. 1 Johannstrasse is an interesting **Heimatmuseum**, devoted to the history and folk art of the region.

Rohrau 26

Road map G3. *1,260.* *Bad Deutsch Altenburg, Petronell.*

East of Vienna lies the small town of Rohrau, with two attractions: Haydn's birthplace and the Harrach family **castle**. The pretty house in which the composer and his brother Michael were born, is now a small **museum** devoted to both composers.

The nearby Harrach castle is one of the most beautiful private art galleries in Austria with a splendid collection of 17th- and 18th-century paintings, mainly from Spain and Naples, but also some work from the Netherlands. There are also interesting porcelain pieces. The castle dates from the 16th century but was rebuilt in the 18th century.

Bust of the composer Joseph Haydn, Rohrau

Geburtshaus Joseph Haydns (Museum)
Tel (02164) 2268. *10am–4pm Tue–Sun.* *Mon, 1 Jan, 24 Dec.*

Harrach'sche Gemäldegalerie (Harrach Castle)
Tel (02164) 22538. *Easter–Nov: 10am–5pm Tue–Sun.* *Mon.*

Hainburg 27

Road map G3. *5,700.* *Bad Deutsch Altenburg, Badgasse 17 (02165) 62900-11.*

Hainburg on the Danube was once a fortified border town of the Eastern Margravate, and it is still a gateway into Austria from the east. The ruins of an 11th-century castle and three substantial town gates remain from this period. The small town has many historic sights, such as the Romanesque cemetery chapel and the Rococo Marian column in Hauptplatz. The best way to travel to Hainburg is along the Danube. The marshy area around the town is a nature reserve, and home to rare bird species no longer seen elsewhere. The area west of Hainburg is preserved as a unique nature reserve.

The Pagan Gate in the Carnuntum Archaeological Park near Hainburg

Environs: 38 km (24 miles) east of Vienna is the village of **Petronell**, where archaeologists unearthed a Roman town, **Carnuntum**, and the remains of a military camp.

The sights open to visitors include a Roman triumphal arch known as Heidentor (pagan gate), public baths, a reconstructed town villa and two huge amphitheatres. The ruins of ancient Carnuntum, the former capital of the Roman province of Pannonia, extend to nearby Bad Deutsch-Altenburg, where many of the unearthed objects are on display in the Museum Carnuntinum.

Archaeological Park Carnuntum
Petronell Carnuntum, Hauptstrasse 296 (02163) 3370. *21 Mar–15 Nov: 9am–5pm daily.* **www**.carnuntum.co.at

Museum Carnuntinum
Bad Deutsch-Altenburg, Badgasse 42. ***Tel*** *(02163) 3370.* *21 Mar–31 Oct: 9am–6pm daily.* **www**.carnuntum.co.at

Schloss Hof 28

Road map G3. Imperial Festival Palace Hof. ***Tel*** *(02285 20 0000).* *Apr–Oct: 10am–6pm daily.* **www**.schlosshof.at

After extensive renovation, Schloss Hof is now one of the most appealing destinations for an excursion from Vienna. From 1725 Prince Eugene of Savoy made it into his principal country seat and laid out a formal country garden which survives to this day.

Extended a generation later under Empress Maria Theresa, the palace contains state and private rooms from both these periods. The Schloss Hof complex also includes an idyllic Manor Farm with herb gardens, craft workshops, and numerous attractions for the young such as rare breeds and pony and carriage rides.

The enchanting nature reserve around Hainburg

For hotels and restaurants in this region see pp294–7 and pp325–7

Neusiedler See ㉓

The jewel of Burgenland, Neusiedler See is the largest steppe lake in Central Europe. On the border between Austria and Hungary (a small section – around one-fifth of its total area – at the southern end belongs to Hungary) it covers an area of 320 sq km (124 sq miles) and has no natural in- or outlets apart from the Wulka River. The water is slightly saline and never more than 2 m (6½ ft) deep, so it warms up quickly in summer. The banks are densely overgrown with reeds which make ideal nesting grounds for birds, while the lakeside beaches are popular with visitors. In 2001, the lake and the surrounding countryside were declared a World Heritage Site by UNESCO.

Neusiedler See
Neusiedler See, Vienna's "seaside", attracts visitors with its wide range of water sports facilities and enchanting, melancholy landscapes.

★ Rust
This attractive town on the western lakeshore has a perfectly preserved old town with many Renaissance and Baroque buildings. Star sights include the town hall and Fischerkirche.

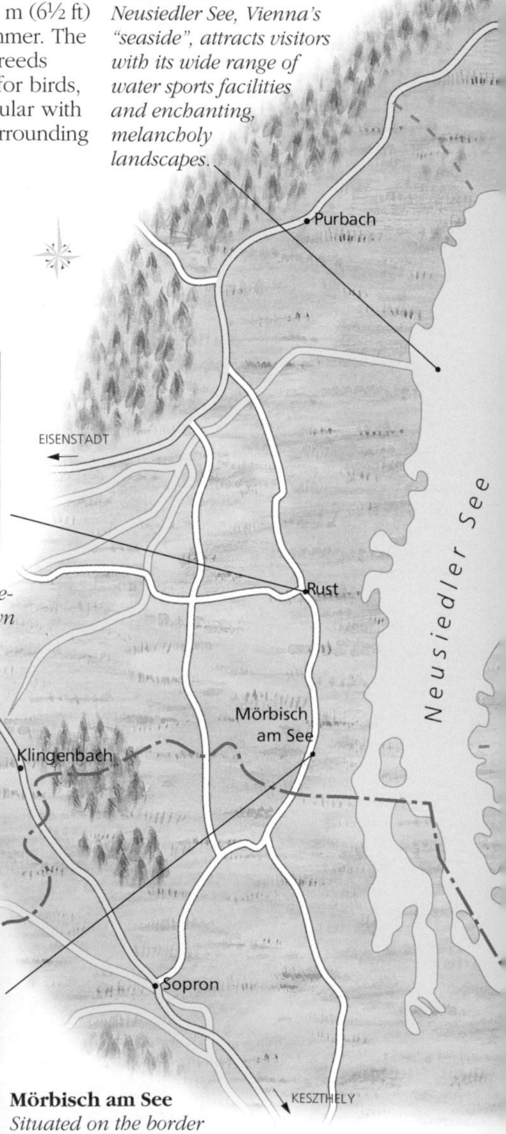

Mörbisch am See
Situated on the border with Hungary, this village produces an excellent white wine. Its charming, whitewashed houses, laden with flowers, create a truly unique atmosphere.

For hotels and restaurants in this region see pp294–7 and pp325–7

Neusiedl am See
A well-known resort and agricultural centre, Neusiedl is situated at the northern end of Neusiedler See. It has a museum devoted to local fauna and flora, and a small ruin.

VISITORS' CHECKLIST

Road map G3. *Rust (02685) 202; Neusiedl am See (02167) 2229; Illmitz, Nationalparkhaus (02175) 34420; Neusiedlersee Tourismus (02167) 8600.* **www**.neusiedlersee.com.

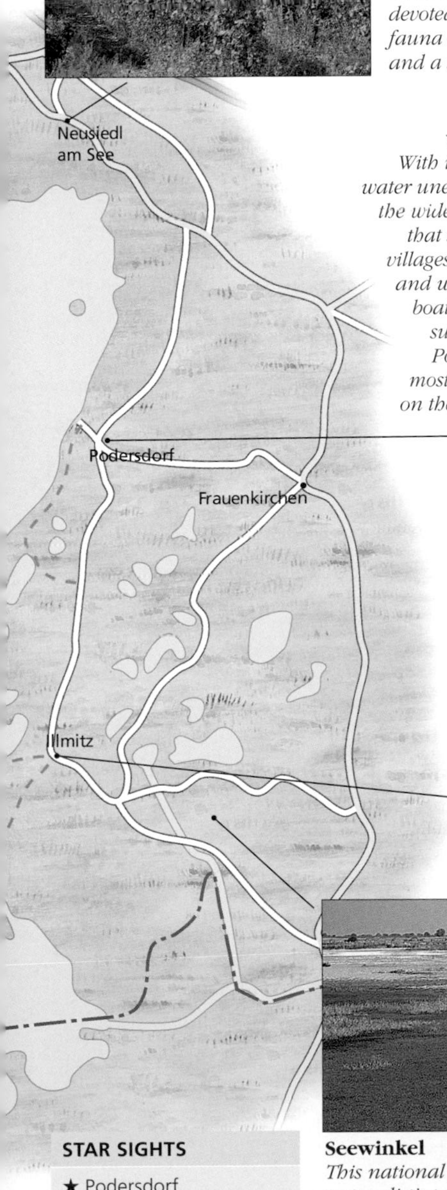

★ Podersdorf
With its access to the water unencumbered by the wide band of reeds that separates other villages from the lake, and with swimming, boating and windsurfing facilities, Podersdorf is the most popular resort on the lake's eastern shores.

Illmitz
Situated amid the marshes of the Seewinkel national park, this is a good base for exploring the surrounding grass- and wetlands.

Seewinkel
This national park, a naturalist's paradise of reedbeds, small lakes and marshes, is home to over 250 different bird species.

STAR SIGHTS

★ Podersdorf

★ Rust

KEY

- Motorway
- Major road
- Minor road
- Walking route
- National border
- River

Eisenstadt ㉔

This small town in Burgenland lies on the southern slopes of the Leitha Hills, 50 km (31 miles) south of Vienna. It became the capital of Burgenland province in 1925, when the larger and more notable Ödenburg – today the Hungarian town of Sopron – ended up on the other side of the border. From this date the town underwent a remarkable growth, and today it is an important transport hub, and wine-making centre. Eisenstadt is mainly associated with the Hungarian Esterházy family and their famous choirmaster, Joseph Haydn. Another great musician, Franz Liszt, was born on the Esterházys' estate, in the village of Raiding *(see p150)*.

Ornamental grille on Joseph Haydn's tomb in the Bergkirche

Exploring Eisenstadt

Above all, Eisenstadt is the town of Haydn, and the main tourist trails retrace his footsteps. Most of the town's historic sights are clustered around the inner town centre, south of Schlosspark. Only the Bergkirche, with its calvary, and the Jewish quarter of Unterberg are situated further to the west.

Bergkirche

Kalvarienbergplatz. **Haydnmausoleum** *Apr–Oct: 9am–5pm daily; Nov–Mar: groups only.*

In 1715, Prince Paul Esterházy ordered a hill to be created to the west of the Schloss and of Eisenstadt's centre. He then had a church built on top of that hill, dedicated to the Visitation of the Virgin Mary, with a Way of the Cross made up of 24 stations. The Passion figures are life-size and each tableau stands in a specially laid out room. The rather theatrical, Baroque-style figures are carved from wood or stone. The north tower of the church contains the most-visited attraction of the church: the tomb of Joseph Haydn. In 1932, on the 200th anniversary of the composer's death, a small mausoleum was built here by the Esterházys for the marble sarcophagus containing Haydn's remains.

Jüdischer Friedhof

Unterbergstrasse.

Jewish Museum Unterbergstrasse 6. ***Tel*** *(02682) 65145.* *May–Oct: 10am–5pm Tue–Sun; Nov–May: 9am–4pm Mon–Thu, 9am–1pm Fri; groups only.*

Until 1938, the Unterberg district of Eisenstadt was the base of the Jewish population, established in the 17th century by the Esterházys. It remained under their protection and played an important role in the life of the town. Inhabitants of the district included the Chief Rabbi of the Hungarian Jewry, banker Samson Wertheimer, and Sandor Wolf, a famous art collector. Eisenstadt was one of a handful of towns where old traditions were still observed, such as the closing of the district for Sabbath, and the chains that were once used for that purpose are preserved to this day. The two Jewish cemeteries in Eisenstadt are among the best-preserved in Austria. The adjacent house, which once belonged to Samson Wertheimer, now houses the **Jewish Museum.**

Burgenländisches Landesmuseum

Museumgasse 1–5. ***Tel*** *(02682) 600 1234.* *9am–5pm Tue–Sat, 10am–5pm Sun.*

This museum houses a large collection of objects associated with the history and art of the Burgenland province. Its geological collection comprises minerals and exhibits on the local Ice Age fauna. Archaeological findings include the Drassburg Venus, items from burial mounds in Siegendorf and objects which represent the Hallstatt and Roman cultures.

Jug from Burgenländisches Landesmuseum

Schloss Esterházy

Esterházyplatz.

Tel *(02682) 63854-12.*

Jan–Mar: 9am–5pm Fri–Sun; Apr–Oct: 9am–5pm daily; Nov–Dec: 9am–5pm Thu–Sun.

The Esterházy Castle was built around 1390, on the site of earlier fortifications, remains of which were discovered in the course of excavations. In 1663–72, Carlo Martino Carlone transformed the castle into a magnificent Baroque palace. The main attraction inside is the Haydnsaal, a concert hall

Tombstones in one of the Jewish cemeteries in Unterberg

Prince's apartments in Esterházy Castle

beautifully decorated with frescoes and boasting truly amazing acoustics. Joseph Haydn once used to conduct the castle orchestra here.

Today, the larger part of the castle is leased to the Burgenland provincial authorities. The castle is surrounded by a beautiful English-style park.

🏠 Domkirche
Pfarrgasse.
This late-Gothic church was built in the 15th century on the site of an earlier medieval structure. As with many other churches in this part of Austria, its builders were conscious of the permanent threat of Turkish invasion, and its lofty steeple is therefore full of loopholes which leave no doubt as to their purpose. The

eclectic-style interior features some medieval tombstones and a relief in the church's vestibule depicting the Mount of Olives. The pulpit and the beautiful organ are Baroque, as are the two altar paintings by Stephan Dorfmeister. The large bronze sculpture of the Pietà is the work of Anton Hanak. The Domkirche was given cathedral status in 1960.

🏠 Franziskanerkirche
Joseph-Haydn-Gasse.
The Franciscan church of St Michael was built between 1625 and 1630, but its interior hails from a later period. The magnificent reliefs in the altarpiece date from 1630. Beneath the church you will find the crypt of the powerful local dynasty, the Esterházy family.

🏛 Haydn-Haus
Joseph-Haydn-Gasse 21. **Tel** (02682) 719 3900. ☐ 1 Apr–11 Nov: 9am–5pm daily ☑ **www**.haydnhaus.at
The house where Joseph Haydn lived 1766–78 is now a small museum displaying a number of the composer's possessions. From 1761,

VISITORS' CHECKLIST

Road map G3. 👥 *12,400.* 🚆
🚌 ℹ *Schloss Esterházy, Esterházyplatz (02682) 63854-12.* 🎷 *Fest der 1000 Weine (Wine Festival, late August), Internationale Haydntage (Haydn Festival, Sept).* **www**.eisenstadt.at

Haydn was employed by the Esterházy family as their Kapellmeister (music director), and in the evening he conducted the court orchestra for performances of his own music. Many of his beautiful compositions were first heard in Eisenstadt.

Haydn's home for 12 years, now a museum devoted to the composer

EISENSTADT CITY CENTRE

Bergkirche ①
Burgenländisches Landesmuseum ③
Domkirche ⑤
Franziskanerkirche ⑥
Haydn-Haus ⑦
Jüdischer Friedhof ②
Schloss Esterházy ④

0 m ___ 250
0 yards ___ 250

Key to Symbols *see back flap*

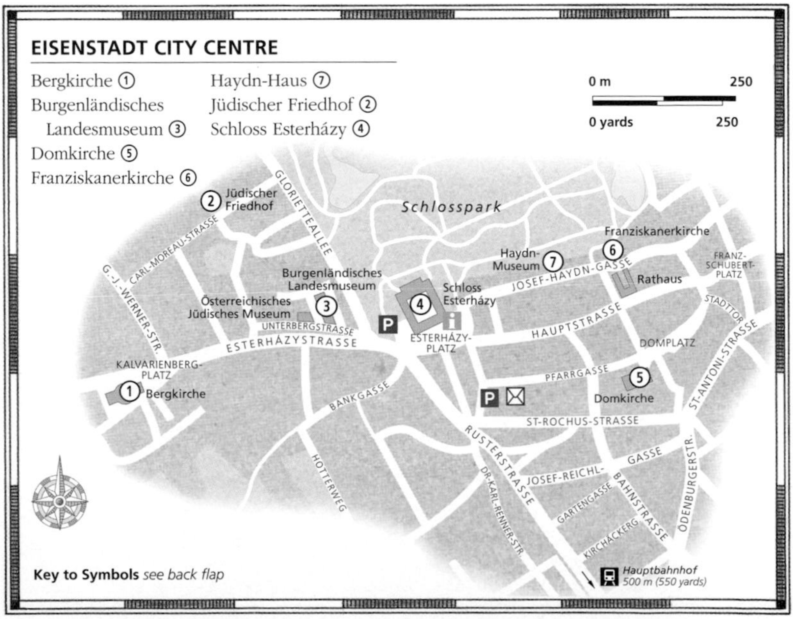

STYRIA

Austria's second-largest province, in the country's southeast, Styria has a population of 1.2 million. It is dominated by forests, meadows and vineyards covering some three-quarters of its total area of 16,387 sq km (6,327 sq miles). It is also an area of iron ore extraction and processing, and Erzberg (Iron Ore Mountain), glittering in every hue of red and brown, is a major tourist attraction.

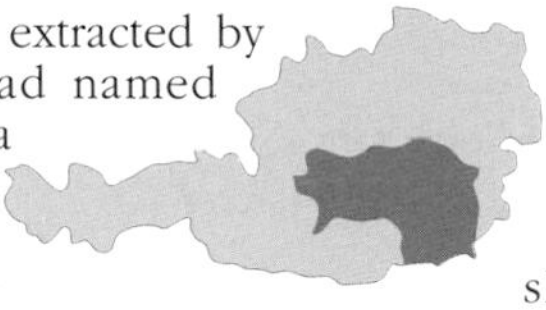

Iron ore was already extracted by the Romans, who had named this part of Austria the Roman province of Noricum. The mineral shaped the history of this province through the centuries, and its traces survive to this day. Following the highs and lows of the early Middle Ages, Styria fell into the hands of the Habsburg dynasty in the 13th century and shared in its fate and fortunes. The province was repeatedly ravaged by Hungarians and Turks, and, after having staved off the Turkish threat, also became susceptible to attacks by the French. A legacy of these times are its numerous hilltop castle strongholds and imposing fortified abbeys. Some have survived intact, others have been meticulously restored to their former splendour to capture the imagination of visitors to the region.

Styria's great attractions include the south-facing slopes of Raxalpen, its gentle climate and its rural idylls – it is known as "the green heart" of Austria. In the west, along its border with the Salzburger Land, the area is dominated by the lofty peaks of the Salzburg Alps and Lower Tauern. Here you will find excellent winter sport centres around Schladming, and at the foot of Dachstein, the highest peak in the region, with the best cross-country–skiing trails. The Salzkammergut in the north is a stunningly beautiful lake district. The province's main rivers are the Mur, which flows through Graz, its tributary the Mürz, and the Salza.

Bad Blumau, an architectural complex based on Franz Hundertwasser's designs

◁ **Rothenfels Castle near Oberwölz**

Exploring Styria

Styria, or Steiermark, is rich in attractions and its capital, Graz, is Austria's second largest city. The west of the province offers excellent winter sports facilities; in the north lie the beautiful Mur and Mürz valleys, and many lakes. The quiet, agricultural southeast is covered with vineyards. Special sights are the National Austrian Open-Air Museum in Stübing, the Lipizzaner stud Piber, and the Mariazell Basilica, the country's largest Marian sanctuary.

SEE ALSO

- ***Where to Stay*** pp297–9
- ***Where to Eat*** pp327–9

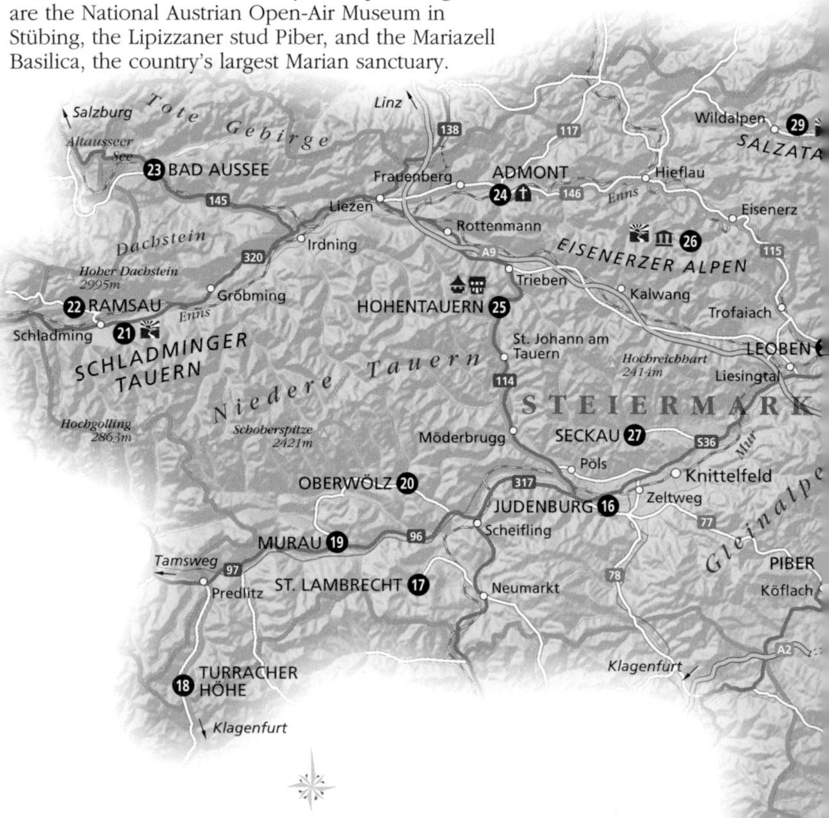

Tobacco, one of the products grown in eastern Styria

One of the grand villas in the spa town of Bad Gleichenberg

GETTING THERE

Graz has a passenger airport, though most international flights go to Vienna. The Province of Styria extends either side of the main road and rail connections crossing Austria from north to south. Local rail and road networks are also fairly well developed.

Watermill in Mureck on the Mur river

Statue of St Roch in the Wine Museum in Kitzeck, near Graz

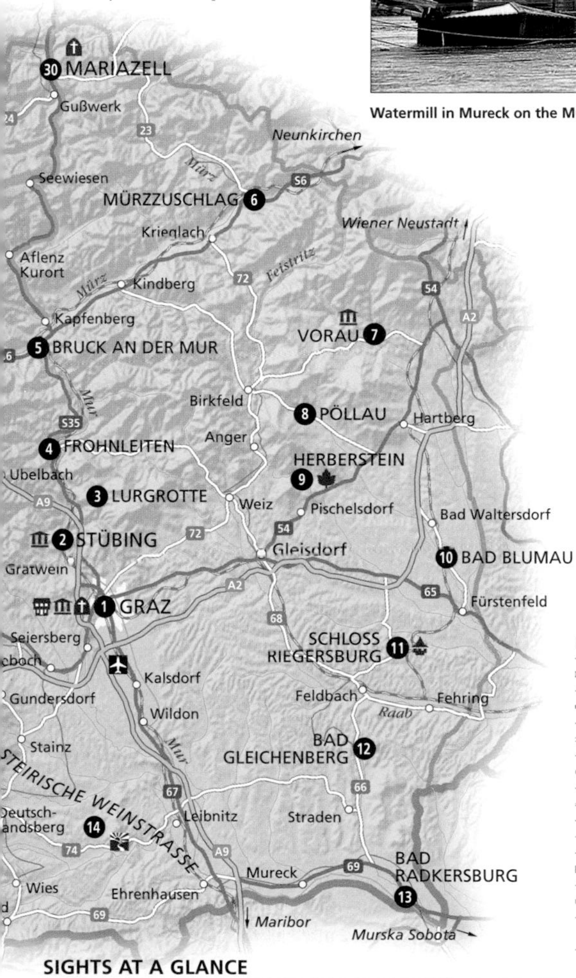

KEY

- Motorway
- Major road
- Minor road
- Scenic route
- Main railway
- Minor railway
- International border
- Province border
- Summit

SIGHTS AT A GLANCE

Admont 24
Bad Aussee 23
Bad Blumau 10
Bad Gleichenberg 12
Bad Radkersburg 13
Bruck an der Mur 5
Castle Riegersburg 11
Eisenerzer Alpen 26
Frohnleiten 4
Graz pp160–65 1
Herberstein 9
Hohentauern 25
Judenburg 16
Leoben 28
Lurgrotte 3
Mariazell pp184–5 30
Murau 19
Mürzzuschlag 6
Oberwölz 20
Piber 15
Pöllau 8
Ramsau 22
Seckau 27
Schladminger Tauern 21
St. Lambrecht 17
Stübing pp166–7 2
Turracher Höhe 18
Vorau 7

Tours

Salzatal Tour 29
Steirische Weinstrasse Tour 14

Graz: Street-by-Street ❶

Graz, the capital of Styria, is the second largest city in Austria. During the Middle Ages it was the seat of a junior branch of the Habsburg family, and later of Emperor Friedrich III. The legacy of the Habsburgs is Graz's lovely Altstadt (old town), one of the best preserved in Central Europe and a UNESCO World Heritage Site. Graz was also a stronghold against Turkish attack.

The modern city extends from the foot of Castle Mountain, on both sides of the Mur river. Graz is famed for its universities, architecture, cultural attractions and culinary traditions. It hosts two classical music festivals each year, one in the summer at the Music College and the "Styriarte", as well as the avant-garde "Styrian Autumn".

Haus am Luegg
This town house at Nos 11 & 12 Hauptplatz (c.1690) has a striking façade, with Renaissance frescoes and early Baroque stucco work.

Rathaus
The new town hall, built in the late 19th century on the southern side of Rathausplatz, replaced the smaller Renaissance palace that previously stood on the same site.

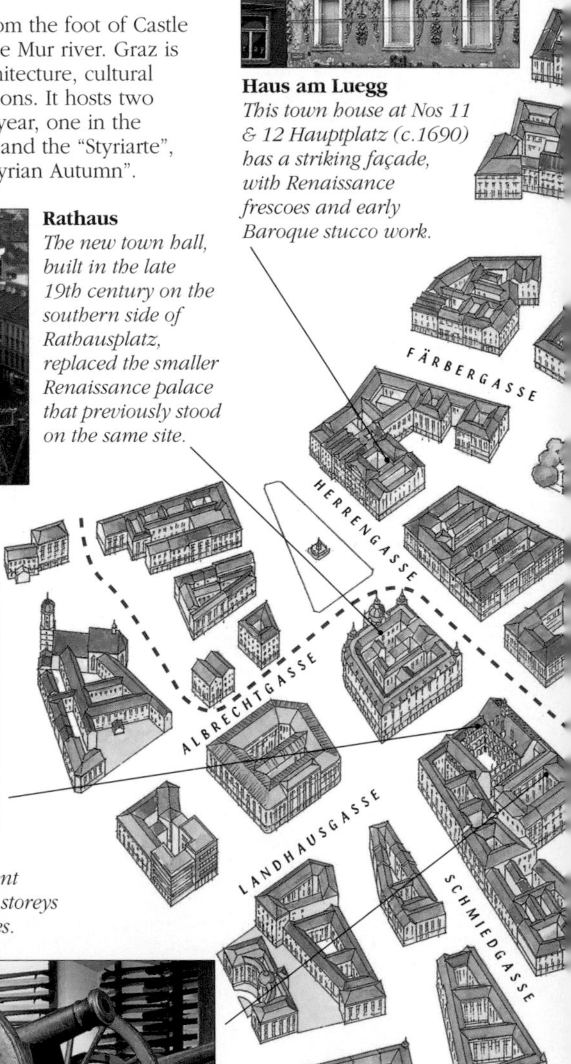

★ Landhaus
The courtyard in this government building has three magnificent storeys of arcaded Renaissance galleries.

★ Landeszeughaus
The jewel of this old armoury, the largest in the world that has been preserved intact, is the collection of weapons from Austria's 16th- and 17th-century Turkish wars (see pp164–5).

KEY

— — — Suggested route

Burg
The impressive double spiral staircase was built in 1499 on the orders of Maximilian I. He extended this vast Gothic castle built by his father, Friedrich III, who had made Graz one of his three capitals.

VISITORS' CHECKLIST

Road map F4. *254,000.* *Graz Tourismus, Herrengasse 16, Graz (0316) 8075-0.* *Jun–Sep: 9am–7pm Mon–Fri, 9am–6pm Sat, 10am–6pm Sun; Oct–May: 9am–6pm Mon–Fri, 9am–6pm Sat, 10am–3pm Sun.* **www**.graztourism.at

Dom
The beautifully carved reliquary chests in the choir of the cathedral were originally made to hold the dowry of Paola di Gonzaga, Duchess of Mantua.

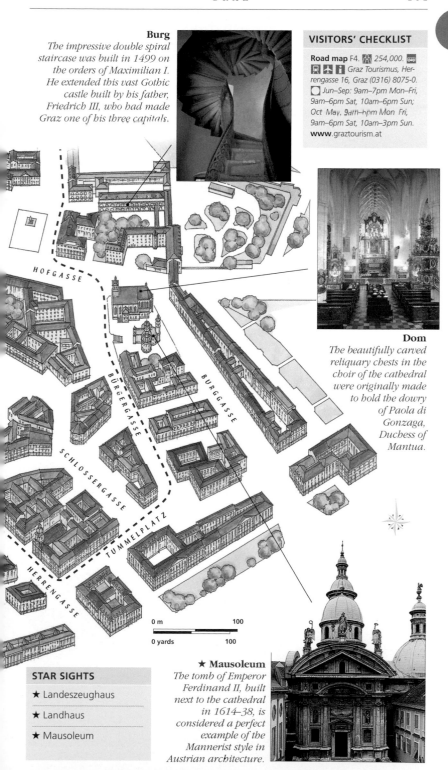

★ Mausoleum
The tomb of Emperor Ferdinand II, built next to the cathedral in 1614–38, is considered a perfect example of the Mannerist style in Austrian architecture.

STAR SIGHTS

★ Landeszeughaus

★ Landhaus

★ Mausoleum

View of the city of Graz and Mur river from the Clock Tower

Exploring Graz

The town is built on both banks of the Mur river; the Altstadt, with most of the tourist sights, is on the left bank. It can be reached by tram from the railway and bus stations. The Island in the Mur is Graz's newest attraction.

Schlossberg

Hofgasse.

At the north of the Altstadt rises the 473-m (1552-ft) high Schlossberg. The top can be reached by a funicular or by a 20-minute walk. The 28-m (92-ft) high Clock Tower (1561), one of the symbols of Graz, offers splendid views over the city. It houses a museum.

Dom

Hofgasse.

The cathedral is a former castle church, built between 1439 and 1464 for Emperor Friedrich III. Its west portal bears the Emperor's coat of arms and his famous motto, AEIOU *(see p38)*. Originally, the cathedral was built as a defensive church on the outskirts of town. It has survived almost intact to this day and the interior still features some original elements, including Gothic frescoes showing life during the plague, although most of the decorations stem from the Baroque period.

Franziskanerkirche

Franziskanerplatz.

The church once belonged to the Minorite Friars, but in 1515 it was handed over to the Franciscans. Inside, the St James's chapel dates from 1320–30, and there are also Gothic cloisters with beautiful tombstones. The interior was redesigned after World War II, and the combination of the restored vault and modern stained-glass windows with earlier details creates a very striking effect. Next to the church is a monastery with a distinctive tower. Both the church and monastery are in an unusually shaped square, surrounded by many interesting buildings with Baroque façades.

Hauptplatz

The triangular square at the heart of the Old Town is an excellent starting point for exploring the city of Graz. It is surrounded by many original town houses from different periods, including the famous Haus am Luegg with its Renaissance and Baroque façade decorations. At No. 4 stands Graz's oldest pharmacy, in a house dating from 1534 with some earlier features. The north side of the square is occupied by the neo-Renaissance town hall, built in the 1880s. In the middle of the square stands the fountain of Archduke Johann, who contributed much to the city's development. The four female figures around it symbolize Styria's four main rivers: the Mur, the Enns, the Drau and the Sann.

Universalmuseum Joanneum

Old Gallery in Schloss Eggenberg (see below). ***Tel*** *(0316) 583264-9770.* *10am–6pm Tue–Sun.*
New Gallery Mariahilferstrasse 2–4. ***Tel*** *(0316) 80170.* *10am–6pm Tue–Sat.* **www**.neuegalerie.at
Schloss Eggenberg Eggenberger Allee 90. ***Tel*** *(0316) 583264-9532.* *Apr–Oct: 10am-6pm Tue–Sun (5pm Nov–Mar).* **www**.museum-joanneum.at

Ducal coronet from the Joanneum collection

The memory of Archduke Johann remains alive in Graz to this day. The grandson of Maria Theresa, he played an important role in the political life of the country and participated in military campaigns, until he finally settled in Graz to devote time to his favourite pursuit of scientific research.

Hauptplatz, the distinctive triangular main square in Graz's centre

For hotels and restaurants in this region see pp297–9 and pp327–9

The Italianate galleried courtyard in the Landhaus

He founded the Technical University as well as the Joanneum, Austria's first public museum, which is named after him. Today the Joanneum has 17 departments and holds several exhibitions, some bequeathed by the Archduke.

The Old Gallery, the most interesting display, is located in the lovely Baroque Eggenberg Palace, 3 km (2 miles) west of Graz, and contains some magnificent medieval paintings by Cranach, Brueghel, and Styrian 17th- and 18th-century artists. Another department, holding a collection of coins and medals and various interesting historic objects is also to be found there. The most valuable exhibit in the museum is the Strettweg chariot, which dates from the 7th century BC.

The New Gallery, a collection of 19th- and 20th-century paintings, drawings and sculptures, previously housed in the Rococo Herberstein Palace, is now part of the Joanneum Quarter.

Landhaus

Herrengasse 16.

The Landhaus, one of the most beautiful Renaissance buildings in Styria, was once the seat of the Styrian diet which under Habsburg rule also covered areas that are now part of Slovenia and Italy. Today it houses the provincial parliament.

The building was altered in the 16th century by the Italian military architect Domenico dell'Allio. The stairs on the northwestern side of the courtyard are the work of another Italian, Bartolomeo di Bosio. The front, with its loggia and vast arched windows, is kept in the Venetian style. Well worth seeing is the beautiful courtyard with its three storeys of balustraded galleries linked by a raised walkway, and a fountain topped with a forged bronze cupola. In summer months it serves as a venue for festival events. Inside the Landhaus is the Baroque Landtag conference room, which has beautifully carved doors crowned by allegorical scenes, and ceiling stucco work by Johann Fromentini, depicting scenes from Styrian history. Also worth seeing is the Knight's Hall, which was decorated by the same artist.

Mausoleum

Hofgasse.

This small building, commissioned by Emperor Ferdinand II (1578–1637) as a tomb for himself and his family, is one of the most unusual and magnificent in Graz. A devout Catholic, the Emperor became especially notorious for the extremely harsh measures he took to introduce the Counter-Reformation in his territories, as well as for provoking the outbreak of the Thirty Years' War.

The mausoleum is one of the foremost examples of Austrian Mannerism, successfully blending various different styles. It was designed by an Italian architect, Pietro de Pomis, and completed by another Italian, Pietro Valnegro, who also built the belfry by the eastern apse. Its narrow façade, exuberantly decorated with sculptures, consists of several architectural planes that create an exceptionally harmonious composition. The interior design is the work of Johann Bernhard Fischer von Erlach, who was born in Graz and began his life and career here.

Palais Attems

Sackstrasse 17.

Palais Attems is the city's most attractive Baroque palace. Built in 1702–16, it was probably designed by Johann Georg Stengg. The palace's main features are its monumental staircase with frescoes and stucco ornaments, and its richly ornamented façades (inside and out, beyond the drive). The uniform furnishing of the rooms, with ceiling stuccos and lovely fireplaces and tiled stoves, is considered to be testimony to the Austrian aristocracy's standard of living during the Baroque period.

Grazer Congress

Schmiedgasse 2. ***Tel*** *(0316) 8049-0.*

Next to the town hall stands an old palace which, in 1980, was transformed into a modern congress centre with multiple facilities for arts performances. The building has two magnificent conference suites as well as contemporary entertainment venues furnished with state-of-the art technology. It also houses the city's largest concert hall, the Stefaniensaal.

The opulent main hall and stairs of the Grazer Congress

Landeszeughaus

The Landeszeughaus, or armoury, was built between 1642 and 1645 as a stock of arms to be handed to the local population in the fight against the Turks. Graz was in the vanguard of defending and guarding access to the threatened Austrian provinces of Styria, Carinthia and Carniola, which gave its armoury great importance. With a collection of over 32,000 objects, the Graz armoury today ranks as the world's best-preserved early arsenal. The museum's beautiful Renaissance façade was designed by the Italian Antonio Solari.

Minerva Statue
The Minerva statue in a niche to the right of the entrance, like the Mars statue on the left, is the work of Giovanni Mamola.

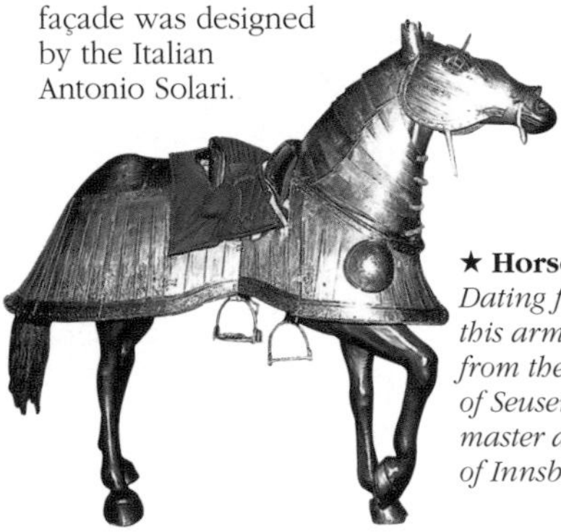

★ Horse Armour
Dating from 1505, this armour hails from the workshop of Seusenhofer, master armourer of Innsbruck.

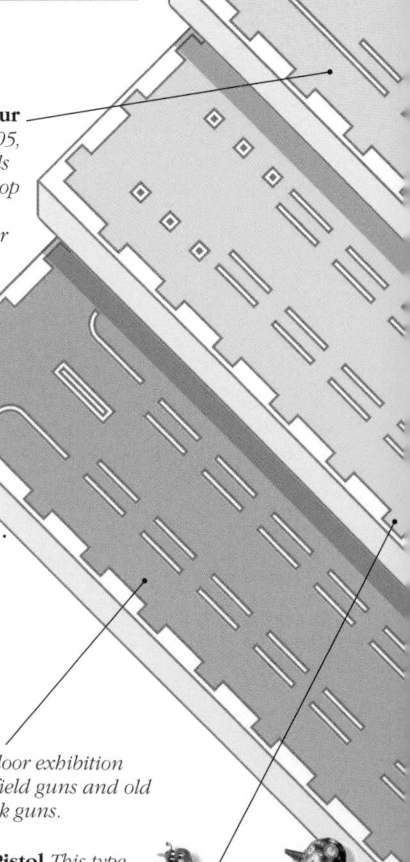

MUSEUM GUIDE

The first floor is devoted to heavy guns, flintlock pistols and rifles. The second floor holds the store of armour used by infantry and cavalry units, and pistols. The third floor displays the armour used by nobles and in tournaments. The fourth floor is devoted to side arms; also shown are musical instruments used by military bands. The cloakroom, toilets and museum shop are located on the ground floor.

Cannons
The first-floor exhibition includes field guns and old naval deck guns.

STAR EXHIBITS

- ★ Helmets
- ★ Horse Armour
- ★ Hungarian Sabres

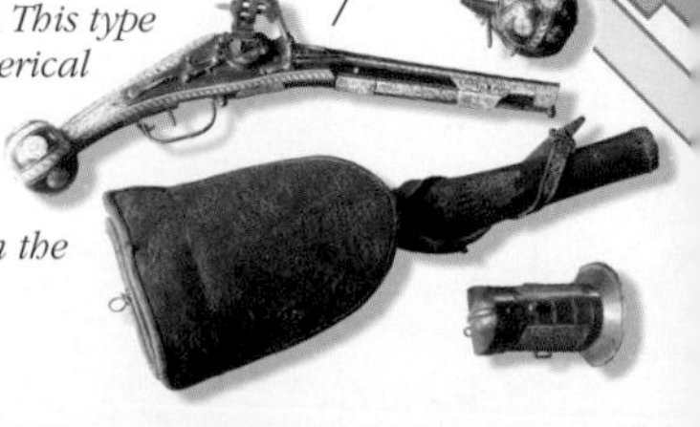

Wheel-lock Pistol *This type of pistol, with a spherical barrel-end, was introduced to the German and Austrian cavalry in the 17th century, and replaced the spear.*

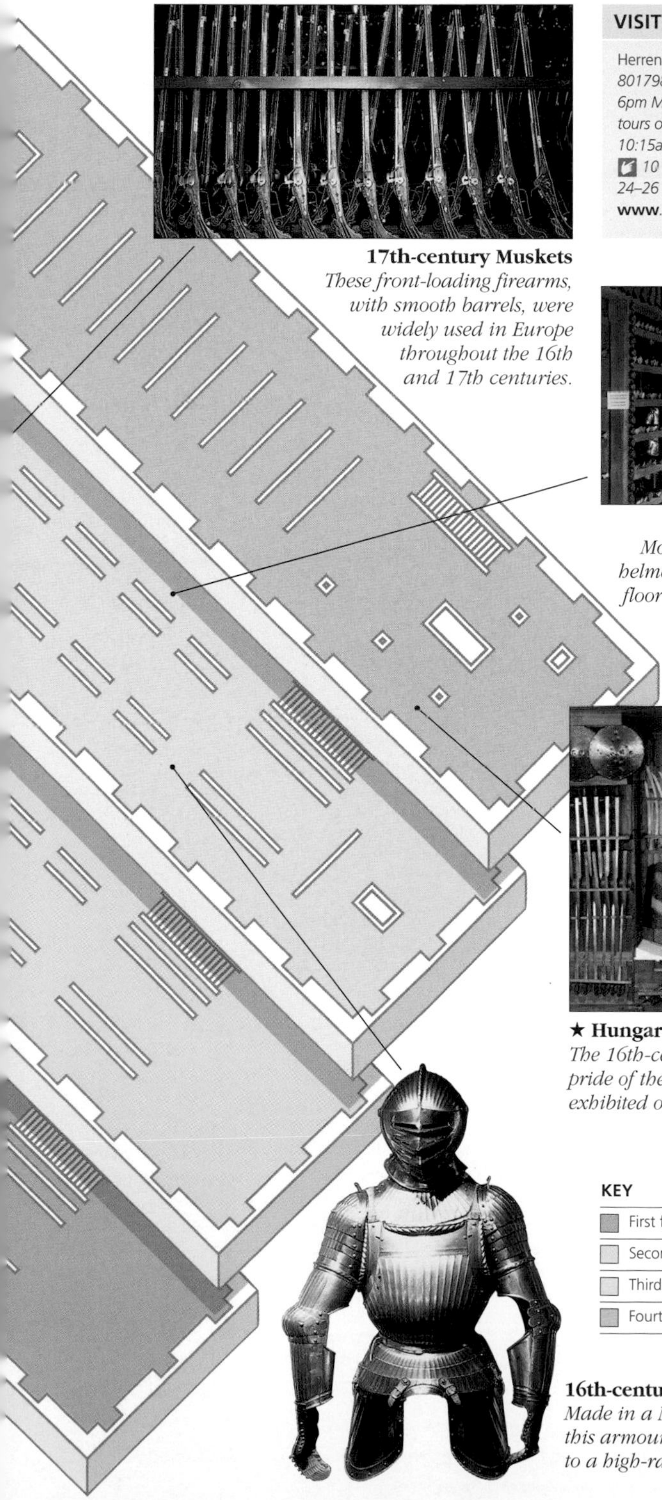

17th-century Muskets
These front-loading firearms, with smooth barrels, were widely used in Europe throughout the 16th and 17th centuries.

VISITORS' CHECKLIST

Herrengasse 16. ***Tel*** *(0316) 80179810.* *Apr–Oct: 10am–6pm Mon–Sun; Nov–Mar: guided tours only, every hour from 10:15am–2:15pm Wed–Mon.* *10 3pm Thu.* *1 Nov, 24–26 Dec, 31 Dec.* **www**.museum-joanneum.at

★ Helmets
Most of the 16th-century helmets adorning the third floor ceiling were made in the Nuremberg and Augsburg workshops.

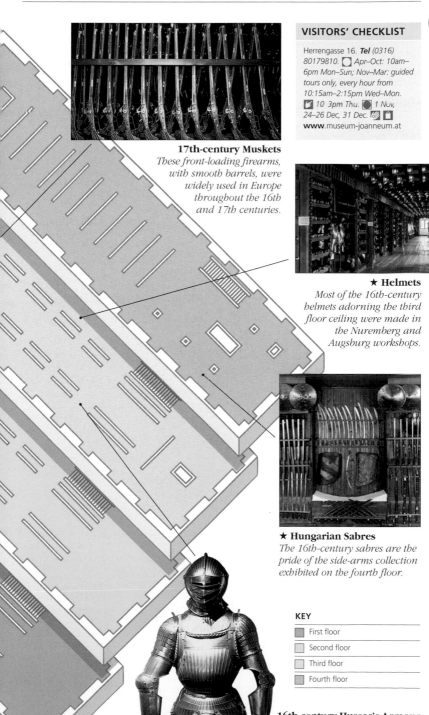

★ Hungarian Sabres
The 16th-century sabres are the pride of the side-arms collection exhibited on the fourth floor.

KEY

- First floor
- Second floor
- Third floor
- Fourth floor

16th-century Hussar's Armour
Made in a Nuremberg workshop, this armour must have belonged to a high-ranking hussar officer.

Stübing ❷

After several earlier attempts, the Österreichische Freilichtmuseum (Austrian Open-Air Museum) was started in 1962, when work was begun in the Styrian village of Stübing by the renowned scholar Professor Viktor Herbert Pöttler. It now occupies an area of 66 ha (24 acres), only 15 km (10 miles) north of Graz. The museum displays are buildings that have been moved here from other parts of Austria. This journey across the country, from east to west, from Burgenland to Vorarlberg, reveals remarkable regional differences in architecture, furnishings and workrooms, and document the everyday life of the houses' former inhabitants.

Farmstead from Alpbach
This Tyrolean farm is called Hanslerhof and dates from 1660. It unites all the essential areas of a farmstead under one single roof.

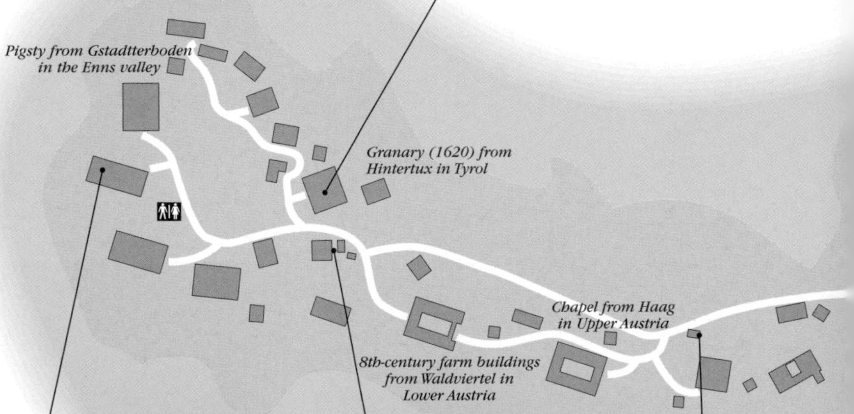

House from Schwarzenberg
This 17th-century building is typical of the rural architecture in Bregenzer Wald (the Bregenz Forest) in Vorarlberg.

Residential House
St. Walburg in southern Tyrol is the original location of this house. It was reconstructed in its present form following a fire in 1811.

STAR SIGHTS

- ★ Farmstead from Western Styria
- ★ Kitchen

Brenner Kreuz
A brick shrine from Ebene Reichenau in Carinthia, this little chapel houses a statue of St. Florian, the patron saint of fire fighters, who is invoked against fire.

MUSEUM ACTIVITIES

Every day, the Open-Air Museum offers activities associated with traditional customs and crafts, in which visitors are invited to participate. You can try your hand at lace-making, or on special days sing folk songs or listen with children to classic fairy tales. *Erlebnistag*, or adventure day, held every year on the last Sunday in September, combines a picnic with instruction into the secrets of traditional craft skills, customs and entertainments.

Traditional needlework display in Stübing

VISITORS' CHECKLIST

Road map F4.
Tel *(03124) 53700.*
Apr–Oct: 9am–5pm daily.
Guided tours on request.
www.freilichtmuseum.at

Crucifix
This cross was taken from a granary in Oberzeiring, which was used as the main food store.

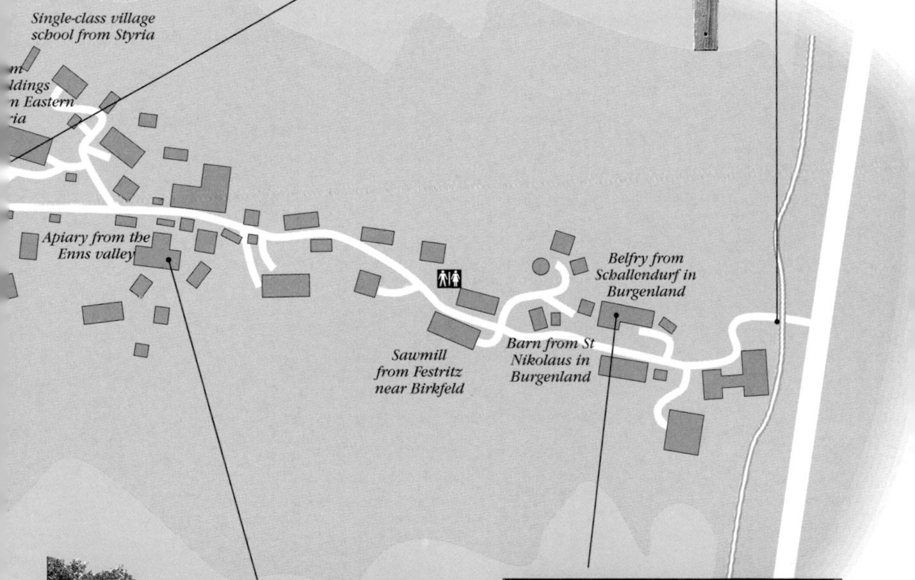

★ Farmstead from Western Styria
The main room in the 16th-century part of this house is the large "black room", where the entire family used to gather around the hearth and stove to cook, eat and socialize.

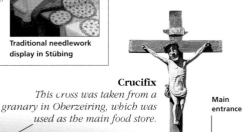

★ Kitchen
This typical kitchen from a house in the Burgenland province, is whitewashed and chimneyless, with an open hearth and traditional bread oven.

The astonishing Lurgrotte caves close to Peggau

Lurgrotte ❸

Road map F4. (03127) 2580. **www**.lurgrotte. com. *Apr–Oct: 9am–4pm daily, Nov–Mar: guided tours on request from Semriach entrance.*

The Lurgrotte is the largest and most interesting cave in Austria, with superb stalactites and stalagmites. A well-lit and clearly sign-posted route leads you through this world of icy wonders, along an underground stream. The largest dripstone, 13 m (43 ft) tall, is nicknamed the "Giant" (der Riese). A railway takes you there from Semriach.

Frohnleiten ❹

Road map F4. *7,350.* *(03126) 2374.* **www**.frohnleiten.at

Set among gentle hills on the Mur river, the town of Frohnleiten is surrounded by a network of clearly marked rambling trails which invite visitors to take long walks.

At one time Frohnleiten was an important transhipment post on the Mur. In 1763, the town almost burned to the ground in a fire. Sights worth visiting include the Servite monastery and the parish church with Rococo figures in the altarpiece by Veit Königer and ceiling frescoes by Josef Adam von Mölk.

Frohnleiten has won several awards for its impressive flower displays, and it has a splendid alpine garden on 90,000 sq m (107,000 sq ft) of land, stocked with some 10,000 species from around the world.

Environs: A short way to the west, in Adriach, is the **St. Georgskirche**, church of St George, with an altarpiece of the martyrdom of St George and four frescoes in the main nave by Josef Adam von Mölk.

Bruck an der Mur ❺

Road map F4. *14,000.* *Koloman-Wallisch-Platz 1 (03862) 890-121.* *Murenschalk (2nd Thu and Fri in Aug).*

This major industrial centre lies at the mouth of the Mürz river, where it flows into the Mur. Bruck flourished during the 14th and 15th centuries, thanks to its trade with Venice, when it had the right to store grain and salt. The small but attractive old town in the fork of the Mürz and Mur rivers dates from this period. Bruck was once a town of blacksmiths and their works are now its chief historical attractions. On the main square stands an iron well (1626) by the local master, Hans Prasser, sporting an intricate wrought-iron canopy. The **parish church of Mariä Geburt** features an interesting door (1500) to the vestry, a beautiful example of Styrian metalwork. This Gothic church was later altered in the Baroque style. The former Minorite church has several important 14th-century frescoes. In the main square, Koloman-Wallisch Platz, stands the town hall with an attractive arcaded courtyard, in a former ducal residence. The town's loveliest building is the late-Gothic **Kornmesserhaus**, built for the ironmonger Kornmess. It has open arcades on the ground floor and a first-floor loggia.

A small distance away, on the other side of the Mur, stands St Rupert's church, with a superb *Last Judgement* fresco (1420), uncovered in the 1930s. Above the town rise the ruins of **Landskron** fortress, whose only remaining feature is the bell tower.

Poster from the Winter Sports Museum in Mürzzuschlag

Mürzzuschlag ❻

Road map F4. *10,700.* *Wiener Strasse 9 (03852) 2555.*

This town on the Mürz at the foot of Semmering Mountain is Austria's oldest winter sports resort. In 1893, Mürzzuschlag hosted the first skiing competitions in the Alps, and in 1934 it was the venue for the Nordic Games that later became the Winter Olympics. The town's first

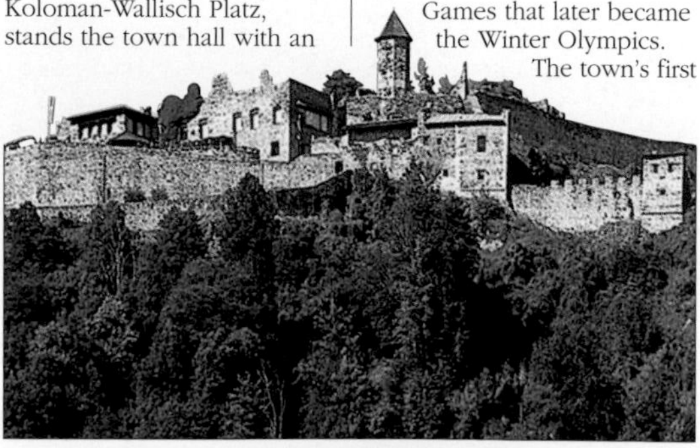

Ruins of Landskron Castle rising above Bruck an der Mur

For hotels and restaurants in this region see pp297–9 and pp327–9

The richly ornamented library in the 12th-century Augustinian Vorau Abbey

historic records date from 1469, when Emperor Friedrich III ordered it to be burned to the ground, following a rebellion led by Count Andreas Baumkircher. Today its main sights of interest are the parish church with a lovely Renaissance altarpiece and its picturesque old houses, including **the house of Johannes Brahms** at No. 4 Wiener Strasse. Also worth visiting is the **Winter Sports Museum** which has the world's largest collection of objects and memorabilia relating to all aspects of winter sports.

Winter Sports Museum
Wiener Strasse 13.
10am–6pm, Tue–Sun.
1 Jan, Shrove Tuesday, 1 Nov, 24–25 Dec, 31 Dec.

Bust of Johannes Brahms, who lived in Mürzzuschlag

Vorau ❼

Road map F4. *1,500.*
Stift Vorau (03337) 2351.

On a remote hill stands the 12th-century Augustinian **Vorau Abbey**. In the 15th century, the abbey was turned into a fortress; its present form is the result of alterations made throughout the 17th and 18th centuries. The main entrance has symmetrical wings on both sides, adjoining two identical towers. One wing contains the cloister; in the other wing are the prelacy and the magnificent fresco- and stucco-adorned library with its low barrel-vault ceiling. On the floor above is the cabinet of manuscripts, decorated with ceiling paintings of the Gods, the Virtues and The Immaculate. It contains some 415 valuable manuscripts, including the oldest annals of poetry in the German language – the Vorauer and the famous Kaiserchronik. The abbey church, dedicated to St Thomas, acquired its sumptuous decor in 1700–1705. It has a main altarpiece by Matthias Steinl, who also created the beautifully ornamented pulpit.

The small nearby town of Vorau also has a fascinating **Open-air Museum** (Freilichtmuseum) with a collection of typical homes and public buildings (school, pharmacy, smithy) from the neighbouring villages, complete with their distinctive furnishings.

Open-air Museum
Tel *(03337) 3466. Easter–Oct: 10am–5pm daily (Jul & Aug: 9am–5pm daily). Nov–Easter.*

Pöllau ❽

Road map F4. *2,200.*
(0335) 4210.
www.naturpark-poellauertal.at

Pöllau lies at the centre of a national park, surrounded by woodland, vineyards and walking trails. The town's main attraction is the former **Augustinian Abbey** and, above all, the lovely **St Veit's church**. Built between 1701 and 1712 by Joachim Carlone of the famous family of architects from Graz, this is a splendid example of Styrian Baroque. The building is vast: the main nave and presbytery measures 62 m (203 ft), the transept 37 m (121 ft) and the dome is 42 m (138 ft) high. The vaults and the inside of the dome are decorated with *trompe l'oeil* frescoes by Matthias von Görz, depicting the four fathers of the church, two Augustinian saints and the 12 apostles. The main altarpiece has a monumental painting by Josef A. Mölk showing the martyrdom of the patron saint St. Veit.

Environs: About 6 km (4 miles) northeast of Pöllau, high up on Pöllauberg Hill, stands the 14th-century Gothic pilgrimage church of **Maria-Lebing**, with vault frescoes by Mölk and two statues of the Virgin Mary – from the 15th and 17th centuries.

Herberstein 9

Road map F4. 300. *Tel (03176) 88250.* *Jan–Mar: 10am–4pm Sat–Sun & hols; Mar–Apr: 10am–4pm daily; May–Sep: 9am–5pm daily; Oct–Mar: 10am–4pm daily.*

Schloss Herberstein, perched on a steep rock amid wild countryside, has remained in the hands of the same family since 1290. Since the Herbersteins still live in the castle, a visit feels a bit like peeping through a keyhole at history.

The medieval fortress, rebuilt numerous times, achieved its present form in the late 16th century. Its most magnificent part is the Florence Courtyard, a lovely arcaded enclosure more reminiscent of Renaissance Italian palaces than of northern European fortresses. Once the castle was a venue for knightly tournaments.

The rooms that are open to visitors today display many items relating to the Herberstein family, and an exhibition that gives a unique insight into aristocratic life in the 18th and 19th centuries. There is even an original kitchen from the 16th century. Temporary exhibitions are organized during the summer.

One of the most interesting places within the castle grounds is the nature reserve, **Tierwet Herberstein**, which is home to wild plants and animals. Its origins can be traced back to the 16th century, when the castle was inhabited by Count Sigmund von Herberstein, the author of pioneering works on the agriculture and geography of Eastern Europe.

The Bad Blumau resort, designed by Friedensreich Hundertwasser

Tierwelt Herberstein
Mar–Nov: 10am–6pm daily; Nov–Mar: 10am–6pm Thu–Sun & hols. **www**.tierwelt-herberstein.at

Bad Blumau 10

Road map F4. *1,500.* *Rogner–Bad Blumau (03383) 51000.* **www**.blumau.com

In eastern Styria, in an area that has long been famed for its crystal-clear mineral waters, is a spa resort that is certainly worth a detour or even a few days' visit. The entire resort of Bad Blumau was designed by the painter and architect Friedensreich Hundertwasser, in a style similar to his building in Vienna *(see pp104–5)*. You will see rounded façades, rippling roofs, colourful walls and irregularly shaped terraces and balconies which transport you into a strange and surreal fairyland. The outside of the complex can be seen with a guided tour. As you stroll along an avenue lined with trees and shrubs that represent the Chinese horoscope, you suddenly realize that the grass you are walking on grows on the roof of a building below.

The main reason for a visit to the spa is, of course, taking the waters. Admission to the complex is available for half and full days, and will prove both an artistic experience and a pleasant way to while away some time.

Castle Riegersburg 11

Road map F5. 2,500. *(03153) 8670.* *Apr & Oct: 10am–5pm daily; May–Sep: 9am–5pm daily.* **www**.riegersburg.com

On a steep basaltic rock high above the Grazbach stream stands Schloss Riegersburg, a mighty medieval fortress, once Styria's most easterly outpost against raiders from Hungary, and then Turkey, and, more recently, a

The medieval fortress of Riegersburg, rebuilt in the 17th century

German stronghold during World War II. The present castle dates from the 17th century. The fortress is surrounded and defended by a 3-km (2-mile) long wall with eleven bastions, seven gates and two moats, and can only be approached by a long steep climb. The castle buildings begin beyond the sixth gate. The first building is the former armoury with a collection of arms and war machines used in the defence of the fortress during a siege. In the courtyard stands a monument to soldiers killed during World War II. Beyond the second moat are the buildings of the castle proper, which houses a museum dedicated to the Liechtenstein family, now owners of the castle and who played an important role in the turbulent history of Austria and Europe.

In the inner courtyard you will find a well surrounded by an intricate wrought-iron enclosure featuring a horseshoe. Is it said that those who succeed in tracing the horseshoe among the intricate decorations may count on good luck. The twelve castle rooms housing the Witches' Museum are devoted to those horrendous times in medieval European history when many women (and some men) were tortured, burned at the stake and otherwise persecuted. The museum has many fascinating exhibits recounting the most gruesome of tales.

Bad Gleichenberg ⓬

Road map F5. *2,100.* *(03159) 2203.*

Once the most popular health resort in Styria, Bad Gleichenberg was developed in 1834 by Count von Wickenburg. When the therapeutic properties of the local spring waters – already known to the Romans – were brought to his attention, he set about developing them. A shrewd businessman, he soon turned this quiet corner of southeastern Styria into a modern resort that attracted visitors with its promise of painless treatments for heart disease, circulatory and respiratory ailments, problems of the digestive tract and rheumatic conditions. Consequently, Bad Gleichenberg became one of the most popular destinations for the health-conscious Austrian aristocracy, who also congregated on the local promenade, and in the magnificent park, which now displays statues of its former visitors hidden among the shrubbery. The town has many surviving villas and Secession-style palaces; one of the most beautiful is the old theatre, now housing a cinema.

Statue of Constantine Wickenburg, in Bad Gleichenberg

Environs: A short way north of the spa town, in Gleichenberg village, stands the medieval **Schloss Kornberg**. Built as a fortress in the 13th century, it was transformed into a residential palace in the 17th century. Today it is a two-storey castle complex with four towers, and a magnificent Renaissance courtyard.

Bad Radkersburg ⓭

Road map F5. *1,600.* *(03476) 2545.*

Bad Radkersburg, on the Slovenian border, was founded as a town in 1265 by the Bohemian King Ottokar. Once a fortified border post as well as an important trade centre and transhipment harbour on the Mur river, today it is a peaceful small town, which still bears many signs of its former glory. In the main square stands the late-Gothic town hall with its octagonal clock tower topped by a belfry. The Marian or Plague Column in the square dates from 1681, and the surrounding houses with their patios and shaded galleries are the former homes of noblemen and rich citizens. The house at No. 9 once belonged to the von Eggenbergs, one of Styria's most powerful families.

Like many of its neighbours, Bad Radkersburg is also a spa town and health resort whose health-giving mineral waters attract numerous visitors.

The octagonal tower of the late-Gothic town hall in Bad Radkersburg

The Plague Column on Hauptplatz in Bad Radkersburg

Steirische Weinstrasse ⓮

Much of southern Styria is given over to vineyards, with vines planted on steep, south-facing slopes. The roads along the foot of the hills run through fields of maize, the region's second crop. The third crop is pumpkins, and pumpkin seeds are used to make *Kürbiskernöl*, a popular salad oil. Visitors following the Styrian wine routes will find many pleasant places to stop for a meal, but more importantly, a chance to sample the local wine and learn about the grape varieties that cloak the gardens of the restaurants.

Gundersdorf ①
At the entrance to the village stands a high pole with four vanes clattering in the wind. This is the *Klapotetz*, a scarecrow that guards the vineyards against birds. There are many such devices throughout the region, but the one in Gundersdorf is the largest.

Stainz ②
This town owes its former wealth to the wine trade. The former Augustinian Abbey was converted into a palace by Archduke Johann and now houses a department of the Graz Joanneum musuem presenting local and regional traditions.

Bad Gams ③
A health resort with iron-rich mineral waters, Bag Gams owes its fame mainly to its superb pottery products.

0 km 5

0 miles 5

KEY

- Suggested route
- Other road
- River, lake
- Viewpoint

Deutschlandsberg ④
This village is the centre of production for Schilcher rosé wine. It is dominated by the ruins of a former castle, whose remaining 12th-century turret affords spectacular views over the valley.

Kitzeck ⑤
In the centre of town, in an old inn between the church and the pub, is a fascinating wine museum. Kitzeck also boasts the highest vineyards in Europe, growing on steep slopes, at an altitude of 564 m (1,850 ft).

AUSTRIAN WINES

Austria can boast some truly excellent wines, in particular its white wines can take their place among the best in the world, and production meets almost the entire domestic demand. The largest wine-producing area is Lower Austria, particularly the Weinviertel and the Wachau Valley. Burgenland, southern Styria and the environs of Vienna are also key regions. The most popular white wines are Grüner Veltliner, Welschriesling and Weissburgunder. The land around Neusiedler See produces white wines, but is famous for its reds: Zweigelt and the full-bodied Blaufränkisch. The light Schilcher comes from Deutschlandsberg in Styria. Eiswein, an Austrian speciality, is a sweet dessert wine from grapes picked after the first frosts.

Label for Austrian red wine from Gumpoldskirchen

Leibnitz ⑥
Several traces reveal earlier Roman settlements in the town of Leibnitz. The archaeological finds are now on display in nearby Seggau Castle.

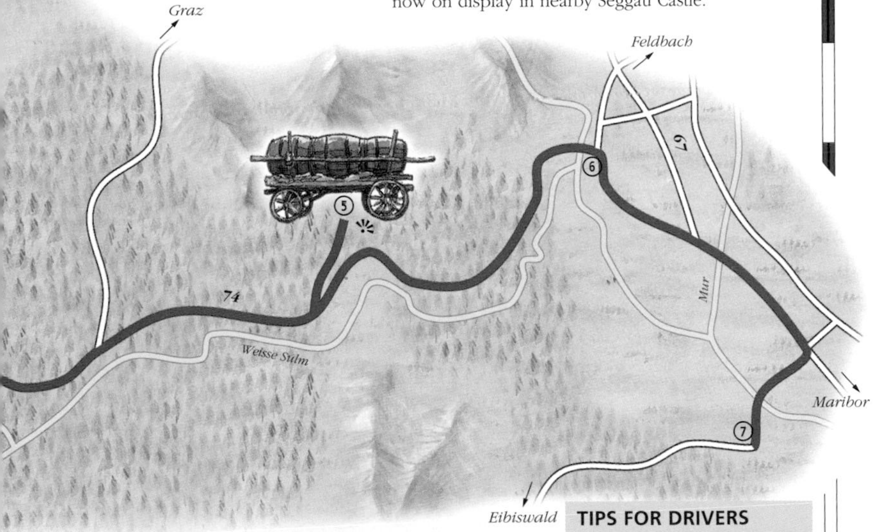

Ehrenhausen ⑦
This historic town makes a good starting point for exploring much of the Styrian wine route. Its greatest attraction is the mausoleum of Rupert von Eggenberg (died 1611), a hero of the Turkish wars, with an interior designed by Johann Bernhard Fischer von Erlach.

TIPS FOR DRIVERS

Length of route: *66 km (41 miles).*
Stopping places: *inns and rooms for rent are dotted along the route.*
Suggestions: *a visit to the Steirisches Weinmuseum (wine museum) Kitzeck, Steinriegel 16.* ***Tel*** *(03456) 2243.* ◯ *Apr–Nov: Sat, Sun, public hols (Aug–Sep: 10am–noon, 2–5pm Tue–Sun & hols); tours on request.*

Piber ⓯

Road map F4. *Köflach.* *500.* ***Tel*** *(03144) 71087.*
Stud *Tel* *(03144) 3323.* *Easter–Oct: 9:30am–5pm daily.*

Piber houses the stud farm for the Spanish Riding School horses. When the town of Lipizza was incorporated into Slovenia after World War I, it was in a former castle in Piber, a small Styrian village, that the famous Lippizaner horses found a new home. The horses are a complex mixture of six different breeds. Born dark-chestnut or black, they acquire their famous white colour between the ages of four and ten. In Piber the initial selection of 5 out of 40 stallions takes place: they are assessed for their suitability and stage talents before five years of training at the Spanish Riding School in Vienna. You can visit the stables here, and watch a film on the history of the stud.

Judenburg ⓰

Road map E4. *10,500.* *(03572) 47127.* **www**.judenburg.com

This town at the fork of a road is an old mercantile centre that took its name from the *Juden*, or Jews, who once lived and traded here. When Emperor Maximilian expelled the Jews in 1496, the town went into decline. Not much remains of the medieval Jewish quarters, but it is worth visiting **Nikolauskirche**, the church of St Nicholas. The only original feature is the presbytery. Rebuilt in 1673 in the Baroque style, the church was subsequently given a Neo-Renaissance facelift during the Neo-Classicist period. Inside are statues of the 12 apostles by the local artist Balthasar Brandstätter. One of the side altars contains a small wooden statue of the Madonna and Child, dating from 1500. The Magdalenenkirche, church of St Mary Magdalene, features lovingly restored Gothic stained-glass windows. Judenburg also has a town museum devoted mainly to the region's history and art.

Environs: East of the town, on the ledge of a rock, stand the ruins of an old Liechtenstein **castle** that was once accessible only by step ladder. In the environs of Judenburg are some of the most interesting archaeological sites dating from prehistoric times. The famous chariot that is now displayed in the Joanneum museum in Eggenberg castle in Graz was unearthed in nearby **Strettweg**.

Image of the patron saint of St. Lambrecht Abbey

St. Lambrecht ⓱

Road map E4. *2,000.* *(03585) 2305.*

St. Lambrecht, a Benedictine Abbey, was founded in the 12th century by Henry III, Duke of Carinthia. The monastery complex was built in 1640 to designs by Domenico Sciassi. The church dates from the 14th century, but it was rebuilt in the Baroque style and today it is a triple-nave basilica with medieval frescoes on the walls and presbytery ceiling, and statues of the church's fathers in the organ enclosure. The main altar (1632) by Valentine Khautt is 16 m (52 ft) high.

North of the church, by the cemetery, stands a 12th-century Romanesque chapel. The abbey also has a magnificent library and an interesting museum with a collection of the old furnishings of church and abbey, including Romanesque sculptures, a 15th-century votive painting, *The Mount of Olives,* by Hans von Tübingen, and 15th- and 16th-century stained-glass panels. The gem of the museum, however, is its collection of birds. Some 1,500 species were assembled in the 19th century by the amateur collector Blasius Hanf.

St. Lambrecht Abbey Museum
Hauptstrasse 1–2.
Tel *(03585) 2305.* *15 May–15 Oct: 10:45am, 2:30pm Mon–Sat, 2:30pm Sun & hols.*

Turracher Höhe ⓲

Road map E5. *60.* *(04275) 8392.*

This small ski resort nestles at an altitude of 1,700 m (5,575 ft) high in the Nocky Mountains, one of Austria's most scenic Alpine ranges on the border between Styria and Carinthia. The town makes a great base for year-round walks in the woods and mountain meadows. Nearby are the remains of an old iron-smelting plant. The blast furnace ended its operation in the early 20th century, but the remains of heavy

The world-famous Lipizzaner horses in a paddock near Piber

For hotels and restaurants in this region see pp297–9 and pp327–9

Splendid autumn colours in the woods around Turracher Höhe

industry create a very striking feature set against the backdrop of the pistes and the beautiful snow-covered hills of the ski resort.

Murau ⑲

Road map E4. *31,000.*
(03532) 2720. **www**.murau.at

Murau sprang up in the 13th century at a crossroads of trading routes on the scenic Mur river and became a local centre for commerce and industry. The historic town centre of Murau lies on the left bank of the Mur river. Its Renaissance houses are dominated by the Gothic **Matthäuskirche**, the church of St Matthew, consecrated in the 13th century and later altered in the Baroque style. The church contains some interesting epitaphs of the Liechtenstein family but its star attraction is the main altar (1655), a magnificent work by local Baroque masters, incorporating a Gothic painting of the Crucifixion (c.1500). Also worth seeing are the medieval frescoes of St Anthony in the transept, and the Entombment of Christ and Annunciation in the main nave.

The castle behind the church, **Schloss Murau**, was founded by the Liechtenstein family and later passed into the hands of the Schwarzenbergs. It has an interesting museum of metallurgy. In **Elisabethkirche**, the church of St Elisabeth, at No. 4 Marktgasse, is a Diocesan Protestant Museum that holds documents relating to the events around the Reformation and Counter-Reformation in these parts of Austria.

Historic buildings in the old town of Murau on the Mur River

Oberwölz ⑳

Road map E4. *1,000.*
(03581) 8420.

This small town, which grew rich through its trade in salt and the smelting of silver excavated in the surrounding hills, has preserved some of its former glory. In the surrounding area many archaeological finds from the Hallstatt period have been unearthed, revealing a long history. Oberwölz once belonged to the bishopric of Freising and up to the time of the Napoleonic wars its envoy resided in the neighbouring **Schloss Rothenfels**.

The town has some well-preserved remains of medieval fortifications, including three turrets and two town gates. Its pride is the Gothic **Stadtpfarrkirche St Martin**, the parish church of St Martin, a triple-nave basilica with an early-Gothic chapel and a 15th-century Gothic vestibule. In 1777, J. A. von Mölk painted the ceiling frescoes in the chapel vault. On the external south wall is a relief from 1500, showing the Last Judgement. Next to the church stands the 14th-century chapel of St Sigismund, with the Way of the Cross by Johann Lederwasch from the turn of the 18th century. In the Cultural Centre is a regional museum with a collection of archaeological finds from the area, and a museum of wind instruments.

Schladminger Tauern ㉑

The small town of Schladming lies at the foot of the Niedere (Lower) Ta uern that extend along the Enns Valley. Rising to 2,800 m (9,200 ft), their gentle slopes provide excellent conditions for downhill skiers, from the beginner to the professional. The scenery is superb, excellent for walking in summer, with an efficient bus network, cable cars and ski lifts in winter. If you are looking for more of a challenge, you can find this in the Dachstein massif close by. But for a relaxing break it is still worth going down to Schladming, with its tempting restaurants and cosy cafés lining the broad promenade.

★ Schladming
The little town of Schladming has a rich history. Once a centre of peasant revolts, it remains to this day the centre of Austrian Protestantism.

★ Ennstal – the Enns Valley
One of Austria's major rivers, the Enns, separates the Niedere Tauern from the Dachstein massif.

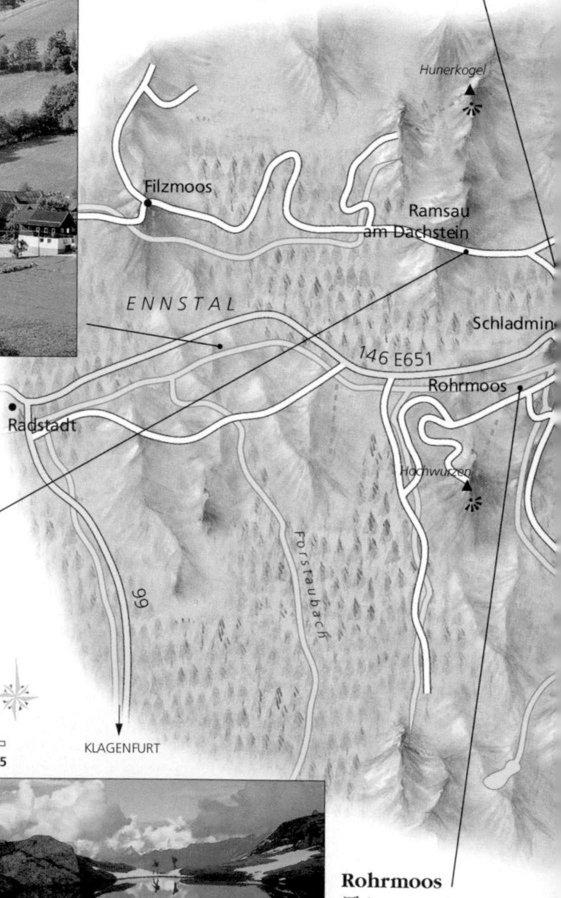

The ascent by cable car from the small village of Ramsau am Dachstein *(see p180)* takes visitors to the tops of Dachstein and Hunerkogel. Climbing instructors also give advice to rock climbers.

0 km 5

0 miles 5

Rohrmoos
This resort, just outside Schladming, is a good base for climbing the neighbouring Hochwurzen and Planai summits.

STAR SIGHTS

- ★ Dachstein Massif
- ★ Ennstal – the Enns Valley
- ★ Schladming

◁ **Mountain lake in Styria in autumn**

★ Dachstein Massif
The highest, most impressive peak is Dachstein itself, which rises to 2,995 m (9,826 ft). A glacier, it is perfect for year-round skiing.

VISITORS' CHECKLIST

Road map D4, E4.
Schladming, Coburgstrasse 45 (03687) 225080.
www.schladming-dachstein.at

Gröbming has an attractive late-medieval church of the Assumption of the Virgin Mary, with a winged altar (1520).

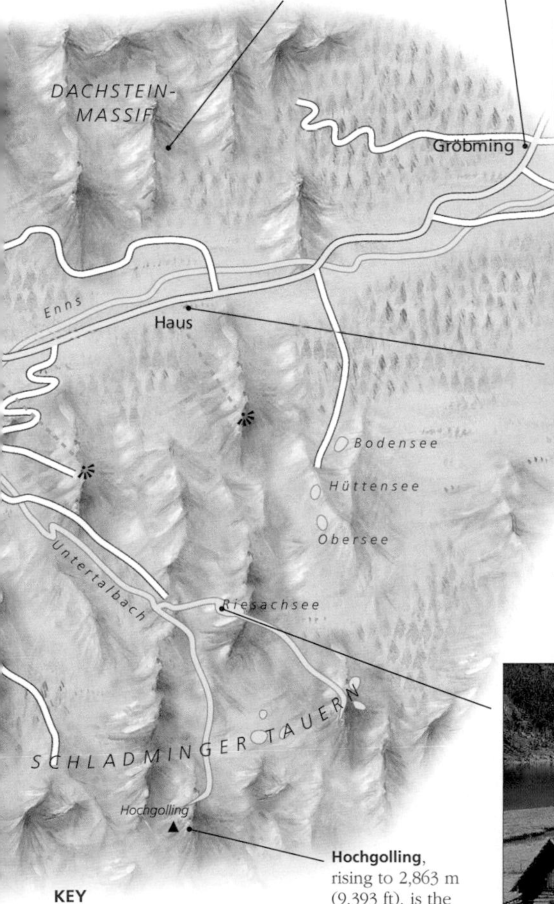

Haus
A resort and winter sports centre, Haus has a beautiful Baroque church. It is a good starting point for mountain walks to the nearby scenic lakes, including Bodensee, Hüttensee and Obersee.

Hochgolling, rising to 2,863 m (9,393 ft), is the highest peak in the Schladminger Tauern. The long, arduous climb rewards with stunning views of the mountains from the top.

KEY

- Major road
- Minor road
- Mountain railway
- River
- Viewpoint

Riesachsee
One of many mountain lakes set amid beautiful scenery, the Riesachsee lies at an altitude of 1,333 m (4,373 ft). It is a perfect spot for trout fishing.

The resort of Ramsau, famed for cross-country skiing

Ramsau ㉒

Road map D4. *2,700.*
(03687) 81833.

At an altitude of 1,000 m (3,280 ft) lies the small town of Ramsau am Dachstein, renowned for its superb cross-country ski runs, extending over some 230 km (143 miles). Snow is almost guaranteed from November until March and the efficient interconnecting system of lifts, cable cars, trains and buses also puts more difficult runs within easy reach. The peaks opposite the Dachstein massif have slopes that are perfectly suited to moderately skilled downhill skiers. In the summer the *Loipen* or cross-country ski runs turn into excellent long-distance walking routes.

From the Ramsau side visitors can ascend the famous Dachstein south face by cable car. A cable car also takes you up the nearby Hunerkogel (2,694 m/8,836 ft), from where a lovely panoramic view of the area unfolds. The descent takes you to nearby Filzmoos, a resort with views of the spectacular Bischofsmütze (Bishop's Mitre).

Ramsau has two museums. **Heimatmuseum Grahhof** is dedicated to local folklore, handicraft and the history of the Reformation, which was very active in this area. The **Alpinmuseum** illustrates the history of mountaineering in the region. There are many other attractions on offer, such as feeding mountain animals in their nurseries and night toboggan runs.

Heimatmuseum Grahhof
Tel *(03687) 81812.*

Alpinmuseum
Tel *(03687) 81522.* *May–Oct: 10am–4pm daily.* *on request.*

Bad Aussee ㉓

Road map D4. *5,000.*
(03622) 54040.

Bad Aussee, the main town in the Styrian part of the Salzkammergut, lies at the fork of the Traun river, which cuts a scenic gorge between the Dachstein massif and the Tote Gebirge (Dead Mountains). The region's original wealth was founded on its salt deposits. Later, Bad Aussee achieved renewed fame when, in 1827, Archduke Johann married Anna Plochl, daughter of the local postmaster. The Archduke, who made many important contributions to the life of Styria, was a grandson of Maria Theresa, the 13th child of future Emperor Leopold II.

The former seat of the Salt Office, in Chlumeckyplatz, is a lovely 14th-century building which now houses the city's regional museum with its exhibition on salt mining. The 13th-century, Romanesque St Paul's church has a notable stone statue of the Madonna.

Environs: A scenic road northwest of Bad Aussee will take you to **Altausseer See** and the Loser peak. On the road is an old salt mine, open to the public. During World War II it was reputedly used to hide works of art.

Admont ㉔

Road map E4. *2,800.*
(03613) 2164.

At the centre of the village of Admont stands a Benedictine Abbey whose importance once reached far beyond the region. Built in the 11th century and often rebuilt, it burned down in 1865, but the fire spared its priceless collection: with nearly 160,000 volumes, it is said to hold the world's largest monastic library. The present Rococo interior of the library was designed by Gotthard Heyberger in 1774, the work carried out by Josef Hueber. The large hall holding two-storey cabinets is 72 m (236 ft)

A picturesque street in Bad Aussee

For hotels and restaurants in this region see pp297–9 and pp327–9

Richly ornamented interior of Admont library

long. The ceiling frescoes by Bartolomeo Altomonte show vast allegorical scenes of the arts, the natural sciences and religion. The abbey's south wing has been converted into a museum showcasing both historic treasures and modern art.

Benedictine Abbey
Tel (03613) 23120.
Apr–Nov: 10am–5pm daily; Nov–Mar: by request.
www.stiftadmont.at

Environs: 5 km (3 miles) beyond Admont, high above the Enns river, stands the 15th-century pilgrimage church **Frauenberg**, rebuilt in the Baroque style. It has a beautiful altarpiece by Josef Stammel.

Hohentauern 25

Road map E4. *550.*
(03618) 335.

Hohentauern (1,274 m/ 4,180 ft) is the highest village in the Rottenmanner Tauern, surrounded by more than 20 peaks higher than 2,000 m (6,560 ft). This mountain range is part of the Niedere (Lower) Tauern, which extend also to Salzburger Land. Other ranges in the Niedere Tauern include Radstätter *(see p228)*, Schladminger *(see pp178–9)* and Wölzer Tauern.

Hohentauern was founded by the Celts. From the 12th century it became important as a commercial centre along Hohentauernpass, the mountain pass connecting the Enns and Mur valleys. St. Bartolomäus Church has magnificent carvings by Josef Stammel.

The Hohentauernpass crosses the range at 1,260 m (4,134 ft) height. A drive along Hohentauern-passstrasse is one of the best ways to enjoy the superb mountain scenery. From the north, you pass through **Rottenmann** with its old city walls; **Möderbrugg**, a former centre of the metal industry; **Oberzeiring** and its disused salt mine; and **Halfelden**, with its large ruined castle. Nearby is the ruined **Schloss Reifenstein**.

Eisenerzer Alpen 26

Road map E4.
(03848) 3700.

You can reach the Eisenerzer Alpen (iron ore alps) by following the steep, narrow valley of the Enns river. This gorge, called Gesäuse, begins a short distance from Admont, near Hieflau. The entrance to the gorge presents great views of the river and the Hochtor massif, rising 2,369 m (7,772 ft) above. The surrounding area is used as a training ground for advanced mountaineering and as a base for expeditions to the neighbouring peaks. Easily the most famous mountain in the Eisenerzer Alpen is **Erzberg**, which has has been exploited for its large iron ore deposits since ancient times. It looks like a stepped pyramid, the red pigment contrasting with the green forests and meadows.

The area around Erzberg is the largest iron ore basin in this part of Europe. In the summer, visitors can explore one of the mines. **Eisenerz**, an old mining town at the foot of Erzberg, has a mining museum where visitors can take an underground "adventure trip" with Hauly, a vast truck. The village also has a lovely old town and the fine fortified 16th-century church of St Oswald.

Stadtmuseum
Eisenerz, Schulstrasse 1. ***Tel*** *(03848) 251166. May–Oct: 9am–noon, 2–5pm Mon–Sat. Sun.*

The shimmering Erzberg – the red iron-ore mountain in the Eisenerzer Alpen

Salzatal Tour ㉙

The small Salza river, a tributary of the upper Enns, cuts its way across the eastern end of the High Limestone Alps. A journey along the Salza Valley is an expedition through a thinly populated area of entrancing beauty. The trail leads along the foothills of the Hochschwab massif, beside wild mountain streams, small barrier lakes and through dense woodlands. The river flows through virgin mountain terrains and its waters are so crystal clear that you can see every detail reflected in its stream.

Prescenyklause ③
Beyond a rock gate is an old dam that once held back the waters of the Salza river so rafts could carry timber to the valleys.

Brunnsee ②
Beyond the village of Wildalpen, a magnificent view opens onto the valley and the lake at the very heart of the Hochschwab massif. The northern slopes of the mountains present themselves in their full glory.

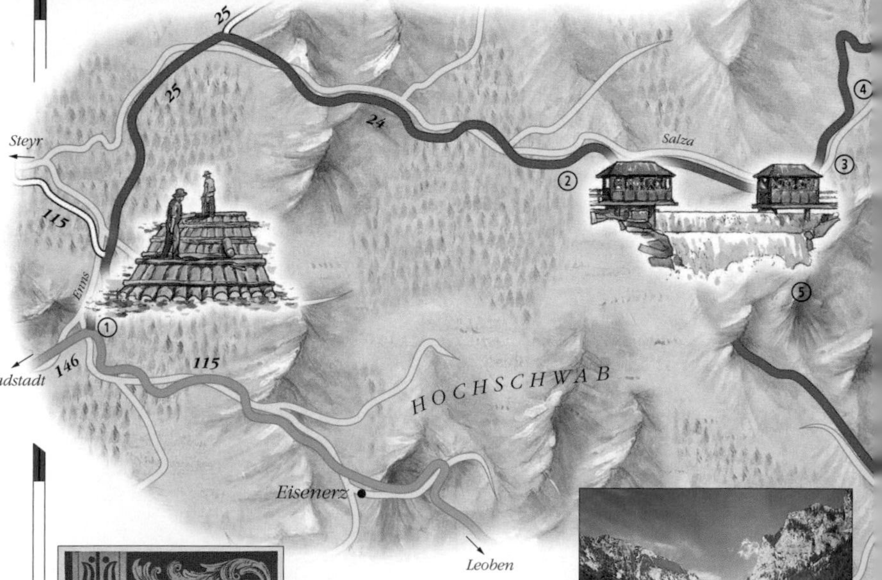

0 km 5

0 miles 5

Hieflau ①
This former centre of the metal industry is hidden amid dense forests. The local village museum displays objects associated with the region's history.

KEY

- Suggested route
- Scenic road
- Other road
- River, lake

Hochschwab ⑤
The highest summit in this vast mountain range is the 2,277-m (7,470-ft) high Hochschwab, the destination of both summer and winter excursions.

TIPS FOR DRIVERS

Length of route: *100 km (60 miles).*
Stopping places: *the only overnight accommodation is available at Weichselboden.*
Suggestions: *a visit to the Köhlerzentrum (Charcoal centre)* ***Tel*** *(03634) 505. May–Oct: 10am–noon, 3–5pm daily.*

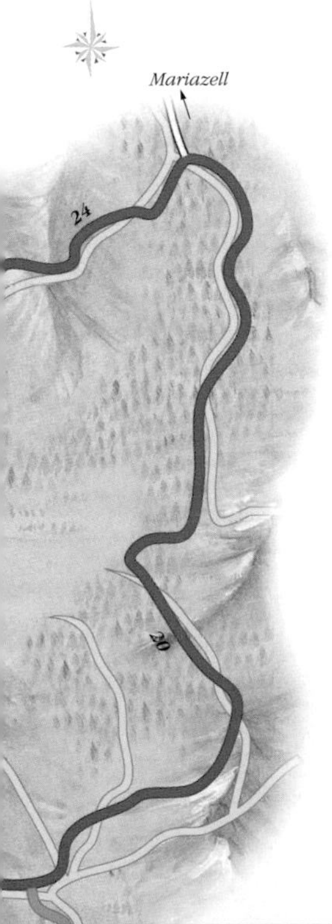

Weichselboden ④
It is worth stopping off in this small village, one of very few along this route, to visit its lime-tree–shaded church. A very small old hotel invites visitors to stay.

The main nave of the abbey church in Seckau Abbey

Seckau ㉗

Road map E4. *1,400.* *(03514) 5234-0.*

The small town of Seckau, established in the 13th century, has some interesting houses and the late-Gothic chapel of St Lucia in the town square. But the main claim to fame lies with **Seckau Abbey**, originally Augustinian and taken over by the Benedictines in the 19th century. Its present shape, dating from the 17th century, is the work of P.F. Carloni, but the abbey's basilica of the Assumption of the Virgin Mary has maintained its original late-Gothic character. Among its treasures is the Crucifixion group in the presbytery, highly expressive figures from the 12th and 13th centuries. The lion figures in the portal and the Madonna and Child in the church vestibule are Romanesque or early Gothic, and on the south wall, 13th-century frescoes were discovered.

Leoben ㉘

Road map F4. *29,000.* *Hauptplatz 12 (03842) 40620.* **www**.leoben.at

Leoben, Styria's second largest town, is an industrial and academic centre. Beautiful mansion houses line Hauptplatz (main square), and the adjacent streets bear witness to the town's early wealth derived from the local iron deposits. There is a lovely old town hall with coats of arms, and the Hacklhaus has a glittering red façade.

Also worth seeing in the old town is the **Pfarrkirche St. Xaver**, the church of St. Xaver, built in the 17th century by the Jesuits, with its beautiful Baroque main altar and a Romanesque crucifix on the south wall. On the other side of the bridge across the Mur river stands the Gothic church of **Maria am Waasen**, with original stained-glass windows in the presbytery. On the southern outskirts, in the district of Göss, stands Styria's first Benedictine **Abbey**, built around 1000 by Archbishop Aribo. It is mainly 16th-century with some earlier elements. The church's main nave is a monument to Styria's late-Gothic architecture. Other original features include 14th-century frescoes in the presbytery and an 11th-century, early-Romanesque crypt.

Austria's most famous brewery, Gösser, a short way from the abbey, is also open to the public. In the city centre, at No. 6 Kirchgasse, is a museum of fine arts.

The elegant Baroque façade of the Hacklhaus in Leoben

Mariazell 30

Virgin and child

The earliest records of the church devoted to the Birth of the Virgin Mary date from 1266, but it is believed to have been established in 1157 and its 850th anniversary was celebrated in 2007. Mariazell is the main pilgrimage centre for the Roman Catholic population in this part of Europe. Pilgrims arrive all year, but highpoints are Assumption (15 Aug) and the Birth of the Virgin (8 Sep). Mariazell became famous in the 14th century, when King Louis of Hungary founded Gnadenkapelle (chapel of mercy) to thank for victory over the Turks.

View of the Church
In the 17th century, the church was extended to accommodate the growing number of pilgrims, and the central tower was supplemented by two Baroque side towers.

Church Interior
The basilica was originally a Gothic hall church, which is still apparent despite the Baroque-style alterations carried out in the late 17th century by Domenico Sciassi.

STAR FEATURES

- ★ Gnadenkapelle
- ★ Main Altar
- ★ Treasury

★ Treasury
The treasury is home to various precious objects, including liturgical vessels, a wooden statuette of the Madonna and Child and an ivory relief – both from the 14th century.

Madonna and Child
Magna Mater Austriae – *the Great Mother of Austria, a late-Romanesque statue of the Madonna and Child – is the main object of veneration by pilgrims to Mariazell.*

VISITORS' CHECKLIST

Road map F4. *1,750.* *Hauptplatz 13.* **Tel** *(03882) 2366.* **Basilica** *Kardinal-Tisserant-Platz 1.* **Tel** *(03882) 2595.* *7am–8pm daily.* **Treasury** *May–Oct, 11am–3pm Tue–Sat, 11am–3pm Sun & hols.* **www**.basilika-mariazell.at

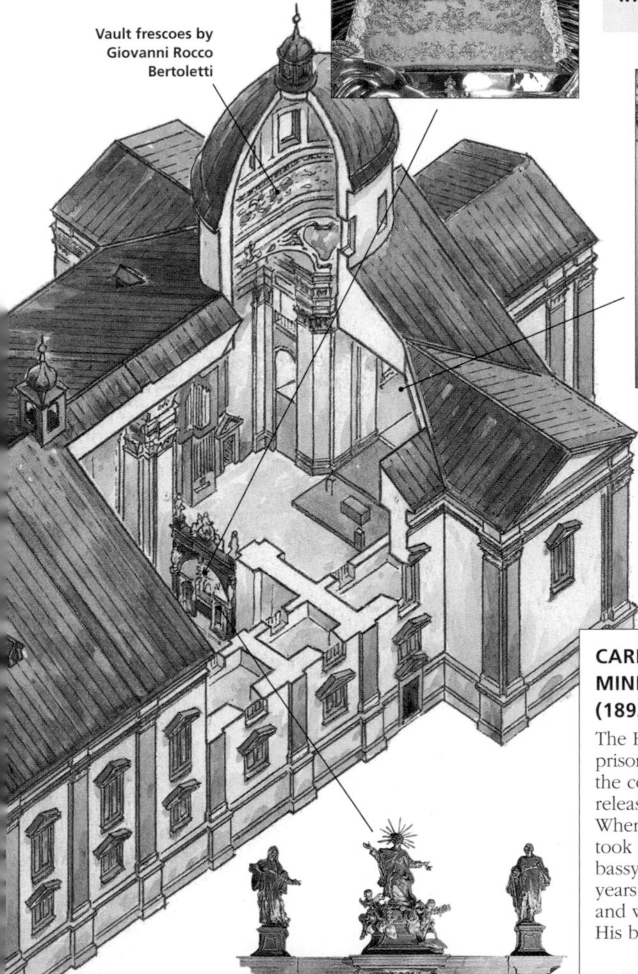

★ Main Altar
The monumental altar showing the Crucifixion is the work of Johann Bernhard Fischer von Erlach. The silver figures on the altar were created by Lorenzo Mattielli.

★ Gnadenkapelle
The chapel, with a statue of the Virgin Mary, was probably founded by King Louis of Hungary and was decorated in Baroque style by Fischer von Erlach the Younger and Lorenzo Mattielli.

CARDINAL JOSEPH MINDSZENTY (1892–1975)

The Hungarian Primate, imprisoned for his opposition to the communist regime, was released in the 1956 uprising. When this was crushed, he took refuge in the US Embassy in Budapest for 15 years. He later lived in Austria and was buried in Mariazell. His body is now in Hungary.

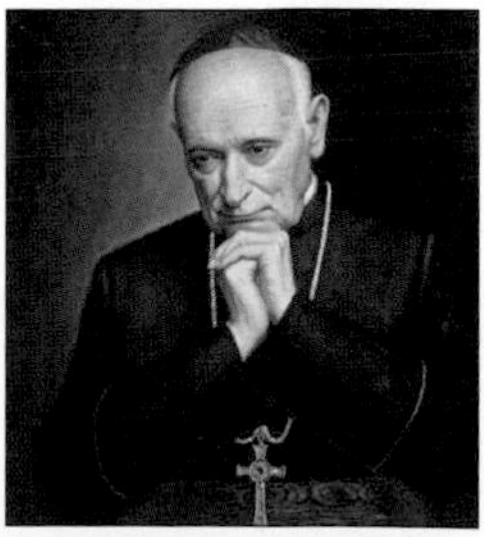

UPPER AUSTRIA

Upper Austria, so called because of its location in the upper reaches of the Austrian Danube, occupies an area of about 12,000 sq km (4,600 sq miles) and has 1.4 million inhabitants. Its borders are marked by the rivers Enns to the east and Inn to the west. To the north, the Czech Republic is its neighbour, to the south there are Styria and the Salzburger Land, to the west is Germany.

Upper Austria is, after Vienna, the most industrialized Austrian province and has remained the richest area of the country since the time when Austria was part of the Roman province of Noricum. In later years, Upper Austria joined Bavaria. Then, under Babenberg rule in the 13th century, it became the cradle of the great future empire, in conjunction with neighbouring Lower Austria.

Historically, the province of Upper Austria is divided into five districts: Mühlviertel, which stretches south to the Danube and occupies the Czech Massif, with Freistadt its largest town; the westernmost district of Innviertel, which lies in the foothills of the Alps, and includes the towns of Ried and Braunau; the Hausruckviertel is named after the Hausruck Massif and Vöcklabruck is its largest town; Traunviertel, which includes the Salzkammergut, one of the most picturesque and popular natural areas in Austria. The Danube Valley is generally considered to be a separate region, with scores of small towns, lofty fortresses and magnificent abbeys, including the most glorious of them all, St. Florian, a jewel of Austrian Baroque architecture.

The province's capital, Linz, is Austria's third largest city, comprising an important industrial centre, the largest Austrian Danube port, and a major transport hub. It is beautifully situated in an extensive valley, surrounded by gently rolling hills, and has a charming old town district.

View from the Krippenstein peak across to the imposing Dachstein massif

◁ **Houses rising up from the banks of the glorious deep blue Hallstätter See**

Exploring Upper Austria

Upper Austria is an exceptionally diverse province, with something to interest everyone. Linz, the capital city, has both the oldest church in Austria and a state-of-the-art virtual technology museum. On the banks of the rivers Danube and Enns rise the magnificent abbeys in Kremsmünster, Steyr and St. Florian. The caves in the Dachstein range are fascinating natural monuments. However, Upper Austria's greatest attraction are its glorious lakes set amid limestone peaks in the beautiful Salzkammergut. The mild climate and therapeutic facilities attract visitors to small resorts, and Bad Ischl was once the summer home of the Emperor.

Steyr's trademark – the Gothic Brummerlhaus with its steeply pitched roof

SIGHTS AT A GLANCE

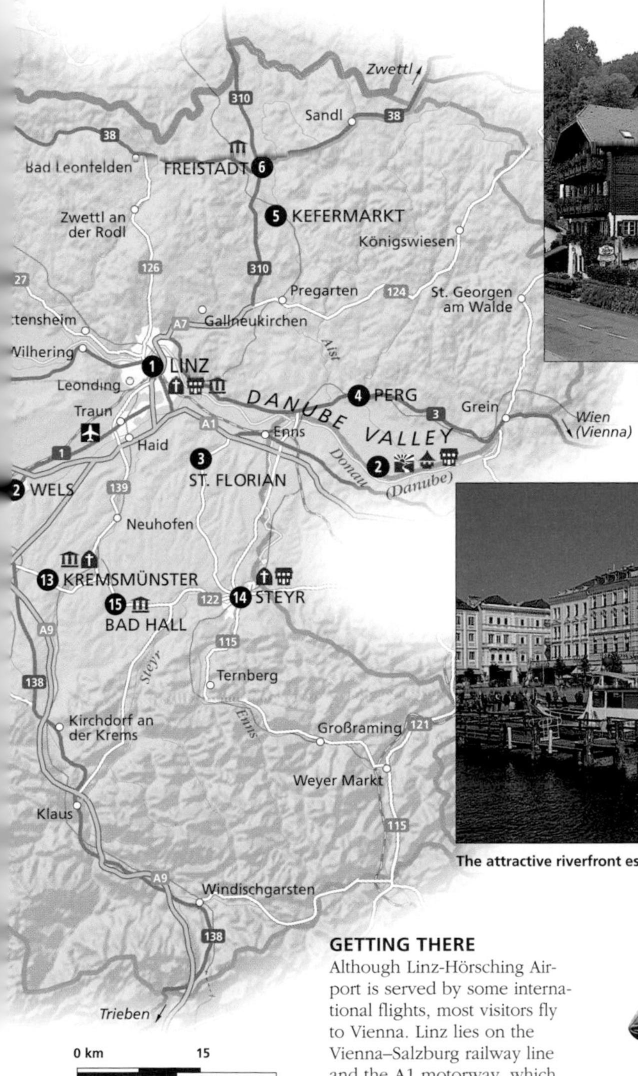

Houses with flower-decked balconies in St. Wolfgang

The attractive riverfront esplanade in Gmunden

KEY

- Motorway
- Major road
- Minor road
- Scenic route
- Main railway
- Minor railway
- International border
- Province border

GETTING THERE

Although Linz-Hörsching Airport is served by some international flights, most visitors fly to Vienna. Linz lies on the Vienna–Salzburg railway line and the A1 motorway, which traverses the province, east to west, and also connects with the southern A9 motorway. There is a dense network of roads and bus routes throughout. From spring until autumn, boats on the Danube River connect Passau with Linz and Linz with the Wachau Valley.

SEE ALSO

- ***Where to Stay*** pp299–301
- ***Where to Eat*** pp330–31

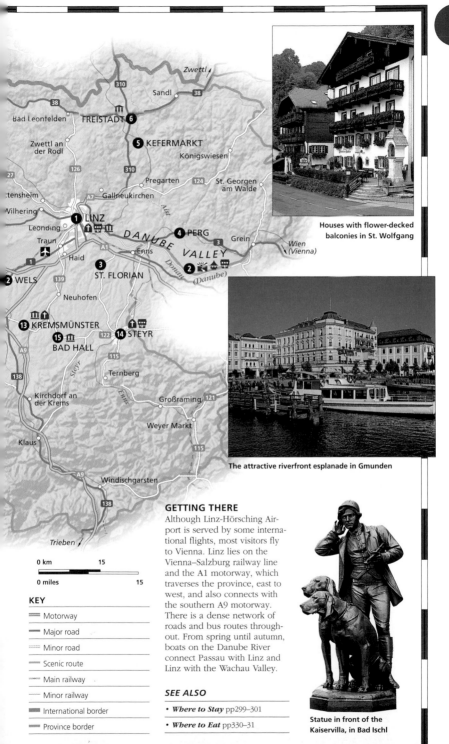

Statue in front of the Kaiservilla, in Bad Ischl

Linz ❶

Straddling the Danube in a scenic spot, Linz owes its former importance and wealth to its location at an intersection of waterways – salt and iron ore were transported along the rivers Traun and Enns, and further along raw materials and finished products travelled down the Danube to Vienna or Passau. This strategic position led the Romans to found a substantial settlement called Lentia on the site. Since the 15th century, Linz has been the capital of Upper Austria. A major industrial centre, it is also a hub of culture with numerous galleries, museums, and the futurist Ars Electronica Center. The composer Anton Bruckner was also associated with Linz in his early career.

A birds-eye view of the town on the banks of the Danube

Exploring Linz

The town sprawls across both banks of the Danube, with the historic old town on the right (south) bank, in the bend of the river. The vast Hauptplatz is regarded as one of Austria's most beautiful architectural complexes. It is also worth taking a trip to a nearby hill, the Pöstlingberg, from where there are splendid views over the town and river. The Ars Electronica Center is situated on the left (north) bank of the Danube.

Martinskirche

Römerstrasse/Martinsgasse.
Tel *(0732) 777454.*

A modest façade hides Austria's oldest surviving church, dedicated to St Martin. It was first mentioned in the 8th century, during the times of Charlemagne, as part of the Carolingians' former royal residence. The Gothic windows and portals date from the 8th century. There was an older Roman wall on the same site, and ten Roman tombstones, together with other ancient stones, were used as building material to erect the church. The interior also dates from the Carolingian period, the only later addition being the Neo-Gothic presbytery. The rainbow arch that separates the nave from the presbytery and the north wall of the church are adorned with 15th-century frescoes of the Virgin Mary on a throne. Much of the interior can only be seen with a guide.

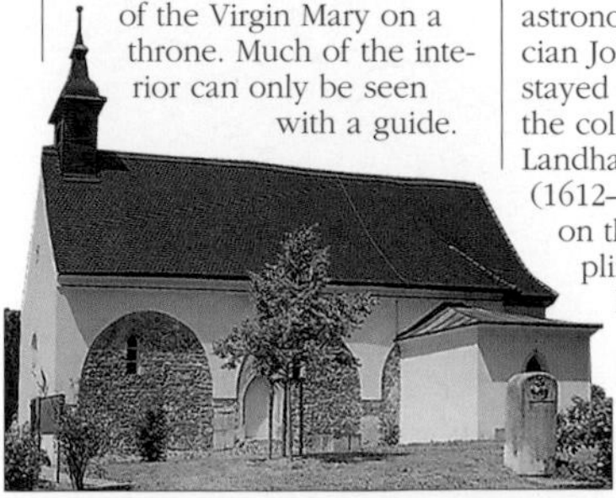

The tiny Martinskirche, Austria's oldest church

Linzer Schloss

Schlossberg 1. ***Tel*** *(0732) 774419.*
9am–6pm Tue–Fri, 10am–5pm Sat, Sun, public holidays.

In the 15th century, Emperor Friedrich III built his residence on the Römerberg (Roman Mountain), on the foundations of an earlier structure. The castle acquired its present shape between 1600 and 1607, during the times of Rudolf II, and since that time its distinctive silhouette has become one of the most famous sights in Linz. Since 1966, this former imperial residence has housed a museum, a branch of the Oberösterreichisches Landesmuseum. Exhibits include paintings and sculptures from early medieval times to the 19th century and the Secession, 12th–18th-century arms, 16th–19th-century musical instruments, furniture and handicrafts, golden, ceramic and glass objects, and a permanent archaeological exhibition. Part of the museum is devoted to folk traditions; there's a reconstructed physics laboratory from the Jesuit school in Linz and the Schloss Weinberg pharmacy (c.1700). From the castle, there are superb views over Linz.

Landhaus

Klosterstrasse 7.
Tel *(0732) 7720-11130.*

The regional government is based in a Renaissance palace built on the site of a former Minorite monastery. Its north portal, from Klosterstrasse, is a beautiful marble work by Renaissance artists. The inner courtyard is surrounded by a colonnade. Here you will find Planetenbrunnen (Fountain of the Planets), built to commemorate the outstanding astronomer and mathematician Johannes Kepler who stayed in Linz and lectured at the college, then based in the Landhaus, for 14 years (1612–26). The seven figures on the fountain's bronze plinth show the planets known at the time.

Close by is the Minoritenkirche, a former Minorite Church, the earliest documented record of which is in the

The Planet Fountain in the inner courtyard of the Landhaus

town chronicles of 1288. Altered in the Baroque style in 1751–8, the church has an unusual façade with oval telescopes between the storeys. The lovely Rococo interior is decorated with charming stuccowork and paintings by Martin Johann Schmidt and Bartolomeo Altomonte.

Hauptplatz

Hauptplatz, in Linz's Old Town, is one of Austria's finest squares and considered to be one of the foremost achievements of town planning. It is 220 m (720 ft) long and 60 m (200 ft) wide, and overall it creates a much stronger impression than its component parts would suggest, although many of its buildings are worth a closer look. The Gothic Altes Rathaus (Old Town Hall) at No. 1 was built around 1513, and still has the original octagonal tower with an astronomical clock. In the 17th century, the town hall was given a new façade supported by columns. Other interesting buildings are the Gothic and Baroque houses, including Feichtingerhaus, a former mail inn (No. 21), a Gothic building with an early-Baroque façade. The Plague Column (1723) in the centre of the square was funded jointly by the local council and all citizens, in thanksgiving for sparing Linz and the Linzers from three deadly disasters: war, fire and the Black Death plague.

VISITORS' CHECKLIST

Road map E3. *186,000.* *Hauptplatz 1 (0732) 7070-2009.* **www**.linz.at *Pflasterspektakel (end Jul); Brucknerfest (Sep); Ars electronica (Sept)*

Hauptplatz with its Baroque Plague Column

LINZ CITY CENTRE

Alter Dom ⑤
Ars Electronica Center ⑪
Hauptplatz ④
Landesmuseum ⑦
Landhaus ③
Martinskirche ①
Neuer Dom ⑩
Schloss ②
Seminarkirche ⑨
Stadtmuseum Nordico ⑧
Stadtpfarrkirche ⑥

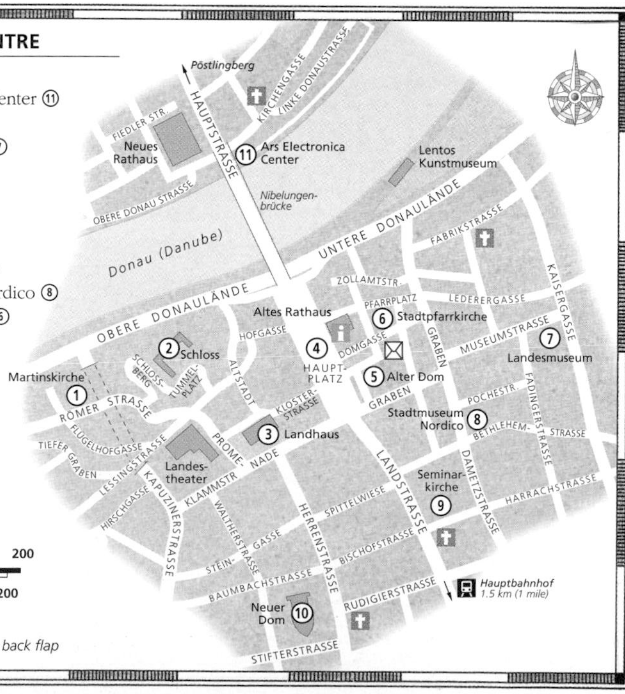

0 m 200
0 yards 200

Key to Symbols *see back flap*

The towers of Alter Dom in Domgasse

Alter Dom

Domgasse 3. ***Tel*** *(0732) 770866-0.* *7am–noon, 3–7pm daily.*

Thanks to reforms, the capital of the archbishopric of Upper Austria was established at Linz, and in 1785 the former Jesuit church was chosen as the cathedral. Ignatiuskirche, the church of St Ignatius, was built in the second half of the 17th century to designs by Pietro Francesco Carlone, and today its green façade and onion-dome–topped twin towers are distinctive features in the town panorama. The simple, modest elevation of the church conceals a beguiling Baroque interior. The wide main nave has three side chapels on each side. Particularly fascinating are the beautifully engraved stalls in the presbytery, where local artists carved the figures of dwarfs and monsters peeping out from behind the backrests and armrests.

From 1856 until 1868 the composer Anton Bruckner was the cathedral's organist. The present organ, by the famous master Krismann, was altered according to Bruckner's own instructions.

Stadtpfarrkirche

Pfarrplatz 4. ***Tel*** *(0732) 776120–0.*

The parish church of the Assumption of the Virgin Mary (Mariä Himmelfahrt) was built in the 13th century as a triple-nave basilica with Gothic presbytery, and altered in the 17th century, when it received a new interior and further chapels. The presbytery includes the tombstone of Emperor Friedrich III, who resided in Linz for a while. The urn containing his heart is concealed behind a marble slab in the church wall to the right of the altar. In the eastern end of the south nave is the chapel of St John of Nepomuk. Its lovely Baroque interior is decorated with frescoes and an altar by Bartolomeo Altomonte. St John of Nepomuk was one of the most revered saints in the Austrian empire. Many towns erected statues to him, and the Stadtpfarrkirche in Linz houses two of these. In the external chapel by the presbytery is a figure, probably created by Georg Raphael Donner. The chapel's architecture and dome shape are the work of another Austrian master of the Baroque, Johann Lukas von Hildebrandt.

Landesmuseum

Museumstrasse 14. ***Tel*** *(0732) 774482-0.* *9am–6pm Tue–Fri, 10am–5pm Sat, Sun & hols.*

The Landesmuseum building is reminiscent of the Viennese houses along Ringstrasse, which is hardly surprising since they were built at the same time and designed in the same spirit of historicism. The museum's architect was a German from Düsseldorf, Bruno Schmitz. The museum was named Francisco-Carolinum Museum in honour of Archduke Francis Karl. Originally it was meant to house the collection of the Museum Society of Upper Austria, established in 1833 by Anton Ritter von Spaun. Today, the museum shows mainly modern Austrian art, with a particular emphasis on artists from Upper Austria. It also holds a collection of works by the renowned Bohemian illustrator, Alfred Kubin, and presents exhibitions of its natural history treasures or relating to the province's past.

Illumination in a Psalter, Landesmuseum

Stadtmuseum Nordico

Dametzstrasse 23. ***Tel*** *(0732) 7070-1900.* *10am–6pm Tue–Sun, (to 9pm Thu).* **www**.nordico.at

In 1675, this 17th-century Baroque complex was the home of the college known as "Nordisches Stift", which had as its aim the education of young boys from nordic countries – hence the name – and their transformation into good Catholics. Today, this imposing building, now owned by the council, houses the Nordico Town Museum, with its collection of objects relating to the history of Linz from ancient times onwards, including a model of the town from 1740. The top floor is given over to temporary exhibitions, mainly of Modern art.

Seminarkirche

Harrachstrasse 7. ***Tel*** *(0732) 771205.* *7am–5pm daily.*

The former Deutschordenkirche (church of the Teutonic Order) is now a seminary church. Artistically, this is the most valuable historic church building in Linz. It was built in the early 18th century, to a design by Johann Lukas Hildebrandt. Its beautiful Baroque façade is topped with the decorative coats of arms of the Harrach family. The tower, crowned with a distinctive flattened dome, is surrounded by sandstone statues

For hotels and restaurants in this region see pp299–301 and pp330–31

The impressive Neuer Dom, Austria's largest cathedral

depicting the virtues expected of a Knight of the Order. The interior is in the shape of an ellipse and is covered with an oval dome. The Crucifixion in the main altar is the work of Martin Altomonte. To the right of the entrance stands a statue of St John of Nepomuk, facing which is a painting of the death of St Joseph. The beautiful ceiling relief shows God the Father reigning among a host of angels on a sky adorned with filigree leaf ornaments.

Neuer Dom

*Herrenstrasse 26. **Tel** (0732) 946100. 7:30am–7pm Mon–Sat, 8am–7pm Sun.*

Construction of the New Cathedral started in 1862, but it was not completed until 1924. Its architect was Vinzenz Statz, the builder of Cologne cathedral. The Neo-Gothic Neuer Dom is Austria's largest sacred structure, with a capacity of 20,000 faithful. It is said that only one condition was stipulated by the local council, and that was that the steeple must not be taller than that of the Stephansdom in Vienna *(see p59)*. Statz complied with the request and the tower in Linz is 134 m (440 ft) high – 3 m (10 ft) lower than its counterpart. The interior was designed by Josef Gasser. The most interesting feature of the cathedral are its modern, colourful stained-glass windows, which depict often complex scenes, such as the history of the city.

Sebastian, mascot of Pöstlingberg's train

Ars Electronica Center

*Hauptstrasse 2. **Tel** (0732) 7272-0. 9am–5pm Tue, Wed, Fri, 9am–9pm Thu, 10am–6pm Sat & Sun.* **www**.aec.at

At the entrance to the Nibelungenbrücke (Bridge of the Nibelungs), on the north bank of the Danube, stands one of Austria's most unusual museums, or rather exhibition centres. The Ars Electronica Center is a highly original museum of virtual worlds, created with the help of modern computer technology. It demonstrates the latest computer wizardry and virtual-reality simulations of space and time travel. Visitors can, for example, journey inside various parts of the universe, visit imaginary Renaissance towns or see a flying saucer disappear into space. There is also a 3D virtual space in the basement where you can explore other worlds with special headsets.

Lentos Kunstmuseum

Ernst-Koref-Promenade 11. ***Tel** (070) 70703614. 10am–6pm Tue–Sun (to 9pm Thu). 1 Jan, 24–25 Dec.* **www**.lentos.at

This brand-new museum on the south bank of the Danube houses a major collection of paintings, sculptures and prints, concentrating on international and Austrian art from the early 20th century to the present day, featuring Expressionism (Kokoschka, Klimt), Op and Pop Art (Warhol), Pluralism and Austrian photography.

Pöstlingberg

A short distance from the centre of Linz, on the extensive plateau of Urfahr on the north bank of the Danube, rises the 537-m (1,762-ft) Pöstlingberg. The electric mountain train, built in 1898, that climbs almost to the top, was once acclaimed as a wonder of technology. The route is 2.9 km (2 miles) long, and the incline reaches a staggering 10.6 per cent.

On the mountain's summit stands the Wallfahrtskirche zu den Sieben Schmerzen Mariens, the pilgrimage church of Our Lady of Seven Sorrows, which is regarded as one of the main symbols of Linz.

Pilgrimage church built between 1738–47 on Pöstlingberg

The Danube Valley ❷

The beautiful blue Danube, extolled by writers and composers, is an extraordinary river. It passes through eight countries, and four capital cities have been built on its banks. The Danube enters Austria as a mountain river right after Passau at Achleiten and leaves 360 km (240 miles) further along, beyond the Hainburg marshes, heading for Bratislava. In Upper Austria, many magnificent towns have been built along its routes; historically, scores of fortresses, abbeys and churches arose on its steep banks (Clam, Melk). The majestic river is an important transport route, and to visitors it offers an excellent network of bicycle routes, with special hotels for cyclists alongside.

Burg Clam
The romantic silhouette of Clam Castle rising above a deep ravine has remained virtually unchanged since the 12th century.

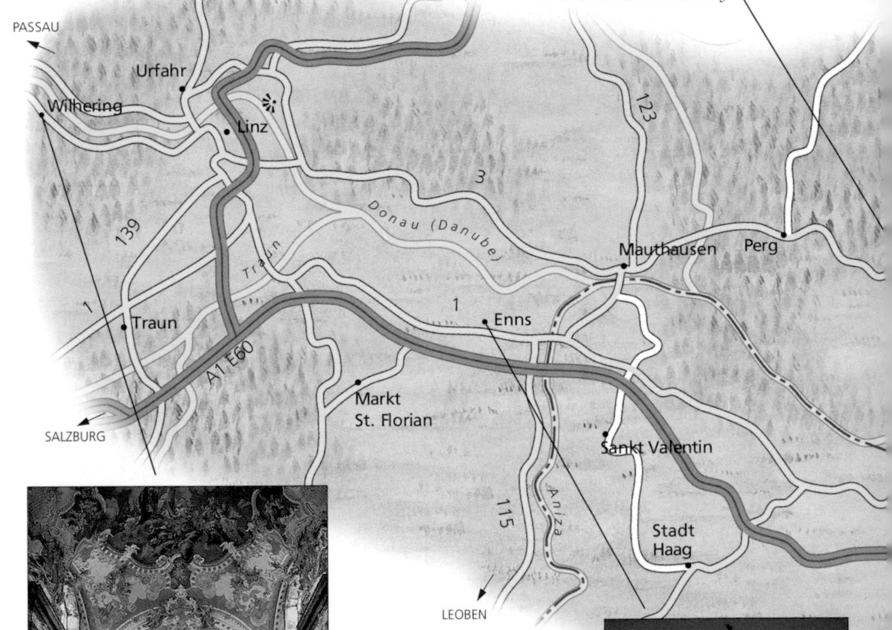

★ Wilhering
The collegiate church of the 12th-century Cistercian Abbey in Wilhering has a beautiful Rococo interior with frescoes by Bartolomeo Altomonte.

★ Enns
The Renaissance municipal tower of Enns was built in 1565–8. It stands on Hauptplatz, on the left bank of the Enns River, just before it joins the Danube.

STAR SIGHTS

★ Enns

★ Wilhering

For hotels and restaurants in this region see pp299–301 and pp330–31

Grein
In the town hall is an original Rococo theatre, but Grein's most popular sight is its late-Gothic castle, extended in the 17th century.

VISITORS' CHECKLIST

Road map E3.
Lindengasse 9, 4040 Linz. (0732) 7277 800. For full details of hotels, restaurants and cycling tours. **www**.danube.at

St. Nikola an der Donau
The Danube ends its journey through Upper Austria near St. Nikola, an area of outstanding natural beauty.

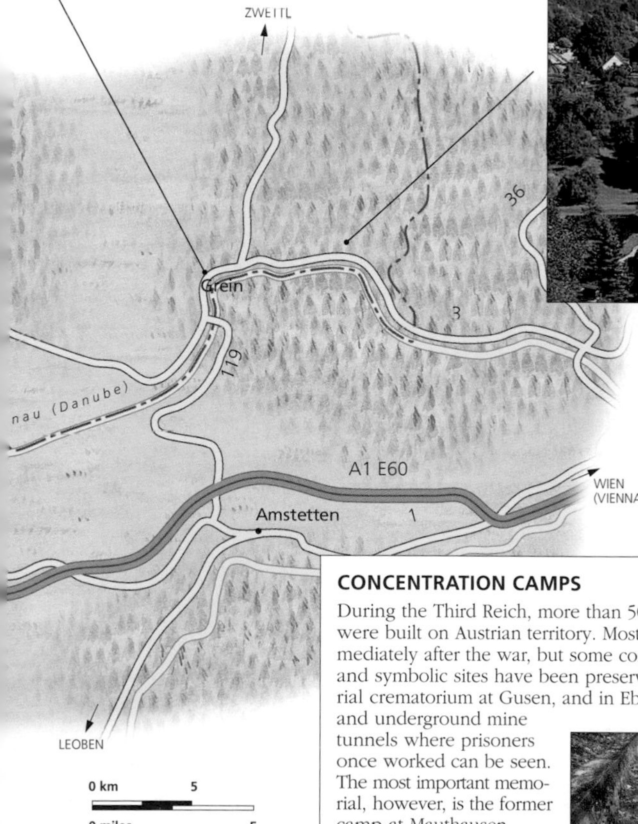

KEY

Motorway
Major road
Minor road
River
Bundesland (province) border
Viewpoint

CONCENTRATION CAMPS

During the Third Reich, more than 50 concentration camps were built on Austrian territory. Most were destroyed immediately after the war, but some commemorative plaques and symbolic sites have been preserved: there is a memorial crematorium at Gusen, and in Ebensee the cemetery and underground mine tunnels where prisoners once worked can be seen. The most important memorial, however, is the former camp at Mauthausen, where the quarry, original buildings and the "ash dump" have been preserved. Just outside the camp is a visitors' centre and musuem operated by the Austrian Government. Each year the liberation is celebrated on the Sunday nearest 8 May.

Mauthausen Todesstiege (Stairway of Death) between quarry and camp

One of the magnificent emperor's rooms in St. Florian Abbey

St. Florian ❸

Road map E3. *3,000.* *(07224) 5690.* **Stift:** *Guided tours: 11am, 1, 3pm.* **Bruckner organ:** *11 May–12 Oct: 2:30pm Wed-Fri, Sun, Mon.*

Florian, the prefect of the Roman Noricum Province, converted to Christianity and was tortured and thrown into the Enns river as a result in 304. His body was retrieved and, in the 11th century, a magnificent abbey and a church were built on the site of his burial place by Augustinian monks; they remain the keepers of St. Florian to this day. The present appearance of the abbey and church is the work of two outstanding Baroque architects: Carlo Carlone and Jakob Prandtauer.

St. Florian is an impressive complex of buildings, with monks' quarters, reception rooms and a church with an adjoining chapel of the Virgin Mary. The main feature in the large courtyard is the Adlerbrunnen (Eagle Well), built in 1603. The east wing houses the library with its vast collection of over 140,000 volumes, incunabula and manuscripts. The ceiling painting by Altomonte shows the marriage of Virtue with Knowledge. Next to the library is the Marble Hall with its vast columns, designed by Jakob Prandtauer. The grand staircase in the west wing, also by Prandtauer, leads to the emperor's apartments where important guests stayed. Adjacent is the room of Anton Bruckner, who was associated with St. Florian for many years.

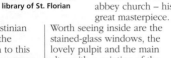

Alter Codex **from the library of St. Florian**

Carlo Carlone remodelled the abbey church – his great masterpiece. Worth seeing inside are the stained-glass windows, the lovely pulpit and the main altar with a painting of the Assumption of the Virgin Mary flanked by columns of pink Salzburg marble. The abbey also has an art gallery.

Perg ❹

Road map E3. *7,000.* *(07262) 53150.*

Perg, a small town with a long history situated 30 km (19 miles) east of Linz, was once owned by the mighty von Perg family, whose last member died in the 12th century, during the Third Crusade. Until the 19th century Perg was the largest centre of millstone production; it is also the home of Manner, the largest manufacturer of sweet wafers in the world. Worth seeing today are some attractive houses on Herrengasse, a 1683 Baroque pillory in the main square and St Jacob's church (1416), which has retained its Gothic interior.

In Perg's environs, graves and numerous remains of the Hallstatt civilization have been unearthed. The Heimathaus at No. 1 Stifterstrasse exhibits finds from that period. It also documents the production of millstones and has an interesting collection of 16th–17th-century ceramics, decorated using a special local technique.

Kefermarkt ❺

Road map E3. *2,200.* *(07947) 75700.*

The main attraction in this little town is its 15th-century Wallfahrtskirche (pilgrimage church), built by Christoph von Zelking, the master of Kefermarkt's castle, Schloss Weinberg. He also commissioned its altar dedicated to his favourite saint, St Wolfgang (died 994), Bishop of Regensburg and Henry II's tutor. We do not know who created the altar, but the result is a masterpiece of medieval art. Entirely carved from limewood, it was probably once painted, but now the original texture and colour of the wood are revealed. Its centre is made up of the figures of Saints Peter, Wolfgang and Christopher. On the wings of the altar the unknown artist has placed scenes of the Annunciation, the Birth of Christ, the Adoration of the Magi and the Death of Mary. The altar was once riddled with woodworm and only narrowly escaped total destruction. It was carefully restored in 1852–5, under the supervision of Adalbert Stifter, a writer and school inspector for Upper Austria.

For hotels and restaurants in this region see pp299–301 and pp330–31

It is to his dedication and appreciation of great art that we owe the altar's survival. There is also an interesting permanent exhibition in the church called "Jesus on the road".

A statue on the splendid wooden altar in Kefermarkt church

Freistadt ❻

Road map E3. 7,400. (07942) 72506-0. **www**.freistadt.at

Freistadt, the largest town in the Mühlviertel region, was once the last border fortress on the route leading from the alpine countries to Bohemia. Much of the medieval **town wall** has survived to this day, including several bastions and two impressive gateways; one of these, the late-Gothic Linzer Tor, is the symbol of the town. The focal point of the old town centre, the rectangular Hauptplatz, is lined with historic houses. On its east side stands the town hall, with a carved fountain.

The 15th-century **Katharinenmünster**, the church of St Catherine, on the southwest side of the square, was altered in the Baroque style by Johann Michael Prunner. The altar paintings are the work of Carlo Carlone. The castle, not far from the main square, was built in 1397 for the widow of Prince Albert III. It was devastated by a fire in 1888 and subsequently turned into a military barracks. The building now houses the **Schlossmuseum**, a regional museum holding Austria's largest collection of glass paintings.

Schlossmuseum
Schlosshof 2.
Tel (07942)72274.
9am–noon, 2–5pm Mon–Fri, 2–5pm Sat, Sun, public holidays.

JAKOB PRANDTAUER (1660–1726)

Austria's outstanding architect of the Baroque, Prandtauer specialized in sacred buildings and shaped the present look of several medieval abbeys. His greatest masterpiece is generally agreed to be the Benedictine Abbey in Melk. He also created the church of the Carmelite nuns in St. Pölten, and gave a Baroque face to the Augustinian abbey in St. Florian and the Benedictine abbey in Kremsmünster. Distinctive features of his work are the variety of forms he used, and the vigorous way in which he blended architecture with the surrounding countryside.

Schärding ❼

Road map D3. 5,050. (07712) 4300. **www**.schaerding.at

This town on the banks of the Inn River was, until 1779, owned by the Bavarian family of Wittelsbach, whose influence can be seen in the local architecture. Schärding's most beautiful feature is its **Stadtplatz**, the central square cut in half by buildings. At the north end of the upper square, **Silberzeile** is a row of beautiful houses with gabled roofs. It is overshadowed by the vast Church of St George's with a grand steeple. Little apart from the gateway and moat remains of the old castle here. The gateway houses a regional museum with a late-Gothic Madonna, a beautiful crucifix and sculptures by Johann Peter Schwanthaler (1720–95).

Silberzeile, a row of pretty and colourful gabled houses in the Stadtplatz in Schärding

Baroque house façades in Obernberg

Obernberg am Inn ❽

Road map D3. *1,600.* *(07758) 22550.*

Until the late 18th century, Obernberg belonged to Bavaria and was ruled by the bishops of Passau. In 1779, it transferred to Austria. The old market town has preserved its lovely **Marktplatz**, the central town square, lined with pretty houses with exceptionally beautiful, richly ornamented stucco façades. Particularly interesting are the façades of the houses at Nos 37, 38 and 57, with decorations attributed to the prominent Bavarian artist, Johann Baptist Modler. A fountain in the centre of the square is surrounded by sculptures. When visiting the Annakapelle, the parish church of Obernberg, it is worth taking a closer look at the 16th-century wood-carving of the Holy Family.

A castle, once owned by the bishops of Passau, has stood in Obernberg since the 12th century, but little remains of it.

Environs: Near Obernberg, 15 km (9 miles) to the southwest, is the largest town of the province, **Ried im Innkreis**, an agricultural centre and the home town of the Schwanthaler family of sculptors. Many members of the family were outstanding artists, active in the region from 1632 to 1838. The local museum, at No. 13 Kirchenplatz, exhibits some of their works.

Figure from fountain in Obernberg town square

Braunau am Inn ❾

Road map D3. *16,500.* *Stadtplatz 12 (07722) 62644.*

Braunau is a substantial border town on the Inn River and one of the prettiest spots in the entire region. It was built by the Dukes of Lower Bavaria, who ruled it for a long time. Originally intended as a bridgehead in their battles with the East, the town remained one of the best-fortified towns in this part of Europe until the 17th century. In 1779 it passed to Austria, together with the rest of the province. The Baroque fortifications were dismantled by Napoleon, but some sections survived, including the remains of several medieval buildings.

The centre of this Gothic town is occupied by the unusually elongated **Stadtplatz**, surrounded by historic houses. At No. 18 Johann-Fischer-Gasse, built in 1385, an old bell-foundry has survived almost intact. Together with the former ducal castle at No. 10 Altstadt next door, it is now the home of the regional museum, showing art, handicrafts and traditions of the Inn region. The town's symbol is the stone tower of the **Stephanskirche** (parish church of St Stephen) which is nearly 100 m (330 ft) tall. Construction began in 1492, but the Baroque cupola dates from a later period. Inside the church is a lovely stone pulpit. The only surviving parts of the original altarpiece by Michael Zürn are figures of the Madonna with Child and Saints Stephen and Laurence. The altar itself dates from 1906; it is a Neo-Gothic copy of Michael Pacher's altar in St. Wolfgang *(see p205)*. Among the tombs outside the church is one of Hans Staininger, who is shown with a curly beard that reaches to his toes – and was said to have been the cause of his untimely death.

Braunau was also the birthplace of Adolf Hitler, who lived at No. 15 Salzburger Vorstadt until he was two.

The birthplace of Adolf Hitler in Braunau am Inn

Schmiding ❿

Road map D3. *Haiding.*

Upper Austria's largest zoo, covering an area of some 120,000 sq m (30 acres), is based at Schmiding, 7 km (4 miles) north of Wels. This modern zoo, with giraffes, monkeys, crocodiles, exotic birds and 1,500 other animal species, is famous for its walk-in aviary with birds of prey – the world's largest. A huge tropical house, an African savannah and Austria's biggest colony of flamingoes are further highlights of the zoo. Children love the 5-m (16-ft) high platform which

Flamingoes in the zoo at Schmiding

allows them to come face to face with the giraffes.

The park lies at the foot of a castle dating from 1405. After World War II the castle served as a military hospital; it has since been restored and converted into apartments.

Schmiding Zoo
Tel (07249) 46272. Mar–Nov: 9am–7pm daily.

Lambach ⓫

Road map D3. *3,500.* *(07245) 283550.*

Lambach, conveniently located on the left bank of the Traun River, grew rich in the Middle Ages thanks to the flourishing salt trade. Around 1040 Count Arnold II Wels-Lambach and his wife Regilinda transformed the family seat into a monastery. Their son, Bishop Adalberto, who was later canonized, invited Benedictine monks here in 1089. In the same year, the Lambach monks established a second monastery at Melk which, eventually, was to surpass the mother abbey in terms of status and beauty. The abbey church was mostly rebuilt in the 17th century; rebuilding of the abbey itself was completed 50 years later.

The Baroque interior of the church is very beautiful, but Lambach owes its fame primarily to the Romanesque frescoes, probably dating from the 11th century. Unique in Austria, they are considered to be one of Europe's most resplendent examples of Romanesque art. At their centre is the Madonna with Child, to the left the Adoration of the Magi, who present gifts to the Holy Infant. The south vault depicts Jerusalem and Herod's palace. The abbey treasury also holds the Romanesque chalice of Bishop Adalbert and precious monstrances and chasubles. Also on view are ceiling paintings by Martino Altomonte and Martin Johann Schmidt. The musical archives hold a copy of Mozart's *Lambacher Symphonie*, which the composer reputedly created while staying here. Lambach also has a beautifully preserved Rococo theatre.

Romanesque frescoes in Lambach Abbey

Wels ⓬

Road map E3. *56,700.* *Kaiser-Josef-Platz 22 (07242) 43495.* **www**.wels.at

The history of Wels dates back to Roman days, as testified by numerous excavations. Some of the objects discovered are on display in the former Minorites' Abbey, including the famous Wels Venus, a bronze statuette from the 1st–2nd century AD and the oldest early-Christian epitaph in Austria, from the first half of the 4th century.

Today Wels is a centre of agriculture and industry, and the venue of an annual agricultural fair of international importance. Many historic features have also been preserved. **Stadtplatz**, the main square in the old town, is entered through a Baroque gate, the **Ledererturm**. Many houses in Stadtplatz have attractive façades, such as the Rococo **Kremsmünstererhof** with its arcaded courtyard, which for 400 years belonged to Kremsmünster Abbey. Adjacent to it stands a water tower (1577) and a two-house complex forming the late-Baroque town hall. Also in Stadtplatz is the Stadtpfarrkirche, the parish church of St John the Evangelist, with an original Romanesque portal and magnificent 14th-century stained-glass windows in the presbytery. **Burg Wels**, the imperial palace first documented in 776, is now a lively cultural centre and home of the regional museum.

The galleried courtyard of Kremsmünsterhof in Stadtplatz, Wels

Kremsmünster 13

Road map E3. *6000.* *Rathausplatz 1 (07583) 7212.*

Perched high above the Krems river stands the 8th-century Benedictine Abbey of Kremsmünster, its present appearance dating mostly from the 17th century. The abbey was completed by Jakob Prandtauer, to designs by Carlo Carlone. Two of its most remarkable features are the 17th-century fish ponds, surrounded by columns, corridors and sculptural fountains, and the unusual **Sternwarte**, a 50-m (165-ft) high observation tower, which holds collections of palaeontology, physics, anthropology, astronomy and zoology. The **Stiftskirche** (abbey church) has rich stucco decorations and angel statues. The abbey museum comprises works by Austrian and Dutch masters from the Baroque and Renaissance periods, wood carvings and gold objects. The pride of Kremsmünster are its earliest exhibits; these include the gilded-copper chalice and candelabras of Duke Tassilo, the legendary founder of the abbey, and the *Codex millenarius* (c.800), an illuminated gospel manuscript.

The Tassilo Chalice in Kremsmünster

Kremsmünster
Tel *(07583) 5275-0.* **www**.stift-kremsmuenster.at *Jan–Apr & Nov–Dec: guided tours 11am, 2, 3:30pm daily; May–Oct: 10, 11am, 2, 3, 4pm Mon–Fri, 10, 11.30am, 2, 3, 4pm Sat, Sun.* **Sternwarte:** *guided tours on request.*

Steyr 14

Road map E3. *40,000.* *Stadtplatz 27 (07252) 53229.*

Steyr, one of Austria's largest industrial centres, is also a very attractive town which has managed to preserve its old town almost intact. The townscape is punctuated in the north by the turrets of the castle and in the south by the towers of the Stadtpfarrkirche, the parish church at Brucknerplatz. The centre of town is the elongated Stadtplatz (town square) with most of the historic sights.

The **Brummerlhaus** (1497) at No. 32, is a well preserved medieval house with a high-pitched roof and three arcaded courtyards, that is now a bank. The Rococo **Rathaus** (town hall), with its slender steeple, was designed by Johann Gottfried Hayberger. The inner courtyards of houses around the square are also worth seeing.

The **Stadtpfarrkirche**, built in 1443, was remodelled in the Neo-Gothic style, but it has preserved some elements of its original 15th-century decor, the work of Hans Puchsbaum, builder of the Stephansdom in Vienna, as well as some lovely wrought-iron grilles. The south wall has magnificent 15th-century stained-glass windows; the sculptures in the north portal and the former cemetery chapel of St Margaret (1430), also by Hans Puchsbaum, date from the same period.

The **Schloss** (castle), first mentioned in 10th-century annals, stands in the oldest part of the town. Today it has a Baroque façade and a mostly Rococo interior. The house at No. 26 Grünmarkt, formerly a granary, is now a museum.

Environs: In **Gleink**, a northern suburb of Steyr, stands a worthy Benedictine Abbey. Some 3 km (2 miles) west of the town centre, in the suburb of **Christkindl**, is the church of the same name (meaning "Infant Christ"), the joint work of Giovanni Battista Carlone and Jakob Prandtauer. In 1695, a devout person placed a wax figure of the Infant Jesus in the hollow of a tree and prayed there every day for a cure. His prayers were answered and soon the crowds of pilgrims drawn to the site of the

Steyr town panorama as seen from the river

miracle were so large that in 1702 the abbot from nearby Garsten decided to build a church. The main object of adoration is the wax figurine of Jesus, kept in a beautifully decorated glass cabinet. The cabinet itself is part of a composition symbolizing the Holy Trinity. Christkindl has its own post office, using the coveted "Christkindl" postmark showing the Infant Jesus. It operates only in the pre-Christmas period, and millions of letters, supposedly from the Infant Jesus, are sent around the world from here.

Christkindl Church
Christkindlweg 69. ***Tel*** *(07252) 54622.*

The façade of the Christkindl church, on the outskirts of Steyr

Bad Hall ⓯

Road map E3. *4,300.*
Kurpromenade 1 (07258) 7200.

Bad Hall, a health resort between Steyr and Kremsmünster, lies on the so-called "Romantic Route", but the idyllic scenery is just one of its attractions: it also boasts the richest iodine springs in Central Europe. A highly modern resort surrounds the springs, which are used to treat eye, circulatory and heart diseases. The lovely Kurpark (spa park), with its excellent sports facilities, makes convalescence a real treat. There is also a Rococo church which belongs to the abbey at Kremsmünster.

The lovely scenery around the resort of Bad Hall

Another sight worth visiting is the fascinating **Forum Hall Museum**, which holds a superb collection devoted to the development of traditional folk handicrafts in Upper Austria, as well as to the history of the local springs.

Forum Hall Museum
Eduard-Bach-Strasse 4.
Tel *(07258) 4888.* *Apr–Nov: 2–6pm Thu–Sun.*

Stadl-Paura ⓰

Road map D3. *5,080*
Marktplatz 1 (07245) 28011-0

Stadl-Paura, a small town on the right bank of the Traun River 2 km (1 mile) south of Lambach, has an imposing **Dreifaltigkeitskirche** (church of the Holy Trinity). Construction of the church was started in 1714 in thanksgiving for the sparing of the town from the plague. In its design, the church represents the Holy Trinity – everything is in triplicate. There are three façades, three portals, three towers and three altars. The church was built by the Linz architect, J. M. Prunner. In the design of the interior decorations some clever false architectural perspectives have been incorporated, creating unusual effects. The paintings in the altarpieces are by Carlo Carlone, Martino Altomonte and Domenico Parodi.

The house at No. 13 Fabrikstrasse, once an orphanage for the children of sailors who lost their lives in the waters of the Traun river, is now a museum of shipping.

The Dreifaltigkeitskirche, pilgrimage church of the Holy Trinity in Stadl-Paura

Schwanenstadt ⓱

Road map D3. *4,400.*
Stadtplatz 54 (07673) 2255-22.

This small town, situated between Lambach and Vöcklabruck, is today an important economic centre. In the centre of town stands a Neo-Gothic parish church with a 78-m (256-ft) spire, built in 1900 on the site of an earlier Gothic church. Worth seeing inside are a late-Gothic statue of the Virgin Mary, a 15th-century relief of the Mourning for Christ and 18th-century Baroque statues of the 12 apostles.

The town hall houses a regional museum which exhibits, among other things, Roman and Bavarian archaeological finds.

In front of the town hall is a 13th-century well; the square is lined with attractive houses with Renaissance and Baroque façades.

SCHLECKER

The riverside townscape of the health resort of Gmunden, on the banks of the Traun river

Vöcklabruck ⓲

Road map D3. *12,000.*
Hinterstadt 14 (07672) 26644.

In 1134, Wezelo von Schöndorf built a bridge over the Vöckla River, and next to it a church and a hospital. Soon a trading settlement sprang up which later became a large town. The only original structures that have survived are two medieval towers.

At the centre of town stands the small, 15th-century, late-Gothic **St. Ulrichkirche** (church of St Ulrich), which has a Baroque interior. The site of the 12th-century hospital and chapel is occupied by the magnificent Baroque **St. Ägiduskirche**, designed by Carlo Carlone, with sculptures by Giovanni Battista Carlone. The ceiling frescoes depict scenes from the lives of Christ and the Virgin Mary.

The former parish house, at No. 10 Hinterstadt, now houses a regional museum with a room devoted to Anton Bruckner.

The south of the town is dominated by the unusual silhouette of **Mariä Himmelfahrtskirche** (church of the Assumption of the Virgin Mary). It has a Neo-Gothic altarpiece with a beautiful 15th-century statue of the Virgin, and stained-glass windows behind the main altar from the same period.

Environs: West of Vöcklabruck, about 12 km (7 miles) away, is the small town of **Gampern**. Its Remigiuskirche (church of St Remigius) has an attractive late-Gothic polyptych (1507) carved in wood.

Gmunden ⓳

Road map D3. *15,000.*
Toscanapark 1 (07612) 64305.

This lakeside town, on the northern end of Traunsee, established itself as a trading post in the salt trade. Today, it is a popular and well-run health resort, and it is also known for its fine ceramics. Gmunden's old town centre is situated between the lake and the left (western) bank of the Traun river. Its Hauptplatz boasts a Renaissance town hall with a small, arcaded tower and a carillon that plays a regular tune. The **Stadtpfarrkirche** (parish church) has a two-fold dedication: the Virgin Mary and the Three Kings. The Magi are also depicted in the main altarpiece, one of the most beautiful works by Thomas Schwanthaler. The figures of Saints Elizabeth and Zacharias were carved by Michael Zürn. Each year on Epiphany Eve (5 Jan), a barge travels along the Traun river, bringing the Three Kings to town, who solemnly proceed to "their" church. A ceramic fountain decorated with a figure of a salt miner stands adjacent to the church. The local **museum**, based at No. 8 Kammerhofgasse in the Renaissance building of the former Salt Mines Authorities, has exhibits on the history of the town and its salt production, a collection of local ceramics as well as displays relating to the composer Johannes Brahms and the German playwright Friedrich Hebbel. At No. 4 Traungasse is the **Sanitärmuseum**, with its amusing displays of locally made sanitaryware, toilet bowls and chamber pots.

A detail from Gmunden town hall

In Traunsee stands the water fortress of **Lake Castle Ort**, built in the 15th and 16th centuries and rebuilt inn 1634. It has an enchanting triangular, arcaded courtyard and remnants of Renaissance frescoes. A popular TV series is set in the castle.

Traunkirchen ⓴

Road map D3. *1,800.*
Ortsplatz 1 (07617) 2234.

Precariously perched on a rocky promontory, the small village of Traunkirchen is one of the most popular tourist destinations in Salzkammergut

Picturesque Johannesbergkapelle above Traunsee in Traunkirchen

◁ **The picturesque town of Hallstatt and Christuskirche rising above the Hallstatter See**

(see p209). It creates a lovely picture, clinging to the west shore of Traunsee, Austria's deepest lake, with views of the lake's wild southern shore and the Traunstein peak on the eastern shore, the highest mountain of the region rising to 1,691 m (5,548 ft). Above the village towers the pretty Johannesbergkapelle. On the northern end of the headland stands the Jesuit **Pfarrkirche**, rebuilt after a fire in 1632. It has an unusual fishermen's pulpit shaped like a fishing boat, with the apostles drawing nets filled with fish. Since 1632 Traunkirchen has also hosted the annual Corpus Christi boat procession.

Salzkammergut Lakes ㉑

See pp206–7.

The steam mountain railway leading to the top of Schafberg

Schafberg ㉒

Road map D4.

One of the most picturesque peaks in the area, Schafberg (Sheep Mountain) rises to 1,783 m (5,850 ft) between Attersee and Wolfgangsee. A mountain railway with steam locomotives takes visitors to the summit, although you have to walk the last bit.

The views from the top are truly unforgettable, embracing the most beautiful lakes of the Salzkammergut: Mondsee, Attersee and Wolfgangsee. Visible in the background are the towering mountain ranges running up to the Dachstein massif in the south, and, beyond Salzburg, you can see the Bavarian Alps on the German-Austrian border.

St. Wolfgang ㉓

Road map D4. *2,800.* *Markt 127 (06138) 8003.*

On the northern shore of Wolfgangsee lies the popular town of St. Wolfgang. According to legend it arose around a chapel built by Wolfgang (died 994), Bishop of Regensburg in Germany and teacher of Emperor Henry II. Although he died a hermit, Wolfgang was an extremely popular figure in his day, and was later canonized. His chapel became a much visited place of pilgrimage. In the 15th century it was replaced by a church with room for a much larger number of pilgrims. It was around that time that the Abbot of Mondsee commissioned the famed South Tyrolean artist, Michael Pacher, to create an altar for the **pilgrimage church**.

Pacher's high altar, combining sculpture, painting and architecture, is acclaimed as one of the most beautiful works of the late-Gothic era. The four scenes visible on the wings of the altarpiece when they are closed (on weekdays) depict events from the life of St. Wolfgang, patron saint of the church. The saint is shown holding a model of the church and is flanked by the figures of the Saints George and Florian. On Sundays, the wings of the altar are opened to reveal eight painted scenes from the life of Christ. They are striking in their coloration, the dynamics of their life-like figures and, above all, in the architectural perspective employed by the artist. The brightly gilded, sculpted centrepiece depicts the Coronation of the Virgin Mary attended by Christ, St Benedict and St. Wolfgang.

The church of St. Wolfgang also has a lovely Baroque altarpiece by Thomas Schwanthaler, depicting the Holy Family on their journey to Jerusalem. The three side altarpieces on the north wall and the magnificently ornate pulpit are the works of a Mondsee master, Meinrad Guggenbichler.

St. Wolfgang is also popular with tourists who come to see the hotel "Weisses Rössl" which inspired an operetta of the same name, *White Horse Inn*, by Ralph Benatzky.

Bad Ischl ㉔

Road map D4. *13,900.* *Auböckplatz 5 (06132) 27757.* **www**.badischl.com

Unusually potent saltwater springs were discovered in this region as early as the 16th century, but Bad Ischl did not become a popular health resort until the early 1800s, when the court doctor ordered saline treatments for the infertile Archduchess Sophie. Soon, she started producing babies. The most famous of these was Franz Joseph I, the future emperor, who spent all his summer holidays with his wife Elizabeth at the **Kaiservilla**. It was also here that he signed the declaration of war with Serbia, on 1 August 1914, signalling the start of World War I.

Many aristocrats and artists have been attracted to the spa, among them the composer Franz Lehár, who lived at No. 8 Lehárkai, which is now a museum devoted to him.

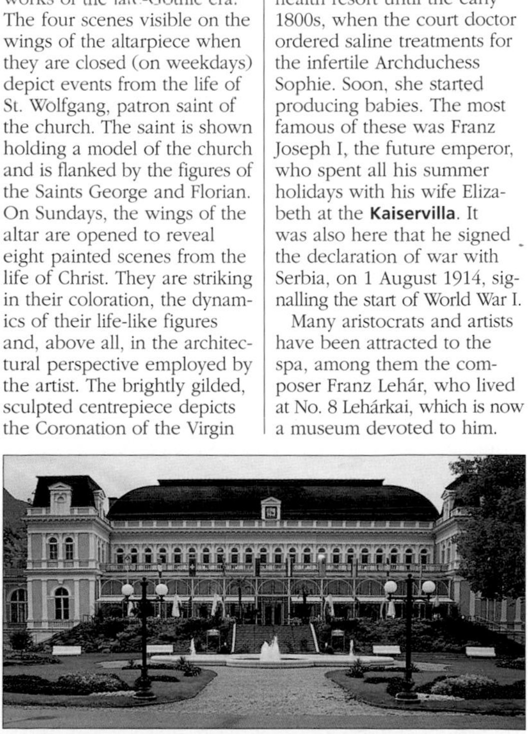

The imposing Spa House in the popular resort of Bad Ischl

Salzkammergut Lakes ㉑

This corner of Austria, which belongs to the Salzkammergut region, is worth visiting at any time of the year. With more than 70 lakes surrounded by mountains, it boasts breathtaking scenery as well as a unique climate, and offers excellent facilities for winter and summer holidays. This is also one of the few areas in Europe to preserve many original folk customs, including the tradition of placing a crib in front of the house at Christmas.

Mondsee
The warmest of the Salzkammergut lakes, at the foot of craggy mountains, is famous for its windsurfing. The little town of the same name arose around a Benedictine abbey, which dominates it to this day.

★ St. Wolfgang
The main attraction in this charming small town and holiday resort is the parish church with its beautiful altarpiece by Michael Pacher (see p205).

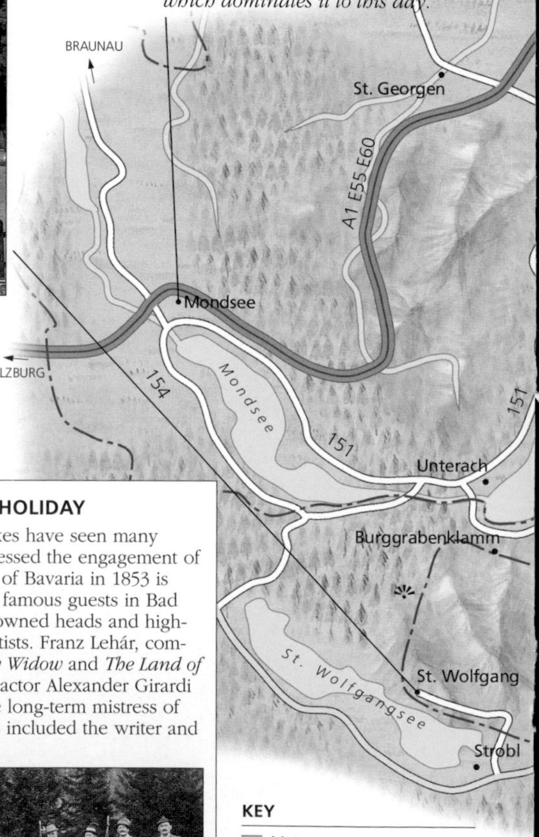

POLITICIANS AND ARTISTS ON HOLIDAY

The shores of the Salzkammergut lakes have seen many famous visitors. The house that witnessed the engagement of Emperor Franz Joseph I to Elizabeth of Bavaria in 1853 is now a museum with memorabilia of famous guests in Bad Ischl. There were scores of them: crowned heads and high-ranking aristocrats were joined by artists. Franz Lehár, composer of operettas such as *The Merry Widow* and *The Land of Smiles*, had his villa here; so did the actor Alexander Girardi and the actress Katharina Schratt, the long-term mistress of Franz Joseph I. Other regular visitors included the writer and actor Johannes Nepomuk Nestroy, the painter Rudolf von Alt, and musicians Johannes Brahms, Anton Bruckner, Johann Strauss and Imre Kálmán. In the late 20th century many politicians spent their holidays in St. Wolfgang, including both the former Austrian and German Chancellors.

Franz Joseph I and his hunting party

★ Attersee
The largest of the Salzkammergut lakes, Attersee is dominated by the Höllengebirge (Mountains of Hell). This popular lake is a great base for boating holidays.

VISITORS' CHECKLIST

Road map D3, D4.
Salzkammergut Tourism Salinenplatz 1, A-4820 Bad Ischl.
Tel *(06132) 26909.*
info@salzkammergut.at
www.salzkammergut.at
"Glöcklerlauf" (Bell walk) Night Procession, Traunsee Jan 5

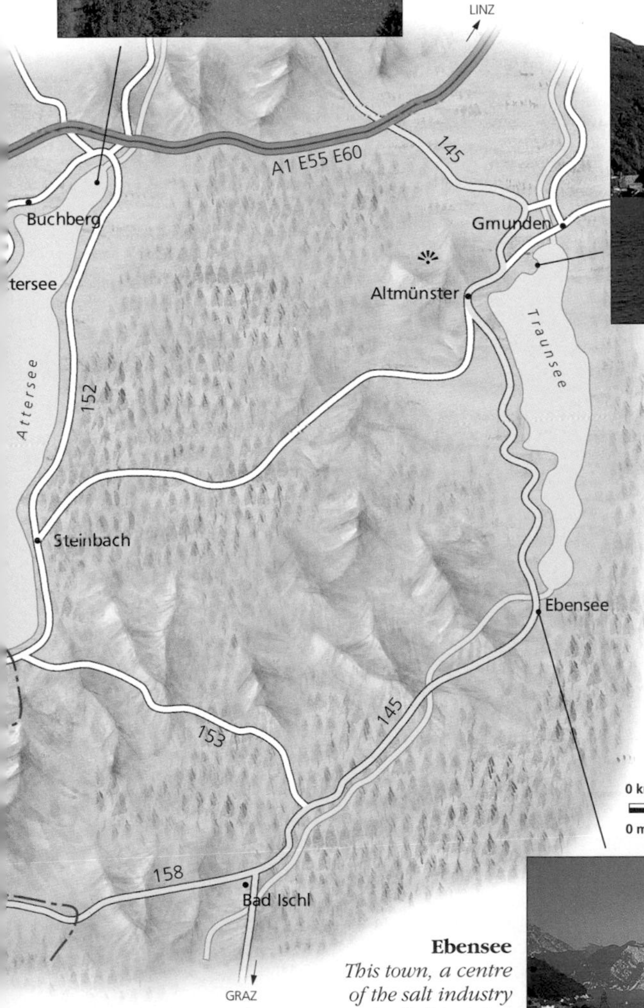

Seeschloss Ort
The pretty lakeside castle, built on an island, has a quadrangular tower topped by an onion dome. One of its last owners was Franz Joseph's nephew, Johann Salvator, a colourful character whose political life displeased the court.

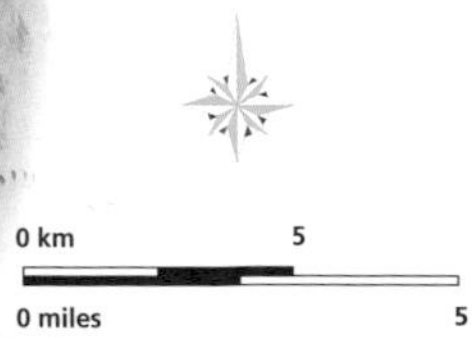

Ebensee
This town, a centre of the salt industry scenically located at the southern end of Traunsee at the bottom of Höllengebirge, is famous for its carnival festivities.

STAR SIGHTS

★ Attersee

★ St. Wolfgang

Bronze-age finds in Hallstatt's World Heritage Museum

Hallstatt ㉕

Road map D4. 1,000. Seestrasse 169 (06134) 8208.

The small town of Hallstatt is one of the loveliest tourist destinations in the Salzkammergut. The steep drop of the Dachstein massif provides a scenic backdrop for the town and adjacent Hallstätter See. The houses are clustered together so tightly that many are accessible only from the lakeside, while the old street runs above the rooftops. Even the local Corpus Christi procession is held on the lake, in festive, decorated boats. Rising above the town on a rocky headland is the pagoda-like roof of the **Pfarrkirche**. Its stepped dome dates from a later period, but the church was built in the 15th century and to this day contains many original features, including the carved wooden altarpiece of the Virgin Mary, sometimes compared to Pacher's altar in St. Wolfgang *(see p205)*. The figure of the Madonna at its centre is flanked by the Saints Barbara, patron of miners, and Catherine, revered by woodcutters. Depicted on the inner wings are scenes from the lives of Mary and Jesus. The altar is guarded by the statues of two knightly saints, George and Florian.

Painted skulls in the Beinhaus chapel of Hallstatt's Pfarrkirche

In the cemetery surrounding the church stands the **Beinhaus**, a chapel that serves as a storehouse for some very bizarre objects. This former mortuary now holds some 1,200 human skulls, painted with floral designs and in many cases inscribed with the name, date and cause of death of the deceased. Shortage of space in the graveyard had meant that some ten years after a funeral, when a body had decomposed, the remains were moved to the chapel to make room for the next coffin to be buried, resulting in this unusual depository.

A short distance below the Catholic Pfarrkirche stands a Neo-Gothic Protestant church, with a slender steeple.

Vertically above the town, about 500 m (1,640 ft) higher, is **Salzwelten**, probably the oldest salt mine in the world, which can be reached by cable car. Salt was mined here as early as 3,000 BC and then transported to the Baltic Sea and the Mediterranean.

In 1846, a large cemetery yielding some 2,000 graves was uncovered in Hallstatt. Rich burial objects dated mainly from the Iron Age but some dated even further back in time, to the Bronze Age. The Hallstatt finds proved so important archaeologically that the Celtic culture of that period (800–400 BC) was named the **Hallstatt civilization**. Its influence reached far into France, the Slav countries and Hungary. Today, Hallstatt treasures can be seen in many Austrian museums, with the bulk of them held at Schloss Eggenberg, near Graz *(see p162)*. The few finds that stayed in Hallstatt are kept in the **World Heritage Museum**. The entire Hallstatt region has been declared a World Heritage Site by UNESCO.

Salzwelten Hallstatt
Lahnstrasse 21. ***Tel*** *(06132) 200 2400.* *Apr–mid-Sep: 9:30am–4:30pm daily; mid-Sep–Oct: 9:30am–3:30pm daily (to 4pm 5–26 Oct).* **www**.salzwelten.at

World Heritage Museum
Seestrasse 56. ***Tel*** *(06134) 828015.* *Jan–Mar: 11am–3pm Mon, Wed–Sun; Apr, Oct: 10am–4pm daily; May–Sep: 10am–6pm daily; Nov–Dec: 11am–3pm Wed–Sun.* **www**.museum-hallstatt.at

Gosauseen ㉖

Road map D4. *Gosau (06136) 8295.*

You cannot truly appreciate the unique charms of the Salzkammergut without visiting this outstandingly beautiful alpine area. The Gosauseen are two small mountain lakes – Vorderer Gosausee and Hinterer Gosausee – both are beautifully situated in limestone rocks intercut with deep gorges. Vorderer Gosausee lies at an altitude of 933 m (3,061 ft). An undemanding walk around the lake will reward you with superb views of the surrounding mountains and over the Dachstein range with its many glaciers.

The most picturesque mountain, with zigzag peaks and a sheer drop, is Gosaukamm (2,459 m/8,068 ft high). This is the easternmost part of the Alps where the snow stays on the ground all year round. The road to Hinterer Gosausee climbs steeply among thick forest. From this lake, 1,154 m (3,786 ft) high, you can climb some of the adjacent peaks.

For hotels and restaurants in this region see pp299–301 and pp330–31

A mountain stream racing through a gorge in the Dachstein range

Dachsteinhöhlen 27

Road map D4. *Winkl 34, Obertraun am Hallstättersee (06131) 5310.* **www**.dachstein.at

The caves in the slopes of the Dachstein range are among Austria's most beautiful and fascinating natural monuments. The vast caves, one of the largest systems on Earth and millions of years old, are covered by 500-year-old permafrost. After the last Ice Age, underground waters created strange ice mountains, glaciers and frozen waterfalls. The most interesting of these is the **Rieseneishöhle** (Giant Ice Cave). The caverns in this surreal underground ice-world are named after King Arthur and the Celtic heroes, Parsifal and Tristan. The most arresting cavern formation is the so-called Ice Chapel.

A little further along, also in a limestone wall of Dachstein, is the entrance to a second system of caves, known as **Mammuthöhle** (Mammoth Caves), so named because of their size rather than after the prehistoric mammal. These caves do not have ice formations, but there is a spectacular light show.

Both networks of caves can be reached via paths starting from the first cable-car station. The sightseeing route leads through a labyrinthine network of tunnels, gorges and chambers that stretch over 44 km (27 miles), with a 1,200 m (4,000 ft) change in altitude. Individual caverns have been given evocative names such as the Realm of Shadows or Midnight Cathedral. Also worth seeing is a third cave, **Koppenbrüllerhöhle**, which has a giant water source and is considered to be the largest water cave in the Dachstein massif.

All caves are open to the public only during the spring and summer seasons (May to Oct; Koppenbrüllerhöhle May to Sep). When visiting the caves, especially the ice caves, make sure you take plenty of warm clothing.

Dachstein ice caves in Obertraun

THE SALZKAMMERGUT

For centuries, the name Salzkammergut applied only to the area around the Hallstätter See and Traunsee lakes, and to the towns of Bad Ischl, Hallstatt and Gmunden. Salt has been excavated here since prehistoric times, ensuring the long-term wealth and development of the entire region. Salt mines exist in the area to this day. In the second half of the 19th century the area became famous for its therapeutic springs, and with time the term Salzkammergut came to refer to the entire land of lakes and mountains that is now Austria's most popular tourist destination. It includes the eastern part of the Salzburg Alps, with the picturesque mountain ranges of Dachstein (eastern part), Totes Gebirge (Dead Mountains) and Höllengebirge (Mountains of Hell). Between the mountains lie 76 lakes, the largest and most famous of which are Traunsee, Mondsee, Attersee, Hallstätter See and Wolfgangsee. For historical reasons, the "land of salt" straddles three Austrian provinces. The largest part is in Upper Austria, a small area in the south belongs to Styria, whilst almost all of Wolfgangsee and the St. Gilgen resort are part of the Salzburger Land.

The much-loved Salzkammergut, land of lakes and mountains

SALZBURGER LAND

The province of Salzburg, a region of high mountains, covers an area of 7,154 sq km (2,762 sq miles) and has 450,000 inhabitants. Its neighbours are Germany and the Austrian provinces of Tyrol, Upper Austria, Styria and Carinthia. A narrow wedge of land along the peaks of the Hohe Tauern mountains reaches as far as the Italian border in the south.

Salzburger Land is divided into five regions: Flachgau, Tennengebirge, Pongau, Pinzgau and Lungau. History has made them different in character and traditions; all are great for sports.

Colonization of the Salzach Valley goes back to prehistoric times. The mineral deposits – copper, precious metals and, above all, salt (*Salz* in German) from which both the town and province take their names – were being exploited as early as 1000 BC. It was salt which created the basis for the development of the so-called Hallstatt civilization that spread from here. The Celtic town of Noricum established in the alpine region ultimately became a Roman province of the same name. Christianity arrived here early, and its turbulent progress was halted only by the great Migration of Nations in 5th-century Europe. It was not until the 7th century that monks settled in Mönchsburg, the future Salzburg, which became first a bishopric and then an archbishopric. The entire province was an independent principality for many centuries, governed by an ecclesiastical ruler acting as sovereign prince and, depending on political circumstance and personal preference, associating himself with the Holy Roman Empire, the Austrian Habsburgs or Rome. Following the Congress of Vienna, in 1815, Salzburg became part of Austria. Today, the beauty of Salzburg, inextricably linked with Mozart, makes this province a visitor magnet second only to Vienna.

The Hochkönig alpine meadows in Salzburger Land

◁ Splendid church domes towering above the beautiful Baroque buildings in Salzburg

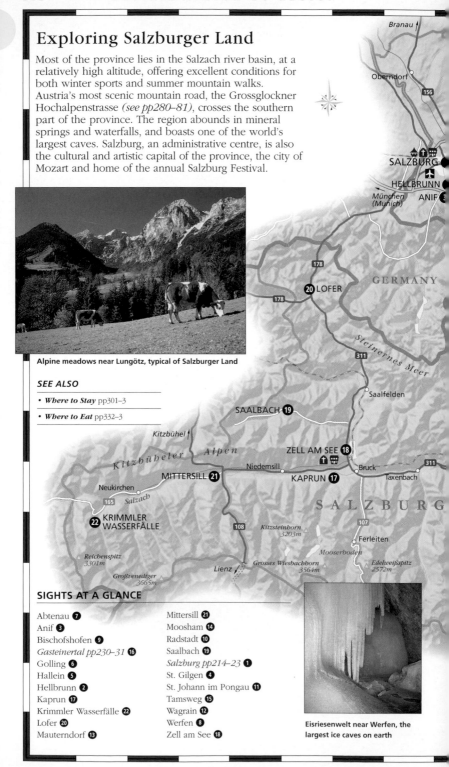

Exploring Salzburger Land

Most of the province lies in the Salzach river basin, at a relatively high altitude, offering excellent conditions for both winter sports and summer mountain walks. Austria's most scenic mountain road, the Grossglockner Hochalpenstrasse *(see pp280–81)*, crosses the southern part of the province. The region abounds in mineral springs and waterfalls, and boasts one of the world's largest caves. Salzburg, an administrative centre, is also the cultural and artistic capital of the province, the city of Mozart and home of the annual Salzburg Festival.

Alpine meadows near Lungötz, typical of Salzburger Land

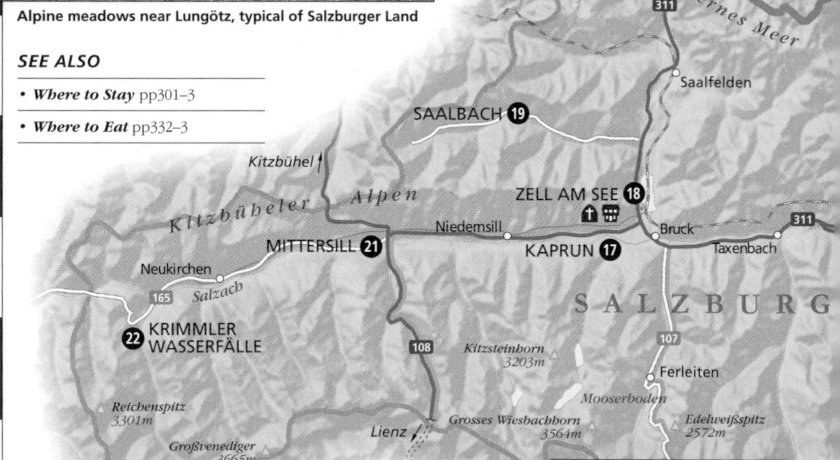

SEE ALSO

- ***Where to Stay*** pp301–3
- ***Where to Eat*** pp332–3

SIGHTS AT A GLANCE

Eisriesenwelt near Werfen, the largest ice caves on earth

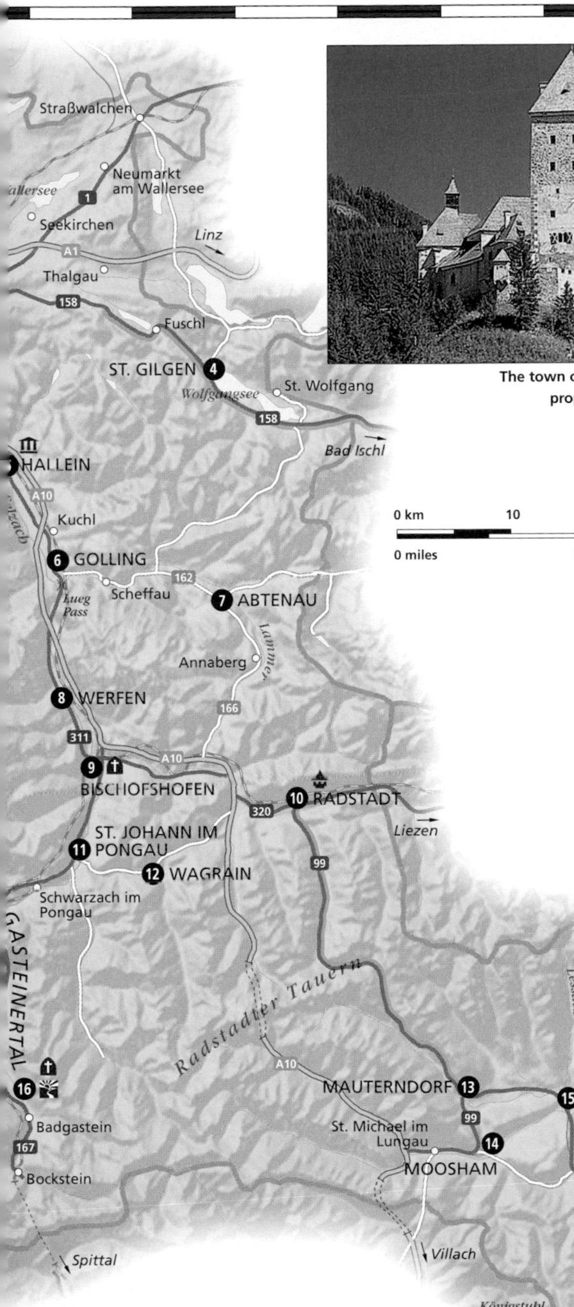

The town of Moosham with its castle, once the property of the archbishops of Salzburg

Side altar in the church of St. Leonard in Tamsweg

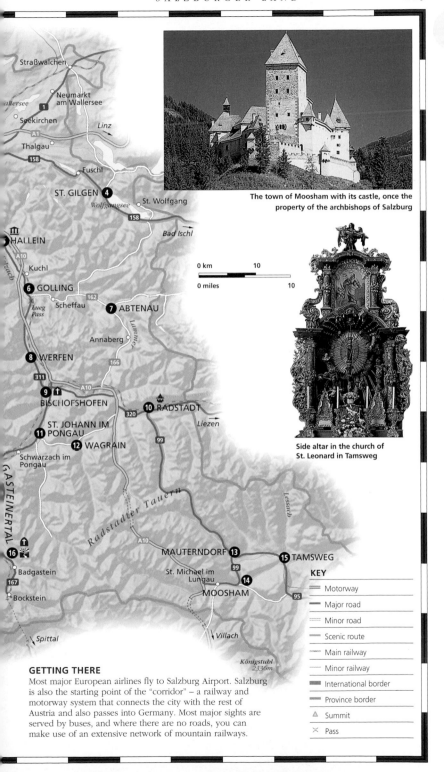

GETTING THERE

Most major European airlines fly to Salzburg Airport. Salzburg is also the starting point of the "corridor" – a railway and motorway system that connects the city with the rest of Austria and also passes into Germany. Most major sights are served by buses, and where there are no roads, you can make use of an extensive network of mountain railways.

Salzburg ❶

According to legend, Salzburg was founded by Bishop Rupert, who arrived with Benedictine monks, and by the Irish Bishop Virgil, who built the town's first cathedral. Salzburg, however, owes its glory and its present appearance to the three archbishops who ruled here after them, between 1587 and 1653: Wolf Dietrich, Marcus Sitticus and Paris Lodron. The most famous creator of the Austrian Baroque, Johann Bernhard Fischer von Erlach, began his career as an architect in Salzburg. It is also the town of Mozart, who was born here in 1756. Today, the prestigious Salzburg Festival attracts participants from around the world.

Tanzmeisterhaus, once the home of Wolfgang Amadeus Mozart

View over the churches of Salzburg and Hohensalzburg fortress

Exploring Salzburg

Salzburg is divided into three distinct areas of interest. The first, including the finest churches, the archbishop's residence and Mozart's birthplace, is on the left bank of the Salzach river. The second area, on the right bank of the Salzach, is the New Town. Its most interesting sights are the Mirabell Palace, the Mozart Conservatoire and Kapuzinerberg. The third area is the mighty former fortress of Hohensalzburg.

Makartplatz

Mozart-Wohnhaus

Makartplatz 8. ***Tel*** *(0662) 874227.* *Sep–Jun: 9am–6pm daily; Jul–Aug: 9am–7pm daily.*

This square was given its current name in memory of the Salzburg-born painter, Hans Makart, whose work greatly influenced contemporary fashion, architecture and interior design in the mid-19th century.

The Tanzmeisterhaus at No. 8 was Wolfgang Amadeus Mozart's home in 1773–87. The original house, destroyed in World War II, was rebuilt, and is a small museum dedicated to the composer.

The Dreifaltigkeitskirche (church of the Holy Trinity), in the northeast corner of the square, dates from 1694 and is one of the earliest works of Johann Bernhard Fischer von Erlach. Built shortly after his return from Italy, it shows signs of Roman influence. Its façade is crowned with sculptures of Faith, Love, Hope and the Church by Michael Bernhard Mandel. The frescoes in the dome vault are by Johann Michael Rottmayr.

Friedhof St. Sebastian

Linzergasse 41. *7am–4pm daily.*

The St. Sebastian cemetery lies just below the church of the same name. All that remains of the old church is a Rococo portal with the bust of its patron saint, and the wrought-iron grille by Philipp Hinterseer. The present, much more modest building, dates from the early 19th century. The cemetery is older, dating from the 15th century. It was designed along the lines of the Italian *campo santo*, with burial sites surrounded by columns, and has magnificent sculptures and tombstones. Next to the entrance, beside the church, is the tomb of the philosopher, physician and father of pharmacology, Paracelsus, who died in Salzburg in 1541.

At the centre of the cemetery stands the chapel of the Archangel St Gabriel that doubles as Archbishop Wolf Dietrich's mausoleum. Nearby are the graves of Mozart's father Leopold and his wife Constanze.

Kapuzinerberg

Kapuzinerberg, a hill on the right bank of the Salzach river opposite the historic Old Town, drops almost down to the river. Steep stairs with 250 steps, known as the Imbertstiege, lead up to the top from Linzergasse – it's well worth the climb. At the half-way point stands the church of St. Johann am Imberg, built in 1681. Its main altarpiece

A gilded figure from the church of St. Sebastian

For hotels and restaurants in this region see pp301–3 and pp332–3

has a painting of the Baptism of Christ. Another interesting feature is the carved pulpit by Johann Georg Hitzl.

A small castle once stood on top of the hill and formed part of the medieval fortifications; later it was partly incorporated into the Capuchin monastery complex whose church was completed in 1602. The monastery has a carved oak door made from the medieval stalls of the earlier cathedral. A short distance away stands a villa that was once the home of the Austrian writer, Stefan Zweig. Below the church, from the top of an old tower, the Hettwä Bastei, you can enjoy superb views over the many domes and spires of Salzburg and its immediate environs.

Putti on the Angels Staircase in Mirabell

Schloss Mirabell

Mirabellplatz. ***Tel*** *(0662) 80720.*
8am–4pm Mon, Wed, Thu, 1–4pm Tue, Fri–Sat.

The site of the present Mirabell Palace was originally used by Archbishop Wolf Dietrich in 1606 to erect a much more modest mansion, which he intended as a home for his mistress Salome Alt. The daughter of a Jewish merchant, she is said to have borne the archbishop 15 children. Dietrich referred to her as his wife and loved her to the end of his life.

In 1727, Johann Lukas von Hildebrandt rebuilt the palace for Archbishop Franz Anton Harrach as a truly royal Baroque home. A fire in 1818 destroyed part of the building, but fortunately the superb Angels Staircase, with sculptures by Georg Raphael Donner, and the Marble Hall, with rich gilt stucco ornaments, were spared. The palace is now a civic administration building. It is surrounded by attractive gardens designed by Johann Bernhard Fischer von Erlach, with groups of sculptures and fountains. The south wing of the orangery today houses a Baroque Museum.

VISITORS' CHECKLIST

Road map D3. *150,000.*
Innsbrucker Bundesstrasse 95 (0662) 85800. *Hauptbahnhof, Südtirolerplatz (0800) 660 600.* *Mozartplatz 5 (0662) 051717.* **www**.salzburg.info.at.
Salzburger Festspiele (late Jul–late Aug).

The beautiful gardens of Schloss Mirabell

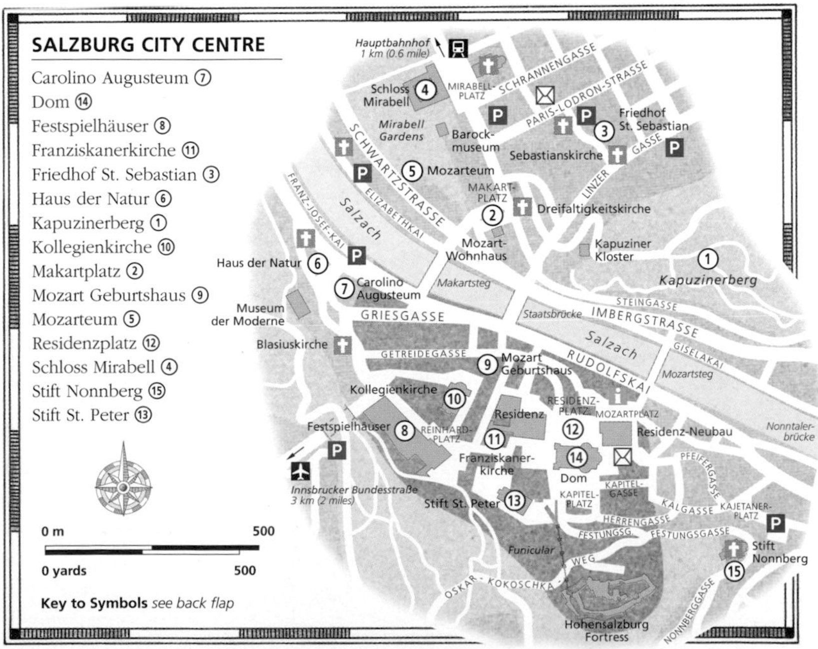

Street-by-Street: Old Town

Salzburg's beautiful Old Town occupies the area between Mönchsberg (Monks' Mountain) and the Salzach river. It has been designated a World Cultural Heritage Site by UNESCO. The town that grew up on the left bank of the Salzach was built almost entirely in the Baroque style and is unusually uniform in appearance. Its ubiquitous Baroque period designs have been faultlessly and seamlessly blended with both earlier and modern architecture.

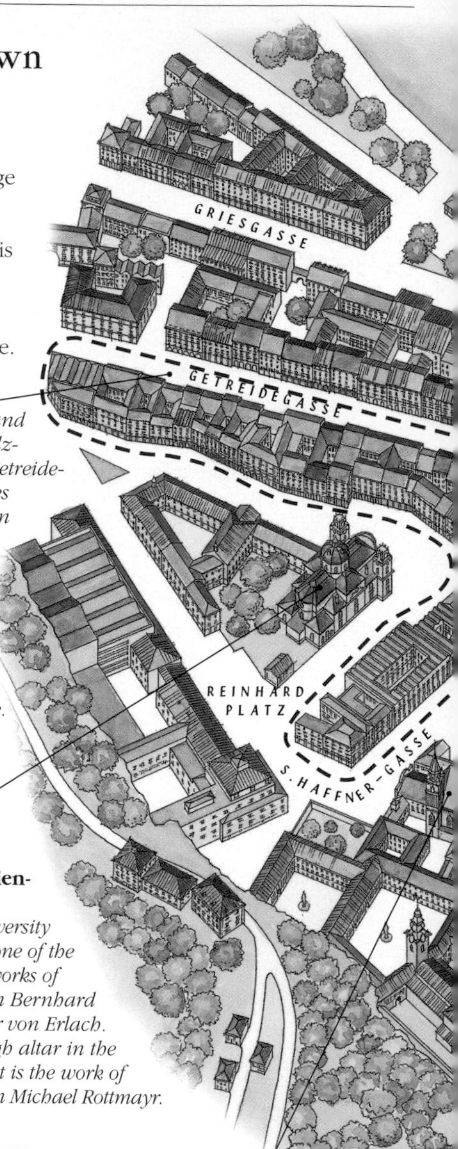

★ Getreidegasse
One of the longest and busiest streets in Salzburg's Old Town, Getreidegasse accommodates present commerce in medieval settings. No. 9 is the house where Wolfgang Amadeus Mozart was born and lived until he was 17; it is now a museum of the composer's life.

Kollegienkirche
The university church is one of the earliest works of Johann Bernhard Fischer von Erlach. The high altar in the transept is the work of Johann Michael Rottmayr.

★ Franziskanerkirche
The Franciscan church has a Baroque altarpiece by Johann Bernhard Fischer von Erlach, which has as its centre an exquisite figure of the Madonna and Child.

0 m 50
0 yards 50

STAR SIGHTS

- ★ Franziskanerkirche
- ★ Getreidegasse
- ★ Residenz

KEY

- - - - Suggested route

For hotels and restaurants in this region see pp301–3 and pp332–3

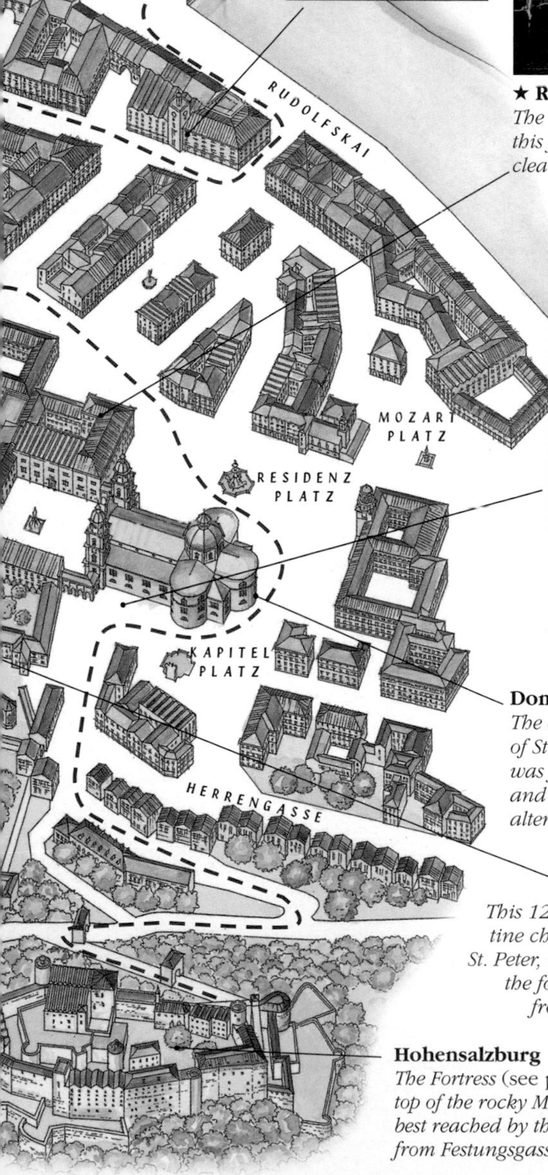

Altes Rathaus
The angular tower of the 15th-century Old Town Hall comes into view at the end of a narrow medieval alleyway.

★ Residenz
The most opulent building in town, this former home of the Archbishop clearly reveals his wealth and power.

Kapitelplatz
The bustling market square has one of Salzburg's most attractive fountains, and offers outdoor games and fun for everyone.

Dom
The cathedral church of St Rupert & St Virgil was first built in 774, and subsequently altered many times.

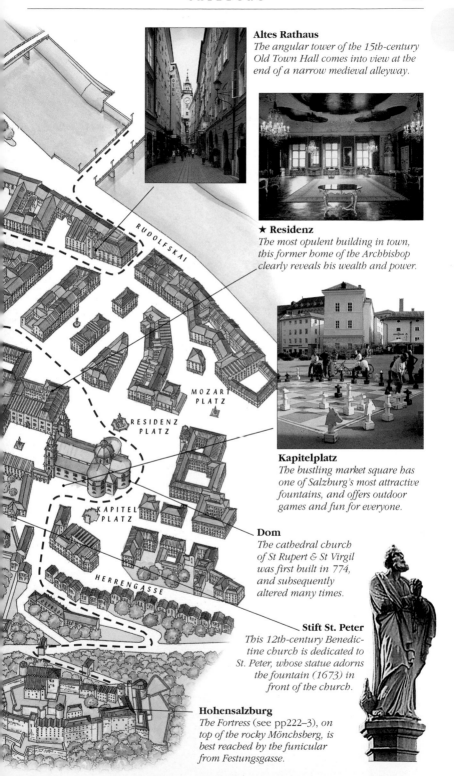

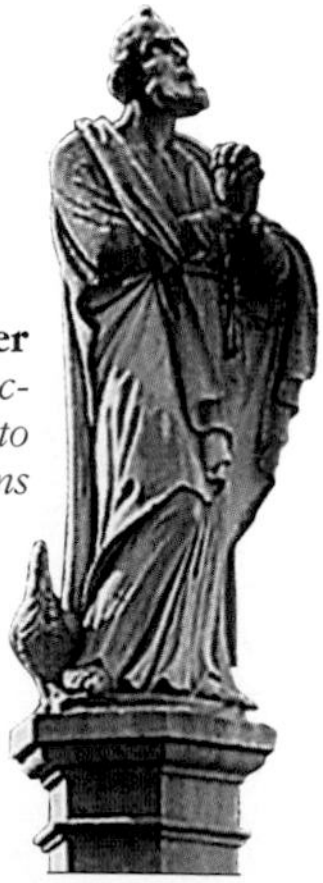

Stift St. Peter
This 12th-century Benedictine church is dedicated to St. Peter, whose statue adorns the fountain (1673) in front of the church.

Hohensalzburg
The Fortress (see pp222–3), *on top of the rocky Mönchsberg, is best reached by the funicular from Festungsgasse.*

The Mozarteum building, Salzburg's Conservatoire

Mozarteum

Schwarzstrasse 26. **Tel** *(0662) 88940.*

In 1842 Mozart's home town erected a monument to the composer and, in 1870, the International Foundation of Mozarteum was established here to promote his music. Today, the Mozarteum holds a collection of his letters, and it is also one of the foremost music schools in Europe. In the grounds of the conservatoire stands the cottage in which Mozart wrote the opera *The Magic Flute*, brought here from Vienna. The main building of the Mozarteum was designed by the architect Richard Berndl, and built in 1910–14. Some departments are housed in the completely rebuilt former palace of Archbishop Lodron next to the Foundation gardens.

Haus der Natur

Museumsplatz 5. **Tel** *(0662) 842653-0.*
9am–5pm daily.

The quarters that were once occupied by the Ursuline Sisters are now the home of the Natural History Museum, one of the most interesting and fun places to visit in Salzburg. The vast complex, consisting of more than 90 rooms arranged on five floors, houses a great variety of fauna. Individual sections of the museum are arranged thematically. In "Sea World", a gigantic aquarium recreates the conditions that closely resemble the natural habitat of various water creatures. The "Reptile Zoo's" 33 terraria house some of the most exciting snakes from around the world. There are also huge rooms simulating the natural habitat of Mississippi alligators and the lost worlds of Jurassic creatures, including ever-popular dinosaurs. Other themes include "men and animals in myths and fairy tales", "the cosmos" and "forest animals". Finally, the treasury room displays equipment needed for gold-panning, as well as crystalline forms of precious gems and stones.

Salzburg Museum

Neue Residenz Mozartplatz.
Tel *(0662) 6208080.* *9am–5pm Mon– Sun, 8pm Thu.*
www.salzburgmuseum.at

This History Museum was founded in 1834 by the amateur collector and treasury official, Vinzenz Maria Süss, who donated his collections to the town. It was named after the Bavarian Princess Caroline Augusta, who, in 1850, took over the stewardship of the museum's collections.

The most exciting items on display date back to Celtic times and include a Celtic pitcher from the Dürnberg area and a Bronze-age helmet from the Lueg Pass. The exhibits from Roman Salzburg, or *Juvavum*, are also interesting; there are fragments of mosaics, including one depicting the abduction of Europa, and numerous architectural features and statues. Also worth seeing are paintings by the Baroque masters, Paul Troger and Johann Michael Rottmayr, as well as those by Hans Makart, who was born in Salzburg in 1840. Separate departments are devoted to handicrafts, coins and musical instruments.

Grosses Festspielhaus

Hofstallgasse 1. **Tel** *(0662) 849097.*
Jan–Mar, Oct–20 Dec: 2pm; Jun, Sep: 2pm & 3:30pm; Jul–Aug: 9:30am, 2pm, 3:30pm. *Guided tours only.*

In 1606, Archbishop Wolf Dietrich von Raitenau

The Pferdeschwemme (horses' trough) fountain in the Grosses Festspielhaus

started building the palace stables on the site of the former barracks. The north façade was designed by Johann Bernhard Fischer von Erlach. The marble fountain, or Pferdeschwemme (horses' trough), in the stable yard, was built in 1695.

In 1917, it was decided that Salzburg should host a theatre and opera festival, and the stables were converted into the Small and Grand Festival Theatres. One of Austria's most outstanding architects, Clemens Holzmeister, supervised rebuilding, carried out during the 1920s, and the greatest artists of that time, Oskar Kokoschka, Anton Kolig, Wolfgang Hutter and Rudolf Hoflechner, designed the interior of the theatres. The Grand Theatre was completed in 1960. Its vast stage is carved deep into the rockface of Mönchsberg; the auditorium can easily accommodate up to 2,400 spectators.

Mozarts Geburtshaus

Getreidegasse 9. **Tel** *(0662) 844313.*
9am–6pm daily (7pm Jul–Aug).

Hagenauerhaus, at No. 9 of the narrow Getreidegasse, is the house where Wolfgang Amadeus Mozart was born on 27 January 1756. The composer's family occupied only one floor of the house.

In 1880, the Mozarteum-Stiftung (International Mozart Foundation) helped to establish a museum here, featuring a collection of Mozart's memorabilia, including family portraits, documents and his first instruments. On the second floor is a delightful exhibition on the theatrical staging of Mozart's operas.

Kollegienkirche

Universitätsplatz. **Tel** *(0662) 841327.*
9am–7pm Mon–Sat, Sun; winter: 10am–dusk.

The Collegiate Church, consecrated in 1707, is one of Salzburg's finest Baroque structures. It was designed by Johann Bernhard Fischer von Erlach, who achieved fantastic and unusual effects by letting natural light shine through windows of various shapes. The paintings on two side altars of the church are by Johann Michael Rottmayr. Italian artisans produced the beautiful stucco work, which decorates the church walls, to a design by Johann Bernhard Fischer von Erlach. The very ornate main altarpiece shows the university as a temple of art and science. It features winged figures symbolizing music, poetry, painting, architecture, theology, philosophy, law and medicine.

The Romanesque south portal of Franziskanerkirche

Franziskanerkirche

Franziskanergasse 5. **Tel** *(0662) 843629. 6am–8pm daily.*

The Franciscan Church seems somewhat out of place in Baroque Salzburg. Repeated attempts at refashioning it in the Baroque style have failed to disguise its Romanesque origins, mixed with Gothic. The 13th-century Romanesque portal leading to the presbytery is particularly fine, with a figure of Christ on the throne flanked by St Rupert and St Peter. The presbytery, with its tall tower and magnificent star-vault, is Gothic. In the 16th century, when the Franciscan Church was temporarily used as a cathedral, it gained an additional Baroque portal, a ring of chapels and many rich interior furnishings. The creator of the new altar, Johann Bernhard Fischer von Erlach, preserved the central statue of the Madonna from the earlier Gothic altar made by Michael Pacher, the outstanding artist of the late-Gothic. The St Francis Chapel has frescoes by Rottmayr, with scenes from the life of its patron saint. On the opposite side of the street are the monastery buildings, which are connected with the church by a bridge.

Residenzplatz

Residenz. Residenzplatz 1.
Tel *(0662) 8042-2690. 10am–5pm daily. 2 weeks before and 1 week after Easter.*
Residenzgalerie. Tel *(0662) 840451.*
9am–5pm Tue–Sun.

The Residenz, seat of the Prince-Archbishop, the religious and secular ruler of the entire province, was built for Archbishop Wolf Dietrich von Raitenau. His successors further extended the building. Following secularization, the building became the seat of the administration. Now one part of the building houses central government agencies and university offices, while the upper storeys are occupied by the Residenzgalerie, which exhibits artworks from the 16th to 19th centuries. Not much remains of its erstwhile decor, but the interior decorations, completed under Lukas von Hildebrandt and carried out by the most prominent artists of the Baroque era, including Johann Michael Rottmayr and Martino Altomonte, still charm visitors to this day. On the forecourt of the palace is the Baroque Residence Fountain, with Tritons and horses spouting water. On the opposite side of the square stands the Residenz-Neubau (New Residence), used as a temporary abode while the bishop's seat was being rebuilt. It has a carillon – the bells can be heard at 7am, 11am and 6pm from Mozartplatz, where a statue of the great composer stands.

Statue of Mozart in Mozartplatz

Sculptures decorating the façade of the Dom

Stift St. Peter

St. Peter Bezirk. ***Tel*** *(0662) 844576-0.* *8am–noon, 4:30–6:30pm.*

Salzburg's Benedictine Abbey was founded in the 7th century by St Rupert, who is said to have resurrected the town after the Great Migration of Nations. It is the only abbey in this part of Europe that has survived intact since then. The present church and monastery complexes were built in the 12th and 13th centuries, but remodelled during the Baroque era, in the 17th and 18th centuries. However, some of the old sculptures have survived, including the early 15th-century *Beautiful Madonna*. The majority of Baroque altar paintings are by Kremser Schmidt. The abbey interior is an impressive display of Baroque opulence.

In the cemetery, Salzburg's oldest, are the final resting places of Mozart's sister Nannerl and of Johann Michael Haydn, brother of Joseph.

Dom

Cathedral Domplatz 7. ***Tel*** *(0662) 80477950.* **Cathedral Museum** ***Tel*** *(0662) 80471860.* *May–Oct: 10am–5pm Mon–Sat, 11am–6pm Sun & hols; Nov–Jan: 10am–5pm daily.*

The first cathedral church in Salzburg, the Dom was built in the 8th century. Following several remodellings and a fire in 1598, the archbishops set out to build an almost entirely new church, designed by the Italian architect, Santino Solari, on the site of the earlier one. The new cathedral, consecrated in 1628, became a model of Baroque church architecture north of the Alps. The façade is decorated with the vast sculpted figures of the cathedral's patron saints, Rupert and Virgil, and Saints Peter and Paul. The cathedral was designed to accommodate 10,000 worshippers, more than the entire population of Salzburg. Its monumental interior is still impressive today. Stairs lead from the transept to the crypt where several prince-archbishops have been laid to rest. Mozart himself played the Baroque organ (1703) here. Today, the great Mozarteum choir often holds concerts of his music in the cathedral. The church's treasures are on show in the **Cathedral Museum**.

Stift Nonnberg

Nonnberggasse 2. ***Tel*** *(0662) 8416070.* *Summer: 7am–7pm daily; winter: 7am–5pm.*

The Benedictine nunnery on the slope of Mönchsberg, now known as Nonnberg (Nuns' Hill), was founded in 714 by St Rupert, who established his niece, St Erentrude, as Mother Superior.

The pilgrimage church Maria Plain on Plainberg

Her tomb lies in the crypt of the church. Emperor Henry II and his wife Kunegunde had the convent and the church extended in the 11th century. A fire in 1423 destroyed most of the buildings and, in the 15th century, a new convent was built on the same site, with a church devoted to the Assumption of the Virgin Mary and to St Erentrude. The Roman tympanum above the main door shows the Virgin Mary accompanied by John the Baptist and St Erentrude.

A true jewel of Nonnberg is its late-Gothic main altarpiece, brought from Scheffau and reputedly produced to sketches by Albrecht Dürer. Behind the main altar, in the central window of the apsis, is an interesting stained-glass panel by Peter Hemmel, one of the most renowned stained-glass artists in the late-Gothic style. Original 12th-century Romanesque frescoes are preserved in the niches. The adjacent chapel of St John has a Gothic altarpiece taken from the earlier cathedral; its creator was visibly influenced by the school of Veit Stoss.

Fresco (1150) in Stift Nonnberg

Environs: On top of Plainberg, a hill north of Salzburg, stands the pilgrimage church of **Maria Plain**, built by Giovanni Antonio Dario and consecrated in 1674. In 1779, Mozart composed the *Coronation Mass* in celebration of the miraculous picture of the Madonna and Child. The interiro was designed by famous Austrian Baroque artists, including Kremser Schmidt and Thomas and Franz Schwanthaler.

Further north, in the village of **Oberndorf**, the carol *Silent Night* was first performed in 1818. Franz Xaver Gruber, a local teacher and organist, wrote the music, and Joseph Mohr the words.

On the southwestern outskirts of Salzburg is **Schloss Leopoldskron**, since 1918 the home of Max Reinhardt, theatrical innovator and founder of the Salzburg Festival.

For hotels and restaurants in this region see pp301–3 and pp332–3

The Salzburg Festival

The Salzburger Festspiele, the largest and most important opera and theatre festival in Europe, was initiated by three people. The eminent writer, Hugo von Hofmannsthal, the composer and conductor Richard Strauss, and the greatest theatrical innovator of the 20th century, the director Max Reinhardt, decided to honour the memory of Mozart by organizing a festival devoted to his work. It was to be held in his home town and be a celebration of theatre and opera. The first festival was held in Salzburg in 1920. Today, it is the most all-embracing event of its type in Europe. The festival programme has become increasingly rich, and the former court stables were converted to create two festival theatres. Performances are held in the Makartplatz theatre, in Schloss Mirabell and in many open-air venues around town. Theatre troops come from all over the world, often with original performances prepared specifically for the festival. Tickets tend to be sold out several months in advance (*see pp346–7*).

The stage in front of the cathedral *in Salzburg is where the Salzburger Festspiele performances begin each July. Max Reinhardt pioneered the idea of open-air performances at the festival, and theatre troops now play to large audiences.*

Herbert von Karajan *(1908–89), born in Salzburg and one of the most outstanding 20th-century conductors of symphonies and operas, was the musical director of the Salzburg Festivals for almost 30 years.*

The Grosses Festspielhaus *is adorned with a Baroque portal by Johann Bernhard Fischer von Erlach. The modern building of the Grand Festival Theatre was completed in 1960 by Clemens Holzmeister* (see pp218–19).

The Fire Dance *is one of the most beautiful performances staged regularly during the Salzburg Festival. As soon as night falls, the whole town comes alive with the lights of the spectacle.*

Since its very first staging *the festival has opened with a performance of Hugo von Hofmannsthal's morality play* Jedermann *("Everyman").*

Hohensalzburg Fortress

Hohensalzburg, the fortress perched on the rocky peak of Festungsberg, was built in the 11th century, during the wars between the Holy Roman Empire and the Papacy, and was gradually extended. The castle served as a refuge for Salzburg's archbishops whenever they felt threatened. Archbishop Leonhard von Keutschach gave it its present look in the 16th century; Archbishop Paris Lodron introduced further architectural changes. A military barracks in the late 19th century, it is today a major tourist attraction.

An interesting feature in the fortress courtyard is a well dating from 1539.

The Glockenturm, through which the castle's residential quarters can be reached, has a bell case created by Hans Reichert in 1505.

Early Cannons
Aimed at the town, many cannons can be seen among the numerous bastions, bulwarks and walkways.

Salzburg Coat of Arms
The coat of arms is placed above the wicket leading to the inner courtyard in front of the old castle.

Archbishop
Johann Jakob Khuen-Belasy (1560–86) carried out the final remodelling of the old fortress. His portrait hangs in one of the rooms of the old castle.

STAR FEATURES

★ Goldene Stube

★ Torture Chamber

Schulhaus and Kuchlturm

Schoolhouse and Kitchen Tower are the remains of fortifications built outside the castle in the 16th century during a revolt against the archbishops.

VISITORS' CHECKLIST

Mönchsberg 34. **Tel** (0662) 842430-11. ☐ Jan–Apr & Oct–Dec: 9:30am–5pm; Easter & Advent weekend: 9am–6pm; May–Sep: 9am–6:30pm. 🖼 🖋

★ Goldene Stube

The richly ornamented Golden Chamber, with its large tiled stove in Gothic style, is one of the loveliest rooms in the castle.

Small Courtyard

In a small square on the castle ramparts stand an old salt warehouse (former stables), and two towers, Hasenturm (Hares' Tower) and Schwefelturm (Sulphur Tower).

★ Torture Chamber

Reckturm, the corner tower, was once a prison and torture chamber. Prisoners were still being tortured at Hohensalzburg up until 1893.

Portrait of Archbishop Marcus Sitticus in Schloss Hellbrunn

Hellbrunn ❷

Road map D4. *(0662) 820372-0.* *Apr–Oct: 9am–4:30pm; May, Jun, Sep: 9am–5:30pm; Jul–Aug: 9am–9pm daily.* **www**.hellbrunn.at

Schloss Hellbrunn, once a summer residence of Salzburg's Archbishop Marcus Sitticus, stands about 4 km (2 miles) south of Salzburg. Sitticus was a nephew of Wolf Dietrich von Raitenau, with an Italian mother. He spent most of his life in Italy, and so it is hardly surprising that his small, suburban castle resembles a Venetian villa. It has an interesting state room with architectural paintings and a tall, octagonal music room. However, the most interesting and popular feature is its garden with ornamental fountains and scenic grottoes, including a mechanical theatre, with trick fountains and moving figures powered by water.

Anif ❸

Road map D4. *4,200.* *(06246) 72365.*

Another 2 km (1 mile) beyond Hellbrunn, also south of Salzburg, stands the small Neo-Gothic castle of Anif. Once a suburban residence, it now lies virtually within the limits of the town Anif. Its earliest historic records date from the 15th century, but it bears signs of an earlier, late-Gothic structure. Once the summer estate of the Salzburg rulers, it belonged to the Chiemsee bishops from 1693 to 1803. After the secularization of the province, it was put up for sale and passed to Count Alois Arco-Stepperg. This new owner had the summer residence converted into a romantic English-style Neo-Gothic castle that has survived unchanged to this day. Its rectangular turret is proudly mirrored in the waters of the lake; the interior is furnished in the English fashion of the day. At the end of World War I, on 13 November 1918, the last king of Bavaria, Ludwig III, signed his abdication in Anif. As the castle is privately owned, visitors can only see its high outside walls.

St. Gilgen ❹

Road map D4. *3,400.* *Mondsee, Bundesstrasse 1A 1 (06227) 2348.* **www**.wolfgangsee.at

St. Gilgen is the largest resort in the Salzburg area of the Salzkammergut. Set on the western shores of the warm Wolfgangsee, amid mountain scenery, this is one of the most attractive health resorts in Austria. St. Gilgen was the birthplace of Mozart's mother, Anna-Maria Pertl. Later, the composer's sister, Nannerl, lived here with her husband, a local office worker. These Mozart-related facts are commemorated by a plaque on the court building. In 1927, the Mozart Fountain was erected in the town square.

The local church of St Giles (St. Ägyd) shows hints of an earlier structure. It was extended in the 18th century and given three Rococo altars with paintings by Peter Lorenzoni.

St. Gilgen is a major water sports centre and harbour, with cruises on Wolfgangsee aboard the steamer *Emperor Franz Joseph* that has been in continuous service since 1873. Not far from St. Gilgen, on the shores of the neighbouring Fuschlsee, stands **Schloss Fuschl**, a small hunting lodge that now houses a luxury hotel.

Hallein ❺

Road map D4. *18,300.* *(06245) 85394.*

The town of Hallein was founded in the 13th century, but salt was mined here way back in prehistoric times. The long association with the salt trade is apparent from the town's name: *hall* is the Celtic word for "salt". The "white gold", as it was called, brought wealth to the entire region for many centuries, until the 18th-century Counter-Reformation led to the emigration of the predominantly Protestant salt miners.

Hallein's Old Town, on the left bank of the Salzach river, is mainly 18th-century in appearance, following much remodelling. The church of St Antonius has a Gothic presbytery, but the rest is much newer. The painting of the Birth of Christ in the main altarpiece is by the last court painter of the Salzburg rulers, the Neo-Classical Andreas Nesselthaler. Hallein was the home of Franz Xaver Gruber who wrote *Silent Night*, and he is buried here. His house at No. 1 Gruberplatz is now a small museum. The most interesting sight in

Poster of the fascinating Keltenmuseum in Hallein

For hotels and restaurants in this region see pp301–3 and pp332–3

Hallein, however, is the **Keltenmuseum** with its unique collection of Celtic objects which relate to the history of salt-mining in the area.

Keltenmuseum
Pflegerplatz 5. ***Tel*** *(06245) 80783.*
9am–5pm daily.

Environs: From the southern end of Hallein you can drive to the top of Dürrnberg, which has some of the most interesting prehistoric finds in Austria. The remains of the settlements that grew up around the rich local salt deposits can be seen to this day. The spa of **Bad Dürrnberg** has a show-mine open specifically for tourists, who are offered rides on an underground salt lake. In the village stands a 14th-century Marian church, now a Baroque structure. The altarpiece contains a miraculous picture of the Madonna, once visited by pilgrims.

Logo of salt mine in Dürrnberg

Golling 6

Road map D4. *4000.*
(06244) 4356.

South of Hallein lies the small town of Golling. At its centre stands the Church of St John the Baptist and St John the Evangelist, with a Gothic main nave and remodelled Baroque side naves. A small medieval castle, devoid of any ornaments and adjoined by a chapel with a Rococo altar, now houses a regional museum.

Environs: There are many natural features of interest near Golling, including the **Lueg Pass** with the spectacular, 100-m (328-ft) deep Salzach river gorge, and the Schwarzbacher Wasserfall, better known as **Gollinger Wasserfall** (100 m/328 ft), much beloved by romantic painters of natural scenes. Also worth a detour is a visit to two interesting churches in the vicinty – St Ulrich's in **Scheffau** and the late-Gothic St Nicholas's Church near **Torren**, which stands high up on a rocky shelf.

The Gollinger Wasserfall, a favourite theme for painters

Abtenau 7

Road map D4. *5,600.*
(06243) 40400.

Abtenau, a summer resort situated in the Salzburg Dolomites, is surrounded by the mighty peaks of the Tennengebirge. The church in the valley was built around 1500. Its main nave is guarded by figures of St George and St Florian. On the north wall, an original late-Gothic fresco can be seen, but the new main altar and side altars are built in the Baroque style.

The enchanting winter landscape of Abtenau

It is worth taking a walk upstream along the Lammer river, which cuts a scenic valley between the Tennengebirge and the craggy wall of the Dachstein.

Werfen 8

Road map D4. *3,200.*
(06468) 5388.
www.eisriesenwelt.at

The little town of Werfen has several interesting churches. St James's Church is mentioned in 14th-century records, but its present style dates from a 17th-century Baroque conversion. The Marian Church was built in the early 18th century.

Environs: There are two fascinating sights near Werfen. Hohenwerfen fortress, built on a rocky outcrop, dates back to the 11th century. Today, it is an interactive museum with many displays, including late-Romanesque frescoes and an exhibition of weapons. It also includes Austria's first museum of falconry.

Eisriesenwelt (giant ice world) is one of the world's largest cave systems. It has dramatic ice formations and superb ice galleries. Some 42 km (26 miles) have been explored so far. A scenic walk or bus or cable car journey will take you from Werfen to the entrance in the western wall of the Hochkögel peak. Inside it is very cold (so take warm clothes). It is open from May to October.

Bischofshofen ❾

Road map D4. *10,000.*
(06462) 2471.

The Celtic settlement that stood on the site of the present Bischofshofen was once a centre of the copper mining trade; the area was also rich in salt mines. Colonization of the region started well before recorded history and traces of ancient cultures can be found everywhere.

The town is dominated by the spire of **St Maximilian's Church**, reputedly built on the site of an older church established by St Rupert, founder of Salzburg. The walls are decorated with 15th-century frescoes, and next to the Neo-Gothic side altarpieces stand the original Gothic figures of St Rupert and St Virgil. In the south arm of the transept stands a Baroque altar with a picture of St Anna attributed to Lienhart Astel (c.1520) and a relief on the predella of Christ and the 12 apostles dating from the same period. The most valuable historic relic in the church is St Rupert's crucifix. This simple, gilded cross, encrusted with precious stones, was given to Bischofshofen in the 12th century by the Archbishop of Salzburg.

St Rupert's Crucifix, Bischofshofen

Bischofshofen is renowned for its excellent ski-jumping hills. Every year, on 6th January, the final event of the world-famous Four Hills Ski-Jumping event takes place on the largest of the slopes.

Radstadt ❿

Road map D4. *4,800.*
(06452) 7472.

The small town of Radstadt grew up around a 13th-century fortress on the banks of the Enns river. Its wealth hailed from its propitious location on the road to Venice, and its monopoly position in the wine trade. Radstadt also had a licence to stock iron and salt. Its medieval fortifications, built by the archbishops of Salzburg, have remained intact.

The surrounding area boasts many small, beguiling castles, including Renaissance **Schloss Tandalier**, southwest of the town. **Schloss Lärchen**, in the centre of town, shows some traces of original, 13th-century architecture; today it houses a regional museum.

Environs: East of Bischofshofen runs **Radstädter Tauernstrasse**, one of the most scenic roads in the Alps. A vast skiing area extends on both sides. The **Rossbrand** (1,770 m/ 5,807 ft), rising north of Radstadt and accessible by car via the Rossbrand Panorama Street, offers astonishing views of more than 150 alpine summits on a clear day.

St. Johann im Pongau ⓫

Road map D4. *10,200.*
(06412) 6036-0.

The largest town in the region, St. Johann im Pongau is a popular resort, visited for its excellent skiing conditions in winter and its plentiful facilities for swimming and walking in summer.

Little remains of its original buildings due to a series of fires in the 19th century; the present town was almost entirely rebuilt. The Neo-Gothic **Domkirche**, the cathedral of St John the Baptist (1861), is acclaimed as the most outstanding work of Neo-Classicism in the Salzburg area. Its architects were Georg Schneider and Josef Wessiken. The charming carved altarpiece (1530) in adjacent St Anna's Chapel has late-Gothic wooden figures of saints. Some 5 km (3 miles) south of the town run the torrential waters of **Grossarler Ache**, a rapid mountain stream that winds through the scenic **Liechtensteinklamm**.

Wagrain ⓬

Road map D4. *3,000.*
(06413) 8448.

Wagrain, situated at an altitude of 800 m (2,625 ft), is the centre of a highly developed winter sports area known as **Ski Alliance**. This vast terrain extends between the Tennengebirge and Radstädter Tauern mountain ranges, and includes several villages connected by good public transport links, funiculars and buses. One ski pass is valid throughout the entire area, giving the holder access to some 260 ski lifts and 860 km (534 miles) of pistes, suitable for intermediates and beginners.

Year-round fun in the water is guaranteed by the Amadé Water World's all-weather pool. The most interesting place is **Zauchensee**, the highest village in the region

View of the town and cathedral in St .Johann im Pongau

◁ **The snowy Alpine peaks from Kitzsteinhorn, near Kaprun**

Rushing stream in the Liechtensteinklamm, near Wagrain

(1,361 m/4,465 ft). It is also worth going inside the Gothic church in Altenmarkt im Pongau. Wagrain itself has a museum devoted to Joseph Mohr, who wrote the words for *Silent Night*, and to the popular 20th-century Austrian writer and humorist Karl Heinrich Waggerl.

The views from the tops of Schwarzkopf, Rosskopf and Mooskopf are stunning and worth a detour.

Mauterndorf ⓭

Road map D4. 1,600. (06472) 7949.

Strategically positioned on the road connecting Salzburg with the Hohe Tauern passes, this little town owed its former wealth to the road tolls it was able to collect. Mauterndorf's greatest attraction is its **Schloss**, built in the 13th century and extended in the 16th century, under Archbishop Leonhard von Keutschach. Scenically located and well proportioned, it is an attractive medieval structure. The rooms are richly decorated with stuccowork and provide interesting interiors. The castle's best feature, however, is the lovely chapel devoted to St Henry (Emperor Henry II), with superb 14th-century frescoes of the Coronation of the Virgin Mary on the rainbow arch, and a 15th-century carved altarpiece. The castle was well restored in the 20th century, and is now a museum and cultural centre. Mauterndorf also has excellent summer and winter sports facilities.

Moosham ⓮

Road map D4. **Schloss** Moosham 12. ***Tel*** *(06476) 305.* *Apr–Oct: 9am–4pm Tue–Sun (daily Aug); Dec–Mar: 11am, 1, 2pm (guided tours only).* *Nov.*

Near the southern end of Radstädter Tauernstrasse, high above the Mur river, towers Schloss Moosham, which also belonged to the Archbishops of Salzburg. The structure probably dates from the 13th century and consists of an upper and a lower castle. Following the secularization of the archbishop's principality, the castle fell into ruin. But in 1886 it passed to Count Hans Wilczek, who fully renovated it. Among the remaining original features are the Baroque roadway, Gothic stained-glass windows in the presbytery of the castle chapel and a collection of items relating to the local arts, which are kept in the castle museum. The coach house and the armoury are also of interest. Some rooms are open to the public, such as a torture chamber, and a Gothic bedchamber with a panel listing the supposed characteristic traits of various European nationalities.

Bedchamber in Schloss Moosham

Below the castle is the popular resort of St Michael, with an interesting Gothic church

A stained-glass window in the church of St Leonard in Tamsweg

Tamsweg ⓯

Road map E4. *5,600.* *(06474) 2145.* *Samson Procession (late Jun, Jul, Aug).*

The largest town in the isolated Lungau region, Tamsweg is famous for its curious Samson Processions, when an effigy of Samson and other figures are paraded around town. Tamsweg owes its past wealth to the iron and salt trade. Fine town houses, such as the 15th-century Mesnerhaus and the 16th-century turreted town hall, line the market square. The 18th-century Post House has frescoes by Gregor Lederwasch, who also painted the pictures in Heiliger Jakobus (St James's Church) built in 1741, to a design by Fidelis Hainzl. The original Rococo interior has been preserved. The 15th-century Church of St Leonard, towering above the town, is one of Austria's foremost pilgrimage churches. It has beautiful stained-glass windows, such as the famous Golden Window (1430–50). The interior furnishings are almost entirely late medieval.

For hotels and restaurants in this region see pp301–3 and pp332–3

Gasteinertal ⓰

The therapeutic properties of the radon-rich mineral springs in and around Badgastein were known to the Celts and Romans, and this was when the first settlements grew in the valley of the Gasteiner Ache stream. The valley flourished in late medieval times and more recently it has become a popular spa, with a long list of clients including royalty, politicians and artists. A cure is sought by those suffering from cardiac and gastric ailments, rheumatism and allergies. At the same time, the valley has developed into a fabulous winter sports centre, with skiing for all levels and snowboarding.

Gasteinertal
This well-developed valley, surrounded by modest mountains, is a popular skiing, snowboarding and summer walking area.

Bad Hofgastein
The late-Gothic parish church was built in the 15th and 16th centuries. The carved tombstones found in its niches show the skills of gold- and silversmiths using locally excavated metals.

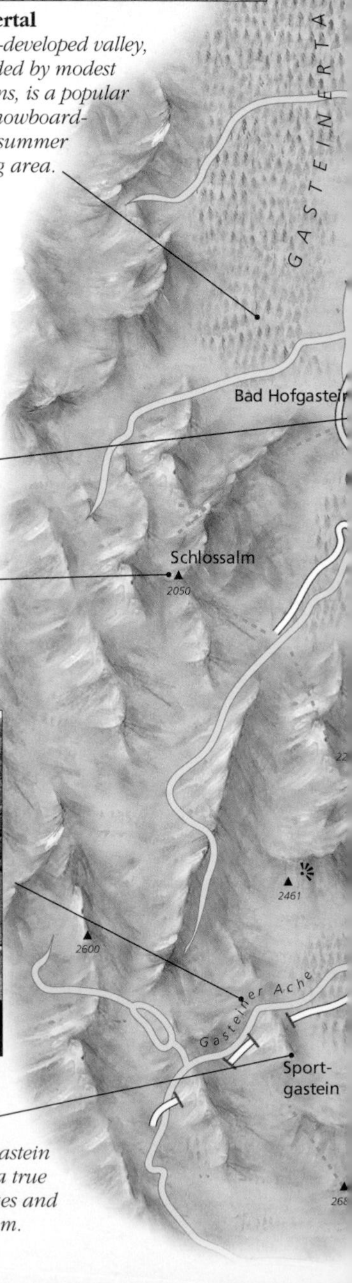

The summit of Schlossalm has a viewing platform at 2,050 m (6,726 ft), providing panoramic views of the neighbouring peaks. It can be reached by funicular.

The Gasteiner Ache
The stream runs along a scenic valley, down from the Hohe Tauern mountains, finishing as a tributary of the Salzach, the principal river of Salzburger Land.

★ Sportgastein
The wide valley near Sportgastein has been transformed into a true mountain gorge, with bridges and viaducts spanning the stream.

For hotels and restaurants in this region see pp301–3 and pp332–3

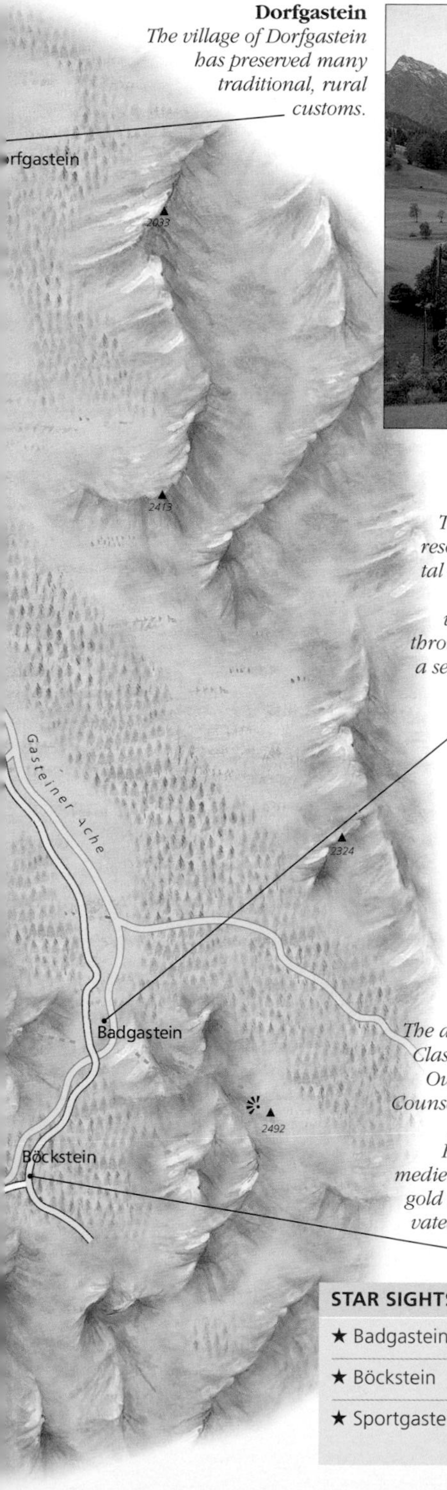

Dorfgastein
The village of Dorfgastein has preserved many traditional, rural customs.

VISITORS' CHECKLIST

Road map D4.
A-5630-Bad Hofgastein, Gasteinertal Tourismus GmbH, Tauernplatz 1.
(06432) 3393-0.
www.gastein.com

0 km 2
0 miles 2

★ Badgastein
The most popular resort in Gasteinertal is crossed by the Gasteiner Ache, which runs right through its centre in a series of attractive waterfalls.

KEY

- Major road
- Minor road
- Funicular
- River
- Viewpoint

★ Böckstein
The altar in the Neo-Classical Church of Our Lady of Good Counsel is the work of Johann Baptist Hagenauer. The medieval mine where gold was once excavated now houses a sanatorium.

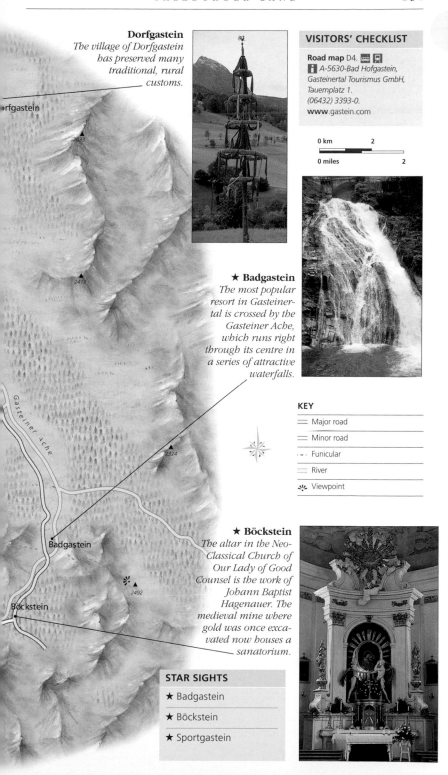

STAR SIGHTS

★ Badgastein

★ Böckstein

★ Sportgastein

Kaprun ⓱

Road map D4. 3,100.
(06547) 8643-0.

Kaprun is a popular winter sports resort. It is also famous for its sophisticated hydroelectric power station, which is acclaimed as a wonder of technology and one of the greatest achievements of human ingenuity. Work on the construction of the Kapruner Ache power station began in 1938, and was completed in 1951. Its highest reservoir is Mooserboden, a lake situated at an altitude of 2,036 m (6,680 ft) and fed by the melting ice of the Pasterze glacier.

Kaprun power station is not only a technological marvel; it is also a tourist attraction. Artificial lakes, weirs and dams, set amid the rocky limestone peaks of the Hohe Tauern mountain range, create a unique natural environment, with numerous trails and attractive scenery for walkers. Following the building of the power station, Kaprun became one of Austria's foremost sports resorts, especially as the nearby glaciers makes year-round skiing possible.

The town of Kaprun itself lies in a valley accessible by road and public transport. It has some of the most modern facilities in Austria, serving the **Kitzsteinhorn** (3,203 m/ 10,509 ft) to the north, an outpost of Austria's highest mountain range. This summit has year-round pistes and excellent snow. In the year 2000, a fire on the Kitzsteinhornbahn, the funicular railway taking visitors to the slopes, caused a major mountain tragedy. The railway has since been re-routed to run outside the tunnel, providing magnificent views of Austria's highest mountains.

On the western edge of Kaprun stands a 15th-century castle destroyed in the 18th century. The building has been restored and today it is a cultural centre.

Kaprun and neighbouring ski resorts have joined forces to attract visitors to this so-called "Europa Sportregion".

Inside St Hippolytus Church in Zell am See

Zell am See ⓲

Road map C4. *9,000.*
(06542) 770-0.

This picture-postcard town on the western shores of Zeller See has a long history. First recorded as the Roman settlement of Bisontio, in medieval times Zell was a mining centre. Among its more interesting historic sights are the 13th-century Vogtturm, and the Church of St. Hippolytus (St Hippolyte) that once belonged to the Augustinian Order. There are some interesting medieval frescoes: the figures of Saints George and Florian in the western gallery are by an artist from the Danube School. Zell am See is now considered one of the best developed sports resorts in Austria, with excellent facilities for skiing and water sports, as well as a convenient base for long walks.

Charming, flower-bedecked houses in Saalbach

Environs: South of Zell am See is the **Hohe Tauern** mountain range and national park *(see pp278–81)*, to the north the rugged scenery of the Steinernes Meer (Stone Sea) and to the west the Schmittenhöhe, divided into the Sonnkogel and Hirschkogel regions, with its highest peak rising to over 2,000 m (6,562 ft). The **Pinzgauer Spaziergang** is one of the most beautiful walking trails in the Austrian Alps, running at an altitude of about 1,000 m (3,280 ft) above the valley floor, from Zell am See to Saalbach, via Schmittenhöhe (a seven-hour walk).

Saalbach ⓳

Road map C4. *2,900.*
(06541) 6800-0.

At the heart of the Glemmtal lies this small town, marking the border between Salzburger Land and Tyrol. A charming winter resort with guaranteed snow, it provides access to 200 km (120 miles) of pistes, with beginner and more challenging runs right to the village centres. There is a wide range of entertainments on offer including extra-wide carving pistes, ungroomed moguls, a GS-race course, facilities for tobogganing and tubing as well as snow bars, huts and flood-lit slope dances.

To the north of Saalbach the Spielberghorn comes into view, while to the south the Schattberg marks the end of the Pinzgauer Spaziergang. This trail, leading across several passes, affords breathtaking views over the neighbouring mountain range. The view extending from Rohrertörl Pass (1,918 m/6,293 ft) embraces the town of Saalbach and the entire valley.

For hotels and restaurants in this region see pp301–3 and pp332–3

Lofer ⓴

Road map C4. 2,000. *(06588) 8321-0.*

The town of Lofer, in the green Salzach Valley, has retained much of the charm of an old mountain village. It is surrounded by the snow-covered rocky summits of the Loferer Steinberge (Stone Mountains). These limestone mountains hide many caves still waiting to be explored. The Lamprechtsofenloch is said to be the deepest aquiferous cave in the world.

Environs: A short distance south of Lofer is the small town of **Kirchenthal** with its pilgrimage church of St Mary, built between 1693 and 1701 by Johann Bernhard Fischer von Erlach. It is one of the greatest works by this outstanding architect, in which he employed some of the ideas that he had developed earlier in Salzburg. The building is blended into the rocky mountain scenery of the Saalach Valley, and two white towers are prominent against the distant snowy mountains. The Neo-Baroque altarpiece includes the 15th-century miraculous picture of the Madonna that was once the destination of pilgrims. On one of the two altars, created by Jakob Zanussi from reddish-pink Salzburg marble, the parents of the Virgin Mary, St Jacob and St Anne, are depicted.

Mittersill ㉑

Road map C4. 5,500. *(06562) 4292.*

This summer resort at the main cross-roads of the Upper Salzach Valley sprang up around a castle. The castle was built in the 12th century and since then has been rebuilt many times, following its destruction during the Peasant Wars and numerous fires. Today it is the seat of the International Protestant Youth Community, a cultural centre and a hotel.

The chapel (1533) features an interesting late-Gothic polyptych attributed to an Aussee Master. The Heiliger Leonhardkirche (Church of St Leonard), originally Gothic, was remodelled in the 18th century to a design by Johann Kleber. It contains a heavily ornamented Rococo pulpit and some remains of the old decorations, including an early 15th-century stone statue of Leonard.

Mittersill lies at the Salzburg end of a beautiful mountain trail leading from East Tyrol, among the wild scenery of the Hohe Tauern National Park. The road known as Felberntauernstrasse affords lovely views of the rugged slopes of Grossvenediger.

The scenic Krimmler Wasserfälle

Krimmler Wasserfälle ㉒

Road map C4. *(06564) 7212.*

In the northwestern part of the Hohe Tauern National Park *(see pp278–81)*, on the border between the provinces of Salzburger Land and Tyrol, are the famous Krimmler Wasserfälle, the waterfalls of the Krimmler Ache, the stream flowing from the glacier of the same name at an altitude of around 3,000 m (9,850 ft). The water falls in three steps, with a total drop of 380 m (1,247 ft). In winter, the falls freeze over. The journey to the waterfalls can be made by car, but a walk along the Wasserfallweg (waterfall path) will prove a truly unforgettable experience. The best starting points for the walk are the Gerlos Pass or Krimmel village.

View of the Hohe Tauern mountains, near Mittersill

TYROL AND VORARLBERG

Both Tyrol and Vorarlberg lie on a narrow stretch of land west of Salzburg. Their main attractions are the Alps – few areas are below 500 m (1,640 ft) and tourism is their primary source of income. The Tyrol is famous for its magnificent scenery and world-renowned resorts such as Kitzbühel, Seefeld and St. Anton, while Vorarlberg draws visitors seeking a more relaxed, rural environment.

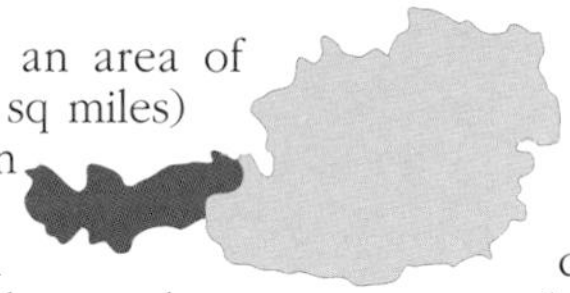

The Tyrol occupies an area of 12,648 sq km (4,883 sq miles) and has a population of 675,000. Its neighbours are Bavaria in the north, Italy in the south, Vorarlberg in the west and Salzburger Land in the east. The Enns is the province's main river, winding its way through the Alpine massifs.

In ancient times Tyrol was inhabited by Rhaetian and Illyrian tribes; it came under Roman rule in the 1st century BC, and later fell to the Bavarians and the Longobards. In the 13th century, it became an independent principality of the Reich. Until 1363 it remained a bone of contention between the Habsburgs and the Bavarians, when it was bequeathed to the Habsburgs. Tyrol was a domain of the family's junior line and as such enjoyed a degree of independence. To this day it has maintained its unique character, music, dialect and even fashion, which has shaped cultural life in the rest of Austria.

The province of Vorarlberg, in contrast, has for many years been culturally fairly separate, largely orientating itself towards its neighbours Germany, Liechtenstein and Switzerland. After Vienna, it is the smallest Austrian province, covering an area of just 2,601 sq km (1,000 sq miles), with 347,000 inhabitants. It was once inhabited by Aleman tribes. From the 15th century the area of present-day Vorarlberg passed gradually into the hands of the Habsburgs, and in 1919 it finally became an independent Austrian province.

The beautiful Lünersee in the province of Vorarlberg, hidden between snow-covered alpine peaks

◁ **A typical Tyrolean scene, with the picture-postcard St Nikolaus church in Orenberg, Tyrol**

Exploring Tyrol and Vorarlberg

Both provinces, in the far west of Austria, are predominantly winter sports regions, although they also offer excellent facilities for summer activities. Among the popular and world-famous tourist centres of Tyrol are Kitzbühel, the area around the Arlberg Pass, and the hinterland of Innsbruck. The latter has twice played host to the Winter Olympic Games, in 1964 and 1976. The capital of the smaller Vorarlberg province is Bregenz, a somewhat sleepy resort located in a romantic spot on the eastern shores of Lake Constance (Bodensee).

Chairlift and ski runs near Zürs

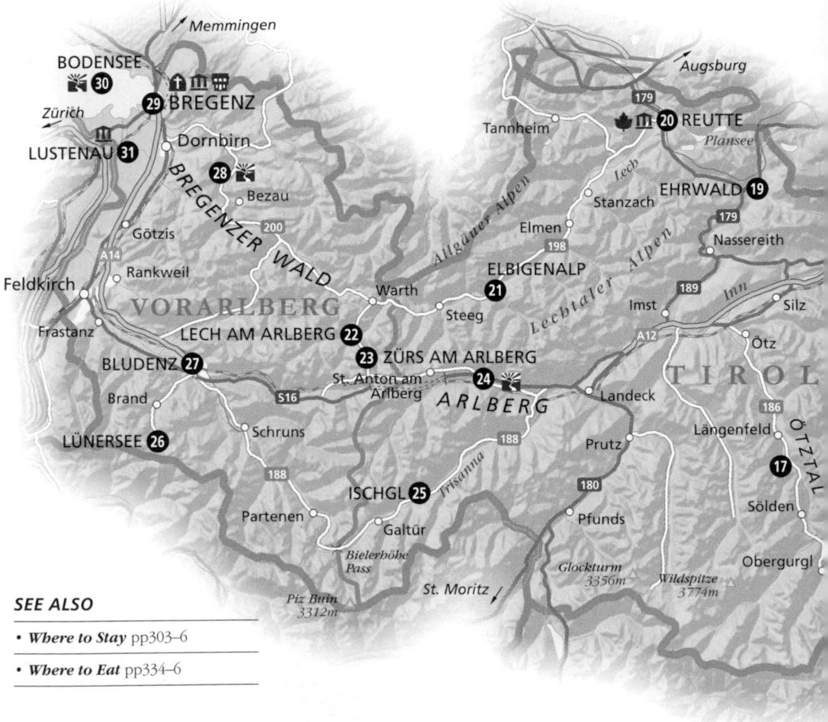

SEE ALSO

- ***Where to Stay*** pp303–6
- ***Where to Eat*** pp334–6

SIGHTS AT A GLANCE

Achensee 7
Alpbach 8
Arlberg pp256–7 24
Bludenz 27
Bodensee 30
Bregenz pp260–61 29
Brenner 15
Ehrwald 19
Elbigenalp 21
Hall in Tirol 3
Igls 2
Innsbruck pp238–43 1
Ischgl 25
Kitzbühel 13
Kufstein 11
Lech am Arlberg 22
Lünersee 26
Lustenau 31
Ötztal 17
Reutte 20
St. Johann in Tirol 12
Schwaz 5
Seefeld 18
Söll 10
Stubaital 16
Tratzberg 6
Wattens 4
Wörgl 9
Zillertaler Alpen pp248–9 14
Zürs am Arlberg 23

Tour:

Bregenzer Wald 28

GETTING THERE

From Innsbruck-Kranebitten Airport flights depart to Salzburg, Vienna and most major European cities. Both Tyrol and Vorarlberg are served by the main railway line from Vienna to Bregenz, and the western motorway reaches Bregenz. Austria's first toll road tunnel passes through the Arlberg massif. Both provinces have a good network of bus routes, although many roads may become impassable in winter. From autumn until spring motorists planning excursions to the mountains need to remember to take winter tyres and snow chains.

The Ballunspitze peak, seen from Paznauntal

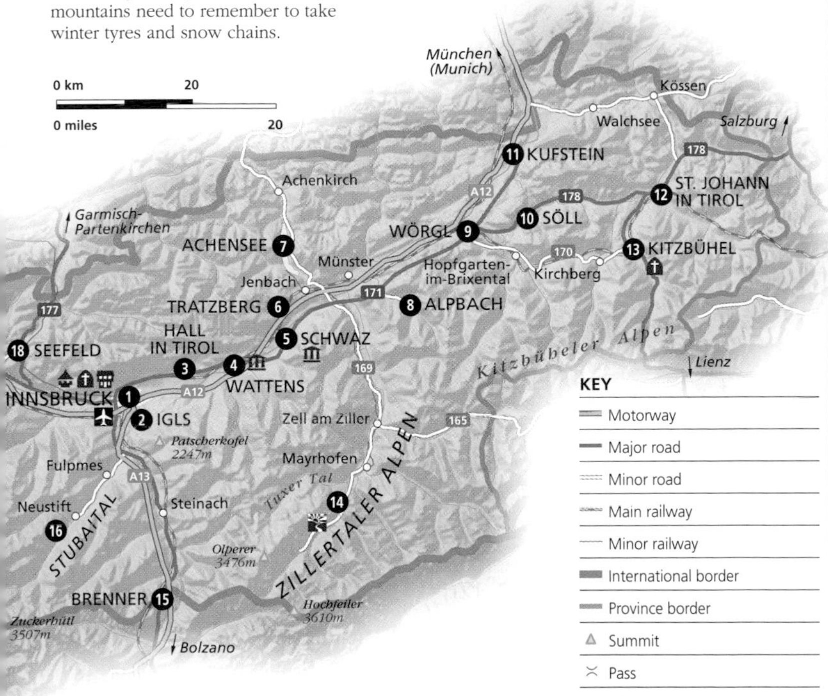

A coat of arms on the 15th-century town hall in Hall in Tyrol

Chapel in the snow-covered valley of Stubai

Innsbruck: Street-by-Street ❶

Innsbruck was built at the confluence of the Sill and Inn rivers and became an important trading post in the Middle Ages. The present district of Wilten was once the site of the Roman camp of Veldidena, but the founders of the city itself are the counts of Andechs, who built a settlement here in 1187. Today Innsbruck is the capital of the province of Tyrol, Austria's most important tourist region. In 1964 and again in 1976 Innsbruck was the host city for the Winter Olympics; many competitions took place in Axamer Lizum, 20 km (14 miles) southwest of the city.

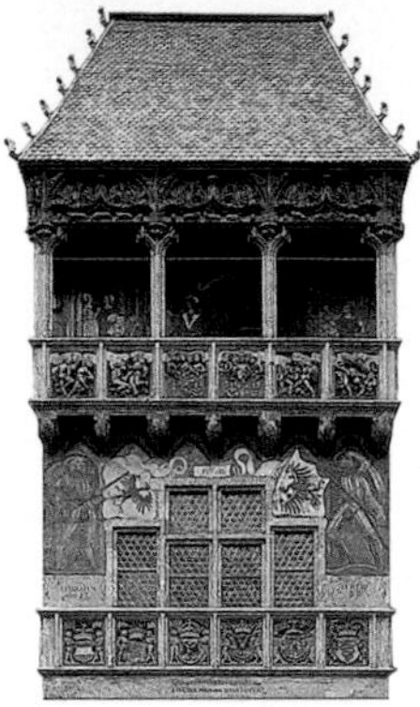

★ Goldenes Dachl
The symbol of Innsbruck, the Golden Roof is an oriel window added in 1500 by Maximilian I to Friedrich IV's former residence. It is covered with 2,657 gilded copper roof tiles.

Herzog-Friedrich-Strasse
The main street of the old town is lined with the attractive façades of numerous Baroque buildings.

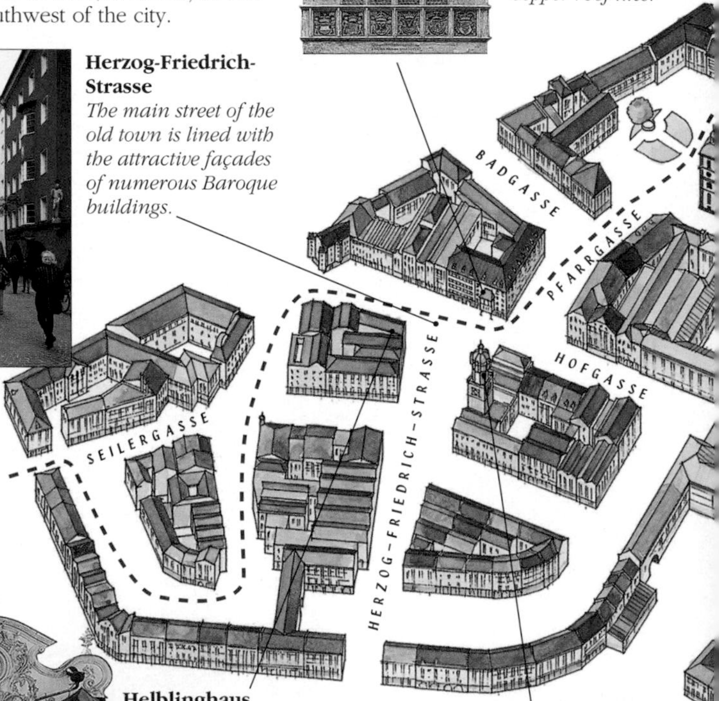

Helblinghaus
The building with an elegant Regency façade at No. 10 Herzog-Friedrich-Strasse was originally a medieval corner house in the Gothic style. In 1725 it was decorated with opulent Rococo stuccowork.

Stadtturm
The 14th-century city tower next to the old town hall acquired its present Renaissance look in 1560. At 56 m (184 ft) high it affords great views.

KEY

- - - - Suggested route

For hotels and restaurants in this region see pp303–6 and pp334–6

★ Dom St. Jakob
The Baroque cathedral has enchanting vault frescoes by Cosmas Damian Asam and a picture of the Madonna and Child *by Lucas Cranach the Elder.*

VISITORS' CHECKLIST

Road map B4. 124,000. *Burggraben 3 (0512) 59850.* **www**.innsbruck.info *Tanzsommer Innsbruck (Jun, Jul), Innsbrucker Festwochen der Alten Musik (Festival of Early Music, Jul, Aug).*

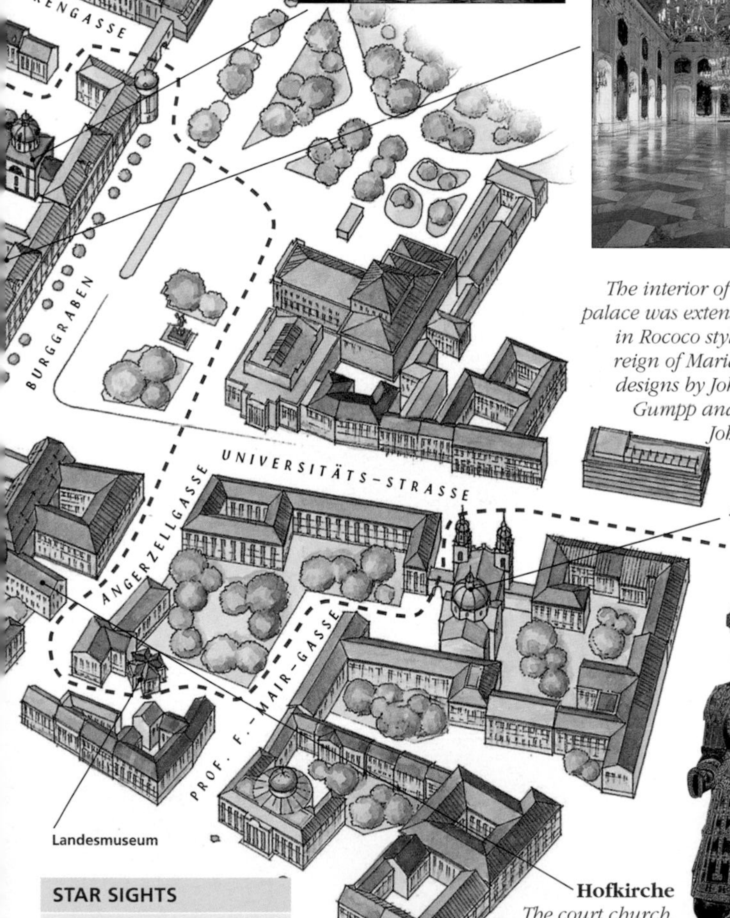

★ Hofburg
The interior of the imperial palace was extensively rebuilt in Rococo style during the reign of Maria Theresa, to designs by Johann Martin Gumpp and Konstantin Johann Walter.

STAR SIGHTS

★ Dom St. Jakob

★ Goldenes Dachl

★ Hofburg

Hofkirche
The court church, built in 1553–63 as a mausoleum for Maximilian I and guarded by large statues (right), *was remodelled in the Baroque style by Georg Anton* Gumpp (see pp242–3).

Exploring Innsbruck

Innsbruck straddles the Inn river. Its Old Town is situated on the right bank, close to the river. Leading up to it is the broad Maria-Theresien-Strasse with the tall column of St Anna (1706). The most impressive historic buildings are found on Herzog-Friedrich-Strasse, Stadtplatz, Hofgasse and Rennweg. Other important sights are Schloss Ambras, on the southern outskirts of the city, and the Panorama of the Battle of Bergisel.

Dom St. Jakob

Domplatz. ***Tel*** *(0512) 583902.*

St James' Cathedral was built in Baroque style in the early 18th century by Johann Jakob Herkomer. Severely damaged during World War II, it was rebuilt in the 1950s, when the church finally acquired the figures for the niches, as well as the equestrian statue of St. Jakob on top of the building, as envisaged in the original designs; the sculptor was Hans André. The fine Baroque interior is the work of Munich artists, the two brothers Cosman Damian (painter) and Egid Quirin (sculptor) Asam. The vault paintings depict scenes from the life of St James (St. Jakob). The picture of *Madonna and Child* in the high altar, which miracles are attributed to, is by Lucas Cranach the Elder.

The old town houses with their rich stucco ornaments, reliefs and frescoes provide an enchanting backdrop to the cathedral, which is regarded as the most magnificent Baroque church building in North Tyrol.

Hofburg

Rennweg 1. ***Tel*** *(0512) 587186.*

9am–5pm daily.

In 1453, Archduke Sigismund embarked on a project to build a princely residence in Innsbruck. His Gothic castle, extended by Maximilian I, survived for several centuries, and to this day the castle dungeons feature the original late-Gothic vaults. A major remodelling took place in 1755, under Maria Theresa, when the plans for the Baroque south wing were prepared by Johann Martin Gumpp, who also remodelled the front of the building and the grand staircase. His work was continued by Konstantin Johann Walter, who is responsible for the palace's uniform, Classicist shape.

The interior of the Hofburg is furnished in Rococo style. The staterooms on the second floor were completed in 1773. The most beautiful of these is the Riesenhalle (the Giants' Hall), embellished with white and gold stucco and a ceiling painting by Franz Anton Maulbertsch, depicting the triumph of the House of Habsburg–Lothringen. The walls are hung with vast portraits of Maria Theresa, her 16 children and other members of the imperial family. The remaining rooms of the south wing also have original Rococo decorations and furnishings.

Riesenhalle, a stateroom in Hofburg

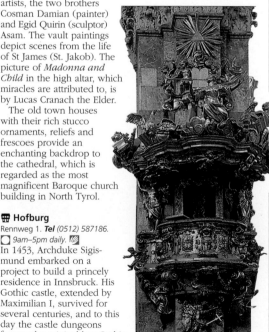

The richly ornamented pulpit in Dom St. Jakob

Goldenes Dachl

Herzog-Friedrich-Strasse 15.

Tel *(0512) 581111. May–Sep: 10am–6pm daily; Oct–Apr: 10am–5pm, Tue–Sun.*

In about 1500 the tall oriel window, with its numerous gilded copper tiles, was added above the balcony of this former residence of the Tyrolean rulers. It created a viewing box from which Emperor Maximilian I could observe street life on the main square of Innsbruck. The two-storey oriel rests on two slender columns. There are six coats of arms under the first-floor windows and the second-floor balustrade is decorated with reliefs; one of these depicts Maximilian I and his two wives: Maria of Burgundy and Bianca Maria Sforza; the second shows the emperor surrounded by court jesters. The building behind the Goldenes Dachl houses the small Maximilianeum, a museum of the emperor's life.

Herzog-Friedrich-Strasse

Herzog-Friedrich-Strasse is one of Innsbruck's loveliest streets. Its main historic sights include the Rococo Helblinghaus (No. 10), the Gothic Old Town Hall, dating from the 14th–15th centuries (No. 21), and its adjacent Stadtturm (city tower), with a viewing terrace.

Many of the other houses along the street also warrant a close look. The four-storey Ottoburg at No. 1, close to the Inn river, has four oriels stacked on top of each other and late-Gothic interior vaults. The Baroque façade of Altes

For hotels and restaurants in this region see pp303–6 and pp334–6

Regierungsgebäude (old governmental building) at No. 3 hides some beautiful rooms including the Claudia-Saal, the Hall of Claudia de Medici, with a late-Renaissance coffered ceiling. At No. 6 is an old inn, *Der Goldene Adler* (Golden Eagle Inn), and the Katzunghaus (at No. 16) has interesting 16th-century reliefs on the oriels.

Altes Landhaus

Maria-Theresien-Strasse 43.
Tel *(0512) 508-0.* *to visitors.*

This 18th-century house, built in 1725–8 by Georg Anton Gumpp and today the seat of Tyrol's provincial government, is regarded as one of Austria's most beautiful secular structures. It has an attractive inner courtyard and its colourful elevations were embellished by Alessandro Callegari. The niches lining the walls of the monumental internal staircase are filled with marble statues and busts of Greek and Roman gods. Ceiling frescoes depict the Tyrolean eagle with an open map of the country. The most opulent room in the building is the Rococo conference hall. Along the same street the Annasäule (1706) rises in front of the Neues Rathaus.

Georg Anton Gumpp's imposing stairwell in Altes Landhaus

Tiroler Landesmuseum Ferdinandeum

Museumstrasse 15. ***Tel*** *(0512) 59489.* *9am–5pm Tue–Sun.*
www.tiroler-landesmuseum.at

Together with the former armoury of Maximilian I at No. 1 Zeughausgasse, this 19th-century building houses the collection of the Tiroler Landesmuseum (the Tyrol Regional Museum), named after Archduke Ferdinand II (1529–95), a Tyrolean ruler and a passionate collector. The museum has individual departments devoted to the natural environment, history, art and handicrafts, and it is also home to a library. Among its most precious exhibits are Gothic panel paintings, sculptures by Michael Pacher, and works by old German and Dutch masters – Lucas Cranach the Elder, Rembrandt, Brueghel and others. The museum also exhibits more recent Austrian art, including works by Klimt, Schiele and Kokoschka.

The impressive, two-tiered 16th-century Schloss Ambras

Schloss Ambras

Schlossstrasse 20. ***Tel*** *(01) 52524-4802.* *10am–5pm daily.*
Nov, 25 Dec.

The castle, on the southeastern city limits, was once the symbol of Tyrol's power and glory. In the 12th century it was the seat of local rulers. The present 16th-century building consists of a lower castle with entrance gate and spacious courtyard, and an upper castle built on the site of an earlier structure. The two parts are connected by the early-Renaissance Spanish Hall, built by Giovanni Luchese in 1571, with original coffered ceiling and inlaid doors.

Archduke Ferdinand II established his own museum at Ambras, but the exhibits ended up in various Viennese museums. Nonetheless, there is still plenty to see, including the Rüstkammer (arsenal), the Kunst- und Wunderkammer (chamber of arts and marvels), and the gallery with portraits of members of the Habsburgs by famous artists such as Lucas Cranach, Peter Paul Rubens and Diego Velázquez.

ANDREAS HOFER (1767–1810)

Andreas Hofer is regarded as Austria's national hero, widely extolled in its literature and poetry. In 1809, he led the Tyrolean uprising against the Bavarian rulers, who were allied with Napoleon's forces. He succeeded in beating the Bavarians, and forced the French army, led by Marshal Lefebvre, to retreat from Tyrol after their defeat on Bergisel, a hill just outside Innsbruck *(see p243)*. Hofer assumed civilian power in Tyrol, but was soon betrayed and captured, and subsequently executed by the French in the town square of Mantua.

Hofkirche

Hofkirche, the court church, was built by Ferdinand I to house the tomb of his grandfather, Emperor Maximilian I. The tomb was designed by Maximilian himself and although his plans were never fully realized, the ensuing structure, completed in 1587, is very impressive indeed and ranks as a masterpiece of Renaissance sculpture. At the centre of the church stands the sarcophagus with a kneeling figure of the emperor. Reliefs on the side panels depict scenes from the emperor's life; the tomb is guarded by larger-than-life cast-iron statues. The tomb is, in fact, empty – Maximilian was laid to rest in Wiener Neustadt, in Lower Austria.

Vaults
The vaults acquired their present form in the early 17th century, when the church was rebuilt in the Baroque style.

★ Tomb of Maximilian I
The cenotaph, at the centre of the church, is guarded by giant figures representing members of Maximilian I's family, including his daughter-in-law, Joanna the Mad, and his spiritual forefathers.

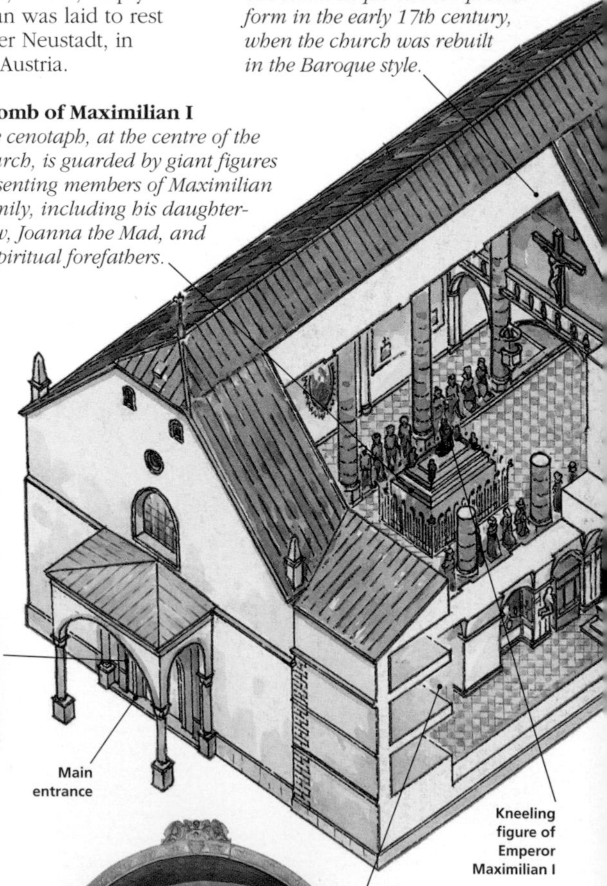

Main Portal
The grand Renaissance portal leading into the church was built in 1553–63 as a tribute to the House of Maximilian I.

★ Silberne Kapelle
The silver chapel holds the tombs of Archduke Ferdinand II and his beloved wife, Philippine Welser, by the Dutch artist, Alexander Colin.

STAR FEATURES

- ★ Silberne Kapelle
- ★ Tomb of Maximilian I

VISITORS' CHECKLIST

Universitätsstrasse 2.
Tel *(0512) 584302.*
9am–5pm Mon–Sat, 12:30–6pm Sun & hols.
www.hofkirche.at

An onion dome crowns the octagonal tower of the church

Charles the Bold
The statue of Charles the Bold, Duke of Burgundy and Maximilian's father-in-law, stands to the right of the tomb, closest to the high altar.

Wilten

In the southeastern suburb of Wilten stands a lovely Baroque church, the Wilten Basilica, built in 1751–6 on the foundations of a former chapel. The church was intended to provide a worthy setting for the picture of *Our Lady at Four Columns,* which miracles were attributed to. It was designed by Franz de Paula Penz and the interior has been kept in the Rococo style. The altarpiece, with its gold, pink and yellow colour scheme, includes a 14th-century painting of the Madonna. It is surrounded by an intricate canopy resting on slender columns. The ceiling paintings are by an Augsburg artist, Matthäus Gündter, and show in the presbytery *Saint Mary Our Advocate* and in the nave *Ester and Judith.*

The Romanesque abbey of Wilten has a church built in the 12th century, devoted to St Lawrence. According to legend, the abbey was built by the giant Haymo, in atonement for the murder of another giant, Thyrsus; both are commemorated by statues. Burned and destroyed several times, the abbey was rebuilt in Baroque style in the 17th–18th centuries.

Bergisel

Tiroler Kaiserjägermuseum am Bergisel Bergisel 1. **Tel** *(0512) 5823 12.* *Apr–Oct: 9am–5pm daily.*
Das Tirol Panorama Bergisel 1. **Tel** *(0512) 59489 198.* *9am–5pm daily.*

On 13 August 1809, Bergisel, or Isel Mountain, in the south of the city, was the scene of a battle fought by Andreas Hofer *(see p241)* and his army of insurgent highlanders, who defeated the combined occupying forces of Bavarians and French. The hill is a popular place for weekend walks among Innsbruck residents.

A monument to Andreas Hofer and the Imperial Fusiliers' Museum (at No. 3 Bergisel) serves as a reminder of the 1809 battle as well as of later battles by this famous regiment.

Statue of Andreas Hofer on Bergisel

In 2011, the Risenrundgemälde, a panoramic painting of the Battle of Bergisel, was moved from its previous home at the bottom of the Hungenburg cable car, to Das Tirol Panorama, a museum on top of Bergisel. Painted by Zeno Diemar in 1896, and measuring 10 x 100 m (33 x 328 ft), the panorama is a *trompe l'oeil* depicting an abbreviated version of the entire battle. The museum also hosts temporary exhibitions alongside its permanent collection of Tyrolean artifacts.

On Bergiselschanze, one of the competitions in the world-famous Vierschanzentournee (four hills' ski-jumping tournament) is held every year on 4 January.

Alpenzoo

Weiherburggasse 37A. **Tel** *(0512) 292323.* *Apr–Oct: 9am–6pm; Nov–Mar: 9am–5pm.*

On the southern slopes of Bergisel is a fascinating alpine zoo, housing a comprehensive collection of alpine fauna. There are some 2,000 animals here, representing more than 150 species typically found in an alpine habitat, including the alpine ibex and bear, and many local birds, fish and reptiles. A cable car from Hungerberg Talstation takes you to the zoo; the ride is free with an entry ticket to the zoo.

An otter in Alpenzoo, on Bergisel south of Innsbruck

The emblematic Mint Tower of Burg Hasegg in Hall in Tirol

Igls ❷

Road map B4. *2,000.* *Hilberstrasse 15 (0512) 377101.*

This small town south of Innsbruck, which had long been popular as a holiday centre and winter-sports resort, was given a new face for the 1976 Winter Olympic Games when modern toboggan and bobsleigh runs were built. The nearby Patscherkofel (2,247 m/7,372 ft high) is a popular destination for winter skiing expeditions and summer rambles. It is served by a funicular, a chair lift and five T-bars. An old salt track, Römerstrasse, runs above the Sill Valley, providing views of the famous Europabrücke (Europe Bridge) *(see p252)*, which spans the alpine gorges and is part of the busiest motorway network connecting northern Europe with Italy.

The **Aegidiuskirche** in Igls, the church of St Giles, probably dates back to the 13th century but has been remodelled in the Baroque period. It has beautiful vault frescoes by Josef Michael Schmitzer.

Near Igls is the interesting pilgrimage chapel Heiligwasser (1662), with attractive stuccowork created in 1720 as well as a wooden statue of the Virgin Mary dating back to the early 15th century.

Hall in Tirol ❸

Road map B4. *12,000.* *Wallpachgasse 5 (05223) 455440.* **www**.hall-in-tirol.at

Hall ranks mostly as a holiday resort, but the Old Town, with much of its original architecture intact, bears testimony to the town's former glory. The symbol of Hall is the twelve-sided tower, known as the Mint Tower, of **Burg Hasegg**. This castle, with its beautiful inner courtyard, once formed a corner section of the town's fortifications. It was the seat of the Tyrolean rulers and, in the 16th century, it became the mint. Today the castle houses the town museum.

In the Old Town, the **Town Hall** with its steep Gothic roof consists of two parts: the 1406 Königshaus (Royal House) with a beautiful debating hall with exposed-beam ceiling; and is a large building on the south side of Oberer Stadtplatz, with a Renaissance portal and a balcony from which the town fathers used to make their proclamations. The 14th-century **Nikolauskirche**, the church of St Nicholas, nearby, has a lovely portal featuring the Sorrowful Christ, the Virgin Mary and St Nicholas, and an attractive Baroque interior. Particularly worth seeing is the Waldlaufkapelle, which is closed off from the rest of the church interior by a wrought-iron grille. It houses a collection of reliquaries.

Coat of arms of Hall in Tirol

Wattens ❹

Road map B4. *7,700.* *(05224) 52904.*

The Swarovski factory of decorative glass and glass jewellery and its museum in Wattens are a unique and fascinating experience. Here you can see the world's largest cut crystal (300,000 carats), and a crystal wall 11 m (36 ft) high, with several tons of glittering semi-precious stones.

Swarovski Crystal Worlds
Kristallweltenstrasse 1. ***Tel*** *(05224) 51080.* *9am–6pm.*

Environs: Volders has an unusual church devoted to St Charles Borromeo, dating from 1620–54.

The entrance to Swarovski Kristallwelten in Wattens

Schwaz ❺

Road map C4. *12,000.* *Franz-Josef-Strasse 2 (05242) 65630.* **www**.schwaz.at

During the 16th century, this busy commercial town in the Inn river valley was the second largest in the Tyrol. Schwaz suffered extensive damage during the battle of 1809, but it has preserved some lovely historic sights.

The imposing Renaissance Schloss Tratzberg

The most impressive of these is the 15th-century **Pfarrkirche**, with its high copper-shingled tower and beautiful, crenellated gables. The most striking elements inside are the stone balustrade of the gallery with intricate lacework (c.1520) and an impressive Baroque organ enclosure. The figures of St Anne, St Ursula and St Elizabeth on the altarpiece are original Gothic decorations. The statues of St George and St Florian, the patron saints of Austria, were added at a later date. The double **cemetery chapel** (1504–7) has a lovely covered staircase leading to the upper chapel, which has a carved wooden altar. The lower chapel has original 16th-century frescoes depicting the Crucifixion and the Mount of Olives.

The late-Gothic **Franziskanerkirche**, the Franciscan church and monastery, has retained its original Gothic interior, clearly visible despite Baroque additions made in the 18th century. The cloister along the south wall of the church was built in 1509–12 by Christof Reichartinger; it shows a series of 16th-century paintings with Passion scenes.

Schwaz was once a major centre for the production of silver, and one of the mines, the **Silberbergwerk**, is now open to the public and can be explored by train and a guided tour on foot.

Silberbergwerk
Alte Landstrasse 3a. ***Tel*** *(05242) 72372-0.* *May–Oct: 9am–5pm daily, Nov–Apr: 10am–4pm Wed–Sun.* **www**.silberbergwerk.at

Tratzberg 6

Road map C4. ***Tel*** *(05242) 6356620.* *Apr–Oct: 10am–4pm daily (to 5pm Jul & Aug).* **www**.schloss-tratzberg.at

A short way from Schwaz, in the Inn river valley, stands the impressive Renaissance Schloss Tratzberg. This castle was once a frontier fortress which guarded Andechs county against the Bavarians. It changed hands many times and is now the private property of the Enzenberg family, with a small museum.

The castle is entered from the west side through a Renaissance portal. The inner courtyard with its heavily decorated low arcades was built in two stages: the first around 1500 and the second in the late 16th century. The most interesting parts of the castle are the armoury, with its tremendous collection of early arms; the Royal Room, with its exposed beam ceiling, once used by Anna of Bohemia, the widow of Duke Henry of Tyrol; and finally the Habsburg Hall, with the family tree of Emperor Maximilian I and 148 portraits. The room has a red marble column at its centre and is covered by a coffered ceiling. The emperor's room on the second floor retains its original intricately carved wooden ceiling, and the bedroom is decorated by a series of 16th-century paintings of a knightly tournament created by Hans Schäufelein. The Fugger family room still boasts its original Renaissance decor. Its best feature is the richly inlaid door dating from 1515.

Achensee 7

Road map C4.

Situated between the Inn and the Isar river basins is Achensee, the largest lake in Tyrol, about 9 km (6 miles) long. On its northern shore the Karwendel mountain range extends up to Innsbruck. On its eastern shore are the Rofan Mountains, with their highest peak, the Rofanspitze, rising to 2,259 m (7,411 ft).

Achensee can be reached by cog-wheel steam train from **Jenbach**. Worth seeing in this village is the church of St. Wolfgang, a late-Gothic structure built in 1487–1500 by Gilg Mitterhofer from Schwaz; its Baroque tower is a later addition. Although repeatedly rebuilt, it still has its late-Gothic side portals and ogival windows; one of the side altars has a late-Gothic statue of the Madonna.

Sailing yachts on Achensee, Tyrol's largest lake

Charming flower displays outside the alpine houses in Alpbach

Alpbach 8

Road map C4. *2,500.* *(05336) 20094.* **www**.alpbach.at

In a high mountain valley on the Alpbach river lies the town of the same name that once a year becomes the intellectual capital of Europe. Every year since 1945, delegates representing the worlds of science, politics, economics and culture have gathered here to discuss the future of the world. Before the fall of communism in the Eastern bloc countries in 1989, Austria's central position in Europe made this the most appropriate place for people from East and West to meet. Today their discussions are rather more academic, yet Alpbach has retained its great importance on Europe's political and intellectual map.

The floral displays outside the alpine houses and chalets in Alpbach rank among the best in the country. The little town also has the interesting **Church of St Oswald**. Its earliest records date from 1369, although it was altered in 1500 and the Baroque interior dates from 1724. The naves have ceiling paintings by Christof Anton Mayr (1751); the sculptures in the presbytery (c.1779) are the work of Franz Xaver Nissel.

Monument to the Battle of 1809 in Wörgl

Wörgl 9

Road map C4. *11,000.* *Bahnhofstrasse 4 (05332) 76007.*

The industrial town of Wörgl, at the fork of Inn river and Brixentaler Ache (a stream), is an important road and rail hub. The earliest settlement on the site, revealed by archaeological finds on the northeastern outskirts of town, date from the Bronze Age. In later years this was the site of a Roman settlement, and in the 4th century a Christian community was founded in the area. In the 13th century Wörgl belonged to Bavaria; during the reign of Maximilian I it finally became incorporated into Tyrol. Wörgl and its environs were the scene of fierce fighting during the Napoleonic wars, when the Tyrolean highlanders fought for their independence from the Bavarians and the French. A monument commemorating the battle now stands in front of **St Lawrence's church**. This church, built in 1748, is Baroque in style and has interesting stucco decorations, vault paintings, a main altar with Baroque sculptures and an attractive medieval statue of the Madonna.

Wörgl's location between the two tourist regions of Kaisergebirge and the Kitzbühel Alps makes it a convenient base for winter and summer expeditions.

Visitors sunbathing on Hohe Salve, near Söll

Söll 10

Road map C4. *3,000.* *(05333) 505210.*

Söll, a small town in the foothills of the Hohe Salve, part of the Wilder Kaiser (Wild Emperor) massif, grew around the **Church of St Peter and St Paul**. Built in 1361 but completely altered in the Baroque style in 1768 by Franz Bock of Kufstein, it contains beautiful vault paintings by Anton Mayr and, by the same artist, a picture of the Madonna in the main altarpiece. The town has many attractive houses with picturesque façades.

The greatest attraction of Söll, however, is the **Hohe Salve** mountain, rising to 1,828 m (5,997 ft) and visible from every point in the town. Two gondolas provide transport to the summit. There is a small chapel here, and the view over Brixental, the Kitzbühel Alps and the High Tauern Mountains in the distance, is truly majestic. Söll lies at the centre of a large skiing region, **Skiwelt Wilder Kaiser-Brixental**, in the southern part of Kaisergebirge, which also includes several other attractive resorts, such as the picturesque town of **Scheffau** nearby.

Kufstein ⓫

Road map C4. 15,000.
(05372) 62207.

The remains of a Stone Age settlement have been found in this health resort and tourist centre on the Bavarian border.

On a rocky hill to the north of the town stands the Feste Kufstein, a mighty fortress with a small barbican and the Emperor's Tower. Today it houses a **Regional Museum** and, on the ground floor of the tower, the Heldenorgel (Heroes' Organ), built to commemorate all who were killed in World War I. The late-Gothic **Church of St Vitus** was rebuilt in the 17th century in the Baroque style, but in the 20th century it was partly returned to its original Gothic appearance. Nearby stands the Holy Trinity Chapel, with a beautiful Baroque altar dating from 1765.

Environs: Hechtsee and Stimmersee, two small, scenic lakes west of Kufstein, are excellent for water sports enthusiasts. About 30 km (22 miles) northeast of Kufstein, beyond the Kaisergebirge ridge known as Zahmer Kaiser (Tame Emperor), is **Walchsee**, a beguiling town and lake of the same name, with many fine houses with picturesque façades and a good water sports centre. The road from Kufstein along the Sparchenbach river leads to Stripsenkopf, at 1,807 m (5,929 ft) the highest peak in the Zahmer Kaiser range, with great views of the Kaisergebirge.

St. Johann in Tirol ⓬

Road map C4. 8,000.
(05352) 63335-0.

St. Johann in Tirol is a popular winter sports resort, boasting good downhill runs on the northern slopes of the Kitzbüheler Horn and splendid conditions for cross-country skiing. The town has several Baroque buildings with picturesque elevations, and the walls of the parish house feature the original frescoes from 1480. The first large Baroque church in the area was built in 1728 by Abraham Milbauer, on the site of an earlier Gothic structure. Inside **Mariä Himmelfahrtskirche** (church of the Assumption of the Virgin Mary) are magnificent vault paintings by one of the great masters of Baroque art, Simon Benedikt Faistenberger.

Kitzbühel ⓭

Road map C4. 8,500.
Hinterstadt 18 (05356) 66660.
www.kitzbuehel.com

Once the undisputed winter sports capital of the country, Kitzbühel now has to share its crown with other resorts. The alpine town is surrounded by several mountain massifs, with scores of well-signposted trails. The best conditions are offered by the Hahnenkamm–Steinbergkogel–Pengelstein group to the southwest, the Kitzbüheler Horn to the north, the Stuckkogel and the Thurn Pass. This is where the famous Hahnenkammrennen, a downhill skiing race, takes place at the end of January each year.

A picturesque snow-covered scene in Kitzbühel

Kitzbühel is more than a sporting resort; untouched by wartime ravages, it has many historic sights. The **Andreaskirche** was built in 1435 on the site of a Romanesque church and in 1785 it was rebuilt in the Baroque style. Inside are late-Gothic columns and 15th-century traceries and frescoes. There is also an interesting main altarpiece, by Simon Benedikt Faistenberger.

Adjacent to the parish church is **Liebfrauenkirche** (church of Our Lady), with a square tower. The main altar is also by Faistenberger. The 14th-century St Catherine's church in the city centre is now a monument to those killed in the two world wars.

The mighty fortress with the Emperor's Tower in Kufstein

Zillertaler Alpen ⓮

The Zillertal, the valley of the Ziller river, extends from Innau to the Austro-Italian border. Initially a wide upland, beyond Mayrhofen it splits into four narrower valleys that cut into the mountain ranges. Artificial lakes and large dams were built into most of the local rivers to provide a power supply for the entire region. The present popularity of winter sports has contributed to the rapid development of Zillertal. Especially popular with skiers are the Tuxer glacier runs, the Mayrhofen-Finkenberg trail and the town of Zell am Ziller. The well-marked trails in breathtakingly beautiful countryside lure ramblers here in the summer, and there are many attractive cycling routes.

Zillertaler Alpen
The Zillertaler Alps, a side range of the High Tauern, are steep crystalline mountains. Their highest peak is the Hochfeiler at 3,510 m/ 11,516 ft.

★ Tuxer Tal
The valley of the Tuxer Bach (Tuxer stream) is picturesque, with many attractive resorts. Tuxer Ferner, the local glacier, offers the best year-round skiing conditions in the entire area.

KEY

- Major road
- Minor road
- Cable car, chairlift
- River
- Viewpoint

Schlegeisspeicher
The largest artificial lake in the area is scenically situated at the foot of the Hochfeiler Massif and the Schlegeis glacier.

STAR SIGHTS

★ Tuxer Tal

★ Zell am Ziller

For hotels and restaurants in this region see pp303–6and pp334–6

★ Zell am Ziller
This beautiful fresco (1779) by Franz A. Zeiller adorns the church of St Vitus. Another sight to see here is the old gold mine.

VISITORS' CHECKLIST

Road map C4. *Zillertal Tourismus Bundesstrasse 27d, A-6262 Schlitters, (05288) 87187.* @ *info@zillertal.at*
www.zillertal.at

Mayrhofen
In this picturesque resort, the most popular tourist destination in the Zillertal, the wide valley narrows and divides into four smaller alpine valleys.

0 km 5
0 miles 5

TYROLEAN NATIONAL COSTUMES

The Tyrolean version of Austria's national costume is not reserved for special occasions – here many people wear it every day. The man's *Tracht* consists of leather shorts (summer) or breeches (winter) held in place by braces and tied under the knees, thick socks and a *Loden* jacket made of thick, woollen cloth, with bone buttons. To this is added a felt hat with a distinctive tuft of coarse animal hair. The woman's *Dirndl* comprises a puffed-sleeve blouse with a bodice and a pleated skirt with an apron. Women also wear hats or scarves.

A young couple dressed in typical Tyrolean outfits

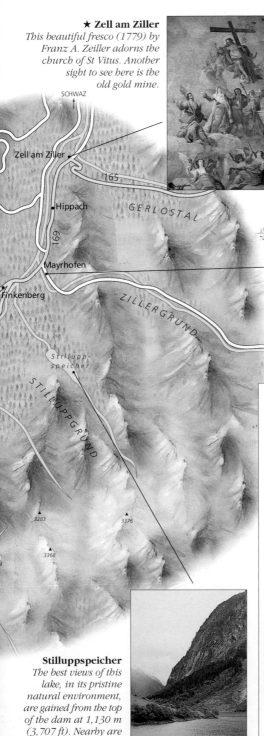

Stilluppspeicher
The best views of this lake, in its pristine natural environment, are gained from the top of the dam at 1,130 m (3,707 ft). Nearby are two waterfalls.

Europabrücke, the highest road bridge in Europe

Brenner ⓯

Road map B5.

At an altitude of 1,374 m (4,508 ft), the Brenner Pass is the lowest passage across the Eastern Alps, and as such one of the most easily accessible routes connecting northern Europe with Italy. Separating the Stubai Alps from the Zillertal Alps, the pass was originally used by the Romans as a trade and military route. A highway suitable for carriage traffic was built in 1772, and the first trans-alpine railway line was opened here in 1867. Today the motorway leading across the wide saddle of the Brenner also boasts the highest and most impressive road bridge in Europe, the Europabrücke, 815 m (2,674 ft) long.

Stubaital ⓰

Road map B4. *Fulpmes, Bahnstrasse 17 (05225) 62235.*
www.stubai.at

Travelling on the Brenner motorway from Innsbruck towards Italy you will pass the Stubai Alps to your right, a high ridge massif with few valleys. The lowest route into the centre of the massif runs along the Stubaital (Stubai Valley), with its busy tourist resorts of Fulpmes and Neustift. The highest peak of the Stubai Alps, Zuckerhütl (Little Sugar Loaf), rises to 3,507 m (11,506 ft). The Stubaital is a very quiet place, particularly when compared with the neighbouring Zillertal, winding its way above a busy motorway. The Stubai glacier provides excellent conditions for all-year skiing and walking.

Fulpmes, a popular tourist centre in the Stubaital

Ötztal ⓱

Road map B4. *Ötz, Hauptstrasse 66 (05252) 6669.*

Following the course of the Ötztaler Ache, a tributary of the Inn river, is the long valley of Ötztal. At its southern end, near the border with Italy, rises the Ötztaler Alpen range, with many peaks above 3,500 m (11,500 ft): the Wildspitze at 3,774 m (12,381 ft) is Tyrol's highest summit.

Nestling within the Ötztaler Alps is also the highest parish in Austria, the ski resort of Obergurgl at 1,927 m (6,322 ft). The largest settlement in the lower part of Ötztal is **Ötz**, an old village with attractive, colourful houses. The paintings on the Star Inn date from 1573 and 1615. On a steep slope stands the church of St George and St Nicholas, which retains some original Gothic features, including a vault and portals.

The largest town at the upper end of the Ötz Valley is **Längenfeld**, where you find the church of St Catherine. It has a 74-m (243-ft) high Gothic tower, a decorative west portal and a Baroque interior.

Ötztal's administrative centre is the old Tyrolean village of **Sölden**. There is good skiing on Tiefenbachferner and superb views from Gaislacher Kogel and Wilder Mann.

In 1991, a frozen human body was discovered on the Italian side of the Ötztal Alps. Although over 5,000 years old, Ötzi, as he was named, was perfectly preserved by the ice, along with some 70 artifacts.

Seefeld ⓲

Road map B4. *3,000.*
Klosterstrasse 43 (05212) 2313.

This small town, occupying a large sunny plateau, is one of the most attractive places near Innsbruck. It is a smart resort, with elegant shops along a wide promenade, and boasts a variety of attractions. In the 1964 and 1976 Winter Olympics, Seefeld was the venue for all the Nordic skiing contests, enhancing

◁ A man-made lake at the foot of Zillertaler Alpen

the town's prosperity and reputation. The local cross-country skiing trails are the longest in the Alps, measuring some 250 km (155 miles).

At the centre of Seefeld stands the huge 15th-century church of St Oswald while at the western end of the town is a chapel built on the orders of Archduke Leopold V to house a crucifix dating from the early 16th century and said to have miraculous powers. The crucifix stands within the altarpiece of this small, circular building with a Renaissance portal and onion dome.

Visitors to Seefeld can also enjoy a trip to the casino, one of the largest in Austria.

View of Zugspitze from the Ehrwald side

Ehrwald ⓳

Road map B4. *2,500.*
Kirchplatz 1 (05673) 2000.

Nestling below the western side of Zugspitze (2,965 m/ 9728 ft), the highest peak of the Bavarian Alps, is the resort village of Ehrwald. On the German side of the mountain is the resort of Garmisch-Partenkirchen, the most popular winter sports centre in that area. Several Austrian and German resorts, including Garmisch-Partenkirchen and Ehrwald, have joined up to form one vast skiing area.

The summit of Zugspitze can be reached from both the German and the Austrian sides. From Ehrwald, you take the cable car from the lower station of Ehrwald/ Obermoos. The upper station affords magnificent views. To the south, beyond the mountain ranges of Kaisergebirge, Karwendelgebirge and Dachstein, you can see the snow-covered peaks of the High Tauern. To the east, there are the Arlberg mountains with Silvretta and Rätikon, with the peaks of the Appenzeller Alpen in between, and the Allgäu and Ammergau mountains in the distance. To the north, Bavaria can be seen.

Clemens Krauss, the founder of the famous Vienna New Year's Day Concerts, lived in Ehrwald and lies buried here.

Reutte ⓴

Road map B4. *6,000.*
Untermarkt 34 (05672) 62336.

Reutte is the largest town in the Ausserfern district, a remote area that was cut off from the world for a considerable time: it is said that the first car arrived here only in 1947. Reutte can be reached from Innsbruck via the Fern Pass, a route first used in Roman times. In the valley of the Lech river, it is today the main town and trade centre of the region. In medieval times it grew rich on the salt trade, and to this day it has some lovely town houses with oriel windows, open staircases and painted façades. Many of the paintings are by Johann Jakob Zeiller, the best-known member of an artistic family that settled in Reutte in the 17th and 18th centuries – they once lived at No. 1 Zeiller Platz.

The 15th-century convent church of St Anna features several interesting works of art. In the main altarpiece is a picture of the Madonna with Child and St Anna (c.1515) and two vast figures of St Magnus and St Afra dating from the early 18th century.

The **Heimatmuseum** (regional museum) has a fine collection of paintings by outstanding masters of the Baroque, mainly of the Zeiller family members, as well as exhibits associated with transport and salt mining.

Specimens representative of the local flora can be seen in the **Alpenblumengarten**, an alpine flower garden on top of the Hahnenkamm, at a height of about 1,700 m (5,577 ft) above sea level.

Heimatmuseum
Grünes Haus, Untermarkt 25.
Tel *(05672) 72304. May–Oct: 1–5pm Tue–Sat (to 7pm Thu); Dec–Mar: 2–5pm Wed–Sat (to 7pm Thu).*

Environs: A short distance east of Reutte is the beautiful, 5-km (3-mile) long **Plansee**, where one of the small pleasure boats can take you on a cruise on the tranquil waters. In winter the entire lake freezes over and becomes one giant ice-skating rink.

Plansee, a tranquil, picturesque lake near Reutte

For hotels and restaurants in this region see pp303–6 and pp334–6

Warth, a town situated within the most famous winter sports region

Elbigenalp ㉑

Road map A4. *850.*
(05634) 5315.

The Lech river valley, which is parallel to the Inn river valley and snakes between mountain passes, cuts a deep ravine between the Allgäuer Alps and the Lechtal Alps. About half-way between the towns of Reutte and Warth lies Elbigenalp, a small village worth visiting for the local **Nikolauskirche** (church of St Nicholas). Built in the 14th century, the church's oldest surviving parts include the Gothic tower, presbytery and font. It was altered in the Baroque style, and the vault and wall paintings as well as the Stations of the Cross are the work of the artistic Zeiller family, who lived in Reutte.

St Martin's cemetery chapel in Elbigenalp has interesting original Gothic frescoes depicting scenes from the life of St Magdalene and the *Dance of Death* by Anton Falger.

Lech am Arlberg ㉒

Road map A4. *1,400.*
(05583) 2161-0.
www.lech-zuers.at

This small resort is situated on a large plateau at an altitude of 1,450 m (4,757 ft), not far from the source of the Lech river. Lech is regarded as one of Austria's most beautiful and most elegant mountain resorts. In order to protect the natural environment, some years ago the local authorities drastically limited the available accommodation, thus creating an exclusive resort. The fame of the resort spread around the world and many celebrities and royals began to spend their winter holidays in Lech, including the late Diana, Princess of Wales.

The town's development has been closely associated with the construction of the Arlberg and Flexen passes, which made Lech accessible in the winter months. Lifts and cable cars were built, and the vast snowy slopes of the Arlberg began to attract winter sports enthusiasts. Summer, too, can be very pleasant here, and there are many beautiful trails for walking or mountain cycling. Sights to see include the 15th-century Gothic **church of St Nicholas**, with an even older tower. In addition, there are swanky hotels, chic shops, smart cafés and restaurants, which combine to make Lech a tourist magnet for the wealthy.

Lech has joined Zürs, Stuben and St Anton to form a large single skiing region.

Zürs am Arlberg ㉓

Road map A4. *130.*
(05583) 2245.

Zürs, a tiny resort some 6 km (4 miles) south of Lech, lies at an altitude of 1,716 m (5,630 ft). Along with

A fabulous scenery of snowy mountain peaks rising above Zürs am Arlberg

neighbouring Lech, Zürs places a great emphasis on the protection of the natural environment. As a rule, the few hotels and pensions accept only regular guests in their very limited number of rooms. The exclusive nature of the resort, its elegant cafés, restaurants and a famous discothèque provide truly world-class après-ski entertainment, while the expansive ski slopes and the fairly heavy snowfalls over many months attract dedicated winter sports enthusiasts. Austria's first chair lifts were built in Zürs in 1937 and the first skiing competitions were held here as early as 1906. Lifts and cable cars take you to a number of excellent viewing points.

Arlberg ㉔

See pp256–7.

Ischgl, one of Austria's most attractive skiing resorts

Ischgl ㉕

Road map A5. *1,500.* *050990-100.* **www**.ischgl.at

Ischgl, on the Trisanna river at the eastern end of the Silvrettastrasse, is one of the loveliest Austrian resorts. An international ski centre, at an altitude of 1,377 m (4,518 ft), it provides access to 200 km (120 miles) of ski runs and 40 lifts within the Silvretta range on the Austrian–Swiss border. The town is also an ideal starting point for a drive along the Silvrettahochalpenstrasse, a hairpin mountain road, often snow-covered – and therefore closed – from November until late May, which connects the Montafon Valley – where Schruns is the best-known resort – and the Ill river with the Trisanna Valley. The road drops by 1,000 m (3,280 ft) over just 15 km (9 miles).

The area around the Silvretta-Stausee, a reservoir on the Bielerhöhe Pass at 2,036 m (6,680 ft), has been made a national park; the ski runs in the Silvretta massif start here. The most beautiful views are to be had from Hohes Rad, 2,934 m (9,626 ft). The high mountain section of Silvrettastrasse ends in Galtür, a lovely village on the Ballunspitze.

Lünersee, a reservoir lake at the foot of Schesaplana

Lünersee ㉖

Road map A5.

Lünersee lies at the foot of the Schesaplana peak (2,965 m/9,728 ft), at an altitude of 1,907 m (6,257 ft). Once this was the largest lake in Eastern Austria, surrounded by rugged mountains criss-crossed with ravines. The dam built here in 1958 raised the water level by 27 m (89 ft), creating an artificial reservoir that now powers Lünersee and Rodund power stations.

Bludenz ㉗

Road map A4. *15,000.* *Werdenbergerstrasse 42 (05552) 63621-260.* **www**.bludenz.at *Chocolate Festival (early Jul).*

Beautifully situated at the confluence of five alpine valleys, the town of Bludenz is now a popular resort with excellent skiing areas in its environs. An 10th-century document survives in which Otto I gives the Bishop of Chur a church "in loco Plutenes". During the reign of Friedrich IV the Poor, the town became an administrative centre and power base for the region.

Despite several devastating fires, Bludenz still has some interesting historic sights. The oldest building is **Oberes Tor** (Upper Gate), which houses the local history museum. Inside St Lawrence church (1514) are two original altars made from black marble and two paintings (1510) showing the Marriage of the Virgin Mary and the Visitation. The seat of the regional authorities is Gayenhofen castle, a medieval building remodelled in Baroque style in 1643 by Franz Andrä von Sternbach.

Today, the town is permeated by chocolate smells from the Suchard factory, producers of the famous confectionery and organizers of an annual chocolate festival.

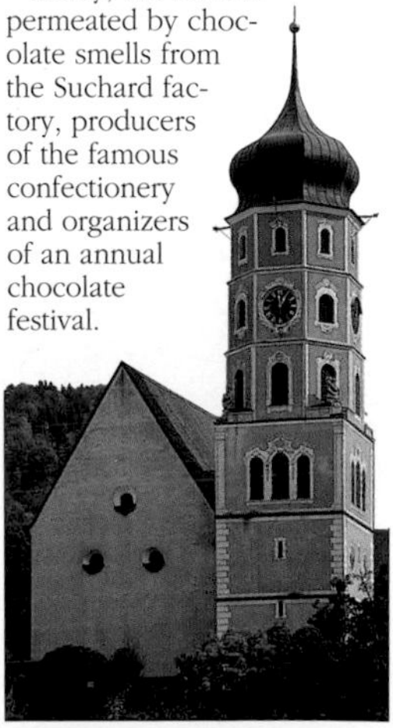

The octagonal tower of the Laurentiuskirche in Bludenz

Arlberg ㉔

The Arlberg Pass in the Eastern Alps is part of the European watershed between the catchment areas of the North Sea, the Black Sea, the tributaries of the Rhine and the Danube. Arlberg used to be completely cut off from the rest of the country, oriented more towards Germany and Switzerland, until the railway tunnel was built in 1880–84, connecting Vorarlberg with the rest of Austria. The tunnel, at an altitude of 1,310 m (4,298 ft), measures 10,238 m (33,589 ft) in length, and was for many years the longest in Austria. Today, the Arlberg region has some of the country's most exclusive ski resorts.

Valluga ⑦
The breathtaking view extending from the summit at 2,809 m (9,216 ft) embraces the Rätikon Mountains, the Montafon Valley as well as the Brenner, Ötztal and Stubai Alps.

Flexenpass ⑥
The pass is surrounded by the Rätikon mountain peaks, including Zimbaspitze and Schesaplana. Thanks to a system of avalanche defences, the road across remains passable in winter.

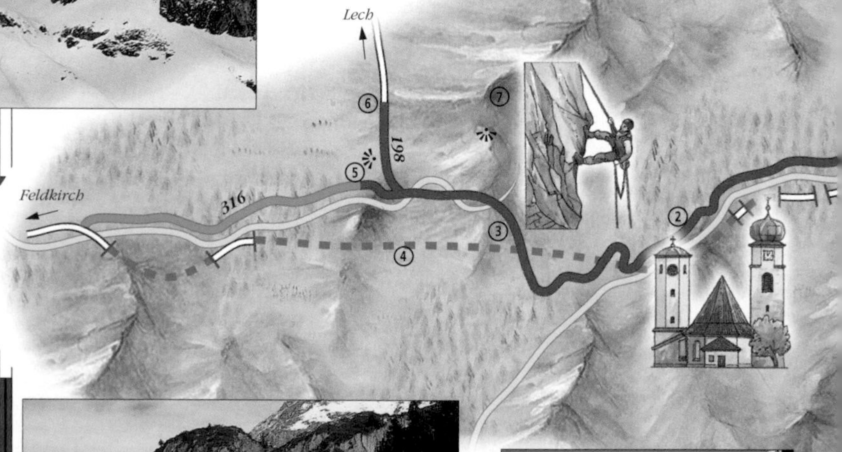

Stuben ⑤
This quiet village at the foot of the Albonagrat (2,334 m/ 7,658 ft) has ski runs leading to St. Anton. The name ("cosy living room") refers to the cabins from where travellers set off on the mountain trails.

Arlbergtunnel ④
The road tunnel underneath the Arlberg Pass, 14 km (9 miles) long, was the longest in the world when it opened in 1978.

Landeck ①
Schloss Landeck, built in about 1200 and rebuilt after a fire, has retained its original grand hall with a late-Gothic vault, and a chapel with early 16th-century frescoes. Today, the castle is the home of the local folk museum.

TIPS FOR DRIVERS

Length of the route: *45 km (28 miles).*
Stopping-off points: *the hotel by the hospice in St. Christoph offers accommodation. There are many restaurants and excellent shops in St. Anton am Arlberg.*

KEY

▦	Motorway
▬	Suggested route
▦	Scenic route
═	Other road
=	River, lake
▪ ▪	Tunnel
✺	Viewpoint

0 km — 5
0 miles — 5

S16 E60
316 E60
188
171
315
①
Innsbruck
Davos

St. Christoph ③
The town's small statue of St Christopher, from the old hospice in St. Christoph, was replaced with a new sculpture after fire damage in 1957. The hospice itself is today a luxury hotel. Austria's first regular ski-school was founded in this town in 1901.

St. Anton am Arlberg ②
The largest tourist resort in Arlberg, St. Anton is surrounded by numerous ski trails, and good snow conditions are guaranteed throughout the season.

Bregenzer Wald ㉘

The Bregenzer Wald (Bregenz Forest) occupies the northern part of Vorarlberg and extends along the Bregenzer Ache valley. This region has maintained much of its individual character. Its inhabitants cherish their traditions, and the architecture, the national costumes and the dialect spoken here differ from those found in the rest of the country. Bregenz Forest has many picturesque resorts with excellent facilities for visitors. Apart from Bregenz itself, two larger urban centres have become established on its borders – Dornbirn, and Feldkirch, the "gateway to Austria", with its beautifully preserved old town.

Schwarzenberg ⑥
This was the home town of Angelika Kauffmann, a prominent artist of the Neo-Classicist period. Her paintings depicting Christ's apostles and disciples can be seen in the local Holy Trinity church.

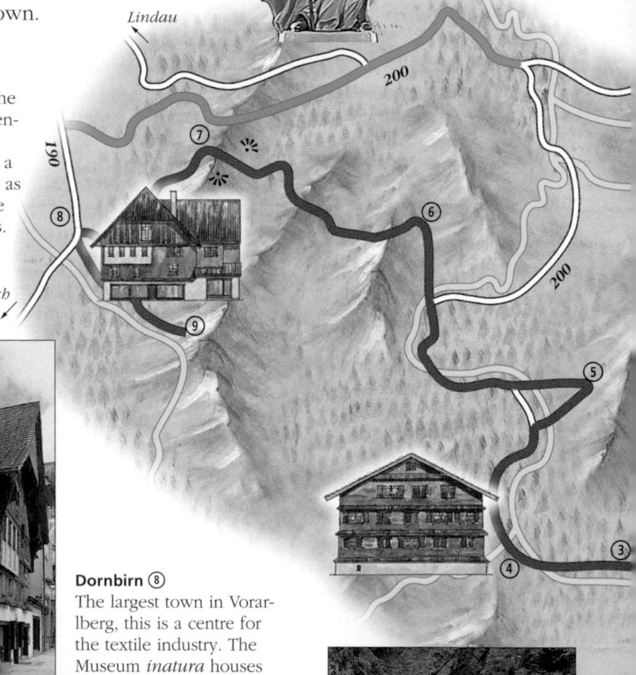

Ammenegg ⑦
From the forecourt of the Sonnblick Inn in Ammenegg visitors can enjoy lovely views which, on a clear day, extend as far as Lake Constance and the peaks of the Swiss Alps.

Dornbirn ⑧
The largest town in Vorarlberg, this is a centre for the textile industry. The Museum *inatura* houses modern displays on the natural environment and the history of the region.

Rappenlochschlucht ⑨
The road to the Rappenloch gorge runs steeply uphill along the Dornbirner Ache stream, and ends at a reservoir.

ANGELIKA KAUFFMANN

Angelika Kauffmann, a Swiss painter (1741–1807) of idealized portraits in sentimental or Neo-Classical style, was associated with German, English and Italian artistic circles. She left many works in Schwarzenberg, where she had family links. The local church has an altarpiece by her and also a small bust. More works by this celebrated artist can be seen in the Vorarlberger Landesmuseum in Bregenz.

Mellau ④
A quiet village on the Bregenzer Ache, Mellau is famous for its wooden houses with shingle-clad roofs, characteristically adorned with flowers.

Bezau ⑤
This picturesque village set among orchards has a lovely church, dating from 1771, and a small but interesting museum devoted to the region's folk art.

Bregenzer Ache ③
The valley of Bregenzer Ache, running from Lechtaler Alpen, is the main axis of the Bregenzer Forest. The river flows between steep rock faces and gentle hills, past pleasant villages, down a long winding gorge, on its way to Bodensee (Lake Constance).

Schröcken ②
The church in Schröcken, at the foot of the Widderstein (2,533 m/8,310 ft), has a richly decorated interior and beautiful stained-glass windows.

Hochtannbergpass ①
The pass between Schröcken and Warth winds its scenic way along the upper Bregenzer Ache, and reaches its highest point near Schröcken at 1,679 m (5,508 ft).

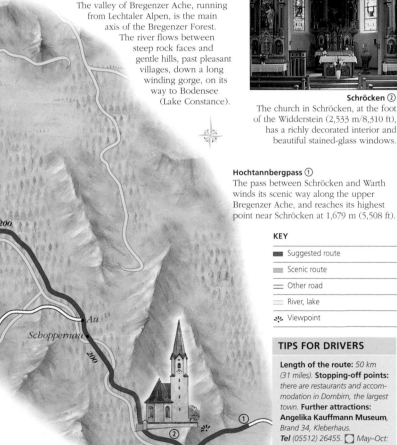

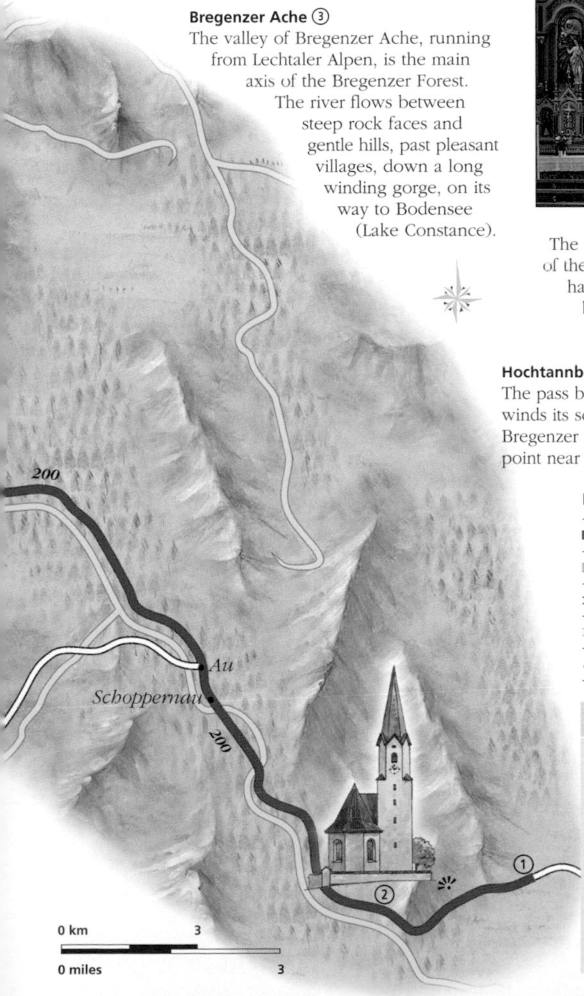

KEY

▬	Suggested route
▭	Scenic route
═	Other road
▬	River, lake
✶	Viewpoint

TIPS FOR DRIVERS

Length of the route: *50 km (31 miles).* **Stopping-off points:** *there are restaurants and accommodation in Dornbirn, the largest town.* **Further attractions: Angelika Kauffmann Museum,** *Brand 34, Kleberhaus.* **Tel** *(05512) 26455.* ☐ *May–Oct: 10am–6pm daily (to 8pm Thu); Nov–Jan: 2–4pm Fri–Sun.* 🖼

0 km 3

0 miles 3

Au
Schoppernau
200

Bregenz ㉙

The capital of Vorarlberg since 1923, Bregenz is strategically – and attractively – situated on the eastern shore of Bodensee (Lake Constance), at the edge of the Rhine valley and the foot of the Austrian and Swiss Alps. It is a meeting point of four countries: Austria, Germany, Switzerland and the Principality of Liechtenstein. The Romans established the settlement of Brigantium, and later it became the Alemanni town of Brancantia. In 1451 and 1523 Bregenz came under Habsburg rule, and during the Thirty Years' War, it was destroyed by the Swedes. Attractions in Bregenz include walks on the nearby Pfänder massif, and boat trips out on the lake.

View of Bregenz, on the shores of Lake Constance

Exploring Bregenz

Oberstadt (upper town) is the oldest part of Bregenz, with a number of well-preserved historic buildings and the remains of 13th-century fortifications. Innenstadt (inner city) is much newer. It has a theatre and an interesting regional museum. The promenades along Lake Constance, always shrouded in a gentle mist, are worth exploring, as are the grounds of the popular Bregenz summer festivals.

Vorarlberger Landesmuseum

Kornmarktplatz 1. ***Tel*** *(05574) 46050.* *until 2013 for major renovation works.* **www**.vlm.at

The Vorarlberg Regional Museum holds collections of prehistoric relics, artifacts dating from the Roman time of the settlement of Brigantium and objects from the days of the Alemanni settlers, all found in Bregenz and its vicinity. A separate department is devoted to regional handicrafts and customs, old weaponry, coins and medals, as well as regional costumes. One particularly fascinating exhibit is the collection of portable organs. The museum also has an art gallery which holds many beautiful portraits by Angelika Kauffmann (1741–1807), whose family came from Bregenzer Wald *(see p258)*. Other interesting exhibits are early artifacts, Roman and Gothic sculptures and paintings, old altarpieces, and beautiful gold and silver ornaments. The jewels of this museum are the 9th-century stone tablet from Lauterach and the early 16th-century crucifix from the collegiate church in Mehrerau.

Rathaus

Rathausstrasse 4.

The former granary built in 1686 became the town's chancellery in 1720 and, in 1810, the seat of the town's authorities. It remains the town hall to this day.

Renaissance altarpiece of 1610, in Seekapelle St. Georg

Seekapelle St. Georg

Rathausstrasse.

The small chapel of St George, known as the Lakeside Chapel, stands close to the church of the same name. Its walls, once lapped by the lake, are now separated from the water by a street and a railway line. The chapel was built in 1445 and altered in the Baroque style in 1690–98, but it has preserved a Renaissance altarpiece, dating from 1615. Depicted at its centre is the Madonna at the foot of the Cross; the side niches show scenes from the Passion.

Martinsturm

Martinsplatz. **Vorarlberger Militärmuseum Martinsturm** Martinsgasse 3. ***Tel*** *(05574) 46632.* *Apr–Nov: 10am–5:30pm Tue–Sun.*

The rectangular St Martin's Tower, the symbol of Bregenz,

The Martinsturm, topped with a Baroque dome

was probably built in the 14th century on earlier Romanesque foundations. Its present look and its staircase date from 1599, while the Baroque cupola was added at a later date. With its Venetian windows and overall muted colour scheme the tower is reminiscent of Moorish architecture. It houses a small museum with displays of arms and weaponry.

In the adjacent St Martin's Chapel, beautiful frescoes can be seen, which date back to 1362 and depict Christ in Mandorla with the symbols of the four evangelists and portraits of the chapel founders, members of the Monfort family.

Altes Rathaus

Oberstadt.

The Old Town Hall, built in 1662 by Michael Kuen, was the seat of the Bregenz municipal authorities until the 19th century. This solid, half-timbered structure stands in the centre of Oberstadt, close to the former town gate, Unteres Tor (Lower Gate). A relief depicts Epona, the Celtic goddess of agriculture who is shown on horseback, holding a horn of plenty.

The 17th-century, half-timbered Altes Rathaus

Zisterzienserkloster Mehrerau

Mehrerauerstrasse 66. ***Tel*** *(05574) 71461.* *8:30–11:45am, 2:30–5:30pm Mon–Sat, 3–4pm Sun.*

To the west of the city centre stands the Zisterzienserkloster Mehrerau, the Cistercian monastery that has been a centre of spiritual and intellectual life since the 11th century.

VISITORS' CHECKLIST

Road map A4.
27,500.
Rathausstrasse 35a (05574) 49590.
www.bregenz.at
Bregenzer Festspiele (mid-Jul–mid-Aug).

The church and monastery complex, originally built for the Benedictines and subsequently taken over by the Cistercians, was remodelled in 1740 in the Baroque style by Franz Anton Beer; the new tower was built using material from the previous Romanesque basilica. It was destroyed in the Napoleonic wars, rebuilt in 1855 and renovated in the 20th century. Inside, two pictures survive with the Stations of the Cross and two late-Gothic statues of the Madonna. The late-Gothic altar in the capitular room dates from 1582.

Adjacent to the reconstructed church and the Romanesque crypt there is now a secondary school, a monastery and a sanatorium.

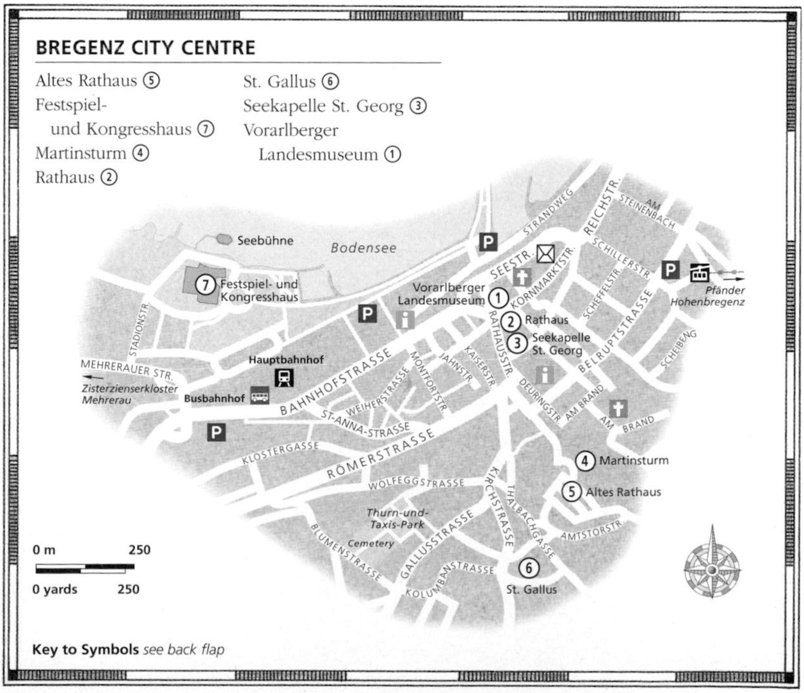

St. Gallus

Kirchplatz 3.

Opposite the city centre, on the banks of the Thalbach stream, stands the Stadtpfarrkirche St. Gallus (the parish church of St Gallus). According to legend, a previous church on this site had been consecrated by Gallus, an Irish missionary who arrived here in the 7th century. The present church was consecrated in 1318, and the sandstone gate tower in front of it was added in the 15th century. Another tower was added in 1672, and in 1738 the church was altered in the Baroque style, to plans by Anton Beer. At that time the nave was raised and a chapel was added in the transept.

The rather modest interior of the church is typical of Vorarlberg's ecclesiastical style and contrasts sharply with the styles of Tyrol and Bavaria, where Baroque opulence is much more in evidence. The main altarpiece includes statues of the saints Gallus, Peter, Paul and Ulrich, while the side chapel has figures of saints Magnus and Nicholas. St Magnus, an 8th-century Benedictine monk from St. Gallen, is the patron saint of the Allgäu, the region between the Tyrol and Vorarlberg; St Nicholas is said to keep a careful watch over the navigation on Bodensee. The beautiful stalls in the presbytery are made from walnut wood. They have deep inlays and the backrests are decorated on the outside with the effigies of saints.

Decorative detail on the wall of Stadtpfarrkirche St. Gallus

Festspielhaus

Platz der Wiener Symphoniker 1.
Tel (05574) 4130.

The Festspielgelände (festival grounds) consists of a complex of buildings created specifically for the Bregenz arts festival that has been held every year since 1946, from late July until late August. The festival events feature theatre and opera performances, as well as symphony concerts and fine art exhibitions. Since 1955, the shows have been staged at the Theater am Kornmarkt, a building in the city centre erected in 1838 as a granary and converted into a theatre in 1955. In 1980, a modern festival and congress complex was opened, including show and concert halls, exhibition rooms and a congress centre. The most spectacular of the festival venues, however, is the famous Seebühne, a floating stage extending far onto the lake. Shows and concerts are staged here and watched by the public on the shore. The summer programme includes opera, operetta, musical and ballet. Behind the festival grounds is the Spielcasino Bregenz.

Seebühne, the floating stage on Lake Constance

Gateway of the ruined Hohenbregenz fortress

Hohenbregenz

The Hohenbregenz fortress, whose ruins stand to this day on Gebhardsberg, was built in the 10th century. In 1338, the recorded owner of the castle was Hugo de Montfort. In 1451, following the death of the last ruler of that line, the castle, together with the town and Bregenz province, were bought by Sigismund of Tyrol. In 1647, the castle was blown up by the Swedish troops of General Wrangel during the Thirty Years' War, leaving only ruins. The original parts still standing today are the gateway, walls, barbican and a single turret.

In 1723, a chapel devoted to the saints Gebhard and George was built on top of Gebhardsberg and it became a popular pilgrimage site. St Gebhard, a 10th-century Bishop of Constance, was the son of Ulrich of Bregenz, born in Hohenbregenz.

Environs: At the foot of the **Pfänder** (1,065 m/3,494 ft), southeast of the present town, stood the Roman settlement of Brigantium. Today, this area is a favourite destination for walkers; you can also reach the top of the hill by cable car. From this summit, there are magnificent views extending across Bodensee (Lake Constance) and all of Bregenz. Far to the south, the ranges of the Allgäuer Alps can be seen on a clear day, as well as the ice-covered Schesaplana massif, the deep ravine of the Rhine and the Swiss peaks of Altmann and Säntis.

Bodensee 30

Road map A4. *Bodensee-Alpenrhein Tourismus, Bregenz, Römerstrasse 2 (05574) 43443.*
www.bodensee-vorarlberg.com

Bodensee, or Lake Constance as it is also known, is one of the largest and best-known European lakes. It divides its waters between the three countries surrounding it: Austria, Germany and Switzerland. Austria actually only claims a very small part of it: the total area of the lake is 538.5 sq km (208 sq miles), of which only 38 sq km (14.7 sq miles) is Austrian. Bodensee is 74 km (44 miles) long, and as such the largest lake in the Alps. Once the lake was much larger, but with time deposits carried by the Rhine have reduced its size. The Rhine flows into the lake in a broad delta, wholly in Austrian territory. Having passed through the entire length of Bodensee, it emerges in a waterfall as a turbulent mountain river near Schaffhausen, in Switzerland. The countryside around the lake benefits from a pleasant, moderate climate. Even before World War II, Bodensee was considered to be one of Europe's most polluted lakes, just as the Rhine was one of the dirtiest rivers. However, for several years now it has met all the standards set for environmental protection.

Today, Bodensee forms not so much a border as a link between the countries that lie on its shores. For Austria it is a highly convenient transport route to western Europe, while for the inhabitants of the surrounding towns and villages, as well as for the visitors that arrive here from the neighbouring countries in great numbers every summer, it provides excellent facilities for water sports and relaxation.

The mountains around the town of Bregenz extend right up to the water, creating a picturesque setting for the countless artistic events that take place here, such as the Bregenz Spring and the internationally acclaimed Bregenz Festival. Many performances take place on the famous Seebühne or floating stage.

A number of interesting towns line the shores of Bodensee, including Lindau, the flower island of Mainau, and Friedrichshafen on the German side, which can be reached by ferry or pleasure craft sailing from Bregenz.

A picturesque sunset over the vast expanse of Bodensee

17th-century lace in the Stickereimuseum in Lustenau

Lustenau 31

Road map A4. *20,000.* *Rathausstrasse 1 (05577) 81810.*

A fairly large town, Lustenau lies 5 km (3 miles) north of the mouth of the Rhine as it joins Bodensee, on the border with Switzerland. It is famous for its beautiful embroidery and lace-making, popular throughout Austria.

It was at Lustenau that the Romans under the leadership of Emperor Constantine II defeated the Alemanni tribes who had risen up against the empire. The earliest historic records date from 887, when the settlement belonged to the Carolingians. Until 1806, it was a free territory within the empire. In 1814, after the Congress of Vienna, Lustenau came under Austrian rule.

During the 19th century, the town developed into one of Austria's most important centres for the textile industry, known primarily for its linen products. One of the most interesting sights in Lustenau is the **Stickereimuseum** (Embroidery Museum) at No. 20 Pontenstrasse, which exhibits both hand-made and modern machine-made embroidery, and some early embroidery machines. Also worth visiting is the Rhine Museum at No. 4 Höchsterstrasse, which documents the history of the local people and the Rhine.

Stickereimuseum
Pontenstrasse 20. ***Tel*** *(05522) 305221.* *3–7pm Thu & Fri.*

CARINTHIA & EAST TYROL

Carinthia and East Tyrol, Austria's two southernmost regions, are bordered by Slovenia and Italy in the south, and Styria and Salzburger Land to the east and north. Between them they have many attractions, including the Carinthian lakes and the Hohe Tauern National Park. East Tyrol is separate from the rest of Tyrol, and has closer transport and cultural links with Carinthia.

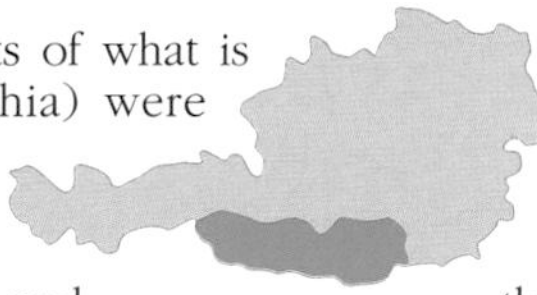

The earliest inhabitants of what is now Kärnten (Carinthia) were the Celtic Carnuni. In the 1st century AD it was part of the Roman province of Noricum, and in the 6th century was overrun by the Slav tribe of the Carantani, from whom it probably took its name. Although Carinthia belonged to the Habsburgs from 1335, a Slav national minority has survived in the area to this day. After World War I the newly-formed state of Yugoslavia tried to annex part of Carinthia from the defeated Austro-Hungarian Empire, but a plebiscite kept the region with Austria. The beauty of its landscape and its pleasant, Mediterranean climate attract many foreign visitors to Carinthia, and numerous Austrians also have second homes here. The most scenic route in the Austrian Alps, the Grossglockner Hochalpenstrasse, separates Carinthia from the East Tyrol, passing through Salzburger Land. Carinthia's two main towns are its capital Klagenfurt, and Villach.

After World War I, the southern part of Tyrol (Südtirol) became an autonomous province of Italy. Thus, georgraphically isolated from other parts of the Tyrol, East Tyrol (Osttirol) grew closer to its Carinthian neighbour than it was to the Tyrolean administration in Innsbruck. The entire province is surrounded by high mountain ranges and much of it is home to the Hohe Tauern National Park. The administrative centre of East Tyrol is Lienz.

A giant relief model of the province of Carinthia in the Schillerpark pavilion in Villach ***(see p274)***

◁ **The hilltop fortress of Hochosterwitz, poised like an eagle's nest above the St. Veit valley**

Exploring Carinthia and East Tyrol

High mountain peaks that descend right down to expansive lakes make these southernmost regions of Austria a paradise for visitors. Excellent on-shore facilities attract water sports enthusiasts, while the mountain glaciers enable committed skiers to enjoy the slopes even in summer. The loveliest parts of the region are the scenic route of Grossglockner Hochalpenstrasse and the Hohe Tauern National Park. While Carinthia is a lake district, East Tyrol is an inaccessible region of high mountains. In winter, cars need to be properly equipped, and not all roads are passable.

The Hohe Tauern National Park, one of the great attractions of the region

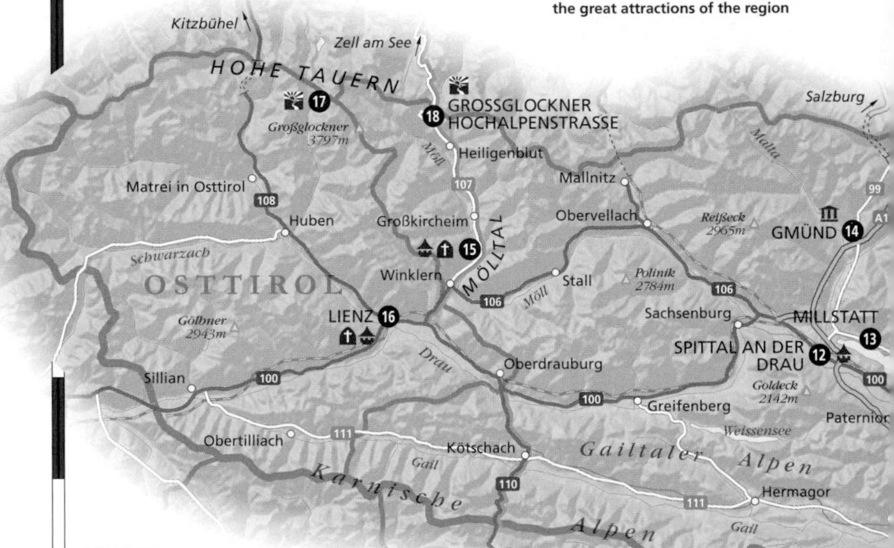

SEE ALSO

- ***Where to Stay*** pp306–7
- ***Where to Eat*** pp336–7

0 km 20

0 miles 20

KEY

- Motorway
- Major road
- Minor road
- Scenic route
- Main railway
- Minor railway
- International border
- Province border
- △ Summit

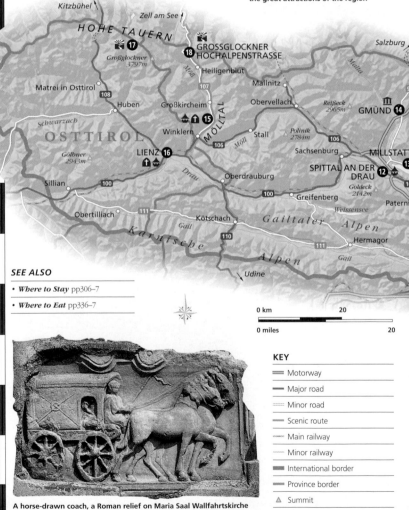

A horse-drawn coach, a Roman relief on Maria Saal Wallfahrtskirche

GETTING THERE

Villach, in Carinthia, is one of Austria's most important road transport hubs. The southern motorway which comes from Vienna passes through Villach and Klagenfurt, Carinthia's capital, which also has a small passenger airport. The easiest way to reach Lienz, in East Tyrol, is via Carinthia. Road and railway tunnels through the mountain ranges provide convenient transport links.

Church in Gratschach, at the foot of Landskron

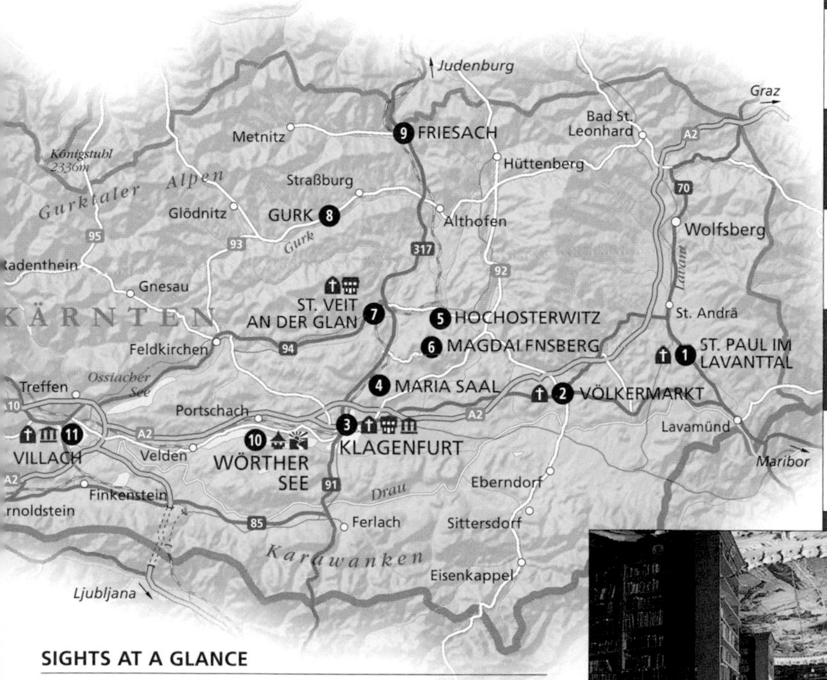

SIGHTS AT A GLANCE

Friesach 9
Gmünd 14
Gurk 8
Hochosterwitz 5
Hohe Tauern National Park (pp278–9) 17
Klagenfurt pp270–73 3
Lienz 16
Magdalensberg 6
Maria Saal 4
Millstatt 13
Mölltal 15
St. Paul im Lavanttal 1
St. Veit an der Glan 7
Spittal an der Drau 12
Villach 11
Völkermarkt 2

Excursions

Grossglockner Hochalpenstrasse 18
Around Wörther See 10

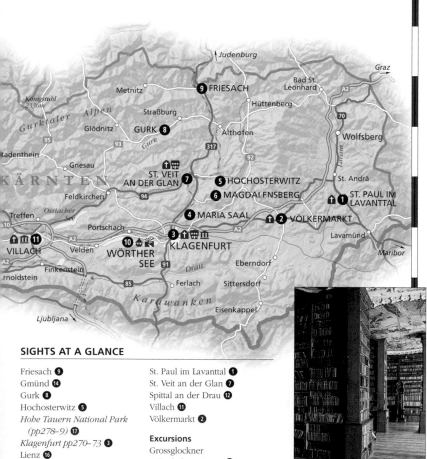

The marvellous library in the abbey of St. Paul im Lavanttal

Late 15th-century fresco in the abbey church, St. Paul im Lavanttal

St. Paul im Lavanttal ❶

Road map E5. *4,000.*
Hauptstrasse 10 (04357) 201722.

On the banks of the Lavant river stands one of the largest churches in Austria, the **Benedictine Abbey of St Paul**. Within the abbey complex is a well-preserved Romanesque church. The apse is decorated with reliefs showing the Adoration of the Magi and the enthroned Christ. Frescoes behind the main altar depict the founders of the abbey and various saints. The abbey museum also houses many magnificent works of art, including early chasubles, an 11th-century cross-shape reliquary that once belonged to Queen Adelaide, and an art collection with paintings by Peter Paul Rubens and Martin Johann Schmidt, and superb woodcuts by Albrecht Dürer and Rembrandt.

Benedictine Abbey of St Paul
Hauptstrasse 1. ***Tel*** *(04357) 201916.*
May–Oct: 9am–5pm.

Völkermarkt ❷

Road map E5. *12,000.*
Hauptplatz 1 (04232) 257147.

This town lies on the banks of a reservoir created by damming the Drau river, 25 km (16 miles) east of the Carinthian capital, Klagenfurt. It grew up around the bridge across the Drau and the 12th-century church of St Rupert, whose Romanesque tower still rises above the town. The **Kirche St. Magdalena** (church of Mary Magdalene), built in 1240 and altered in the 15th century, has a lovely late-Romanesque west portal. Its interior is late-Gothic, with some earlier features, such as the 14th-century frescoes next to the entrance. In one of the side chapels and in the presbytery, details of late-Gothic frescoes can be seen.

In Völkermarkt's Hauptplatz stands a former ducal palace, now the seat of the local authorities, and an arcaded late-Gothic town hall.

The Romanesque portal of Kirche St. Magdalena in Völkermarkt

Klagenfurt ❸

See pp270–73.

Maria Saal ❹

Road map E5. *4,200.*
Am Platzl 7 (04223) 221425.

The first church was erected at Maria Saal in the 8th century, and a secondary Christianization was conducted from here, which is why it became known as the cradle of Carinthia. The pilgrimage church, built in 1430–56, has a stone statue of the Virgin Mary in the high altar from 1420. On the outer walls of the church are two remarkable Roman reliefs, one depicting the cart of Death, the other showing Achilles pulling the body of Hector behind the chariot. The relief on the south wall, showing the Coronation of the Virgin Mary, is the work of Hans Valkenauer.

Opposite the church is a late-Gothic octagonal mortuary and the cemetery chapel. It has beautiful 15th-century vault frescoes with the family tree of Jesus, as well as a late-Gothic altar with scenes from the life of St Mary and an altar of St George slaying the dragon. The Sachsen-Kapelle (Saxon Chapel) is devoted to St Modestus, who founded the church and whose tombstone has survived to this day.

Archaeological excavations near Maria Saal, at the site of the Roman town of Virunum, the capital of Noricum, have yielded relics including the Bronze-Age carved stone throne of the Princes of Carinthia *(see p38)*.

Hochosterwitz ❺

Road map E5. ***Tel*** *(04213) 2020.*
Apr, Oct: 9am–5pm; May–Sep: 8am–6pm.
www.burg-hochosterwitz.com

The fortress of Hochosterwitz, one of the symbols of Carinthia, perches on a rock 160 m (525 ft) high and is clearly visible from afar. Although the origins of the castle can be traced back to Roman times, it was built in the 16th century by Domenico dell'Allio. The present fortress is the result of Renaissance remodelling of earlier Romanesque and Gothic structures. A fief from the mid-16th century, it later became the property of the Khevenhüller family, who own it to this day. Both fortress and fortifications are open to visitors; the access road runs in a loop between the old walls, passing through 14 gates. There is also a local museum.

The turreted fortress of Hochosterwitz is said to have inspired Walt Disney's animated version of *Snow White*.

The slopes of Magdalensberg, site of fascinating archaeological finds

Magdalensberg 6

Road map E5. 2,200. *Deinsdorf 10, Pischeldorf (04224) 2213.*

On top of Magdalene Hill, rising 1,056 m (3,465 ft) from the Glan valley, are the remains of a town believed to be ancient Noricum, dating from the late-Celtic and early-Roman periods. Numerous finds, fragments of statues and the remains of old altars testify to the overlapping nature of Celtic and Roman cultures, with some later Christian additions.

Below the summit are the scant remains of a Roman temple and secular buildings dating from the 1st century AD. In spring and summer, the finds can be viewed in the open-air archaeological park and in the museum.

There is a small church on top of Magdalensberg, with a three-headed stone statue in the nave. This, as well as the hilltop location of the church, indicate the pagan, Celtic origins of the area.

St. Veit an der Glan 7

Road map E5. *13,600.* *Hauptplatz 1 (04212) 5555668.*

From 1174 to 1518, St. Veit an der Glan was the seat of the dukes of Spanheim, who ruled Carinthia during the Middle Ages; it then lost its position to Klagenfurt.

Many historic buildings are preserved in the old town around Hauptplatz, including the beautifully decorated **Rathaus** (town hall) of 1468, altered in the Baroque style. It has a lovely 16th-century arcaded courtyard. The 12th-century **Pfarrkirche St. Veit** (parish church of St Vitus) contains stone carvings from various periods; the altars are made in the Baroque style.

The most recent symbol of St. Veit is the unusual Kunsthotel Fuchs Palast, a modern hotel built in 1998 to designs by the outstanding artist, Ernst Fuchs. It is themed around

Baroque stuccowork on the Rathaus façade, St. Veit an der Glan

the signs of the zodiac. Also worth a visit is the Kärntner Eisenbahnmuseum (Carinthian Railway Museum), which has exhibits and documents on the history of the local railways.

Gurk 8

Road map E5. *1,300.* *Dr. Schnerichstrasse 12 (04266) 812527.* **Cathedral** *(04266) 8236.*

Gurk, the former ecclesiastical capital of Carinthia, is dominated by a cathedral church, built in 1140–1200 by Bishop Roman and one of the most outstanding achievements of Austrian Romanesque architecture. The Gothic vestibule is adorned by stained-glass windows (1340) and Gothic frescoes. The original main portal and door have carved and painted Romanesque medallions. Inside it is a startling combination of pure Romanesque and Gothic, with net vaulting and a Baroque main altar. The striking crypt is supported by 100 columns.

The medieval fortress of Hochosterwitz, one of the symbols of Carinthia

Klagenfurt: Street-by-Street ❸

Situated at the eastern end of Wörther See, the warmest lake in Austria, Klagenfurt, the attractive provincial capital of Carinthia, is an important trade centre and transport hub founded in the 12th century. In 1544, it was almost entirely destroyed by fire and had to be rebuilt. Reconstruction was undertaken mainly by Italian architects and it is highly reminiscent of Italian towns in style. In the 16th century, Klagenfurt was the centre of the Counter-Reformation. During the Baroque period it was extended and partially rebuilt, although most of its historic buildings date from an earlier era. Its historic centre is the district around Alter Platz (Old Square).

Stadtpfarrkirche St. Egid
This Baroque church was built on the site of an earlier church destroyed by an earthquake in 1692. Its spire rises to 91 m (299 ft).

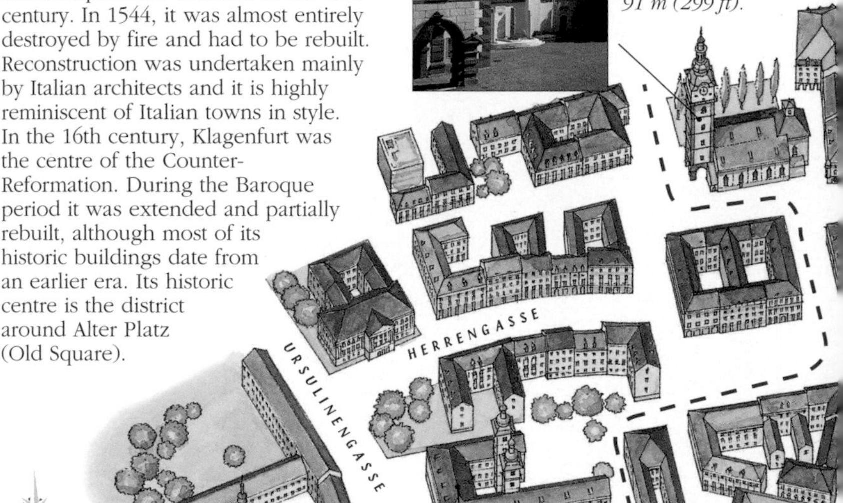

The square is the site of a modern bus station.

Heiligengeistkirche
The church of the Holy Spirit, built in 1355 and altered in 1660, features a beautiful altarpiece by Lorenzo Glaber and an interesting Baroque pulpit.

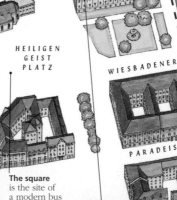

★ Landhaus
The 16th-century Landhaus boasts a lovely galleried inner courtyard and a magnificent heraldic hall with ceiling paintings by Josef Ferdinand Fromiller.

KEY

- - - - Suggested route

Altes Rathaus
One of the most attractive sights is the galleried courtyard of the 17th-century former town hall. Once known as Weltzer Palace, now as Rosenberg Palace, it was the first seat of the Klagenfurt town authorities.

VISITORS' CHECKLIST

Road map E5. 85,000. Annabichl. Rathaus, Neuer Platz 1 (0463) 5372271. Benediktiner Market (every day). Pfarrplatz, for organic produce (Fri). Klagenfurter Stadtfest (end Aug). **www**.klagenfurt.at

Dragon Fountain
In Neuer Platz (New Square) is a fountain with the mythical Lindwurm dragon, created by Ulrich Vogelsang in 1593; a town symbol, it has found its way into the Klagenfurt coat of arms.

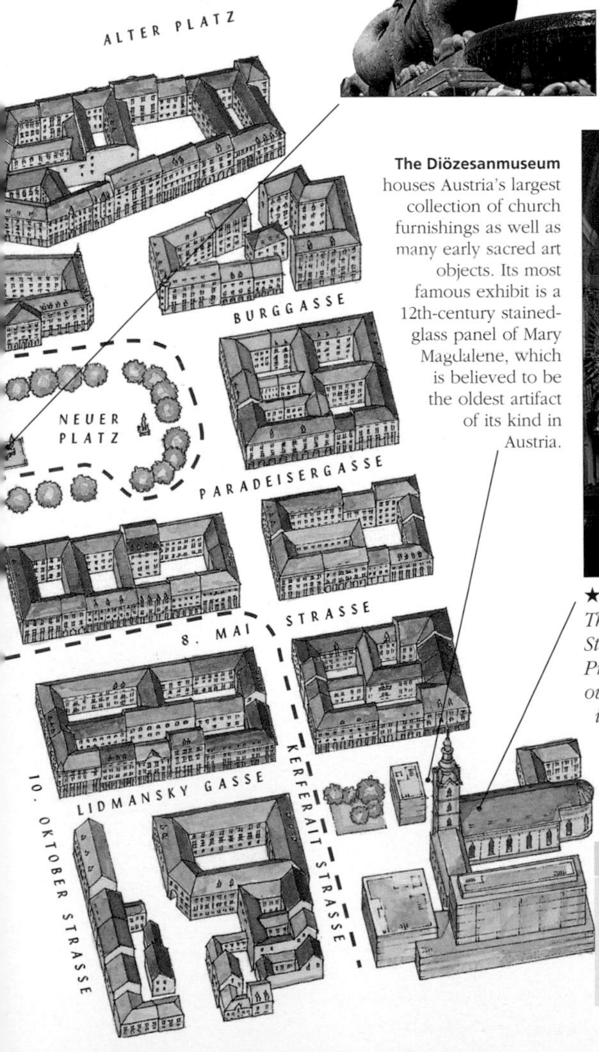

The Diözesanmuseum houses Austria's largest collection of church furnishings as well as many early sacred art objects. Its most famous exhibit is a 12th-century stained-glass panel of Mary Magdalene, which is believed to be the oldest artifact of its kind in Austria.

★ Dom St. Peter und Paul
The Cathedral of St Peter and St Paul, originally built as a Protestant church, was taken over and altered by the Jesuits in 1604, and in 1727 it was completely rebuilt after a major fire. The high altar (1752) is the work of Daniel Gran.

STAR SIGHTS

- ★ Dom St. Peter und Paul
- ★ Landhaus

Market in the historic Old Town of Klagenfurt

Exploring Klagenfurt

Klagenfurt lies south of the Glan river, 30 km (19 miles) from the Slovenian and 60 km (37 miles) from the Italian borders. Its Old Town, laid out on a rectangular grid, extends between Hauptplatz, Alter Platz and Neuer Platz, 4 km (2 miles) from Wörther See. The road to the lake runs through Europapark and the Minimundus exhibition.

Landhaus

Landhaushof. ***Tel*** *(0463) 57757.*
Apr–Oct: 9am–1pm, 2–5pm daily.

The Landhaus, the present seat of the Carinthian provincial government, stands on the western side of Alter Platz. Commissioned by the Carinthian estates, it was built in 1574 on the site of a former ducal palace to designs by Antonio Verda of Lugano and Franz Freymann. The resulting structure is Klagenfurt's most important secular building and a Renaissance gem, with two symmetrically spaced spires, beyond which is an open two-storey, galleried courtyard. The domes crowning the two towers and the decorated elevation date from 1740. The most beautiful room in the Landhaus, the Wappensaal (heraldic hall), dates from the same period. It is almost entirely the work of Josef Ferdinand Fromiller, the foremost Carinthian artist of the day. The walls of the hall display hundreds of Carinthian coats of arms, while the ceiling painting shows the Carinthian nobles paying homage to Charles VI; the flat ceiling is made to look vaulted in this *trompe l'oeil*. The north wing of the Landhaus houses the remains of the armoury.

The attractive, galleried courtyard of the Landhaus

Many old buildings have survived in the town centre nearby, including the Town Hall with a galleried Renaissance courtyard. The Trinity Column in Alter Platz, heart of the shopping district, dates from 1680; the crescent and cross were added after the victory over the Turks (1683).

Neuer Platz

Neuer Platz.

The square is dominated by Lindwurmbrunnen (Dragon Fountain), whose winged beast has become the symbol and crest of the town. The dragon was carved from a single block of stone by Ulrich Vogelsang, in 1593, while the giant who eventually saved the town was added later by Michael Hönel. The unveiling of this monument in 1636 was a great public event.

The Town Hall, formerly the Palace of the Rosenberg family, has been the seat of the municipal authorities since 1918. Built in 1582 and altered in 1650, it has an interesting Renaissance stairway. Originally outside the town walls surrounding Spanheim Castle, it became the centre of the new Renaissance town. In 1764, Neuer Platz was the site of the first monument to be erected to Maria Theresa in Austria. The square is lined on all sides by many 16th- and 17th-century mansions with beautiful façades.

17th-century Old Town Hall in Alter Platz

Dom St. Peter und Paul

Domplatz. ***Tel*** *(0463) 54950.*
7am–7pm daily.

Klagenfurt's cathedral was built in 1578 as a Protestant church by Klagenfurt's Mayor, Christoph Windisch. In 1604, the church was taken over by the Jesuits, and was elevated to the rank of cathedral in 1787, when the bishopric was transferred from Gurk to Klagenfurt. In 1723, following a fire, the late-Gothic interior was rebuilt in the Baroque style. The cathedral was badly damaged in World War II, during the 1944 bombing raids, but has been restored to its former splendour.

Rich stucco decoration on the walls and ceiling blend elements of various architectural styles into one successful composition. The vault frescoes were painted by Josef Ferdinand Fromiller, while the gallery stucco was the work of Kilian Pittner. Daniel Gran painted the main altarpiece in 1752. The vestry holds the last work by Johann Martin Schmidt.

Landesmuseum Kärnten

Museumgasse 2. ***Tel*** *(050536) 30599.* *10am–6pm Tue–Fri (to 8pm Thu), 10am–5pm Sat, Sun & hols.*

The collections of the Regional Museum, founded in 1844, illustrate several centuries of history in Carinthia as well as its art, rooted in Celtic and Roman cultures. The floor mosaic of a young Dionysus surrounded by hedonistic satyrs is a beautiful example of Roman art. One of the museum's curiosities is a "dragon's skull" (in fact a rhinoceros), found nearby, which served as a model for the fountain dragon in Neuer Platz. Its discovery gave credence to the legend that a dragon once tormented the town, demanding the sacrifice of animals and humans.

The museum also holds many works of art and handicraft. One of its most interesting exhibits is a carved altar from the St. Veit school. In the park in front is a small collection of stones, including some Roman stone statues.

Statue on the side altar in the Dom

Minimundus

Villacher Strasse 241. ***Tel*** *(0463) 21194.* *Apr, Oct: 9am–6pm; May–Sep: 9am–7pm.*

Europapark, a large green space west of Klagenfurt, is home to this theme park, with over 170 miniature models of the world's most famous buildings. They are crafted in minute detail to a scale of 1:25, and have been added to since 1959, when a children's charity, *Rettet das Kind*, set up the first architectural miniatures near Wörther See. All the profits go to the foundation. Among the models from all continents are Rome's St Peter's Basilica, Paris's Eiffel Tower, London's Big Ben, Brussels's Atomium, Agra's Taj Mahal and New York's Statue of Liberty. Not surprisingly, Austria's own historic buildings, such as the Stephansdom in Vienna, are heavily represented. Many other achievements and inventions are also represented by miniature models, for example Austrian watermills, Mississippi paddle steamers and the earliest steam trains.

Environs: The town of Klagenfurt is surrounded by lakes and mountains; the closest is **Wörther See** *(see pp276–7)*, which gave the Carinthian capital its byname, Rose of the Wörther See. **Viktring Abbey**, 6 km (4 miles) southwest of Klagenfurt, belonged to the Cistercian monks who arrived in Viktring in 1142. The many castles and palaces in the vicinity testify to the region's prosperity. Sights worth visiting include the fortified castle of **Mageregg** (1590, altered in 1841), surrounded by a zoological park for local animals. The lovely 12th-century **Schloss Hallegg**, which has preserved its old turret, was remodelled in the 16th century and turned into a Renaissance residence with two inner courtyards.

Stained-glass window in the Cistercian Abbey in Viktring

Models of Salzburg Cathedral and Ort Castle, in Minimundus

Friesach 9

Road map E5. 5,500.
Fürstenhofplatz 1 (04268) 4300.

Friesach is Carinthia's oldest town, with a history going back to 860, when the nearby fortress of **Petersberg** was founded. Traces of the town's glorious past have survived to this day, including a moated town wall, 820 m (2,690 ft) long, and several castle towers. Of the fortress itself, only the six-storey keep on Petersberg survives. In the former chapel room, on the fourth floor, the remains of 12th-century frescoes can be seen.

Adjacent to the fortress is **Peterskirche** (church of St Peter), which has a Gothic altar (1525) with a Romanesque statue of the Madonna (c.1200). The **Dominikanerkloster** (Dominican abbey) from 1217 holds a 14th-century Madonna, a wooden crucifix (1300) and other medieval artifacts. The church of St Blaise, built by the Teutonic Knights in 1213 on the ruins of an earlier church, has some original 12th-century frescoes.

Around Wörther See 10

See pp276–7.

Villach 11

Road map E5. 57,000.
Rathausplatz 1 (04242) 2052900.

Carinthia's second largest town is an important tourist centre, health resort and transport hub. The earliest archaeological finds testifying to the region's colonization date from Celtic times. It has a small old town. **Stadtpfarrkirche St. Jakob** (parish church of St Jacob) was built after a powerful earthquake in 1348, and later rebuilt. Its most notable features are the Renaissance chapels of the Görz-Dietrichstein and the Khevenhüller families and the 95-m (312-ft) high tower. The **Municipal Museum**, in a 16th-century building at No. 38 Widmanngasse, covers regional history, archaeology and art. In **Schillerpark** you can see an astonishing 3D-map of Carinthia, at a scale of 1:10,000.

Environs: Lovely 14th-century frescoes and a late-Gothic altar (c.1520) can be seen in the church of **Maria Gail**, 3 km (2 miles) southeast of Villach.

Schloss Porcia's galleries, Spittal an der Drau

Spittal an der Drau 12

Road map D5. 16,000.
Schloss Porcia, Burgplatz 1 (04762) 5650220.

The town of Spittal is dominated by the Goldeck peak (2,142 m/7,028 ft). The history of the town began in the 12th century, when Count Ortenburg founded a church and a *Spittal* or hospice on this site. The town owes its Renaissance character to the vast 16th-century **Schloss Porcia**, which is also known as Salamanca Palace after its builder, the Spanish nobleman Gabriel of Salamanca. The Porcia family, who owned the palace from 1662 until 1918, added to its decor while preserving the original architecture based on Spanish Renaissance palaces. Its most beautiful aspect is the galleried inner courtyard; be sure to have a close look at the rich decorations of its individual storeys. The well-preserved palace now houses a museum of folk art on the two top floors.

The former thermal bath complex in Villach (the new building opens in 2012)

Environs: On a hill near the village of St. Peter in Holz, 5 km (3 miles) northwest of Spittal an der Drau, stand the ruins of an Early Christian church and the **Römermuseum Teurnia**. The hill was settled first by Celts, then by Romans, and the museum exhibits many small items, scripts and coins.

Millstatt 13

Road map D5. 3,400.
Rathaus, Marktplatz 8 (04766) 2010.

The greatest attraction in Millstatt, on the northern shore of Millstätter See, is a **Benedictine Abbey** dating from 1070. From then until 1469 it was run by the Hirsau Benedictines; later the monastery and church passed into the hands of the Order of the Knights of St George, and from 1598 until 1773 it was owned by the Jesuits.

The most beautiful part of the abbey is its Renaissance courtyard surrounded by two-storey arcades. This was built in the 16th century, when the abbey was run by the Order of St George. The monastery is linked with the church by a 12th-century cloister whose pillars, decorated by medieval carvers, display a grotesque world of animals, plants and faces. Even older, dating back to the Carolingian period, are the magical ornaments on the old buildings, possibly representing some pagan spells. An eye-catching feature inside the church is the Romanesque portal, made by master craftsman Rudger in 1170. In the side chapels are the red marble tombs of the Order's Grand Masters. Also worth seeing is a fresco from 1519, depicting the Last Judgement.

Courtyard of the Benedictine Abbey in Millstatt

Gmünd ⓮

Road map D5. *2,600.*
Hauptplatz 20 (04732) 221514.

In the 12th century, the Archbishops of Salzburg who ruled Gmünd began to encircle the town with mighty fortifications, many of which survive to this day, including old gate turrets and bastions. Two castles tower over the town: the older one, **Altes Schloss**, was destroyed by a fire in 1886, but was restored and is now used as a cultural centre. It was commissioned in 1506 by Archbishop Leonhard. The **Neues Schloss** (New Castle) was built in 1651–4 by Count Christoph Lodron. Today the former castle keep houses a school and a concert hall.

An alley in Gmünd, famous for its former Porsche factory

The Austrian-born designer Ferdinand Porsche worked in Gmünd in 1944–50, and 52 of the classic "365" models were hand-made locally. The most famous models and construction frames are displayed in the **Porsche Museum**.

Porsche Museum
Gmünd. ***Tel** (04732) 2471.*
15 May–15 Oct: 9am–6pm, 16 Oct–14 May: 10am–4pm.
www.porschemuseum.at.

Mölltal ⓯

Road map D5.

The Möll river, a tributary of the Drau and overshadowed by Grosses Reisseck peak, runs along the Mölltal, a valley whose upper reaches form a natural extension of the magnificent road known as Grossglockner Hochalpenstrasse. The river meanders scenically between the high mountain peaks. The road along the valley, starting in Winklern, is an important transit route between Carinthia at one end and Lienz and the Dolomites at the other, winding its way between old mills, waterfalls and huts.

The parish of **Grosskirchheim** was once a major mining district, and the 16th-century **Schloss Grosskirchheim** now houses an interesting mining museum.

In **Döllach** you can see the interesting late-Gothic church of St Andrew, and in **Sagritz** the originally late-Gothic church of St George. **Schloss Falkenstein**, near Obervellach, has an unusual tower with a wooden top.

Lienz ⓰

Road map D5. *13,000.*
Europaplatz 1 (050212) 400.

The town has been the capital of East Tyrol since 1919 but its origins date back to the Middle Ages. The **Stadtpfarrkirche St Andrä** (parish church of St Andrew), a triple-nave Gothic basilica, was built in the 15th century; western sections include parts of an earlier Romanesque church. Today, following many alterations, the church is predominantly Baroque in style. Inside are a fresco by J. A. Mölk and a high altar by Franz Engele. The **Franziskanerkirche** (Franciscan church), built around 1350, features original 15th-century frescoes and a Gothic Pietà standing by a side altar.

High above the town sits **Schloss Bruck**, the seat of the Görz Counts, built between the 13th and 16th centuries. The castle has a tall Romanesque turret; its main body contains a Romanesque chapel with 13th- and 15th-century frescoes. Today it also houses a regional museum with Gothic and Baroque artifacts and paintings by the local Tyrolean artist Albin Egger-Lienz (1868–1926).

The Romanesque tower of Schloss Bruck in Lienz

Around Wörther See ⑩

Wörther See is the warmest lake in Austria; in summer, the temperature of its waters reaches 24–28°C. Numerous resorts are lined along its shores; the largest of these is the modern, brash town of Velden, with its casino. Krumpendorf and the exclusive resort of Pörtschach lie on the easily accessible northern shore; quiet Reifnitz is on the southern shore. Not far from Wörther See are other, smaller lakes, including Ossiacher See, in a scenic mountain setting. To the south, the Carinthian lake district extends along the Slovenian border, surrounded by the snowy peaks of the enchanting Karawanken Alps.

Ossiach ①
The former Benedictine Abbey in Ossiach and its church were built in the 11th-century and altered in the early-Baroque style. The oldest monastery in Carinthia, it was burned down by Turkish invaders and is now a hotel.

Schloss Landskron ②
Not much remains of the original medieval castle, but the ruins are nevertheless impressive. Today, the bird of prey show, held on the slopes of the castle hill, and "Monkey Mountain" are the greatest attractions nearby.

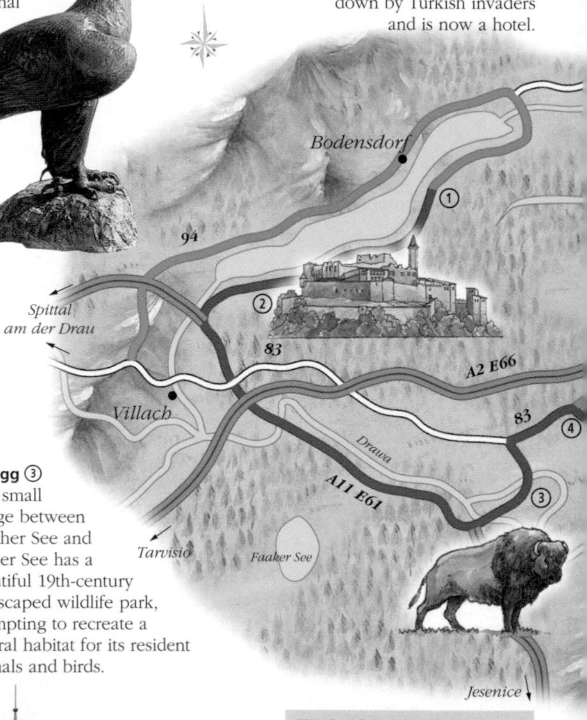

Rosegg ③
This small village between Wörther See and Faaker See has a beautiful 19th-century landscaped wildlife park, attempting to recreate a natural habitat for its resident animals and birds.

Schloss Velden ④
The well-known, swanky resort on the shores of Wörther See boasts an early-Baroque castle, originally built by the Khevenhüller family, which featured as setting for a popular Austrian TV series. It is now an elegant hotel.

TIPS FOR DRIVERS

Length of route: *45 km (28 miles).*

Stopping-off points: *there are several resorts around the lake offering restaurants and hotels; Velden is the largest resort.*

Further attractions: *Wildpark in Rosegg.* ***Tel*** *(04274) 52357.* ◯ *Apr–Nov.*

Maria Wörth ⑤
On a promontory that extends far into the lake, stands a 12th-century church built on earlier foundations and featuring original 11th-century Romanesque frescoes.

Wörther See ⑥
Wörther See is Austria's warmest lake and its shores have become known as the Austrian Riviera. Entertainment here ranges from relaxation to swimming and all sorts of water sports.

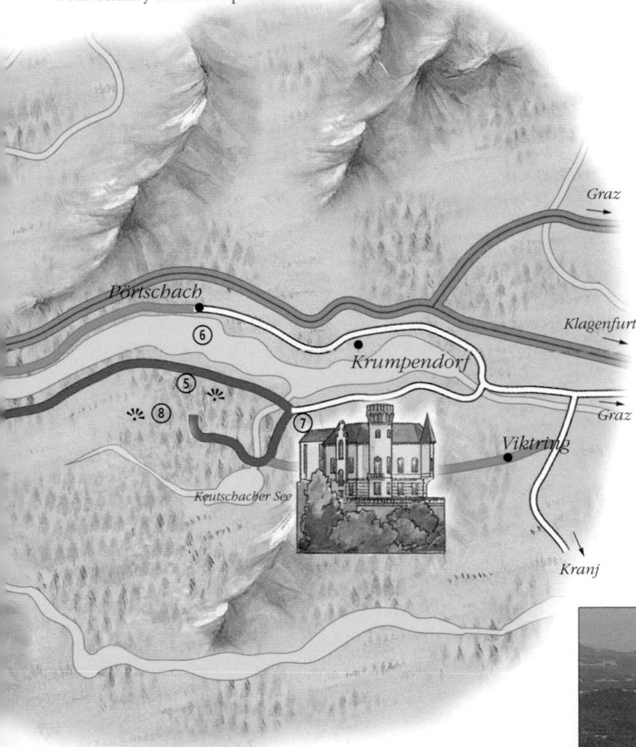

Reifnitz ⑦
Established as early as 1195, this was once one of the mightiest castles in Carinthia. All that remains today are the main body and the castle keep.

KEY

- Motorway
- Suggested route
- Scenic route
- Other road
- River, lake
- Viewpoint

Pyramidenkogel ⑧
From the top of the hill Pyramidenkogel, above the lake, there are stunning vistas of the entire area, including Wörther See itself, with the Karawanken Alps to the south, and several beautiful neighbouring lakes.

Hohe Tauern National Park ⓱

The beautiful area around Austria's highest peak, the Grossglockner, is a national park. The unique landscape, flora and fauna of the region, the Hohe Tauern, is jointly protected by the provincial governments of Salzburger Land, Tyrol and Carinthia. The Hohe Tauern has more than 300 peaks rising above 3,000 m (9,850 ft) and several glaciers – the Pasterze is the longest and most spectacular. This whole national park area is protected by law and visitors are asked to keep to the marked trails. On its edges are many popular tourist resorts such as Badgastein, Kaprun, Zell am See and East Tyrol's capital, Lienz.

Artificial Lakes
One of the great attractions of the Hohe Tauern is its many picturesque reservoirs, gathering the crystal-clear meltwaters from the glaciers high above each spring.

★ Pasterze Glacier
The largest glacier in the Eastern Alps is 10 km (6 miles) long and covers an area of 19.5 sq km (7.6 sq miles). Its far end can be reached by stairs carved into the ice or by cable car.

★ Grossglockner
Austria's highest peak (3,797 m/12,457 ft) towers at the border between Carinthia and East Tyrol, a crucifix marking the summit.

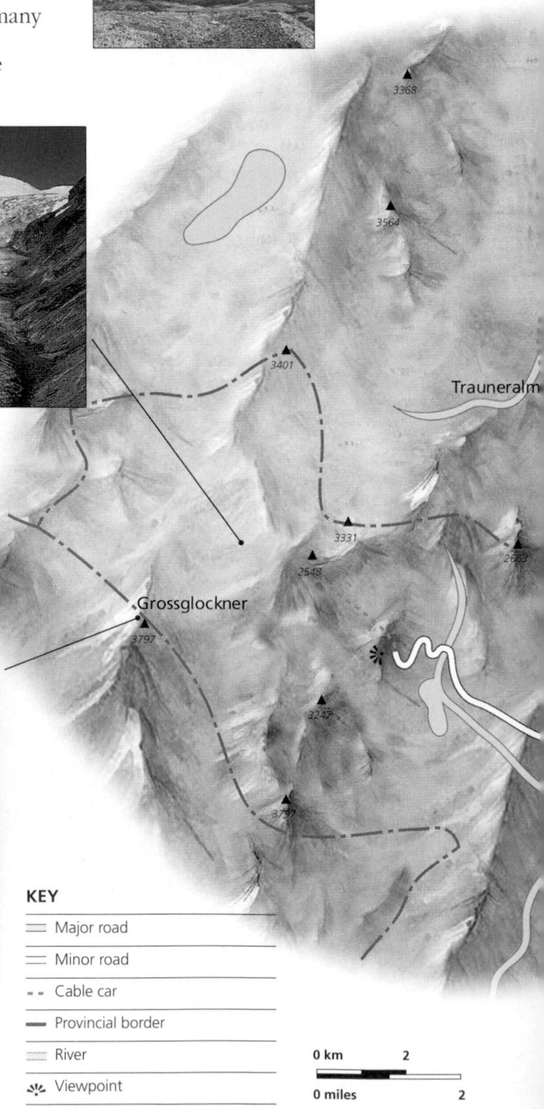

For hotels and restaurants in this region see pp306–7 and pp336–7

Edelweissspitze
Edelweissspitze, 2,572 m/8,438 ft high, is the central peak of the Fusch-Rauriser range. There are amazing views from the viewing tower at the summit.

VISITORS' CHECKLIST

Road map D4. *Nationalpark Hohe Tauern, A-9971 Matrei in Osttirol, Kirchplatz 2. (04875) 5112.*
www.hohetauern.at.

Alpine Flora
An impressive range of alpine plantlife, such as this aromatic alpine tansy (Tanacetum) can be seen in the park at different altitudes.

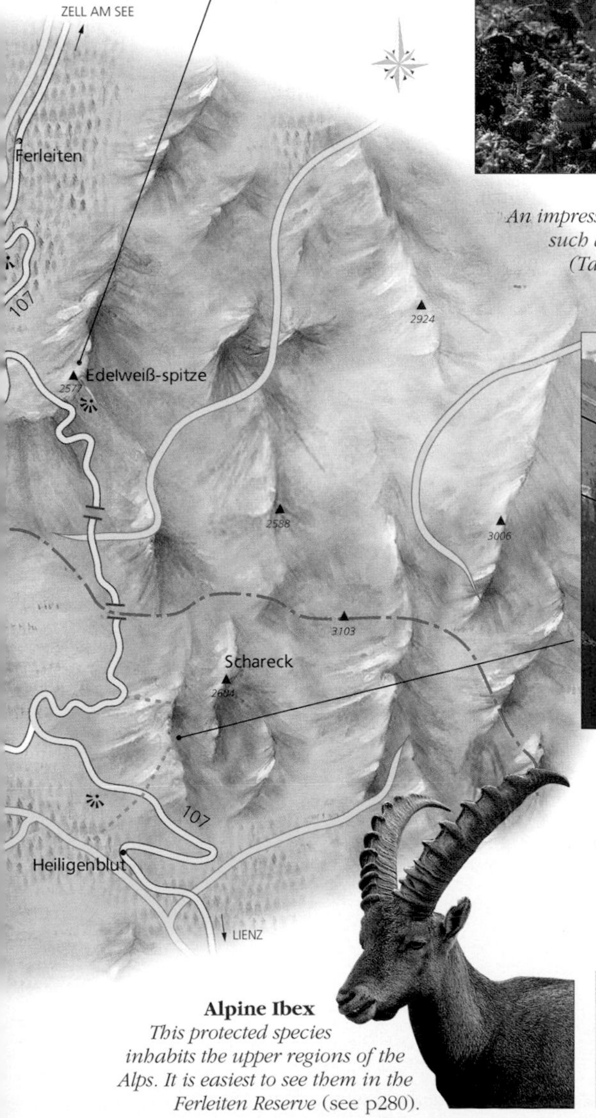

Cable Car to Schareck
Schareck peak (2,606 m/8,550 ft) in the Goldberg-gruppe (Gold Mountains) can be reached by cable car, with one change en route. Schareck is an excellent starting point for excursions into the upper mountains.

Alpine Ibex
This protected species inhabits the upper regions of the Alps. It is easiest to see them in the Ferleiten Reserve (see p280).

STAR SIGHTS

★ Grossglockner

★ Pasterze Glacier

Grossglockner Hochalpenstrasse ⓲

Traversing the Hohe Tauern National Park is the Grossglockner High Alpine Road, regarded as one of the world's most beautiful mountain routes. Completed in 1935, the road was built along the old mountain passes between Bruck in Salzburger Land and Heiligenblut in Carinthia. Measuring 47.8 km (29.7 miles) long, it forms part of a north–south route from Bavaria to Italy. Branching off the main road are two trails leading to viewpoints. The highest point of the route is Hochtor, at 2,505 m (8,218 ft), the lowest is Bruck, at 755 m (2,477 ft). With the 1.5 km (1 mile) rise in altitude, the flora also changes.

Hochtor ⑤
The Hochtor (High Gate) is the highest point along the Grossglockner Hochalpenstrasse. Here the road runs through a tunnel measuring 2.3 km (1.5 miles) in length.

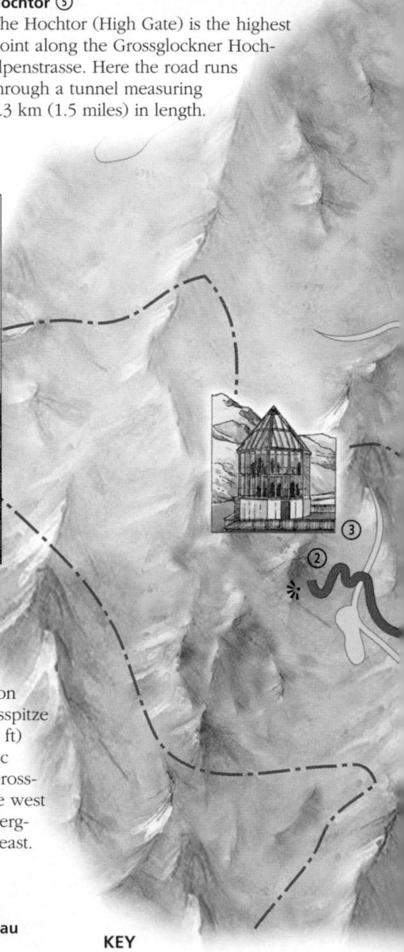

Fuscher Törl ⑥
The road winds its way above steep ravines, offering splendid views on both sides of this ridge to the Goldberggruppe (Gold Mountains).

Viewing Tower on Edelweissspitze ⑦
The tower built on top of Edelweissspitze (2,572 m/8,438 ft) affords fantastic views of the Grossglockner to the west and the Goldberggruppe to the east.

Alpine Naturschau Museum ⑧
Situated at an altitude of 2,260 m (7,415 ft) is a small museum of the local flora, fauna and ecology, offering free admission to visitors. In Ferleiten, to the north, is an alpine animal reserve.

KEY

- Suggested route
- Other road
- Cable car
- River, lake
- Provincial border
- Viewpoint

Schareck ④
The Schareck peak, part of the Goldberg massif, was once mined for gold. From here visitors can see the Schildberg peak and the looming Grossglockner massif to the west, as well as the superb high-altitude ski slopes.

TIPS FOR DRIVERS

Length of the route: *40 km (25 miles).*
Stopping-off points: *you can stay at one of the mountain hostels, and many restaurants also offer accommodation.*
Additional information: *the route is a toll road, open to cars only from May to November.*

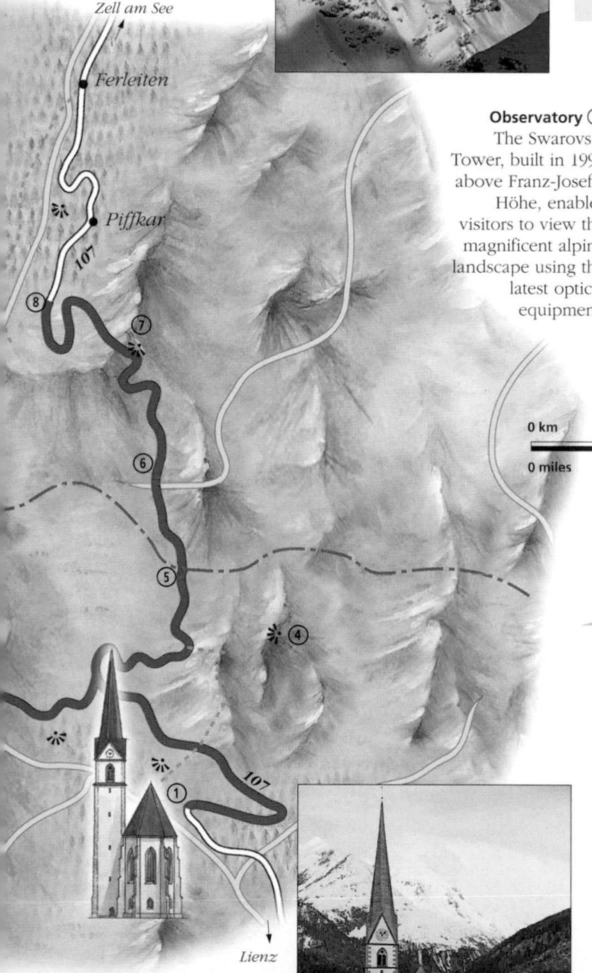

Observatory ③
The Swarovski Tower, built in 1998 above Franz-Josefs-Höhe, enables visitors to view the magnificent alpine landscape using the latest optical equipment.

Heiligenblut ①
The church in Heiligenblut was built in the 15th century by monks from Admont. Inside is a beautiful altar from the workshop of Michael Pacher, and a richly carved tabernacle said to house a phial of Christ's blood.

Franz-Josefs-Höhe ②
Along the Gletscherstrasse (Glacier Road) is a viewing terrace at 2,369 m (7,772 ft), giving fabulous views of both Grossglockner and the Pasterze Glacier.

TRAVELLERS' NEEDS

WHERE TO STAY

Austria has a highly developed infrastructure, and you should find it easy to locate the exact type of accommodation that you are looking for. There is a great number of hotels and pensions, offering different standards of accommodation and service at a range of prices. You can also find friendly private lodgings and good campsites. The rooms are mostly well furnished and comfortable, the staff kind and courteous. Away from towns, where transport is not always readily available, hotel staff may even offer to collect travellers without cars from railway or coach stations. Within the list of hotels on pages 288–307, there is a choice of around 170 hotels and pensions, which represent various price categories and a high standard of service. Information on other types of overnight accommodation can be found on pages 286–7.

A hotel complex in Kampl, in a typically scenic location

THE RANGE OF HOTELS

Hotels and pensions are awarded one to five stars, as in other countries, with the number of stars depending on the facilities offered by the hotel rather than the standard of service. Generally speaking, pensions have fewer facilities but they often offer a more homely atmosphere.

Your choice of hotel will be determined by what you are intending to do during your time in Austria. Visitors who are mainly interested in sightseeing and are likely to be constantly on the move, may prefer to stay in less costly private lodgings or pensions. Sports enthusiasts need to look for hotels that offer the appropriate facilities. Alternatively, you may be seeking peace and quiet, or you may wish to improve your overall health and wellbeing; in this case you'll want to seek out one of the numerous, well-equipped spa hotels. Whatever your plans, you should not be stuck for choice as the choice of hotels is truly vast.

HOW TO BOOK

As in other countries, hotel accommodation can be booked directly by post, telephone, fax, email or through the internet. Reservations can be made directly with the hotel or through a local tourist office. The **Wiener Tourismusverband** (Vienna Tourism Association) or a local tourist centre may be able to assist if you are booking for small groups. They will mail out brochures and leaflets on request, including abroad, and provide detailed information on the accommodation.

It is generally advisable to book some time in advance, particularly for the summer months, Christmas and Easter.

INTERNATIONAL AND AUSTRIAN CHAIN HOTELS

In addition to well-known and popular hotel chains, such as Mercure and **Hilton**, it is also worth considering are **50plus Hotels** which mostly offer spa facilities and access to various health treatments. The largest clusters of such hotels are to be found in the vicinity of Salzburg and in Vorarlberg province. Other hotel chains include Romantik-Hotels, Grand Hotel, Marriott, Bristol, **Austria Trend**, Hotel-Post, Renaissance and **Ibis**. All offer high standards and good service, but only a few have air-conditioned rooms.

A majestic hotel in the elegant ski resort of Badgastein

The impressively grand lobby of the Imperial Hotel (*see p293*)

◁ **Casino and Kurpark by night in Baden**

The cosy, candle-lit interior of the Weismayr Hotel in Badgastein (*see p301*)

HOTELS IN HISTORIC BUILDINGS

Visitors who are looking for something a bit special should consider a stay at one of the many medieval castles that have been converted into hotels. Often the name *Schlosshotel* is used to indicate that an establishment is a hotel within a palace. Some excellent examples of such converted fortresses or palaces are: Burg Oberranna; Hotel Schloss Dürnstein in the Wachau region; Burghotel Deutschlandsberg in Styria; or one of the various Renaissance or Baroque palaces or mansions such as Raffelsberger Hof in Weissenkirchen (in Lower Austria), Schlosshotel Oth in Baden near Vienna, Schloss Feyregg in Bad Hall (Upper Austria) and the Hotel Palais Coburg in Vienna. Each of these offers up-to-date accommodation facilities in luxurious surroundings, richly furnished but exuding the romantic atmosphere of a bygone age. Schloss Fuschl in Hof near Salzburg, for example, is now not only a palace but an entire resort, including a well-equipped health spa. Hunting lodges, usually based in the countryside, are also popular with visitors, and many guests return every year to take part in the hunt.

Sign of the Golden Eagle in Innsbruck

Prices at such historic hotels are often higher than those demanded by other well-known hotels; a single room at the Schwarzenberg Palace in Vienna, for example, will cost you about €250–400 per night, while a similar room in one of the Inter-Continental hotels costs €210–300.

Generally speaking, Vienna is an expensive city to stay in. In the provinces accommodation in palaces and mansions costs around €100–250, with a select few, such as Herrenhaus Tennerhof in the top winter sports resort of Kitzbühel, charging as much as €600–800. Information about accommodation in converted palaces can be obtained from the local tourist offices, which also have all the relevant brochures, catalogues and booking details.

HOTEL PRICES

The price of hotel accommodation is dictated not only by the category of the hotel, but also by its location and local events and traditions. Differences may be significant, even within the same category. Accommodation in Vienna, Salzburg and Graz is often expensive, and many hotels and pensions situated in prime locations are overpriced. You can cut costs by staying outside the main town centres; in Vienna, for example, you can expect to pay approximately a fifth less for a room in an establishment just outside the Ringstrasse, and less still further afield. Staying in provincial towns tends to be somewhat cheaper, but even here you will encounter a wide range of prices. You will find less costly accommodation if you time your visit to fall outside the main tourist season – if, for example, you visit a resort specializing in winter sports during the summer months. In the cities, you may also be able to negotiate discounted room rates for weekend visits or longer stays.

A charming rustic pension in the mountainous region of Lech

HIDDEN EXTRAS

When booking a room you should check in advance if any additional charges, such as *Kurtaxe* (health spa tax) or for cleaning on departure, will be levied. Generally, prices are inclusive of taxes such as *MWSt* (VAT), but occasionally these are separate. In all but the five-star hotels, breakfast is included. Other typical extra costs to watch out for are charges for off-road parking, especially in the larger cities, unfavourable rates of exchange and high costs for making phone calls.

If you have opted for full-board accommodation in a pension, you will need to take the additional cost for lunch and dinner drinks into account, and you should also allow for a small tip.

If you are renting an apartment, it is worth checking whether the cost of electricity is included in the rent or whether it is metered.

A concert at the elegant hotel Schwarzenberg Palace in Vienna

PENSIONS AND GASTHÖFE

Pensions are widespread and popular in Austria. Less formal than a hotel, they are typically run by a family and usually provide modest accommodation, breakfast and a pleasant family atmosphere – guests often meet the owners. Most rooms have *en suite* bathrooms and toilet, some have telephone, TV and a balcony. In smaller towns and villages, the owners often invite their guests to join in at social evenings with music, dancing or a barbecue.

A *Gasthof* is a traditional inn with a restaurant on the ground floor and rooms to rent above. A wide range of establishments is covered by this description, from small, inexpensive, family-run hotels with modestly equipped rooms, to the most luxurious accommodation in an exquisitely restored country inn.

INEXPENSIVE ACCOMMODATION

Relatively inexpensive accommodation can often be found in private homes.

In attractive tourist areas, it is common for owners of larger villas and private houses to rent rooms to tourists. Vacancies are generally indicated by the sign *Fremdenzimmer* or *Zimmer frei*. The standard of furnishing varies; some rooms are *en suite*, for others the bathroom facilities are shared. Breakfast may or may not be included in the room price.

Young people travelling in groups can stay at a *Jugendherberge* (Youth Hostel), the least expensive option for an overnight stay. Most are of a high standard, and some are located in old castles, beautiful villas or other historic buildings. Tourist offices can provide details.

AGROTOURISM

Families with children often enjoy holidays on a farm. There is a large network of such farms, fully adapted to put up guests. Some offer self-catering facilities, in others meals can be provided by the farmer, on a similar basis as in pensions, offering bed and breakfast (*Zimmer mit Frühstück*), half-board (*Halbpension*) or full board (*Vollpension*). The number of rooms for let in a *Bauernhof*, and the prices that are charged, vary. Rooms are of a perfectly acceptable standard, and for children from towns and cities it is an ideal opportunity to observe the daily work on a farm and to have direct contact with farm animals. There may also be the opportunity to go horse-riding, or hire a bike, boat or fishing tackle, so that a full programme of outdoor activities can be enjoyed by the whole family.

Information on *Bauernhof* (farm) holidays with pictures and detailed descriptions and price lists can be obtained from tourist offices. Tourist offices in many provinces also send out free brochures to interested holidaymakers.

A stone statue outside a Salzburg hotel

MOUNTAIN HOSTELS AND SHELTERS

Mountain hostels and shelters can be found along all the major walking trails. They exist even in Vienna: on the banks of the Old Danube, no higher than 155 m (509 ft), stands a picturesque hut, although it is reserved exclusively for groups. Lower Austria has a large number of hostels, some at relatively low altitudes. In the High Alps travellers can find numerous huts or shelters. They usually have rooms for two, three or many more people to share,

A caravan site on the shores of Ossiacher See in Carinthia

A mountain hostel near Schöpfl, in the Vienna Woods

and sleeping is on simple mattresses. The higher in the mountains you climb and the more remote you are, the less luxurious the huts. Hostels can provide you with information on the local hiking trails, current climbing conditions and the weather forecasts.

Depending on the popularity of an area and the season, hostels will be open either all year round or only during the summer months, usually until the end of September or October. Some open only at the weekend, even in summer, or by appointment, or are closed one day in the week, on the *Ruhetag* (rest day). The Österreichischer Alpenverein (ÖAV) or the local tourist bureaux will be able to advise you.

CAMPING

Travelling with a camping trailer, camper van or just a tent is popular in Austria, and there are dedicated campsites in all the larger towns and popular resorts. Generally of high standard, sites are equipped with washrooms and kitchens, and they allow caravan owners to exchange gas bottles and use washing machines, dishwashers and ironing rooms. Some sites have fixed caravans for hire, and almost all have a playground for children. A few are adapted for the needs of disabled people. Restaurants, bars and grocery stores can usually be found nearby.

The average price is typically €7–23 per day for two people sharing; in addition a health resort tax *(Kurtaxe)* may be charged by some, and the use of showers and electricity will be extra.

TRAVELLING WITH CHILDREN

In larger towns, most public squares have some form of playing equipment such as swings, slides or wooden climbing towers. Similar facilities are often provided by hotels and pensions, and even some restaurants may have allocated a separate corner or room for children to play in. In many hotels and pensions it is possible to book a child-minding service. In restaurants, there is usually a children's menu on offer.

Some pensions, particularly those aimed at families with children, organize special activities for young people; these might include all sorts of sport activities, ranging from skiing, skating and tobogganing to horse-riding, tennis, swimming and cycling. Some even offer beginners' rock-climbing lessons and canoeing. Children of all ages will also enjoy visiting Austria's numerous castles and fortresses.

DIRECTORY

INFORMATION ON ACCOMMODATION & RESERVATIONS

Österreich Werbung
Margaretenstrasse 1, Vienna.
Tel *(01) 58866-0.*
www.austriatourism.com

Wiener Tourismusverband
Albertinaplatz, Vienna.
Tel *(01) 24 555.*
www.wien.info

Kärnten Information
Casinoplatz 1, Velden.
Tel *(04274) 5210023.*
www.kaernten.at

Niederösterreich Information
Niederösterreich Ring 2, Haus C, St Pölten.
Tel *(02742) 9000-19800.*
www.niederoesterreich.at

OÖ-Tourismus Information
Freistädtstrasse 119, Linz.
Tel *(0732) 7277100.*
www.oberoesterreich.at

Steiermark Tourismus GmbH
St. Peter-Hauptstrasse 243, Graz.
Tel *(0316) 4003–0*
www.steiermark.com

Tirol Info
Maria-Theresien-Strasse 55, Innsbruck.
Tel *(0512) 72720.*
www.tyrol.com

HOTEL CHAINS

50plus Hotels
www.50plushotels.at

Austria-Trend
www.austria-trend.at

Ibis
www.ibishotel.com

Hilton
www.hilton.com

HOTELS IN HISTORIC BUILDINGS

Schlosshotels und Herrenhäuser in Österreich
Moosstrasse 60, Salzburg.
Tel *(0662) 830 68 141.*
www.schlosshotels.co.at

YOUTH HOSTELS

Österreichischer Jugendherbergs-verband (ÖJHV)
Gonzagagasse 22, Vienna.
Tel *(01) 533 53 53.*
www.oejhv.or.at

MOUNTAIN HOSTELS AND SHELTERS

Österreichischer Alpenverein (ÖAV)
Rotenturm Strasse 14, Vienna. ***Tel*** *(01) 513 10 03.*
www.alpenverein.at

CAMPSITES

Österreichischer Camping Club
Schubertring 1–3, Vienna.
Tel *(01) 713 61 51.*
www.campingclub.at

Choosing a Hotel

Hotels have been selected across a wide price range for facilities, good value, exceptional location, comfort or style. This chart lists the hotels by region, in chapter order. Map references refer either to the Vienna Street Finder on *pp116–21*, or the road map on the inside back cover.

PRICE CATEGORIES
Price categories for a standard double room per night, including breakfast, tax and service:

€ Under €90
€€ €90–140
€€€ €140–180
€€€€ €180–260
€€€€€ Over €260

VIENNA

INNER CITY Suzanne €
Walfischgasse 4, 1010 **Tel** *(01) 513 25 07* **Fax** *(01) 513 25 00* **Rooms** *26* **Map** *2 C5*

This pension is just a few steps from the Kärntner Strasse and the Opera House. A perfect location for shopping and cultural entertainment. The bedrooms, with paintings and comfortable armchairs, reflect old-fashioned Viennese charm. The more expensive rooms have kitchenettes. **www.pension-suzanne.at**

INNER CITY Austria €€
Fleischmarkt 20, 1010 **Tel** *(01) 515 23* **Fax** *(01) 515 23 506* **Rooms** *46* **Map** *2 C3, 3 D3, 3 D4*

A roomy hotel located in a quiet cul-de-sac close to the Old University. The spacious bedrooms are cosily decorated and have high ceilings. Downstairs are a few small sitting rooms and a breakfast room with a fountain. Standard, comfortable bathrooms, with either baths or showers. **www.hotelaustria-wien.at**

INNER CITY Aviano €€
Marco d'Avianogasse 1, 1010 **Tel** *(01) 512 83 30* **Fax** *(01) 512 83 30 6* **Rooms** *17* **Map** *2 B5*

Located only one minute from the Opera House, this four-star pension offers a friendly, welcoming atmosphere with very personalized service. The staff can help organize site-seeing tours and tickets to concerts. Cheerful, well-decorated rooms. Good value for money. **www.secrethomes.at**

INNER CITY Bajazzo €€
Esslinggasse 7, 1010 **Tel** *(01) 533 89 03* **Fax** *(01) 535 39 97* **Rooms** *12* **Map** *2 BC, 2 C2*

A quaint hotel in the centre of town within walking distance to many important sites. The renovated rooms are modern, clean and feature standard amenities. The breakfast room is cheerfully decorated, and the service provided here is personal and friendly. **www.hotelbajazzo.eu**

INNER CITY Kärntnerhof €€
Grashofgasse 4, 1011 **Tel** *(01) 512 19 23* **Fax** *(01) 513 22 28 39* **Rooms** *43* **Map** *2 C4*

This quiet, well-run hotel is located in a cul-de-sac in central Vienna. A gate at the end leads to the lovely Heiligenkreuzerhof where you can park a car. The 19th-century building's best feature is a fine Art Deco elevator, enclosed within a spiral staircase. Rooms have free Internet access. **www.karntnerhof.at**

INNER CITY Marc Aurel €€
Marc-Aurel Strasse 8, 1010 **Tel** *(01) 533 36 40 0* **Fax** *(01) 533 00 78* **Rooms** *31* **Map** *2 C3*

This comfortable hotel with simple but spacious rooms has an on-site restaurant, café and, in the summer, a dining garden. All rooms, including the apartments and suites, can be rented monthly at a discount price. Some rooms feature a kitchenette. Pets are permitted. **www.hotel-marcaurel.com**

INNER CITY Neuer Markt €€
Seilergasse 9, 1010 **Tel** *(01) 512 23 16* **Fax** *(01) 513 9105* **Rooms** *37* **Map** *2 B4*

A pension has existed on this site since the 1920s, and the Neuer Markt continues the tradition in true Viennese style. Plenty of dusty-rose coloured furnishings. Friendly, personal service. For those staying longer than seven nights, a pick-up service upon arrival at the airport or train stations is provided free of charge. **www.hotelpension.at**

INNER CITY Opera Suites €€
Kärntner Strasse 47, 1010 **Tel** *(01) 512 93 10* **Fax** *(01) 512 93 1017* **Rooms** *12* **Map** *2 B5, 2 C5*

Located just opposite the Opera House on Kärntner Strasse in the centre of the city, Opera Suites features tastefully decorated bedrooms that are large and comfortable. Each room has a kitchenette. All bathrooms are generally small, and with showers. Continental breakfast is served in your room. **www.operasuites.at**

INNER CITY Pension Nossek €€
Graben 17, 1010 **Tel** *(01) 533 70 41 0* **Fax** *(01) 535 36 46* **Rooms** *26* **Map** *2 B4*

Located in Vienna's elegant pedestrian street, the Graben, this family-run pension books up well in advance – especially the balconied rooms that overlook the street. The rooms are refined but simple, and line three floors. Most bedrooms have period furniture, tasteful paintings and parquet floors. Standard bathrooms. **www.pension-nossek.at**

Key to Symbols *see back cover flap*

INNER CITY Post €€

Fleischmarkt 24, 1010 ***Tel*** *(01) 515 83 0* ***Fax*** *(01) 515 83 80 8* ***Rooms*** *107* ***Map*** *2 C3, 3 D3*

This traditional hotel is built on the site of a former guest house and inn, whose lodgers included Mozart, Josef Haydn, Richard Wagner and Friedrich Nietzsche. The rooms are comfortable, and there are a number of business rooms with broadband Internet access. A restaurant/café is on the premises. **www.hotel-post-wien.at**

INNER CITY Schlosshotel Römischer Kaiser €€

Annagasse 16, 1010 ***Tel*** *(01) 512 77 51 0* ***Fax*** *(01) 512 77 51 13* ***Rooms*** *24* ***Map*** *2 C5*

This classic example of a Viennese miniature Baroque palace was built for the imperial finance minister Johann Hüber in 1684. The bedrooms are furnished elegantly, and are cheerful and airy. Most bathrooms are in original Gianni Versace design. Bicycles can be rented. **www.hotel-roemischer-kaiser.at**

INNER CITY Zur Wiener Staatsoper €€

Krugerstrasse 11, 1010 ***Tel*** *(01) 513 12 74* ***Fax*** *(01) 513 12 74 15* ***Rooms*** *22* ***Map*** *2 C5*

This small hotel is housed in a tall, narrow 19th-century building on a pedestrian street just off Kärntner Strasse. Its amusing façade features caryatids over the entry and, higher up, reliefs of faces. Inside is the generally comfortable breakfast room, bedrooms and bathrooms with showers. **www.zurwienerstaatsoper.at**

INNER CITY Amadeus €€€

Wildpretmarkt 5, 1010 ***Tel*** *(01) 533 87 38* ***Fax*** *(01) 533 87 38 38* ***Rooms*** *48* ***Map*** *2 C3*

Set in Vienna's historic centre, near the former location of the ancient Roman camp Vindobona and St Stephen's Cathedral, the Amadeus reflects traditional Viennese charm and decor. Somewhat standard, but easy-going and pleasant service. **www.hotel-amadeus.at**

INNER CITY Arenberg €€€

Stubenring 2, 1010 ***Tel*** *(01) 512 52 91* ***Fax*** *(01) 513 93 56* ***Rooms*** *22* ***Map*** *3 D4, 3 E4, 3 E3*

Located directly on the Ringstrasse, the Arenberg is a stylishly elegant establishment. The bedrooms reflect traditional decor and provide comfort and charm as well as sound-proof windows. The bathrooms are modern and gleaming. Offers several good value weekend stay packages. **www.arenberg.at**

INNER CITY Capricorno €€€

Schwedenplatz 3–4, 1010 ***Tel*** *(01) 533 31 04 0* ***Fax*** *(01) 533 76 71 4* ***Rooms*** *46* ***Map*** *3 D3*

Located close to shops, the subway and to the pubs and clubs of Vienna's "Bermuda Triangle", this hotel offers elegantly designed rooms, many of which feature a balcony. Internet access is available. The helpful and friendly staff are available round the clock. **www.capricorno.schick-hotels.com**

INNER CITY Das Tigra €€€

Tiefer Graben 14–20, 1010 ***Tel*** *(01) 533 96 41 0* ***Fax*** *(01) 533 96 45* ***Rooms*** *75* ***Map*** *2 B3*

Parts of this hotel, located near St Stephen's Cathedral, are under landmark protection. Mozart stayed here as a young man, and this is commemorated by a plaque on the building. The rooms today are modern, in warm colours, yet decorated in classic style. Pets are permitted. **www.hotel-tigra.at**

INNER CITY Domizil €€€

Schulerstrasse 14, 1010 ***Tel*** *(01) 513 31 99 0* ***Fax*** *(01) 512 34 84* ***Rooms*** *40* ***Map*** *2 C4, 3 D4*

This comfortable hotel is located in central Vienna, near many shops, restaurants and a even a casino. Room amenities include a TV, telephone, mini-bar, and an in-room safe. A bar is also on site and bicycles are for rent. Pets are permitted. **www.hoteldomizil.at**

INNER CITY Graben €€€

Dorotheergasse 3, 1010 ***Tel*** *(01) 512 15 31 0* ***Fax*** *(01) 512 15 31 20* ***Rooms*** *52* ***Map*** *2 B4*

Since the 18th century, Hotel Graben has attracted literary greats such as Franz Kafka and Max Brod. Perfectly located just off the Graben pedestrian street, it is near numerous galleries and antique shops. It includes a business centre, and an Italian restaurant below. Pets are permitted. **www.kremslehnerhotels.at**

INNER CITY Hilton Vienna Plaza €€€

Schottenring 11, 1010 ***Tel*** *(01) 313 90 0* ***Fax*** *(01) 313 90 22 009* ***Rooms*** *218* ***Map*** *2 B2*

Located on the Ring, the Hilton Vienna Plaza is designed in Art Deco and contemporary styles. Guest rooms are spacious and light, feature marble bathrooms, and offer a full range of amenities. Babysitting, mobile phone rental and business facilities are just some of the services offered. Pets permitted. **www.hilton.at/wienplaza**

INNER CITY Hotel am Parkring €€€

Parkring 12, 1015 ***Tel*** *(01) 514 80 0* ***Fax*** *(01) 514 80 40* ***Rooms*** *58* ***Map*** *3 D4*

Located on the upper floors of a Ringstrasse building, this hotel offers magnificent views of Vienna. Most rooms feature a balcony or a terrace. The hotel's restaurant, Himmelstube, on the 12th floor lives up to its name ("sky parlour") with a superb city panorama. Pets are permitted. **www.schick-hotels.com**

INNER CITY Mailberger Hof €€€

Annagasse 7, 1010 ***Tel*** *(01) 512 06 41* ***Fax*** *(01) 512 06 41 10* ***Rooms*** *40* ***Map*** *2 C5*

Two Gothic houses have merged to create a Baroque palace, this building is owned by the Knights of Malta and is under landmark protection. You can dine in the striking vaulted restaurant. A wide, stone staircase leads to the spacious, tastefully furnished bedrooms. **www.mailbergerhof.at**

INNER CITY Pertschy €€€

Habsburgergasse 5, 1010 ***Tel*** *(01) 534 49 0* ***Fax*** *(01) 534 49 49* ***Rooms*** *55* ***Map*** *2 B4*

This traditional Viennese pension combines Rococo-style decor within an address that dates back to the 14th century. Entry is through old gates to a courtyard and up a wide stone staircase. A walkway connects the bedrooms. The breakfast room is decorated in dark wood, coffee house style. Pets are permitted. **www.pertschy.com**

INNER CITY Radisson Blu Palais Hotel Vienna €€€

Parkring 16, 1010 ***Tel*** *(01) 515 17 0* ***Fax*** *(01) 512 22 16* ***Rooms*** *247* ***Map*** *3 D4, 3 D5*

Housed in two combined former Viennese palaces across from the Stadtpark, this hotel offers tastefully decorated rooms with amenities that include heated bathroom floors. Also provided are a sauna and spa offering massages and other beauty treatments. Pets are permitted. **www.vienna.radissonblu.com/palais-hotel-vienna**

INNER CITY Wandl €€€

Peterplatz 9, 1010 ***Tel*** *(01) 534 55 0* ***Fax*** *(01) 534 55 77* ***Rooms*** *138* ***Map*** *2 B4*

Located close to the Peterskirche, this charming, old-fashioned hotel has been in the same family for generations. Fine stuccoed features are in some of the bedrooms as well as in the covered courtyard that serves as a breakfast room. Other rooms are simpler, but large, and feature parquet floors. **www.hotel-wandl.com**

INNER CITY Alma Boutique Hotel €€€€

Hafnersteig 7, 1010 ***Tel*** *(01) 533 29 61* ***Fax*** *(01) 533 29 61 81* ***Rooms*** *26* ***Map*** *3 D3*

Formerly the Pension Christina, the Alma Boutique Hotel has undergone a complete renovation. The bedrooms have been stylishly decorated in tones of gold, red and brown, and the luxury rooms all boast whirlpool baths. The location is ideal – all the major landmarks are within walking distance. **www.hotel-alma.com**

INNER CITY Am Stephansplatz €€€€

Stephansplatz 9, 1010 ***Tel*** *(01) 534 05 0* ***Fax*** *(01) 534 05 71 1* ***Rooms*** *56* ***Map*** *2 C4*

Designed with ecologically friendly building materials, this hotel features sleek, modern rooms, some with dark, acacia parquet floors and fine leather and veneer furniture. The hotel also uses high-quality Grander water for all purposes. Some non-smoking floors. **www.hotelamstephansplatz.at**

INNER CITY Astoria €€€€

Kärntner Strasse 32–34, 1015 ***Tel*** *(01) 515 77* ***Fax*** *(01) 515 77 58 2* ***Rooms*** *118* ***Map*** *2 B5, 2 C5*

A hotel since 1912, it features a panelled Jugendstil foyer leading to a grand dining room on the first floor. Some of the splendid bedrooms feature their own brass letter boxes. The spacious rooms are traditionally furnished, often with period decor. Ideally located near the Opera House. **www.austria-trend.at/hotel.astoria**

INNER CITY K&K Palais €€€€

Rudolfsplatz 11, 1010 ***Tel*** *(01) 533 13 53* ***Fax*** *(01) 533 13 53 70* ***Rooms*** *66* ***Map*** *2 C3*

Bright, modern rooms are situated in this fine 19th-century building once belonging to Austria's imperial family (the Habsburgs). Very sleek and contemporary interior with an impressive, glass-fronted lobby and marble staircase. Also includes a business lounge and numerous concierge services. **www.kkhotels.com**

INNER CITY Kaiserin Elisabeth €€€€

Weihburggasse 3, 1010 ***Tel*** *(01) 512 26 0* ***Fax*** *(01) 515 26 7* ***Rooms*** *63* ***Map*** *2 C4, 2 C5*

This elegant hotel, named after the indomitable Habsburg empress, is located just off the Stephansplatz. In the 1800s, it played host to many famous musicians such as Wagner and Liszt. The *fin-de-siècle*-style bedrooms are smart, and Persian rugs lie on parquet floors in the public rooms. Pets are permitted. **www.kaiserinelisabeth.at**

INNER CITY König von Ungarn €€€€

Schulerstrasse 10, 1010 ***Tel*** *(01) 515 84 0* ***Fax*** *(01) 515 84 8* ***Rooms*** *44* ***Map*** *2 C4, 3 D4*

Though in a 16th-century building, the hotel has been welcoming guests since 1815; signatures of many famous visitors are found in the guest book. There is a serene, covered central courtyard with an elegant bar/sitting room. Most bedrooms are spacious. Next door, Mozart composed *The Marriage of Figaro*. **www.kvu.at**

INNER CITY Radisson Blu Style Hotel €€€€

Herrengasse 12, 1010 ***Tel*** *(01) 227 800* ***Fax*** *(01) 227 80 79* ***Rooms*** *78* ***Map*** *2 A3, 2 B3, 2 B4*

This conveniently located hotel is contemporary in style and offers uniquely designed rooms with amenities including a flat-panel LCD TV and a CD/DVD player. Also good fitness and beauty treatment facilities. Pets are permitted. Also home to the stylish H12 bar and Sapori restaurant, which serves Italian cuisine. **www.radissonsas.com**

INNER CITY Starlight Suiten Hotel Salzgries €€€€

Salgries 12, 1010 ***Tel*** *(01) 535 92 22* ***Fax*** *(01) 535 92 22 11* ***Rooms*** *49* ***Map*** *2 C3*

Comprised of lovely suites, each with a living room, bedroom, bathroom and work area. Also included is mini-bar, microwave, telephones and TVs – ideal for a long-term stay. Café and sauna on site. Children up to age six can stay for free when accompanied by their parents. **www.starlighthotels.com**

INNER CITY Vienna Marriott €€€€

Parkring 12a, 1010 ***Tel*** *(01) 515 18 0* ***Fax*** *(01) 515 18 67 36* ***Rooms*** *313* ***Map*** *3 D4, 3 D5*

Numerous shops, cafés and bars fill the open-plan atrium of this modern Ringstrasse hotel. A restaurant and a ballroom for 500 people are also featured. Business facilities include 11 meeting rooms. The bedrooms are generally large. There is a swimming pool and a 24-hour fitness centre. **www.viennamarriott.com**

Key to Price Guide *see p288* **Key to Symbols** *see back cover flap*

INNER CITY Ambassador €€€€€

Neuer Markt 5, 1010 ***Tel*** *(01) 961 61 0* ***Fax*** *(01) 513 29 99* ***Rooms*** *86* ***Map*** *2 C5*

With its elegant 19th-century façade, this hotel looks on to the pedestrian shopping street Kärntner Strasse. Marble pillars, tapestries and chandeliers add to the hotel's regal magnificence. Some of the bedrooms have their own sitting rooms. Inside is the highly regarded "Mörwald im Ambassador" restaurant. **www.ambassador.at**

INNER CITY Palais Coburg Hotel Residenz €€€€€

Coburgbastei 4, 1010 ***Tel*** *(01) 518 18 0* ***Fax*** *(01) 512 22 47 66* ***Rooms*** *35* ***Map*** *3 D5*

This 19th-century former Saxe-Coburg-Gotha palace is today a luxury Relais & Chateaux hotel. There are 35 elegant suites, from traditional to contemporary, plus a unique rooftop spa and two fine restaurants. The wine cellar is stocked with one of Europe's finest collections. **www.palaiscoburg.at**

NORTH OF MARIAHILFER STRASSE Academia €

Pfeilgasse 3a, 1080 ***Tel*** *(01) 401 76 55* ***Fax*** *(01) 401 76 20* ***Rooms*** *263* ***Map*** *1 A4, 1 B4*

During the academic year, this establishment serves as a student residence. However, during the summer break (1 July to 30 September), it opens its doors to the public as a hotel. The rooms are modern and airy, and have a telephone. Some feature a balcony. **www.academia-hotels.co.at**

NORTH OF MARIAHILFER STRASSE Andreas €

Schlösselgasse 11, 1080 ***Tel*** *(01) 405 34 88* ***Fax*** *(01) 405 34 88 50* ***Rooms*** *40* ***Map*** *1 C2, 1 C3*

A friendly, family-run hotel that is often visited by university professors and Burgtheater artists. The bedrooms are of a cheerful and simple, no-nonsense standard. Good cyclist facilities. Well-located, close to the city centre. **www.hotelpensionandreas.at**

NORTH OF MARIAHILFER STRASSE Arpi €

Kochgasse 15, 1080 ***Tel*** *(01) 405 00 33* ***Fax*** *(01) 405 00 33 37* ***Rooms*** *20* ***Map*** *1 B2, 1 B3*

This is a family-owned, centrally located hotel and pension. It is a clean and modern establishment with friendly staff, who will assist you in obtaining tickets to theatres and concerts as well as help to arrange sightseeing tours, including to Salzburg and Prague. **www.hotelarpi.com**

NORTH OF MARIAHILFER STRASSE Excellence €

Alser Strasse 21, 1080 ***Tel*** *(01) 407 96 20* ***Fax*** *(01) 407 96 20 11* ***Rooms*** *27* ***Map*** *1 A2, 1 B2*

A clean, modern establishment with elegant cherry wood decor in all of the rooms. Unpretentious, yet comfortable, it also offers a wide range of services and amenities, including a key card lock system, laundry service and international breakfast. Located within a short distance to the city centre. **www.pension-excellence.com**

NORTH OF MARIAHILFER STRASSE Golderner Bär €

Türkenstrasse 27, 1090 ***Tel*** *(01) 317 51 11* ***Fax*** *(01) 317 51 11 22* ***Rooms*** *27* ***Map*** *2 A2, 2 B2, 2 B1*

This is a simple but comfortable hotel located just minutes from the landmark Votivkirche and the Ringstrasse. The rooms are designed in a modern style and feature sound-proof windows. Amenities include free Internet access. The staff are particularly friendly and helpful. **www.goldbaerhotel.com**

NORTH OF MARIAHILFER STRASSE Terminus Hotel €

Fillgradergasse 4, 1060 ***Tel*** *(01) 587 73 86 0* ***Fax*** *(01) 587 73 86 76* ***Rooms*** *45* ***Map*** *4 B1*

Located close to the shopping street Mariahilfer Strasse, this small hotel offers adequate accommodation with the standard range of amenities, such as a TV and telephone. Each room is decorated in a different style. The staff are helpful and pleasant. Pets are permitted. **www.terminus.at**

NORTH OF MARIAHILFER STRASSE Alpha €€

Buchfeldgasse 8, 1080 ***Tel*** *(01) 403 52 91* ***Fax*** *(01) 403 52 91 62* ***Rooms*** *58* ***Map*** *1 C3, 1 C4*

Located close to the Austrian Parliament, City Hall and the Ringstrasse, this hotel is simple yet cosy and modern. All 58 non-smoking rooms feature a telephone, satellite TV and a safe. The breakfast room is light and airy. Internet access is available in the public areas. **www.hotelalpha.at**

NORTH OF MARIAHILFER STRASSE Altstadt Vienna €€

Kirchengasse 41, 1070 ***Tel*** *(01) 522 66 66* ***Fax*** *(01) 523 49 01* ***Rooms*** *42* ***Map*** *1 B5, 4 A1*

Situated in the artistic Spittelberg area, this hotel was built in 1902 in the Ringstrasse style. Traditional rooms provide a clever contrast to the ultra-sleek rooms recently designed by Italian architect Matteo Thun; these feature striking modern furnishings. Free Wi-Fi access. Excellent service and style. **www.altstadt.at**

NORTH OF MARIAHILFER STRASSE Cordial Theaterhotel Wien €€

Josefstädter Strasse 22, 1080 ***Tel*** *(01) 405 36 48 0* ***Fax*** *(01) 405 14 06* ***Rooms*** *54* ***Map*** *1 B4*

Simple but comfortable, modern rooms at this hotel, located close to the famous Theater in der Josefstadt. There is also a bar, sauna and solarium, and a seminar room for 60 people. Breakfast can be served in your room for a small, additional fee. The friendly staff can help with sighteseeing arrangements. **www.cordial.co.at**

NORTH OF MARIAHILFER STRASSE Hotel Fürstenhof €€

Neubaugürtel 4, 1060 ***Tel*** *(01) 523 32 67* ***Fax*** *(01) 523 32 67 26* ***Rooms*** *58*

Very friendly service and clean and comfortable rooms define this family-run hotel. Situated in an early 20th-century building, the rooms are decorated in both traditional and contemporary styles. Some have chandeliers. Conveniently located near the Westbahnhof. **www.hotel-fuerstenhof.com**

NORTH OF MARIAHILFER STRASSE Hotel Kummer €€

Mariahilfer Strasse 71a, 1060 **Tel** *(01) 588 95* **Fax** *(01) 587 81 33* **Rooms** *95* **Map** *4 A1*

This hotel is ideally located on the vibrant shopping avenue Mariahilfer Strasse, and only minutes from the centre of town. The rooms are elegantly furnished, comfortable and offer numerous amenities, including free Premiere movie channels and a trouser press. **www.hotelkummer.at**

NORTH OF MARIAHILFER STRASSE Mercure Josefshof Wien €€

Josefsgasse 4–6, 1080 **Tel** *(01) 404 19* **Fax** *(01) 404 19 15 0* **Rooms** *169* **Map** *1 C4*

This hotel is located in a quiet street, close to Vienna's English Theatre and numerous other sites. The bedrooms are smart with high-quality furniture and parquet flooring, and the tiled bathrooms are gleaming. Pets are permitted. Children under 12 years of age can stay for free when accompanied by an adult. **www.josefshof.com**

NORTH OF MARIAHILFER STRASSE Museum €€

Museumstrasse 3, 1070 **Tel** *(01) 523 44 26* **Fax** *(01) 523 44 26 30* **Rooms** *15* **Map** *1 C4, 1 C5*

Located next to the Kunsthistorisches and Naturhistorisches museums, this is a classic Viennese pension with a Ringstrasse architectural period façade, complete with wrought-iron balconies. Massive, spartan bedrooms feature high ceilings and wooden floors. Ornate fireplaces and chandeliers in the sitting and breakfast rooms. **www.hotelmuseum.at**

NORTH OF MARIAHILFER STRASSE Zipser €€

Lange Gasse 49, 1080 **Tel** *(01) 404 54 0* **Fax** *(01) 404 54 13* **Rooms** *47* **Map** *1 B3, 1 B4*

The poet Ödön von Horváth stayed here in the 1920s, and even mentioned it in his book *Stories from the Wienerwald*. Located in the beautiful Josefstadt area, the hotel offers clean, bright and modern bedrooms – some large ones toward the back feature wooden balconies overlooking an attractive leafy courtyard. **www.zipser.at**

NORTH OF MARIAHILFER STRASSE Rathauspark €€€

Rathausstrasse 17, 1010 **Tel** *(01) 404 12 0* **Fax** *(01) 404 12 761* **Rooms** *117* **Map** *1 C4*

This building was erected in 1880 and was once the residence of renowned author Sefan Zweig. Today, as a fine hotel, it still conveys elegance of the past, but combines it with modern style and conveniences. The upper floor has air-conditioning, and there are three non-smoking floors. Free high speed Internet service. **www.austria-trend.at/rhw**

NORTH OF MARIAHILFER STRASSE Rathaus Wein & Design €€€

Lange Gasse 13, 1080 **Tel** *(01) 400 11 22* **Fax** *(01) 400 11 22 88* **Rooms** *40* **Map** *1 B3, 1 B4*

Located in a historic townhouse, this renovated, highly modern hotel is is dedicated to the culture of wine. Each luxurious double room is named after an Austrian vintner, whose wines are in the mini-bar. The bathroom is stocked with wine cosmetics. Even wine region excursions can be arranged. Truly unique. **www.hotel-rathaus-wien.at**

NORTH OF MARIAHILFER STRASSE Regina €€€

Rooseveltplatz 15, 1096 **Tel** *(01) 404 46 0* **Fax** *(01) 408 83 92* **Rooms** *164* **Map** *2 A2*

With brass chandeliers and classical statues, the hotel's interior recalls the grandeur of 1877, when it was built. Owned by the Kremslehner family since 1896, it is practically a Viennese institution today. The hotel caters to many tourist groups. The bedrooms are somewhat old-fashioned, but comfortable. **www.kremslehnerhotels.at**

SOUTH OF THE RING Clima Cityhotel €

Theresianumgasse 21a, 1040 **Tel** *(01) 515 16 96* **Fax** *(01) 504 35 52* **Rooms** *37* **Map** *5, D3, 5 E3*

Quiet despite its central location, this hotel offers a great view of the city from the upper floors. It is situated close to the beautiful Belvedere Palace and gardens. The bedrooms are clean and modern, though seemingly austere, with good-sized bathrooms. The friendly staff can assist you in obtaining tickets to events. **www.climacity-hotel.com**

SOUTH OF THE RING Am Schubertring €€

Schubertring 11, 1010 **Tel** *(01) 717 02 0* **Fax** *(01) 713 99 66* **Rooms** *39* **Map** *2 C5, 3 D5*

Housed in a building erected during Vienna's Ringstrasse era (1870s), this is one of the city's few hotels reflecting the Belle Epoque and Jugendstil styles. Rooms are furnished according to that period, with many complemented by elegant Persian rugs. Some fine views of St Stephen's Cathedral. Pets allowed. **www.schubertring.at**

SOUTH OF THE RING Mercure Secession €€

Getreidemarkt 5, 1060 **Tel** *(01) 588 38 0* **Fax** *(01) 588 38 212* **Rooms** *70* **Map** *4 C1*

This turn-of-the-century hotel reflects Viennese charm underscored by modern comfort and service. The stylish rooms are brightly coloured and well-furnished. Plenty of services including dry cleaning and ironing, and desks for tourist information and car hire. Pets allowed. Close to tram, subway and bus lines. **www.mercure.com**

SOUTH OF THE RING Hotel Kaiserhof Wien €€€

Frankenberggasse 10, 1040 **Tel** *(01) 505 17 01* **Fax** *(01) 505 88 75 88* **Rooms** *75* **Map** *4 C2, 5 D2*

Located close to the Karlsplatz, this hotel offers plush, warm-coloured rooms, all with modern conveniences and some with Wi-Fi Internet access. Exercise buffs can enjoy a fitness room, sauna, steam room and sanarium, which features special coloured mood lighting. Fine quality and service. **www.hotel-kaiserhof.at**

SOUTH OF THE RING Le Meridien Vienna €€€€

Opernring 13–15, 1010 **Tel** *(01) 588 90* **Fax** *(01) 588 90 90 90* **Rooms** *294* **Map** *2 B5*

This urban chic hotel has rooms tastefully decorated in shades of blue, green and pink and accented in earth shades and light woods. Numerous amenities include bathrobes, slippers and umbrellas. The wellness centre features a Jacuzzi, pool, sauna and steam room. Designed for a sophisticated, first-class stay. **www.lemeridien.com/vienna**

Key to Price Guide *see p288* **Key to Symbols** *see back cover flap*

SOUTH OF THE RING Bristol €€€€€

Kärntner Ring 1, 1015 **Tel** *(01) 515 16 0* **Fax** *(01) 515 16 55 0* **Rooms** *140* **Map** *5 D1*

This traditional, luxurious hotel is located just across from the Opera House, on the Ringstrasse. Numerous celebrities and entrepreneurs have appreciated its opulent marble, gilt, antiques and paintings. The plush bedrooms include top-floor penthouses and superb business suites. **www.luxurycollection.com/bristol**

SOUTH OF THE RING Grand Hotel Wien €€€€€

Kärntner Ring 9, 1010 **Tel** *(01) 515 80 0* **Fax** *(01) 515 13 13* **Rooms** *205* **Map** *2 B5*

This extravagant Ringstrasse hotel dates back to 1870, when it opened as one of Europe's finest establishments. The original façade remains but the rest is modern luxury, with plush bedrooms, excellent restaurants and extensive business facilities. Perfect central location. **www.grandhotelwien.com**

SOUTH OF THE RING Imperial €€€€€

Kärntner Ring 16, 1015 **Tel** *(01) 501 10 0* **Fax** *(01) 501 10 41 0* **Rooms** *138* **Map** *2 B5*

The grande dame of Vienna's luxury hotels, the Imperial has been pampering guests in an air of exclusivity since 1873. Heads of state, international entertainers and royalty often stay in this former palace on the Ring. Silk-lined walls, chandeliered ceilings and marble bathrooms only begin to define the ambience. **www.luxurycollection.com/imperial**

SOUTH OF THE RING Sacher €€€€€

Philarmonikerstrasse 4, 1010 **Tel** *(01) 514 56 0* **Fax** *(01) 514 56 81 0* **Rooms** *152* **Map** *2 B5*

Since 1876, the famous and wealthy have frequented the Hotel Sacher. Today, this Viennese icon is a bastion of tradition combined with modern technology. Amenities are in abundance here. The rooms range from opulent to elegant. This is the home of the original Sacher Torte. **www.sacher.com**

FURTHER AFIELD Arcotel Boltzmann €

Boltzmanngasse 8, 1090 **Tel** *(01) 316 12 0* **Fax** *(01) 316 12 81 6* **Rooms** *70* **Map** *1 C1*

A small, charming hotel in the embassy district, the Boltzmann is also situated close to the romantic Strudelhof Steps. It is surrounded by gardens and parks, and is a short ten-minute walk from the historic centre. The hotel also offers cosy, atmospheric rooms as well as a private garden. **www.arcotel.at**

FURTHER AFIELD Deutschmeister €

Grünentorgasse 30, 1090 **Tel** *(01) 310 34 04* **Fax** *(01) 310 04 80* **Rooms** *52* **Map** *2 A1*

A pleasant establishment with smoking and non-smoking floors. The bedrooms are comfortable, and reflect both traditional and modern decor in warm colours, including golds and greens. Standard amenities. Friendly service. Just a few minutes from the Ring. **www.city-hotels.at**

FURTHER AFIELD Hotel Beethoven €

Millöckergasse 6, 1060 **Tel** *(01) 587 44 82 0* **Fax** *(01) 587 44 42* **Rooms** *36*

This hotel is situated across from the Theater an der Wien, where Beethoven once resided, and a short stroll to the Naschmarkt. The rooms are elegant and comfortable, some with period-style furniture. Internet access and staff assistance for theatre and concert tickets are some of the services provided. Pets permitted. **www.hotel-beethoven.at**

FURTHER AFIELD Hotel Harmonie €

Harmoniegasse 5–7, 1090 **Tel** *317 66 04* **Fax** *317 66 04 55* **Rooms** *68* **Map** *2 A1*

Situated in a quiet location, this hotel offers rooms that are simple but comfortable and designed in a modern style. There is a café and bar, and the staff will assist you in obtaining entertainment tickets. Pets are permitted. Children under the age of 12 can stay for free when accompanied by two adults. **www.bestwestern-ce.com/harmonie**

FURTHER AFIELD Hotel Korotan €

Albertgasse 48, 1080 **Tel** *(01) 403 41 93* **Fax** *(01) 403 41 93 99* **Rooms** *66* **Map** *1 A2*

Part hotel, part student pension, the hotel itself has a very modern, vibrant style, and friendly staff. All rooms are standard and clean, plus have Internet access. Also on the premises are a chapel, library and art gallery, emphasizing a cultural atmosphere. **www.hotel.korotan.com**

FURTHER AFIELD Lindenhof €

Breitenleer Strasse 256, 1220 **Tel** *(01) 734 36 37* **Fax** *(01) 734 29 80* **Rooms** *24*

Family-owned since 1928, this cosy hostelry is located in an 18th-century building and provides simple, comfortable rooms. The proprietors take pride in offering old-fashioned hospitality and plenty of entertainment. There are ample dining facilities, including an indoor restaurant and outdoor terrace. **www.lindenhof-breitenlee.com**

FURTHER AFIELD Mozart €

Nordberg-Strasse 4, 1090 **Tel** *(01) 317 15 37* **Fax** *(01) 317 24 77* **Rooms** *56*

This building once served as quarters for the American Allied troops after World War II. Today, the hotel's rooms, though spacious, are furnished with somewhat standard furniture. The hot water supply is heated by solar energy. A private house bar is available. Pets are permitted. **www.hotelmozart-vienna.at**

FURTHER AFIELD Sophienalpe €

Sofienalpenstrasse 13, 1140 **Tel** *(01) 486 24 32* **Fax** *(01) 485 16 55 12* **Rooms** *70*

Built in 1912, this hotel looks like a grand Habsburg-era country villa: it is located in the middle of the Vienna Woods. The rooms are furnished very comfortably, catering to active guests who want to take advantage of the area's numerous hiking and mountain bike paths. A bus to the city leaves every 1.5 hours. **www.sophienalpe.at**

FURTHER AFIELD Gartenhotel Glanzing €€

Glanzinggasse 23, 1190 **Tel** *(01) 470 42 72 0* **Fax** *(01) 470 42 72 14* **Rooms** *14*

Built in the 1930s, this lovely, ivy-festooned hotel is located in a leafy area near the Vienna Woods and several *Heurigen*. Bedrooms are large and comfortable, and the main room hosts a grand piano. Fitness facilities are open 24 hours. Children under age 15 can stay for free when accompanied by an adult. **www.gartenhotel-glanzing.at**

FURTHER AFIELD Grinzinger Hof €€

Grinzinger Allee 86, 1190 **Tel** *(01) 320 63 13* **Fax** *(01) 320 63 13 4* **Rooms** *10*

More of a guest house than a hotel, the Grinzinger Hof is located in the village of Grinzing, part of the city's 19th district. Nearby are some of Vienna's finest *Heurigen* as well as vineyards. A very personal service is offered at the hotel, and it happily caters to cyclists. **www.grinzing.com**

FURTHER AFIELD Hotel Erzherzog Rainer €€

Wiedner Hauptstrasse 27–29, 1040 **Tel** *(01) 501 11 0* **Fax** *(01) 501 11 35 0* **Rooms** *84* **Map** *4 C3*

Traditional Austrian hospitality defines this hotel, located near the Künstlerhaus. The rooms are large, decorated tastefully, and are quiet with sound-proof windows. There is also a comfortable coffee house and bar. The restaurant, Wiener Wirtschaft, serves delicious Viennese food. Pets are permitted. **www.schick-hotels.com**

FURTHER AFIELD Hotel Jäger €€

Hernalser Hauptstrasse 187, 1170 **Tel** *(01) 486 66 20 0* **Fax** *(01) 486 66 20 8* **Rooms** *17*

Owned and operated by the Jäger family since 1911, this boutique hotel offers friendly, first-class service. Accommodation includes two apartments, each with a kitchen. Children under age 12 can stay for free when accompanied by two paying adults. Pets permitted. **www.hoteljaeger.at**

FURTHER AFIELD Landhaus Fuhrgassl-Huber €€

Neustift am Walde, Rathstrasse 24, 1190 **Tel** *(01) 440 30 33* **Fax** *(01) 440 27 14* **Rooms** *38*

This quaint, family-run hotel lies in the wine village Neustift am Walde, at the edge of Vienna. The building dates to 1795, but the renovated rooms are furnished elegantly and in warm colours. Next door is a *Heuriger*, and walking in the vineyards can be enjoyed. A bus to Vienna stops outside the hotel. **www.fuhrgassl-huber.at**

FURTHER AFIELD Parkhotel Schönbrunn €€

Hietzinger Hauptstr 10–20, 1130 **Tel** *(01) 878 04 0* **Fax** *(01) 878 04 3220* **Rooms** *394*

Originally built as a guest house of Emperor Franz Josef I in 1907, the Parkhotel Schönbrunn still evokes an imperial aura with its period-style furniture, chandeliers and even its grand ballroom. Located directly across from the elaborate park of Schloss Schönbrunn. Ideal for large groups and business stays. **www.austria-trend.at/paw**

FURTHER AFIELD Tourotel Roter Hahn €€

Landstrasser Hauptstrasse 40, 1030 **Tel** *(01) 713 25 68 0* **Fax** *(01) 713 25 68 19 0* **Rooms** *48*

This hotel is in a building protected as a historic national monument. Each of the rooms is uniquely decorated and has plenty of amenities. The friendly staff can provide assistance in obtaining tickets to sites and events in town. Pets are permitted.

FURTHER AFIELD Hotel Stefanie €€€

Taborstrasse 12, 1020 **Tel** *(01) 211 50* **Fax** *(01) 211 50 16 0* **Rooms** *126* **Map** *3 D1*

Dating back to 1703, this is the oldest four-star hotel in Vienna. And it is conveniently located just across the Danube canal, a few minutes from St Stephen's Cathedral. The bedrooms are in either traditional Viennese or contemporary styles. Some have Wi-Fi Internet access. Pets are permitted. **www.schick-hotels.com**

FURTHER AFIELD Mercure Grand Hotel Biedermeier €€€

Landstrasser Hauptstrasse 28, 1030 **Tel** *(01) 716 71 0* **Fax** *(01) 716 71 5 03* **Rooms** *201* **Map** *2 C5*

This hotel is located in a superbly restored heritage-style Biedermeier arcade, just off one of Vienna's main shopping streets. The bedrooms, most of which look down to the cobblestone passage, are spacious and quiet. Bicycles are available to rent. Pets are permitted. **www.accorhotels.com**

FURTHER AFIELD InterContinental Wien €€€€

Johannesgasse 28, 1037 **Tel** *(01) 711 22 0* **Fax** *(01) 713 44 89* **Rooms** *453* **Map** *2 C5*

This modern, cosmopolitan chain hotel is just a 2-minute walk from the Ringstrasse and the Stadtpark gardens. More than half of the rooms available are non-smoking. Classical music is played nightly in the bar area of the elegant, chandeliered foyer. Numerous amenities. **www.vienna.intercontinental.com**

LOWER AUSTRIA AND BURGENLAND

BAD TATZMANNSDORF Landhaus Pannonia €€€

Parkstrasse 20, 7431 **Tel** *(03353) 82 48* **Fax** *(03353) 82 48 30* **Rooms** *27* **Road map** *G4*

In Bad Tatzmannsdorf's oldest inn, this small, family-friendly establishment offers large bright guest rooms with modern en-suite bathrooms and TV. Substantial breakfast buffet, and a pleasant sun terrace with a café serving delicious home-made pastries are also part of this inn's charm.

Key to Price Guide *see p288* **Key to Symbols** *see back cover flap*

BAD TATZMANNSDORF Reiter's Supreme Hotel €€€€

Am Gofplatz 1, 7431 **Tel** *(03353) 88 41 607* **Fax** *(03353) 88 41 138* **Rooms** *177* **Road map** *G4*

A sprawling luxurious thermal spa resort with indoor and outdoor pools, whirlpool, steam bath and saunas, and a bar by the pool. The guest rooms and suites are furnished with modern flair, and most overlook the golf course and all rooms have a balcony. **www.burgenlandresort.at**

BADEN Hotel Admiral am Kurpark €€€

Renngasse 8, 2500 **Tel** *(02252) 86 79 9* **Fax** *(02252) 86 79 98* **Rooms** *22* **Road map** *G3*

This hotel has modern conference facilities, several suites and a luxury penthouse. Comfortably furnished rooms feature well-appointed bathrooms, whirlpools, telephones, TV, radio and fax facilities. Also a bridge room, reading room, Internet corner, sauna, steam bath and solarium. **www.hotel-admiral.at**

BADEN Grand Hotel Sauerhof €€€€

Weilburgstrasse 11–13, 2500 **Tel** *(02252) 41 25 10* **Fax** *(02252) 43 62 6* **Rooms** *90* **Road map** *G3*

A delightful *palais* designed in the Biedermeier style, this grand hotel sits amid its own serene park. True to its aristocratic roots, accommodations are opulent and spacious. There are 90 rooms and suites, an elegant restaurant, bar, and historic wine cellar dating to 1419. Splendid indoor pool and spa. Golf nearby. **www.sauerhof.at**

DURNSTEIN Hotel Schloss Dürnstein €€€€€

Dürnstein 2, 3601 **Tel** *(02711) 21 20* **Fax** *(02711) 21 23 0* **Rooms** *41* **Road map** *F3*

This dreamy castle is the ultimate romantic address. Dine on the terrace overlooking the Danube River and sleep in a four-poster bed fit for royalty. This Relais et Chateaux property offers an endless range of silver-service dining possibilities, and breathtaking indoor and outdoor pools. **www.schloss.at**

EGGENBURG Stadthotel Eggenburg €

Kremser Strasse 8, 3730 **Tel** *(02984) 35 31* **Fax** *(02984) 35 31 101* **Rooms** *27* **Road map** *F2*

This family-run hotel is located in the centre of the medieval town of Eggenburg. Quiet, comfortable rooms with modern amenities and traditional touches. There is a restaurant as well as a cosy guest lounge. Conference room and meeting hall available. **www.tiscover.com**

EISENSTADT Hotel Burgenland €€€

Schubertplatz 1, 7000 **Tel** *(02682) 69 6* **Fax** *(02682) 65 53 1* **Rooms** *87* **Road map** *G3*

Located in the centre of Eisenstadt, a few minutes from the Esterhazy Palace. Rooms and suites are equipped with radio, TV and telephone. There is restaurant and bar, café, indoor swimming pool and sauna. Adjoining the hotel is a conference centre. Private garage. **www.austria-hotels.at**

EISENSTADT Hotel Ohr €€€

Ruster Strasse 51, 7000 **Tel** *(02682) 624 60* **Fax** *(02682) 64 26 09* **Rooms** *29* **Road map** *G3*

A family hotel, standing some distance from the town centre, which makes it quiet and relaxing. The elegant, modern rooms are functionally equipped. The restaurant specializes in typical Austrian dishes and regional cuisine. Horse-riding is on offer. **www.hotelohr.at**

FEUERSBRUNN Mörwald Hotel Villa Katharina €€€

Feuersbrunn, 3483 **Tel** *(02738) 22 98* **Fax** *(02738) 22 98 60* **Rooms** *10* **Road map** *F3*

The kitchen is king at this celebrated chef's hotel, though every other need is carefully tended to as well. Award-winning chef Toni M. delivers fresh and exciting menus. Cooking courses available. Some rooms are cleverly named and designed around grape varietals. **www.moerwald.at**

GOSING Alpenhotel Gösing €€€

Gösing an der Mariazellerbahn, 3221 **Tel** *(02728) 21 7* **Fax** *(27282) 17 11 6* **Rooms** *73* **Road map** *F4*

Built in the early 20th century, this large four-star country hotel has great charm and a traditional Austrian woodwork interior and furnishings. Some rooms include lavish bathrooms and a private steam bath and sauna. Indoor swimming pool. **www.goesing.at**

KREMS Am Förthof €€

Förthofer Donaulände 8, 3504 **Tel** *(02732) 833 45* **Fax** *(02732) 833 45 40* **Rooms** *41* **Road map** *F3*

A romantic gourmet hotel in the midst of Austria's wine region. Private gardens enjoy Danube views. The charming restaurant features light and creative cuisine, an extensive wine menu and wine tastings. Special six-course menu with 12 wines. Bicycles are free of charge. Outdoor pool. **www.hotel-foerthof.at**

KRONBERG Landgut Kronberghof €€

Am Russbach 3, 2123 **Tel** *(02245) 43 04* **Fax** *(02245) 43 04 4* **Rooms** *15* **Road map** *G3*

A small country house hotel on a lake that specializes in horse riding. A choice of handsome horses for beginners and experts, as well as lessons and numerous riding arenas. Pleasant rooms with whirlpool baths and there is an attractive outdoor swimming pool. **www.kronberghof.at**

LOIPERSDORF Pension Krainz €€

Henndorf-Therme 2, 8282 Loipersdorf **Tel** *(03329) 466 11* **Fax** *(03329) 466 11 30* **Rooms** *15* **Road map** *G5*

Close to the large thermal spa centre of Loipersdorf, this family-, golf- and tennis-oriented hotel offers numerous reductions for children on room rates and activities. Standard and superior rooms are spacious and sunny. The restaurant has an extended dinner between 5–10pm to accommodate families. **www.krainz-loipersdorf.at**

MAUERBACH Berghotel Tulbingerkogel €€€

Tulbingerkogel 1, 3001 ***Tel*** *(02273) 73 91* ***Fax*** *(02273) 73 91 73* ***Rooms*** *46* ***Road map*** *F3*

Part old traditional, part contemporary design hotel. Glorious forest views from floor-to-ceiling guest room windows. Inviting outdoor pool overlooking manicured gardens. There is an excellent restaurant and an impressive wine collection with more than 1,200 wines from around the world. **www.tulbingerkogel.at**

MOLLERSDORF Hotel-Restaurant Holzinger €€€

Teichgasse 2, 2513 ***Tel*** *(02252) 52 45 5* ***Fax*** *(02252) 52 45 54.* ***Rooms*** *35* ***Road map*** *G3*

Simple family-run hotel with modern singles, doubles and suites with en-suite, satellite TV, telephone and radio. There are two restaurants serving typical Austrian fare, with a cosy garden attached, especially pleasant in the summer. **www.hotel-holzinger.at**

NEUSIEDL AM SEE Hotel Wende €€€

Seestrasse 42 ***Tel*** *(02167) 81 11 0* ***Fax*** *(02167) 81 11 64 9* ***Rooms*** *105* ***Road map*** *G3*

This child-friendly hotel in the national park Neusiedlersee-Seewinkel has been renovated several times. Comfortable guest rooms with balconies, relaxation area with an indoor pool and well-equipped seminar rooms. Restaurant with light and airy winter garden. **www.hotel-wende.at**

PAMHAGEN Vila Vita Hotel und Feriendorf Pannonia €€€€

Storchengasse 1, 7152 ***Tel*** *(02175) 21 80 0* ***Fax*** *(02175) 21 80 44 4* ***Rooms*** *160* ***Road map*** *G3*

A large holiday resort 80 km (50 miles) from Vienna in the heart of a park. There are many rooms as well as numerous well-appointed bungalows, some with thatched roofs, accommodating up to six people. Indoor pool and heated outdoor pool, beauty treatments and massage. **www.vilavitahotels.com**

PODERSDORF Seewirt Haus Attila €€€

Podersdorf am See, Strandplatz 1, A-7141 ***Tel*** *(02177) 24 15* ***Fax*** *(02177) 24 15 30* ***Rooms*** *70* ***Road map*** *G3*

Lakeside resort hotel just one hour from Vienna. Lavish four-course dinners are served in the restaurant with wine pairing. Most rooms have balconies with lake views, and it is a lovely region to borrow the hotel bikes for rides through the vineyards. Spa area as well as sailing, swimming and horseriding. **www.seewirtkarner.at**

RETZ Hotel Althof Retz €€€

Althofgasse 14 Retz, 2070 ***Tel*** *(02942) 37 11* ***Fax*** *(02942) 37 11 55* ***Road map*** *F2*

Formerly a castle in the Middle Ages, now a modern country lodge. Warm colours in individually decorated rooms and suites. There is a sauna, steam bath, solarium, whirlpool, romantic castle garden and a 17th-century wine cellar. Packages include wine tasting and tours. **www.althof.at**

RUST Hotel Sifkovits €€

Am Seekanal 8, 7071 ***Tel*** *(02685) 276 or 360* ***Fax*** *(02685) 36 01 2* ***Rooms*** *34* ***Road map*** *G3*

Charming and personal, each of the 34 rooms is furnished in its own style. Extensive breakfast buffet with organic produce and a restaurant serving regional and international dishes. There is a large garden with sun chairs for relaxing and an inviting lobby. **www.sifkovits.at**

RUST Seehotel Rust €€€€

Am Seekanal 2–4, 7071 ***Tel*** *(02685) 38 10* ***Fax*** *(02685) 38 14 19* ***Rooms*** *110* ***Road map*** *G3*

A large holiday complex that houses modern rooms in six categories from standard to apartment. Located right on the waters of the Neusiedlersee, there are two restaurants, a bar, wellness centre, playground, tennis courts and beach volleyball as well as a private beach for guests. **www.seehotel.rust.at**

SEMMERING Belvedere €€€€

Hochstrasse 60, 2680 ***Tel*** *(02664) 22 70* ***Fax*** *(02664) 22 67 42* ***Rooms*** *39* ***Road map*** *F4*

Pretty, traditional-style hotel with a warm atmosphere, located right in the village. Handy for mountain sports, and offers an indoor swimming pool with a glass-covered roof, sauna, steam bath, solarium and a large sunny garden. Typical Austrian cuisine is served using local produce. **www.semmering.com/hotel-belvedere**

ST POLTEN Austria Trend Hotel Metropol €€

Schillerplatz 1, 2680 ***Tel*** *(02742) 707 00* ***Fax*** *(02742) 707 00 133* ***Rooms*** *87* ***Road map*** *F3*

The Hotel Metropol is a modern business hotel located at the entrance to the pedestrian zone. All rooms come with en-suite bathroom, telephone, modem link, minibar, cable and Pay TV. There is a sauna, steam bath and a plentiful breakfast buffet. The restaurant is open for lunch and dinner on weekdays. **www.austria-trend.at/hotel-metropol**

STEGERSBACH Allegria Hotel €€

Golfstrasse 1, 7551 ***Tel*** *(03326) 50 00* ***Fax*** *(03326) 50 08 00* ***Rooms*** *86* ***Road map*** *G4*

A large thermal spa resort where accommodation comes in the form of six modernised chalets or a cool elegant development with 50 double rooms, maisonettes and suites. Two thermal springs feed the spa, at which a wide variety of baths, treatments and daily activities are offered. **www.dietherme.com**

STEGERSBACH Larimar Hotel-Therme-Spa €€€€

Panoramaweg 2, A-7551 Stegersbach ***Tel*** *(03326) 55 10 0* ***Fax*** *(03326) 55 10 09 90* ***Rooms*** *200* ***Road map*** *G4*

Stylish modern wellness hotel that offers thermal waters, spa facilities and nearby golf. Guest rooms are furnished in cool, clean lines with earth, fire, water and air themes. Thermal pools are large and sunny with underwater music, and the spa offers various Oriental-influenced treatments. **www.larimarhotel.at**

Key to Price Guide *see p288* **Key to Symbols** *see back cover flap*

WACHAU Gartenhotel & Weingut Pfeffel €€

Dürnstein 122, A-3601 ***Tel*** *(02711) 20 6* ***Fax*** *(02711) 20 68* ***Rooms*** *40* ***Road map*** *F3*

Pretty garden courtyard with flowering trees where drinks and simple meals are served. Guest rooms are handsomely furnished in a traditional Austrian motif. The host serves wine from his own terraced vineyard. Outdoor pool and sauna. **www.pfeffel.at**

WEISSENKIRCHEN/WACHAU Hotel-Weingasthof Donauwirt €€

Wachaustrasse 47, 3610 ***Tel*** *(02715) 22 47* ***Fax*** *(02715) 22 47 47* ***Rooms*** *11* ***Road map*** *F3*

A cheerfully decorated family-run hotel with a sophisticated restaurant that serves exciting award-winning cuisine and home-made produce such as bread and jam. Impressive wine cellar with a large choice of Austrian vintages. Some guest rooms have balconies. **www.donauwirt.at**

ZWETTL Hotel Schwarz-Alm €€

Gschwendt 43, 3910 ***Tel*** *(02822) 53 17 3* ***Fax*** *(02822) 53 17 31 1* ***Rooms*** *38* ***Road map*** *F2*

A sizeable country hotel amid an oasis of green forest where guests can enjoy an assortment of activities including hiking, mountain biking and fishing. A wellness centre offers various saunas, steam baths and waterbeds to relax in. There is a brewery nearby. **www.schwarzalm.at**

STYRIA

BAD AUSSEE Hotel Erzherzog Johann €€€€

Kurhausplatz 62, 8990 ***Tel*** *(03622) 52 50 7* ***Fax*** *(03622) 52 50 76 80* ***Rooms*** *62* ***Road map*** *D4*

This modern spa hotel achieves a warm feeling thanks to the use of natural materials and stylish design. A decadent wellness centre offers a salt water pool, various sauna and steam baths, and pine divan beds in front of an open fire. Local Styrian dishes are served with international flair. **www.erzherzogjohann.at**

BAD BLUMAU Rogner-Bad Blumau €€€€€

Blumau 100, 8283 ***Tel*** *(03383) 51 00* ***Fax*** *(03383) 51 00 80 8* ***Rooms*** *243* ***Road map*** *F4*

Welcome to the Alice in Wonderland of spa hotels. Designed by renowned Austrian artist Friedensreich Hundertwasser, this fanciful hotel can not fail to delight. Its hot spring has the highest mineralization of any Austrian spa region. Guests may take part in smudging ceremonies, fire meditation and trance dances. **www.blumau.com**

BAD GLEICHENBERG Hotel Stenitzer €€€

Stefanie-Stenitzer-Schulstrasse 51, 8344 ***Tel*** *(03159) 22 50* ***Fax*** *(03159) 22 50 60* ***Rooms*** *30* ***Road map*** *F5*

An elegantly furnished four-star property with extensive wellness facilities and varied massage treatments. Double rooms and suites are reached via a grand staircase. A romantic terrace looks on to the formal gardens. Special spa packages are available. **www.hotel-stenitzer.com**

BAD RADKERSBURG Thermenhotel Radkersburger Hof €€

Thermenstrasse 11, 8490 ***Tel*** *(03476) 356 00* ***Fax*** *(03476) 35 80* ***Rooms*** *121* ***Road map*** *F5*

A traditional four-star thermal spa resort, with water fitness classes, group sports and a range of water therapies, pools and saunas. Physiotherapy and acupuncture are available. A traditional café serving typical Austrian cakes is also part of the daily regime. Comfortable rooms with en-suite facilities. **www.radkersburgerhof.at**

BAD RADKERSBURG Das Kurhotel im Park €€€

Kurhausstrasse 5, 8490 ***Tel*** *(03476) 25 71 0* ***Fax*** *(03476) 20 85 45* ***Rooms*** *160* ***Road map*** *F5*

Choose from ten varying styles of rooms and suites furnished with subtle Mediterranean influences. A sprawling hotel with extensive grounds, including a landscaped garden with a romantically lit pool. Thermal water emanates from deep below the ground here, and is used in some treatments in the lavish wellness centre. **www.hotel-im-park.at**

BAD WALTERSDORF Hotel & Spa Der Steirerhof Bad Waltersdorf €€€€€

Wagerberg 125, 8271 ***Tel*** *(03333) 32 11 0* ***Fax*** *(03333) 32 11 44 4* ***Rooms*** *160* ***Road map*** *F4*

Splendidly located amid large park grounds, this luxurious five-star spa hotel offers calming thermal baths and indulgent treatments. Its 160 rooms are furnished with organic materials, and special rooms are designed for allergy sufferers. Tennis courts, bicycle routes and a daily fitness programme including yoga and Pilates. **www.dersteirerhof.at**

BRUCK AN DER MUR Hotel Landskron €€

Am Schiffertor 3, 8600 ***Tel*** *(03862) 58 45 80* ***Fax*** *(03862) 584 58-6* ***Rooms*** *45* ***Road map*** *F4*

A modern business-style hotel with numerous conference rooms, two suites and many guest rooms. All rooms have bath tubs, TV, Internet and a desk. There is a restaurant, as well as a sauna and steambath, which are available to guests. **www.hotel-landskron.at**

DEUTSCHLANDSBERG Koralpenblick €

Rostock 15, Trahütten, 8530 ***Tel*** *(03461) 21 0* ***Fax*** *(03461) 21 04* ***Rooms*** *16* ***Road map*** *F5*

A relaxed family-oriented country hotel, well suited for long walks in the gentle mountains that surround and for relaxing in the sauna and steambath afterwards. Guest rooms are pine-panelled and cosy. The dining room serves home-made breads, cakes and juices, and locally reared organic Styrian beef. **www.koralpenblick.at**

FELDBACH Familienhotel Etmisslerhof €

Etmissl, 8622 ***Tel*** *(03861) 84 44* ***Fax*** *(03861) 84 44 40* ***Rooms*** *26* ***Road map*** *F4*

A large country hotel that has both romantic and family appeal: children's playground, outdoor swimming pool and petting zoo. Comfortable rooms and apartments for up to five people. Some of the rooms have canopy beds. Also has a fine restaurant, sauna, whirlpool and steambath. **www.etmisslerhof.at**

FOHNSDORF Hotel Schloss Gabelhofen €€€

Schlossgasse 54, 8753 ***Tel*** *(03573) 55 55 0* ***Fax*** *(03573) 55 55 6* ***Rooms*** *57* ***Road map*** *E4*

Splendidly atmospheric castle hotel with individually designed rooms in the towers or in the main castle. The two-storied tower suite has a separate entrance and private terrace. There is a sumptuous dining room, and tastings are held in the wine cellar. A thermal water park is situated next door. **www.gabelhofen.at**

FROHNLEITEN Hotel Frohnleitnerhof €€

Hauptplatz 14a, 8130 ***Tel*** *(03126) 41 50* ***Fax*** *(03126) 41 50 55 5* ***Rooms*** *29* ***Road map*** *F4*

Perched on the scenic edge of the Mur River, this hotel is conveniently located in the centre of the village. Its restaurant serves regional specialities. There are TVs and telephones in the rooms and an outdoor terrace overlooking the water. **www.frohnleitnerhof.at**

GRAZ Hotel Daniel €€

Europaplatz 1, 8021 ***Tel*** *(0316) 71 10 80* ***Fax*** *(0316) 07 11 08 5* ***Rooms*** *110* ***Road map*** *F4*

Cool, minimalist design sets the tone in this young, hip hotel. Rooms are compact but efficiently planned. All have air-conditioning, CD and DVD, TV, telephone and rain shower. Guests can rent a Vespa from €15 per day. There is an extra charge for breakfast. **www.hoteldaniel.com**

GRAZ Hotel Zum Dom €€

Bürgergasse 14, Graz, 8010 ***Tel*** *(0316) 82 48 00* ***Fax*** *(0316) 82 48 00 8* ***Rooms*** *29* ***Road map*** *F4*

A unique boutique hotel incorporating modern luxuries within the structure of the handsome historic building. Well located in the picturesque old city and close to shopping, restaurants and bars. Its 29 rooms and suites have striking pieces of art, decadent baths and a real sense of style. **www.domhotel.co.at**

GRAZ Austria Trend Hotel Europa Graz €€€

Bahnhofgürtel 89, 8020 ***Tel*** *(0316) 70 76 0* ***Fax*** *(0316) 70 76 60 6* ***Rooms*** *114* ***Road map*** *F4*

Handy for the train station, the clean modern lines and neutral colour scheme makes this a confortable holiday or business choice. The rooms and suites are equipped with en-suite bathrooms, air-conditioning, telephone, radio, cable TV, safe, minibar and allergy-tested pillows. Breakfast offers both hot and cold choices. **www.austria-trend.at/en**

GRAZ Erzherzog Johann €€€€

Sackstrasse 3–5, 8010 ***Tel*** *(0316) 81 16 16* ***Fax*** *(0316) 81 15 15* ***Rooms*** *62* ***Road map*** *F4*

Elegant old-world hotel which was an inn since the 16th century, and a grand *palais* during the 18th century. The beautifully crafted interior iron work dates from this period. Rooms and grand suites are furnished with lovely antiques and parquet floors. There is an elegant winter garden restaurant and Viennese-style café. **www.erzherzog-johann.com**

GRAZ Grand Hotel Wiesler €€€€

Grieskai 4–8, 8020 ***Tel*** *(0316) 70 66 0* ***Fax*** *(0316) 70 66 76* ***Rooms*** *113* ***Road map*** *F4*

A five-storey Art Nouveau jewel, this centrally located city hideaway features 96 air-conditioned rooms and 17 sumptuous suites with elegant marble baths. Many rooms offer city views including Castle Hill and the clock tower. The Wiesler Restaurant is decorated with Philippe Starck furniture. **www.hotelwiesler.com**

KAPFENBERG Hotel Böhlerstern €€

Friedrich-Böhler-Strasse 13, 8605 ***Tel*** *(03862) 25 55 96 37 5* ***Fax*** *(03862) 25 55 96 16 5* ***Rooms*** *37* ***Road map*** *F4*

Constructed in 1919, a classical exterior belies the contemporary design of the hotel interior. The hotel has cool modern touches. In addition to a fitness room and sauna, a restaurant serves traditional dishes prepared with a lighter touch. **www.boehlerstern.at**

LEOBEN / NIKLASDORF Brücklwirt €€

Leobener Strasse 90, 8712 ***Tel*** *(03842) 817 27* ***Fax*** *(03842) 817 275* ***Rooms*** *70* ***Road map*** *F4*

A modern hotel near to the motorway to Leoben. The rooms, although not large, are comfortable and the tiled bathrooms are light and spotlessly clean. There is a sauna, solarium and steam bath. The restaurant serves excellent local cuisine and a candle-lit dinner on the terrace is a truly unforgettable experience. **www.bruecklwirt.co.at**

MARIAZELL Hotel Drei Hasen €€

Wiener Strasse 11, 8630 ***Tel*** *(03882) 24 10* ***Fax*** *(03882) 24 10 80 0* ***Rooms*** *45* ***Road map*** *F4*

Friendly, family-run, three-star hotel at the foot of the cable car handy for skiing. Simple comfortable rooms with en-suite facilities, TV and mountain views. Drinks are enjoyed in a lovely traditional wood-panelled stube. Hearty Austrian meals in the cosy restaurant. **www.dreihasen.at**

MARIAZELL Hotel Schwarzer Adler €€€€

Hauptplatz 1, 8630 ***Tel*** *(03882) 28 63 0* ***Fax*** *(03882) 28 63 50* ***Rooms*** *32* ***Road map*** *F4*

Traditional and cheerfully painted hotel in the town centre, convenient for hiking in the surrounding hills. Regional and Austrian cuisine is available in the restaurant, and there is a café with a billiard table. The graciously decorated rooms come with en-suite bathrooms and TV; larger family suites are also available. **www.hotelschwarzeradler.at**

Key to Price Guide *see p288* **Key to Symbols** *see back cover flap*

RAMSAU Peter Rosegger €€€

Ramsau 233, 8972 ***Tel*** *(03687) 81 22 30* ***Fax*** *(03687) 81 22 38* ***Rooms*** *12* ***Road map*** *D4*

Comfortable rooms with natural pine furniture and stunning views of the Dachstein Tauern mountains. In addition to a cosy restaurant, there is a guest lounge, reading room, TV room, playroom and a private garden. Pets are welcome. **www.tiscover.at/peter.rosegger**

RAMSAU-KULM Wander-und Langlaufhotel Almfrieden €€

8972 Ramsau am Dachstein ***Tel*** *(03687) 81 75 3* ***Fax*** *(03687) 81 75 36* ***Rooms*** *80* ***Road map*** *D4*

Large, child-friendly mountain resort hotel with double, single and family-rooms with shower or bath, WC, TV and balcony. There is a children's playground and welcoming sun terrace. The centre of the village is about 2 km (1 mile) away so using the bus or hiring a car is recommended. **www.almfrieden.at**

SCHLADMING Gasthof Kirchenwirt €€

Schladminger Hauptplatz 27, 8970 ***Tel*** *(03697) 224 35* ***Fax*** *(03697) 224 35-16* ***Rooms*** *16* ***Road map*** *D4*

This hotel, in the centre of an old mountain village near Planai, is an excellent base for active holidays. It has a cosy, old-fashioned bar and a stylish restaurant serving regional specialities. Rooms are comfortable and some have four-poster beds. Very friendly service. **www.kirchenwirt-schladming.com**

SCHLADMING Posthotel Schladming €€€

Hauptplatz 10, 8970 ***Tel*** *(03687) 22 57 1* ***Fax*** *(03687) 22 57 18* ***Rooms*** *40* ***Road map*** *D4*

Located in the heart of the pedestrian zone and a 3-minute walk to ski and hiking lifts, this attractive 400-year-old house has been revamped with all of today's comforts. Enjoy typical Styrian dishes in the region's oldest inn, the Knappnstubn. **www.posthotel-schladming.at**

TURRACHER HOHE Schlosshotel Seewirt €€€

Turracher Höhe 33, A-8864 ***Tel*** *(04275) 82 34* ***Fax*** *(04275) 82 34 21 5* ***Rooms*** *42* ***Road map*** *D4*

Originally a simple guest house built at the turn of the 19th century, this four-star romantic hotel was renovated to an excellent standard throughout. Its rooms and suites are individually furnished while preserving its historical atmosphere. Indoor pool, massage, gym and a special sauna built from an old farm house. **www.schlosshotel-seewirt.com**

UPPER AUSTRIA

ALTMUNSTER Gasthof Pension "Urzn" €

Gmundnerberg 91, 4813 ***Tel*** *(07612) 87 21 4* ***Fax*** *(07612) 89 92 7* ***Rooms*** *19* ***Road map*** *D3*

A cosy, family-run mountain hotel with comfortable rooms that have a shower, WC and heating. There is a casual lounge, and a terrace, with striking views of the lake and mountains, where hot food is available all day. A popular region for hiking, mountain biking and sailing. **www.urzn.at**

BAD ISCHL Austria Classic Hotel Goldenes Schiff €€

Adalbert Stifter-Kai 3, 4820 ***Tel*** *(06132) 24 24 1* ***Fax*** *(06132) 24 24 15 8* ***Rooms*** *56* ***Road map*** *D4*

Located in Bad Ischl, the former summer retreat of the Austrian monarchy, the building dates back to the 17th century when it was originally a public house. Today the four-star hotel is designed in a light and sophisticated style. A terrace overlooks the Traun River. **www.goldenes-schiff.at**

BAD LEONFELDEN Kurhotel Bad Leonfelden €€€

Spielau 8, 4190 ***Tel*** *(07213) 63 63* ***Fax*** *(07213) 63 63 29 2* ***Rooms*** *88* ***Road map*** *E3*

A four-star health resort in Bad Leonfelden, a town with a long spa history specializing in water, kneipp and mud therapy. Treatments include massage and physical therapy, combined with diet, sports and recreation. Cosmetic treatments are also available. **www.daskurhotel.at**

GMUNDEN Austria am See €

Sparkassegasse 1, 4810 ***Tel*** *(07612) 72239* ***Fax*** *(07612) 72239* ***Rooms*** *7* ***Road map*** *D3*

Centrally located in the village of Gmunden, next to the waters of the Traunsee. Rooms are quiet and comfortable. The reading room was formerly part of the Grand Hotel. Breakfast is available in the Wiener Café, with castle views, or the stylish Schubert Café. Equipped with all modern conveniences. **www.traunsee.at/panorama-appartments**

GMUNDEN Seehotel Schwan €€

Rathausplatz 8, 4810 ***Tel*** *(07612) 63 39 1* ***Fax*** *(07612) 633 918* ***Rooms*** *35* ***Road map*** *D3*

A comfortable pretty hotel sitting on the edge of the Traun River. All rooms have a shower and bath, TV, and some enjoy lake views from their separate sitting areas. The restaurant specializes in fish and regional dishes. **www.seehotel-schwan.at**

GMUNDEN Schlosshotel "Freisitz Roith" €€€€

Traunsteinstrasse 87, 4810 ***Tel*** *(07612) 64 90 5* ***Fax*** *(07612) 64 90 51 7* ***Rooms*** *19* ***Road map*** *D3*

The castle hotel Freisitz Roith is one of the oldest estates around lake Traunsee. Operating as a hotel since the 1960s, records trace its noble lineage to the 16th century. This gracious style lives on in the spacious rooms and elegant suites, and in the award-winning restaurant. **www.schlosshotel.at**

HALLSTATT Seehotel Grüner Baum €€€

Marktplatz 104, 4830 ***Tel*** *(06134) 82 63* ***Fax*** *(06134) 82 63 44* ***Rooms*** *20* ***Road map*** *D4*

The lakeside hotel dates to at least 1700, its splendid façade dominating the quaint Hallstatt marketplace. An inviting terrace looks directly on to the lake. An impressive guest list includes Empress Elisabeth (Sissy) of Austria and Agatha Christie. Rooms are charmingly furnished with a mixture of contemporary and antique pieces. **www.gruenerbaum.cc**

LAKE WOLFGANGSEE Hotel Berau €

Schwarzenbach 16 ***Tel*** *(06138) 25 43 0* ***Fax*** *(06138) 25 43 5* ***Rooms*** *15* ***Road map*** *D4*

On the shores of Lake Wolfgangsee, with a private bay and just a 10-minute walk from atmospheric St Wolfgang. Comfortable family atmosphere with rooms furnished to a high standard. Fitness and leisure facilities and plenty of green space. **www.landhotels.at/berau**

LINZ Hotel Ibis Linz €

Kärntner Strasse 18–20, 4020 ***Tel*** *(0732) 69 40 1* ***Fax*** *(0732) 69 40 19* ***Rooms*** *146* ***Road map*** *E3*

Functional and modern, this hotel is well located opposite the train station and in the city centre. There rooms are air-conditioned and have wireless Internet connections. The bar serves snacks 24 hours a day. Public covered pay-parking close to the hotel. **www.ibishotel.com**

LINZ Arcotel Nike €€

Untere Donaulände 9, 4020 ***Tel*** *(0732) 76 26 0* ***Fax*** *(0732) 76 26 2* ***Rooms*** *176* ***Road map*** *E3*

The River Danube makes an idyllic backdrop for this modern, efficiently appointed hotel. A 5-minute walk from the old centre, its rooms are furnished in a clean, modern style. A restaurant and café as well as wellness centre with hammam, indoor pool, sauna and steam bath are in house. Bright conference rooms. **www.arcotel.at**

LINZ Courtyard by Marriott Hotels Linz €€

Europaplatz 2, 4020 ***Tel*** *(0732) 69 59 0* ***Fax*** *(0732) 60 60 90* ***Rooms*** *236* ***Road map*** *E3*

Minutes from the historic main square and close to the Danube River. Rooms and suites include mini-bar, individual climate control, satellite TV and Internet. Restaurant Europe offers international and Austrian fare. Fitness centre, event facilities and underground parking. **www.marriott.at/lnzcy**

LINZ Hotel Opera €€

Scharitzerstrasse 7 ***Tel*** *(0732) 65 60 47* ***Fax*** *(0732) 65 60 47 10 3* ***Road map*** *E3*

Located in a quiet side street in the centre of Linz near the railway station, shops and the Donau cycle path. Guest rooms are simply equipped with shower or bath as well as TV and wireless Internet. There is a breakfast buffet and a restaurant serving simple dishes from afternoon until evening. **www.hotel-opera.at**

LINZ Austria Trend Hotel Schillerpark €€€

Schiller-Platz 2–4, 4020 ***Tel*** *(0732) 69 50 0* ***Fax*** *(0732) 69 50 9* ***Rooms*** *111* ***Road map*** *E3*

This rectangular glass and steel designed building offers functional modern rooms and suites with en-suite bathrooms, air-conditioning, TV, Pay-TV, minibar and safe. All single rooms feature double beds. Rooms located on the executive floor are more luxuriously equipped. There is a restaurant and several cafés and bars. **www.austria-trend.at**

MONDSEE Seegasthof Weisse Taube €

St. Lorenz 116, 5310 ***Tel*** *(06232) 22 77* ***Fax*** *(06232) 39 01* ***Rooms*** *45* ***Road map*** *D3*

Simple hotel pleasantly situated on the shores of the Mondsee, close to the town centre. Some of the guest rooms have balconies with beautiful lake views. Half board or breakfast is available. Rooms are basic, yet comfortable. **www.seegasthof-weisse-taube.at**

MONDSEE Seegasthof-Hotel Lackner €€€

A-5310 Mondsee ***Tel*** *(06232) 23 59 0* ***Fax*** *(06232) 23 59 50* ***Rooms*** *16* ***Road map*** *D3*

A family-owned inn since 1919, just a few steps from the warm Mondsee yet close to Salzburg. In addition to water pursuits, there is a welcoming bar, sunny terrace and a sophisticated and creative chef, who also offers cookery classes. Extensive wine collection. **www.seehotel-lackner.at**

SALZKAMMERGUT Landhotel Agathawirt €

St Agatha 10, 4822 Bad Goisern ***Tel*** *(06135) 83 41* ***Fax*** *(06135) 75 57* ***Rooms*** *29* ***Road map*** *D3*

Built in 1517, this cultural landmark provides an atmospheric setting. Relax in the garden in summer or by a wood-burning fireplace in the winter. Solar-heated pool, sauna and steam bath. Rental bikes are available as are guided hikes and mountain bike tours. À la carte restaurant in historic room with garden. **www.agathawirt.at**

SCHARDING Schärdinger Hof €

Innbruckstrasse 6–8, 4780 ***Tel*** *(07712) 44 04 0* ***Fax*** *(07712) 44 08* ***Rooms*** *42* ***Road map*** *D3*

Located in one of Austria's prettiest Baroque towns, this hotel blends in with neighbouring brightly painted façades. The restaurant serves menus inspired by old Austro-Hungarian recipes. All rooms have shower and bath, TV and radio. Daily cultural excursions are organized through the hotel. **www.schaerdingerhof.at**

SCHARDING Stiegenwirt €

Schlossgasse 2–6, 4780 ***Tel*** *(07712) 30 70 0* ***Fax*** *(07712) 30 70 84* ***Rooms*** *26* ***Road map*** *D3*

One of many pretty painted Baroque façades in the city, the hotel has been owned by the same family since 1910. It is located in the centre and features a charming dining room and comfortable double and singe rooms. Bicycles are available for rent. **www.stiegenwirt-schaerding.at**

Key to Price Guide *see p288* **Key to Symbols** *see back cover flap*

ST GEORGEN IM ATTERGAU Söllinger's Attergauhof €€

Attergaustrasse 41, 4880 **Tel** *(07667) 64 06* **Fax** *(07667) 64 06 15* **Rooms** *28* **Road map** *D3*

Simple rooms with en-suite facilities as well as several family rooms and an apartment are available. Warm Austrian meals served all day, and a number of different local beers are available on tap. There is a bar and a late-night dance club located right in the hotel. **www.attergauhof.at**

ST WOLFGANG Hotel Weisses Rössl €€€€

Markt 74, 5360 **Tel** *(06138) 23 06 66* **Fax** *(06138) 23 06 41* **Rooms** *72* **Road map** *D4*

Long a destination for Christian pilgrims, St Wolfgang is now a hotspot for those looking for luxurious relaxation beside the lake. Rooms are decorated in modern or romantic style, with 17th-century wooden ceilings. An impressive lake pool is heated to the perfect temperature and appears to float at the lake's edge. **www.weissesroessl.at**

ST WOLFGANG Landhaus Zu Appesbach €€€€€

Aupromenade 18, 5360 **Tel** *(06138) 22 09* **Fax** *(06138) 22 09 14* **Rooms** *26* **Road map** *D4*

Formerly a private mansion, now a small exclusive hotel with beautiful rooms, suites and roomy apartments. The grandest is the Windsor Suite, where the Duke of Windsor stayed. Lovely gardens and a private beach leads on to shimmering Lake Wolfgang. Elegant reading room, bar and restaurant. **www.appesbach.com**

TRAUNKIRCHEN Hotel Post €€

Ortsplatz 5, 4801 **Tel** *(07617) 23 07 0* **Fax** *(07617) 28 09* **Rooms** *54* **Road map** *D3*

Traditional four-star hotel in the centre of Traunkirchen on the shore of Lake Traunsee. All rooms have en-suite facilities, radio, TV, telephone. Spa with sauna, solarium and whirlpool. Local and international menus in its restaurant with a patio and garden opening onto the Johannesberg mountain. **www.hotel-post-traunkirchen.at**

WEISSENBACH AM ATTERSEE Hotel Post €€

Ischlerstrasse 1, 4854 **Tel** *(07663) 81 41* **Fax** *(07663) 81 42 45* **Rooms** *37* **Road map** *D3*

Idyllically located in a spacious park, with its own beach on the shore of Lake Attersee, this hotel offers a relaxed environment with the amenities of four-star luxury. Single and double rooms, as well as family suites, all with en-suite bathroom, telephone, radio and satellite TV. Playroom, bar and reading room. **www.hpw.at/attersee**

WINDISCHGARSTEN Berggasthof Zottensberg €

Edelbach 55, 4580 **Tel** *(07566) 309* **Fax** *(07566) 309-3* **Rooms** *24* **Road map** *E4*

Typical alpine hotel at an altitude of 900 m (2,953 ft). It is situated only 10 km (6 miles) from a skiing centre. The large, rustic dining room is subdivided into many cosy corners and niches affording excellent privacy. There is also an alpine hut to rent, a game reserve to explore and horses. **www.zottensberg.at**

SALZBURGER LAND

ANTHERING Gasthof Hammerschmiede €€

Acharting 22, A-5102 Anthering/Salzburg **Tel** *(06223) 25 03* **Fax** *(06223) 25 03 77* **Rooms** *20* **Road map** *D4*

This four-star hotel enjoys a peaceful location amid an idyllic forest setting. Sun chairs in the meadow, a lovely garden terrace and a rushing Alpine stream, which provides bathing opportunites and Kneipp activities. One dining room is both a blacksmith museum and a banquet room. **www.hammerschmiede.at**

BADGASTEIN Hotel Weismayr €€€

Kaiser-Franz-Joseph-Strasse 6, 5640 **Tel** *(06434) 25 94 0* **Fax** *(06434) 25 94 14* **Rooms** *77* **Road map** *D4*

This grand four-star hotel built in turn-of-the-century style began its life as the villa of a Prussian general. All the comforts of an imperial provincial retreat remain, including formal dining room, salon, beer keller, spa with indoor pool, gym and treatments. Tennis, horseriding, walking and skiing available. **www.weismayr.com**

BADGASTEIN Arcotel Elisabethpark €€€€

Kaiser-Franz-Joseph-Strasse 5, 5640 **Tel** *(06434) 25 51 0* **Fax** *(06434) 25 51 10* **Rooms** *115* **Road map** *D4*

Part of a chain with sister hotels in Germany, Austria and Eastern Europe, this property offers two room categories: modern classic and traditional, in its unrefurbished wing. Rooms feature either south-facing park or northerly mountain views. Private thermal indoor pool, three saunas, spa and wellness centre. **www.elisabethpark.at**

EUGENDORF Landgasthof Holznerwirt €€

Dorfstrasse 4, 5301 **Tel** *(06225) 82 05* **Fax** *(06225) 82 05 19* **Rooms** *57* **Road map** *D4*

Atmospheric flower-bedecked hotel which combines appealing touches of feather beds, traditional *Kachelofen* heating and wood decoration. Also, modern bathrooms, a wellness centre, conference rooms and dining room specializing in Salzburger cuisine. Small enough for a personal welcome, large enough for groups. **www.holznerwirt.at**

FILZMOOS Pension Geierberg €

Neuberg 196, 5532 **Tel** *(06453) 87 88 0* **Fax** *(06453) 78 88 31* **Rooms** *7* **Road map** *D4*

Well situated next to the Geierberg ski lift and close to the free Filzmooser Wanderbus. Individual rooms with attractive carved wooden cabinetry, shower and WC, telephone, TV, radio and balcony. Apartments with two or three bedrooms are well suited for active family holidays. All guests have use of sauna, steambath and solarium. **www.geierberg.at**

FILZMOOS Tannenhof €

Filzmoos 84, 5332 **Tel** *(06453) 82 02* **Fax** *(06453) 84 60* **Rooms** *25* **Road map** *D4*

Cosy bed and breakfast nestled in the mountains and ideal for relaxed family outdoor pursuits. Rooms have TVs and functional en-suite facilities with bath or shower. Some rooms have balconies. There is no restaurant but the café serves lovely home-made cakes. **www.sieberer.at/tannenhof**

FILZMOOS Hubertus €€€

Am Dorfplatz 1, 5532 **Tel** *(06453) 82 04* **Fax** *(06453) 82 04 6* **Rooms** *14* **Road map** *D4*

A sparkling star in the firmament of *haute* Austrian cuisine, the hotel and restaurant of Johanna Maier has earned two Michelin stars. Elegant deluxe and standard doubles and junior suites. Cookery courses from the celebrity chef are available, as is fly fishing in summer with the patron. **www.hotelhubertus.at**

FUSCHL AM SEE Hotel Seewinkel €€€

Seestrasse 31, 5330 **Tel** *(06226) 83 44* **Fax** *(06226) 83 44 18* **Rooms** *32* **Road map** *D4*

Splendid lake panorama over the Fuschlsee, complete with private bathing beach, accessed across the gardens. Sailing and windsurfing on the lake is available as is a rowing boat, for free use by guests. Single, double and multi-bed rooms and suites, plus more lavish suites in the adjacent fairytale-inspired Schlössl. **www.seewinkel.com**

FUSCHL AM SEE Hotel Schloss Fuschl €€€€€

Hof bei Salzburg, 5322 **Tel** *(06229) 22 53 0* **Fax** *(06229) 22 53 53 1* **Rooms** *84* **Road map** *D4*

This castle, dating to 1450, has played host to movie stars and empresses. It overlooks one of Austria's grandest lakes and has a state-of-the-art spa and swimming pool with lake views. Private boats and Rolls-Royces for your entertainment. Choice of rooms, suites and pretty lakeside cottages. **www.schlossfuschl.at**

GROSSARL Alte Post €€

Marktplatz 24, 5611 **Tel** *(06414) 20 7* **Fax** *(06414) 20 71 15* **Rooms** *40* **Road map** *D4*

Spacious, family-friendly hotel on the market square. Extensive activity programme including children's walks, bowling, playroom, bikes, and skiing and snowshoeing in winter. Most rooms have balconies. Studio accommodation for three to five people available. Satellite TV and Internet connection in rooms. Prices are higher in the winter. **www.altepost.cc**

KLEINARL Pension Viehhof €

Kleinarl 190, 5603 **Tel** *(06418) 24 0* **Fax** *(06418) 24 03 1* **Rooms** *15* **Road map** *D4*

Traditional chalet style guest house with attractive pine decoration, located on the wide valley floor right next to the ski lift. Rooms, as well as apartments for four with full kitchens. A sauna and solarium are available, as well as a children's playroom. Well placed to access quiet summer walking trails and winter ski pistes. **www.pension-viehhof.at**

KLEINARL Gästehaus Keil €€

Kleinarl 173, 5603 **Tel** *(06418) 61 8* **Fax** *(06418) 61 84 0* **Rooms** *18* **Road map** *D4*

A small yet elegant chalet-style guest house with a wellness centre that comes equipped with an indoor pool, solarium, fitness room, sauna and steam bath. Stylish touches, such as the winter garden relaxation area, make this is a relaxing choice for a low-key mountain retreat. **www.keil.at**

SAALBACH Hotel Bauer €€

Oberdorf, 5 5753 **Tel** *(06541) 62 13 0* **Fax** *(06541) 62 13 5* **Rooms** *40* **Road map** *C4*

Located in the pedestrian zone and a stone's throw away from the lifts and ski slopes, the family-run hotel is an inviting choice for both active and relaxing holidays. Pretty winter garden and popular *après* ski hut. There is also a wellness area. **www.saalbach-hotel-bauer.at**

SALZBURG Bergland €€

Rupertgasse 15, 5020 **Tel** *(0662) 87 23 18 0* **Fax** *(0662) 87 23 18 8* **Rooms** *18* **Road map** *D3*

Located in a quiet street just 10-minutes walk to the centre, this small hotel has been in the family since 1912. Bathrooms are large and stylish, and downstairs a music room with piano and small English library make a cosy spot. Bicycles are available to hire. Rooms are non-smoking and have satellite TV. **www.berglandhotel.at**

SALZBURG NH Salzburg City €€€€

Franz-Josef-Strasse 26, 5020 **Tel** *(0662) 88 20 41* **Fax** *(0662) 87 42 40* **Rooms** *140* **Road map** *D3*

This sleek, stylishly designed hotel serves both business and holiday travellers looking to be near the historical centre and Mirabell Gardens. The hotel offers access to wireless Internet and concierge services. There is an underground garage as well as public parking. The train station is 2 km (1 mile) away. **www.nh-hotels.de**

SALZBURG Hotel Goldener Hirsch €€€€€

Getreidegasse 37, 5020 **Tel** *(0662) 80 84 0* **Fax** *(0662) 84 33 49* **Rooms** *69* **Road map** *D3*

A luxury hotel dating from 1407 in the Baroque centre of Salzburg with an array of hand-crafted furnishings and antiques. Renowned restaurant Goldener Hirsch features Austrian and international specialities among intimate candlelit tables. Romantic charm in each of the rooms, blended with modern amenities. **www.goldenerhirsch.com**

SALZBURG Hotel Sacher Salzburg €€€€€

Schwarzstrasse 5–7, 5020 **Tel** *(0662) 88 97 7* **Fax** *(0662) 88 97 71 4* **Rooms** *118* **Road map** *D3*

Residing here in five-star splendour comes with unlimited access to Sachertorte, the chocolate cake Austria is famous for. The turn-of-the-century hotel offers state-of-the-art luxury paired with grand tradition. Rich red interiors, bright marble bathrooms and splendid views of the Salzach River and the Old Town. **www.sacher.at**

Key to Price Guide *see p288* **Key to Symbols** *see back cover flap*

SALZBURG Hotel Schloss Mönchstein €€€€€

Mönchsberg Park 26, 5020 ***Tel*** *(0662) 84 85 55 0* ***Fax*** *(0662) 84 85 59* ***Rooms*** *23* ***Road map*** *D3*

An enchanting 14th-century castle hotel situated on top of the Mönchsberg and surrounded by its own park. Unparalleled view over the rooftops of Salzburg, and the Old Town is within 7 minutes via the Mönchsberg lift. Book a room, or the entire castle is available to rent. **www.monchstein.at**

SALZKAMMERGUT Hotel Bergrose €€

A-5350 Strobl, 162 ***Tel*** *(06137) 54 31* ***Fax*** *(06137) 54 31 5* ***Rooms*** *30* ***Road map*** *D4*

A quiet location surrounded by mountains and meadows. Individually furnished rooms and suites are decorated in wood and antiques. Indoor pool with waterfall, sauna, salt water-enriched steambath, whirlpool and Rasul bath. In addition to apartments there is a chalet for two, the Almhütte. **www.bergrose.at**

ST GILGEN Pension Seeblick €

Pöllach 29, 5340 ***Tel*** *(06227) 26 82* ***Fax*** *(06227) 26 82* ***Rooms*** *14* ***Road map*** *D4*

This small, pleasant, typically alpine pension on the shores of Wolfgangsee in the Salzkammergut region, has been run by the same family for three generations. Rooms are simple and clean. Double rooms have balconies and beautiful views of the lake. A relaxing and friendly pension. Golf is available nearby. **www.pensionseeblick.at**

ST GILGEN Parkhotel Billroth €€€

Billrothstrasse 2, 5340 ***Tel*** *(06227) 22 17* ***Fax*** *(06227) 18 25* ***Rooms*** *45* ***Road map*** *D4*

This calm lakeside retreat invites long walks around the edge of pretty Wolfgangsee or into the green hills that surround. Of course, the less adventurous can admire the same panorama from the grand dining room and sun terrace. Rooms offer lake or garden views, bath or shower and separate WC. **www.billroth.at**

ZELL AM SEE Grand Hotel Zell am See €€€

Esplanade 4–6, A-5700 Zell am See ***Tel*** *(06542) 65 42 78 80* ***Fax*** *(06542) 78 83 05* ***Rooms*** ***Road map*** *D4*

A grand white confection perched on the lakeside of one of Austria's most serene water settings. A small private beach gives access to swimming and boating. The wellness centre is elegant and state of the art with an array of saunas and pools. Numerous dining options are correspondingly opulent. **www.grandhotel-zellamsee.at**

ZELL AM SEE Sporthotel Alpenblick €€€

Alte Landesstrasse 6, 5700 ***Tel*** *(06542) 54 33* ***Fax*** *(06542) 54 33 1* ***Rooms*** *70* ***Road map*** *D4*

Over the years, this family-run hotel has grown and extensively expanded its spa area. You can swim directly from the indoor to the outdoor pool all year round, unwind in various saunas and treatments, and then relax on a waterbed for two. The restaurant boasts a light and healthy version of Austrian cooking. **www.alpenblick.at**

TYROL AND VORARLBERG

AU IM BREGENZER WALD Hotel Rössle €€€

Lisse 90, 6883 ***Tel*** *(05515) 22 16* ***Fax*** *(05515) 22 16 6* ***Rooms*** *32* ***Road map*** *A4*

This traditional mountain hotel has spacious rooms with balconies, as well as an elegant wood-panelled restaurant that specializes in Austrian and international cuisine. There are bicycles available to explore surrounding mountains paths, and the ski lift is nearby. A disco is located in the hotel, as well as steam bath, sauna and massage. **www.roessle-au.at**

AU IM BREGENZER WALD Krone in Au €€€€

Jaghausen 4, 6883 ***Tel*** *(05515) 220 10* ***Fax*** *(00551) 22 01 20 1* ***Rooms*** *68* ***Road map*** *A4*

Attractive large resort hotel, 5 minutes from centre. Cosy hall and lounge with traditional tile oven. Amusements include table tennis, billiards, children's playroom, indoor swimming pool, saunas, steam bath, free bike hire. Extensive breakfast buffet with local organic fare. Daily activities include cultural walk and guided hikes. **www.krone-au.at**

BEZAU Gasthof Sonne €€

Kriechere, 6870 ***Tel*** *(05514) 22 62* ***Fax*** *(05514) 29 12* ***Rooms*** *30* ***Road map*** *A4*

Rooms are decorated in clean modern lines with either a private balcony or panoramic windows. The public rooms are done in a more traditional wood-crafted style. Daytime activities revolve around the wellness centre, guided hikes, rafting and outdoor pursuits. In the evenings, five-course dinners are events in themselves. **www.gasthof-sonne.at**

BLUDENZ Schlosshotel Dörflinger €€

Schlossplatz 5, 6700 ***Tel*** *(05552) 630 16* ***Fax*** *(05552) 63 01 68* ***Rooms*** *45* ***Road map*** *A4*

High on a hill, the centre of Bludenz is only five minutes away from this large hotel offering rooms and several apartments for up to six people. A covered terrace overlooks the mountains. Regional specialities are served in the panoramic dining room. Road and mountain bikes are available free of charge. **www.schlosshotel.cc**

BREGENZ Kaiser Hotel Bregenz €€

Kaiserstrasse 2, 6900 ***Tel*** *(05574) 52 98 0* ***Fax*** *(05574) 52 98 2* ***Rooms*** *8* ***Road map*** *A4*

A small, romantic hotel dating from the 15th century with rooms featuring whirlpool baths and feather beds. The suites have canopied beds, heated floors and CD players. Some of the original features are still visible. An Italian café is located downstairs. **www.kaiser-hotel.at**

BREGENZ Messmer Hotel €€€

Kornmarktstrasse 16, 6900 ***Tel*** *(05574) 423 56* ***Fax*** *(05574) 423 56 6* ***Rooms*** *81* ***Road map*** *A4*

The white-peaked façade of the Messmer makes an imposing site in Bregenz. A home from home for music lovers during the Bregenzer Music Festival, the four-star property offers a fully modernized business and holiday stay. The rooms feature spacious en-suite baths and conference facilities are available. **www.hotel-messmer.at**

BREGENZ Weisses Kreuz €€€€

Römerstrasse 5, 6900 ***Tel*** *(05574) 498 80* ***Fax*** *(05574) 49 88 67* ***Rooms*** *44* ***Road map*** *A4*

Weisses Kreuz combines over 100 years of hospitality with glamorous rooms that are air-conditioned and come with digital flatscreen TVs and delightful touches like exposed beams and ornate cornices. Minutes walk from Lake Constance and shops, cafés and restaurants. Non-smoking rooms available. **www.hotelweisseskreuz.at**

FELDKIRCH Hotel-Gasthof Löwen €

Feldkirch-Nofels, Kohlgasse 1, 6800 ***Tel*** *(05522) 3583* ***Fax*** *(05522) 35 83 55* ***Rooms*** *68* ***Road map*** *A4*

A favourite with hikers, cyclists and motorbikers, this typical Vorarlberg inn features comfortable rooms and hearty local menus. A sauna or steambath will help guests relax before a drink in the cosy Stuble bar, on the terrace or in one of several restaurants. **www.hotel-loewen.at**

FELDKIRCH Central Hotel Löwen €€

Schlossgraben 13, 6800 ***Tel*** *(05522) 720 70* ***Fax*** *(05522) 720 70-5* ***Rooms*** *71* ***Road map*** *A4*

Brightened by the paintings of local artist Matthias Baumgartner, this aptly named hotel is in the middle of the old town, well placed for business and the popular Lake Constance cycle route. Its modern rooms feature bathrooms, cable TV and modem connection. Spa and pool facilities at its partner hotel Holiday Inn Feldkirch. **www.central-hotel-loewen.at**

FINKENBERG Sport- und Wellnesshotel Stock €€€€€

Dorf 142, 6292 ***Tel*** *(05285) 67 75* ***Fax*** *(05285) 67 75-421* ***Rooms*** *75* ***Road map*** *C4*

A destination resort hotel with so many trimmings that checking out is a challenge. An endless array of romantic rooms and suites some offering terraces, private sauna, elegant tiled ovens and marble tubs for two overlooking the mountain tops. **www.sporthotel-stock.com**

FONTANELLA/FASCHINA Hotel Faschina €€€

Faschina 55 ***Tel*** *(05510) 224* ***Fax*** *(05510) 224 26* ***Rooms*** *39* ***Road map*** *A4*

Dip into the biosphere reserve of the Walsertal from this comfortable mountain retreat. An elegant yet relaxed restaurant serves regional and international cuisine. A delightful spa features an open fire in its wood-panelled relaxation room and hay baths using local fragrant herbs and grasses. **www.hotel-faschina.at**

FONTANELLA/FASCHINA Hotel Walserhof €€€

Faschina 66, 6733 ***Tel*** *(05510) 21 7* ***Fax*** *(05510) 21 71 3* ***Rooms*** *39* ***Road map*** *A4*

Surrounded by mountains and located at 1, 500 m (4921 ft), this comfortable four-star family hotel is equipped with a swimming pool and wellness centre, as well as facilities for children, including a playroom and babysitting service. Rooms are decorated with pine furnishings and lots of natural light. **www.walserhof.at**

FULPMES Waldhof €€€€

Gröbenweg 19, 6166 ***Tel*** *(05225) 62 17 5* ***Fax*** *(05225) 64 28 3* ***Rooms*** *52* ***Road map*** *B4*

Mountain hideaway with Tyrolean ambience and luxurious amenities. Comfortable rooms with shower/WC, balcony, telephone, radio and cable TV. Panoramic views of the glaciated Stubai mountains. Hotel bar, fireplace lounge and original Tyrolean wood-panelled lounge. Breakfast buffet and regional specialities. **www.waldhof-stubaital.at**

HALL IN TIROL Austria Classic Hotel Heiligkreuz €€

Reimmichlstrasse 18, 6060 ***Tel*** *(05223) 57 11 4* ***Fax*** *(05223) 57 11 45* ***Rooms*** *35* ***Road map*** *B4*

A hotel has been on this site since the 16th century, though the current incarnation is strictly modern. The four-star property has standard and superior rooms. There is a small wellness area, where guests can drink spring water from the stone well, which has its source underneath the hotel. **www.heiligkreuz.at**

IMST Schloss-Hotel Post €€

Eduard-Wallhöfer-Platz 3, 6460 ***Tel*** *(05412) 66 55 5* ***Fax*** *(05412) 66 51 95 5* ***Rooms*** *30* ***Road map*** *B4*

The splendid Sprengenstein Castle, which dates from 1450, is now the most romantic address in the valley. Enjoy fine cuisine in the grand historic dining room and drinks in the comfortable parlour, the old vaults, or the romantic veranda. Singles, doubles and gracious suites. Chlorine-free indoor pool. **www.romantikhotel-post.com**

INNSBRUCK Altpradl €€

Pradler Strasse 8, 6020 ***Tel*** *(0512) 34 51 56* ***Fax*** *(0512) 34 51 56* ***Rooms*** *33* ***Road map*** *B4*

This hotel is centrally located on the edge of the historic old town. Standing on a junction all rooms have a sunny aspect and offer town views. Rooms are clean and comfortable and the staff are friendly. The sauna and steam room are particularly relaxing after a day of skiing. Free ski bus available in winter. **www.hotel-altpradl.at**

INNSBRUCK Goldener Adler €€

Herzog-Friedrich-Strasse 6, 6020 ***Tel*** *(0512) 57 11 11* ***Fax*** *(0512) 58 44 09* ***Rooms*** *34* ***Road map*** *B4*

Located in the heart of the old town, this is one of the first inns in Europe, built in 1390. The rooms are named after former guests, which have included emperors, kings and Mozart himself. Several restaurants serve fine Tyrolean cuisine. The Goethe Stube is a fine place to drink in living history. **www.goldeneradler.com**

Key to Price Guide *see p288* **Key to Symbols** *see back cover flap*

INNSBRUCK Parkhotel Leipzigerhof €€

Defreggerstrasse 13, 6020 **Tel** *(0512) 34 35 25* **Fax** *(0512) 39 43 57* **Rooms** *55* **Road map** *B4*

A fully modernised, family-owned, four-star hotel in the centre of Innsbruck. Bright en-suite bathrooms, elegant traditional restaurant, plus recreation centre with sauna and solarium. Rooms are equipped with high-speed Internet. **www.leipzigerhof.at**

INNSBRUCK Hotel Sailer €€€

Adamgasse 8, 6020 **Tel** *(0512) 5563* **Fax** *(0512) 53637* **Rooms** *93* **Road map** *B4*

Tended to by two generations of the Sailer Family, this modern hotel offers large rooms decorated in a simple, fresh style. There is a lovely atmospheric Tyrolean restaurant, which serves regional cuisine. The location is excellent, just a 2 minute walk from the train station. **www.sailer-innsbruck.at**

INNSBRUCK Schlosshotel Igls €€€€€

Viller Steig 2, A-6080 Igls **Tel** *(05123) 77 21 7* **Fax** *(05123) 77 21 71 98* **Rooms** *18* **Road map** *B4*

At this luxurious and discreet mountain castle every guest is treated royally. The elegant Blue Saloon serves as breakfast room, and the mahogany-panelled restaurant offers fine seasonally influenced menus. Each of the bedrooms is uniquely furnished. Combined indoor-outdoor pool, sauna, steam-bath, solarium and massage. **www.schlosshotel-igls.com**

KIRCHBERG IN TIROL Hotel Sportalm €€€€

Brandseitweg 26–28, 6365 **Tel** *(05357) 27 78* **Fax** *(05357) 33 47 30* **Rooms** *27* **Road map** *C4*

Amid the rolling Kitzbuhel Alps, this hotel is well located at the base of the Fleckalmbahn cable car. Beautifully furnished in the Tyrolean style. In addition to standard rooms, there are several suites and apartments. There is an extensive spa area with pool, and ballroom dancing and lessons are available. **www.hotel-sportalm.at**

KIRCHBERG IN TIROL Tyroler Hof €€€€

Möselgasse 11, 6365 **Tel** *(05357) 26 66* **Fax** *(05357) 26 65 65* **Rooms** *25* **Road map** *C4*

Welcoming family-run, four-star hotel that offers ski and golf packages with special rates. Full breakfast buffet with home-made products and a four-course gourmet dinner menu. Vital Centre with sauna, steam bath, Jacuzzis and solarium. Situated in Kirchberg, a quiet alternative to nearby Kitzbuhel. **www.tyrolerhof.at**

KITZBUHEL Hotel Zur Tenne €€€

Vorderstadt 8–10, 6370 **Tel** *(05356) 64 44 40* **Fax** *(05356) 64 80 35 6* **Rooms** *51* **Road map** *C4*

Centrally located, this cosy hotel is an exquisite Tyrolean country house with style of its own. The winter garden restaurant provides a lively view of the town. Cosy, luxurious rooms and suites, some with furnished balconies. **www.hotelzurtenne.com**

KITZBUHEL Goldener Greif €€€€€

Hinterstadt 24, 6370 **Tel** *(05356) 64 31 1* **Fax** *(05356) 65 00 1* **Rooms** *35* **Road map** *C4*

This hotel dates back to the 13th century and has the prettiest painted façade in Kitzbuhel, though the hotel's entrance is now at the back of the building. Rooms have beautifully appointed wood interiors and ceiling frescoes. Bright large bathrooms and an excellent sense of hospitality from the staff. **www.hotel-goldener-greif.at**

KITZBUHEL Schloss Lebenberg €€€€€

Lebenbergstrasse 17, 6370 **Tel** *(05356) 690 10* **Fax** *(05356) 64 40 5* **Rooms** *109* **Road map** *C4*

A medieval castle with a modern extension, this imposing hotel sits high above the village – though walking back up is a hike. Many marked trails lead right from the door. Elegant rooms, some with canopy beds and French doors on to a terrace. **www.austria-trend.at/hotel-schloss-lebenberg**

KLEINWALSERTAL/RIEZLERN Hotel-Pension Widdersteinblick €€

Eggstrasse 24, 6991 **Tel** *(05517) 56 01* **Fax** *(05517) 34 58* **Rooms** *15* **Road map** *A4*

Intimate and traditional, this chalet-style mountain hotel has good access to walking and skiing in the scenic Kleinwalsertal area. Sauna, whirlpool and steam bath provide good relaxation options. Hearty dinners are served and a full buffet at breakfast. **www.hotel-widdersteinblick.de**

MAYRHOFEN Hotel Berghof €€

Dursterstrasse 220, 6290 **Tel** *(05285) 62 25 4* **Fax** *(05285) 62 25 49 0* **Rooms** *100* **Road map** *C4*

For over 100 years, this gracious four-star hotel has been a Mayrhofen focal point. The Moigg Family added a garden restaurant with live music and barbecues, and refurbished four pretty dining rooms offering a range of cuisine and formality. Comfortable, cheerful rooms. **www.berghof.cc**

MAYRHOFEN Elisabeth €€€€

Einfahrt Mitte 432, 6290 **Tel** *(05285) 67 67 0* **Fax** *(05285) 67 67 67* **Rooms** *32* **Road map** *C4*

Exquisitely appointed five-star hotel with attention paid to every detail. A near endless array of cosy panelled corners, elegant bars and fine dining rooms serving artful Austrian and Italian menus. Dine like an empress in the new Sissi Stube, member of the prestigious international gourmet club Chaine des Rotisseurs. **www.elisabethhotel.com**

MUTTERS Hotel Altenburg €

Kirchplatz 4–6, A-6162 **Tel** *(0512) 54 85 24* **Fax** *(0512) 54 85 24 6* **Rooms** *34* **Road map** *B4*

A building that dates back to the 16th century, this hotel has been affectionately renovated and offers Tyrolean hospitality and comfortable rooms. Innsbruck is easily reached by car in ten minutes. Rooms have bath or shower and WC, radio, telephone and TV. There is an indoor swimming pool, sauna and steam room. **www.altenburg.com**

OBERLECH Hotel Montana €€€€€

Oberlech, 6764 ***Tel*** *(05583) 2460* ***Fax*** *(05583) 246038* ***Rooms*** *43* **Road map** *A4*

A hotel of top-notch ski pedigree, owned by the family of former world-champion ski racer Patrick Ortlieb, and located on the edge of the piste in Oberlech. Ideal for luxury-orientated and sporty families, couples and mountain lovers. Elegant ambience. Babysitting and children's ski school. **www.montanaoberlech.at**

PERTISAU Hotel Post am See €€€€€

Pertisau 82, 6213 ***Tel*** *(05243) 52 07* ***Fax*** *(05243) 52 11 80* ***Rooms*** *63* **Road map** *C4*

Open since 1906, this hotel sits just steps from the Achensee. Perfect for both active or relaxing holiday experiences, including boating and skiing. All rooms and apartments are finished in warm wood with feather beds, balcony, satellite TV and high-speed Internet. Full wellness facilities and beauty treatments. **www.post-pertisau.com**

TIROL Hotel Post €€

A 6363 Westendorf ***Tel*** *(05334) 62 02* ***Fax*** *(05334) 21 49 5* ***Rooms*** *40* **Road map** *B4*

Traditional three-star mountain hotel offering numerous amenities and typical Tirolean hospitality. Its rooms are decorated with carved wood decor and have en-suite facilities. Generous breakfast buffet and hearty Austrian cuisine. A few times each week there is live zither music. **www.hotelpost.co.at**

CARINTHIA AND EAST TYROL

BAD BLEIBERG Der Bleibergerhof €€€

Drei Lärchen 150, 9530 ***Tel*** *(04244) 22 05* ***Fax*** *(04244) 22 05 70* ***Rooms*** *80* **Road map** *E5*

This spa hotel promises a world of well-being in the southernmost high-altitude thermal valley in Austria. A cool palette of soothing colours and modern design throughout. In addition to a full menu of state of the art wellness facilities, guests can rent their own spa area and enjoy tailormade treatments. **www.falkensteiner.com/bleibergerhof**

BAD KLEINKIRCHHEIM Hotel Die Post €€€€

Dorfstrasse 64, 9546 ***Tel*** *(04240) 21 2* ***Fax*** *(04240) 65 0* ***Rooms*** *99* **Road map** *E5*

A pretty pension with an altitude of 750 m (2,460 ft) allowing for stunning views of Ossiacher See, about 2 km (1 mile) away. Numerous terraces, incuding outside dining space. Rooms have a typical alpine-style interior. Children are well catered for with a fun playroom. **www.diepost.com**

BODENSDORF Stofflwirt €

Deutschberg 6, 9551 ***Tel*** *(04243) 69 20* ***Fax*** *(04243) 69 25* ***Rooms*** *8* **Road map** *E5*

An attractive hotel that combines traditional materials with modern style. All rooms and suites are south-facing with garden and Kaiserburg mountain views. A spa as well as massage and cosmetics rooms are available to guests. Six different pools with different temperatures. **www.stofflwirt.at**

FAAK AM SEE Pensionen-Ferienwohnungen Waldruh-Tannenheim €

Halbinselstrasse 1–3, 9583 ***Tel*** *(04254) 22 95* ***Fax*** *(04254) 22 95 4* ***Rooms*** *16* **Road map** *E5*

Complex of buildings at the edge of a forest, on a promontory in Faaker See, with views over the surrounding mountains. Hores-riding, fishing, bicycle hire and table tennis are are available. Summer barbecues are held in the garden. Apartments are also available. **www.tiscover.at/waldruh-tannenheim**

FELD AM SEE Hotel Lindenhof €€

Dorfstrasse 8, 9544 ***Tel*** *(04246) 22 74* ***Fax*** *(04246) 22 74 50* ***Rooms*** *23* **Road map** *E5*

Idyllic lakeside setting in the heart of the Nockberge mountains.This four-star hotel stresses individuality, offering fine cuisine and wines in a region known for mountain biking, hiking and skiing. A small water world includes a spring-water pool, sauna, jet tub and beauty treatments. **www.landhotel-lindenhof.at**

FINKENSTEIN Finkensteiner Hof €€

Mallestiger Platz 1, 9584 ***Tel*** *(04254) 21 76* ***Fax*** *(04254) 21 76 80* ***Rooms*** *42* **Road map** *E5*

Situated in the centre of Finkenstein, there is both a solar-heated pool with water slide, waterfall and massage jets and a flat and sandy private beach at the lake. Hiking is popular and bikes are free of charge. Comfortable and bright rooms. **www.finkensteinerhof.at**

HEILIGENBLUT Hotel Post €€

Hof 1, 9844 ***Tel*** *(04824) 22 45* ***Fax*** *(04824) 22 45 81* ***Rooms*** *50* **Road map** *D4*

Just opposite the Grossglockner lift, this hotel has access to skiing in winter and is hiking paradise in summer. A casual atmosphere pervades and advice on the day's activities is available from the proprietor, a certified mountain guide. Come back to a relaxing sauna, steam bath, indoor pool and massage. **www.landhotel-post.com**

KLAGENFURT Arcotel Moser Verdino €€

Domgasse 2, 9020 ***Tel*** *(0463) 57 87 80* ***Fax*** *(0463) 51 76 5* ***Rooms*** *71* **Road map** *E5*

An address that combines Carinthian charm with Mediterranean flair. Built on the original site of the door to the medieval city wall, this historical Art Nouveau gem has been updated to incorporate trendy interior features dominated by dark wood, white table cloths and open architecture. **www.arcotelhotels.com**

Key to Price Guide *see p288* **Key to Symbols** *see back cover flap*

KLAGENFURT Hotel Palais Porcia €€

Neuer Platz 13, 9020 **Tel** *(0463) 5115 900* **Fax** *(0463) 5115 9030* **Rooms** *35* **Road map** *E5*

Elegant hotel in a historical city palace. Opulent, uniquely decorated rooms with plush carpets, rich red furnishings, some with four-poster beds, and all modern amenities, including marble and granite bathrooms, TV, telephone, fax connection and air-conditioning. **www.hotel-palais-porcia.com**

LIENZ Best Western Hotel Sonne €€

Südtiroler Platz 8, 9900 **Tel** *(04852) 63 31 1* **Fax** *(04852) 63 31 4* **Rooms** *62* **Road map** *D5*

Centrally located Lienz hotel, not far from the Dolomite Mountains and fishing, hiking, biking or sightseeing. A modern, family-orientated hotel with spacious guest rooms, including roof-garden views to the Dolomites and Alps. Complimentary full breakfast. Conference facilities and underground garage. **www.hotelsonnelienz.at**

LIENZ Parkhotel Tristacher See €€€

9900 Lienz **Tel** *(04852) 67 66 6* **Fax** *(04852) 67 69 9* **Rooms** *45* **Road map** *D5*

Perched on the edge of Tristach Lake, to the south of the picturesque Dolomite town of Lienz. Ideal for scenic walks before settling into the cosy Tyrolean-style restaurant or the terrace overlooking the lake. In addition to excellent regional wines, mineral water from the hotel's own spring is served. No bus parties or package tours. **www.parkhotel-tristachersee.at**

LIENZ Traube €€€

Hauptplatz 14, 9900 **Tel** *(04852) 64 44 4* **Fax** *(04852) 64 18 4* **Rooms** *51* **Road map** *D5*

Romantikhotel Traube provide spacious, individually furnished rooms, some with antiques. A cosy tavern offers specialities from Italy and East Tyrol. There is a day bar, sauna and indoor swimming pool, with a view over the roofs of Lienz. **www.hoteltraube.at**

MARIA WORTH Hotel Wörth €€€

Seepromenade 12, 9082 **Tel** *(04273) 22 76 0* **Fax** *(04273) 22 76 57* **Rooms** *35* **Road map** *E5*

Stunning scenery overlooking crystal waters of the Wörthersee and picturesque Maria Worth. Private beach and nearby access to water skiing, boating and parasailing. Vast breakfast buffet on the sun terrace. Wellness centre is open to guests. Rooms and suites with balconies and forest or lake views. **www.hotelwoerth.com**

MILLSTATT Hotel Seevilla €€€

Millstatt in Kärnten, A-9872 **Tel** *(04766) 21 02* **Fax** *(04766) 22 21* **Rooms** *42* **Road map** *D5*

A warm and inviting property with a personal touch and classic style. Set amid park grounds at the edge of a lake, there is a large sunbathing lawn and a separate children's swimming pool. Guests can also swim from the charming lakeside boathouse with sauna, solarium, Turkish steam bath and massage room. **www.see-villa.at**

OSSIACH Gasthof Ossiacherhof €€

Alt-Ossiach 12, 9570 **Tel** *(04243) 22 09* **Fax** *(04243) 22 09* **Rooms** *50* **Road map** *E5*

Colourful flower-festooned balconies on this homely three-star hotel. The cosy rooms and several apartments make this a comfortable retreat for families. Lounge, TV room, and children's playground. Located on a small pleasant lake. **www.ossiacherhof.at**

OSSIACH Strandgasthof Seewirt €€

Josefine Köllich, 9570 **Tel** *(04243) 22 68* **Fax** *(04243) 31 68* **Rooms** *12* **Road map** *E5*

A pleasant pension on the shores of Ossiacher See, next to the church where concerts are held as part of the Carinthian Summer festival. In the summer, the restaurant tables are placed outdoors under the shade of the trees. The pension owns 8 hectares (20 acres) of the lake, where guests can fish. **www.seewirt-ossiach.at**

PORTSCHACH Schloss Leonstain €€€

Leonstainerstrasse 1, 9210 **Tel** *(04272) 28 16-0* **Fax** *(04272) 28 23* **Rooms** *32* **Road map** *E5*

Brahms was enchanted enough to write a violin concerto here. Located at a lively seaside resort by the Wörthersee, the castle was built in 1492 and now offers a balance between old-world charm and modern amenities. All the rooms, maisonettes and suites are individually furnished with antiques. Discounts on nearby golf for guests. **www.leonstain.at**

PORTSCHACH Schloss Seefels €€€€

Pörtschach/Töschling, 9210 **Tel** *(04272) 23 77* **Fax** *(04272) 37 04* **Rooms** *73* **Road map** *E5*

Originally a palace built in 1860, this hotel is situated on a splendid waterside location on the Wörthersee, near golf courses, with grand belle époque features. Five-star luxury with amenities that include indoor and outdoor pools, sauna, hammam and herbal baths, tennis and childcare centre. Member of Relais et Chateaux. **www.seefels.at**

SEEBODEN Hotel Bellevue €€€

Am Waldrand 24, 9871 **Tel** *(04762) 813 46 0* **Fax** *(04762) 813 46-86* **Rooms** *53* **Road map** *D5*

A fair-sized hotel on the western shore of the Millstätter See in a truly peaceful location. Typically alpine architecture, all rooms have balconies with stunning views of the lake and mountains. The restaurant has a sun-terrace for outdoor dining. Guests can enjoy golf, fishing and watersports. **www.bellevue.or.at**

VELDEN Casinohotel Mösslacher €€€€

Am Corso 10, 9220 **Tel** *(04274) 51 23 3* **Fax** *(04274) 51 23 0* **Rooms** *38* **Road map** *E5*

Sleep beneath a giant royal flush or black and white teddy bear in these funky individually designed spacious rooms. Free Internet access, flat screen TV and views of lake Wörth. A modern wellness-area and a private beach will help guests unwind after a night at the tables. **www.casino-hotel.at**

WHERE TO EAT

Austrian cuisine, although not known as one of the top-ranking in the world, nevertheless produces delicious country foods, innovative modern dishes, and a wonderful array of cakes and desserts. Shaped by the culinary traditions of many nationalities, it includes elements of Italian, Polish, Hungarian and Czech cuisines. In the larger cities, as well as the local cuisine, you are also likely to find Italian, Greek, Turkish and Chinese restaurants – eating out is a popular pastime here. Nearly all Austrian eateries – whether restaurant, café, *Gasthaus* or *Heuriger* – serve a version of the world-famous *Schnitzel*.

Mozartkugeln, decorated with a portrait of Mozart

The restaurants listed on pages 318–37 have been selected from the best on offer, across all price ranges. They are organized by region and price. The phrasebook *(p392)* will help you order a meal; some restaurants will have English menus.

A beautifully illuminated restaurant on the shores of Bindsee

WHAT TO EAT AND WHEN

For breakfast Austrians tend to eat a roll or two with butter and jam, accompanied by coffee. Most hotels have a self-service breakfast bar. Breakfast is generally served throughout the day, and even small bakeries usually have a few tables where you can quietly enjoy your pastries.

Most restaurants serve lunch from noon to 2 or 3pm. Many offer a *Tagesmenü* (fixed-price menu of the day), or a *Tagesteller* (dish of the day), as one of the best-priced options.

In Austrian homes, dinner is eaten early, at about 6pm. In restaurants, however, food is generally served throughout the evening. Wine, fruit juice or water are normally drunk with the meal, and stronger drinks, such as one of the locally produced fruit brandies, may be served as a *digestif*. Some establishments serve food throughout the day.

OPENING HOURS

A few small grocery stores, bakeries and coffee houses open as early as 7am in the morning; most open between 8am and 10am.

Restaurants serve as meeting points for socializing with family and friends as much as for eating, and many places will stay open as late as 2am, sometimes later. If the atmosphere is particularly friendly, often in smaller restaurants, guests may even stay until dawn the following day.

Many places close for one day a week (the Ruhetag), and may also be closed on public holidays. At a country inn it may be difficult to order a meal after 9pm. Your hotel or pension will advise you of their serving times.

TYPES OF RESTAURANTS AND SNACK BARS

A wide range of restaurants, bars and snack bars offer modest or grand meals any time of day. There is a large number of luxurious restaurants, often based within the luxury hotels, which serve first-class international menus prepared by top chefs.

A *Wirtshaus* is a country inn, a *Gasthaus* a slightly more sophisticated restaurant, both typically concentrating on local cuisine. The best-known and best-liked of all

Tables set in front of a typical *Wirtshaus* inn, in Lech

Interior of a *Gasthaus* in St. Christoph

Austrian restaurants is the *Heuriger*, a simple, often seasonal wine bar in the wine-growing villages, with light meals at low prices. Here, wine is served at your table in a glass mug, and you fetch your food from a buffet. If fir branches are displayed outside it means the *Heuriger* is open and serving the home-pressed vintage.

In cities you can get basic fare at a *Beisl* (snack bar) or a *Würstelstand*, a street kiosk serving a variety of sausages with bread and mustard, with quality varying from simple and dull to innovative and stylish. At an *Imbiss-Stube* you can get a light snack such as a bowl of soup, or order the daily set menu. This is usually displayed on a blackboard outside. Many cafés also serve good food, but you should watch the prices, as they can be higher than in restaurants.

DRESS CODE

The older generation of Austrians tend to dress formally when going out to eat at a good restaurant, but more casual clothes are also acceptable. In luxury or hotel restaurants it is wise to err on the side of conservatism. In the grander restaurants in the cities, smarter clothes (jacket and tie for men, or evening wear) are invariably expected. At a *Heuriger*, the locals let their hair down, and you can wear what you feel comfortable in. Swimwear is acceptable only in lakeside beach bars.

RESERVATIONS

In general it is wise to make a reservation if you wish to eat in a particular restaurant, especially if any kind of entertainment is on offer, if the restaurant is in a popular spot or if its cuisine is highly recommended. During the high season and in busy tourist areas it is often essential to book. Even a simple snack bar such as a *Beisl* may have a faithful local clientele and you may be disappointed if you wander in and expect to find a free table. If you are going to a *Heuriger* in a group you will need to book a table.

PRICES AND TIPS

It is difficult to generalize about prices. Lunch at an average restaurant should cost about €8–12 per person. For an evening meal you need to allow two or three times that price, or more if drinks are included. Self-service establishments usually charge by the size of the plate.

In the more expensive restaurants, the bill may include *Gedeck*, the cover charge, or a cover charge may be made for the bread served at the table.

Although a service charge is almost always included in the bill, you are expected to leave an additional sum of up to 10 per cent for service.

Credit cards are accepted in most luxury and hotel restaurants, but the majority of snack bars accept only cash.

CHILDREN AND VEGETARIANS

Some restaurants offer smaller servings for children and light eaters, but these may be only marginally less expensive than the regular portions – it might be cheaper to buy a regular meal to share if you have more than one child. Many restaurants, however, do have a special children's menu with the usual favourites such as french fries and burgers.

Austrians are avid meat-eaters, but most popular restaurants in the main tourist areas do offer vegetarian dishes. Pasta, mixed vegetables or a *Salatplatte* (mixed salad) with bread or *Salzstangerl* are popular. Many places, such as the *Heurigen*, offer buffets with a selection of vegetarian dishes to choose from.

A *Heuriger* awaiting its guests, in the vicinity of Mörbisch

The Flavours of Austria: Savoury Dishes

Austrian cuisine is a direct legacy of the country's imperial past, when culinary traditions from many parts of Europe influenced Viennese cooks. As a result, it is far more varied and flavoursome than most people realize. There are Italian and Adriatic influences, Polish- and Hungarian- inspired dishes, and even a rich seam of Balkan flavours running through much of the Austrian kitchen repertoire. *Schnitzel*, for example, may have come to Austria via Milan, which was once under Austrian control, while *gulasch* is the Austrian version of a Hungarian dish that became popular in Vienna in the 19th century.

Chanterelle mushrooms

Cheese stall at a local Austrian farmers' market

MEAT, POULTRY & DAIRY

Beef is narrowly ahead of pork as the nation's favourite meat. Austrian cattle farmers have a long and proud heritage of producing fine beef, which is used in many dishes, such as paprika-rich *Gulasch*. That most famous of Austrian dishes, *Wiener Schnitzel*, is traditionally made with veal. Pork is used primarily to make hams and sausages. The classic Austrian way with pork is to cure it, smoke it and leave it to mature for months in the clean air of the high Alpine pastures. The result is called *Speck*. Lean speck is similar to Italian *prosciutto*, though with a distinctive smoky tang, while fattier cuts are more like *pancetta* or streaky bacon. *Bratwurst*, made with beef, pork and veal, are Austria's preferred sausages, but other types such as *frankfurters* are also common. Chicken is almost always served breaded, but *Grillhendl* is a whole chicken roasted over an open fire, or on a spit. Duck *(Ente)* is often served with sweet sauces, but sometimes with sour accompaniments such as pickled red cabbage. Roast goose *(Gänsebraten)* is also popular, as are

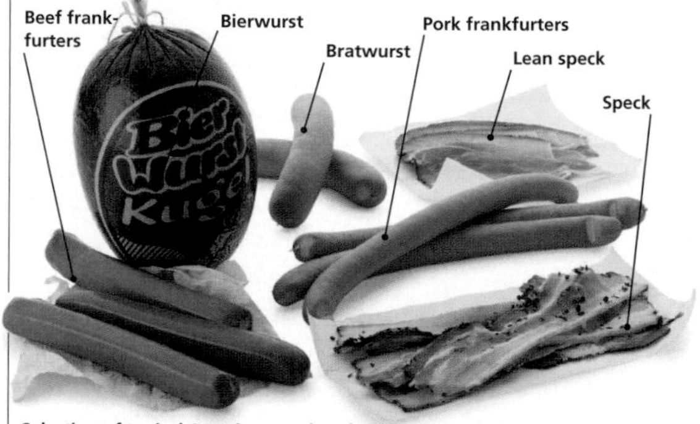

Selection of typical Austrian cured pork, sausages and salami

AUSTRIAN DISHES AND SPECIALITIES

Paprika

While most classic Austrian dishes (especially those originating in Vienna) are found all over the country, there are some regional differences. *Knödel* are more popular in the east, as are carp, game and pork, while beef and lamb appear more often the further west (and higher up the mountains) you travel. Beef is essential for *Tafelspitz*, often called the national dish. *Speck* is used to make *Speck Knödel*, small, dense dumplings, but the one part of the pig that Austrians do love to eat uncured is the knuckle, called *Stelze*, roasted and served chopped with heaps of sauerkraut. *Fischgröstl* is a mix of fish and seafood, fried together with onion, potato and mince (usually leftovers). It is rarely found on menus, but you may be lucky enough to try it in an Austrian home.

Tafelspitz *is silverside of beef, boiled with root vegetables and served thickly sliced with gherkins and sauerkraut.*

Spectacular array of vegetables on display in a Viennese market

goose livers. The milk of Austrian dairy cows, grazed on sweet Alpine pastures, produces some excellent artisan cheeses, such as fruity Wälder.

FISH

While not great seafood lovers, Austrians have developed a number of their own fish dishes. Trout *(Forelle)* is the most popular fish, usually served grilled with boiled potatoes. Herring *(Hering)* is pickled and eaten as an appetizer. *Heringsschmaus*, a smoked herring and apple salad, is hugely popular at Easter. Carp *(Karpfen)* is a favourite Christmas dish, but is eaten all year, as is plaice (*Scholle* or *Goldbutt*), which is often served with a rich vegetable-based sauce.

VEGETABLES

Vegetables in Austria are of the highest quality and so, while imported produce is available all year round, seasonality is still important to Austrians. That is truest of

Bunches of pale spears of Austrian *spargel* (asparagus)

all for the nation's favourite vegetable, asparagus *(Spargel)*. Only local produce is used, and so is found on menus only during the harvesting season, which runs from the end of April to early July. Austrians use asparagus in every way imaginable at this time of year. Wild mushrooms are another seasonal prize, especially chanterelles *(Eierschwammerl)*. Potatoes *(Erdäpfel)* feature widely, sometimes in the form of *Knödels* (dumplings, which may be savoury or sweet). Cabbage *(Kohl)* is popular: the white variety is often pickled (*Sauerkraut*) and red (*Rotkraut*) served with venison and game dishes.

SAVOURY SNACKS

Liptauer: Goat's or sheep's milk cheese is mixed with paprika, caraway seeds, capers, mustard, chives and onions to create this paste, a staple of Austrian wine bars.

Maroni: Roast chestnuts are a winter treat; the aroma of them, toasting over a brazier on a snowy day, is somehow quintessentially Vienna.

Saure Blunzen: Blood sausage is marinated in vinegar and thinly sliced and served with brown bread. A popular "beer snack".

Schmaltzbrot: Brown bread spread thickly with beef or pork dripping, and eaten with onions and pickles.

Wiener Schnitzel *should classically be veal, breaded and fried. In Austria it is never served with sauce.*

Rindsgulasch *is the beef version of Hungarian goulash, a rich stew flavoured with paprika and caraway.*

Forelle Blau, *literally "blue trout", is made by poaching an unscaled fish in stock, which gives it a blueish hue.*

The Flavours of Austria: Cakes and Pastries

Few cities in the world can rival Vienna's devotion to all things sweet. The Viennese enjoy cakes mid-morning or afternoon, and set aside time for between-meal snacks. The finest *torten* (gâteaux), pastries and cakes tend to be found in *Konditoreien* and are usually consumed with a cup of coffee. Traditional Viennese desserts can be found in all good restaurants, and are typically rich. From the classic Viennese *Apfelstrudel* to *Gugelhupf* from the Tirol, Austrian desserts all carry a regional influence. In Vienna, pastries take pride of place while, to the west, the Italian influence is strong and cakes, ice creams and meringues are preferred.

Poppy seeds

Relaxing over coffee and cake in an elegant Viennese café

CAKES

The Austrian tradition of cake-baking goes back centuries, with competition fierce between towns and cities to produce the finest. Even in small villages, bakeries would try to outdo each other with their sweet creations. Almost every Austrian city now has its trademark cake, with its citizens quick to boast that theirs is the best. The most famous Austrian cake is a Viennese creation, the *Sachertorte*, a rich chocolate cake invented by chef Franz Sacher for Chancellor Metternich in 1832. The signature dish of many an Austrian chef, it should be the first cake the visitor tries – with so much choice on offer, it will be difficult to decide on the second. While the Viennese rave about *Sachertorte*, over in Linz the locals insist their own *Linzertorte* – an almond based cake usually topped with raspberries – is superior. The people of Linz also say that the *Linzertorte* is older, dating back – legend has it – to the 17th century. Around the Hungarian border, they are proud of their *Dobostorte*, named for the Budapest chef who created it in the 19th century. Its layers of sponge

Some of the many mouthwatering Austrian cakes available

VIENNESE DESSERTS

Hazelnuts

From *Topfentascherl* (curd cheese envelopes) to *Kastaniereis* (chestnut purée), Vienna's dessert cuisine uses rich and varied ingredients. Fruits such as plums and apples fill featherlight dumplings, pancakes, fritters and strudels, and although *Mehlspeisen* (puddings) translates literally as "dishes without flour", ground hazelnuts or almonds can be used in its place. Nuts play a key role, especially hazels and pine nuts, the latter often featuring in *Apfelstrudel*. More unusual desserts include sweet "pasta" served with poppyseeds to create *Mohnnudeln*, and *Bohmische Omeletten* (Bohemian omelettes) served with whipped cream and prune sauce. Conversely, *Palatschinken* may also be a savoury snack.

Mohr im Hemd, *a hazelnut and chocolate pudding, is served with chocolate sauce and whipped cream.*

Display of traditional pastries and cakes in a *Konditorei*

and chocolate butter cream are topped with a caramel glaze. From Salzburg, the cake of choice is baked meringue, known as *Salzburger Nockerl*, or Salzburg Soufflé. *Esterházy-torte* also features meringue, layered with a rich hazelnut cream. Stollen is a marzipan-filled fruit bread originally from Germany and now an integral part of an Austrian Christmas. Regional or not, you'll now find all these classic cakes in Vienna and across the country.

PASTRIES

In the perfect global village, a place on the main street would always be reserved for an Austrian pastry and coffee shop. That the French collective name for sweet pastry is *Viennoiserie* underlines the noble Viennese tradition of sweet baking. Austrian legend has it that the nation's café habit began when the Turks left all their coffee behind as they abandoned Vienna after the failed siege of 1529. The *Kipfel*, a light, crescent-shaped pastry (which later became famous as the croissant) also dates from the time of the Turkish siege, its shape being based on the crescent moon in the Ottoman flag. While such symbolism is often lost today, the importance of the café in Austrian society is not. Modern-day Austrians view cafés as extensions of their home, and spend hours reading, chatting and even watching television in them. Treats on offer in cafés will generally include a classic *Apfelstrudel*, *Cremeschnitte* (slices of puff pastry filled with custard and glazed with strawberry fondant), and *Punschkrapferl*, a calorie-packed, pink-fondant-topped pastry laced with rum.

Entrance to one of the world-famous Mozart chocolate shops

MOZARTKUGEL

Fine chocolates, presented in colourfully decorated boxes carrying the portrait of Mozart, are probably the quintessential Austrian souvenir. Known in Austria as *Mozartkugel*, the chocolates originated in Salzburg, where Mozart lived while composing *Cosi fan Tutti*, the opera in which he worships chocolate. In 1890, master confectioner Paul Fürst made the first Mozart chocolates by forming small balls of marzipan which he coated in a praline cream and then dipped in warm chocolate. Viennese confectioners soon adopted the technique and even today producers vie with one another as to whose *Mozartkugel* are the best and most authentic.

Apfelstrudel *rolls paper-thin pastry with apple, sultanas, cinnamon and sometimes pine nuts or poppyseeds.*

Palatschinken *are fat, fluffy crêpes that may be filled with fruit or jam, or served with vanilla or chocolate sauce.*

Topfenknödel *are light curd cheese dumplings rolled in breadcrumbs, fried and served with fruit compôte.*

Cafés and Bars in Vienna

The café has been an ingrained part of Viennese life for centuries, and there are plenty of traditional cafés found throughout the city. The majority of the popular cafés are found in central Vienna, where they are best seen as architectural ambassadors from the days of the Habsburg monarchy. But Vienna is not all about history and tradition: many sleek cafés and bars have opened up, adding a new dimension to a city that not long ago was still in a post-World War II slumber; yet now it is a vibrant European Union capital.

The spacious Café Central with its fine Neo-Gothic vaulted ceiling

THE VIENNESE CAFE

It may be an exaggeration to call Vienna's cafés the heart of the city, but they are certainly one of its lifelines. Following the Turkish invasions of the 16th and 17th centuries, cafés in Vienna have been important meeting places, and have traced the history of this remarkable city. In Vienna's oldest café, the **Frauenhuber**, Mozart himself once performed; in **Café Central**, once a gathering spot for intellectuals, Leon Trotsky made some revolutionary plans for Russia; Sigmund Freud often took therapy breaks at the traditionally elegant **Café Landtmann**, and the Bohemian-esque **Café Bräunerhof** provided inspiration for renowned writer Thomas Bernhardt.

CAFE CULTURE

One of the best advantages of Vienna's cafés is that you can linger at your table for several hours by ordering just one cup of coffee. You can also read local and international newspapers and magazines, provided free of charge, and depending on the establishment, enjoy a host of other offerings. At **Café Prückel**, for example, the bridge tables are set up, while **Café Sperl** is ideal for billiard playing. And literary readings are a favourite at the 200-year-old **Café Dommayer**.

Architecture- and design-gazing is highly important, too. **Café Museum**, built in 1899, shows off the talent of Art Nouveau functionalist Adolf Loos. The **Kleines Café** (*Kleines* meaning "little") is a wonder with its nearly Lilliputian proportions. And the splendidly painted Neo-Gothic vaulting is the main feature of **Café Central**.

At Cafe Prückel diners can enjoy a game of bridge with their coffee

TYPES OF COFFEE

In most of Vienna's finer cafés, a tuxedoed waiter will serve your coffee, along with a glass of water, on a silver metal tray. But ordering coffee in the first place may be no easy task, as there are at least 20 different types to choose from. Some variations are:

Kleiner Brauner: small coffee with milk
Grosser Brauner: large coffee with milk
Kleiner Schwarzer: small espresso
Grosser Schwarzer: double espresso
Melange: light Grosser Brauner with steamed milk
Mokka: strong black coffee
Kapuziner: black coffee with frothed milk
Franziskaner: lighter version of the Kapuziner
Milchkaffee: half coffee, half milk
Verlängerter: espresso with a dash of hot water
Einspänner: large glass of Mokka with whipped cream on top and sometimes sprinkled with cocoa
Eiskaffee: cold, black, with vanilla ice cream and topped with whipped cream

Coffee is elegantly served on a silver tray with a glass of water

WHAT TO EAT

Café fare can range from sausages to soups to cakes and pastries. Lunch at **Café Landtmann** and the mirror-laden **Café Schwarzenberg** can include traditional *Wiener Schnitzel*, while **Demel**, formerly the confectioners to the Habsburg Court, offers fancy salads and an array of tantalizing sweets. **Café Diglas** never runs out of over-sized portions of strudels and cream cakes, while **Café Hawelka** is famous for its *Buchteln* (jam-filled buns) served late into the evening.

The elegant interior of the sophisticated Blaue Bar

VIENNA'S BARS

Vienna has an exciting bar scene, with several modern bars, serving as buzzing alternatives to the more traditional establishments. Fabulous views of the Stephansdom, plus fine mixed drinks, can be had at the rooftop **Skybar** on the pedestrian Kärntnerstrasse. Cocktails, including tasty martinis, are served just down the street at the sophisticated **Loos Bar**. For sumptuous elegance there is nothing like the **Blaue Bar** inside the venerable Hotel Sacher. For a taste of old-fashioned 1950s nightclub glamour, **Eden Bar** is the place to go.

AUSTRIAN WINES IN VIENNA

Today, Austria produces some of the finest wines in the world, from whites such as Grüner Veltliner and Riesling from the Wachau and Kamptal regions, to reds including Blaufränkisch from Mittelburgenland and Zweigelt from Neusiedlersee, and luscious dessert wines (in styles such as Eiswein and Trockenbeerenauslese) from around the towns of Illmitz and Rust. Vienna, a wine-growing area in its own right, produces excellent Gemischte Satz, a traditional dry white varietal blend. Most bars in Vienna feature Austrian wines. **Weinbar Coburg** in Palais Coburg offers a fine range by the glass as does **Wein & Co**, which has several branches around the city.

AUSTRIAN BEERS

An array of beers are produced in Austria, with the light-bodied Märzen as the most common. There is also Weissbier (wheat beer), and even the alcohol-free beer, Null Komma Josef, which is made by Vienna's Ottakringer brewery. Also produced from this brewery are the soft Gold Fassl brand, plus a pilsner and an unfiltered Zwickl beer. The cosy, vaulted-ceiling **Bierhof** serves these and other fine Austrian beers. Most order either a Seidl (0.3 litre glass) or the half-litre Krügel, but there is also the tiny 0.2 litre Pfiff, which is a must served with the single-face sandwiches at **Trzesniewski**.

DIRECTORY

CAFES

Café Bräunerhof
Stallburggasse 2,
1010 Vienna.
Tel *(01) 512 38 93.*
Map 2 B4.

Café Central
Palais Fers,
Herrengasse 14,
1010 Vienna.
Tel *(01) 535 99 05.*
Map 2 B3.

Café Diglas
Wollzeile 10,
1010 Vienna.
Tel *(01) 512 57 65.*
Map 2 C4.

Café Dommayer
Dommayergasse 1,
1130 Vienna.
Tel *(01) 877 54 65.*

Café Hawelka
Dorotheergasse 6,
1010 Vienna.
Tel *(01) 512 82 30.*
Map 2 B4.

Café Landtmann
Dr. Karl-Lueger-Ring 4,
1010 Vienna.
Tel *(01) 241 00 111.*
Map 2 A3.

Café Museum
Friedrichstrasse 6,
1010 Vienna.
Tel *(01) 586 52 02.*
Map 4 C1.

Café Prückel
Stubenring 24,
1010 Vienna.
Tel *(01) 512 61 15.*
Map 2 D4.

Café Schwarzenberg
Kärntner Ring 17,
1010 Vienna.
Tel *(01) 512 89 98 13.*
Map 4 D1.

Café Sperl
Gumpendorferstrasse 11,
1060 Wien.
Tel *(01) 586 41 58*

Demel
Kohlmarkt 14,
1010 Vienna.
Tel *(01) 535 17 17.*
Map 2 B4.

Frauenhuber
Himmelpfortgasse 6,
1010 Vienna.
Tel *(01) 512 83 83.*
Map 2 C4.

Kleines Café
Franziskanerplatz 3,
1010 Vienna.
Map 2 C4

BARS

Bierhof
Haarhof 4,
1010 Vienna.
Tel *(01) 533 44 28.*
Map 2 B4.

Blaue Bar im Sacher Hotel
Philharmonikerstrasse 4,
1010 Vienna.
Tel *(01) 514 56 840.*
Map 2 B5.

Eden Bar
Liliengasse 2,
1010 Vienna.
Tel *(01) 512 74 50.*
Map 2 C4.

Loos Bar
Kärntner Durchgang 10,
1010 Vienna.
Tel *(01) 512 32 83.*
Map 2 C4.

Skybar
Kärntner Strasse 19,
1010 Vienna.
Tel *(01) 513 17 12 12.*
Map 2 C4.

Trzesniewski
Dorotheergasse 1,
1010 Vienna.
Tel *(01) 512 32 91.*
Map 2 B4.

Wein & Co
Jasomirgottstrasse 3–5,
1010 Vienna.
Tel *(01) 535 09 16 12.*
Map 2 C4.
(One of several branches)

Weinbar Coburg
Coburgbastei 4,
1010 Vienna.
Tel *(01) 518 18 830.*
Map 2 D5.

What to Drink in Austria

Austria is a source of excellent wine and good rich beers. Austrian wine is mainly white, though there are excellent local red wines. The wine is drunk before it has finished maturing: *Most*, available from late summer, is the product of the first fermentation of the grapes. In early autumn, this is followed by *Sturm*, a gently fizzing, low-alcohol drink produced by the next stage of grape fermentation. Finally, the *Heuriger*, new-vintage wine, is served. Sweet *Eiswein* is made from grapes left on the vines until the first frosts. Some first-class brandies are also produced – fruit brandies and *Schnaps* are typical drinks.

Vineyards beyond the villages north and west of Vienna, producing *Heuriger* wines

Chardonnay from Styria and sparkling wine from Lower Austria

AUSTRIAN WINES

The most popular wine in Austria is Grüner Veltliner *(see below)*; a grape variety that also makes an excellent *Eiswein*. Other varietal wines include superb dry Rieslings, especially from the Wachau, and rich Weissburgunders (Pinot Blanc), Chardonnays and Traminers. Red wines tend to be soft and lush – robust reds come from the Blaufränkisch and Zweigelt grapes.

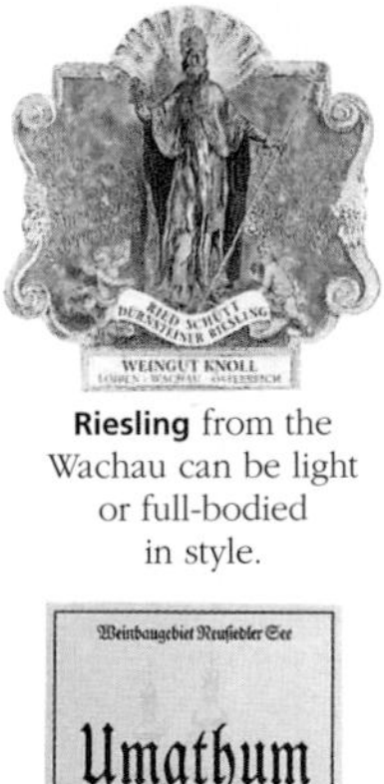

Riesling from the Wachau can be light or full-bodied in style.

Producer's name
Grape variety
Level of ripeness
Style (dry)
Vintage
Producer's address
Alcohol content
Quantity
Wiener Wein
WIENINGER
Grüner Veltliner
1991
Kabinett
Auckenthal
Weingut Wieninger, 1210 Wien, Stammersdorfer Straße 78
Qualitätswein mit staatlicher Prüf-Nr. K 0005392, 11,0 %vol
ÖSTERREICH trocken e 0,75l

Grüner Veltliner is a fresh, fruity white grape. It makes a dry wine that is widely available.

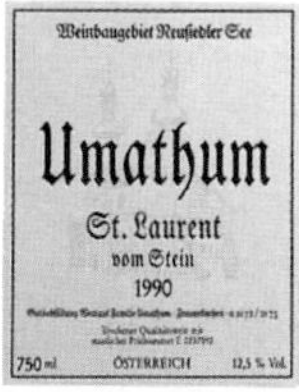

St Laurent is a soft red wine from the Neusiedler See region; it is rich and stylish.

Blaufränkisch is a quality red wine – the best is produced in Burgenland.

Krügel or 0.5-litre tankard

Seidl or standard 0.3 litre measure

Krügel or 0.5-litre of pale beer

Pfiff, the smallest measure of beer, a 0.2-litre glass

Kaiser is a light beer

Weizengold wheat beer

Gösser Spezial, a rich beer

AUSTRIAN BEERS

Good malty beers have been produced in Austria for more than 150 years. The most popular beers are made by the Gösser brewery in Styria – light *Gösser Gold*, stronger *Gösser Spezial* and dark, sweet *Gösser Stiftsbräu*. One of the oldest breweries, based in Schwechat, Lower Austria, produces a variety of pale beers and a slimming beer (so it is claimed) – *Adam Schlank & Rank*. In Vienna, beer from the local brewery in the Ottakring district, the pale sweet *Gold Fassl*, is popular although Bavarian-style wheat beers such as *Weizengold* are also available. The most popular alcohol-free beer in Austria is *Null Komma Josef*.

Bierhof beer mat advertising a pub in the Haarhof.

Null Komma Josef, (Nought Point Joseph), an alcohol-free beer.

OTHER AUSTRIAN DRINKS

Austria offers a good range of non-alcoholic fruit juices such as *Himbeersaft* (raspberry juice) or *Johannisbeersaft* (blackcurrant juice). *Almdudler* (alpine pasture yodler), a herbal lemonade, is also a speciality. Fruit is the basis of many types of schnaps (sometimes called *Brand*). This powerful eau-de-vie is distilled from berries such as juniper or fruits such as apricots *(Marillen)* and quince *(Quitten)*. It is worth paying the extra to sample the schnaps from specialists. Mixer drinks are popular: they include *Radler* (cyclist), a beer with lemonade. An innkeeper is said to have invented this drink on a hot day when, almost out of beer, he served it to thirsty cyclists.

Apricot schnaps

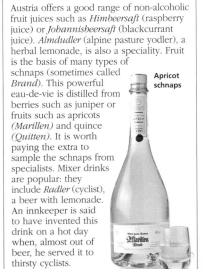

Wiener Rathauskeller, a popular beer-drinkers' haunt

Choosing a Restaurant

The restaurants in this guide have been selected across a wide range of price categories for their good value, exceptional food and interesting location. This chart lists the restaurants by region, in chapter order. Map references refer either to the Vienna Street Finder on *pp116–21*, or the road map on the inside back cover.

PRICE CATEGORIES
Price categories are for a three-course meal for one person, without drinks, including tax and service:

€ Under €20
€€ €20–35
€€€ €35–45
€€€€ €45–55
€€€€€ Over €55

VIENNA

INNER CITY Art of Life — €

Stubenring 14, 1010 ***Tel*** *(01) 512 55 53* — ***Map*** *3 D4*

Affordable and no limits on how much you can pile on the plate with the set-price buffet menu. It is therefore particularly popular with backpackers and students, both visiting and resident. A great meeting place, it is famous for its vegetarian and fish menus, and vegan ice cream, in vegan sugar cones. Organic wines. Closed Sun.

INNER CITY Rosenberger Markt — €

Maysedergasse 2, 1010 ***Tel*** *(01) 512 34 58* — ***Map*** *2 B5*

Moderately priced self-service buffet restaurant near the Opera House and the Sacher Hotel. On the basement level it has a wide variety of foods: meats, sausages, potatoes, salads, soups, desserts and drinks, great breads and even sushi, too. Frequented heavily by tourists.

INNER CITY Weibel 3 — €

Riemergasse 1–3, 1010 ***Tel*** *(01) 513 31 10* — ***Map*** *2 C4*

One of three highly rated city restaurants operated by this engaging and eponymous kitchen master, locally renowned for his artistic flair. Intimate inside, with only a few outdoor tables, the restaurant has nonetheless an extensive collection of wines. The motto is: we're not very big, so we have to be better.

INNER CITY Zu den 3 Hacken — €

Singerstrasse 28, 1010 ***Tel*** *(01) 512 58 95* — ***Map*** *2 C4*

Said to be the oldest tavern in Vienna, it has pavement tables painted green to match the green and white striped awning. Inside are four wood panelled stube dining rooms, one dedicated to the composer Schubert (a regular guest in his day). Small tasting room in the wine cellar. Classic Viennese cooking in a friendly ambience. Closed Sun.

INNER CITY Cantina e l'arte — €€

Dr Karl-Lueger Ring 14, 1010 ***Tel*** *(05 0505) 41490* — ***Map*** *2 A3*

An Italian restaurant near the university with the ambience of an Italian *osteria*. Specializing in the cuisine and wines of Friuli, a region of Italy which along with Venice and Trieste used to belong to Austria. Dishes include *frico* (baked potatoes and cheese) and *centopelle* (a tripe recipe). Non-smoking section. Closed Sat & Sun; Jul–Aug; 25 Dec.

INNER CITY Expedit — €€

Wiesingerstrasse 6, 1010 ***Tel*** *(01) 512 33 13* — ***Map*** *3 D3*

A simple, often crowded, bar and restaurant with something of a cult status. Known for its friendly service and youthful and enthusiastic staff. The cuisine is Ligurian, after the Italian province on the Mediterranean around Genoa. Ligurian foods are also for sale in the deli. In the basement there is a full-size sand *boccia* (bowls) pitch. Closed Sun.

INNER CITY Figlmüller — €€

Wollzeile 5, 1010 ***Tel*** *(01) 512 61 77* — ***Map*** *3 D4*

This is a cosy restaurant and wine tavern that specializes in traditional Austrian fare. It is most famous for its huge *Wiener Schnitzels*, perfect accompanied by a large glass of house red. Meals for a gluten-free diet are also available. Pets are permitted. Closed end Jul–early Aug.

INNER CITY Hansen — €€

Wipplingerstrasse 34, 1010 ***Tel*** *(01) 532 05 42* — ***Map*** *2 B2*

Twin restaurant of the Vestibühl, it is located in the basement of the former stock exchange. Deliberate attempts have been made to recreate an old Roman ambience, with skylights and terracotta pottery, not to mention abundant plant life from the florist shop next door. Renowned for its breakfasts. Small patio. Limited menu.

INNER CITY Harry's Time — €€

Dr Karl-Lueger Platz 5, 1010 ***Tel*** *(01) 512 45 56* — ***Map*** *3 D4*

Something for everyone: light meals at the bar, a summer garden and a fixed price menu offering no-limits servings of starters, pasta, main courses and desserts. Ultra modern decor with a light and open atmosphere. Over 200 choices of wine, most Austrian. The cuisine is creative Austrian with international dishes as well.

Key to Symbols *see back cover flap*

INNER CITY Immervoll €€

Weihburggasse 17, 1010 ***Tel*** *(01) 513 52 88* ***Map*** *2 C4*

Hip and trendy "scene" restaurant with only 15 tables, it features a charming 17th-century interior with wood everywhere and an antique tiled stove. The cuisine starts with classic Viennese dishes, then adds a creative touch. Loyal clientele, so not always easy to get a table. Reservations advised. Open daily until midnight.

INNER CITY Kanzleramt €€

Schauflergasse 6, 1010 ***Tel*** *(01) 533 19 09* ***Map*** *2 B4*

This is the most likely place to spot Arnold Schwarzenegger on a visit to his native country. Adjacent to the federal government offices, the "Chancellery" is the hangout for Austria's movers and shakers. Try tempting little snacks like goose liver or *Topfenkaiserschmarren* (a Viennese cheese pancake speciality). Closed Sun & hols.

INNER CITY Lebenbauer €€

Teinfaltstrasse 3, 1010 ***Tel*** *(01) 533 55 56* ***Map*** *2 A3*

This is an award-winning, popular, comfortable and airy vegetarian and natural foods restaurant. Here, you can select from a wide variety of attractively served healthy meals. Fish is also available. A pleasant outdoor patio is available for warmer weather dining. Reservations are recommended. Closed Sat, Sun & hols.

INNER CITY Nirvana €€

Rotenturmstrasse 16–18, 1010 ***Tel*** *(01) 513 30 75* ***Map*** *2 C3*

An authentic Indian restaurant consciously embracing the cuisine of the entire country from the north (chicken tikka) to the south (*masala dosa*), even including Goa. It is a modern restaurant housed in a commercial building, but perhaps attempts to squeeze one or two too many tables into the available space. Glassed garden area. Closed Sun.

INNER CITY Ofenloch €€

Kurrentgasse 8, 1010 ***Tel*** *(01) 533 88 44* ***Map*** *2 B3*

Classic Viennese dishes are served in this historic restaurant with a traditional *Wirtshaus* (tavern) interior. The dishes are prepared using only the very best local products, which are largely organically grown. Weather permitting, diners can eat outside on one of Vienna's oldest streets. Closed Sun.

INNER CITY Reinthaler's Beisl €€

Dorotheergasse 2–4, 1010 ***Tel*** *(01) 513 12 49* ***Map*** *2 B4*

Handy for the busy shopping district of Graben in the old part of Vienna, Reinthaler's offers tired tourists a chance to sit down at its few tables on the pavement outside. A typical *Beisl* (modest restaurant), it serves Austrian and Viennese classic dishes. Menus in English.

INNER CITY Schimanszky €€

Biberstrasse 2, 1010 ***Tel*** *(01) 513 45 43* ***Map*** *3 D4*

Part of a culinary empire which includes vineyards and a hotel in the woods, this downtown restaurant is attractively decorated in green and white, and offers inspired renditions of classic Austrian dishes like *Tafelspitz* (boiled beef). Tables are set outside in summer. A catalogue is available to order wine, kitchen tools and oils, among other things. Closed Sun.

INNER CITY Cantinetta Antinori €€€

Jasomirgottstrasse 3–5, 1010 ***Tel*** *(01) 533 77 22* ***Map*** *2 C4*

Part of an upmarket restaurant chain with locations in Italy, Switzerland and Russia, this restaurant offers classic Tuscan dishes, including pasta and fish, and wine from its own vineyards, which produce some of the finest Chianti. Both the ambience and service have a discreet Italian stylishness. Reservations are required.

INNER CITY Indochine 21 €€€

Stubenring 18, 1010 ***Tel*** *(01) 513 76 60* ***Map*** *3 D4*

An Asian restaurant with a cuisine which ranges across Vietnam, Laos and Cambodia and which is self-consciously interpreted for the 21st century (hence the name) with considerable French flair. Long list of seriously exotic cocktails. Some very expensive wines as well as moderately priced ones. Restaurant open daily until midnight, bar until 4am.

INNER CITY Plachutta €€€

Wollzeile 38, 1010 ***Tel*** *(01) 512 15 77* ***Map*** *3 D4*

This is the flagship restaurant of the Plachutta chain and the unrivalled headquarters of Austria's famous *Taflspitz* dish of boiled beef. The Plachutta restaurants are dedicated to keeping Viennese traditional cooking alive, using classic ingredients and methods. Open daily until midnight. Closed late Jul–mid-Aug.

INNER CITY Trattoria Martinelli €€€

Freyung 3, Palais Harrach, 1010 ***Tel*** *(01) 533 67 21* ***Map*** *2 B3*

The priority of this elegant restaurant in the historic Harrach palace is to offer fine and authentic Tuscan cuisine in an Italian atmosphere. Among the specialities are the celebrated *osso buco* and the delicious and unique wild duck ravioli. Opulent decor and Baroque ambience. Romantic dining in the palace courtyard. Good choice of Italian wines.

INNER CITY Vestibül im Burgtheater €€€

Dr Karl-Lueger-Ring 2, 1010 ***Tel*** *(01) 532 49 99* ***Map*** *2 A3*

Opulence and magnificence, as one would expect of this one-time Imperial entrance to the theatre. Marble pillars, frescoed ceilings, arches and vast spaces – if it's all too much, there is also a restful garden. The menu far exceeds imperial ambitions (Emperor Franz Joseph ate boiled beef every day). Creative and eclectic cuisine. Closed Sun & hols.

INNER CITY Walter Bauer V €€€

Sonnenfelsgasse 17, 1010 **Tel** *(01) 512 98 71* **Map** *3 D4*

Upmarket city restaurant of great appeal and with above average prices. Very popular but with limited seating. Elegant interior with a vaulted ceiling and red walls with a white trim. Refined and creative takes on classic French cuisine. Excellent lobster. Good selection of European wines. Reservations advised. Closed Sat & Sun.

INNER CITY Wirtshaus im Palais Kinsky €€€

Freyung 4, 1010 **Tel** *(01) 535 34 35* **Map** *2 B3*

This modern restaurant is found in one of Vienna's most important Baroque palaces, and the quiet courtyard setting is a welcome retreat from the hustle and bustle of the Innere Stadt. The menu has both Austrian and international dishes with an emphasis on seasonal specialities. Try the goose liver crème brûlée or the delicious *Wiener Schnitzel*.

INNER CITY Wrenkh V €€€

Bauernmarkt 10, 1010 **Tel** *(01) 533 15 26* **Map** *2 C3*

Famous for years as Vienna's premier strictly vegetarian restaurant, Wrenkh's now serves chicken and fish as well, though tofu still figures prominently on the menu. Its unique "happy cuisine" philosophy tries to take the seriousness out of *haute cuisine*, and is demonstrated in cooking workshops open to the public. Menus in English. Closed Sun.

INNER CITY Zum Schwarzen Kameel V €€€

Bognergasse 5, 1010 **Tel** *(01) 533 81 25* **Map** *2 B3*

This popular, family-owned restaurant, bar and café serves both international and regional cuisine, with classics such as *Tafelspitz* (boiled beef) competing with lighter fare, such as delicious ham sandwiches. There are daily fish specials. The Art Deco dining room is a particularly enjoyable place to sit. Closed Sun & hols.

INNER CITY Do & Co V €€€€

Stephansplatz 12, 1010 **Tel** *(01) 533 39 69* **Map** *4 C4*

Part of a catering empire as well as a Viennese institution, Do & Co is on the 7th floor of the Haas-Haus building and has a striking view of the Stephansdom. Excellent international and regional dishes are served, and the specialities include kebabs. Reservations are required.

INNER CITY Le Siècle V €€€€

Parkring 16, 1010 **Tel** *(01) 515 173 440* **Map** *3 D5*

Gourmet restaurant of the Radisson SAS Palais Hotel that serves award-winning Viennese and international cuisine in the heart of the city. Le Siècle has tremendous views out over the Stadpark. For lighter and less expensive meals, try the Palais Café, an all-day dinning restaurant in the Winter Garden, as well as a bistro bar serving bar meals.

INNER CITY Mörwald im Ambassador V €€€€

Kärntnerstrasse 22, 1010 **Tel** *(01) 961 61 161* **Map** *2 C5*

Located in the Ambassador Hotel, this restaurant serves traditional and modern Viennese fare and is popular with locals as well as tourists. Specialities incude pork and veal dishes. There is a range of unique desserts, including dumplings and pancakes with fruit. Reservations are required.

INNER CITY Zum weissen Rauchfangkehrer €€€€

Weihburggasse 4, 1010 **Tel** *(01) 512 34 71* **Map** *2 C4*

Wherever the name the "White Chimneysweep" came from (allegedly from visits to the baker's daughter), this attractive stone building is indeed painted all white. A favourite with restaurant critics, it offers four panelled dining rooms, two of which are non-smoking. Excellent wines. Reservations essential. Closed Sun–Mon.

INNER CITY Meinl am Graben V €€€€€

Graben 19, 1010 **Tel** *(01) 532 33 34 6000* **Map** *2 B4*

Meinl is the biggest name in Austria for food. The downstairs wine bar always has 30 open wine varieties to taste. The café with attached garden offers unlimited blends of coffee beans. And naturally the restaurant is one of the best in the country, and is applauded for its creativity and superb presentation. Reservations are required.

INNER CITY Palais Coburg V €€€€€

Coburgbastei 4, 1010 **Tel** *(01) 518 18 800* **Map** *2 C5*

Award-winning gourmet restaurant and wine bar bistro of the palatial Coburg Palace hotel. The cuisine is advertised as "clear, modern and purist", disdaining fads and emphasizing the interplay between food and wine. Spectacular glass garden pavilion, and a bar with views into the wine cellar. Popular champagne brunch every Sunday.

NORTH OF MARIAHILFER STRASSE Arnes €

Westbahnstrasse 28, 1070 **Tel** *(01) 523 27 68*

Popular cheap and cheerful snack bar with tasty light meals, some highly spiced. Serves both Greek and Kurdish cuisine as well as a large choice of vegetarian selections. Good meeting place for backpackers and young people who enjoy the likes of Greek salads and appetizers, several types of kebabs and fried vegetables. Open daily until midnight.

NORTH OF MARIAHILFER STRASSE Das Möbel V €

Burggasse 10, 1070 **Tel** *(01) 524 94 97*

The "Furniture" is an actual furniture shop, with an added café and small restaurant. Good coffee and light meals, particularly quiche. However, food takes second place to the furniture. The theme is that no two pieces of furniture are the same. If you like the chair you are sitting on (all creations of Austrian designers) you can buy it.

Key to Price Guide *see p318* **Key to Symbols** *see back cover flap*

NORTH OF MARIAHILFER STRASSE Die Wäscherei €

Albertgasse 49, 1080 ***Tel*** *(01) 409 23 75 11* **Map** *1 A3*

Witty and popular "scene" restaurant for the young crowd, which sponsors musical events and creates a cultural centre at the bar and restaurant. Offers to "wash your thirst and iron your hunger away". Great cocktails, bar food and burgers. Open Mon–Sat until 2am, Sun until midnight.

NORTH OF MARIAHILFER STRASSE Spatzennest €

St Ulrichsplatz 1, 1070 ***Tel*** *(01) 526 16 59* **Map** *1 B5*

This quaint *Beisl* (tavern) is in a pleasant location near St Ulrich's church and close to the lively Spittelberg pedestrian area with its eateries and stalls. It offers appetizing, traditional Viennese and regional specialities, including *Wiener Schnitzels*, smoked pork dumplings and roasted chicken. Daily specials are particularly good value. Closed Fri & Sat.

NORTH OF MARIAHILFER STRASSE Adam's Gasthaus €€

Florianigasse 2, 1080 ***Tel*** *(01) 408 01 12* **Map** *1 C3*

Restaurant and coffee bar which refuses to take itself seriously, and is openly eccentric and carefree. Extremely congenial atmosphere but serious cooking, offering both classic Viennese and a good variety of vegetarian dishes. Large outdoor garden for 120 guests. Dogs welcomed. Closed Sat, Sun & hols.

NORTH OF MARIAHILFER STRASSE Glacis Beisl €€

Museumsquartier, Zugang Breitegasse 4, 1070 ***Tel*** *(01) 526 56 60* **Map** *2 A5*

Moderately priced restaurant in the museum district that has a huge aquarium at the entrance. A popular restaurant with tourists it offers carefully chosen dishes of meats, dumplings, pasta and fish. Shady summer garden for fine weather as well as an enclosed winter garden. Menu in English. Open daily until 2am.

NORTH OF MARIAHILFER STRASSE Salz & Pfeffer €€

Joanelligasse 8, 1060 ***Tel*** *(0664) 405 33 35* **Map** *4 B2*

A hot spot for night owls, food and drink is served non-stop until 8am, and is therefore popular with the young and insomniacs. Wide-ranging menu, including Romanian specialities. Totally non-smoking. Modestly priced wines, including riojas from Spain and vintages from South Africa, which are seldom found in Austria.

NORTH OF MARIAHILFER STRASSE Schnattl €€

Lange Gasse 40, 1080 ***Tel*** *(01) 405 34 00* **Map** *1 B3*

A popular restaurant that features Stryian (southern Austrian) fare. The Schnattl emphasizes healthy organic produce. Try the salad with pumpkinseed oil dressing or game during the autumn hunting season. The interior is in the post-modern style. Styrian wines are featured. Good value daily lunch specials. Reservations are advised. Closed Sat & Sun; Aug.

NORTH OF MARIAHILFER STRASSE Steman €€

Otto/Bauer Gasse 7, 1060 ***Tel*** *(01) 597 85 09*

Comfortable and homely guest house, modernised but retaining historic features. Diners eat family-style at long tables in a dining room of panelled wood with old oil paintings. The Viennese dishes produced have won favourable comment in the local press. Closed Sat & Sun.

NORTH OF MARIAHILFER STRASSE Stomach €€

Seegasse 26, 1090 ***Tel*** *(01) 310 20 99* **Map** *2 A1*

The choice of food in this restaurant is eclectic and the portions are large. Standard fare is Viennese with some international and seasonal selections. Located in a Biedermeier house, the courtyard is one of the most attractive in Vienna for summer dining. Reservations are recommended. Closed Mon, Tue & lunch Wed–Sat.

SOUTH OF THE RING Demi Tass €

Prinz-Eugen-Strasse 28, 1040 ***Tel*** *(01) 504 31 19* **Map** *5 E2*

An award-winning, upmarket Asian restaurant featuring the cuisine of northern India. The dining room is attractively decorated with oriental tapestries and prints. Typical chicken and lamb meat dishes, with Indian breads, salads and sauces. Good choice of vegetarian dishes. Interesting Indian drinks with yoghurt, mango and vodka. Closed Sun.

SOUTH OF THE RING Engel am Naschmarkt €

Naschmarkt Stand 232/235, 1040 ***Tel*** *(01) 586 66 07* **Map** *4 C1*

Located in the Naschmarkt, an eclectic bazaar that draws all sorts of people, the Engel is famous for its all-day Saturday breakfasts. The restaurant and kitchen are very small, and the cooking is something of a performance art. Each day is a new, very inexpensive, lunch special. Take away is also available. Closed Sun.

SOUTH OF THE RING Kunsthallencafé €

Treitlstrasse 2 Karlsplatz, 1040 ***Tel*** *(01) 587 00 73* **Map** *5 D1*

Concept restaurant of the art museum, designed as an event centre as well as an eatery, offering snacks and light meals. A contemporary design and floor-to-ceiling glass walls, which provide views of the sculptures outside. Live music events with DJs occasionally. Large outdoor area with tables on open-paved area. Open daily until 2am.

SOUTH OF THE RING Naschmarkt Deli €

Naschmarkt Stand 421/436, 1040 ***Tel*** *(01) 585 08 23* **Map** *4 C1*

Unique in Austria, this restaurant focuses on the cuisine of both Turkey and the US. On good days sit outside at the handful of small tables on the paved area outside the market stalls. Inside there is more seating, with tables jammed together café-style. Excellent breakfasts are available. Hugely popular. Closed Sun.

SOUTH OF THE RING Rioja Club €
Paulanergasse 7, 1040 **Tel** *(0676) 534 90 50* **Map** *4 C2*

Spanish tapas and wine bar with a lively ambience. There are special inexpensive evening buffets Mondays and Tuesdays, Tuesdays being reserved for non-smokers. The shop sells all manner of Spanish foodstuffs both fresh and preserved, and offers the largest selection of Spanish wines and spirits in Austria. Closed Sun.

SOUTH OF THE RING Salm Bräu €
Rennweg 8, 1030 **Tel** *(01) 799 59 92* **Map** *5 E1*

A bustling and convivial ambience prevails in this family-run restaurant with its own in-house brewery. The decor is rustic in these renovated stables of the monastic buildings flanking the Salesianerinnenkirche. Good value regional cooking. The *Surstelze* (smoked pork joint) for two is a speciality, and is ideally accompanied by the home brew.

SOUTH OF THE RING Ubl €
Pressgasse 26 **Tel** *(01) 587 64 37* **Map** *4 C2*

This is an old-fashioned simple restaurant of considerable charm and hospitality, featuring old parquet floors, dark panelling, lovely blue tablecloths and huge arched windows that let in plenty of light. Traditional dishes are cooked traditionally and Viennese specialities are always on offer. Open daily until midnight.

SOUTH OF THE RING Fischrestaurant Umar €€
Naschmarkt Stand 79/79, 1040 **Tel** *(01) 587 04 56* **Map** *4 C1*

In the market where you can buy anything, this fish stand has fresh deliveries three times a week from Dubai and India, and deliveries daily of European fish. Mediterranean fish are a speciality, and all are cooked fresh in the pan. Tables are on the pavement outside, and locals swear you can't find cheaper, or better, fish anywhere. Closed Sun.

SOUTH OF THE RING Gusshaus €€
Gusshausstrasse 23, 1040 **Tel** *(01) 504 47 50* **Map** *5 D2*

A restaurant and bar near the Vienna Technical University and behind the Karlskirche. The ambitious cuisine covers traditional Viennese dishes but also tackles recipes from France, Spain and Italy. The main dining room has the decor of an elegant drawing room. There are two other stube rooms and a *vinothek* wine room. Closed Sat lunch, Sun & hols.

SOUTH OF THE RING Motto Club Restaurant-Bar €€
Schönbrunner Strasse 30, 1050 **Tel** *(01) 587 06 72* **Map** *4 B3*

A variety of dishes starting with Austrian traditional cuisine and ranging onwards to Asian and Mediterranean cooking styles is provided in this chic and cosy restaurant and bar. Try the spinach salad or teriyaki tofu dish for a unique treat. Also worth trying is the mousse for dessert. DJ music is played nightly.

SOUTH OF THE RING Pan e Wien €€
Salesianergasse 25, 1030 **Tel** *(01) 710 38 70* **Map** *5 F1*

Sister restaurant to the Pan e Giardin *(see below)*, it is also Italian and has the same menu. Great choice of Italian vintages. Wines ready for drinking are displayed in an attractive wooden cabinet with cubby holes, as one used to see in old Italian wine bars a century ago. The mellow all-wood dining room features a fireplace. Closed Sun.

SOUTH OF THE RING Pan e Giardin €€€
Strohgasse opposite Nr 16, 1030 **Tel** *(01) 710 38 70* **Map** *5 E1*

One of two such Pan restaurants honouring the god of wine, this one with a lovely patio garden, covered by large umbrellas and with comfy chairs. The cuisine consists of some fish dishes but mostly pasta and meats. Good desserts, including Toblerone mousse. Extensive choice of Italian wines and selected Austrian vintages. Closed Sun.

SOUTH OF THE RING Steirereck €€€€€
Meierei im Stadtpark, 1030 **Tel** *(01) 713 31 68* **Map** *3 D5*

With its atmospheric location, fabulous service and culinary artistry, this restaurant may be one of the best in Vienna. Menus of stunning flair show both Austrian and international influences. If you appreciate a meal that is staged as a performance, this is the place for you. Reservations are required. Closed Sat & Sun.

FURTHER AFIELD Café-Restaurant Piccolo €
Gredlerstrasse 10, 1020 **Tel** *(01) 216 12 83* **Map** *3 D3*

Not to be confused with three other Vienna area eateries with the same name. This one is a sports bar, where regulars, many expatriates, come to play darts or backgammon and watch games on the big bar TV. Menus are in English. Limited range of snacks and light meals. Open daily until midnight.

FURTHER AFIELD Chang Asian Noodles €
Waaggasse 1, 1040 **Tel** *(01) 961 92 12* **Map** *4 C2*

One of four popular Chang restaurants in the Vienna region, and one of two specializing in noodles. Clean, modern decor with a counter bar for quick service. Rather crammed inside. Very price-conscious, creative menus, which change every week. Noodles and soups particularly good. Tables outside on the pavement in summer. Closed Sun.

FURTHER AFIELD Gergely's €
Schlossgasse 21, 1050 **Tel** *(01) 544 07 67* **Map** *4 B3*

A restaurant concept, heartily endorsed by hip, young Viennese, Gergely's is one of several restaurants in the Schlossquadrat complex. Novelties include presenting four different dishes on one square plate and cooking meats at the table on a hot stone. Wine, cocktails and bio-organic health drinks are served. Tables outside.

Key to Price Guide *see p318* **Key to Symbols** *see back cover flap*

FURTHER AFIELD Kiang €

Landstrasser Hauptstrasse 50, 1030 ***Tel*** *(01) 715 34 70* ***Map*** *3 F5*

One of three Kiang Asian restaurants in the city, it serves up grilled prawns, noodles and other Asian dishes like sushi and Thai curry. Cramped inside, though pleasant modern industrial-style decor. Huge glass front allows natural light to flood the dining area. Very popular and price conscious. Take away available. Open daily until 11:30pm.

FURTHER AFIELD Schweizerhaus €

Prater 116, 1020 ***Tel*** *(01) 728 01 52*

Regional and Eastern European fare is served up in generous, good value portions in this very popular and often crowded restaurant with a large beer garden inside the Prater Park. Try the beef stew or Slovakian cabbage soup. Beer-lovers may want to sample the Czech Budweiser Budvar beer. Closed Nov–mid-Mar.

FURTHER AFIELD Soosser Weinhaus €

Karmelitergasse 11, 1020 ***Tel*** *(01) 214 48 70* ***Map*** *3 D2*

Little frequented by tourists, this is a typical Vienna *Beisl* both in that it is an unpretentious and modestly priced eating house and that it is a drinking spot for local people. Good home cooking, particularly on Thursdays, when the special is *Wiener Schnitzel*. Daily lunchtime specials. Closed Sun & hols.

FURTHER AFIELD Wieninger €

Stammersdorfer Strasse 78, 1210 ***Tel*** *(01) 292 41 06*

Classic *Heuriger* (wine tavern) in the north-eastern suburbs of Vienna not far from the wine-growing area. Standard Austrian cooking, with buffets ranging from standard to gourmet, all of which are good value. Five dining rooms, one non-smoking, including an old wine press cellar. Large courtyard garden with umbrellas and picnic tables.

FURTHER AFIELD Altes Presshaus €€

Cobenzlgasse 15, 1190 ***Tel*** *(01) 320 02 03* ***Map***

A "press house" has nothing to do with newspapers and is actually where wine is made. And this one claims to be the oldest in the area. There is a restaurant as well as a *Heuriger* wine bar. The name traditionally denotes a bar where only wine grown in Vienna itself is served. Popular, so book ahead. Closed Jan–Mar.

FURTHER AFIELD Benkei €€

Ungargasse 6, 1030 ***Tel*** *(01) 718 18 88*

An authentic Japanese restaurant with a wide-ranging menu. Prices vary from very modest to expensive, depending on menu choice. Inexpensive soups and tasting menus for sushi beginners. There are three *tatami* rooms in traditional Japanese decor. Reservations recommended on weekends. Open daily until 11:30pm.

FURTHER AFIELD Contor €€

Leopoldskrongasse 51, 1020 ***Tel*** *(01) 219 63 16*

A small Spanish restaurant with live music, tapas and an engaging ambience. Inexpensive daily lunchtime specials. Typical Spanish cuisine but also some standard Austrian dishes. A few tables outside on the pavement in summer. Small shop selling Spanish wine and delicatessen items. Dogs are permitted in the restaurant. Closed Sun & hols.

FURTHER AFIELD Gmoa-Keller €€

Am Heumarkt 25, 1030 ***Tel*** *(01) 712 53 10* ***Map*** *3 D5*

Featuring both regional Austrian fare and seasonal dishes, this is a popular restaurant. Among the specialities are soups, veal and beef, plus fruit or chocolate pancakes for dessert. It is a friendly place that is much favoured by the musical fraternity from the nearby concert halls. Closed Sun.

FURTHER AFIELD Jumbo Wok €€

Keilgasse 6, 1030 ***Tel*** *(01) 966 19 91.*

Simple but surprisingly spacious Asian restaurant with dark wood floors and evocative Chinese prints on the walls. The cuisine ranges from Cantonese to Thai, with corresponding degrees of spiciness. Some standard international dishes as well. Very tasty soups. The beef in black bean sauce is recommended. Closed Mon.

FURTHER AFIELD Leopold €€

Grosse Pfarrgasse 11, 1020 ***Tel*** *(01) 218 22 81* ***Map*** *3 D1*

A "scene" bar and restaurant popular with trendy young people, it is contemporary in style with very high ceilings. Inexpensive light meals include bar snacks such as potato wedges with chilli sauce, or tasty appetizers such as buffalo mozzarella and rocket salad. Inexpensive main courses, but limited choice. Famous for its schnapps. Closed Sun dinner.

FURTHER AFIELD Lusthaus €€

Freudenau 254/Prater Hauptallee, 1020 ***Tel*** *(01) 728 95 65*

The *Lusthaus* is a house of culinary pleasures. A former imperial hunting pavillion, it serves seasonal Viennese and Austrian cuisine according to old recipes. Located in the Prater amusement park, the restaurant is very popular and sometimes overcrowded at weekends. Booking advised. Closed Wed.

FURTHER AFIELD Mayer am Pfarrplatz €€

Pfarrplatz 2, 1190 ***Tel*** *(01) 370 33 61*

An authentic *Heuriger* (tavern selling local wines), this whitewashed inn on the edge of Heiligenstadt was once the home of Beethoven. It has a cobbled courtyard for outdoor dining and atmospheric panelled rooms inside. Simple buffets of cheese, sausage and meats complement superb regional wines.

FURTHER AFIELD Osteria Stradina €€

Praterstrasse 40, 1020 **Tel** *(01) 212 18 12.* **Map** *3 E2*

The sign outside says, "Pasta, Wine and Music" and that's exactly what's on offer. Inexpensive daily specials and classic Italian comfort food like *bruschetta* (grilled bread with olive oil), but no pizzas. Italian Moretti beer and Italian coffee add fuel to what is a very lively ambience. All wines, including sparkling *spumante*, are exclusively Italian.

FURTHER AFIELD Pancho €€

Blumauergasse 1a, 1020 **Tel** *(01) 212 58 69* **Map** *3 E1*

Popular and lively authentic Mexican restaurant, which also has another branch called Mas! with a huge summer terrace. Cramped quarters in what used to be a garage, but modest prices make up for the lack of elbow room. All you can eat Sunday brunches. Menus in English. Half-price cocktails during Happy Hours 6–7pm & 11pm–midnight.

FURTHER AFIELD Schuppich–Cucina Triestina €€

Rotensterngasse 18, 1020 **Tel** *(01) 212 43 40* **Map** *3 E2*

Unusual fusion of Austrian cooking with the cuisine of the Trieste region of Italy. Menus only in Italian or German, but English-speaking waiters will translate. The *saltimbocca* (veal) and chicken *cacciatore* are welcome changes from *schnitzel*, even for Austrians. Some good, and not expensive, Italian wines. Reservations advised.

FURTHER AFIELD Seidl €€

Ungargasse 63, 1030 **Tel** *(01) 713 17 81*

An unpretentious restaurant of the traditional *Beisl* (cosy pub) type, with the menu chalked up on black boards outside, and a typical Viennese *Schanigarten* (tables set out on the pavement). Dark wood panelling inside. Good value daily lunch specials which attract a loyal clientele. Dogs permitted. Non-smoking section. Closed Sat–Sun & hols.

FURTHER AFIELD Silberwirt €€

Schlossgasse 21, 1050 **Tel** *(01) 544 49 07* **Map** *4 B3*

Silberwirt is part of a complex of eateries built on the site of Schloss Margareten, which was devastated by the Turks during the 1683 siege of Vienna. Time-hallowed Viennese dishes are cooked with care and flair, and served in a relaxed ambience. A variety of Austrian wines are on offer, too. Reservations are recommended.

FURTHER AFIELD Stadtwirt €€

Untere Viaduktgasse 45, 1030 **Tel** *(01) 713 38 28* **Map** *3 E4*

This is a bustling restaurant, popular with locals, that has cosy corner seats and tables for groups. Also provided is superb Viennese and regional cooking at affordable prices, plus house wines, draught beer and brandies. Very friendly service. Menus only in German. Reservations are required. Closed Sat lunch & Sun.

FURTHER AFIELD Taverna Lefteris €€

Hörnesgasse 17, 1030 **Tel** *(01) 713 74 51*

Lively Greek restaurant featuring the cuisine of Crete and including a wide selection of Greek wines, as well as *retsina* and ouzo. Greek bread is baked on the premises as well as *mezedes* starters and a moussaka advertised as the best in town. Boisterous Tuesday evenings, with live Greek music and dancing. Reservations essential. Closed Sun & hols.

FURTHER AFIELD Zur Goldenen Glocke €€

Schönbrunnerstrasse 8, 1050 **Tel** *(01) 587 57 67* **Map** *4 B2*

An old-fashioned restaurant, of the kind which is fast disappearing, that serves classic Viennese cuisine. In addition to simple tables in the bar, there are four exquisite dining rooms, each like a museum of different periods in Vienna's history. Large walled garden for summer dining. Closed Sun dinner.

FURTHER AFIELD Niky's Kuchlmasterei €€€

Obere Weissgerberstrasse 6, 1020 **Tel** *(01) 712 90 00* **Map** *3 E3*

Ornate Baroque decor, including large wall tapestries and lavish red carpet. Theme rooms include a distillery, for tasting schnapps, and wine cellar for candlelit dinners. Guests can dine in a medieval Knight's Chamber, the Library Room or on the heated terrace. Lunchtime buffets during the week. Mediterranean and creative Austrian cuisine.

FURTHER AFIELD Plachutta Hietzing €€€

Auhofstrasse 1, 1130 **Tel** *(01) 877 70 87*

A short walk from Schönbrunn Park, this is a haven for meat eaters, the restaurant being particularly proud of its *Tafelspitz* (boiled beef) served with apple sauce and horseradish. Each day there is a different beef dish offered as a special. Very popular. Outdoor tables on the pavement. Reservations advised. Open daily until 11pm.

FURTHER AFIELD Tempel €€€

Praterstrasse 56, Innenhof, 1020 **Tel** *(01) 214 01 79* **Map** *3 E2*

Smart dining room with dark wood polished floors, oil paintings and a vaulted ceiling. French-influenced cuisine ranges from fish to beef, with Austrian veal dishes, too. Some French wines in addition to standard Austrian vintages. Vegetarian, even vegan, menus. Set weekday menu is excellent value. Small garden for 20 diners. Closed Sun–Mon.

FURTHER AFIELD Vincent €€€

Grosse Pfarrgasse 7, 1020 **Tel** *(01) 214 15 16* **Map** *2 D1*

The name bespeaks the owner's passion for modern art, specimens of which adorn the walls. The excellent organic fare is a nouvelle cuisine influenced version of Viennese cooking, and decidedly creative. When available, try the mussels or the veal kidneys cooked in port wine. Reservations are required. Closed Sun & lunch.

Key to Price Guide *see p318* **Key to Symbols** *see back cover flap*

LOWER AUSTRIA AND BURGENLAND

ALLAND Zur Grube €€

Groisbach 24, 2534 ***Tel*** *(02258) 2361* ***Road map*** *F3*

Although not much to look at from the outside, the parking lot of this modern guest house is almost always filled, with locals who come for the warm service and excellent home cooking at very modest prices. Meat and noodle dishes frequent the menu, and a tempting array of desserts. The summer garden seats 50 diners.

AMSTETTEN Stadtbrauhof €€

Hauptplatz 14, 3300 ***Tel*** *(07472) 628 00* ***Road map*** *E3*

Cheerful bar and restaurant, much frequented by young people. Daily specials are written on the blackboard outside. Far more beer than wine is consumed, and the large beer garden seats 200 guests. Live music from rock bands and local folk groups. Vegetarian menu as well as classic Austrian dishes.

BADEN Grand Hotel Sauerhof €€€€

Weilburgstrasse 11–13, 2500 ***Tel*** *(02252) 412 51 183* ***Road map*** *G3*

The Rauhenstein is the house restaurant of the magnificent 19th-century Biedermeier palace, which houses the Grand Hotel Sauerhof, a tourist attraction in itself. The dining room is, unexpectedly, more cosy than ornate and palatial. The menu, too, is not over the top, stopping just short of gourmet status but tasty nonetheless.

BADEN Primavera €€€€€

Weilburgstrasse 3, 2500 ***Tel*** *(02252) 855 51* ***Road map*** *G3*

Award-winning gourmet restaurant rated by both Michelin and GaultMillau. In the centre of Baden, housed in an attractive yellow stone house, the elegant dining room has an impressive vaulted wine cellar with 200 international vintages. The Mediterranean and French cuisine is of a very high calibre. Closed Sun–Mon; Jul–Aug.

DONNERSKIRCHEN Vinarium im Leisserhof €€

Haupstrasse 57, 7082 ***Tel*** *(02683) 86 36* ***Road map*** *G3*

A cultural centre as well as restaurant and winery. The cuisine is promoted as Pannonian, which refers to an ancient region today covering parts of Austria, Hungary and the former Yugoslavia. Pannonian cooking is increasingly fashionable in Burgenland and uses local game, fish and vegetables, many of which are grown wild. Closed Mon–Tue; Jan–Feb.

DURNSTEIN Loibnerhof €€€

Unterloiben 7, 3601 ***Tel*** *(02732) 828 90* ***Road map*** *F3*

Family-run restaurant in a 17th-century house of immense charm. In spring and summer everyone eats in the huge garden under the spreading chestnut trees. The cooking of largely regional dishes is superb, and the atmosphere is warm and familial. Excellent desserts. Closed Mon–Tue.

DURNSTEIN Schloss Dürnstein €€€€

Dürnstein, 3601 ***Tel*** *(02711) 212* ***Road map*** *F3*

It is difficult to imagine anywhere more scenic than the terrace of this castle restaurant overlooking the blue Danube. Truly palatial decor, both in the Yellow banqueting room and in the Rose dining room. The main restaurant has huge oil paintings and oriental carpets. Impeccable service and international cuisine. Open daily until 10pm.

GAADEN Meierei Gaaden €

Anningerstrasse 5, 2531 ***Tel*** *(02237) 81 43* ***Road map*** *F3*

Light meals feature on the menu at this coffee house and *Jausenstation*, loosely translated as a snack bar. Choose from breakfast on the sunny terrace, sandwiches, sausages or potato salad later, then apple strudel or other pastries. Good selection of wines and beers. Non-smoking section and playground for kids. Closed Tue–Thu.

GRAFENEGG Schloss Grafenegg €€€

Grafenegg 12, 3485 ***Tel*** *(02735) 2616–0.* ***Road map*** *F3*

Managed by the Mörwald restaurant chain, which offer some of the best dining spots in the region, this castle is a tourist attraction in itself. Just sitting in the dining rooms is a treat, as is dining on the patio in good weather. Expect a mix of international and Austrian cuisine with excellent presentation and a high standard of service. Closed Mon & Tue; Dec–Apr.

HAAG-STADT Mitter €€€

Linzer Strasse 11, 3350 ***Tel*** *(07434) 424 26* ***Road map*** *E3*

Substantial yellow stone townhouse containing restaurant, pub and hotel rooms. The old-fashioned, simple stube dining room offers inexpensive meals, mostly regional. The themed menu offers seasonal fare: goose, asparagus or game, for example. Summer garden seats 80 guests. Dogs permitted. Closed Thu.

HALBTURN Knappenstöckl €€

Schloss Halbturn, 7131 ***Tel*** *(02172) 82 39 0* ***Road map*** *G3*

This is the restaurant and coffee house of the magnificent Castle Halbturn. The main dining room is of museum quality. Tables to accommodate tour groups are tucked away literally under the stairs and spread out on to the terrace. It is possible to taste and buy the castle wine, and to visit the wine cellars. Closed Mon.

HINTERBRUHL BEI MODLING Hexensitz €€€

Johannesstrasse 35, 2371 ***Tel*** *(02236) 229 37* ***Road map*** *G3*

Simple single-storey yellow stone building offering the best of Austrian country cooking. Dedicated staff and devoted service. Most of the menu items are familiar. Rather than flair and creativity, there is attention to getting classic dishes right. Each day there is fresh fish from the market. Shady garden for 60 diners. Closed Mon.

KREMS Mörwald Kloster Und €€€

Undstrasse 6, 3500 ***Tel*** *(02732) 704 93 0* ***Road map*** *F3*

Atmospheric dining inside the walls of a 17th-century Capuchin monastery with an international menu meriting Relais Gourmand classification. The wine cellar has frequent tasting events and outside dining is available in the courtyard and garden. Cuisine courses are also offered. Non-smoking section. Closed Sun–Mon.

MARIA TAFERL Krone–Kaiserhof €€

Maria Taferl 24, 3672 ***Tel*** *(07413) 63 55* ***Road map*** *F3*

Popular hotel in an area of outstanding beauty, much frequented by golfers and bikers. The Donauterrasse restaurant offers magnificent views over the eponymous river and to the Alps beyond. The Smaragd gourmet restaurant has wall-to-ceiling glass windows, for the same views. Worth visiting is the brick vaulted wine cellar for free wine tastings.

MAUTERN Nikolaihof Wachau €€

Nikolaigasse 77, 3512 ***Tel*** *(02732) 829 01* ***Road map*** *E4*

Nikolaihof is the oldest wine estate in Austria. Schnapps, mustard and jams are produced and sold on the estate. Diners have a choice of Baroque dining rooms indoors or the huge shaded garden. Exceptional menu, including an inexpensive buffet option. Organic produce is used. Closed Sun–Tue & Nov–Apr.

MAYERLING Hanner €€€€€

Mayerling 1, 2534 ***Tel*** *(02258) 23 78* ***Road map*** *F3*

Less than half an hour from downtown Vienna this Relais Gourmand restaurant is part of a sports hotel complex built in the early 20th century. Visitors are invited to inspect the extremely high tech kitchens, said to be unique in Austria. There is a casual dining area, open until midnight, as well as the exciting gourmet restaurant.

MICHELBACH Schwarzwallner €

Untergoin 6, 3074 ***Tel*** *(02744) 82 41* ***Road map*** *F3*

Rustic charm and good home cooking in a farm house setting where guests can dine in the open garden in summer or the conservatory in winter. The main dining room is simple, but has a huge antique tiled *Kachelofen* oven. Waitresses dress in traditional costume. Local specialities include *Blunzl* (fried black pudding). Closed Tue–Wed.

MODLING Babenbergerhof €€€€

Babenbergergasse 6, 2340 ***Tel*** *(02236) 222 46 405* ***Road map*** *E3*

Restaurant, café and bistro attached to the upmarket Hotel Babenbergerhof. A special menu features lots of protein, little fat and lots of vitamins. Fried goose liver, *Tafelspitz* (boiled beef) and other courses are always available, too. The Wirtsthaus Pub offers tapas and full meals, and there are snacks and tastings in the wine cellar.

NECKENMARKT Zur Traube €€

Herrengasse 42, 7311 ***Tel*** *(02610) 422 56* ***Road map*** *G4*

Traube refers to the grape, but at least as much beer as wine is consumed in this convivial family restaurant attached to a modestly priced hotel. The two dining rooms are functional and are good for families with children (as is the cooking). Regular theme menus feature lamb, local beef, asparagus and game. Summer garden with picnic tables.

NEUSIEDL AM SEE Landgasthaus am Nyikospark €€

Untere Hauptstrasse 59, 7100 ***Tel*** *(02167) 40222* ***Road map*** *G3*

Regional gourmet cooking in a contemporary ambience. A modern twist on classic dishes, presented with a lighter touch that attracts hordes of diners to the restaurant. Summer dining on the outdoor patio shaded by walnut trees. Conservatory garden in winter. Gourmet cooking classes available. Non-smoking area. Closed Mon–Tue.

NEUSIEDL AM SEE Mole West €€

Strandbad, Westmole, 7100 ***Tel*** *(02167) 202 05* ***Road map*** *G3*

This stunning restaurant on the water is partly a dock and partly a piece of sculpture. The interior is all modern wood, with huge picture windows out to the lake. Innovative cuisine and one of the largest wine collections in the region. This is the perfect place to watch sunsets on the lake and is immensely popular, so booking is advised.Closed Nov–Dec.

PODERSDORF Dankbarkeit €€

Haupstrasse 39, 7141 ***Tel*** *(02177) 22 33* ***Road map*** *G3*

A country restaurant with its own vineyards and guest house. Home cooking makes use of local sources of fish, lamb and geese. The asparagus, which grows near the vineyard, is also recommended. In addition to the estate's own wine, 50 other vintages are on offer. The shady summer garden caters for 65 guests. Closed Wed–Thu; Nov–Jan.

POTTSCHING Der Reisinger €€

Hauptstrasse 83, 7033 ***Tel*** *(02631) 22 12* ***Road map*** *G3*

One of three stylish local restaurants owned by the same family, which offers good regional cooking with flair. The White Tomato Mousse is not to be missed. A good choice of, mostly Austrian, wines is available. Very popular restaurant, especially for the good value Sunday brunches. Closed Mon–Wed.

PURBACH Kloster am Spitz €€€

Waldsiedlung 2, 7083 ***Tel*** *(02683) 55 19* **Road map** *G3*

Part of a complex including a restaurant, vineyard and modern hotel. The menu is deliberately kept limited to a choice of six main courses, according to the best seasonal ingredients. Great views of lake Neusiedler from the large garden terrace. Wines from the attached vineyard. Closed Mon–Tue; Nov–Mar.

RITZING Horvath €€€

Lange Zeile 92, 7323 ***Tel*** *(02619) 672 29* **Road map** *G4*

Simple cottage-style country restaurant with its own gardens. Good for game, lamb and mushrooms. Several dining rooms, the modern Speisasaal being the most attractive. Outdoor dining is available on the terrace and summer garden, or in the enclosed Mediterranean-themed winter garden. Closed Mon–Tue.

RUST Inamera €€€

Oggauer Strasse 29, 7071 ***Tel*** *(02685) 64 73* **Road map** *G4*

Young, dynamic and innovative are the words local residents use to describe the team at Inamera. The very creative cuisine matches the contemporary décor of white paint, white tablecloths and abstract art on the walls. Phenomenal wine list, mostly Austrian, but with some top vintages from the New World. Closed Mon–Tue.

RUST Mooslechners Rusterhof €€€

Rathausplatz 18, 7071 ***Tel*** *02685) 60 79-3* **Road map** *G4*

Country restaurant and hotel that serves a range of Mediterranean cuisine alongside more regional dishes. The summer patio caters for 40 guests, and bar food is also available. Reservations are essential as there are no fixed days of closure, which are at the discretion of the owner. Closed Oct–Mar.

SCHUTZEN/GEBIRGE Restaurant Taubenkobel €€€€€

Hauptstrasse 33, 7081 ***Tel*** *(02684) 22 97* **Road map** *G3*

One of Austria's most interesting award-winning restaurants. Set in the countryside next to a pond, the restaurant is housed in a small white washed 19th-century house. There is no point describing the menu, because it changes as frequently as the celebrated chef's creative juices flow. Closed Mon–Tue.

ST MARGARETHEN Eselmühle €€€

St Margarethen, 7062 ***Tel*** *(02680) 28 00* **Road map** *G3*

This old hamlet is a very popular excursion for families with children, where the main feature is the Donkey Mill restaurant. Regional dishes using ingredients from the surrounding organic farm include *carpaccio* of lamb served with goat's cheese and pastry filled with ricotta cheese. Fresh fish and wild mushrooms are recommended. Closed Mon–Tue.

WEIDEN/SEE Zur Blauen Gans €€€€

Seepark, 7121 ***Tel*** *(02167) 75 10* **Road map** *G3*

In what is becoming something of a gourmet zone around the Neusiedler See, the "Blue Goose" has achieved a Michelin star. The cuisine is mainly French, but is infused with many local ingredients. The formal dining room is elegant, and the wooden deck terrace offers views of the boatyard. Cooking courses run each autumn. Closed Tue–Wed; Dec–Mar.

STYRIA

BAD RADKERSBURG Kurhotel im Park €€

Im Kurpark, 8490 ***Tel*** *(03476) 257 10* **Road map** *F5*

Large and lavish spa hotel with many dining options, including less formal options at the bar of the swimming pool or the wine-tasting bar. There is a small gourmet restaurant plus a larger one serving Mediterranean cuisine, and outdoor dining is available in the garden. All dining areas are strictly non-smoking. Open daily until 9pm.

BAD WALTERSDORF Safenhof €€€

Hauptstrasse 78, 8271 ***Tel*** *(03333) 22 39* **Road map** *F4*

Attractive red and white city restaurant with colourful flowerboxes in summer. Very creative and artistic presentation of international cuisine, rated by GaultMillau. The dining room is light and airy, and the service friendly. Menus in English available. Pleasant garden with awnings for summer meals. Playground for children. Closed Mon.

BAD WALTERSDORF Thermenhof €€€

Wagerberg 120, 8271 ***Tel*** *(03333) 28 01 0* **Road map** *F4*

Restaurant of a luxurious spa hotel with its own hot springs. The health-conscious menus focus on organic and fresh ingredients, and smoking is not permitted anywhere except the cigar bar. Asian influence in many dishes, but also traditional Austrian cooking. Wine cellar with 130 vintages, mostly Austrian. Most diners are residents of the hotel.

DEUTSCHLANDSBERG Alpengasthof Koralpenblick €€

Trahütten, Rostock 5, 8530 ***Tel*** *(03461) 210* **Road map** *F5*

Set in rolling farmland with lovely views, the guest house is part of a working farm, and is geared towards families with children. In the restaurant all home-grown products are organic, including the Styrian beef, which appears extensively on the menu. Freshly baked home-made cakes and pastries. Booking for non-guests advised.

ETMISSL Hubinger (Vital-Gasthof) €€€

Etmissl Nr 25, 8622 **Tel** *(03861) 81 14* **Road map** *F4*

This restaurant and small hotel promote relaxation in nature. An unusual and impressive ancient fortified house, built in stone set in the foothills of the Hochscwab, they offer "Green cuisine", meaning that all bread, ham, vegetables and milk products come from the farm and kitchens on site. Children are warmly welcomed. Reservations advised.

FISCHBACH Zum Forsthaus €€

8654 Fischbach, 8654 **Tel** *(03170) 201* **Road map** *F4*

Award-winning restaurant in a 17th-century guest house. The dining room is simply decorated but with timeless charm, added to by the high vaulted ceilings and wood panelling. Creative cooking with a light touch. Wines limited to Austrian vintages. Children's menus and playground. Dogs permitted. Closed Wed.

FROHNLEITEN Frohnleitnerhof €€

Hauptplatz 14a, 8130 **Tel** *(03126) 41 50-0* **Road map** *F4*

A restaurant with its own brewery and hotel attached. The brewery has a pub dining area that serves bar snacks and light meals. The restaurant offers a five-course gourmet tasting menu emphasizing authentic Styrian dishes prepared with bio-organic ingredients. Sometimes special menus focus on lamb, fish and asparagus according to season.

FURSTENFELD Das Leitgeb €€

Ledergasse 13, 8280 **Tel** *(03382) 53 039* **Road map** *G4*

In a characterful old pink stone building with white columns, this restaurant wins rave reviews from the local press. Interesting menu, blending traditional Austrian fare with more adventurous cooking styles. Good choice of local wines, but guests can bring their own bottle, too. Barbeques every Thursday. Lovely garden. Closed Wed.

GAMLITZ Jaglhof €€€

Sernau 25, 8462 **Tel** *(03454) 66 75* **Road map** *F5*

In the heart of wine country, this contemporary design hotel and restaurant celebrate the grape, not least by opening the scenic terrace to diners whenever weather permits. Also, each item on the menu comes with a specific suggestion of which Austrian vintage best accompanies it. Excellent for fish. Closed Tue–Wed.

GAMLITZ Sattlerhof €€€

Sernau 2a, 8462 **Tel** *(03453) 44 54 0* **Road map** *F5*

With rolling hills and steeper vine terraces, the Sattlerhof is both a wine estate itself and a hotel with restaurant. Admirably, the restaurant wine list extends to 200 vintages from around the world, not limiting itself to the local vines. Renowned for reasonably priced Styrian dishes. Closed Sun–Mon & mid-Dec–mid-Mar.

GRAZ Häuserl im Wald €€

Roseggerweg 105, 8044 **Tel** *(0316) 39 11 65* **Road map** *F4*

Particularly cosy and comfortable guest house in the green belt area of Graz. Ideal for diners with children, as there is a playground and a small petting zoo on the grounds. The dining room is cluttered with antique lamps, flowering plants and knick knacks. Good home-cooking of classic Austrian dishes and reasonable prices. Closed Mon.

GRAZ Mayers €€

Sackstrasse 29, 8010 **Tel** *(0316) 81 33 91* **Road map** *F4*

Unashamedly claiming to have the best view in Graz, Mayers does indeed have floor-to-ceiling picture windows, part of its sleek modern design. The cuisine is Mediterranean but with Asian influences. Also open for coffee and tea, and outdoor dining is available on the terrace. Dogs permitted.

GRAZ Ohnime €€

Purbergstrasse 56, 8044 **Tel** *(0316) 39 11 43* **Road map** *F4*

Large, contemporary design restaurant divided into several rooms and sections, including some alcove areas with vaulted ceilings. Austrian and Italian dishes dominate the menu, but little choice of wines other than Austrian. Awarded 13 GaultMillau points for good bourgeois cooking. The summer terrace has lovely views. Closed Mon–Tue.

GRAZ Wintergarten €€

Sackstrasse 3–5, 8010 **Tel** *(0316) 81 16 16* **Road map** *F4*

Spacious and spectacular atrium restaurant built into the old courtyard of the majestic palace hotel Erzherzog Johann. The glass-roofed dining area is overflowing with vegetation. The classic Austrian cuisine is enlivened by influences from Italy. Ideal setting for afternoon coffee and cakes. Tables are limited, so reservations advised. Closed Mon–Tue.

GRAZ Iohan €€€

Landhausgasse 1, 8010 **Tel** *(0316) 82 13 12* **Road map** *F4*

One of the busiest and most popular eating spots in Graz, especially for the young and hip. One reason is the stunning architecture of the ancient Landhaus building. Squat stone columns support vaulted ceilings under which acres of white tablecloths are spread. There is also a courtyard terrace for summer dining. Eclectic cuisine. Closed Sun–Mon & hols.

GRAZ Mod (Hotel zum Dom) €€€€

Bindergasse 1, 8010 **Tel** *(0316) 82 48 00-41* **Road map** *F4*

Mod is the contemporary restaurant of the venerable Hotel Dom. Where the hotel is classic and understated, the Mod (Dom spelled backwards) restaurant is stripped down and minimalist. Its cross-over cuisine has won 14 GaultMillau points, and diners are queuing to get in. Small garden and terrace. Reservations advised. Closed Sun.

GROBMING Landhaus St Georg €€€

Kulmweg 555, 8962 ***Tel*** *(03685) 22 7 40* ***Road map*** *E4*

Modern family hotel in the Dachstein-Tauern ski and summer resort region. The fitness and beauty theme extends to the menu, where vital ingredients like mushrooms and berries are prominent. Good range of vegetarian dishes, but also the likes of beef and noodles. Open daily until 10pm.

HART BEI GRAZ Hirschenwirt €€€

Rupertistrasse 115, 8075 ***Tel*** *(0316) 46 56 00* ***Road map*** *F4*

Very popular with Graz residents for its mix of traditional Austrian cooking and Styrian specialities. Special price business lunch menu on weekdays. Romantic meals can also be arranged, if booked in advance. Summer garden seats 50 people. Dogs permitted in the restaurant. Reservations advised. Closed Sun–Mon.

HARTBERG Abend Restaurant im Schloss €€

Herrengasse 1, 8230 ***Tel*** *(03332) 618 50* ***Road map*** *F4*

Its name "Evening Restaurant in the Castle"does not do justice to this experience, which often extends to the early hours of the morning (the kitchen is open to 2am). Claiming to have the best desserts in Styria, it is equally famous for its venison and regional Styrian wines. Excellent vegetarian menu. Lively music. Closed Sun.

HOHENTAUERN Passhöhe €€€

Hohentauern 110, 8785 ***Tel*** *(03618) 219* ***Road map*** *E4*

Very popular with a large number of loyal customers, this family-run restaurant and hotel merits 13 GaultMillau points for its menu of mostly Styrian specialities. The wine list, too, is almost exclusively limited to Styrian vintages. Non-smoking sections, but not closed off from smokers. Small summer garden for 35 diners.

IRDNING Hirsch'n Wirt €€€

Aigner Strasse 22, 8952 ***Tel*** *(03682) 224 45* ***Road map*** *E4*

Not often in Austria, especially in a restaurant trumpeting venison in its name, does one get offered a first course of sushi or sashimi. The creative menu changes frequently and is constrained to no barriers other than the chef's imagination. There are two small traditional stube dining rooms, the Stüberl being for non-smokers. Summer terrace.

KITZECK Kirchenwirt €€

Steinriegel 52, 8442 ***Tel*** *(03456) 22 25* ***Road map*** *F5*

Evocative old cottage-style house set in a historic village in the heart of Styria's wine-growing region. The summer terrace, with views of the church tower and vineyards, is said to be the highest in Europe. Two non-smoking, old-fashioned stube dining rooms. Menu features local Styrian organic lamb, poultry, beef and fish. Closed Sun–Tue; Dec–Mar.

KNITTELFELD Forellenhof Gursch €€

Flatschach 6, 8720 ***Tel*** *(03577) 22 0 10* ***Road map*** *E4*

The name Forellenhof promises that this is the place for trout. Indeed, fresh trout do come from the private lake just outside. But Styrian beef, pork and lamb served with fresh vegetables from the garden are equally tempting. Romantic candlelit dinners in a private room can be booked. Enclosed non-smoking area. Closed Mon.

MURAU Hotel Gasthof Lercher €€

Schwarzenbergstrasse 10, 8850 ***Tel*** *(03532) 24 31* ***Road map*** *E4*

Modernised 18th-century hotel and restaurant in the village centre, within walking distance of the ski slopes. The dining room, mostly populated by hotel guests, is attractively painted in white, with a dark polished wooden floor. The menu favours Styrian beef dishes and Austrian standards. Fresh trout from the local rivers is always on the menu.

RAMSAU/DACHSTEIN Pehab-Kirchenwirt €€

Raumsau 62, 8972 ***Tel*** *(03687) 817 32* ***Road map*** *D4*

Well-equipped, family-run hotel, very popular with skiers in winter. The decor is a modern Austrian farm house style and the menu offers classic Austrian dishes, with attention to fresh ingredients and seasonal offerings. Creative use of herbs and spices in the kitchen, including pumpkin oil and "bear's garlic".

REIN Landgasthof Schaupp €€€

Rein/Tallak 53, 8103 ***Tel*** *(03124) 517 32* ***Road map*** *F4*

A functional modern rectangular building of no particular charm, the Schaupp guest house and restaurant is nonetheless hugely popular with the local population, particularly for its buffets of Italian dishes. Each month there is a culinary theme: asparagus and beef steaks in May, for example. Closed Tue–Wed.

ST SEBASTIAN/MARIAZELL Lurgbauer €€€

Lurg 1, 3224 ***Tel*** *(03882) 37 18* ***Road map*** *F3*

Guest house with a working farm attached, which is known locally for its hearty breakfasts. Aberdeen Angus cows are the pride of the farmyard, and the menu. The small dining room seats only 16 and service is family style. Special culinary weeks are offered with room and board. Reservations required. Closed May–Oct: Mon–Tue; Nov–Apr: Mon–Thu.

TURNAU Wirtshaus Steirereck €€€€

Pogusch 21, 8625 ***Tel*** *(03863) 2000 or 5151* ***Road map*** *F4*

Wirtshaus Steirereck advertises itself as being for "ultra-cool kids, philosophers and people who know their way around a farmyard". Expect an enthusiastic welcome and creative cooking of local specialities, with a good vegetarian menu and fresh fish. The staff all dress in local peasant style. Summer garden and terrace. Closed Mon–Wed.

UPPER AUSTRIA

AIGEN-SCHLAGL Bärnsteinhof €€€

Marktplatz 12, 4160 **Tel** *(07281) 6245* **Road map** *E2*

Family-run spa hotel in the centre of a small village with a country house ambience. The award-winning cuisine ranges from Viennese to farm house in style but also focuses on spa cuisine featuring vegetarian dishes and organic ingredients. Old stone wine cellar with vaulted roof for tastings. Outdoor dining on roof terrace.

ATTERSEE Seegasthof Oberndorfer €€€

Haupstrasse 18, 4864 **Tel** *(07666) 78640* **Road map** *D3*

Popular family hotel on the edge of lake Attersee, with mountain views in the distance. Fresh fish and typical Austrian dishes like *schnitzel* are supplemented by a menu of vegetarian, organic and spa cuisine items. English speaking staff. Large garden as well as wooden deck on the lake for light meals.

ATTNANG-PUCHHEIM Christian's €€€

Gmundner Strasse, 4800 **Tel** *(07674) 646 33* **Road map** *D3*

Off the beaten track in the small village of Attnang-Pucheim, with views of the castle and massive basilica, Christian's Restaurant in the castle market area is winning a growing local reputation for its superbly presented menu of fresh-water fish dishes. Traditional local specialities are also on offer. Friendly English-speaking service. Closed Fri.

BAD GOISERN Landhotel Agathawirt €

St Agatha 10, 4822 **Tel** *(06135) 83 41* **Road map** *D3*

This countryside hotel was built centuries ago, and its dining room has many period features. The cuisine focuses on fresh ingredients and the menu changes often, though traditional regional dishes are always available. Organic lamb prepared in the local manner is a favourite. Summer garden dining under a chestnut tree.

BAD ISCHL Villa Schratt €€€€

Steinbruch 43, 4820 **Tel** *(06132) 235 35* **Road map** *D4*

Once owned by a mistress of the Austrian emperor, this old wooden house with gingerbread-style balconies looks like somewhere Hansel and Gretel might have stopped for lunch. The garden is particularly inviting. The cuisine is hearty, helpings copious, but this is fine cuisine, not *burgher* food. Good wine list. Closed Mon–Wed.

EFERDING Landgasthof Dieplinger €€

Brandstatt 4, 4070 **Tel** *(07272) 23 24* **Road map** *E3*

Countryside inn with pale yellow walls and attractive red tiles, once an ancient fortified house. The landlord farms the surrounding land, described as Austria's prime vegetable growing soil, as well as distilling his own fiery liqueurs. Emphasis on bio-organic lamb, asparagus and local fish from the river Danube. Closed Thu.

GMUNDEN Schloss Freisitz Roith €€€

Traunsteinstrasse 87, 4810 **Tel** *(07612) 649 05* **Road map** *D3*

Historic old castle hotel with sloping grass front on to the lake Traunsee. The castle owner is also the cook, one of the most celebrated in the region. The terrace restaurant, with romantic views, is glassed in during winter (always non-smoking). Freshwater fish is of course a speciality. Good choice of Austrian wines. Closed Jan.

GREIN Zur Traube €€

Greinburgstrasse 6, 4360 **Tel** *(07268) 312* **Road map** *E3*

Very popular local restaurant in the picturesque village of Grein, noted for its medieval buildings with painted façades. The name denotes a toast "to the grape!" and the wine list includes a reasonable choice of Austrian vintages. Charming dining area with antique *Kachelofen* oven. Traditional Austrian cuisine. Reservations advised. Closed Thu; 2nd week Jan.

GRIESKIRCHEN Waldschänke €€€

Kirchdorf 15, 4710 **Tel** *(07248) 623 08* **Road map** *D3*

From the outside Waldschänke looks like a simple, modern era guest house, and inside the decor is neither old fashioned nor elaborate. The menu changes every day: Monday, for example, is *Knödeltag* (noodle day). Wide choice of vegetarian dishes, but wild game when in season as well. Hearty desserts. Closed Mon–Tue.

HALLSTATT Gasthof Zauner-Seewirt €€

Marktplatz 51, 4830 **Tel** *(06134) 82 46* **Road map** *D4*

Don't be surprised if the food is a bit salty. This town boasts the world's oldest salt mine. The trademark *Salzfürstenplatte* includes both savoury boar and fish. The Seewirt dates back to 1893, and fish has always been the main item on the menu. An all-wooden interior, and very attentive service. Closed 5 Nov–3 Dec.

LINZ Stieglbräu Zum Klosterhof €€

Landstrasse 30, 4020 **Tel** *(0732) 77 33 73* **Road map** *E3*

Regional cuisine can be enjoyed in this historic building close to the main shopping street. Seasonal ingredients used include mushrooms, venison and goose. Live music on Fridays and Saturdays. The spacious outdoor area is a popular spot with diners when the weather is fine.

Key to Price Guide *see p318* **Key to Symbols** *see back cover flap*

LINZ Chizuru €€€

Untere Donauländе 21–25, 4020 ***Tel*** *(0732) 77 27 79* ***Road map*** *E3*

An authentic Japanese restaurant in Linz with a real sushi bar, where diners sit close up to the chef slicing and dicing. The interior is somewhat spartan in decor and limited in space; however, in summer there is garden seating for an additional 60 guests. Reservations are advised, as Chizuru is very popular with local residents. Closed Sun.

MONDSEE Seegasthof Lackner €€€€

Mondseestrasse 1, 5310 ***Tel*** *(06232) 23 59* ***Road map*** *D3*

A seaside hotel on the Mondsee with ample outdoor dining areas in summer. The bar has a bistro feel; the lakeside terrace has its own grill for barbeques. There are regular cooking courses for aspiring gourmet chefs. Pies and terrines to take away, as well as wild boar broth, are on sale from the kitchen.

NUSSDORF/ATTERSEE Bräugasthof Aichinger €€

Am Anger 1, 4865 ***Tel*** *(07666) 80 07* ***Road map*** *D3*

A family hotel where many diners are resident guests. The bar keeps the iced wines in an ancient stone baptismal font. Seemingly unchanged for centuries, the stube features carved wooden benches. The formal dining room is open and airy, with a typical *Kachelofen* ceramic oven. Traditional menu. Good choice of local beers. Closed Mon; Jan–Feb.

SCHARDING Stiegenwirt €€

Schlossgasse 2–6, 4780 ***Tel*** *(07712) 30 70* ***Road map*** *D3*

This family-run hotel and restaurant is located on a pretty Baroque square. The menu features regional Austrian cuisine such as veal offal and *Tafelspitz*, and seasonal dishes include duck and venison. Smaller portions are available at reduced prices for those who don't want to over-indulge. Closed Thu.

ST FLORIAN Zur Kanne €€

Marktplatz 7, 4490 ***Tel*** *(07224) 42 88* ***Road map*** *E3*

With a quiet location on a cobbled street, this yellow-coloured, two-storey hotel and restaurant was once a bakery. There are two stube dining areas as well as an artfully modernised vaulted wine cellar. Vegetarian meals are always available. Special menus and festive occasions in the seasons for game, asparagus and local fish.

ST WOLFGANG Im Weissen Rössl €€

Mark 74, 5360 ***Tel*** *(06138) 23 06 0* ***Road map*** *D4*

The "White Horse" is a large lakeside complex where food is just part of the romantic and health-conscious ethos. You can eat almost anywhere: by the swimming pools, on the terrace by the water, on the pavement terrace, in the wine cellar or in one of two restaurants inside. Traditional Austrian cuisine predominates.

ST WOLFGANG Lachsen €€€

Ried 5, 5360 ***Tel*** *(06138) 24 32* ***Road map*** *D4*

The name refers to salmon, and fish is naturally a speciality of this charming inn highly regarded by local residents. Typical Austrian cuisine is served with some flair and the wine list consists of almost exclusively Austrian vintages. Sun terrace and garden shaded by lime trees with views of the lake. Dogs permitted. Open daily until midnight.

STEYR Mader €€€

Stadtplatz 36, 4400 ***Tel*** *(07252) 533 58* ***Road map*** *E3*

Advertising tradition with flair, this historic city centre hotel dates from the 17th century. Among a choice of dining areas, the wine cellar with its huge vaulted stone ceiling is most atmospheric. Outside dining in the flagged courtyard is a summer treat. Traditional gourmet dishes as well as lighter health-conscious menus. Closed Sun, hols.

TRAUNKIRCHEN Das Traunsee €€

Klosterplatz 4, 4801 ***Tel*** *(07617) 22 16* ***Road map*** *D3*

An unrelenting lakeside theme dominates the menu of this upmarket hotel right on the water. The motto is: "Traunsee fish will swim three times – in water, in butter and in wine". Every seat in the restaurant has views of the lake. Outdoor terrace and wooden deck at lake level for snacks. Closed Oct–Apr.

TRAUNKIRCHEN Symposionhotel Post €€

Ortsplatz 5, 4801 ***Tel*** *(07617) 230 70* ***Road map*** *D3*

Traditional old coaching inn on the shores of the Traunsee, in the centre of tranquil Traunkirchen. The restaurant boasts "the absolute peak of classic Austrian cooking". Among regional specialities, the menu encompasses a range of vegetarian dishes and a section covering "spa cuisine". Tour bus groups are welcomed.

WELS Maxlhaid €€

Maxlhaid 9, 4600 ***Tel*** *(07242) 467 160* ***Road map*** *E3*

A most unusual and interesting restaurant, part of a working farm, museum and hotel complex which used to be part of a horse-drawn freight route. Horses are still kept, and the menu offers some traditional dishes from the days of the horse railway. Extensive gardens, playground for kids. Closed weekends.

WEYREGG/ATTERSEE Restaurant Kaisergasthof €€

Weyregger Strasse 75, 4852 ***Tel*** *(07664) 22 02* ***Road map*** *D3*

On the eastern shore of lake Attersee is the Kaisergasthof, once the Imperial Post Station and now a delightful hotel and restaurant. The menu focuses on traditional Alpine and Adriatic cuisine, with particular emphasis on seasonal specialities such as asparagus and game. Closed Mon–Tue; Oct–May.

SALZBURGER LAND

ANIF Schlosswirt zu Anif €€

Salzachtalstrasse 7, 5081 **Tel** *(06246) 721 75.* **Road map** *D4*

A treat for the eyes as well as the taste buds. This 17th-century fortified house in yellow stone takes you back to an unhurried era. The summer garden is shady and green, the dining room is homey, with chintz curtains and flowers, and the food is traditional Salzburger fare, hearty and plenty of it. Closed Sun.

BERGHEIM Gmachl €€€

Dorfstrasse 35, 5101 **Tel** *(0662) 45 21 24* **Road map** *D3*

It started as a butcher's shop, but now the hotel spa complex spreads over acres of park land just outside Salzburg. There are five dining rooms, each with a different menu, as well as an attractive garden for summer dining. Fitness menus feature vegetarian and organic meals, but traditional meat dishes are also available.

BRUCK/GLOCKNERSTRASSE Zacherlbräu €€€

Glocknerstrasse 14, 5671 **Tel** *(06545) 72 42* **Road map** *D3*

Locally renowned for its home-made cheeses and schnapps, this historic inn by the village church also offers visiting diners a spot of fly fishing on the river. Carrying on the self-sufficiency theme, all vegetables and salads come from the kitchen garden. Two dining rooms, all in wood, a beer cellar and a garden for summer dining.

EUGENDORF BEI SALZBURG Don Carlos €

Schamingstrasse 17 (Golfplatz), 5301 **Tel** *(06225) 871 11* **Road map** *D3*

A taste of Italy in Salzburgerland. A popular spot for the young sporty set. In addition to pizzas and other Italian fare, there is a good selection of traditional Austrian dishes, served with flair and enthusiasm. A large awning-covered terrace sits right on the golf course. Open daily until 9:30pm. Closed Nov–Mar.

FILZMOOS Hubertus (Geniesserhotel) €€€€€

Am Dorfplatz 1, 5532 **Tel** *(06453) 82 04* **Road map** *D4*

Advertised as a haunt of epicures, this elegant guest house also offers visiting diners the chance to do some fly fishing on the local river. Fixed price gourmet menus as well as a choice of individual dishes. Fresh trout and game according to season. Creative cuisine. Cooking courses available. Closed Mon–Tue.

FUSCHL AM SEE Brunnwirt €€

Wolfgangseestrasse 11, 5330 **Tel** *(06226) 82 36* **Road map** *D3*

Picture postcard 15th-century farm house in pink stone in an idyllic setting of woods and lake. Salzburg and Austrian cuisine is served. The summer garden has tables by the lake and the charming dining room has a *Kachelofen* ceramic oven. Separate banquet area. Cakes not to be missed. Non-smoking section. Dogs permitted. Reservations advised.

FUSCHL AM SEE Schlick €€

Seestrasse 12, 5330 **Tel** *(06226) 82 37* **Road map** *D3*

Romantic setting in a small village on the shores of lake Fuschl. The dining room has views out over the lake, as does the large summer garden with kiosk serving snacks and tables under awnings for evening meals. Austrian and Salzburg dishes dominate the menu, with good freshwater fish always available. Reservations advised. Closed Nov.

FUSCHL AM SEE Ebner's Waldhof Wellnesshotel €€€

Seestrasse 30, 5330 **Tel** *(06226) 82 64* **Road map** *D3*

A large complex of buildings in pastoral countryside right on the edge of lake Fuschl. Wide choice of dining areas, including by the swimming pool or in the gardens. Separate Waldhofalm chalet-style restaurant on the golf course. Highly rated Gütl Gourmet Restaurant serving Austrian traditional fare. Most diners are hotel guests.

GOLDEGG/SEE Hecht €€€

Hofmark 8, 5622 **Tel** *(06415) 81370* **Road map** *D4*

Good cooking, rated at 15 GaultMillau points, at this hotel restaurant in the ski and summer resort of Goldegg. Modern guest house built in old farm house style with considerable charm and cosiness. Traditional dishes are served with excellent presentation. Intimate dining room with tiled *Kachelofen* stove. Large summer garden.

GOLDEGG/SEE Zum Bierführer €€€

Hofmark 19, 5622 **Tel** *(06415) 81 02* **Road map** *D4*

Goldegg am See is a charming village, set on a sunny plateau with its own small lake. The Bierführer is a modern family-run hotel with a high reputation for good bourgeois home-cooking. Regional dishes and Austrian traditional favourites dominate the menu. Good value. Small dining room decorated with antiques. Closed Mon; Nov.

GOLLING AN DER SALZACH Bürgerstube Döllerer €€€€€

Markt 56, 5440 **Tel** *(06244) 422 00* **Road map** *D4*

The Bürgerstube is a gourmet restaurant which has won a Michelin star for its creative and inspired cooking. Favourites include Pinzgau game and lamb, Attersee ox, trout and char from the Blutnau Valley. Extensive collection of international wines. Closed Sun–Mon.

Key to Price Guide *see p318* **Key to Symbols** *see back cover flap*

HALLEIN/TAXACH Hohlwegwirt €€€€
Salzburger Strasse 84a, 5400 ***Tel*** *(06245) 824 15* ***Road map*** *D4*

A small but exquisitely furnished guest house where the landlord is passionate about his cooking. With an enviable local reputation, the restaurant is generally packed with Salzburger residents. Pasta and terrine, both made using local freshwater fish, are superb. Theme menus according to season. Enclosed non-smoking area. Closed Mon.

HALLWANG / SALZBURG Zum Pfefferschiff zu Söllheim €€€€€
Söllheim 3, 5300 ***Tel*** *(0662) 66 12 42* ***Road map*** *D3*

One of Austria's most celebrated restaurants, the "Pepper Ship" offers Austrian and international cuisine served in an elegant drawing room-style dining room with antique ceramic *Kachelofen* oven and polished wood floors. In summer the garden, with tables under umbrellas and leafy chestnut trees, is superb. Reservations required. Closed Sun–Mon.

KAPRUN Zur Mühle €€
Nicolaus Gassnerstrasse 38, 5710 ***Tel*** *(06547) 8254-0* ***Road map*** *D4*

The restaurant of the hotel and summer camping grounds of the hotel Mühle has a typical wooden farm house decor in the dining area, with a *Kachelofen* ceramic oven. The menu consists of standard Austrian and regional dishes, mostly meat and noodles. Children's menu and playground. Reservations for non-guests advised.

MAISHOFEN Schloss Kammer €€
Kammererstrasse 22, 5751 ***Tel*** *(06542) 682 02* ***Road map*** *D4*

Relaxed dining in a historic castle, or in the old horse stables, which serve as a banqueting hall. In addition to the castle, there are also guest rooms in a nearby wooden house of great charm. A working farm, the castle features its own beef on the menu. There is also a shooting range available to visiting diners. Closed Nov.

MITTERSILL Meilinger Taverne €€
Stadtplatz 10, 5730 ***Tel*** *(06562) 42 26* ***Road map*** *C4*

This looming three-storey red building with white trim is impossible to miss. Dating back to the early 18th century, the Meilinger Taverne is a lively meeting place for local people, thanks to its emphasis on typically Austrian dishes, friendly service and reasonable prices. Small outside dining area on pavement in summer.

SALZBURG Die Gersberg Alm €€
Gersberg 37, 5020 ***Tel*** *(0662) 64 12 57* ***Road map*** *D3*

Just outside Salzburg in an extensive park on a hill. The menu features organic beef, fresh fish and a wide range of mouth-watering pastries. Mostly Austrian wines, with many local schnapps. One of the most enticing garden areas in which to eat in the Salzburg region: leafy and spacious and with a fountain. Open daily until midnight.

SALZBURG Stieglbräu €€
Rainerstrasse 14, 5020 ***Tel*** *(0662) 87 76 94* ***Road map*** *D3*

Restaurant, beer garden and bar in a Best Western hotel within walking distance of the train station and most tourist attractions in downtown Salzburg. Typical hotel menu of international dishes and standard Austrian specialities. The bar is a popular meeting place. The beer garden is lively in summer and attracts many local citizens.

SALZBURG Alt Salzburg €€€
Bürgerspitalgasse 2, 5020 ***Tel*** *(0662) 84 14 76* ***Road map*** *D3*

In the historical centre of Salzburg, a popular and lively restaurant with a high reputation for good food at a reasonable price. Three dining areas, including one carved out of solid rock at the rear. The menu concentrates on standard Austrian and Salzburg favourites. No menus in English, but waiters are happy to translate. Closed Sun.

SALZBURG Hölle €€€
Dr Adolf-Altmann Strasse 2, 5020 ***Tel*** *(0662) 82 07 60 0* ***Road map*** *D3*

Popular and attractive city hotel, part of the Austrian Classic Hotels association. Three dining areas, all of character and featuring rich old wood. Mostly Austrian cuisine, with special theme menus featuring free-range duck and geese, for example. Large garden for 150 guests, also open in winter. Dogs permitted. Open daily until midnight.

SALZBURG Hotel Sacher Salzburg €€€€
Schwarzstrasse 5–7, 5020 ***Tel*** *(0662) 88 97 70* ***Road map*** *D3*

The Hotel Sacher is no place to contemplate starting a diet. Home of the famous chocolate cake of the same name, the hotel emphasizes that nothing you eat elsewhere can compare. The recipe remains a secret since it was created in 1832. Among three restaurants, one a grill and one for local specialities, is the opulent gourmet room, the Zirbelzimmer.

ST JOHANN IM PONGAU Oberforst Alm €€
Alpendorf 12, 5600 ***Tel*** *(06412) 63 96* ***Road map*** *D4*

A large modern chalet-style building set in the woods in the hills. Several large dining areas including a huge sun terrace. Separate downstairs area with toys for children. Austrian cuisine, with regional Pongau dishes and special theme weeks featuring game, for example. Evenings can become very lively, with dancing and folklore music.

ZELL AM SEE Zum Hirschen €€€
Dreifaltigkeitsgasse 1, 5700 ***Tel*** *(06542) 774 0* ***Road map*** *D4*

A smart, modern hotel restaurant in the centre of the ski and summer resort of Zell. Parquet floors, an old *Kachelofen* ceramic oven and carved wooden tables and chairs make for a genuine farm house feel. Service by English-speaking staff is very friendly. Typical Austrian and international fare. Good wines. Closed Apr–May; Oct–Dec.

TYROL AND VORARLBERG

BEZAU Gams €€€

Platz 44, 6870 **Tel** *(05514) 22 20* **Road map** *A4*

Creative and light cooking is the theme, as befits this luxury spa resort. The Romantik dining room echoes an elegant French villa. The Wirthaus is a cube of ancient polished wood, serving regional pub fare, while the small 20-seat Gourmet Restaurant serves more exotic, and more expensive delights. Superb wine list.

BEZAU Post €€€

Brugg 35, 6870 **Tel** *(05514) 22 07* **Road map** *A4*

Part of an international chain of 13 luxury spa resorts, the Post is an indulgence of all the senses, not least culinary. The restaurant merits 16 GaultMillau points. Mushrooms from the nearby Bregenz forest and cheeses from neighbouring farms are some of the natural products used in a cuisine which is constantly innovative.

BRAZ/BLUDENZ Rössle €€€

Arlbergstrasse 67, 6751 **Tel** *(05552) 28 10 50* **Road map** *A4*

A charming old-fashioned village centre guest house with window boxes overflowing with flowers in summer. The low-ceilinged dining room features parquet floor and walls panelled in carved wood. Prices are moderate, but the presentation of regional specialities shows immense attention to detail. Dogs permitted. Closed Mon.

BRAZ/BLUDENZ Traube €€€€

Klostertaler Strasse 12, 6751 **Tel** *(05552) 281 03-0* **Road map** *A4*

An award-winning village centre old-fashioned, family-run guest house. Three typical stube dining rooms, all in old wood. The Jägerstube has a vaulted wooden ceiling with deer antler decorations. The Bienstube has old, unfinished pine walls and ceiling. The menu features regional dishes and standard international fare. Open daily until midnight.

BREGENZ Gebhardsberg €€€

Gebhardsberg 1, 6900 **Tel** *(05574) 42 515* **Road map** *A4*

Commanding the heights overlooking Bregenz, this castle restaurant claims culinary ties with Italy dating back to the 17th century. The menu features beef from the Vorarlberg, fish from Lake Constance and local suckling pig. Summer dining outdoors under the ancient trees. Very popular with local residents. Reservations advised. Closed Mon (Oct–Apr).

BREGENZ Deuring-Schlössle €€€€€

Ehre-Guta-Platz 4, 6900 **Tel** *(05574) 478 00* **Road map** *A4*

Gourmet dining in a gorgeous castle; in autumn the walls are covered with red ivy. Summer gourmet festivals in the castle garden. Casual meals are served in the lounge, in front of the fireplace. The creative bio-cuisine emphasizing natural ingredients is widely praised in the local press. Cooking classes available. Closed Sun.

DORNBIRN Hirschen €€€

Haselstauderstrasse 31, 6850 **Tel** *(05572) 26 363* **Road map** *A4*

Characterful old guest house in the centre of a small village, with contemporary furnishings inside, the bar being particularly minimalist. Small garden dining area with umbrellas. Good presentation, and good value meals with a choice of local dishes as well as vegetarian and health-conscious organic fare. Special menus for children. Closed Sun; 25 Dec.

DORNBIRN Rickatschwende €€€

Bödelestrasse, 6850 **Tel** *(05572) 253 50-0* **Road map** *A4*

Large, somewhat institutional looking, hotel and spa in the woods above the lake. The Schwende Stüble restaurant terrace has superb views over the lake and countryside and features an open fireplace. The cuisine is standard international fare, focusing on light and healthy ingredients. Many diners are hotel guests. Closed Mon.

EBBS Gourmetrestaurant Unterwirt €€

Wildbichlerstrasse 38, 6341 **Tel** *(05373) 42 288* **Road map** *C4*

Lovingly restored 15th-century inn with vaulted ceilings and period furnishings in a small village just off the main A93 highway. The Gourmetrestaurant offers inexpensive regional dishes as well as international cuisine. Choice of exquisitely panelled dining rooms. Leafy garden dining area with children's playground. Closed Tue; mid-Nov–mid-Dec.

EICHENBERG Schönblick €€€€

Dorf 6, 6941 **Tel** *(05574) 459 65* **Road map** *E4*

High on a verdant alpine pasture, with the lake in the near distance, the Schönblick lives up to its name, "lovely views". The restaurant aims to offer good value, especially for families, with its varied menu. Wine and cheese tastings in the brick vaulted wine cellar are available. Closed Mon.

ELLMAU Der Bär €€€

Kirchbichl 9, 6452 **Tel** *(05358) 23 95* **Road map** *C4*

Cocktails as well as an extensive wine list provide ample liquid refreshment in the bar with its lush red leather banquettes. Healthy and fresh ingredients are the theme in the strictly non-smoking dining room. Presentation of the minimalist-inspired gourmet dishes is excellent.

Key to Price Guide *see p318* **Key to Symbols** *see back cover flap*

ELLMAU Kaiserhof €€€

Harmstätt 8, 6452 ***Tel*** *(05358) 20 22* ***Road map*** *C4*

Sprawling modern spa hotel in open countryside with stunning mountain views. The dining rooms all overwhelm with old-fashioned Austrian charm, including carved ceilings and ancient ceramic ovens. The Kaiser Bar is spacious and elegant. Award-winning cuisine, based on fresh regional produce, organic whenever possible. Closed Sun–Tue.

FELDKIRCH Alpenrose €€

Rosengasse 4, 6680 ***Tel*** *(05522) 721 75* ***Road map*** *A4*

Much praised for retaining the charm of a 16th-century merchant's house, this pale pink city hotel in the old town offers a number of dining areas, not least outside under wide umbrellas. Tables are generously spaced apart from each other in the salon-style main dining room. Wildfowl and game are recommended. Closed Sun.

HIPPACH Sieghard €€

Johann Sponring/strasse 83, 6283 ***Tel*** *(05282) 33 09* ***Road map*** *C4*

Attractive village centre hotel in the Zillertal area, which with its turret looks a bit like a wedding cake. Cuisine with a long-standing local reputation, based on local fresh ingredients and changing often with seasonal offerings. In-house cooking courses are offered. The chocolate mousse is highly recommended. Open daily until 9:30pm.

INNSBRUCK Kapeller €€

Philippine-Welser-Strasse 96, 6020 ***Tel*** *(0512) 34 31 06* ***Road map*** *B4*

Tastefully appointed and recently modernised historic guest house in the centre of Innsbruck. The Dorfstube offers intimacy and Tyrolean traditional dishes. The Nickolaustube is a masterpiece of carved wood. Most attractive is the small dining terrace, partly covered in glass, in an interior courtyard with views of the old town. Closed Sun & hols.

INNSBRUCK Koreth €€

Hauptplatz 1, 6020 ***Tel*** *(0512) 26 34 59* ***Road map*** *B4*

An architectural as well as culinary delight, this white-painted, four-storey guest house in the Mühlau area dates from 1449. Lovingly preserved wood panelling and period furnishings create an atmosphere evocative of the past. But the cooking is very contemporary, being health-conscious and guided by seasonal ingredients. Closed Sun–Mon; Jan.

INNSBRUCK Schwarzer Adler €€

Kaiserjägerstrasse 2, 6020 ***Tel*** *(0512) 58 71 09* ***Road map*** *B4*

Restaurant of the "Romantik Hotel", which also claims to be the perfect business hotel. The rooftop terrace restaurant, with enchanting views over Innsbruck, is certainly romantic, though reserved only for hotel guests. Indoors, the narrow Adler Stube is the oldest dining room. The cuisine is health-conscious and elegantly presented.

INNSBRUCK Goldener Adler €€€

Herzog-Friedrich-Strasse 6, 6020 ***Tel*** *(0512) 57 11 11* ***Road map*** *B4*

Restaurant of the Best Western Hotel Goldener Adler, centrally located and one of the oldest inns in Europe, dating from 1390. Mozart is said to have eaten here. Five dining areas, including intimate and cosy stube rooms. Outdoor dining on the pavement outside the hotel. Open daily until midnight, but kitchen closes at 10:30pm.

ISCHGL Trofana Royal €€€

Haus Nr 334, 6561 ***Tel*** *(05444) 600* ***Road map*** *A5*

A large five-storey spa hotel in the centre of Austria's most lively ski resort. The restaurant features period panelled walls and an old ceramic *Kachelofen* oven and has been awarded an impressive 18 points by GaultMillau and one star by Michelin. A visit to the brick vaulted wine cellar is a must. Cooking courses on request.

KELCHSAU Fuchswirt €€€

Oberdorf 11, 6361 ***Tel*** *(05335) 40 111* ***Road map*** *C4*

A traditional three-storey, chalet-style guest house in the centre of Kelchsau, yet with cows grazing just outside. Families and children are welcome: special menus and a playground for kids. Large summer garden dining area. Tyrolean dishes as well as standard international fare. Loyal clientele, especially skiers. Closed Tue.

KITZBUHEL Tennerhof €€€€€

Griesenauweg 26, 6370 ***Tel*** *(05356) 631 81* ***Road map*** *C4*

Gourmet cuisine, with one Michelin star and 17 GaultMillau points, in the luxurious Relais et Châteaux Hotel Tennerhof. Unquestionably one of the best restaurants in Austria. Produce, in summer, comes from gardens behind the hotel, the meat from bio-organic farms nearby. Dining terrace with mountain views.

LANDECK Schrofenstein €€

Malserstrasse 31, 6500 ***Tel*** *(05442) 623 95* ***Road map*** *B4*

Historic hotel with lavish reception rooms, including period furniture and huge oil paintings. Wide-ranging menu including Tyrolean dishes such as garlic cream soup as well as Asian-influenced items such as black tiger prawns with sesame-parmesan chips. Garden dining in summer. Live accordion music. Open daily until midnight.

LECH Hotel-Gasthof Post €€€€€

Dorf 11, 6764 ***Tel*** *(05583) 22 06 0* ***Road map*** *A4*

Traditional guest house in Austria's most chic and sophisticated ski resort with exceptional service and cuisine. A Relais et Châteaux hotel, the restaurant has been awarded by both Michelin and GaultMillau for the traditional Austrian menu, not least the *Kalbs Beuscherl* (a veal offal dish). Four dining rooms and large garden under the trees.

SEEFELD Habhof €€€

Brochweg 1, 6100 ***Tel*** *(05212) 47 11* ***Road map*** *B4*

Award-winning restaurant of the aptly named Gourmethotel Habhof. Emphasis is on Tyrolean dishes and fresh local ingredients. Large Panorama Terrace with superb valley and mountain views, but open only at lunchtime to diners who are not hotel guests. Be sure to leave room for the mouth-watering home-made strudels and cakes. Closed Tue.

ST CHRISTOPH AM ARLBERG Hospiz Alm €€€

Arlberg 1, 6580 ***Tel*** *(05446) 26 11* ***Road map*** *A4*

At 1,800 m (5,900 ft), this is one of the most celebrated restaurants in the Alps and arguably the oldest mountain restaurant in the world. Favourite haunt of skiers from Lech and St Anton in winter. Large sun terrace in summer and winter. Huge wine cellar. Evocative ambience rivalled only by the impeccable cuisine. Reservations essential.

STUMM/ZILLERTAL Landgasthof Linde €€

Dorf 2, 6272 ***Tel*** *(05283) 22 77-0* ***Road map*** *C4*

A pastoral idyll, this 16th-century guest house with red and white shutters is set in a tiny village next to the church and castle with woodlands and pastures all around. An exceptional feature is the garden dining area with a gingerbread-style summer house. Extensive list of Austrian wines, including Styrian classics. Closed Mon–Tue; Jun; 15 Nov–10 Dec.

VOLDERS/WATTENS Ross-Stall-Taverne €€€

Bundesstrasse 5, 6111 ***Tel*** *(05224) 552 60* ***Road map*** *B4*

Awarded 13 GaultMillau points, this modest tavern is a haven of old-time charm and creative cuisine. Mixing dishes from both the Tyrol and Carinthia, the menu invites diners to linger and to experiment. Emphasis is on local production and season ingredients. Special menus for children. Dogs permitted. Closed Sun–Tue.

CARINTHIA AND EAST TYROL

BAD BLEIBERG OB VILLACH Der Bleibergerhof €€€€

Drei Lärchen 150, 9530 ***Tel*** *(04244) 22 05* ***Road map*** *D5*

Exceptional setting in Austria's most southerly alpine valley. Part of a luxury spa and golf hotel complex. The emphasis of the menu is on bio-natural foods, especially vegetarian and regional fruits and berries. More hearty Carinthian meat dishes are also available. Dogs allowed in the dining area. Kitchen closes early, at 8:30pm.

DROBOLLACH Schönruh €€

Seeblickstrasse 40, 9580 ***Tel*** *(04254) 21 92* ***Road map*** *E5*

A modern family holiday hotel built in traditional style on the edge of the Faaker See and set in rolling countryside. The restaurant is mainly geared towards hotel guests. The menu is typical of the region, with standard Austrian and international dishes, including local fish. Open daily until 9:30pm. Closed Jan–Feb.

DROBOLLACH/FAAKER SEE Seehotel Ressmann €€

Strandbadstrasse 69, 9580 ***Tel*** *(04254) 22 10* ***Road map*** *E5*

A modern hotel and restaurant on the shores of the Faaker See. The hotel offers a weekly package with half-board, gala dinner and excursions to local vinters for wine-tastings. The menu features contemporary regional cuisine prepared from local produce and there is a cheese buffet three times a week. Closed Nov–Mar.

FELD AM SEE Landhotel Lindenhof (Vinum) €€

Kirchenplatz 2, 9544 ***Tel*** *(04246) 22 74* ***Road map*** *D5*

Upmarket lakeside hotel and spa, much frequented by touring cyclists. An eclectic mix of Carinthian and Mediterranean cuisine, with emphasis on light and wholesome ingredients. Rated by both GaultMillau and Michelin restaurant guides. Renowned for its wine collection. Enclosed non-smoking section. Closed Mon.

FERLACH Antonitsch Glainach €

Glainach 12, 9170 ***Tel*** *(04227) 22 26* ***Road map*** *E5*

Advertised as a real old-fashioned Carinthian guest house, the inn is actually a modern structure encompassing traditional architectural features. The modest prices and warm welcome are indeed old-fashioned as are the regional dishes. Very popular with local diners. Outdoor dining in fine weather for 60 people. Closed Mon–Tue.

HERMAGOR Bärenwirt €€

Hauptplatz 17, 9620 ***Tel*** *(04282) 20 52* ***Road map*** *E5*

The motto of this characterful city guest house in the centre of the old town is "from the region, for the region". Fresh vegetables from the garden and seasonal changes to the menu do not displace the ever-present Carinthian noodles, however. Loyal local clientele. Cosy wooden interior. Open daily until midnight.

KLAGENFURT Felsenkeller €€

Felkirchner Strasse 141, 9020 ***Tel*** *(0463) 420130* ***Road map*** *E5*

Advertised as a major attraction on the *biercult* (beer cult) circuit, this cosy guest house has a surprising collection of wines and liqueurs (among the latter is a cherry port). Along with Austrian wines are many from the New World. The menu is bistro-like, with Carinthian noodles and meat dishes predominating. Open daily until midnight.

KLAGENFURT St Petersburg €€

Waagplatz 3, 9020 ***Tel*** *(0463) 59 12 18* ***Road map*** *E5*

As the name suggests, an unusual taste of Russian cuisine is mixed here with traditional Carinthian fare, making for hearty meals washed down with a good selection of local wines – and vodkas imported directly from Russia. Menus are in German but English-speaking staff are available to translate. Closed Sun.

KOTTMANNSDORF Plöschenberg €€

Ploschenberg 4, 9071 ***Tel*** *(04220) 22 40* ***Road map*** *E5*

A large yellow hillside guest house in a tranquil setting with mountain views. Good cuisine at moderate prices, aiming at the family market. The large garden dining area has a playground with swings and toys for children. Most of the meat served comes from the inn's own farm. Excellent presentation. Closed Mon–Tue; Jan.

KRUMPENDORF Hudelist €€€

Wieningerallee 12, 9201 ***Tel*** *(04229) 2681* ***Road map*** *E5*

Set in the vicinity of lake Wörther See in a quiet garden, yet near the village centre, this attractive family inn has an enviable local reputation for fine cuisine. The wide-ranging menu incorporates local Carinthian dishes as well as Italian and, most surprisingly, Finnish specialities. Children's menus and playground area. Dogs permitted. Large garden.

LIENZ Parkhotel Tristachersee €€€€

Tristachersee 1, 9900 ***Tel*** *(04852) 676 66* ***Road map*** *D5*

Unimpeachable setting in the woods and on the edge of lake Tristachersee. Tranquillity and romance are enhanced by a ban on tour buses. Freshwater fish, including Zander (pike-perch), pike, catfish, carp, trout and char, are part of an extensive menu that includes Italian as well as Austrian dishes. Large outdoor terrace. Open daily until 10pm.

MATREI Rauter €€€€

Rauterplatz 3, 9971 ***Tel*** *(04875) 66 11* ***Road map*** *C5*

Highly recommended cuisine in a modern family-run luxury hotel set in scenic surroundings, with the unusual possibility of fly fishing for your own dinner. Choice of two dining rooms: the elegant Herr'n Zimmer with an international menu or the rustic Rauterstube with more traditional Tyrolean dishes. Reservations required. Open daily until 10pm.

MILLSTATT Hotel See-Villa €€€

Seestrasse 68, 9872 ***Tel*** *(04766) 21 02* ***Road map*** *D5*

A fairytale pale yellow turreted fortified house right on the water, the See-Villa demands a visit. The lakeside garden is perfect for afternoon strudel and coffee. The evening buffets are sumptuous, with a variety of freshwater fish. But overall the cooking is described as *burgher*-like, the way the Carinthians like it. Closed Oct–Apr.

PORTSCHACH Leon in Schloss Leonstain €€€

Pörtschach, 9210 ***Tel*** *(04272) 28 16-81* ***Road map*** *E5*

Dating from 1492, the Castle Leonstain enchants with its storybook setting. Brahms was inspired to write both a concerto and a symphony here, though it is not known if he ate in the restaurant. The menu is international, with some Asian influences. Large enclosed patio for outdoor dining. Smoking permitted after 10pm. Closed Oct–May.

PORTSCHACH Schloss Seefels €€€€

Töschling 1, 9210 ***Tel*** *(04272) 23 77* ***Road map*** *E5*

Choice of four dining areas and menus in this lavish Relais et Châteaux period hotel on the Austrian Riviera shores of the Wörther See. La Terrasse Restaurant has both inside and outdoor tables looking over the lake. The Porto Bello is outside on a deck lakeshore. The Orangerie is the main gourmet restaurant. And the Schlossbar is for snacks.

RADENTHEIN Die Gartenrast €€

Gartenraststrassse 9, 9545 ***Tel*** *(04246) 20 17* ***Road map*** *D5*

A turn-of-the-century farm house inn, with charming interiors in painted wood and a genuine feel of hospitality. Chicken is advertised as being the best in the region. The owner is also a connoisseur of fine cigars and single malt whiskies. Summer garden. Non-smoking rooms. Pets and children welcome.

SPITTAL/DRAU Edlingerwirt €€

Villacher Strasse 88, 9800 ***Tel*** *(04762) 51 50* ***Road map*** *D5*

Regional cooking and a largely local clientele. Strict adherence to using only local products. Menus are only in German but English-speaking staff are generally on hand to translate. Relaxed atmosphere, so not for tourists looking for a quick meal. Small garden for 24 guests. Enclosed non-smoking area. Closed Sun.

STRASSBURG Das Herrenhaus €

Am Hauptplatz 3, 9341 ***Tel*** *(04266) 22 51* ***Road map*** *E5*

Picture postcard townhouse in pedestrian zone in the village centre with large open courtyard. There are a number of dining areas in the hotel. The menu infuses traditional regional dishes, all prepared from local ingredients, with "a breath from our southern neighbour, Italy". Popular with locals and tourists alike. Closed Mon.

VELDEN Sternard's Restaurant Pavillon €€€

Seecorso 8, 9220 ***Tel*** *(04274) 511 09* ***Road map*** *E5*

Chef Stefan Sternard has created a name for himself with his unpretentious style of cooking, which concentrates on regional products and seasonal dishes. The menu features Carinthian salmon and char, asparagus with wild garlic and lamb with mushrooms as well as game and goose. Closed Jan–Mar; Oct–Mar: Tue–Wed.

SHOPPING IN AUSTRIA

Until quite recently, shops in Austria kept to strict opening and even stricter closing hours. Around lunchtime or after 6 pm for example, no self-respecting Austrian would dream of doing any shopping, even in Vienna. The *Wochenende* (weekend) was even more sacrosanct – at many shops it started on Friday evening. Today though, opening hours have become liberalized, and now it is much more common for shops to stay open at lunchtime and for longer in the evenings.

Bust of Emperor Franz Joseph I

Markets, ranging from international fairs to street and flea markets, are widely popular with visitors, and there is an excellent range of goods to buy. Check out traditional crafts and clothes, speciality foods and drinks, as well as exquisite ceramics and glassware.

OPENING HOURS

Shops usually open at 8:30 or 9am and close at 6pm or later. Supermarkets open from 8am to 7pm, and until 5pm on Saturdays. The Mercur and Billa supermarkets are open late on Fridays, until 7:30pm, and Billa branches at Vienna's Nordbahnhof railway station and at the airport open seven days a week.

Smaller shops still close at lunchtime for an hour or so. In provincial towns opening hours may vary from those in Vienna and be more suited to the local needs.

MARKETS AND FAIRS

Markets and fairs are a firm part of tradition in Austria. The country hosts many international fairs, where anything from household items and construction machinery to modern jewellery or Austrian folk art, wines and spirits are exhibited.

Shop window, displaying typical souvenirs in Innsbruck

For holiday-makers there are countless charming street markets, which are often held in the main square of small villages. On Friday and Saturday mornings, some streets close to traffic and fill with market stalls offering produce straight from the farm, including fruit, vegetables, flowers, meat products and freshly baked goods. The market is often surrounded by historic buildings, allowing you to combine shopping and sightseeing.

The Naschmarkt near Karlsplatz in Vienna is the biggest street market in Austria, and besides food and clothes, there is also a flea market on Saturdays. The dates and venues for other flea markets or antiques fairs are published in the daily papers.

Wine shop in a private vineyard in Mörbisch

VAT REFUNDS

Except for citizens of other EU countries, visitors to Austria are entitled to reclaim *Mehrwertsteuer* (abbreviated as MwSt), the equivalent of VAT, on their purchases. The rate is 20% on industrial goods and 10% on food products. You need to tell the vendor that you are buying the goods for export. Larger department stores will be able to provide you with the appropriate form; alternatively, you can get it from customs. Fill in the form and present it together with the receipt when you leave Austria. You may be asked to show the goods, which must still be in their original packaging, unopened and unused. If the money is not refunded at the border, you can apply for it by writing to Global Refund Austria, A-1030 Vienna, Trubelgasse 19 (tel 01–79 84 4 00, fax 79 840-44) and have it sent by post or transferred to your bank account.

A typical market selling a wide range of goods in Deutschlandsberg

END-OF-SEASON SALES

Twice a year, the shopping scene is enlivened by seasonal price reductions; the *Winterschlussverkauf* (winter sales) start in the last week of January, and the *Sommerschlussverkauf* (summer sales) at the end of July. This is a good time to buy clothes, sports equipment and shoes. Look for much reduced skis, an anorak or a warm coat; or you could find a lovely dress or a lightweight suit at half its original price or less. Occasionally a shop will sell all its stock at the same price in order to make room for new collections.

Different rules apply to electronic goods, for which price reductions are governed by supply and demand. Large department stores tend to reduce some prices in late autumn, particularly on electrical goods, but this depends on individual establishments.

There is no fixed season for food price reductions, which may occur at any time. If you are looking for a bargain, keep an eye out for the promotional leaflets issued by most supermarkets.

CERAMICS AND CRYSTAL GLASS

Austria is famous for its beautiful porcelain from the Augarten factory, based in the Viennese park, where Johann Strauss once played his waltzes. The decorations on vases, jugs, boxes and tableware reflect the artistic trends of past centuries, from Baroque through Neo-Classical and Biedermeier right up to the present day. Porcelain goods can be purchased in the shop in Graben or from the factory, which is open to visitors. Also worth buying is the attractive hand-painted pottery from Gmunden, with colourful Biedermeier-style flowers, dots and other ornamentation.

BILLA

Billa supermarket logo

Glassware – including superb chandeliers and delicate tableware – tends to be highly original, although expensive. Many people also collect imaginative crystal ornaments such as dogs and cats made by Swarovski.

CRAFTS AND FOLK ART

Hand-embroidered items, such as tablecloths, are also in great demand. The true works of art in this field are ladies' evening purses, miniature pictures and even jewellery, embroidered in *petit point* with 300 to 2,500 stitches per sq cm (2,000 to 16,000 stitches per sq inch). This work, carried out with the aid of a magnifying glass, is so exhausting that it can be done only for a maximum of three hours a day.

Folk costumes are another popular purchase. They vary in the detail, but the woman's *Dirndl* always consists of a skirt with an apron, a waistcoat and a white, often embroidered blouse, while the man's *Tracht* includes short or calf-length leather trousers and a distinctively cut felt jacket. All this is topped by a jaunty hat adorned with feathers or goats' beard.

ALCOHOLIC DRINKS

Most supermarkets stock a good selection of Austrian wines, but if you head to one of the vineyards you can try before you buy. Visit one of the many vineyards in the Wachau Valley or among the hills of Burgenland, and you can sample the wine, and even buy direct. One of the stronger drinks would also be a good souvenir – try *Weinbrand* (cognac), *Slivovitz* (plum brandy), *Obstler* (fruit brandy) or *Marillenbrand* (apricot liqueur).

SPECIALITY FOODS

The most popular purchases from the food counter are Austrian chocolates in their many guises. You can buy good-quality confectionery at most supermarkets; popular chains include Billa, Merkur, Inter-Spar, Eurospar, Zielpunkt and Hofer, with the latter charging the lowest prices. There are also smaller food stores, especially in the large cities, but these are generally more expensive.

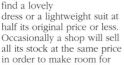

Sweets and confectionery in front of a shop in Salzburg

What to Buy in Austria

Ad for folk fashion shop

The range of souvenirs worth buying in Austria is vast, ranging from the unashamedly kitsch to the exquisite and delicate. The most typical purchases are chocolates and all kinds of alcoholic drinks which are often attractively packaged. Quality purchases include Tyrolean costumes and warm winter coats made of loden as well as attractive porcelain or glassware made in Austria, including the stunning Swarovski crystal chandeliers.

Sissi Figurines
The Austrian people's love for "Sissi", Emperor Franz Joseph's unhappy wife, knows no bounds. It is evident to this day from the many statuettes of the Empress Elisabeth, on sale all over the country.

SOUVENIRS

In a country as reliant on tourism as Austria, the souvenir industry naturally plays an important role, with market stalls, shops and motorway service stations all offering an enormous selection of *Andenken* (souvenirs) designed to help you remember your stay in one of Austria's provinces – and hopefully make you come back for more.

Glass Snowstorms
Glass snowstorms with swirling snowflakes may be considered as kitsch by some, yet they remain very popular with tourists, and children are particularly keen on them. Inside, you can see any number of famous Austrian landmarks such as the Big Wheel in the Prater, a symbol of Vienna.

Wanderhut
The Tyrolean "walker's hat" is popular with mountain walkers. In winter it protects against the cold; in summer it provides shade from the sun, which can be surprisingly fierce in the mountains.

Augarten Figurines
An attractive souvenir from the Augarten porcelain makers are the delicate, hand-finished porcelain figurines of the famous white Lipizzaner stallions and riders from the Spanish Riding School in Vienna.

Bells
In the autumn, the cattle of Tyrol and Vorarlberg are driven down from the Alm, the summer mountain pastures, and the bells around their necks have always fascinated visitors. The bells come in all shapes and sizes, often highly decorated. They make, of course, a great souvenir.

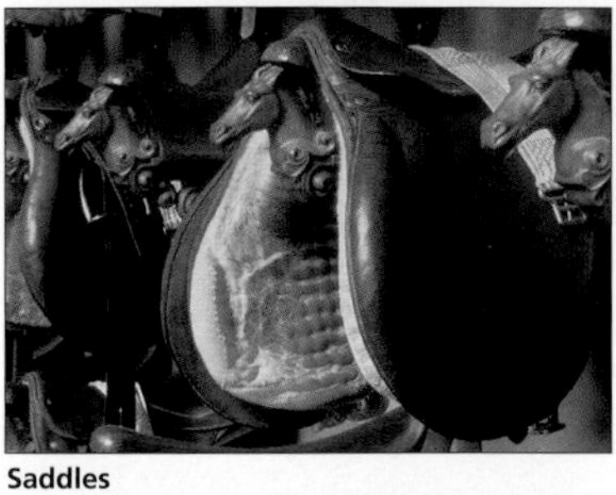

Saddles
One of the more unusual gifts you can find are intricately made miniature horses with tack and saddles, often copies of items seen in the collections of armouries and arsenals.

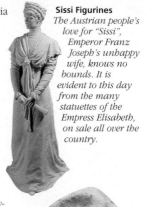

Handicrafts and Folk Art
Austria is deservedly proud of its local crafts traditions. In specialist shops or markets you can find delicate embroidery and lacework or great wood carvings, such as this mask.

CERAMICS

Austria is famous for its traditional and modern ceramics. Whether you choose a fine porcelain figure from Augarten or a hand-painted, ornamental faience from Gmunden, they will add elegance to your home. Many factories also produce less costly items, such as busts of the famous.

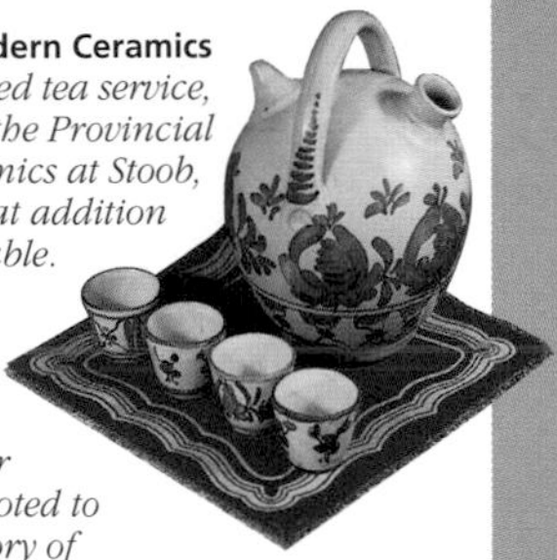

Modern Ceramics
This curiously shaped tea service, produced at the Provincial College for Ceramics at Stoob, would make a great addition to any tea-time table.

Bust of Mozart
Mozart memorabilia such as this bust are sold all over Salzburg, a city devoted to marketing the memory of Wolfgang Amadeus Mozart.

Dinner Service
Attractive ceramic tableware, such as this colourful dinner service from Klagenfurt, would make a welcome present to bring home or a useful and practical addition to your own household collection.

CONFECTIONERY

Austrian confectioners, of whom many were suppliers to the Imperial Court, look back with pride on centuries of tradition. The *Sachertorte* has a particularly distinguished history, but there are numerous other specialities worth bringing back for friends and family – if you can bear to share!

Christmas decorations in a confectionery shop window

Mozartkugeln
This speciality chocolate from Salzburg, produced in various shapes and wrapped in silver foil, always bears the portrait of the famous composer.

Gingerbread
Gingerbread hearts are decorated with a variety of mostly romantic messages and intricate patterns in coloured icing. This one says "Because I love you".

ALCOHOLIC DRINKS

Many Austrian wines have come a long way and are now highly regarded by connoisseurs. The country produces some excellent white dry and dessert wines, as well as the heavier Rieslings. Among the reds, Styrian Schilcher and Blaufränkisch from Burgenland can both compete with Italian and Spanish wines. Austria also produces other alcoholic beverages, including fruit brandies and liqueurs.

Glass tankards, an excellent present for beer lovers

Wine
Specially sealed and bottled at the vineyard where it is produced, a bottle of Austrian wine makes an unusual but welcome present.

Beer
Although they are little known abroad, Austria produces some very fine beers. Try some of the local brands and take home a few bottles – you won't easily find them elsewhere.

ENTERTAINMENT IN AUSTRIA

Witty, fun loving and charming, the Austrians manage to defy pretty much every cliché of what it means to be Germanic. Their sense of *Gemutlichkeit*, or good times, comes alive in the music, festivals, cafés and bars that pulse across the country. *The Sound of Music* may now be one of its most renowned attractions, but you are sure to find more than a few of your favourite things in Austria. From a lederhosen-lined folk dance in an old-world village, to extreme sports on mountain tops, to a classical music concert beneath the stars, it's a variety show of amusements. Against the setting of breathtaking lakes and mountains, an array of entertainment choices await, both formal and informal. Inevitably, excellent regional cuisine, wine and the ubiquitous beer are also part of the experience.

Body-painted street performer

Mozart's opera *Apollo Et Hyacinthus*, performed at the Salzburg Festival

INFORMATION SOURCES

Austria is an information-friendly destination. Each province, city and indeed nearly every village of any size boasts a full-service tourist bureau at the ready for walk-in and online information. Here you can find events calendars and background information on anything and everything taking place in the way of music, theatre, festivals and holiday events. Posters announcing current events from concerts to exhibitions are widely displayed in town squares and café windows. The events listing magazine **Falter** is widely available across the country. For personalized tours, Austria's superb network of professionally accredited English-speaking **tour guides** are highly recommended. Before travelling, be sure to look at **www.austria.info**, the website of the **Austrian National Tourist Office**. It's also worth checking out the event and entertainment listings website **www.whatsonwhen.com**.

BOOKING TICKETS

All the big music festivals offer online booking for seats. Some of them, like the Salzburg Festival, sell out months in advance. It is also possible to buy tickets, sometimes last minute, from ticket agencies.

Money-saving discount cards are available for sightseeing and public transport in all the major cities, including Innsbruck, Linz, Salzburg and Vienna. For a small price, these cards offer significant discounts, or in some cases completely free access to public transport, sightseeing, shopping, dining, and museums. The cards can be purchased upon arrival at your destination, and if you are planning to travel around a lot and take in many of the sights, they can prove to be very economical.

FREE EVENTS

While particular museum and gallery exhibits may charge an entrance fee, access to most churches, markets and galleries in Austria is free of charge, offering a wealth of great architecture, art and history at no cost whatsoever. Attending an organ recital or choir-led mass at one of the country's many Baroque cathedrals is an unforgettable experience. Many churches also offer complimentary guided tours; a small tip for the guide at the end of the tour is customary.

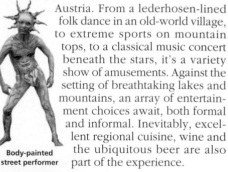

Guided tour of Salzburg Cathedral with its fine Baroque architecture

FACILITIES FOR THE DISABLED

Most large concert halls and theatres have reserved areas for wheelchairs and seats for people with mobility problems. These must be reserved in advance when booking. Many music and theatre venues also provide help for those with hearing difficulties. Be sure to make your needs very clear when booking tickets. Information about disabled access to accommodation, and to public and leisure facilities is provided by **IBTF** (Information for Barrier Free Tourism in Austria). Regional guides, providing advice on disabled access, are available online.

RELIGIOUS CELEBRATIONS

A predominantly Catholic country, Austrian religious celebrations are pageants of colour in which everyone can join in. Starting at the end of November through to Christmas Day, Christmas markets spring up in towns and cities, offering handicrafts, seasonal foods, mulled wine and heaps of atmosphere. In the streets you may see St Niklaus accompanied by a scary devil figure, Krampus, who threatens to beat naughty children. This procession is called Perchtenlauf. Every November Austria's biggest Krampus festival is held in Schladming, Styria.

Fasching is the Austrian version of a carnival, and is a let-loose party that takes place just before Lent with masked balls and socially sanctioned outrageousness. At Easter, real eggs are hand-painted and hung on plants or twigs, called Palmkatzerln. At Palm Sunday processions, children carry tall sticks decorated with streamers and pretzels.

TRADITIONAL MUSIC AND DANCE

When your neighbour lives on the next mountaintop, communicating is a challenge – hence the rise of yodelling as an art form. The melodic throat singing relies on echo and yips and yells, which are impressive performed solo, and mesmerising when sung *en masse*. Traditional folk celebrations often include the Schuhplattler, a gymnastic dance developed by Tirolean men in order to impress young maidens. The Ländler,

Local brass band playing at an Austrian beer festival

an adaptation of which was performed in *The Sound of Music*, is danced by couples amid much stomping and clamping. The Polka and, ever the pride of Vienna, the Waltz, are classic dances performed both professionally and at private celebrations.

THEATRE

Each summer, since 1920, the weaving cobblestone streets of Salzburg swell with the thousands attending the **Salzburg Festival**. No less than 220,000 spectators arrive to enjoy the 170 performances of classical music, opera and drama. The main festival halls are located in prime location in the old town. From Shakespeare and Moliere, to Mozart and Beethoven, the Salzburg Festival represents the *non plus ultra* of high culture in Austria. Booking ahead is imperative, and that includes accommodation.

CASINOS

A dozen casinos across the country, from Bad Gastein to Vienna, offer an assortment of games of chances – from traditional roulette, blackjack and baccara – to modern day Texas Hold 'em. The minimum age for entrance is 18 years. Blackjack, poker, even slot machine tournaments are held regularly. The elegant and atmospheric architecture in **Badgastein** and **Baden** add a distinctly James Bond element to the thrill.

NIGHTLIFE

Austrian nightlife does not start and stop in Vienna by any means. The provincial capitals certainly hold their own in the party department. There is a wide choice of relaxed pubs, trendy bars, discos and nightclubs that stay open till 4am. For world-class clubbing, DJs Kruder & Dorfmeister have put Austrian electronic music on the map. Linz boasts some 80 night spots open until well after midnight; its "Bermuda Triangle" bars stay open until the small hours. University towns like Innsbruck and Graz have a young vibrant feel. In the countryside there is action, especially in summer, at the discos and bars round Austria's lakes. All the best late nights culminate in a snack at a Würstlstand, where the party crowd congregate alongside late-night truck drivers.

Viennese Christmas Market, capturing the essence of Christmas spirit

Beer garden and restaurant by Wolfgang Lake, Wolfgangsee

BEER GARDENS & CAFES

Café culture is its own form of entertainment and the Austrians are rightfully proud of theirs. People watching, reading newspapers mounted on traditional wooden sticks and chatting are the norm – all accompanied by strong coffee and tasty cakes. *Café und Kuchen* hour falls between lunch and dinner, and goes nicely with a visit to the *Heurige* (taverns where young, "early" wine is served).

Drinkers sit comfortably out in the open under trees drinking a glass of wine or a *G'spritzn*, a mixture of wine and soda water. As a point of etiquette, when toasting Austrians always look each other directly in the eyes; those failing to do so risk seven years of bad sex or bad weather – take your pick.

FESTIVALS

From spring to autumn, hundreds of festivals celebrate food, wine and the harvest up and down the country. Austrians are proud of their traditional farming methods, and its resulting quality organic products. At the Festival of 1,000 Wines in Burgenland, winemakers showcase their best wines and local food in the picturesque orangerie of Esterhazy Castle. Winemakers of Lower Austria's **Wine Route** offer local wine, food and culture at various regional wine festivals throughout the summer, with live music, exhibitions, children's programmes and wine tastings. Similarly, a variety of summer festivals are devoted to an assortment of pumpkins, cheeses, hams, chocolate, even a **Dumpling festival** in St Johann am Tirol, where the world's longest dumpling table takes rolly-polly centre stage. One of the most charming of the autumn traditions is the annual **Herding festivals**, where the animals from the high-alpine, where they graze free all summer, are brought down to the village to spend the winter in barns. The animals are paraded through the villages festooned with flowers and bells. In Styria, the famous **Lipizzaner Horse Procession** bring down the horses from their mountain pastures in this way to the delight of onlookers. Not to be outdone by the animals, humans as performance art are the focus of the **European Body Painting Festival** at Millstättersee. Also, Europe's largest **Harley Meeting at Faaker See** attracts its fair share of tattooed bodies as well.

Cattle decorated with flowers and bells, grazing in pasture

SPECTATOR SPORTS

As national interests go, skiing and snow boarding take bronze, silver and gold in the hearts of Austrians. Don't let the possibility that you're not actually taking part stop you from getting in on the excitement. The season kicks off with the ski **World Cup** opening race at Solden in late October, which attracts thousands of enthusiasts. The most famous ski race in the world is held in Kitzbühel each January, the **Hahnenkamm**, a weekend of street parties and music.

Ski contestant at Kitzbühel, the most famous ski race in the world

More than 10,000 people come to the major ski season ending bash at Ischgl for the **Top of the Mountain** concert. In past years, the free April outdoor concert has featured Elton John, Tina Turner, Sting, Lionel Richie, Jon Bon Jovi, Alanis Morisette, Bob Dylan and Enrique Iglesias.

While it definitely plays second fiddle to skiing, football is still a popular sport. As host of UEFA EURO 2008 the cities of Vienna, Klagenfurt, Salzburg and Innsbruck all have welcoming stadiums and the opportunity to watch a professional match should not be missed. The Ernst Happel Stadion in Vienna is home to Austria's national team.

SPAS

Part entertainment, part just what the doctor ordered, spa holidays are more than a mere indulgence, and have the added bonus of being regarded as a necessity to good health. Austria's more than 100 mineral spas have a long tradition of healing all manner of complaints from rheumatism to respiratory illness. **Badgastein**'s water contains Radon, a gas whose powerful properties require that patients produce a doctor's certificate before participating. Others offer full regimes of medical supervision, tailored fitness programmes, and of course the more run of the mill massage and beauty treatments.

Rogner-Bad Blumau Hotel, designed by Friedensreich Hundertwasser

The clean, cool lines of Maria Alm's post-modern **Haller Hotel** is a stylish venue for classic sports massage. In Leogang's **Krallerhof Wellness Hotel** a full menu of cool and warm, wet and dry saunas and pools bubble and simmer.

Many of the most lovely wellness hotels are located in the mountains, like the five-star splendour of the spa at **The Hospiz** in St Christoph.

High-tech, architecturally ambitious waterworlds are sprouting up across the country: the post-modern minimalism of Langenfeld **Aqua Dome**, two thermal slopeside baths at **Römerbad** and **St Kathrein-Therme** in Carinthia and the spectacular **Felsentherme** in the Gastein Valley. The dreamscape of Friedensreich Hundertwasser's **Rogner-Bad Blumau** thermal spa resort is unforgettable.

DIRECTORY

INFORMATION SOURCES

Austrian National Tourist Office
www.austria.info

Falter Magazine
www.falter.at

Tour Guides
www.austriaguides.at
www.whatsonwhen.com
www.viennaticketoffice.com

BOOKING TICKETS

www.oeticket.com
Tel (01) 1 96 0 96.

www.ticketonline.at
Tel (01) 188 0 88.

www.viennaclassic.com
Tel (01) 1 982 13 51.

FACILITIES FOR THE DISABLED

IBTF
www.ibft.at/en/lists/vereine

www.handicap.tirol.at

www.nobatravel.at

www. steiermark.com/fueralle

www.oberoesterreich.at/nohandicap

TRADITIONAL MUSIC AND DANCE

Viennese Balls
www.vienna.info

THEATRE

Salzburg Festival
Tel (0662) 8045 500.
www.salzburgerfestspiele.at

Vienna State Opera
Tel (01) 5144 2250.
www.wiener-staats-oper.at

Volksopera
Tel (01) 1 51444 3670.
www.volksoper.at

CASINOS

Baden Casino
www.casinos.at

Badgastein Casino
www.badgastein.casinos.at

FESTIVALS

Cheese Festival
Tel (04715) 8516.
www.kaese-festival.at

Dumpling Festival
Tel (05352) 633350.
www.knoedelfest.at

Gail Valley Speck Festival
Tel (0463) 3000.
www.speckfest.at
www.kaernten.at

Harley Meeting at Faaker See
www.europeanbikeweek.com

Herding Festivals
www.austria.info

International Milka Giant Chocolate Festival
Tel (05552) 62170.
www.bludenz.at

Lipizzaner Horse Procession
www.austria.info

Wine Route
www.weinstrassen.at

SPECTATOR SPORTS

Hahnenkamm Ski Race
www.kitzbuehel.com

Top of the Mountain Concert
www.ischgl.com

World Cup Ski Opening Solden
www.soelden.com

SPAS

Aqua Dome Spa
Tel (05253) 6400.
www.aqua-dome.at

Badgastein
Tel (06432) 33930.
www.gastein.com

Felsentherme
Tel (06434) 2535.
www.felsentherme.com

Haller Alpine Wellness Hotel
Tel (06584) 2100.
www.hotel-haller.at

Hospiz
Tel (05446) 2611.
www.arlberghospiz.com

Krallerhof Wellness Hotel
Tel (06583) 82460.
www.krallerhof.com

Rogner Bad Blumau
Tel (03383) 51000.
www.blumau.com

Römerbad
Tel (04240) 8282201.
www.roemerbad.com

St Kathrein-Therme
Tel (04240) 8282301.
www.therme-badkleinkirchheim.at

Live Music and Concerts

It's true: the hills are alive with the sound of music. However, there is much more to be enjoyed musically in this tuneful land than the Rogers and Hammerstein song with angel-voiced siblings. Dozens of annual classical music festivals attract the world's premier artists and musicians to stunning venues where the music was often originally performed. Whether in Mozart's Innsbruck or Haydn's Eisenstadt, the settings are as spectacular as the melodies. Also, it is possible to leap out of the cradle of classical music and straight into a leather-lined folk evening, a vibrant electronic music scene or club DJs who are famous across Europe, such as DJ Ötzi. Music programmes vary each year but each of the following summer festivals is an annual extravaganza of sound.

OPERA AND OPERETTA

Though Vienna's reputation for opera is renowned, the rest of the country's operatic contribution is not to be forgotten. There is no better example of a perfect harmony of space and sound than the **Bregenz Festival**. Its dramatic 20 m (66 ft) stage floats atop the dark waters of Lake Constance and past audiences have enjoyed the strains of Puccini's *Tosca* and Verdi's *The Troubador*. As well as the headline performance, other musical works are performed in the Festival Hall.

Also on a floating stage, the **Mörbisch Festival on the Lake** celebrated its 50th anniversary of operetta in the open air with *Vienna Blood* by Johann Strauss in 2007.

In Upper Austria, opera lovers flock in large numbers to Bad Ischl, the former summer hunting retreat of Emperor Franz Josef, for the **Lehar Festival**. Also nearby is the extraordinary Roman quarry of St Margarethen – the backdrop for the **Burgenland Opera Festival** with productions like Verdi's *Nabucco*.

The **Tiroler Festspiele Erl** is held in the lowlands of the Tyrol every July. Founded by the conductor Gustav Kuhn, the festival features a mix of opera and chamber music.

Lighter fare is also on the menu for those new to opera. The **Steyr Music Festival** highlights the musical *Les Misérables* and the reform opera *Orpheus and Eurydike*.

CLASSICAL CONCERTS AND FESTIVALS

The concert halls of Austria are the mainstay of classical music in the country, and you will find concerts in both small towns and the grand provincial capitals. Perhaps most famous is the **Salzburg Festival**, the internationally recognized festival celebrating classical music, opera and drama. Every summer thousands come from around the world to listen to the world's greatest plays and music. The main *festspielhaus* (festival hall) has been impressively refurbished. Lesser known is the **Salzburg Whitsun Festival**, which offers delightful opera buffa pieces. In 2007, the Salzburg Whitsun Festival began a co-operation with the celebrated conductor Riccardo Muti, which lasted until 2011. The festival takes place on a yearly basis.

The **Haydn Festival** in Eisenstadt each September is a high point of the concert season calendar. The works of Joseph Haydn are performed against the works of other composers to show contrast in programmes expertly selected by artistic director Dr Walter Reicher. In 2009, Burgenland commemorated the 200th anniversary of Hadyn's death with many musical events. In September a splendid series of concerts dedicated to the works of Johannes Brahms takes place in Styria, home to the Brahms Museum and the **International Brahms Festival**.

Many festivals guarantee a feast for the ears and eyes. **Allegro Vivo**, Lower Austria's most traditional music festival, opens its doors every summer to thousands of music lovers who revel in the beautiful castles and Baroque abbeys, which form the backdrop for the events. Matinees at Schloss Esterházy offer a wonderful chance to experience the music of Haydn in the very rooms where the composer himself worked and where many of his compositions were first performed. In Radstadt's Renaissance palace of Höch near Flachau, **Paul-Hofhaimer Days** offers early music and new sounds. Past festivals have provided a mixed bag of the oratories, varying from *The Four Seasons* by Haydn to *King David* by Honecker. Since 1978, the **Innsbruck Festival of Ancient Music** has delighted concert-goers with its grand halls and diverse programmes.

In addition to mixing music with grand architecture, other pleasing combinations are on offer. **Schloss Grafenegg** music festival, the brain child of top contemporary pianist Rudolf Buchbinder, combines tastings from Austria's top vineyards with musical programmes. Similarly, the **Brucknerfest Linz** features a dynamic combination of classical music and modern media art.

The rural charm of the Bregenzerwald region goes well with the music of Schubert and his contemporaries. The annual **Schubertiade** in Schwarzenberg boasts some 70 events including chamber concerts, song evenings, readings and master classes. More than 70,000 fans also come for the Schubertiade; the little sister to this is Steyr's Schubert Festival, offering a smaller cross-section of Schubert and his contemporaries.

For lovers of something a little edgier, Nikolaus Harnoncourt's Styrian festival of classical music, **Styriarte**, is probably the most avant-garde Austria has to offer outside Vienna. "A connoisseur's choice" is the description often heard.

ROCK, POP, JAZZ AND ALTERNATIVE

It is outdoor rock surrounded by outdoor rocks at the mountain-ringed city of Salzburg's massive outdoor **Frequency Festival**. The annual Salzburg outdoor music fest means 3 days, 3 stages and 40 bands worth of hard rock. It's a full camping experience, with showers and earplugs available. Previous headliners have included The Kaiser Chiefs. Graz buzzes during **Springsix**, Austria's largest festival for electronic art and music. International electronic acts, DJs and visual artists transform the city into a massive party zone.

Blues and boogie are the vibe at the **Kitzbühel Summer Concerts** on five stages across this pretty medieval mountain resort town. A few dozen peaks over in Montafon, the cultural **Montafon Summer** festival comprises some 20 events including concerts ranging from opera to jazz to classical music, as well as children's entertainment. The best of the international jazz scene meets at the **Jazz Fest in Saalfelden** amid the excellent acoustics of the Congress Center main stage, plus "short cuts" at the Kunsthaus Nexus, and free concerts in the town square.

The **Ramsau Festival** stages a pick and mix of culture. Previous years have welcomed the Vienna State Opera Ballet, choreographed by Renato Zanella; the Bratislava Symphonic Orchestra, conducted by Mario Kosik; the L'Orfeo Baroque Orchestra, with light installations by Stefan Knor; Austria's best accordion player Otto Lechner and many others.

Of course, no discussion of Austrian popular music is complete without mention of **Hansi Hinterseer**, former World Cup ski racer turned aging pop idol. He plays venues across Austria year round, with the stamina one expects of a ski racer.

FOLK MUSIC

You'll find many folk music concerts in Austrian towns and villages throughout the year. Of the annual ones, St Anton's **Folk Music Time** is a favourite. The charming mountain town's pedestrian zone provides the perfect setting for authentic alpine music, attracting traditionally costumed ensembles from Austria, South Tirol, Bavaria and Switzerland.

THE SOUND OF MUSIC

It has been more than 40 years since actor Julie Andrews put Salzburg on the (modern) musical map. The Von Trapp odyssey has become an industry in Salzburg, yet most Austrians have never heard of it. **Sound of Music** tours (of which there are many every day in Salzburg) take in all the big backdrops, and a musical dinner theatre plays all the favourites live.

DIRECTORY

OPERA AND OPERETTA

Bregenz Festival
Tel 43 5574 4076.
www.bregenzerfestspiele.com

Burgenland Opera Festival
Tel 43 2680 2100.
www.ofs.at

Lehar Festival
Tel 43 6132 23839.
www.leharfestival.at

Mörbisch Festival on the Lake
Tel 43 2682 662100.
www.seefestspiele-moerbisch.at

Steyr Music Festival
Tel 43 664 407 2122.
www.musikfestivalsteyr.at

Tiroler Festspiele Erl
Tel 43 512 578888.
www.tiroler-festspiele.at

CLASSICAL CONCERTS AND FESTIVALS

Allegro Vivo
www.allegro-vivo.at

Brucknerfest Linz
Tel 43 732 76120.
www.brucknerhaus.at

Haydn Festival
Haydn & Esterházy.
Tel 43 2682 61866.
www.schloss-esterhazy.at
www.haydnfestival.at

Innsbruck Festival of Ancient Music
Tel 43 512 57 1032.
www.altemusik.at

International Brahms Festival
Tel 43 3852 3434.
www.brahmsmuseum.at

Paul-Hofhaimer Days
Tel 43 6452 7150.
www.radstadt.com

Salzburg Festival
Tel 43 662 8045 500.
www.salzburgerfestspiele.at

Salzburg Whitsun Festival
Tel 43 662 889870.
www.salzburg.info

Schloss Grafenegg
Tel 43 2735 5500.
www.grafenegg.com

Schubertiade
Tel 43 5576 72091.
www.schubertiade.at

Styriarte
Tel 43 316 8129410.
www.styriarte.com

ROCK, POP, JAZZ AND ALTERNATIVE

Frequency Festival
www.frequency.at

Hansi Hinterseer
www.hansi-hinterseer.at

Jazz Fest in Saalfelden
Tel 43 6582 70660.
www.jazzfestsaalfelden.at

Kitzbühel Summer Concerts
Tel 43 5356 777.
www.kitzbuehel.com

Montafon Summer
Tel 43 5556 722530.
www.montafon.at

Ramsau Festival
Tel 43 3687 81833.
www.ramsau.com

Springsix
www.springsix.at

FOLK MUSIC

Folk Music Time
Tel 43 5446 22690.
www.stantonamarlberg.com

THE SOUND OF MUSIC

Sound of Music
Tel 43 662 889870.
www.salzburg.info

OUTDOOR ACTIVITIES

Austria is an ideal country for sports enthusiasts all year round. For winter sports you can find some 22,000 perfect pistes for downhill skiing and 16,000 km (10,000 miles) of dedicated trails for cross-country skiing in the Alps as well as some 14,000 km (9,000 miles) of walking trails, which are cleared of snow so that you can admire the stunning mountain scenery unimpeded. The countless lakes are perfectly suited for water skiing, sailing and wind surfing, and of course for swimming in summer, while the Tyrolean Alps are a paradise for rock climbers and mountaineers.

Downhill run on a snowboard

Throughout Austria there are also superb facilities for more unusual sports, such as glacier climbing, snowshoe walking, rafting, canoeing, bungee jumping or paragliding.

SKIING

The main sport in the Alps is, of course, skiing. Visitors have a choice from skiing on the gentlest family slopes to braving rough runs down the steep slopes of the high Alps, from staying in the deep, fresh snow of the nursery slopes to venturing onto extremely difficult "black" downhill runs. Even nighttime skiing is possible, since some of the runs are illuminated at night.

The best areas for skiing are in Upper and Lower Austria and in Styria. Around Innsbruck, one of Austria's largest winter sports areas, year-round skiing is possible, for example in the Stubaital, Glungezer, Axamer Lizum and Mutterer Alm.

The Salzburg region has some 860 km (530 miles) of ski trails and 270 ski lifts, and resorts such as Filzmoos and Kleinarl regularly host many famous skiing contests. The permanent glaciers, such as those in the Ötztal Alps, welcome skiers all year round.

Most Austrian winter sports centres sell passes which give access to all the local ski facilities. If you wish to experience the thrill of skiing down the route that has been used in the World Cup since 1972, go to the Planai slopes in the Styrian resort of Schladming.

The Baroque monastery in Stams in Tyrol has a skiing college whose graduates include several international champions. Those who are more interested in the high life among Europe's aristocracy and in the pleasures of *après-ski*, should make for the pistes in Lech and Zürs am Arlberg, in Voralberg, and in Kitzbühel, in Tyrol.

Langlauf, nordic or cross-country skiing, is also well catered for in Austria, with numerous attractive routes, called *Loipe*. Almost all cross-country routes also have sprint sections, where you can try out your steps.

Downhill skiing – Austria's most popular sport

A skier studying an information board in the mountains

SNOWBOARDING

Snowboarding is one of the most popular winter activities in Austria after skiing. The sport arrived in Europe from the United States and was originally no more than a teenage craze. It has long since turned serious – Austria was one of the first countries to hold contests in the discipline, and the annual event in Seefeld, Tyrol, has become a meeting ground for the world's snowboarding elite. Austrians won many medals in the last two Olympic Winter Games, both in the parallel slalom and the half pipe (something between a ski piste and a bobsleigh run), and one of the first snowboarding champions, Stefan Gimpl, enjoys great popularity in his country.

Tyrol is the snowboarder's paradise and it used to be the home of the International Snowboarding Federation. Young people from all over the world come here to participate in the Powder Turns, in Kaprun or Saalbach-Hinterglemm.

SLEIGHS AND TOBOGGANS

As well as skiing, almost all Austrian winter sports centres have facilities for bobsleigh and toboggan rides. Resorts such as Ischgl, in western Tyrol, are famous for their excellent tobogganing facilities. There are also several summer sleigh runs, for example in northern Tyrol. Sleigh hire costs between €3 and €5 per day. In some places it is possible to carry your sleigh up the hill on the mountain lift, but you cannot carry it down again – you have to ride it along the track.

If you're not too keen on racing down the mountain, you can enjoy the romantic and more leisurely pursuit of admiring the countryside while being transported in a horse-drawn sleigh, for €12 to €15 per person. The hire of a whole carriage costs between €40 and €70.

MOUNTAINEERING

Wherever there are mountains you will always find rock climbers and mountaineers. In Austria, the largest organization for climbers is the **Österreichischer Alpenverein**. It has more than 190 regional divisions all over Austria, with its headquarters in Vienna. Besides selling maps, books and guides, the association also runs a library and hires out equipment, it maintains mountain hostels and walking trails, organizes skiing courses and runs a

Mountaineering – a sport for the brave and determined

Ramblers on one of the many mountain trails in summer

school of mountaineering. Members of the Alpenverein enjoy many discounts, for example on accommodation in mountain huts. There is also a meteorological phoneline, giving information about current and expected weather conditions, including any avalanche warnings, which allows rock climbers to make the appropriate arrangements for their expedition.

WALKING

Rambles on the mountain trails are a popular activity, enjoyed by Austrians and visitors alike. The Rosengartenschlucht, a ravine northwest of Imst whose sides reach 100 m (328 ft) in height, is a particularly attractive walk; you walk along the valley of the Ötz River and get to see the Stuibenfall, Tyrol's tallest waterfall, created by a fallen rock. Many rambling trails can also be found in the region of Eben im Pongau. In Kleinarl, one of the attractions are the *Fackelwanderungen*, nighttime walk with torches. In the Salzkammergut, a lift takes visitors to the top of the Grünberg or Feuerkogel mountains, where many long tourist trails grant walkers views of the fairy-tale landscape of the alpine lakes.

There are walking trails all over the country, and they are all clearly signposted and marked on tree trunks by black-and-white signs. As with the ski runs, the level of difficulty is indicated by a colour. Local tourist offices have detailed maps of the area. And, if you don't trust your map-reading skills, you can always hire a mountain guide or join a rambling group.

CYCLING

On the flat, bicycles are an ideal and inexpensive way of getting around. In the mountains, cycling becomes more of an endurance test. Nonetheless, mountain-biking is popular and every holiday resort and most hotels offer bikes for hire. St. Johann, in the highest part of the Alps, plays host to various international cycling races. In June and September, cyclists meet in East Tyrol to compete in an arduous race around the Lienz Dolomites. Less ambitious cyclists choose the scenic *Radwege* along rivers such as the Danube or Drau. In Vienna, despite heavy car traffic, cyclists can be seen everywhere. In towns and suburbs, many cycle routes have been marked; you can see them on maps available in any bookshop.

Visitors on a winter mountain biking expedition

Yachting marina in Mörbisch

WATER SPORTS

Snow is not the only element attracting sports enthusiasts to Austria – an abundance of rivers and lakes offer much to the summer visitor, whether it's in the form of relaxation or active holidays. The lovely lakes in the Salzkammergut, especially, are worth exploring.

Austrian lakes come in all shapes and sizes, but most are suitable for swimming and sailing. The largest and most famous are Bodensee (Lake Constance) and Neusiedler See. The latter, easily accessible from Vienna, is a 40-km (25-mile) long lake on the Hungarian border, and the venue every weekend for an Olympic-standard regatta. There are sailing and windsurfing schools on many Austrian lakes, and on the larger ones waterskiing and paraskiing are also on offer.

Scuba-diving is also possible at certain times of the year and in designated areas of some lakes, particularly in the Salzkammergut.

Many mountain rivers, particularly those in the western part of Austria, flow through narrow ravines and tumble down in numerous waterfalls – thus creating endless thrills for canoeists and competitors in the annual white-water rafting contests. An especially popular rafting event takes place along a gorge, the Imsterschlucht.

Even in Vienna you can enjoy watersports – along the Old Danube many places hire out water skis, rowing or sailing boats, without the need to prove any special expertise.

Lastly, the lakes and rivers are perfect for fishing. Local tourist offices will be able to advise you on where the best spots are, and sell you a licence.

HORSE RIDING

Horse riding, while not as popular as skiing, also has many followers. Lower Austria has a number of studs which offer a variety of riding holidays. Some hotels, too, own their own horses or have an arrangement with a local riding centre which allows guests to use its facilities. In many resorts, riding lessons can also be booked in indoor arenas, which is especially useful during bad weather or in the winter months.

Even if your visit only takes you to Vienna, you still don't have to forego the pleasures of horse riding – the Prater funfair, once the favourite riding course of the Empress Elisabeth, is open to this day to lovers of the sport.

Horse riding is one of the more costly activities, but it is not exorbitant; in the Tyrol, for example, one hour's riding in winter costs about €15 per person – about the same as you would have to pay for hiring a tennis court.

Horse riding along the shores of Neusiedler See

TENNIS

Indoor tennis courts, which are also open in winter, can be found in any of the larger resorts and in many hotels; outdoor courts are available in most cities. They are less common in the mountain resorts which specialize in other sports. Prices vary; in Styria the cost of hiring a court for one hour is around €13–17 during the day, or €18–19 in the evening.

Hang-gliding – a spectacular sport, enjoyed in Stubaital

EXTREME SPORTS

So-called extreme sports, such as rafting, canyoning, speedboat racing, paragliding, hang gliding, bungee jumping or free climbing, are all well represented in Austria. New companies open every day, offering equipment hire and organized events to tempt the adventurous who are seeking an adrenaline kick.

DIRECTORY

SKIING, SNOWBOARDING, TOBOGGANING

Dachstein Gletscherbahn
Ramsauerstrasse 756, 8970 Schladming. **Tel** *(03687) 23310.* **www**.planai.at

Zell am See/ Kaprun Information
Bruckner Bundesstrasse 1a, 5700 Zell am See. **Tel** *(06542) 770.*

Österreichischer Bob- und Skeletonverband
Haus des Sports, Stadionstrasse 1, 6020 Innsbruck. **Tel** *(0512) 20 02 50.* **www**.bobskeleton.at

Tourismus-gemeinschaft Mölltaler Gletscher
9831 Flattach. **Tel** *(04785) 615.* **www**.flattach.at

Tourismusverband Neustift im Stubaital
6167 Neustift. **Tel** *(0501) 8810.* **www**.stubai.at

Tourismusverband Ötztal Arena
6450 Sölden. **Tel** *(05720) 200.* **www**.soelden.com

Tourismusverband Pitztal
6473 Wenns. **Tel** *(05414) 869 99.* **www**.pitztal.com

Tourismusverband Tux
Lanersbach 401. 6293 Tux. **Tel** *(05287) 8506.* **www**.tux.at

ROCK CLIMBING, MOUNTAINEERING

Österreichischer Alpenverein
Olympiastrasse 37, 6010 Innsbruck. **Tel** *(0512) 595 47.* **www**.alpenverein.at

Österreichischer Touristenklub
Bäckerstrasse 16, 1010 Vienna. **Tel** *(01) 51 23 844.* **www**.oetk.at

Verband Alpiner Vereine Österreichs
Bäckerstrasse 16, 1010 Vienna. **Tel** *(01) 512 54 88.* **www**.vavoe.at

WALKING, RAMBLING

Europa-Wanderhotels
9773 Irschen 10. **Tel** *(04710) 2780.* **www**.wanderhotels.com

CYCLING

Mountain Bike Holidays
5751 Maishofen. **Tel** *(06542) 80 480-22.* **www**.bike-holidays.com

Radtouren in Österreich
Freistädterstrasse 119, 4041Linz. **Tel** *(0732) 221022.* **www**.radtouren.at

WATERSKIING, SAILING

Austrian Water Ski Federation
Leitergraben 34, 3060 Leonding. **Tel** *0676 4283305.* **www**.oewsv.at

Österreichischer Segelverband
7100 Neusiedl am See. **Tel** *(02167) 40243-0.* **www**.segelverband.at

HORSE RIDING

Reiten in Österreich Reitarena Austria
4121 Altenfelden. **Tel** *(07282) 55880.* **www**.tiscover.at/reiten **www**.reitarena.com

Urlaub am Bauernhof
Gabelsbergerstrasse 19, 5020 Salzburg. **Tel** *(0662) 88 02 02.* **www**.farmholidays.com

EXTREME SPORTS

Absolute Outdoor
8940 Liezen. **Tel** *(03612) 253 43.* **www**.rafting.at

Action Club Zillertal
6290 Mayrhofen. **Tel** *(0664) 4413074.* **www**.action-club-zillertal.com

Adventure Club Tuxertal
6293 Tux. **Tel** *(05287) 87 287.* **www**.natursport.at

Aktiv-Zentrum
6874 Bizau. **Tel** *(05514) 31 48.* **www**.aktiv-zentrum.at

Austria-Adventure Sportagentur Klappacher
Hofzeile 7–9/3/16, 1190 Vienna. **Tel** *(01) 368 76 17 or (0664) 460 75 83.* **www**.outdoor-experts.at.

Austria-Adventure Sportagentur Raab
Mairenben 30, 4452 Ternberg. **Tel** *(0664) 503 13 72.* **www**.austria-adventure.at

Club Aktiv Mölltal
9832 Stall/Mölltal 13. **Tel** *(04785) 410.* **www**.cam.at

Club Montée Adventure Center
Anger 10, 5324 Faistenau. **Tel** *(06228) 30008.* **www**.montee.com

Dachstein Tauern Balloons
8972 Ramsau a.12. **Tel** *(03687) 80863.* **www**.dachstein-tauern-balloons.at

Feelfree
Platzleweg 5, 6430 Ötz. **Tel** *(05252) 603530.* **www**.feelfree.at

Flugschule Salzkammergut
Flachbergweg 46, 4810 Gmunden. **Tel** *(07612) 730 33.* **www**.paragleiten.net

Freelife
8923 Palfau. **Tel** *(07230) 79160.*

Gesäuse Sportagentur
Holzäpfeltal 108. **Tel** *(03636) 515.* **www**.salza.at

Jauntal Bungy & Event GmbH
9113 Ruden. **Tel** *(04234) 222.* **www**.bungy.at

Kormoran (Canyoning)
3125 Stanzendorf. **Tel** *(02786) 30065.* **www**.kormoran.at

Outdoor Leadership
Steinach 3, 4822 Bad Goisern. **Tel** *(06135) 6058.* **www**.outdoor-leadership.com

Österreichischer Aero Club
Prinz Eugen-Strasse 12, 1040 Vienna. **Tel** *(01) 505 10 28.* **www**.aeroclub.at

SKI-DEP
ATOMIC
ATOMIC
HEAD

SURVIVAL GUIDE

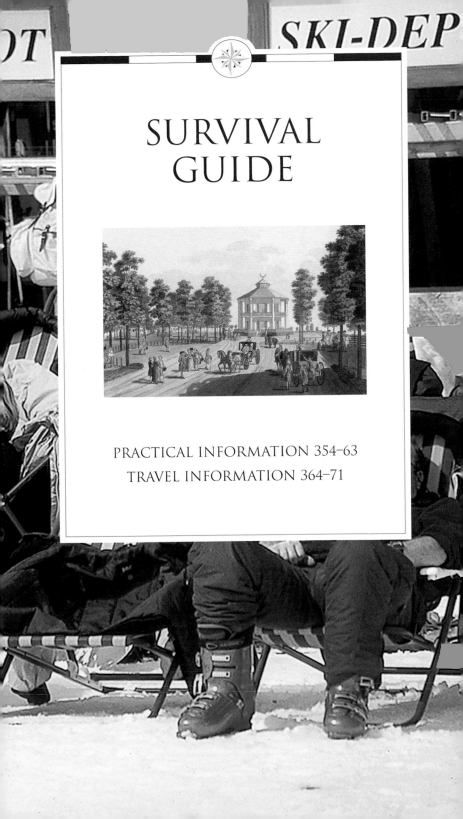

PRACTICAL INFORMATION

Austria is a fantastic holiday destination, for both winter and summer. It features numerous attractions, from well-equipped alpine skiing centres to quaint and charming villages, from fascinating historic sights in the towns to the superb collections of its museums – there is something on offer for every taste and budget. Visitors will have no problems finding suitable accommodation, interesting restaurants or enjoyable cultural events, and the tourist offices in most towns and villages will be only too pleased to furnish you with all the information you require. Alternatively, you can find useful details on the Internet. Many larger towns and all major sights post helpful hints and fascinating facts on their own websites.

Sign for tourist information

Visitors crowding around a cable car station in Ischgl

WHEN TO VISIT

There is no such thing as a low season in Austria – the tourist season continues virtually all year round. Most hotels divide the year into two main parts: spring–summer (1 May–30 Sep) and autumn–winter (1 Oct–30 Apr). The winter season peaks at Christmas and again from the end of January to the beginning of March. Only small hotels and pensions far from winter sports facilities close for the winter. Ski enthusiasts can enjoy the Alps from Christmas until Easter, while walkers are best advised to visit in the spring, when there is a breeze in the air and the mountain slopes display a rich tapestry of colourful flowers.

The peak of the summer season is between June and August, and this period coincides with the greatest number of cultural events, festivals and village fairs all over the country. At any time of year you will be able to discover and explore new sides of this multi-faceted country.

IMMIGRATION AND VISA FORMALITIES

Nationals from most European and many overseas countries do not need a visa to enter Austria. You will need a national identity card or, in the case of Britain which does not have an identity card, a valid passport. Citizens of EU countries can stay as long as they like. Visitors from the US, Canada, Australia or New Zealand are welcome for up to three months, or longer with a visa obtained from the Austrian Embassy or Consulate in their home country before the first date of entry.

Dogs and cats require a current rabies vaccination certificate; motorists need a green card as proof of third-party insurance.

CUSTOMS REGULATIONS

Nationals of EU countries, including Britain and Ireland, may take home unlimited quantities of duty-paid alcoholic drinks and tobacco goods as long as these are intended for their own consumption, and it can be proven that the goods are not intended for resale.

Citizens of the US and Canada are limited to a maximum of 200 cigarettes (or 50 cigars) and one litre of spirits (or 2¼ litres of wine or 3 litres of beer). Regulations for residents of Australia and New Zealand vary slightly from these guidelines.

If you are in doubt, consult the customs offices in your own country before you travel to Austria.

Up-to-date information on what may be brought into Austria can be found on the Internet at www.bmf.gv.at and in the *Zollinfo* brochure, available at the border.

A useful orientation board and map of the local area in Zell am See

◁ **Visitors relaxing at Kitzsteinhorn Glacier, Kaprun, Salzburger Land**

EMBASSIES AND CONSULATES

The Embassies for all countries, including the UK, are based in Vienna. Some larger cities have consulates where you can turn for help *(see p357)*.

TOURIST INFORMATION

There are many local tourist offices all over Austria, offering useful advice to visitors on accommodation, restaurants, excursions and cultural events *(see p287)*. Offices are sign-posted with the white letter "i" against a green background *(see opposite)*. Every province also has its own tourist information centre, where you can turn for help. Most of the local tourist offices offer their services free and hand out free leaflets, maps and information booklets.

You can plan your trip in advance by getting in touch with travel agencies or the representatives of **Österreich Werbung** (the Austrian National Tourist Office) directly. For cheaper accommodation and information about youth hostels or pop concerts, the multilingual team at **Jugendinformation Wien** will provide assistance.

Sign of a pension in Lofer

OPENING HOURS

This guide provides the opening times for each individual sight you may want to visit. Most businesses start work at around 8am and close at about 4pm. On Fridays, many close early and, even if they do not, it may be hard to get anything done. Most shops are open from Monday to Friday, 8am to 6pm (sometimes 7:30pm) and on Saturdays from 8am mostly until 5pm (in larger cities). Shops also close on Sundays and public holidays, and in the countryside some close on Wednesday afternoons.

Banks in many towns are open from 8am until 3pm (5:30pm on Thursdays); smaller branches close at lunchtime. All banks remain closed on Saturdays, but you can change money at the airport, the main railway stations or in bureaux de change, or use an automatic teller machine.

MUSEUMS AND HISTORIC MONUMENTS

The national list of palaces, castles and ruins comprises a staggering 2,000 sights, and this does not even include Austria's countless churches, monasteries or abbeys. Vienna alone has more than 60 museums, and Styria over 200; of these only 58 are state-owned; the remainder belong to associations, churches, companies or private individuals.

Opening hours vary and depend on the local tourist seasons. Generally speaking, museums are open from 10am until 4pm or 7pm. Once a week they stay open longer, some until 9pm or even midnight. Some museums close for one day in the week, usually on a Monday.

Signposts help visitors find the way to the alpine huts

A group of sightseers admiring historic buildings in Innsbruck

Check times, special events and arrangements for guided tours locally. For groups of 10 people or more it is often possible to arrange the time of their visit in advance – and you may be eligible for a group discount. At the end of a guided tour it is customary to leave a small tip.

ADMISSION PRICES

Museum entrance fees can vary from €2 to €8. Admission to historic houses costs about €10–15. Children up to the age of 6 (in some museums, up to the age of 7) are admitted free, and 6–15 year-olds pay half price, as do senior citizens (60 and over). There are also reductions for students. Some museums offer family tickets (admitting for example two adults and three children); a few allow free admission on a particular day in the week.

An adult cinema ticket costs around €7–10. Some cinemas sell tickets at lower prices at the beginning of the week. For theatre tickets you will need to set aside €30–40 or more; musicals cost upwards of €40. Concert tickets start at around €14. The three-day *Wien-Karte* entitles you to unlimited use of all public transport facilities for 72 hours as well as reduced admission to some museums, and discounts in selected shops and restaurants.

A range of foreign-language newspapers and magazines on street stands

INFORMATION FOR DISABLED VISITORS

Austria is better prepared to receive disabled visitors than many other countries, and many trams and buses can accommodate wheelchairs. At train stations, you need to ask about lifts when you get your ticket. Facilities vary at underground stations, so it is best to check first. In some regions the facilities are fairly basic, but concessions on tickets are available for disabled visitors.

Special parking spaces are set aside for disabled drivers and are clearly marked as such; if your car displays the appropriate sticker, parking is also free of charge.

All public toilets have special wide cubicles for the wheelchair-bound. Information about facilities for the disabled can be obtained from the local tourist information offices.

Most of the main sights have access ramps. Contact the museums in advance so they can organize help with wheelchairs if needed.

Some of the larger 5-star hotels have special facilities for disabled guests, such as rooms where the beds are equipped with handgrips and similar aids exist in bathroom and toilet. Some also have extra-wide showers that allow easy wheelchair access. Some few restaurants have access ramps for wheelchairs.

TRAVELLING WITH CHILDREN

Many hotels offer a free stay or reduced rates for children under the age of 12 who share a room with their parents. Children up to the age of 15 pay half fare on public transport; on Sundays, public holidays and during the summer vacations they travel for free. They are also entitled to reduced admission when visiting museums and historic sights. The large supermarkets and also chemists have a department with essential items for babies as do the Drogeriemarkt and Bipa Stores.

INFORMATION FOR YOUNG PEOPLE

Students holding an international student card and a valid college ID are entitled to discounts on railways and municipal public transport, as well as reduced admission to cinemas, museums and sports events. They will also be offered accommodation in a *Jugendherberge* (youth hostel) at a lower price. Up-to-date information on accommodation in student dormitories and youth hostels can be obtained from any tourist office.

RELIGION

Austria is a predominantly Catholic country – as is apparent from the large number of Catholic churches; Protestants make up just 5 per cent of the population. There is also a fair-sized immigrant population from various national backgrounds and following various religious faiths; probably the largest group among them are the Muslims. In Vienna, there is a sizeable Jewish community, which has its own synagogues, while the cemeteries are communal.

LANGUAGE

Although all Austrians officially speak German, in reality they speak "Austrian". While this variety of Low German does not differ from High German as markedly as Swiss German, its pronunciation and even some rules of grammar and vocabulary may make it seem like a different language.

Added to this are several Austrian dialects, which differ from province to province. Austrians are the first to admit that it would be impossible to learn them all in their countless regional varieties. For instance, visitors who know a little German find *Tirolerisch,* the dialect spoken in Tyrol, completely incomprehensible.

You will have few problems making yourself understood in English, especially in the larger cities and main tourist centres. English is also spoken by most young people who learn it at elementary school.

Information board on a building in Innsbruck

EVERYDAY CUSTOMS

Peace and quiet are highly valued by Austrians who live outside the cities. They are friendly and easy-going people who tend to keep up their traditions, especially in the mountainous regions. Austrians, especially the older generation, tend to be very courteous, and they expect the same from visitors.

When asked for directions, Austrians will always do their best to help. The Austrians like polite formalities, though hand-kissing is no longer the norm. It is the exception to go on to first-name terms immediately. Forms of address such as Herr

Doktor and Herr Ober (head waiter) can be used liberally.

It is worth knowing a few phrases, too, such as, when meeting someone, *Wie geht es Ihnen?,* to enquire after their health. In the morning, *Guten Morgen* is the standard greeting, at lunchtime *Mahlzeit*, later in the day *Guten Tag*. Everywhere and at any time *Grüss Gott* is used, literally "greet the Lord".

NEWSPAPERS AND RADIO

The most popular dailies, the *Kurier* or the *Kronen Zeitung* give detailed TV, radio, cinema and theatre listings, information on concerts, lectures, meetings, flea markets, as well as weekend excursions. *Die Presse* and *Der Standard* provide serious political commentaries. The most popular weekly magazine is the *News*, and the leading monthly *Profil*. There are also countless illustrated women's magazines. German magazines and newspapers are available everywhere.

Foreign-language papers, such as *The Times, Financial Times, Guardian International, The Herald Tribune* or *Le Monde* are available from central kiosks in the larger towns. In Vienna, foreign newspapers and magazines can also be bought at all railway stations or at the Morava bookshop at No. 11 Wollzeile *(see map 2 C4).*

Tourist information for students and young travellers

Austria has two main radio stations. Ö1 plays classical music and transmits the news in English and French on weekdays at 8:15am. Ö3 plays popular music and transmits regular traffic bulletins. Radio FM4 broadcasts in English from 1am to 2pm daily on 103.8 MHz. It covers regional and international news as well as cultural events. There are also several private radio stations playing mainly pop music. Cable stations carry the BBC World Service around the clock.

ELECTRICAL ADAPTORS

The voltage in Austria is 220V AC. Plugs have two small round pins. It is a good idea to buy a multi-adaptor before coming to Austria, as they are not easy to find here. Some of the more expensive hotels may offer guest adaptors, but usually only for use with electric shavers.

TIME

Austria uses Central European Time (GMT plus one hour). Clocks move forward one hour on the last Sunday in March and back on the last Sunday in October.

DIRECTORY

EMBASSIES & CONSULATES

Australia
Mattiellistrasse 2–4, 1040 Vienna. ***Tel*** *(01) 50674.*
www.australian-embassy.at

Canada
Laurenzerberg 2, 1010 Vienna.
Tel *(01) 531 383 000.*
www.kanada.at

Ireland
Rotenturmstrasse 16–18, 1010 Vienna.
Tel *(01) 715 42 46.*

New Zealand
Salesianergasse 15/3, 1030 Vienna.
Tel *(01) 318 85 05.*

United Kingdom
Jauresgasse 12, 1030 Vienna.
Tel *(01) 716130.*
www.britishembassy.at

United States of America
Boltzmanngasse 16, 1090 Vienna.
Tel *(01) 31339.*
www.usembassy.at

TOURIST OFFICES

Wiener Tourismusverband
corner of Albertinaplatz & Tegetthoffstrasse, 1010 Vienna.
Tel *(01) 24555, 211140.*
www.wien.info

WienXtra-Jugend-Info
Babenbergerstrasse 1, 1040 Vienna.
Tel *(01) 400084-100.*
www.jugendinfowien.at

Österreich Werbung – Austrian Holiday Information
Margaretenstrasse 1, 1040 Vienna.
Tel *(01) 58866-0/0810 101818.*
www.austria.info

TOURIST OFFICES ABROAD

London
PO Box 2363, London W1A 2QB.
Tel *0845 101 1818.*
www.austria.info/uk

New York
P.O. Box 1142, New York, NY 10018-114.
Tel *(212) 944 6880.*
www.austria.info/us

Sydney
36 Carrington Street, 1st floor, Sydney, NSW 2000.
Tel *(02) 9299 3621.*
www.austria.info.au

Toronto
2 Bloor Street East, Suite 3330, Toronto, Ontario M4W 1A8.
Tel *(416) 967 3381.*

Personal Security and Health

Austria is one of Europe's safest countries. Tourists are unlikely to encounter any violence (though there has been an increase in petty crimes such as pickpocketing in busy tourist areas) and the police and emergency services are easy to contact. Pharmacists are respected and their advice is often sought by locals. A visit to the pharmacy, unless the problem is serious, is probably the easiest choice if you are feeling unwell. Above all, this is a peaceful country, a land of historic sights, works of art, and beautiful, stunning scenery.

DIRECTORY

EMERGENCY TELEPHONE NUMBERS

Ambulance
Tel *144.*
Tel *50 50 (Graz).*
Tel *69 200 (Linz).*

Emergency Medical Assistance
Tel *141.*
Can be consulted evenings, nights, Saturdays, Sundays and public holidays.

Fire Service
Tel *122.*

Flying Ambulance Service
Tel *401 44-0.*

Mobile Telephone Emergency Line
Tel *112.*

Police
Tel *133.*

Roadside Assistance
Tel *120.*

POLICE

In Vienna, in the provincial capitals, and in all the larger towns, public order is maintained by the *Polizei*. The police also run lost property departments *(Fundbüro)*, which can be found in any district police station. In the provinces, policing is carried out by the *Gendarmerie*.

PERSONAL SECURITY AND PROPERTY

There are few places in Austria to steer clear of, even at night. However, it is as well to be careful. Avoid areas around stations at night and pay extra attention at funfairs or large gatherings. Don't become an easy target for thieves: never leave items visible in a car; carry money and documents safely. Women should avoid placing bags on the floor in cafés and restaurants.

In case of a theft, report it without delay to the nearest *Polizeiwache* (police station). If you lose traveller's cheques, seek help at the nearest bank, which will stop them. Credit and debit card thefts should be reported immediately to your credit card company or bank. Contact your consulate if you lose your passport, or if it is stolen.

LOST PROPERTY

Go to the nearest police station in the first instance. If they do not succeed in restoring your property within seven days, then try the lost property bureau *(Fundbüro)*. For property lost on railways or the Schnellbahn, go to the Westbahnhof in Vienna and enquire in person.

SOS sign on a U-Bahn platform

ACCIDENTS AND EMERGENCIES

Britain has a reciprocal arrangement with Austria whereby emergency hospital treatment is free if you have a British passport. Visits to doctors, dentists or outpatient departments are also free of charge, but getting free treatment can involve a lot of bureaucracy. Britons should be sure to get a European Health Insurance Card, available from post offices, before travelling. It is also a good idea to take out full health insurance. Visitors from other countries should establish what is required to cover their medical treatment either with their home embassy or with their medical insurance company.

If you are ill, it is best to go to a clinic at a state hospital. In Vienna, the main hospital (and the largest in Europe) is the **Allgemeines Krankenhaus** (General Hospital) in the ninth district. People without insurance or money to pay for medical services are cared for at the **Krankenhaus der Barmherzigen**

Police motorcycle

Policeman

Fire engine

Police car

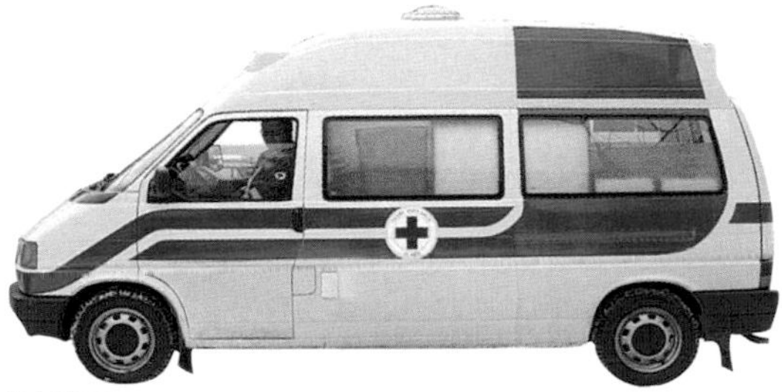
Ambulance

Brüder (Brothers of Mercy Hospital), which also runs a free emergency dental clinic. In a medical emergency, call an ambulance *(Rettungsdienst)*.

Policewoman

Fireman

HEALTH PRECAUTIONS

Tick-Borne Encephalitis is a possible danger wherever there are deciduous trees in Austria. Only a tiny proportion of ticks carry the disease, which may cause brain damage and in some cases lead to death. Most Austrians and foreign residents are inoculated against it. Inoculation is done in several stages, but is not usually recommended for holidaymakers. The risk of infection is minimal, but to be on the safe side, if you are bitten, do not remove the tick but go to an outpatients department.

PHARMACIES

If it is not an emergency, it is best to go to an *Apotheke* (pharmacy) for advice on medicines and treatment. Pharmacies display a red "A" sign and operate a night rota system. Any closed pharmacies will display the address of the nearest one open, and the **Pharmacy Information Line** also has details of some which are open.

Apart from medicines, pharmacies also sell some herbal remedies. *Reformhäuser* specialize in such products and natural healthcare.

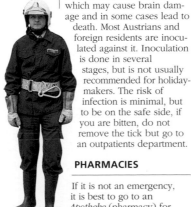

Façade of a typical *Apotheke* (pharmacy) in Vienna

DIRECTORY

HOSPITALS

Allgemeines Krankenhaus
Währinger Gürtel 18–20, 1090 Vienna.
Tel *(01) 404 00-0.*

Krankenhaus der Barmherzigen Brüder
(Brothers of Mercy Hospital), Grosse Mohrengasse 9, 1020 Vienna.
Tel *(01) 211 210.*

IMPORTANT TELEPHONE NUMBERS

Dental Emergency Service
(at night, weekends, public holidays) Vienna.
Tel *(01) 51 22 078.*

International Pharmacy
Kärntner Ring 17, Vienna.
Tel *(01) 512 28 25.*

Lost Property Office
Bastiengasse 36, 1180 Vienna.
Tel *(01) 4000-8091.*

Pharmacy Information Line
Vienna. ***Tel*** *(01) 15 50.*

Banking and Currency

Bank Austria
UniCredit Group

Bank Austria logo

Austrian banking services are very accessible. Money-changing machines (ATMs) can be found in all the major cities (*see directory*), and most shops, hotels and restaurants accept credit cards, although some still only take cash. You can take any amount of money into Austria, in euros or in other currencies. The largest Austrian banks, including Bank Austria Creditanstalt, BAWAG and Raiffeisenbank, have branches in most of the provincial cities.

MONEY EXCHANGE

The best place to change money is at a bank; there is a minimum handling fee of about €3.60 per transaction. Although you can use travel agents and hotels, the banks give you a better rate and charge less commission. Railway station *Wechselstuben* (bureaux de change) charge 4 per cent on the exchanged sum. Exchanging a larger amount of money at one time can save on commission. You can also exchange pounds sterling for euros at an automatic money-changing machine.

Most banks are open from 8:30am to 12:30pm and from 1:30pm to 3pm Monday to Friday (to 5:30pm on Thursdays). A few, such as the main Creditanstalt bank in Vienna, Bank Austria and some banks in the provincial capitals as well as those in the busier tourist resorts or close to railway stations and airports, have extended opening hours.

BEZIRKSBAUERNKAMMER ZELL AM SEE

Logo of a bank in Zell am See

CREDIT CARDS

The banks operate a large network of ATMs, many of which take foreign credit cards with PIN codes. This facility will be clearly stated on the front of the machine – just look for the logo of your card. Instructions are often given in English and other languages.

At most hotels, shops and restaurants you can pay by credit or debit card, although some do not take all cards. It is best to always carry some cash on you. Some establishments also set a minimum sum that can be paid for by credit card. Make sure you report lost or stolen cards to your own or nearest Austrian bank without delay.

TRAVELLER'S CHEQUES

Traveller's cheques are the safest way to carry large sums of money. Choose a well-known name such as American Express, Visa, Thomas Cook or cheques issued through a bank. Cheques can be cashed at any bank or bureau de change, and some larger shops and hotels will also accept payment by traveller's cheque.

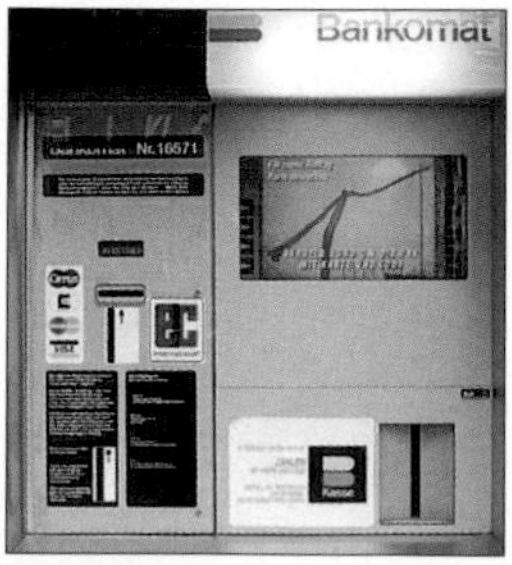

A Bankomat automatic money-dispensing machine

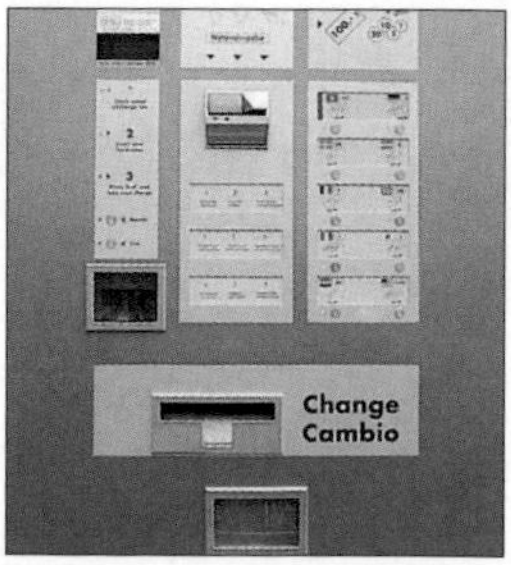

Currency conversion machine that accepts foreign banknotes

DIRECTORY

BUREAUX DE CHANGE (WECHSELSTUBE)

Vienna
Westbahnhof, Europaplatz 1.
7am–10pm daily.
Schwechat Airport.
6am–10:45pm daily.

Graz
Bankhaus Krentschker, Hamelingasse 8.
Main station, Platform 1.

Innsbruck
Main station, Südtiroler Platz.

Melk
Babenberger Strasse1.

Salzburg
Bundesstrasse 95.
Main station, Südtiroler Platz.
Airport, Innsbrucker Residenzplatz 9.

AUTOMATIC MONEY-CHANGING MACHINES

Vienna
Kärntner Strasse 32.
Kärntner Strasse 51.
Michaelerplatz 3.
Operngasse 8.
Rotenturmstrasse 27.
Schottenring 1.
Stephansplatz 2.

Feldkirch
Leonhardsplatz 4.

Krems
Obere Landstrasse 19.

Kufstein
Georg-Pirmoser-Strasse 2.
Unterer Stadtplatz.

Salzburg
Getreidegasse 1.

Schönberg
Europabrücke.

St. Wolfgang
Aberseestrasse 8.

Velden
Am Korso.

THE EURO

The Euro (€) is the common currency of the European Union. It went into general circulation on 1 January 2002, initially for 12 participating countries. Austria was one of those 12 countries taking the Euro in 2002, with the Austrian schilling phased out in the same year.

EU members using the Euro as sole official currency are known as the Eurozone. Several EU members have opted out of joining this common currency.

Euro notes are identical throughout the Eurozone countries, each one including designs of fictional architectural structures and monuments. The coins, however, have one side identical (the value side), and one side with an image unique to each country.

Bank Notes

Euro bank notes have seven denominations. The grey €5 note is the smallest, followed by the pink €10 note, blue €20 note, orange €50 note, green €100 note, yellow €200 note and purple €500 note. All notes show the stars of the European Union and architectural motifs.

€5 note

€10 note

€20 note

€50 note

€100 note

€200 note

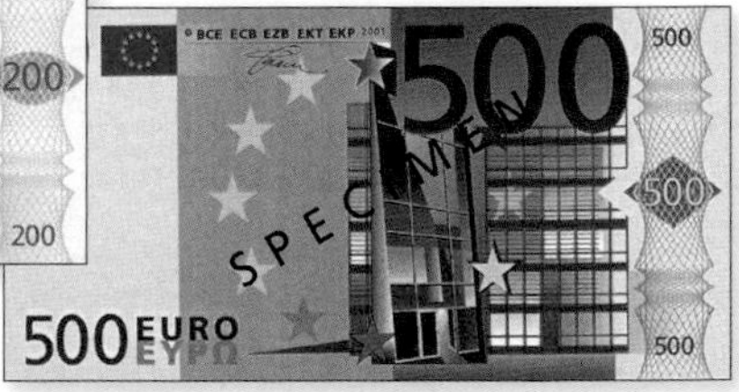

€500 note

€2 coin

€1 coin

50 cents

20 cents

10 cents

Coins

The euro has eight coin denominations: €1 and €2; 50 cents, 20 cents, 10 cents, 5 cents, 2 cents and 1 cent. The €2 and €1 coins are both silver and gold in colour. The 50-, 20- and 10-cent coins are gold. The 5-, 2- and 1-cent coins are bronze.

5 cents

2 cents

1 cent

Using the Telephone

The Austrian telephone system underwent a process of modernization in the late nineties; the privatized company Telekom Austria lost its monopoly and other foreign companies entered the market. As a result, prices have been modified, and there are now four different time tariffs for domestic and international calls. To phone outside Austria, you may find it more convenient to use a telephone booth at a post office, as you will be able to pay at the counter rather than using coins.

Coin-operated phone

Emergency phone sign

Sign for cardphone

TYPES OF TELEPHONES

There are two types of payphones in Austria, card- or coin-operated phones. Most phones carry instructions in English and other languages. Coin-operated telephones accept 10-, 20- and 50-cent as well as 1- and 2-euro coins. In card phones you can use a magnetic phonecard known as *Telefon-Wertkarte*, which may be purchased at newsagents and post offices. Austria has one of the most expensive telephone systems in Europe, so make sure you have plenty of change.

On some older phones, a red or black button needs to be pushed once the coins have been accepted and the call has been answered – otherwise the recipient will not be able to hear you.

USING THE TELEPHONE

International and domestic dialling codes can be found in the first volume of the telephone directory. Directories are usually available in telephone boxes, but may be too tatty to use. Post offices have directories in good condition, or contact directory enquiries *(see Reaching the Right Number below)*.

You can phone from hotels, pensions, restaurants, post offices, and booths in the street or at railway stations. For international calls it is best to avoid hotels as they tend to charge a hefty premium rate for calls.

Cheap-rate calling times for international calls from Austria is between 6pm and 8am and at weekends; for domestic calls it is between 8pm and 6am, and weekends.

USING A CARD PHONE

1 Lift the receiver and wait for the dialling tone.

2 Insert the credit card as shown by the arrow, or use a phone card *(below)*.

3 Wait for the value of available credit to be displayed.

4 Key in the phone number required.

5 Replace the receiver at the end of the call and withdraw the card.

2 Instead of a credit card, you can use a phone card in this slot.

USING A COIN-OPERATED PHONE

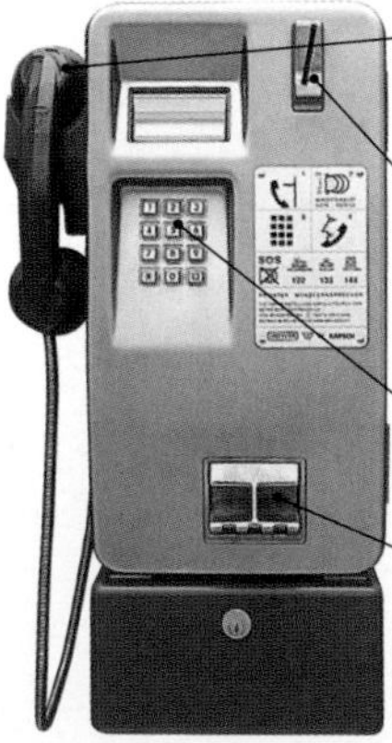

1 Lift the receiver.

2 Insert coins (10 cents minimum, no change given). Wait for the dialling tone.

3 Key in the phone number required.

4 Replace the receiver at the end of the call and collect any unused coins. A display shows how much money is left.

REACHING THE RIGHT NUMBER

- International dialling code for Austria is +43.
- For Austrian directory enquiries, dial 11811. For international directory enquiries, dial 0900 118877 (EU and neighbouring countries 118877).
- Railway timetable information: 05 17 17.
- Road conditions and snowfall: 15 84.
- Central Post Office Information (Zentrale Postauskunft): (0810) 010 100.
- To ring home from Austria, dial the appropriate country code, followed by the number. Omit the 0 from the local area code.
- For the **UK** dial 0044.
- For the **Irish Republic** dial 00353.
- For the **USA** dial 001.
- For **Australia** dial 0061.
- For **New Zealand** dial 0064.
- For international or national telegrams, dial 0800 100 190.

Mail and Postal Services

Decorative stamp

Besides buying postage stamps *(Briefmarken)* and arranging for the delivery of letters, parcels and telegrams, you can also make telephone calls, send moneygrams and send or receive fax messages at a post office. You can collect correspondence marked *Postlagernd (poste restante)* but you will need proof of identity. In addition, the post office sells phonecards and collectors' stamps and cashes traveller's cheques; some also exchange currency.

Post office sign

OPENING HOURS

The opening hours for post offices vary. In Vienna, the main post offices open 8am–6pm Monday to Friday, 8am–10am on Saturdays. Sub-post offices open 8am–noon and 2–6pm Monday to Friday.

In other provinces, opening hours are adapted to the local needs – in smaller resorts the post office is only open in the morning. The addresses of post offices can be found in local telephone directories, or ask at your hotel.

SENDING A LETTER

You can buy postage stamps at post offices, which also have stamp-vending machines. Letters for Europe weighing up to 20 g cost 65 cents, as do postcards. A registered letter costs around €2. In the address, add the standard country code, as used on car number plates, before the town or post code, for example GB for Britain, F for France.

Postboxes are yellow. Those with a red band are emptied at night, weekends and on public holidays, as well as on weekdays.

In order to send a parcel, registered letter or express package, you need to fill in a form which is available at the post office. A parcel weighing less then 2 kg may be sent more cheaply as a letter. The post office also sells suitable cardboard boxes for posting parcels.

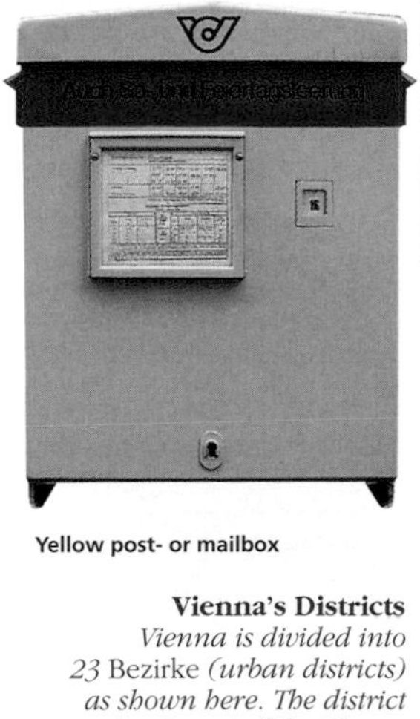

Yellow post- or mailbox

MAIN POST OFFICES

In all large towns, the main post offices and those in the railway stations open for longer hours in the evening, as well as on Saturdays, Sundays and bank holidays; they may, however, only offer a limited range of postal services after their normal opening hours.

In Vienna, the following post offices remain open all week: Fleischmarkt 19, Westbahnhof, Franz-Josefs-Bahnhof and Schwechat Airport. In Innsbruck, the main post offices are at No. 2 Maximilianstrasse and at the Hauptbahnhof railway station. The post office at the Hauptbahnhof railway station at No. 17 Südtiroler Platz in Salzburg stays open from 6am to 11pm every day of the week.

INTERNET AND EMAIL

Internet facilities are readily available in Austria. Most post offices have Internet services, there is an increasing number of coffee shops offering Wi-Fi to their customers and there are Internet cafés, called Speednet-Café or Internet-Café. Here you can sit in comfort at a computer terminal while enjoying a cup of coffee, and surfing the Internet. Charges are generally reasonable, about €3 per hour, depending on the number of users.

Vienna's Districts

Vienna is divided into 23 Bezirke *(urban districts) as shown here. The district number is part of the Vienna postcode. For example, the 23rd district is written as A-1230. The inset shows the area covered by our Street Finder maps 1-5 (see pp117–21).*

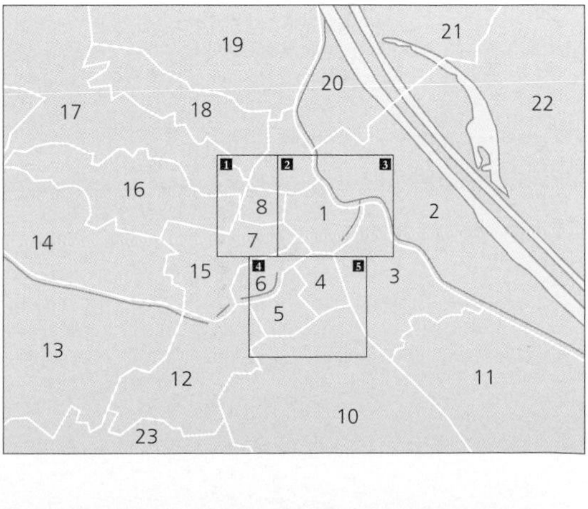

GETTING TO AUSTRIA

As a popular tourist destination, Austria is well served by both air and rail. The major cities – Vienna, Linz, Graz, Innsbruck, Salzburg and Klagenfurt – have international airports and there are direct flights from all main European cities as well as from the USA, Canada, Japan and Australia. Vienna is a key transit point between West and East, and about eight million passengers a year pass through its Schwechat airport.

An Austrian Airlines aircraft

There are good rail and coach links, too, but from Britain this involves a long journey, often overnight, and is not significantly cheaper than air travel. The motorway network linking Austria and the rest of Europe is extensive, and the roads are clearly signposted and well maintained.

The transit area at Schwechat International Airport in Vienna

AIR TRAVEL

There are several flights a day between London's Heathrow and Vienna's Schwechat Airport, which are operated by British Airways and by Austria's national airline Austrian Airways. Austrian Airways also serves Innsbruck from London Gatwick and Vienna from Manchester. Of the "low-cost" airlines Ryanair tends to be good value for money and flies from London Stansted to Graz, Klagenfurt, Linz, Bratislava and Salzburg, with connections from Glasgow and Dublin; and British European flies from Birmingham and London Gatwick to Salzburg.

If you wish to fly from the United States, there are direct flights with Delta from New York and Orlando. Lauda Air runs flights from Los Angeles, and Austrian Airlines from Chicago. There are also direct flights from Sydney and Toronto.

Thanks to its central location Vienna's Schwechat Airport is a major European transit airport, meaning that all the major airlines have offices here. The airport is located 19 km (12 miles) from Vienna's city centre, and is easily accessible by train or bus. A modern airport, Schwechat is very easy and quick to use.

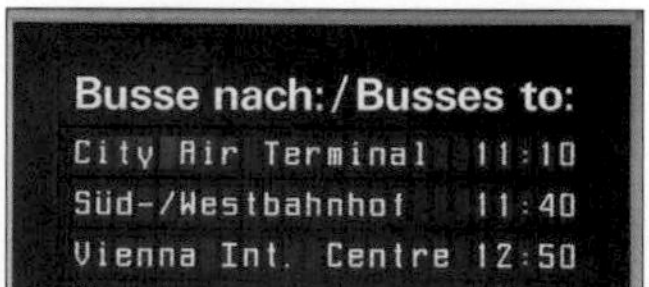

Busse nach: / Busses to:
City Air Terminal 11:10
Süd-/Westbahnhof 11:40
Vienna Int. Centre 12:50
Bratislava 13:20

Bus transfer information board

DOMESTIC FLIGHTS

Domestic flights within Austria are operated by Tyrolean Airways, part of the Austrian Airlines Group. There are daily flights from Vienna to Graz, Klagenfurt, Innsbruck, Salzburg and Linz. Air travel in Austria is expensive and, with extra time needed for checking in, the journey to and from the airport and for retrieving your luggage, it is not always the fastest and best way of getting to another destination in Austria.

SPECIAL DEALS

It is not necessary to pay full price for a scheduled ticket. There are good deals if you shop around the discount agencies and the Internet. You can usually get APEX tickets if you book at least two weeks in advance and if you can travel at days other than the weekend. Charters are available at very competitive rates. Weekend package offers, including the price of two nights at a good hotel, can be excellent value, sometimes costing less than the economy-ticket price. In addition, budget airlines often have special extra-low deals.

Frequent travellers with British Airways or Austrian Airlines enjoy many privileges if they join the respective frequent fliers' programmes. including priority on standby lists and upgrades to business class. Such programmes also often award points for car hire from major companies such as Avis, Europcar, Hertz or Sixt, as well as overnight stays at major hotel chains such as the Hilton, Holiday Inn or Marriot.

Travellers with special needs, for example wheelchair users, should notify the airlines of their requirements. Children up to and including the age of two travel free (or at

The modern building of Schwechat International Airport near Vienna

10 per cent of the price). Children aged three years and over pay the same price for flights as adults on all airlines.

AUSTRIAN AIRPORTS AND TRANSFERS

Many business travellers to Vienna never leave the airport: opposite the terminal building is the five-star luxury hotel Astron, and next to it the vast World Trade Centre, where many companies have their head offices. Vienna's airport has all the facilities that a traveller might need: information desks, service desks, shops, automatic money-exchange machines, bureaux de change and banks (though the rates for exchanging money at the airport are less favourable than elsewhere).

The taxi journey from the airport to the centre of Vienna costs around €35. Flughafentaxi Neudeck also has vans available in its fleet. Alternatively, you can hire a car at the airport, from companies such as Avis, Budget, Europcar, Hertz or Thrifty. All you need when hiring a vehicle is a driver's licence, a passport and a credit card for the deposit.

The CAT (City Airport Train: www.cityairporttrain.com) leaves every half hour and takes you to Wien-Mitte Station. The journey time is 16 minutes and the fare (one way) is around €9. Buses go to Schwedenplatz and Westbahnhof. They depart every 25 minutes and the 30-minute journey costs about €8 one way.

Logo of Austrian Airlines

The cheapest means of transport into the city is the suburban railway line, the *Schnellbahn*, which operates a half-hourly service.

Salzburg Airport, which is at No. 95 Innsbrucker Bundesstrasse, is situated extremely close to the town centre, a mere 4 km (2 miles) to the west. It can be reached by bus or taxi. Innsbruck Airport is also located near the town centre (4 km/ 2 miles) and the transfer by taxi or bus "F" takes 10–15 minutes. Buses from Klagenfurt Airport run every 30 minutes and take approximately 15 minutes to reach the centre of town.

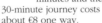

Shopping centre inside Vienna's Schwechat International Airport

DIRECTORY

AUSTRIAN AIRLINES

Airport Information
Tel *(01) 7007-22233.*
www.viennaairport.com

Offices in the UK
5th & 6th Floor, 10 Wardour Street, London W1D 6BQ.
Tel *(020) 7434 7350.*

Reservations
Kärntnerring 18, 1010 Vienna.
Tel *(0) 51 789.*
www.aua.com

OTHER AIRLINES

British Airways
Tel *(0845) 7733377.*
www.britishairways.com

british european
Reservations for UK passengers:
Tel *(0871) 7000535.*
www.flybe.com

KLM
Tel *(01) 795 67 232.*
www.klm.com/at-ge

Ryanair
Tel *From Ireland: (0818) 303030.*
From the UK: (0871) 246 0000.
www.ryanair.com

Tyrolean Airways
Tel *051789.*
www.tyrolean.at

CAR HIRE

Avis
Tel *(01) 587 6241 or 7007 32700.*
www.avis.at

Hertz City
Tel *(01) 512 8677 or 7007 32661.*
www.hertz.at

Travelling by Train

Situated in the heart of Europe, with Vienna as its main railway hub, Austria has excellent rail links with every important centre on the Continent, and there is a good network of lines within the country itself. The trains are comfortable, clean and safe; they run frequently and regularly. Punctuality is one of the main benefits – the old adage that you can set your watch by an Austrian train is largely true, although a few minutes' delay can occur. Unfortunately railway tickets are expensive. The largest railway line is the ÖBB – Österreichische Bundesbahnen, the Austrian Federal Railway Lines, and there are also 12 smaller, private railway lines.

Vienna's Franz-Josefs-Bahnhof, the terminal for trains from the north

TRAINS

Österreichische Bundesbahnen – ÖBB – runs several types of services. The modern EuroCity trains (marked with the letters EC) cover long-distance routes in record time. Night passengers travel on the EuroNight (EN) or CityNight-Line, with sleeping cars and couchettes. Comfortable InterCity (IC) and SuperCity trains connect major towns and tourist resorts. Every seat on the InterCity Express has a radio with headphones installed, and the first-class carriages are equipped with videos as well as power points for laptop computers. Domestic lines are also served by the D-Züge (D), long-distance trains running every day, at greater or lesser speed. More recently, the local routes have acquired modern, double-decker City Shuttle trains.

Bundesbahn logo

Motorists can also travel by rail with their cars between Mallnitz in Carinthia and the Gastein Valley. The cost of transport is about €10.

SEAT RESERVATIONS

In Austria, it is not compulsory to reserve a seat, even on express or international routes. It is entirely up to you, though trains can become busy, particularly during the peak tourist season in summer or when there is snow.

Reservations can be made at the ticket offices of any of the larger stations, at the ÖBB Reiseservicecenter or online at www.oebb.at The computerized system allows staff to check which seats are still available on any given train. Reserved seats are marked on the door of each compartment; you should take note of your carriage number when you are boarding, and again at the compartment door. Seat reservations are included in the price of first-class tickets.

Railway line passing right by the stunning Melk Abbey

RAILWAY STATIONS

The German word for a railway station is *Bahnhof*, and the main railway station is *Hauptbahnhof*. The capital city of each province has a *Hauptbahnhof*, Vienna has two. Railway stations are sometimes sited away from the city centre. They have bureaux de change, luggage deposits and information desks, with English-speaking staff. If there is no ticket office, you can buy a ticket from the machine on the platform.

ARRIVING FROM BRITAIN

The most direct form of rail travel to Austria from Britain is by Eurostar from London to either Paris or Brussels. From Paris you can take a German sleeper train to Munich and connect there for travel on to Graz, Innsbruck, Klagenfurt, Salzburg or Vienna. From Brussels, take a Thalys train to Cologne then travel on to either Linz or Vienna on a CityNight-Line overnight sleeper. For further details visit www.seat61.com/Austria.htm. The travel agency (Reisebüro) at Westbahnhof is open from 8am to 7pm on weekdays and 8am to 1pm on Saturdays; staff will be able to provide information as well as help with the booking of hotel rooms or other accommodation.

Construction is underway for a new main train station in Vienna. Hauptbahnhof Wien, located on Südtirolerplatz, is due to open in 2015 and will serve all international routes and provide access to the U1 subway. The Südbahnhof station has closed and all trains that previously used this station now leave and terminate at Meidling Philadelphiabrücke (on the U6 subway line). Most trains from Germany still arrive at Westbahnhof, which will eventually serve domestic routes only. Trains from the north arrive at Franz-Josefs-Bahnhof; this is served by the Schnell-bahn and the cross-city tram "D", which takes you to the Ringstraße in the centre.

TICKETS

Railway tickets are not cheap. A second-class ticket from Vienna to Salzburg, 300 km (190 miles) away, costs around €40 and this price is not influenced by the speed of the train. Prices are not calculated by the time it takes to reach your destination but according to the class of travel. Up to two children under six years, accompanied by an adult, travel for free. Each additional child, and children aged 6–15 years, pay half price.

The Schnellbahn, Vienna's suburban train line

Railway viaduct near Mattersburg

Ticket offices can be found in all larger railway stations. They also sell tickets for international routes. You can book a ticket on the phone with ÖBB Reiseservicecenter (05 17 17) or online. International tickets, with only a few exceptions, are valid for two months; domestic tickets, for journeys over 100 km (62 miles), are valid for one month.

There are many types of tickets, such as group, family and tourist travel, with or without concessions. When buying a ticket, seek advice at the ticket office of the Reiseservicecenter as to which is best for you.

Young people up to the age of 26 years may travel at a lower cost at certain times and on some types of trains. Further information may be obtained from a ticket office, the ÖBB Reiseservicecenter or via the Internet (www.oebb.at). If you are in possession of a credit card or *Vorteilscard* (advantage card) you may have your ticket printed straight away. It is then valid in conjunction with proof of age and identity.

A large number of different *Vorteilscards* are available at low prices, giving reductions on rail travel – Classic gives a 45 per cent reduction on all Austrian ÖBB trains and the majority of private lines, for one year; senior citizens get a further reduction on the Classic card. There is a family version *(Vorteilscard Familie)*, one for young people up to the age of 26 *(Vorteils-card<26)*, for the disabled *(Vorteilscard Spezial)*, and for the blind *(Vorteilscard Blind)*. When buying these cards, you will need to have with you proof of identity and a recent photograph. Alternatively, holders of a *Vorteilscard* can buy tickets on the phone, via text message or through the Internet *(see above)*.

RAILWAY NETWORK MAP

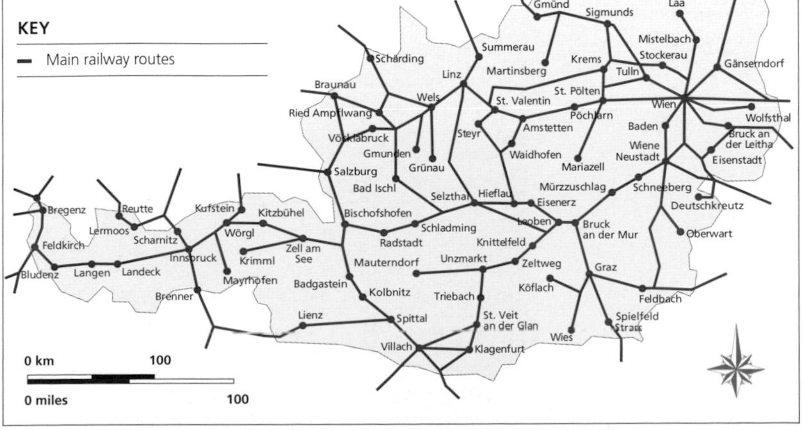

Travelling by Car

Travelling by car on Austrian roads can be a real pleasure. The road surfaces are in good condition and Austrians tend to comply with the traffic laws. Even in crowded cities, the traffic is relatively calm – you are forbidden to sound your horn other than to warn others of a danger. Routes are generally well signposted, but even so the motorists should carry an accurate map of the area. Motorways are marked with the letter A (for *Autobahn*) or E (for European motorway route); in addition, there are fast-traffic roads and a network of secondary roads that often pass through very scenic regions.

The spectacular Grossglockner Hochalpenstrasse *(see pp280–81)*

DRIVING IN AUSTRIA

Visitors arriving by car can make use of any of a number of border crossings. Those with nothing to declare are directed toward the green channel; when importing goods on which duty is to be paid, you will have to pass through the red channel.

A toll is charged on the motorways and some other fast-traffic roads (in urban areas as well as the countryside). It is collected via a prepaid disc, known as *Autobahnpickerl*, which can be bought at border crossing points, and from kiosks and petrol stations in Austria. The stickers, valid for 10 days, two months or one year, currently cost €7.90, €23 or €76.50 respectively. A 10-day sticker is valid from 9am on the day of issue until midnight of the ninth day thereafter. Stick the sticker to the top left corner of your car windscreen. The sticker does not entitle the driver to use any private pay-roads, of which fortunately there are very few; usually such roads are situated at high altitudes. You will also be asked to pay a separate charge for going across alpine passes and through tunnels.

WHAT TO TAKE

Visitors travelling by car in Austria need to carry a valid passport and driver's licence as well as their vehicle's registration document and green card (insurance policy). The vehicle must have a plaque showing the country of registration, and it must also be equipped with a first-aid box and a red warning triangle. In winter, it is obligatory to have winter tyres and snow chains, which are essential for driving on the mountain roads.

ROADS AND SIGNPOSTS

Motorways *(Autobahnen)* and the slip roads leading to them are signposted with white lettering on blue boards; on maps, motorways are shown as yellow lines between two thinner lines. An inn near a turning is indicated by a short sign with black lettering on white background.

Fernstrassen (long-distance roads) or *Bundesstrassen* (federal roads) are marked in red, and *Landstrassen* (country roads) in yellow. On the road, traffic signs are black-and-white. The written ones you may need to know are: *Stau* – traffic jam, *Schnee* – snow, *Umleitung* – diversion, and *Baustelle* – road works. All the remaining road signs follow the European standard.

ROAD TRAFFIC REGULATIONS

In Austria, motorists drive on the right-hand side of the road. The speed limit on motorways is 130 km/h (81 mph), and on other roads 100 km/h (62 mph). In towns and built-up areas the limit is 50 km/h (31 mph), but only 30 km/h (19 mph) in Graz. Lorries, caravans and cars with trailers are restricted to 100 km/h (62 mph) on motorways. While not everyone follows the prescribed speed limits, Austrian police carry out checks with infra-red guns and can fine you on the spot. Drivers and passengers are obliged to wear seatbelts

A toll station at the entrance to a pay-road in the mountains

at all times. Children up to the age of 15, or until they reach a height of 1.5 m (5 ft), are not allowed to travel in the front seat, unless the car is equipped with a special child restraint.

DRIVING IN TOWNS

Finding a place in which to park is not easy, especially in the centre of the larger towns; it is often best to use a multi-storey car park which is indicated by the word *Parkhaus*. *Frei* means that parking spaces are available.

Cars left in a controlled parking zone, indicated by blue lines on the road, must display a parking ticket or be parked validly near a meter (see below for how to buy a parking ticket from a meter). In most parts of Vienna parking is restricted to resident permit holders. Visitors may park for up to 2 hours, if they display a parking card (from newsagents).

It is never worth leaving your car in a prohibited area – a traffic warden will arrive immediately, impose a fine and arrange for your car to be towed away. Retrieving an impounded car is a lengthy, costly and difficult procedure.

A road hugging the edge of the Seidewinktal valley

Sign informing motorists of the need to fit wheel-chains

CAR HIRE

Major car hire firms, such as Autohansa, Avis, Denzel, Europcar, Hartl, Hertz and Trendcar, all have offices in Austria. Car hire is more expensive at the airport, but it is the only place where you will be able to hire a car late at night or at weekends.

To hire a car you must be 19 or over, and for some car companies the age limit is 25; you must also hold a valid passport and a driver's licence as well as a credit card or charge card from an approved company. (A charge card can sometimes be obtained from selected tourist offices, inside or outside Austria.)

A car may be hired for any duration and dropped off at any agreed point, to be collected by the hire company Not all destinations, however, have suitable drop-off points. Cars may be taken outside Austria to approved EU countries. You may also take hired cars to some, but not to all Eastern Europe countries, only with special permission from the hiring company.

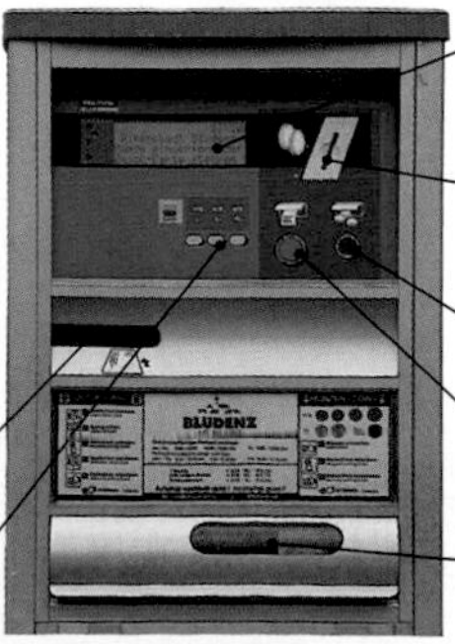

Parking meters
In many towns you will have to obtain a ticket from a parking meter to park your car. Display it on the windscreen.

ARRIVING BY COACH

Eurolines runs coaches from London Victoria to Wien Mitte. This is also the terminal station for routes to major European cities such as Bratislava, Budapest, Zurich, Paris, Brussels, Milan and Copenhagen, plus domestic routes from eastern Austria.

Coaches are equipped to the European standard and tickets may be cheaper than rail travel, but the journey from the UK is long and fares are not particularly cheap. Often, budget airlines offer a more convenient way to travel at a comparable cost *(see p364)*.

TRAVELLING BY COACH

The entire country is served by an excellent coach network, allowing you to reach almost any destination including some remote places not connected to the rail network. Prices are similar to those charged for rail travel.

HITCHHIKING

It is not always easy to get a lift in Austria; few drivers are willing to take hitchhikers. If you decide to thumb a lift, the best point to wait is by the exit road from a town. Young people waiting there often carry cardboard notices stating their desired destination. As anywhere, women travelling alone should take extra care. In some provinces, children below the age of 16 are forbidden to hitchhike.

Getting Around Towns

Finding your way around an unfamiliar town, even with a map, is often difficult. One-way traffic systems, pedestrianized areas and parking restrictions are all designed to keep car traffic out. Walking is the easiest and most enjoyable way to get around the compact city centres, where most of the historic sights are to be found. Austrian towns generally have a well-developed public transport system, including buses and, in most cities, trams. Vienna also has an underground network (metro) – the quickest way to reach any destination. In some cities, travel cards give you unlimited travel on all local transport facilities for a specified number of days.

WALKING

Pedestrians have priority, even on roads – but you should never rely on this. Try to use subways or crossings where there are signals, especially when crossing wide roads with fast-moving traffic. Visitors from the UK and Australia need to remember that motorists drive on the right. Do not cross a road when the red signal shows even if there is no traffic – you may be spot-fined for jay walking. Watch out also for cyclists who share the pavement with pedestrians.

In larger cities, guided walking tours are available during the summer months, which will take you past all the sights. Exploring themes such as the Baroque, or Vienna 1900, they are available in English and other languages. For information contact the local tourist offices.

Tourists strolling through a mountain village

BICYCLES

Cycle routes usually run on the pavement and are clearly marked with lines and arrows. Pedestrians need to take extra care not to stray into the cycling area. Where there is no cycle route, cyclists join the road traffic and are obliged to adhere to all normal traffic rules. There are special posts on pavements and in public squares for parking and securing bicycles. In Vienna, bike paths take you around the Ringstrasse and past many of the sights. Bikes may also be hired from some stations, at a discount if you have a train ticket.

One of the most scenic long-distance cycling routes is the *Radweg* (cycle track) along the Danube river.

Horse-drawn carriage trip in Salzburg

TAXIS

You can recognize a taxi by the TAXI sign on the roof. They are usually saloon cars, often Mercedes. If a taxi is for hire, the sign will be illuminated. In the centre of a city it is easier to get a taxi at one of the taxi ranks, rather than hailing it in the street. Taxi ranks can be found near railway stations and large hotels. Alternatively, you can book a taxi by phone. In the rush hour it may be faster to travel by underground or by tram. All taxis have meters and charges are calculated per kilometre travelled. Additional charges are made for more than one passenger, luggage, late night and weekend journeys. In Vienna, a taxi to the airport will cost about €35. It is usual to tip 10 per cent of the fare, rounding up the fare to the nearest euro.

BUSES

Many city centres are served by hopper buses, while larger buses take visitors to the inner suburbs. Municipal bus lines are often extensions of tram lines. This is signalled by a letter in the number of the bus, thus bus No. 46A extends the route of tram No. 46, making it easy to find the correct line.

TRAMS

Along with buses and the underground, trams are the most convenient form of transport in the cities. It is easy to track your progress as each stop is announced by a pre-recorded voice and all carriages display the route map, indicating the stops.

The doors are released by pressing a button. Make sure you press the button to signal your intention to get out – trams or buses may continue without stopping if no one is waiting at the station.

TICKETS

Tickets can be bought at newsagents, in blocks of five or ten, or in suburban railway stations where blocks of two or four are also available. You should always buy a ticket before travelling, since it is not always possible to buy one from the driver or the ticket machine inside the vehicle. Having boarded the bus, tram or train you need to stamp your ticket at the start of your journey; you will not need to stamp it again if you change to a different line or different mode of transport.

The tickets are valid for travel on all forms of transport within a town, within varying time limits. For a *Kurzstrecke* or short distance, which is clearly marked on the route maps, you need a half-price *Kurzstreckenfahrschein*, which will entitle you to travel only within a stated zone. Besides single tickets, you may also buy a 24-hour pass, a *Streifenkarte* (strip of tickets) valid for three or eight days, a *Wochenkarte* valid for one week, a *Monatskarte,* valid for one month, or a *Jahreskarte,* which permits you to travel for one year.

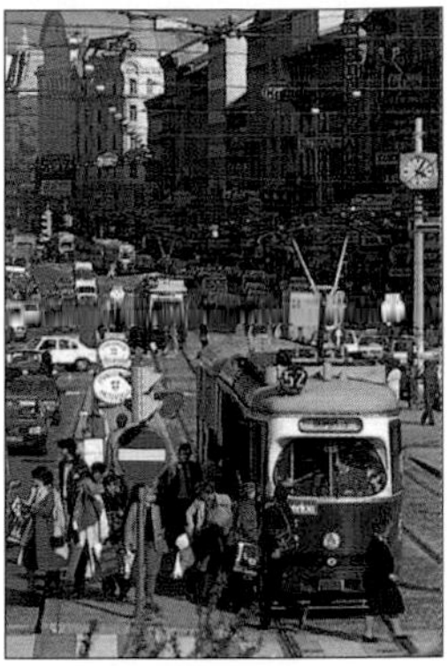

A typical red-and-white tram in one of Vienna's busy streets

The rules of public transport vary between the provinces in Austria. Tourist offices and hotels will be able to advise you on local regulations.

MAKING A JOURNEY BY UNDERGROUND

1 To determine which line to take, travellers should look for their destination on a U-Bahn map. The five lines are distinguished by colour and number (U1, U2, U3, U4 & U5). Simply trace the line to your destination, making a note of where you need to change lines. Connections to other forms of transport are also shown.

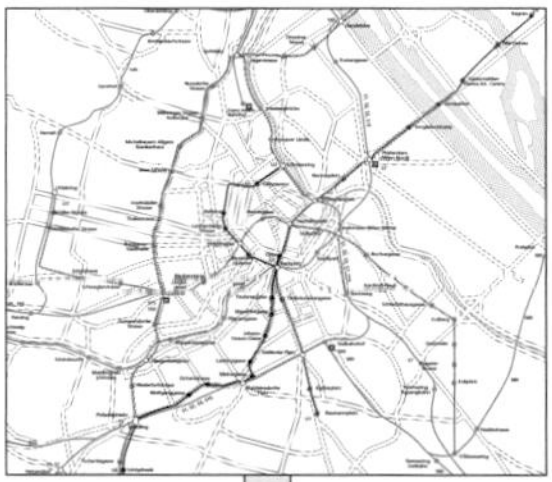

Pull handle to open door

The door opens out to the side

2 Tickets can be bought from a newsagent, ticket vending machines or ticket offices. To get to the trains, insert your ticket into the ticket-stamping machine in the direction of the arrow. Wait for the ping indicating that it is validated, and pass through the barrier. Follow the signs (with the number and colour of the line) to your platform.

3 Once you are on the platform, check the direction and destination of the train on an electronic destination indicator.

Sign showing stops on line 3 of the U-Bahn, including the connecting stops

4 Stops along the line are shown on a plan. A red arrow in the corner shows the direction in which the train enters the station.

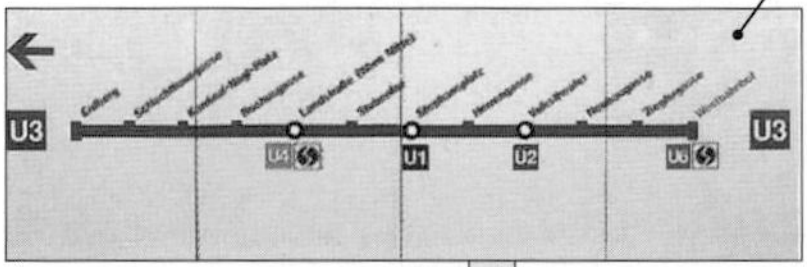

6 At stations with more than one exit, use the map of the city to check which street or square you will come out at.

5 At your destination follow the *Ausgang* signs to reach street level.

General Index

Page numbers in **bold** type refer to main entries.

A

B

C

L

Q

R

S

U

V

Acknowledgments

Dorling Kindersley would like to thank the following people whose contributions and assistance have made the preparation of this book possible.

Consultant
Gerhard Bruschke

Additional Contributors
Helen Harrison, Darrel Joseph, Doug Sager, Leslie Woit

Additional Photography
Maciej Bronarski, Dip. Ing. Walter Hildebrand, Renata and Marek Kosińscy, Piotr Kiedrowski, Ian O'Leary, Peter Wilson, Paweł Wroński

Cartography
An Bundesamt Eich- und Vermessungwesen, Lundesaufnahme (BEV), Uma Bhattacharya, Mohammad Hassan, Jasneet Kaur

DTP
Vinod Harish, Vincent Kurien, Azeem Siddiqui

Reader
Judith Meddick

Fact-Checkers
Martina Bauer, Melanie Nicholson-Hartzell

Proofreader
Emily Hatchwell

Indexer
Helen Peters

Senior Editor
Jacky Jackson/Wordwise Associates Ltd.

Managing Art Editor
Kate Poole/Ian Midson

Publishing Manager
Helen Townsend

Design and Editorial Assistance
Jo Cowen, Conrad Van Dyk, Mariana Evmolpidou, Karen Fitzpatrick, Anna Freiberger, Rhiannon Furbear, Juliet Kenny, Carly Madden, Hayley Maher, Alison McGill, Sam Merrell, Kate Molan, Sangita Patel, Marianne Petrou, Marisa Renzullo, Sadie Smith, Susana Smith, Rachel Symons

Additional Picture Research
Ellen Root

Special Assistance
Wiedza i Życie would like to thank Mr. Roman Skrzypczak of the Austrian Tourist Information Centre for his help in obtaining materials and for facilitating contacts with other Austrian institutions.

The publisher would also like to thank all the people and institutions who allowed photographs belonging to them to be reproduced, as well as granting permission to use photographs from their archives:

Agencja Forum (Krzysztof Wójcik)
Artothek (Susanne Vierthaler and Holger Gehrmann)
Basilika Mariazell, Benediktiner-Superiorat (P. Karl Schauer OSB, Superior)
Brahms Museum, Mürzzuschlag
Burgenländisches Landesmuseum, Eisenstadt (Julia Raab and Gerard Schlag)
Corbis (Gabriela Ściborska)
Chorherrenstift Klosterneuburg-Stiftsmuseum (Mag. Wolfgang Huber)
Die Österreich Werbung, Bildarchiv (Dr. Dietmar Jungreithmair)
DK Library
FIS Wintersportmuseum, Mürzzuschlag (Mag. Hannes Nothnagl)
Festung Hochensalzburg
Heeresgeschichtliches Museum in Arsenal (Peter Enne)
Kunsthistorisches Museum, Wien (Elisabeth Reicher)
Lurgrotte Peggau
Museum Schloss Greillenstein (Elisabeth Kuefstein)
Museumsverein Schloss Rosenau, Österreichisches Freimaurermuseum
Naturpark Grebenzen Büro St. Lambrecht (Frater Gerwig Romirer)
Österreichischen Freilichtmuseum, Stübing bei Graz (Egbert Pöttler)
Rathaus w St. Pölten (Andrea Jäger)
Salzburger Burgen und Schlösser, Betriebsführung
Stadtmarketing Eisenstadt, Schloss Esterházy (Guenter Schumich)
Stift Melk, Kultur and Tourismus (Maria Prüller)
Wien-Tourismus (Waltraud Wolf)
Zefa (Ewa Kozłowska)

Picture Credits

Key: a = above; b = below/bottom; c = centre; f = far; l = left; r = right; t = top.

Alamy Images AA World Travel Library 10tc; Pat Behnke 344tl; blickwinkel/McPHOTO 11cb; Colinspics 343tc; Rob Crandall 98bl; Danita Delimont/Walter Bibikow 345tc; David Noble Photography 313tl; FAN travelstock/Michael Schindel 314cla; imagebroker/ Christian Handl 311tl; INSADCO Photography/ Martin Bobrovsky 311c; Rainer Jahns 11tr; Jon Arnold Images/Jon Arnold 10bl; Barry Mason 313cb; mediacolor's 312cl; Pictures Colour Library 343br; Charles Ridgway 342crb; Robert Harding Picture Library

Ltd/Richard Nebesky 310cl; Westend 61/ Hans Huber 344bc.
ARTOTHEK Chr. Brandstätter 29c; Photobusiness 29t; Ernst Reinhold 28b.
AV MEDIENSTELLE DER ERZDIÖZESE WIEN 36b.
BASILIKA MARIAZELL 184-185
BENEDIKTINERSTIFT ST. LAMBRECHT 174t.
BRAHMS MUSEUM (Mürzzuschlag) 168c.
BRONARSKI, MACIEJ 339b.
BURGENLÄNDISCHES LANDESMUSEUM (Eisenstadt) 24bl, 154tr.
CAFE PRUCKEL 314bc.
CORBIS: 46cr; AFP 47c, 47t, 47b; Archivo Iconografico 40b, 43c, 45t; Bettmann 43t, 46br; Jonathan Blair 31t; Corbis Sygma 31b; Wolfgang Kaehler 143c; Bob Krist 221bl, 221br; Massimo Listri 142t, 242t; Ali Meyer 29b, 41t; José F. Poblete 10cr; Leonard de Selva 46t; James A. Sugar 160cla.
FESTUNG HOHENSALZBURG (Salzburg) 223cra.
FREILICHTMUSEUM STÜBING 167t, 167br.
GETTY IMAGES AFP/Josch 342cl; Sean Gallup 342tc; Joe Klamar 344cr; Photographer's Choice/Josef Fankhauser 11cl.
HEERESGESCHICHTLICHES MUSEUM, WIEN 39c, 44b, 46bl; Österreichische Galerie 44t.
HOTEL SACHER, WIEN 314bc.
KIEDROWSKI, PIOTR 341brb.
KOSIŃSCY, RENATA AND MAREK 17b, 22tl, 22bl, 23t, 23cla, 23cl, 23cr, 23cb, 23bl, 23dc, 23br
KUNSTHISTORISCHES MUSEUM, WIEN 40t, 40cra, 40cb, 42c, 84–87.
LURGROTTE, PEGGAU 168t.
MUSEUM SCHLOSS GREILLENSTEIN 141tl.
MUSEUMSVEREIN SCHLOSS ROSENAU, ÖSTERREICHISCHES FREIMAURERMUSEUM 141br.
ÖSTERREICH WERBUNG: 16b; Ascher 19t; Bald 17c; Bartl 3, 51c, 92t, 115t, 132t, 340clb; Bohnacker 162b, 197b, 206t; Carniel 208t; W. Daemon 81b; Diejun 1, 38c, 182tlb, 183bla, 340tl, 340br; Fankhauser 34t, 249br 349br; Gottfried 263b; H. Graf 67t; Gruenert 200t, 233b, 253b; Haider 23b, 44cl, 76b; Haller 45cra; Herzberger 114t, 221tr, 341clb, 367t; Hinterndorfer Ch. 146b; Imprima 134b; Jalain 35b; Jellasitz 155t; Jezierzański 140t, 175t, 179c; Kalmar 77t, 77b, 108t, 340cla, 340bl; Kneidinger 19c, 181b, 193t; Lamm 175b, 178c, 178b, 179b; Landova 199t; R. Liebing 18b, 286b; Mallaun 212t, 233t, 252t, 256t, 257t, 348b, 349bl; Markowitsch 32t, 33b, 104t, 127t, 179t, 181t, 221tr, 241c, 247t, 341tl; Mayer 59b, 246t; Nechansky 259tl; A. Niederstrasser 2–3, 246b; OEW-Bildarchiv 146t, 340cra, Robert Pfeifer 71b, Pigneter 190t, 191b, 207t; G. Popp 148-149, 182br, 350b; Porizka 193b, 207b, 209b; Ramstorfer 42bl; Salzburger Burgen/S/B 217ca; Schmeja 341tr; Simoner 24t, 147b, 156; Storto 42br 205t, 253t; Trumler 24cla, 25t, 25cl, 25crb, 36, 37br, 37bl, 39t, 40cla, 42t, 43b, 65cb, 111b, 134c, 140bl 141bl, 145tra. 145cl, 145cr, 145b, 183t, 192b, 194bla, 195b, 196, 197tlb, 199bl, 206b, 239c, 240t, 270brb, 273tra 340tr; W. Weinhaeupl 207c, 213t, 225b, 272t; H. Wiesenhofer 19b, 32c, 32b, 33t, 35t, 41crb, 138t, 145glw, 154b, 161t, 162t, 162c, 163b, 169t, 183brb, 201t, 254b, 270bla; Winderer 34b.
RATHAUS (St. Pölten) 132b.
REUTERS 30b, 30t, 30c.
STIFT MELK 142cla, 142clb, 142br 143t, 143bl, 143br.
UNICREDIT BANK AUSTRIA AG: 360tl.
WROŃSKI, PAWEŁ 230t, 285t, 285c, 308t, 338c, 341bl, 341bra.
WINTERSPORTMUSEUM (Mürzzuschlag) 168c.
WIEN MUSEUM 62bc.
WIEN-TOURISMUS 48–49, 58tr, 59t, 64tlb, 64b.
ZEFA: Damm 176-177, 234; Kalt 12; Mathis 235b; K. Meier 210; Raga 214c; Rose 22-23c, 201t; Spichtinger 180t; Weir 178t.

JACKET: Front: ALAMY IMAGES: nagelestock.com. Back: ALAMY IMAGES: Ian G Dagnall clb, imagebroker/FB-Rose cla, David Noton tl, Robert Harding Picture Libary Ltd/Gavin Hellier bl. Spine: ALAMY IMAGES: Ian G Dagnall t.

All other images © Dorling Kindersley
For further information: www.dkimages.com

Phrase Book

In Emergency

Help!	**Hilfe!**	**hilf**-er
Stop!	**Halt!**	**hult**
Call	**Holen Sie**	**hole**'n zee
.....a doctor	**...einen Arzt**	...**ine**'n **artst**
.....an ambulance	**...einen Krankenwagen**	...**ine**'n **krank**'n**varg**'n
.....the police	**...die Polizei**	...dee pol-its-**eye**
.....the fire brigade	**...die Feuerwehr**	...dee **foy**-er-vair
Where is a telephone?	**Wo finde ich ein Telefon?**	voh **fin**-der ish ine tel-e-fone?
Where is the hospital?	**Wo ist das Krankenhaus?**	voh ist duss **krunk**'n-hows?

Communication Essentials

Yes	**Ja**	**yah**
No	**Nein**	**nine**
Please	**Bitte**	**bitt**-er
Thank you	**Danke vielmals**	dunk-er **feel**-malse
Excuse me	**Gestatten**	g'**shtatt**'n
Hello	**Grüss Gott**	groos got
Goodbye	**Auf Wiedersehen**	owf **veed**-er-zay-ern
morning	**Vormittag**	**for**-mit-targ
afternoon	**Nachmittag**	**nakh**-mit-targ
evening	**Abend**	**ah**b'nt
yesterday	**Gestern**	**gest**'n
today	**Heute**	**hoyt**-er
tomorrow	**Morgen**	**morg**'n
here	**hier**	**hear**
there	**dort**	**dort**
What?	**Was?**	**vuss**?
When?	**Wann?**	**vunn**?
Where?	**Wo/Wohin?**	**voh**/vo-**hin**?

Useful Phrases & Words

Where is...?	**Wo befindet sich...?**	voe b'**find**'t zish...?
Where are...?	**Wo befinden sich...?**	voe b'**find**'n zish...?
How far is it to...?	**Wie weit ist...?**	vee **vite** ist...?
Do you speak English?	**Sprechen Sie englisch?**	**shpresh**'n zee **eng**-glish?
I don't understand	**Ich verstehe nicht**	ish fair-**shtay**-er nisht
I'm sorry	**Es tut mir leid**	es toot meer lyte
big	**gross**	**grohss**
small	**klein**	**kline**
open	**auf/offen**	**owf**/**off'**n
closed	**zu/geschlossen**	tsoo/g'**shloss'**n
left	**links**	**links**
right	**rechts**	**reshts**
near	**in der Nähe**	in dair **nay**-er
far	**weit**	**vyte**
up	**auf, oben**	**owf**, **obe**'n
down	**ab, unten**	**up**, **oont**'n
early	**früh**	**froo**
late	**spät**	**shpate**
entrance	**Eingang/Einfahrt**	**ine**-gung/**ine**-fart
exit	**Ausgang/Ausfahrt**	**ows**-gung/**ows**-fart
toilet	**WC/Toilette**	vay-**say**/toy-**lett**-er

Making a Telephone Call

I'd like to place a long-distance call	**Ich möchte ein Ferngespräch machen**	ish **mer**-shter ine **fairn**-g'shpresh mukh'n
I'd like to call collect	**Ich möchte ein Rückgespräch machen**	ish **mer**-shter ine **rook**-g'shpresh mukh'n
local call	**Ortsgespräch**	**orts**-g'**shpresh**
Can I leave a message?	**Kann ich etwas ausrichten?**	kunn ish **ett**-vuss **ows**-rikht'n

Staying in a Hotel

Do you have a vacant room?	**Haben Sie ein Zimmer frei?**	**harb**'n zee ine **tsimm**-er fry?
double room	**ein Doppelzimmer**	ine **dopp**'l-tsimm-er
twin room	**ein Doppelzimmer**	ine **dopp**'l-tsimm-er
single room	**ein Einzelzimmer**	ine **ine**-ts'l-tsimm-er
with a bath/shower	**mit Bad/Dusche**	mitt **bart**/**doosh**-er
key	**Schlüssel**	shlooss'l
I have a reservation	**Ich habe ein Zimmer reserviert**	ish **harb**-er ine **tsimm**-er rezz-er-**veert**

Sightseeing

bus	**der Bus**	dair **booss**
tram	**die Strassenbahn**	dee **stra**-sen-barn
train	**der Zug**	dair tsoog
art gallery	**Galerie**	gall-er-**ee**
bus station	**Busbahnhof**	booss-**barn**-hofe
bus (tram) stop	**die Haltestelle**	dee **hal**-te-shtel-er
castle	**Schloss, Burg**	**shloss**, **boorg**
palace	**Schloss, Palais**	**shloss**, pall-**ay**
post office	**das Postamt**	dee **pohs**-taamt
cathedral	**Dom**	**dome**
church	**Kirche**	**keersh**-er
garden	**Garten, Park**	**gart**'n, **park**
museum	**Museum**	moo-**zay**-oom
information (office)	**Information**	in-for-mut-**see**-**on**

Shopping

How much does this cost?	**Wieviel kostet das?**	**vee**-feel **kost**'t duss?
I would like...	**Ich hätte gern...**	ish **hett**-er gairn...
Do you have...?	**Haben Sie...?**	**harb**'n zee...?
expensive	**teuer**	**toy**-er
cheap	**billig**	**bill**-igg
bank	**Bank**	**bunk**
book shop	**Buchladen**	**bookh**-lard'n
chemist/pharmacy	**Apotheke**	App-o-**tay**-ker
hairdresser	**Friseur/Frisör**	freezz-**er**/freezz-**er**
market	**Markt**	**markt**
newsagent	**Tabak Trafik**	tab-**ack** tra-feek
travel agent	**Reisebüro**	**rye-z**er-boo-roe

Eating Out

Have you got a table for... people?	**Haben Sie einen Tisch für... Personen?**	harb'n zee ine'n tish foor... pair-**sohn**'n?
The bill please	**Zahlen, bitte**	**tsarl**'n **bitt**-er
I am a vegetarian	**Ich bin Vegetarier**	ish bin vegg-er-**tah**-ree-er
Waitress/waiter	**Fräulein/Herr Ober**	**froy**-line/hair **oh**-bare
menu	**die Speisekarte**	dee **shpize**-er-kart-er
wine list	**Weinkarte**	**vine**-kart-er
breakfast	**Frühstück**	**froo**-shtook
lunch	**Mittagessen**	**mit**-targ-ess'n
dinner	**Abendessen**	**arb**'nt-ess'n

Menu Decoder

Ei	**eye**	egg
Eis	**ice**	ice cream
Fisch	**fish**	fish
Fleisch	**flysh**	meat
Garnelen	**gar**-nayl'n	prawns
gebacken	g'**buck**'n	baked/fried
gebraten	g'**brart**'n	roast
gekocht	g'**kokht**	boiled
Gemüse	g'**mooz**-er	vegetables
vom Grill	fom **grill**	grilled
Hendl/Hahn/Huhn	**hend**'l/**harn**/**hoon**	chicken
Kaffee	kaf-**fay**	coffee
Kartoffel/Erdäpfel	kar-**toff**'l/**air**-dupf'l	potatoes
Käse	**kayz**-er	cheese
Knödel	**k'nerd**'l	dumpling
Lamm	**lumm**	lamb
Meeresfrüchte	**mair**-erz-froosh-ter	seafood
Milch	**milhk**	milk
Mineralwasser	minn-er-**arl**-vuss-er	mineral water
Obst	**ohbst**	fresh fruit
Pfeffer	**pfeff**-er	pepper
Pommes frites	pomm-**fritt**	chips
Reis	**rice**	rice
Rind	**rint**	beef
Rostbraten	rohst-**brart**'n	steak
Rotwein	**roht**-vine	red wine
Salz	**zults**	salt
Schinken/Speck	**shink**'n/shpeck	ham
Schlag	**shlahgg**	cream
Schokolade	shock-o-**lard**-er	chocolate
Schwein	**shvine**	pork
Tee	**tay**	tea
Wasser	**vuss**-er	water
Weisswein	**vyce**-vine	white wine
Wurst	**voorst**	sausage (fresh)
Zucker	**tsook**-er	sugar

Road Map of Austria

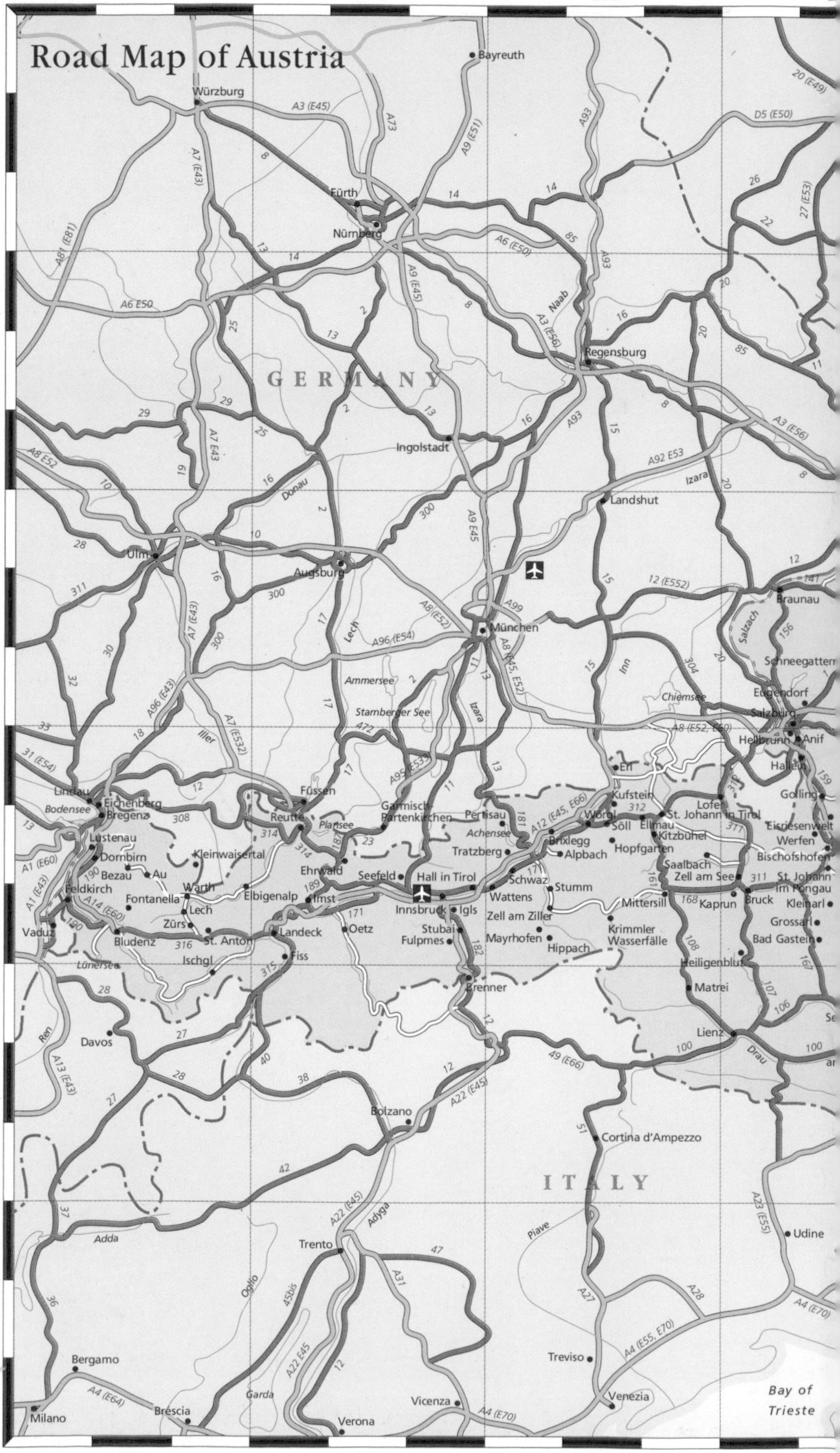